THE BOOK OF VISIONS

THE BOOK OF VISIONS

An Encyclopaedia of Social Innovations

Edited by

Nicholas Albery

Assisted by

Valerie Yule

Foreword by

Anita Roddick

This edition first published in Great Britain in 1992 by
Virgin Books
an imprint of Virgin Publishing Ltd
338 Ladbroke Grove
London W10 5AH

Material collected, typeset and laid out by
The Institute for Social Inventions
20 Heber Road
London NW2 6AA
tel 081 208 2853
fax 081 452 6434

All royalties from this book are going to the Institute for Social Inventions, a registered educational charity, towards its workshops in schools and other activities. The Institute is grateful to all the hundreds of people around the world who freely contributed items and is apologetic to any whom it failed to trace or acknowledge. Please send all corrections, updates and additions to the Institute at the above address. The Institute is especially grateful to: The Body Shop and Anita Roddick for their support for this book and for the last three years of the competition; to Valerie Yule in Australia for her help with the preliminary sorting of the material; to Richard Doust for his free design consultancy for the book's lay-out; to Yvonne Ackroyd, Roger Knights and Marion Schmidt for their research help; to Nicholas Saunders and his Neal's Yard DeskTop Publishing Studio and to a number of foundations, particularly the Joseph Rowntree Charitable Trust, for their financial support to the Institute for Social Inventions over the years.

A catalogue record for this book is available from the British Library

ISBN 0 86369 601 5

Printed and bound in Great Britain by BPCC Wheatons Ltd, Exeter

FOREWORD

Anita Roddick
founder of The Body Shop

In West Sussex, not far from where I live, an 18th Century quote carved in the wall of a country church reads:

> 'A vision without a task is but a dream, a task without a vision is drudgery, a vision and a task are the hope of the world.'

That is why I am so fond of the Institute for Social Inventions. We all have visions of a better world. Far too often we treat them as mere dreams, precisely because they are not linked to tasks. The Institute gives voice to the many incremental but bold tasks people have invented to take us towards our visions – to make hope in this world.

Inspired by the Institute, The Body Shop now has its very own Department of Social Inventions. We aim to train at least one 'specialist' in social inventions in each of our 700 shops worldwide.

I am thrilled by this book. It is a wonderful collection of inspired ideas. But its power lies beyond that. I encourage you to use this book in your own community; in your own way – commit yourself to carrying out at least one of the ideas and use the book to dislodge yourself from the mental ruts a society like ours can leave you in. At its core this Encyclopaedia of Social Inventions is a mating call to social entrepreneurs. Be one.

CONTENTS

Chapter one

SOCIAL INNOVATIONS – PAST AND PRESENT

Ideas Wanted!

Nicholas Albery, Chairman of the Institute for Social Inventions

I define a social innovation or social invention as a new and imaginative way of tackling a social problem or improving the quality of life. Unlike a technological invention, it tends to be a new service, rather than a product or patentable process, and there tends to be no money in it. This Encyclopaedia consists of hundreds of donated contributions from so-called 'ordinary people', social inventors in disguise.

The Institute for Social Inventions, the organisation which collected these visions, ideas and projects, was launched in 1985 with just this aim – of encouraging the innate inventiveness of the British public and collecting, researching, publicising and carrying out the best ideas.

> 'Every man and woman in the country should be encouraged to observe, tackle and help to overcome those anomalies and inefficiencies of which he or she has first hand knowledge'

The first person I know of who raised the need for an organisation such as ours was Clavell Blount. Back in the 1950s he persuaded an MP to promote a debate in the House on the topic of 'Ideas into Action' and wrote a book of this name, in which he urged that every effort should be made to collect the suggestions of members of the public. As he wrote:

'It seems to me that we have reached a point in our history where we are faced by a choice between two alternatives:

'EITHER we believe it would be best to leave our fate to a few "master minds" who will decide just how the industrial and social life of this nation is to run, and who will issue their directives through their chains of command;

'OR we think it best that the national "problem of survival" should be broken down into its smallest practical elements and that, by means of psychological and material incentives, every man and woman in the country should be encouraged to observe, tackle and help to overcome those anomalies and inefficiencies of which he or she has first hand knowledge.'

> '£1,000 in prizes to be won (see the final pages of this book for details)'

The main such incentive that the Institute has been able to offer so far has been that of dangling the bait of our annual competition, judged in June of each year, offering a minimum £1,000 in prizes and a variable amount of publicity (see the final pages of this book for details).

This competition is merely a lure to entice the punter by the finger so that the rest of the body will follow. The Institute then encourages the senders-in-of-ideas to take matters further themselves, often giving hints on whom to approach and how. Some ideas the Institute does take up itself. Most of these are described more fully in this volume.

The Institute has launched a social inventions workshop programme in many state schools; and it promotes Community Counselling Circles as a way of training large groups (and has published a book on this). It has helped a number of its own pet schemes get going, including a Natural Death Centre ('to improve the quality of dying' and to support those who are dying at home); an Adopt-a-Planet competition (where school classes caretake a vandalised part of their local neighbourhood); a Hippocratic Oath for Scientists (signed by many Nobel-prize-winning scientists); a Universal Declaration of the Rights of Posterity; a rating scheme for gurus and spiritual masters; a rating scheme for advertisements; and Forum Theatres (to help resolve children's disputes).

With help from the Network for Social Change, the Institute has also been active in Eastern Europe, helping found the East Europe Constitution Design Forum which brings together (at international symposia and by fax) the key constitution designers and politicians from Eastern Europe and the ex-Soviet Union, in an attempt to use constitutional and electoral models as a way of defusing some of the ethnic turmoil resulting from the decolonisation of the Soviet empire. The Institute has published a timely book 'Can Civil Wars Be Avoided?' which argues that Local Balance Representation might be a suitable model for many of the emerging democracies (and for Northern Ireland). In this electoral system, parties are penalised and begin to lose seats they would otherwise have won, if they fail to get a minimum number of votes in all areas of the country, thus encouraging them to appeal to all of the various ethnic groupings.

But the Institute's primary interest is in helping members of the public to put their own ideas into action – examples in this volume include the Prison Ashram Trust (to encourage meditation by prisoners), the Pathfinder Clubs for schoolchildren set up by Eileen Chandler of Leicester; the Wildlife Areas around Hospitals initiated by Pat Hartridge of Oxford (and now spreading to a number of hospitals); the agroforestry Forest Garden model demonstrated by Robert Hart in Shropshire (now copied in many other places and described in an Institute booklet); and Guy Yeoman's State Dowry project for Kenya (financial incentives to encourage women to have fewer children, now the subject of a small feasibility study). The 92 award winners in the Institute's competitions find a place in this book, and many of these show signs of progress.

My personal preference is for projects at the neighbourhood level, where there is still a human scale – indeed the Institute shares with the Prince of Wales the aim of helping to restore this sense of scale to our overblown 'giantist' societies, where most problems are insoluble (or at least beyond the reach of 'ordinary' people) until the scale has been reduced. It is anyway more productive concentrating on neighbourhood schemes at this stage, until the Institute gains leverage as it becomes more weighty and established. It is dispiriting work putting pressure on government ministries, which routinely resist new ideas from outside.

One of the greatest pleasures of working with the Institute is watching over the emergence of an international network of social inventors. The Institute itself is part of an educational charity and is backed by Sir Peter Parker, Lord Young of Dartington, Edward de Bono and others. Anita Roddick and her Body Shop colleagues have been especially encouraging with their own ideas and projects and with their help for our competition and for this book. Nor could the Institute have survived without the help of the Joseph Rowntree Charitable Trust and of Nicholas Saunders, who is the founder of most of the businesses in Neal's Yard, Covent Garden. He is one of the Institute's five directors; it also has sixteen consultants and some 500 members and subscribers, 'eyes and ears' around the world. There are now Social Invention centres modelled on ours successfully under way in Russia, Sweden and Germany. Many of the people within this network are natural social inventors, as even casual browsers through this volume will realise, for the same names crop up again and again – Clive Akerman, Fred Allen, Margaret Buckley, Steven Burkeman, Cairns Campbell, David Chapman, Margaret Chisman, Guy Dauncey, Alec Dickson, Robert Hart, Conrad Hopman, Tony Judge, Frances Kendall, Roger Knights, Marilyn Mehlmann, Phyllis O'Rourke, John Papworth, John Seymour, Meredith Thring, Gregory Wright, Michael Young, Valerie Yule and John Zube. These are a few of the great social inventors; to me they are the unsung heroes of our times. Rather than an obsession with one particular scheme, the ideal social inventor has a track record of successful projects, with plenty of ideas for more.

One of the chief theoreticians of social innovations has been George Fairweather. Writing in the early seventies, he argued that not only was our survival on earth threatened as never before, but also that revolution and non-violent protest were unlikely to bring about the social transformations required. In his view, there needed to be organisations that could deal with problems before they became crises, and that could set up, test, compare and evaluate small-scale innovative solutions before applying them more widely:

'What was good enough to create social change in the sixteenth century,' he wrote, 'is not good enough in the late twentieth and twenty-first centuries. It seems inescapable that a mechanism for social change that involves innovation, advocacy and preparing the culture for the future needs to be created so that continuous problem-solving can occur. Experimental social innovation transcends revolution because it creates continous problem-solving social change.' It is as if Fairweather were drawing up a blueprint for our Institute, although we had not in fact heard of his work before our launch.

Anyone who is at all inspired by any of the ideas in this Book of Visions, please join in our adventure – join the Institute as a member (see details below), contribute to the Journal, become a social inventions workshop leader or whatever suits your talents. You will I hope find at least a few ideas in this volume that appeal to you as being not only new and imaginative but also feasible. Anything you can do to help implement them within your profession or sphere of competence, please do. Some of the ideas are evidently not feasible as they stand, but have been included for their provocation value. The trick is not so much to demonstrate your critical faculties by picking holes in the ideas, but, as in brainstorming, more to prove your ingenuity by imagining an improvement or an entirely revamped scheme that would work.

> ## 'The trick is not so much to demonstrate your critical faculties by picking holes in the ideas, but, as in brainstorming, more to prove your ingenuity by imagining an improvement'

A reminder: towards the back, you will find details of next year's competition. There is satisfaction, modest glory and £1,000 to be won, and places to be filled in the next edition of this Encyclopaedia. I feel like a recruiting poster: 'Your Country (whichever country it may be) Needs You and Your Ideas.'

• *'Ideas Into Action' by Clavell Blount, published by The Clair Press, London, 1962. Clavell Blount can be contacted at 36 Station Road, Thames Ditton, Surrey KT7 ONS (tel 081 398 2117).*

• *'Social Inventions' by Stuart Conger, published by Information Canada, Prince Albert, 1974. Stuart Conger can be contacted at 572 Highcroft Avenue, Ottawa, Canada K1Z 5J5 (tel 613 729 4913).*

• *'Social Change: the Challenge to Survival' by George Fairweather, published by General Learning Press, Morristown, N.J. 07960, USA, 1972*

• *Membership of the Institute for Social Inventions, including discounts on books and meetings, a 'Who's Who of Social Inventors' and a journal, costs £15 p.a. (£9 concessionary rate for full-time students, hard-pressed OAPs and UB40 unemployed; £17 by Visa or Mastercard for those outside the UK). Apply to the Institute for Social Inventions, 20 Heber Road, London NW2 6AA (tel 081 208 2853; fax 081 452 6434).*

The history of social inventions

Stuart Conger

The following is extracted from a longer article which first appeared in the Futurist. Conger was responsible for setting up a Canadian Social Inventions Centre called Saskatchewan NewStart. This ran on an experimental basis from 1967 to 1972 and focused on developing new methods of counselling and training adults.

What is a Social Invention?

A social invention is a new law, organisation or procedure that changes the way in which people relate to themselves or to each other, either individually or collectively. Examples of laws that are social inventions include:

1. The Poor Law of 1388, which first gave the poor the right to relief;

2. The Indenture of Children Act of 1601, which spelled out the terms under which children were bound to another person or family;

3. The English Bill of Rights of 1689;

4. The Compulsory School Attendance Act in Prussia in 1717;

5. The Swiss Unemployment Insurance Act of 1789;

6. The laws against cruelty to children that were enacted in the United States after 1875, at which time the New York Society for the Prevention of Cruelty to Animals demonstrated that it was possible to prosecute parents for the abuse of children under laws against cruelty to animals. (We had laws to protect animals before we had them to protect children.)

Social procedures v. social organisations

Social inventions include both organisations and procedures.

A *procedure* is a method that might be used by many organisations in many contexts. For example: examinations, instructional methods, curriculum design, mental tests, guidance, probation, instructional TV, programmed instruction and behaviour modification.

Organisational social inventions are typified by schools, service clubs, Boy Scouts, mental health associations, women's institutes, child guidance clinics, jails, community colleges, the YMCA and churches.

'Once an organisation is invented it seldom concerns itself with inventing new procedural methods for the delivering of its services or objectives'

Once an organisation is invented it seldom concerns itself with inventing new procedural methods for the delivering of its services or objectives. Instead, it becomes consumed with developing methods of self-maintenance and extension. The restriction of employment to teachers in educational institutions, to social workers in welfare agencies, etc, is intended to preserve territorial imperatives and prevents cross breeding of ideas or methods. Thus, the invention of teachers' contracts, teacher training institutions, jurisdictions, etc, becomes the focus for social inventions in organisations. Therefore, most instrumental social inventions can be expected to be made outside the institutions in which they should be utilised. This is why we need social invention centres that are separate from service delivery institutions. It is because of the inherent threat to the latter of a new procedure, however, that they do not advocate such research centres. A very interesting example is the College of Education that conducts research on teaching – even on new methods – but does not implement the new methods in its own institutions. The difficulty of a social institution in adopting new ways does suggest the value of establishing alternative social institutions and removing the monopoly given to most existing social institutions.

'Most instrumental social inventions are made outside the institutions in which they should be utilised'

Examples of *organisations* that were important social inventions would include the following:

- schools in Sumer, 2500 BC;
- law courts in the same country, 2400 BC;
- House of Commons, 1300 AD;
- labour union in England, 1696;
- penitentiaries in Rome, 1700;
- adult schools in Wales, 1754;
- Children's Aid Society in New York, 1853;
- teachers' colleges in New York, 1894;

Procedures that represent social invention would include:

- charity, 2100 BC;
- democracy, 510 BC in Athens;
- municipal system, 100 BC in Rome;
- licensing of teachers, 362 AD;
- training of lawyers, 1292;
- oath to tell the truth in courts, 1327;
- Hansard, 1608;
- formal steps in teaching, 1838;
- probation in Boston, 1841;
- IQ tests in Paris, 1905;
- programmed instruction in US, 1957;
- computer assisted instruction in US, 1960.

A social invention such as the law court, school, municipal government or prison, spawns many ancillary inventions that ultimately create a social system. For instance, the social system developed around the civil law court includes the judge, jury, lawyer, plea, coroner, justice of the peace, code of law and law schools. Each component of the system was itself an invention, but adapted to fit the system.

Each social system comprises a series of social inventions. Some systems, such as education, are relatively developed, while other systems, such as intergroup relations, have so few methods to rely on that the system is more a constellation of problems than a cluster of solutions.

Medicine has developed a system for inventing better methods of curing and preventing disease, and people recognise this when they support medical research. By contrast, education does not have a well-developed system for the invention of new methods of education. Other social systems such as welfare and corrections are very stable as far as their technology is concerned because they have not established research laboratories at all, and hence, improvements in these areas can hardly be expected, except at a very slow rate.

(continued on page 6)

Some examples of social inventions through the ages

Social Invention	When	Where	Who	Why
Book	2800 BC	Egypt	Egyptians	Since papyrus was easier to work with, the 'book' must have been invented in Egypt soon after writing had been introduced.
Taxation	2700 BC	Sumer	King, Temple Officials	Priests let out part of the temple lands to private individuals. This permitted the accumulation of wealth in private hands. As a result both king and priests taxed citizens on all aspects of life and death.
School	2500 BC	Sumer	Priests	First established for purpose of training the scribes required to satisfy the economic and administrative demands of the land, primarily those of the temple and palace. Often attached to temple.
Courts of Law	2400 BC	Sumer	Priests	The law courts were but a department of the divine government and would therefore be directed by the god's servants; and further, since all land in theory, and a vast proportion in fact, belonged to the god, most economic questions would be of direct concern to him and would be regulated by priests.
Mail – letters	2200 BC	Sumer	Ur-Nammu	Letters carried by royal messengers kept the king informed on state matters.
Medical code of ethics	1800 BC	Babylon	Hammurabi	Hammurabi collected all the codes of law in existence and set down one general code, establishing for the first time the concept of the penal and civil responsibility of the physician.
Alphabet	1500 BC	Ugarit – Palestine	Phoenicians – Canaanites	Began as a tool of traders and men of business who were looking for a simpler method of keeping books. Came into general use after priests and merchants agreed on the sound associated with each character.
Coinage	700 BC	Asia Minor	Lydians	The need for pieces of metal of a fixed shape and standard weight stamped and guaranteed by the state as to both quality and weight for use in trade brought on invention of coinage.

'Origins of mail service: Letters carried by royal messengers kept the king informed on state matters'

More examples of social inventions through the ages

Social Invention	When	Where	Who	Why
Hospital	600 BC	Epidaurus Greece	Priests	The temple at Epidaurus was one of the first to be built, dedicated to the Greek healing god Asclepius. A hostel was attached to this temple where sick people could come and be treated by the priests.
Museum	629 BC	Athens	Athenians	Originally a place connected with the muses or the arts inspired by them.
Democracy	510 BC	Athens	Cleisthenes	After gaining back control of Athens, Cleisthenes instituted sweeping constitutional changes.
Political Party	1641 AD	England		The abolition of episcopacy was proposed to parliament and two parties stood opposed to one another in the House of Commons, not merely on some incidental question, but on a great principle of action which constituted a permanent bond between those who took one side or the other.
Labour trade union	1699 AD	England Newcastle	Keelmen: Lighter men, coal industry	Workmen began to combine for purposes of mutual insurance against sickness, old age or death.
Employment agencies	1891 AD	New Zealand	Government	The New Zealand Government established exchanges as long ago as 1891. The municipal and state systems of Germany, established before the turn of the century, served as a model for the British agencies.
Group therapy	1905 AD		Joseph Pratt	Though foreshadowed as early as 1905 by Joseph J. Pratt's group treatment of tuberculosis patients, group therapy was forced on psychiatrists by the large numbers of World War II soldiers needing treatment. The use of group methods proved so effective that they then developed rapidly.
Psychodrama	1918–23 AD	Germany	Moreno	In this method, patients more or less spontaneously dramatise their problem before an audience of fellow patients and therapists, some of whom also participate in the dramatic production itself. The dramatisation is followed by discussion with the audience.

'A hostel was attached to this temple where sick people could come and be treated by the priests'

(Continued from page 3)

Some of our social problems in Canada do not even have a system of social technologies to provide relief and hence we can anticipate continued frustration with little hope of improvement. A critical example is the burgeoning problem of racial and lingustic discord in Canada. The social technology for dealing with this problem does not exist and no real efforts are being made to develop it. Among the needed approaches are vastly improved methods of (1) teaching languages, (2) overcoming prejudice, (3) creating and sustaining dialogue, and (4) fostering equality between groups. The present methods that are available are so crude that while they may be used to force progress in one area, they create backlash in another. For instance, efforts to make more people bilingual apparently increase prejudice, and, therefore, our programmes in the entire area of racial and linguistic reconciliation amount to a zero sum game. The elements or components of the system act to maintain the set status quo rather than to encourage progress.

Our present systems of law, education, welfare and municipal government can be directly traced back two, three, four or five thousand years, and changes over the years have modified the system, but not created entirely new systems. Furthermore, social systems as a rule operate as monopolies which, of course, tend to be less susceptible to change or replacement. The citizen cannot choose whether to attend a school, jail, court or welfare agency.

Slow adoption

If you consider transportation, you find the citizen has several separate choices of systems that he can select, e.g. bus, train, car, snowmobile and motorcycle. Each is separately owned and operated, or manufactured and sold, thus giving the citizen real choice. A prime invention spawned each system: the car, for instance, prompted the invention of motels, credit cards, paved highways, service stations, drive-ins, driver training schools, traffic police, parking meters, shopping centres and automobile associations.

'It takes about 50 years for a new educational invention to come into use in half the schools'

When we look at education today we see signs of people chafing at the monopolistic education system which includes schools, universities, colleges of education, departments of education and teachers' unions. These act as a constellation interacting in mutual maintenance and stability. Studies have shown that it takes about 50 years for a new educational invention to come into use in half the schools. Other social institutions take just as long to adopt new improved methods.

Because of the monopolistic nature of our social institutions and systems, and their difficulty in adapting to new circumstances or achieving a significant measure of self-renewal, it may be as necessary to invent new social institutions as to invent new laws or procedures.

At the same time, however, our social problems are growing in severity and people are no longer docile about being in jail, unemployed, poor and discriminated against, and they are using television, strikes, boycotts, demonstrations and even violence to draw attention to their problems.

Agencies cannot adapt

Present organisations that are almost overwhelmed by the sheer demand to provide services on a minimum budget cannot be expected to invent new methods. Sometimes such agencies are not able to adapt sufficiently to accept new social inventions. A similar situation would have been to expect railways to invent a better alternative means of transportation. They were not even prepared to adopt the car when it was invented. We would still be in the railway age, and the car would still be an awkward means of transportation, if the automobile had been given to the railways to develop.

Yet, this is precisely what is done with our social problems and innovations. If a new educational method, such as programmed learning, is invented, which does not require a stand-up teacher, it is assigned to stand-up teachers to try it out, and naturally, they find it is not very good.

'Better methods of penal reform will be devised only by people who have no direct or indirect interest in maintaining the present system'

For the same reasons, there has been little progress in the reformation of criminals since Pope Clement invented penitentiaries in 1700. Research and innovation in prisons has been assigned to prison officials, and they are no more likely to develop a new method than the railways were to have invented the car. Better methods of penal reform will be devised only by people who have no direct or indirect interest in maintaining the present system.

Need new 'improved' product

It is a fact of commercial life that it is necessary to come up with a 'new improved' product each year. Sometimes an innovation is an improvement of substance, sometimes of style. Sometimes the improvement represents a new generation of the product, and sometimes it fails abysmally. The Ford Motor Company devoted huge amounts of technical and consumer research to design the Edsel, but the car was not popular with the public. As a company, Ford was able to discontinue the Edsel, but if the Edsel had been developed by a governmental agency, it would still be in production and would be given to under-developed countries as foreign aid or as a bonus for buying our wheat.

When the Edsel failed, Ford did not give up its consumer and technical research, but used them to develop other cars such as the Thunderbird and Mustang, which proved successful.

We must do the same with our social programmes. We must see them as stages in the evolution of truly valuable and important social technologies.

One of the problems that we face in stimulating social inventions is the general lack of a recognition that they are necessary. People recognise that cancer can be cured only by medical research, but they do not yet realise that intergroup relations can be resolved through inventing better social methods, and the thing that really is needed is a number of social invention centres to invent these better methods on a continuous basis.

People enjoy being 'guinea pigs'

Some people believe that it is wrong to experiment with human beings. They argue that a researcher who uses people for his own purposes denies them freedom, dignity and self-direction and is probably tricking them into believing or doing certain things that are contrary to their nature or integrity.

> **'It is a fact of commercial life that it is necessary to come up with a "new improved" product each year. We must do the same with our social programmes'**

There is a popular notion that people do not want to be treated as 'guinea pigs', but the notion is wrong. People enjoy the special attention that they get when they are the subjects in an experiment. People want to be treated as individual human beings. Workers on the assembly line do not receive this treatment. Typists in a clerical pool seldom get it. A child in a class of 40 students does not get it. But subjects in social experiments do get the special attention of someone (the researcher), who pays special attention to them and is genuinely interested in their reactions. Indeed, the good feeling that the experimenter creates in his human guinea pigs, because he is really interested in them, has been known to ruin some experiments.

Experimenting with people means that you assess them at some point in time, try a new programme with some, and an old programme with others, then you assess the subjects again to see if those who followed the new programme are any better off than those who took part in the old. Technically, you are not experimenting with people but with programmes, because if you find that the people are no better off for participating in the new programme, you fault the programme and say we have to develop a better programme.

We can be assured that people do not mind being subjects in human experiments. They will give their cooperation in the project for the privilege of being treated as human beings.

Saskatchewan NewStart has experimented with up to 110 people in its laboratory at one time. Our programme has traded two things for the cooperation of these adults: (a) a commitment to help them meet their objectives in further education and (2) some greater attention to them as people.

At the present time we in Canada are doing little to invent better methods of reducing poverty and other social ills. These age-old problems are getting more serious and there is an immediate need for new methods of resolving social problems. The methods can only be invented by a process of action research which conceives, conducts and evaluates new approaches in real-life situations, in other words, social invention centres.

The methods that are used today to solve social problems are about 4,000 years old, whereas the methods used to solve medical, agricultural, transportation and industrial problems are about 25 years old. If we can establish social invention centres, we can create solutions to our age-old social problems, and can rid society of racial strife, mental illness, crime and poverty. This is a goal worth working for.

Stuart Conger, 572 Highcroft Avenue, Ottawa, Canada K1Z 5J5 (tel 613 729 4913).

Who are the social inventors?

Alec Dickson

Extracted from a speech made by Alec Dickson, founder of CSV and VSO, when presenting the 1988 Social Inventions Awards.

Who are social inventors, where are the Red Adairs who respond to human needs?

In my lifetime I think of Frank Laubach, the missionary working amongst the Moro people in the Philippines who devised the 'Each One Teach One' approach as a simple way by which the barely literate might help others to learn to read.

I think of Chad Varah, founder of the Samaritans, perceiving how the telephone could be a lifeline for those on the brink of suicide.

I salute those who pioneered the kibbutz movement as a new approach to family living – and those in Toronto today who have made some involvement in community service a precondition for Barmitzvah, just as elsewhere in North America the Mormons require their young people to engage in service to others as part of the process of being accepted as adults.

I honour Cecily Saunders and others in the Hospice movement who have shown how to bring dignity to the dying and relief from suffering.

I pay tribute to Lisa and Curtis Sliwa who have mobilised the Guardian Angels, initially among young Hispanics in New York, to combat mugging on the subway at night – and who are now reaching out to contend with prostitution and drug addiction.

I greet erstwhile colleagues in CSV who convinced the Home Office of the capacity of Borstal boys, of young prisoners and even children-in-care to help others (and themselves) as volunteers – demonstrating that you do not have to be good to do good.

I congratulate those who have discovered that the appointment of carefully chosen equivalents of a concierge to apartment blocks can reduce vandalism and promote neighbourliness.

I express gratitude to the nurses in one hospital who will not let patients be wheeled away to the operating theatre until they have grasped what it is intended shall happen to them – a compassionate insistence on the patient's right to know.

I think of Molly Barrett at Walkden School getting her pupils to devise an alarm clock for the deaf; Professor Thring at Queen Mary College challenging engineering students to design a wheelchair capable of climbing stairs; and Sinclair Goodlad at Imperial College inspiring internationally able students to tutor slow-learning pupils of maths in Pimlico and Stockwell – all demonstrating what can be achieved through the humane application of knowledge, in a partnership of service and learning.

These are some of the 'models' which come to my mind. But there are other yardsticks by which we can value the role of social inventors. The Institute believes that in most of us there lies a capacity for social invention. This can be nurtured by discovering what others are creating, by brainstorming, by exercising the imagination and opening the mind's eye, as Margaret Chisman has shown us how to do.

Alec Dickson, 19 Blenheim Road, London W4 IVB (tel 081 994 7437). 'Exercising the Imagination' and 'Opening the

Mind's Eye' are both booklets by Margaret Chisman, available from the Institute for Social Inventions, 20 Heber Road, London NW2 6AA (tel 081 208 2853; fax 081 452 6434).

A lifetime's work

Michael Young

The following self-portrait of a social inventor – the Institute for Social Inventions' honorary fellow, Lord Young of Dartington – is adapted from the epilogue to a compendium of Young's writings entitled 'The Social Scientist as Innovator' (published by Abt Books, 55 Wheeler Street, Cambridge, MA 02138, USA, 1983).

Throughout my life, my work and writing have reflected an interest in the future, that is, in the changing anticipations at different points in the century. They also express two dominant moods. The first is radical, restless and optimistic. For the six years from 1945 to 1951, I was the head of the Labour Party's Research Department and involved in policy making for the most radical democratic government of the century. The Manifesto for the 1945 Election, which I helped to write, was called 'Let Us Face The Future.' It reads now very much as a period piece, and of course it is; but it worked – the entire programme was put into action – and the experience gave me a taste both for conjecture and acting on it. Our particular brave new world of those years was no dystopia. A better future for Britain was in the offing, and likewise for the British territories in the Indian, Asian and African continents which the Labour Government propelled towards independence.

My Labour Party pamphlet, 'Small Man, Big World', belonged to that period. I thought that big government, like big business or big unionism, was a threat to democracy, since democracy could flourish best in small groups built to the scale of the individual. But I still had faith that one only had to hammer away at such obvious truths and in the end governments would have to give way, that is, give away some of their power.

'The Association's journal, Which?, has become a somewhat farouche national institution'

The faith did not seem outlandish at the time. The government to which I was appealing from the party office *was* effective. Even so, it lost its momentum and was defeated at the General Election of 1951. It was succeeded by a long, drawn-out yawn. But I believed (and still do believe) that reform is both needed and possible, with the impetus coming not so much from within political parties as from without. This happened with the Consumers' Association. I wanted to copy the Consumers Union of U.S.A but to make the copy a good deal more lively than the original – which I think it has been so far. The Association's journal, 'Which?', has become a somewhat farouche national institution. I put the proposal that such a consumer body should be established into Labour's Manifesto for the 1950 Election, and, luckily, nothing was done to implement it, leaving the way open for a private initiative. The success of the Consumers' Association has in its turn led to many new Acts of Parliament intended to protect consumers and to the naming of Ministers for Consumer Affairs in both Labour and Conservative governments. It has become one of a number of non-party pressure groups dedicated to reform.

I formed another, to get the Open University set up – this was unfortunately too expensive for anyone except the government to finance – so we campaigned for the government to do just that, which eventually it did. I was prompted to push for it partly by the satire, intended to be deadly serious as well as funny, embodied in my book, 'The Rise of the Meritocracy.' The meritocratic elite of the future was to be open only to those who could as children sail through one examination after another. The Open University was, and is, to be open to anyone, with or without qualification.

These two campaigns have been successful. Not so one launched, as a follow-up to the Open University, by the International Extension College. Under its aegis a small chain of new colleges has been started in Africa, consultancy work done in dozens of Third World countries, and a World Refugee College established in 1980 as an offshoot. But the goal was perhaps too ambitious. It was to create as an alternative to orthodox schools a dense network of 'radio colleges' which would be open to anyone and which would also not be exam-ridden. The people to benefit would be the hundreds of millions of children and adults, who, as things are, get no schooling at all. But how can they be organised? If there is a way we have not found it yet.

Single-issue politics cannot, however, ever oust ordinary humdrum politics. I have never completely abandoned my hopes for the latter, and, whether with hopes or without them, the state of political life of any nation must never be neglected. This was without any longer expecting any worthwhile general reforms to come from either of the established parties. A new progressive party was different. I put in a plea for one in 1960 and helped to found one in 1981: the Social Democratic Party. Less institutionalised than the old parties, with roots not going so deep in history, the new party was intended to be more receptive to new thinking.

My other mood is less aerated, less optimistic, more concerned with the prevention of further decline than with the achievement of further progress. The purpose is conservation. This mood was first struck in my books on the family. 'Family and Kinship in East London' was about the threat posed by 'progress' to extended families which, until they became the victims of housing policies, had proved their resilience, as I hope they will again. The immediate family has also been under threat, and, if it were not able to resist, the whole of our marvellous civilisation would crumble within a generation or two. Nothing is more important than the conservation of the family and what remains of active community life. The broader conservationist or ecological movement needs to encompass them both.

'I am left mainly with a sense of wonder'

It is always difficult to remember what the future seemed to hold at any moment in the past. But futuristic memories are one of the keys to the understanding of any age. Looking back through the marches of the century to what I thought would happen, what I hoped would happen, and what did happen, I am left mainly with a sense of wonder. It has been as marvellously true of our age as of any other, that, in Blake's words: 'Eternity is in love with the productions of time.'

Chapter two

CHILDREN AND EDUCATION

Chanting in pregnancy and childbirth

Frederick Leboyer, author of 'Birth Without Violence' which saw childbirth for the first time through the eyes of the newborn, is attempting to launch a second revolution in the way childbirth is envisaged – this time by encouraging the mother to take up Indian chanting and thus to transform pregnancy and childbirth into a spiritual experience.

In essence, Leboyer is suggesting that the mother breathe in deeply and slowly from the belly, chanting a loud pure sound on the outbreath and with the contraction; and then waiting at the end of the outbreath for the contraction to be over, before breathing in again. Leboyer learned the chanting from the Indian teacher, Savitry Nayr.

Nicholas Albery interviewed Leboyer about this new approach:

Albery: Is there any culture or society on earth that you know of where chanting has been used by the mothers in pregnancy or birth?

'This new connection of pure sound with birth is opening the gate for women into a totally unknown experience'

Leboyer: No. This new connection of pure sound with birth is opening the gate for women into a totally unknown experience.

When a woman is giving birth she is reborn herself. She goes back to her own birth and can go beyond herself. Her little self merges with the real self, the totality, the one and all. Going through this frightening experience, she comes to the limitations of the small 'I', the ego collapses. She's both herself and the totality.

Albery: Are there signs that the unborn child in pregnancy appreciates the chanting of the mother?

Leboyer: Yes. Very often when the woman has a restless child in the womb, it signifies that the child is unhappy. With the chanting, the mother knows, 'My child is different now.' She knows because the child moves around less.

Albery: Can you imagine groups of pregnant women getting together to practise chanting?

Leboyer: No. It needs to be a one to one relationship, almost like psychoanalysis, it is so intimate.

Some women believe you can take six quick lessons before birth, like before taking a car for a drive. But there are things which cannot be taught. All inner experiences are a matter of getting attuned. Little by little you awaken. The disciple is trying to understand, and reading about it may say 'Ah yes', but the teaching can only be the confirmation of personal understanding, it has only this value.

Albery: Does it need to be the specific type of Indian chanting you are describing?

Leboyer: Some people say, 'It is very nice to have music in labour, what would you like, Vivaldi or what?' But listening to pure sound is different, a perfect sound includes all its harmonies, it is all sounds put together, just as the rainbow includes all colours. With pure sound you can touch absolute perfection. You need to let the sounds open and awaken within yourself. If women can connect with this level of themselves, the experience of childbirth has another dimension.

'This kind of childbirth cannot happen in hospitals. It is only for a few. The doctor stops the woman from going on her journey'

This kind of childbirth cannot happen in hospitals. It is only for a few. The doctor stops the woman from going on her journey. He is so afraid. I would never advise women to have a home birth. That is not my business. However, if the woman says, 'This is what I want,' I would encourage her. There is no right way of giving birth. Everything is itself.

Birth is not something sweet. It is the most intense experience a person can go through. But as long as you fight it, you're finished. Just as the mystics tell of the joy of getting drunkenly flooded with excessive energy, so for the woman it is possible to go through the storm of labour like this, instead of containing the contractions or bearing the pains.

In childbirth, breath is the ultimate. The breathing and contraction get completely attuned. It is a matter of becoming aware that breath and contraction are one and the same movement, in time with the cosmic breath, the breath of the universe. The breath is breathing you, it is a holographic concept of one in the whole, each part a reproduction of the whole.

And during the months of pregnancy, the woman who is so-called 'expecting' is not expecting any more. She is beyond time. It is a state of grace. There is a field energy around the body. But once pregnancy is institutionalised, the magic is gone, it becomes like a supermarket. It is no longer sacred.

Frederick Leboyer, 8 Warner House, Priory Walk, London SW10 9RE (tel 071 373 1695). See 'The Art of Breathing' by Leboyer, published by Element Books, 1986. Leboyer also has a film on this subject, entitled 'The Rite of Birth.'

Prenatal University

Extracted from the American 'Brain/Mind Bulletin.'

A team of medical practitioners in Northern California has formed a 'prenatal university' – a systematised programme of prenatal stimulation for parents. Manuals and cassette tapes suggest techniques for interaction with a foetus.

In a follow-up study of 500 babies born after the programme, the researchers found enhanced physical and mental development, including easy birth, early speech, physical agility and healthy parent-child bonding.

Prenatal University, 27225 Calaroga Avenue, Hayward, California 94545, USA.

Dolphin midwives

Extracted from a piece by Vicki Mackenzie in the Daily Telegraph.

Igor Charkovsky, the Russian male midwife, is known for helping pregnant women give birth underwater in the Black Sea 'aided' by dolphins. 'Dolphins have an affinity with the baby in the womb and are automatically attracted to pregnant women. They sense when a woman is about to give birth and gather round. They give both the mother and child a sense of protection and safety,' says Charkovsky.

> ## 'Dolphins sense when a woman is about to give birth and gather round. They give both the mother and child a sense of protection and safety'

'Sometimes when the baby is born the dolphins muzzle it to the surface to help it breath.'

Charkovsky began to experiment with dolphins and children in 1979 at a dolphin research station. He discovered that 9ft mammals were exceptionally gentle with the children, aged between eight days and eight years, allowing them to ride on their backs, and handling them with extraordinary care, understanding and purposefulness.

More specifically he realised how powerfully beneficial the animals were for the newborn, who lay peacefully sleeping in the sea with the dolphins swimming around them. He concluded that dolphins through their benign energy take the stress off the baby and mother alike, during and after the birth.

Igor Charkovsky, 127254 Moscow, Rustaveli 15a, Kv61, CIS (tel 7095 219 5937). See also 'Dolphin Therapy' in this book, in the chapter on 'Death and Dying.'

Planning for small children

With her colleagues, Julia Jaspert produced 'Under Threes Welcome', a free guide for parents of young children in Camden, which is in its sixth edition (and has now been imitated in some two hundred other areas of the UK). Jaspert introduced the concept to restaurants and shops, awarding them a sticker through a 'We Welcome Small Children' campaign. She writes:

'Next we thought that too many shops, restaurants and public places forget the architectural side of providing access to parents with small children. The result was another book: *Thinking of Small Children, Access, Provision and Play*, funded by Camden Council, but aided by our voluntary efforts.'

> ## 'Too many shops, restaurants and public places forget the architectural side of providing access to parents with small children'

In an ideal world, the needs of young children would be considered in all new developments. This book is aimed at planners, architects and other professionals, and is full of advice, some of which would not be obvious to the non-parent. For instance, 'at present it is difficult to find small lifts, eight persons or less, with 900mm openings,' big enough to allow access to double pushchairs. Lift manufacturers please note. Some of the advice would not be expensive to follow, as in the section on cafes and restaurants:

The following would be helpful:
* A willingness to heat baby milk/food.
* Child portions or a spare plate to enable children who eat very little to share the adult's food.
* Children's plastic cutlery set and beaker or plastic mug.
* Plenty of napkins/paper tissues or even sachets of cleansing wipes.
* A few 'quiet' toys or games.

One well-known method they advocate, which should be universally applied in waiting rooms in hospitals and GPs' surgeries and elsewhere, is that of numbered tickets to be given out to people as they arrive, and the current number displayed, so that you can form an idea of how long you have to wait, and whether you can take your children outside for a while.

* *Julia Jaspert, We Welcome Small Children Campaign, 93 Belsize Lane, London NW3 5AY (tel 071 586 3453; fax 071 586 4622).*
* *'Under Threes Welcome' can be obtained by mail for £1 (p&p) or free by asking any Camden Children's Books Librarian.*

A directory of mothers' rooms

Susan Townend had great difficulty finding quiet and private places to breastfeed her baby when on holiday. Most stores or shops had no facilities for nursing mothers or for parents to change their babies. She was sometimes reduced to feeding her baby whilst sitting on toilets. She also knew mothers who were changing to bottle-feeding so that they could travel and shop more conveniently.

Townend was incensed by this lack of concern for parents, and on her return from holiday, she researched, compiled and published a directory of public places in the UK with 'mothers' rooms.' She was also instrumental in persuading Mothercare to open such rooms in over fifty of their larger stores.

Susan Townend, The Garden House, Back Lane, Allerthrope, York, YO4 4RP (tel 0759 304804). Townend's directory is available from her for £2.

Together time

Nicholas Albery

Here are three ideas for which my son, when younger, was either the guinea pig or the inspiration.

I used to give my son (from about the age of five onwards) a two hour period each week of 'together time' in which I let him take any initiatives for action. The rules we agreed were that during this period he initiated conversation or suggested activities, and I followed, paying him as near 100% attention as I could. I could only refuse to do something if it went strongly against my moral code, or if it involved going shopping, and we had to remain within reasonable 'playing distance' of each other. It is a way for a child to imagine and pre-plan what he or she wants to do at a particular time in the future; to become inventive and to develop personality, and to have more of a feeling of autonomy.

> 'It is a way for a child to pre-plan what he or she wants to do, to become inventive and to develop personality, and to have more of a feeling of autonomy'

Other parents tend to comment that they do something like this anyway most of the time. But I think that there is a crucial difference between giving a child *all* of one's attention rather than *some* of it, and between a period a child can plan for and one that is uncertain.

I got the idea from the American humanistic psychotherapist Alvin Mahrer, who calls it 'Effectance Training' and suggests a half hour period every day, starting in a modified form with the young baby. Mahrer believes that it is vital that children dismantle the parental 'primitive field' which has encompassed them and largely operated their surface personality in the early years. Maintaining the primitive personality undissolved into adulthood is 'the ultimate cause of problems, of psychopathologies, of painful behaviour.' Mahrer argues that the principal route to worthwhile social change lies through such Effectance Training.

> 'Maintaining the primitive personality undissolved into adulthood is the ultimate cause of problems, of psychopathologies, of painful behaviour'

See 'Experiencing, a Humanistic Theory of Psychology and Psychiatry' by Alvin Mahrer (published by Brunnel/Mazel, New York, 1978, pages 627 ff).

Kids' ratings for films

I suggest that all film review editors send some young people along to U, PG, 12 and 15 category movies (how young would depend on the movie) and that they get the young people to give a rating out of 10 for how enjoyable the film was, plus a few words of comments – some of these comments and a numerical 'Rating by the Kids' could then be tagged on to the end of adult reviewers' comments. The films that reviewers hated seemed to be the ones that my son enjoyed most.

Combatting TV tyranny

One experiment to discourage my son from spending too much of his summer holidays consuming endless TV was to insist that for every programme he watched, he had to write in his diary a minimum 40 word review, saying what he liked and did not like about the programme, with a small drawing to go with it. This was not enough of a deterrent to stop him watching a programme he really wanted to watch, but it did make him think twice about just switching on at random. But the main improvement was that it cured me of minding him watching TV, since I knew that now it was helping him to develop his critical faculties, rather than stupefying him.

Nicholas Albery, 20 Heber Road, London NW2 6AA (tel 081 208 2853; fax 081 452 6434).

Magic Circle to enhance children's self-esteem

Murray White

These extracts are taken from an article by Murray White in the Times Educational Supplement. When it was written he was headmaster of Kings Hedges Junior School, Cambridge. He now runs Esteem Workshops, introducing these techniques in schools all over the UK. He is also the British representative on the International Council for Self Esteem.

Research has shown a strong link between a child's self-esteem and his or her academic success; children who feel good about themselves learn more easily and retain information longer. In fact, they do better in every way: if they have a sense of well-being they are much more likely to be able to handle the ups and downs of daily life, including prejudice, abuse, addiction, delinquency and violence.

With this in mind I instituted Circletime for every class in this junior school in 1988. Previous to this, for several years I had been taking classes and groups and spending time discussing behaviour, exploring feelings and playing games, with pleasing results. Staff had commented on the changes the activities had brought about in the children, both individually and collectively. One said, 'My class doesn't like playing yours (addressed to the class teacher) at rounders. They always win. Your class seem to be able to work together so much better.'

I ask all the teachers to begin Circletime each day with the class sitting on the floor in a circle. If possible the teacher will be sitting first, waiting for the circle to form and able to greet each child individually on arrival. Before the register, the day begins with a round. The teacher says an incomplete sentence, gives an example to finish it off, then the child next to her repeats the phrase and puts his or her own ending on it, and so on. It has several purposes. It is a re-establishment of the group, an important joining together into a class. Children can 'pass' if they wish, but few do.

'The teacher says an incomplete sentence, gives an example to finish it off, then the child next to her repeats the phrase and puts his or her own ending on it'

Even in a large class the level of listening to others is clearly high. Some enjoy the chance to be really imaginative and direct in their answers. Many quickly recognise it as a safe environment where they can really say what they are thinking. 'Today I'm feeling ... nervous' said a seven year old, two weeks into term. 'I wish I was with ... my father, if I knew where he was,' admitted a shy 11 year old girl. Sensitive teachers will hear these and respond appropriately later.

Our rounds are about all sorts of things. 'What makes me laugh is ...' Even a round where a child chooses a fruit she would like to be, often reveals much. For the children, self-disclosure in these rounds by the teacher is valuable too. Rounds also help the retiring child to feel included. At the beginning of the term lots of activities are centred on getting to know each other and on the creation of a close warm class identity.

After registration and the opportunity to share with everyone anything that has happened during the time children have been apart, comes the selection of the Special Child for the day. This is universally popular with the children and I would guess for many of them is an unusual experience.

Selection was first made by balloon popping. Balloons were blown up, each child put her name on paper inside one, and they were hung from the ceiling. Each day one balloon was popped and whoever's name appeared was 'Child' for the day. After every child had had a turn another method – riddles – was used, so that each had two special days in the term. Its importance in the children's lives was evident. On the second time round, one nine year old boy said 'It's Wednesday today and it was Wednesday last time I was chosen.' Others chimed in to remember the days of the week when it was their turn.

'The Special Child will be asked to leave the room while a discussion takes place about all the nice things that can be said about her'

There is considerable opportunity for variation of the procedure but the principles of specialness are clear. First the child is presented (often by yesterday's holder) with a badge. In our case it was made of cardboard on string, but on one side it says 'I am Special' and on the other side 'I'm great' or something similar. Then she will be asked to leave the room while a discussion takes place about all the nice things that can be said about her (it is a real delight to me to see smiling children outside doors waiting to be called back) or alternatively she would immediately begin to ask children who volunteered by raising hands to make their comments.

There are always plenty of contributions and the vast majority are genuine. The children receive them with quiet

pleasure. Some make real discoveries. One 11 year old boy was told by others that they admired his ability to deal calmly with other pupils' aggression. The next day the group was discussing 'feeling' words and he suggested 'surprised.' When asked to elaborate he said he had been surprised to find out how much he was liked. He appears to have gained a lot of confidence and joins in discussions much more freely.

Faced with a barrage of compliments it can be difficult to remember or even believe them. It is important to get the children to preface their remarks with phrases like 'I think you ...' or 'I believe that you ...' In this way the recipient accepts it as an opinion and cannot contradict it. Teachers record the comments while they are being said and the sheet is presented to the child.

Also, the child is asked to tell the class which comments mean most to them. 'You are nice to be with' is always a favourite. This part of the ceremony ends with the child being asked to name and tell us one thing about herself of which she is pleased, perhaps proud. It often causes difficulty and here we see the measure of low self-esteem. I shall always remember the capable 11 year old girl who eventually said in a low voice 'I am good at maths' and then in a whisper added 'sometimes.'

Part of the fun of Circletime is that the Special Child is asked if he or she wants to be called by another name for the day. Nicknames used among friends become universally accepted and other children take bigger risks and choose their popular heroes and heroines. Special children are also given, or can claim, other privileges. One very popular one is to elect to sit on a chair in front of assembly; this means the whole school will acknowledge that they are special. The Special Child also chooses the game for the day. A repertoire of games has been built up and incorporated in Circletime. These again have many purposes. One is to act as 'energy raisers.' They are useful at other times as well.

There are three rules in Circletime: only one person speaks at a time; everyone can have fun; no one is to spoil anyone else's fun. It is a time when the children find out a bit more about themselves and what they are capable of and how they relate to each other. There are lots of serious, lively discussions where feelings are discovered, explored and accepted. The children come to realise that if they understand themselves it will help them better to understand others. The value of co-operation and friendship is examined and emphasised using practical exercises.

At least twice a week in Circletime each class splits into groups of three. This is the children's opportunity to talk and be listened to, where they will get close attention from peers to form and exchange ideas and opinions which are then brought back to the big group for an airing.

Of course, arguments, quarrels and other unpleasant situations still abound in school as children follow their old patterns of behaviour in getting their needs met, but there is a growing awareness that there are alternatives. I believe children flourish when in an environment structured by definite controlled limits, but within these they must be encouraged to become responsible for their own decisions and helped to achieve autonomy. Self-esteem develops when children have a basis for evaluating present performance and making comparisons with earlier behaviour and attitudes.

Various sanctions and punishments are used but it is important that these do not harm the child's self-concept. It is essential to differentiate between the doer and the deed. 'I like you but cannot accept your behaviour.'

Recently, two 11 year old boys, not generally known for their community spirit or for their need to tell me anything, told me quite casually in their classroom how they had approached two younger boys in the playground who they knew were frightened of them and said 'OK, we'll be your friends.' Another boy with a reputation for aggression had gone out of his way to make friends with a first year child.

Towards the end of term the emphasis switched to goal-setting and achieving targets. Children were asked to think of small specific targets – things which they thought desirable for them to do or to learn to do, either at home or school – or to keep a daily record. By encouragement from everyone and the use of simple will exercises, the children were helped to realise how they can achieve their potential.

Visitors to Circletime have been numerous and, sitting on the floor in the circle, are readily accepted by the children. Also the children were happy for a video to be made of parts of it, sponsored by the Artemis Trust.

Other activities included taking photographs of every child and displaying them in the entrance hall for all to admire and the making of booklets called 'All About Me.' They have all been aimed at enhancing self-esteem.

The importance of self-esteem is stated very eloquently by Dorothy Corkille Briggs in her book 'Your Child's Self-Esteem' (Doubleday 1970):

'A person's judgement of self influences the kinds of friends he chooses, how he gets along with others, the kind of person he marries, and how productive he will be. It affects his creativity, integrity, stability and even whether he will be a leader or a follower. His feeling of self-worth forms the core of his personality and determines the use he makes of his aptitudes and abilities. His attitude toward himself has a direct bearing on how he lives all parts of his life. In fact, self-esteem is the mainspring that slates each of us for success or failure as a human being.'

> 'A person's judgement of self influences the kinds of friends he chooses, how he gets along with others, the kind of person he marries, and how productive he will be'

'Magic Circles – the Benefits of Circle Time', an account of the enthusiastic reaction of children and teachers who have taken part in this project, and details of workshops and publications describing the procedure are available from: Murray White, 5 Ferry Path, Cambridge, CB4 1HB (tel and fax 0223 65351).

A cassette for uncomfortable feelings

Phyllis Peterson of Illinois has made a sensitive and enjoyable cassette story called 'Louis, the Giant, Invisible Turtle', aimed at helping children aged 7 to 14 to handle difficult and uncomfortable feelings. Louis Timothy is a turtle suffering from giantism – 'angry feelings stuffing him to the point of explosion,' and he has become invisible because he is 'afraid to show people what he thinks and feels.' A stork doctor shows him how to share his sad or bad feelings, how to be angry with what others have done to him without hating these others themselves; and helps Louis Timothy to 'share who he really is, to be real and to feel.'

> 'Louis Timothy is a turtle suffering from giantism – angry feelings stuffing him to the point of explosion, and he is afraid to show people what he thinks and feels'

Peterson believes that many parents teach their boys particularly to 'stuff their feelings', with messages such as 'be a big boy,' 'don't cry' or 'don't be afraid.' This cassette helps counteract such messages. The voices of the turtle and the doctor have a fine humorous edge to them, and the cassette holds the listener's attention.

Peterson writes: 'This story is my gift to the world and any one who wants to help distribute it can buy their own 90 minute blank audio cassette tape and send it with three International Reply Coupons from the post office (or two dollars in cash notes) to cover postage, and a self-addressed envelope; my colleague Ken Heral will send out a copy, which can be copied in its turn.

'I have started a campaign to have people copy it and donate it to schools, churches, support groups, programmes for runaway children, groups that work with prostitutes, social service agencies, drug addiction support groups and others. It is currently being used by Wisconsin Committee for the Prevention of Child Abuse, the Greater Milwaukee Parents Anonymous, Martin House in Rockford, Illinois and Parents Anonymous of Pennsylvania.'

Phyllis Peterson and Ken Heral, 2308 Maple Avenue, Loves Park, Illinois 61111, USA (tel 815 633 0492 h; 608 365 6641 w). This scheme was highly commended in the 1989 Social Inventions Awards.

Co-parents

Angela Murphy

From a letter to the Independent.

My husband and I want a number of close friends to take a long term interest in our child – in other words, to take on all the responsibilities of a godparent, except for religious education.

> 'The tradition of asking close friends or family to take a special interest in children goes back to the fourth century'

Our choice of a name for our son's 'sponsors' was the term 'co-parent.' It seems to contain the right degree of warmth, and also has a historical precedent. The tradition of asking close friends or family to take a special interest in children goes back to the fourth century, and the terms 'commater' and 'compater' (they also carried the meaning of 'intimate friend') first occurred at the end of the sixth century.

Christenings and spiritual kinship were primarily seen as a means of extending and intensifying natural kinship relations in an uncertain world when wider social and family ties were threatened. The religious education of the child was, in those days, its least significant aspect.

Parents would choose people with whom they wished to create a formal state of friendship (just as in rites of blood-brotherhood). Now that the extended family is stretched and scattered, it is even more important to confirm the bonds of friendship. We believe that our celebration has helped us to do this.

Angela Murphy, 21 Leamington Road Villas, London W11 1HS (tel 071 727 4920).

Comment by Valerie Yule

An extension of this idea would be 'community godparents' for local children who have no relatives beyond parents.

Through any agency or family in the local community, parents can ask someone or two people to act as 'community godparents.' Some ritual celebration can be made of this, for example, with a small party, or even a religious blessing.

Such unofficial relatives could be a blessing to single parents and their children.

Valerie Yule, 57 Waimarie Drive, Mount Waverley, Victoria, Australia 3149 (tel 807 4315).

The British Organisation of Non-Parents

The British Organisation of Non-Parents (BON) wants to:
• Eliminate the cultural and media bias against non-parents;
• Challenge the social tendency to glorify and romanticise parenthood;
• Call for responsible parenthood by dispelling myths and emphasising the realities involved in child-raising;
• Provide social contacts and activities for its members and produce a newsletter.

> 'a study has shown that among old people in homes, those with children have less contact with the outside world than those without children'

Their leaflet answers the question 'Who will look after me when I'm old?':

'A study has shown that among old people in homes, those with children have less contact with the outside world than those without children. The sons and daughters rarely visited, while the childless people, who had spent their lives pursuing busy careers and cultivating friendships and interests outside the family were visited by a wide range of friends, ex-colleagues and ex-neighbours.'

Their main assertion is that 'there is nothing wrong in honestly stating that having children is not your ideal way of life. There is, however, something very wrong in having a child you don't really want.'

BON, BM Box 5866, London WC1N 3XX (tel 031 554 2731).

The Parent Network

The Parent Network is an ambitious organisation which aims to involve 20,000 parents within ten years in a national network of parent support groups called 'Parent-Link.' Parents pay between £10 and £70 to meet once a week over a 12 week period and are facilitated by a specially trained parent to learn 'how to communicate more effectively and to improve their relationships with each other and with their children.' In a jargon-free way they are introduced to communications, relationship and assertion skills to use at home with their families.

Parents who have been through the programme are then encouraged to continue to meet in support groups and to become part of a local network. They can go on to train as Coordinators offering Parent-Link to other local parents. In Coordinator trainings which currently cost from £130 they learn how to recruit members for these groups, how group dynamics work, and they get additional practice in listening skills and in facilitating Parent-Link.

The project has been primarily funded by Richard Evans, who made his money in the computer industry, but left this work, deciding to form a charitable trust, the Artemis Trust, to 'support specific projects in the personal and emotional growth fields.'

> 'Network-based, locally available, cheap, non-threatening, showing quick and immediate results and spread by word of mouth by people sharing the same socio-economic and cultural backgrounds'

Evans began by asking himself why the humanistic psychology and personal growth movements have not spread widely in this country. He illustrated the main findings of his research in a slide lecture show which summarised over 3,000 studies of how innovations are best diffused in society. He realised that his most effective strategy would be to work through 'change agents' and 'opinion leaders' to develop a service that would be network-based, locally available, cheap, non-threatening, showing quick and immediate results and spread by word of mouth by people sharing the same socio-economic and cultural backgrounds.

Market research confirmed that workshops aimed at parents would be popular, as long as the focus was on self-help and experiential learning rather than education or therapy. The very week his market research results came through, Evans was approached by Ivan Sokolov, an ex-community development worker and trainer in health and social services, with a plan for parent support groups. 'It was sheer synchronicity,' says Sokolov. 'How it came about was that I had spent a year as a single parent looking after my two sons, aged three and a half and six, and I had tried to establish a more democratic relationship with them. I met more and more families who wanted to relate to their children without being either authoritarian or permissive, in a way that would encourage them to become self-disciplined, with a sense of self-worth, whilst taking their parents' needs into account.'

> 'To provide parents with a real and practical way to choose to relate as they want with their children, rather than be driven by unconscious patterns of behaviour set up during their childhood'

Sokolov studied various models including Parent Effectiveness Training, and began running groups where parents could learn from each other. The continuing demand led him to decide to set up a voluntary organisation to train 'ordinary people' to run the groups. 'People prefer to learn from others like them,' says Sokolov, 'rather than from experts up on a pedestal. For me, the goal of Parent Network is to provide parents with a real and practical way to choose to relate as they want with their children, rather than be driven by unconscious patterns of behaviour set up during their childhood.'

Parent Network now has a staff of seven in its national office with some 150 Coordinators around the country. One of their main objectives is to recruit Coordinators in order to spread Parent-Link more widely.

Sokolov's book, 'The Parents Book – Getting On Well With Our Children' (published by Thorsons, 1988, £5-99) describes many of the skills and exercises. Here, for instance, is a sample item from the book:

The soft no

The next time you find yourself in a situation where your child is demanding something, try the soft no. Stay calm inside, keeping your needs clearly in the forefront of your mind, believing that your child will accept what you say. Be completely straight, do not offer explanations or try to justify your 'no'; instead, if your child gets loud and angry, try getting softer and quieter, even to the point of whispering.

> 'If your child gets loud and angry, try getting softer and quieter, even to the point of whispering'

Jacquie Pearson (director), The Parent Network, 44 Caversham Road, London NW5 (tel 071 485 8535; fax 071 267 4426). This scheme was highly commended in the 1987 Social Inventions Awards.

Toughlove

The following interview comes from the American book 'Local Heros – The Rebirth of Heroism in America' (publishing details below).

Phyllis and David York got involved in community work that arose from personal trauma. One of their three daughters was arrested for robbing a cocaine dealer, the capping point of a history of troubles. They'd tried everything they knew to help her (and they were family therapists themselves in Philadelphia). A threshold had been crossed: they couldn't bring themselves to bail their daughter out of jail.

Instead they turned to their friends for help. They asked for community support, and they got it. Out of that incident,

TOUGHLOVE was born.

TOUGHLOVE is an approach for parents who have trouble raising their teenage children, or whose teenagers are getting into trouble, and usually both. The approach typically involves parent self-help groups which meet regularly to support each other, to change family behaviour, and to set limits, or 'bottom lines.' More than one thousand such groups meet in the States and Canada (with also 75 groups in New Zealand).

> 'The "tough" part means enforcing standards, calmly but unfailingly, up to and including, if necessary, committing the teenager to treatment'

The 'love' part of TOUGHLOVE includes setting reasonable and fair behavioural standards, so that teenagers can grow to be responsible and caring adults. The 'tough' part means enforcing those standards, calmly but unfailingly, up to and including, if necessary, committing the teenager to treatment, refusing to appear in court, and evicting the older teenager from the house. Other TOUGHLOVE parents, if needed, can temporarily take your place.

The Yorks believe that the community has a responsibiilty with parents for the raising of kids. If kids go wrong, it's partly because community standards have been poorly defined or poorly taught. The community has to take care of its own. In that respect TOUGHLOVE is an intentional model for community involvement.

The Yorks started TOUGHLOVE mainly for themselves and for the people around them, not thinking in larger terms until a local magazine story appeared, got spread around, and touched a national nerve. Now it is an international non-profit organisation.

Interviewer: How did things move from calling up a friend and getting support for your daughter to broadening the network?

David: Someone we knew in this local community called us up and said they were having trouble with their son who was seventeen. He'd taken off. He'd taken his father's camel hair coat, and his whisky, and done a whole number on him. And now the father says, 'Now what do I do? I don't know where the kid is, he's somewhere around, but we don't know where he's living.'

So we said, 'Call up the people in your community; call up your friends, your neighbours, and get everybody together, because we know your son's living somewhere in this New Hope vicinity. Let's see if we can track him down and cut off his resources.' And so they got thirty folks together, and that was our first TOUGHLOVE group....

We became like the leaders of this group. That was okay for a while, but after about seven or eight months, it got to be really tiring, to go every week to this meeting. And we began to put a manual together...

Time magazine interviewed us. And the gal that interviewed us had a hard job getting it published; they didn't want to publish it. They thought it was too radical a movement.

Phyllis: Kicking the kids out.

David: Yeah, it runs against the common trend of the poor kids, you know, suffering from terrible parents.

Phyllis: Then when Ann Landers put it in, we got fifteen

hundred letters a day for I don't know how long. Ten days, we got fifteen thousand letters. Over two thousand phone calls in a week. At this little office in Sellersville, with one person, one maniac person, working.

- *TOUGHLOVE, P.O. Box 1069, Doylestown, PA 18901, USA (tel 215 348 7090). Toughlove has spawned books, a newsletter, and a movement; and nowadays there are also 'kids' groups' running in parallel with the parents' groups, where the children tackle problems with the assistance of a trained counsellor. There are no registered groups in the UK yet, but the book 'Toughlove' by Phyllis and David York and Ted Wachtel, is published by Bantam Books, New York and is available from Toughlove for $4.*

- *This interview is excerpted from 'Local Heros – The Rebirth of Heroism in America' which is published by Lexington Books, 125 Spring Street, Lexington, Massachusetts 02173, USA, price $17.95, 1987. Bill Berkowitz, the book's author, is at 12 Pelham Terrace, Arlington, MA 02174, USA (tel 617 646 6319).*

The Friendship Trust

Margie McGregor

There are many organisations concerned with the problems of teenagers who could add to the effectiveness of their work if they focused on the following proven idea:

> 'The simplest remedy for a teenager with problems is if he or she is encouraged to choose and develop a hobby or creative interest, by an adult who is felt to be a friend'

The simplest remedy for a teenager with problems is if he or she is encouraged to choose and develop a hobby or creative interest, by an adult who is felt to be a friend.

The Friendship Trust (registered charity No. 290186) was formed to spread this idea and to encourage friends outside the family to offer at least an hour of their time, with a view to helping the child or teenager reinforce their personal identity by finding their hidden abilities through a self-chosen hobby or interest. Where no such trusted family friend is available, it is intended that families anywhere in the UK should have a link through the Friendship Trust with caring adults in their community. In the last nine years, over 500 adults and 600 children and teenagers in Oxfordshire have been involved with this scheme. For instance:

Ben was 16 years old. He had been through a very disturbed childhood with many moves. He became aggressive at school, in the street and at home.

When asked by Mary, a friend of the family, what interest he would like to share with an adult, he said he had always wanted to be a blacksmith. Mary took it upon herself to go through the yellow pages and to ring several blacksmiths. One of these is Ted, who agreed Ben could work alongside him each Saturday morning.

Although this was very much like 'work experience', in fact it was for Ben far more personal than that. Ted and his family just accepted Ben as another member of their unit. Ben's behaviour changed. His parents and teachers were able to talk about his new interest instead of the usual angry exchanges.

> 'Mary took it upon herself to go through the yellow pages and to ring several blacksmiths. One of these is Ted, who agreed Ben could work alongside him each Saturday morning'

Through my own experience as a parent, I know it is impossible at times to inspire our own children. They are often emotionally too close and too dependent on us even to listen to us if they are going through a personal or family crisis. Adults need to recognise this and to seek an adult friend whom they completely trust, who can encourage the youngster's creativity (standards of craftsmanship are not important).

Our purpose is to rely less on professionals and more on our personal networks. Even an hour spent by a teenager chatting to an adult they feel is a friend can have a massive effect, with an over-night change in a teenager's feelings of self-worth and respect for others. Parents and carers feel very supported.

The Prince's Trust, Northmoor Trust and others are supporting the Friendship Trust for three years for its administrative costs, and a nationwide network of helpers is being established, and many adults' lives have been reestablished because of their involvement in helping with this idea.

We are willing to talk to organisations if a fee and travelling expenses can be met. But many individuals within organisations and potential adult friends could take the idea forward without further help from us, if they could just understand its simplicity.

Margie McGregor, The Friendship Trust, Hordley House, Wootton, Woodstock, Oxon. OX20 1EP (tel 0993 812765).

Bringing hobbies into the school curriculum

Nicholas Gillett

You can judge people best by the way they spend their spare time. A youngster without a hobby is an educational failure however well he does in examinations. As a result of education for leisure at a good school 'everyone is good at something.' These words were used in praise of a Bristol comprehensive school by an old lady working on a conveyor belt in a cake factory.

The National Curriculum focuses the attention of both teachers and learners on what can be measured and thus squeezes extra-curricular activities into nothingness. By contrast in another country after long discussions in the Ministry of Education, extra-curricular activities were put into the curriculum!

With such thoughts in mind the writer, when teaching a bottom stream class of twelve year olds in the thirties, tried out some experiments which, if they had been carried out in a science laboratory and had concerned the pocket rather than the heart, would have received widespread acclaim. Ambitious teachers shun the bottom stream expecting to find there the unsuccessful, the uncooperative, the unloved and even the unteachable. Teachers tend to find what they expect.

> ### 'Every boy and girl would bring something which they had done or made, however humble it might be, and display it in a classroom exhibition'

The experiments sound simple: it was necessary to find out whether every boy and girl would bring something which they had done or made, however humble it might be, and display it in a classroom exhibition. To leave out two or three children would have convinced them that they were failures and alienated them still more. Some of the girls insisted that they did nothing or that they were too busy at home to make something to bring. In the end they brought some of their knitting or made some cakes. A boy was more adamant: 'No, I don't do anything,' he insisted.

'You mean you just do nothing, just prop up the wall?' Having visited all the homes it was easier to insist, so turning to his neighbour the question was put: 'You tell me what he does.'

'Please sir, he roller-skates.'

The diminutive twelve year old brightened up a little and when it was time for writing he managed to finish a whole sentence for the first time. It was, however, the day when he brought his skates and stood in front of the class holding them in his hands and answered the questions of his interested classmates which made the day of the year for him. From then on he was easy to teach. Much later the film 'Kes' was produced following this theme. It showed a boy who never got on at school until the teacher discovered that his secret hobby was caring for a kestrel.

After the war, the Birmingham Federation of PTAs took up the task of demonstrating that such exhibitions make for better teaching, provide much more scope and encouragement for all children – that is for the most gifted as well as the least successful at ordinary school work. Head teachers sometimes said that their children did not do anything. Some of them admitted later that they had been surprised by what turned up from unlikely homes.

The most imaginative or creative exhibits at each participating school were chosen each year for the central exhibition at a department store. Teachers learned that it was worth giving out a notice just before holidays began as a reminder of the exhibition the following term. Children found that they made new friends through discovering common interests and learned from them. Parents found that the ideal medium for parent-teacher cooperation is children's leisure activities. Finally, teachers found that they knew their children better and knew how to motivate them. They made personal relations of an entirely new quality. It was Aristotle who said, 'How shall I learn unless it be from my friend?'

In a later development a teacher was appointed to a secondary modern school to work normally in the classroom for half of his time and to spend the rest of his time with teachers, parents or children improving the quality and quantity of the children's leisure activities in and around the homes. It was an enormous success and the headmaster said, 'If we did not have Mr Preston we'd have to invent him.' The exhibition became more varied and dramatic. On one occasion a pet pig escaped and narrowly avoided upsetting a hive full of bees. Two boys made large telescopes in the metal-work room and wanted eventually to use them to photograph some constellations. They turned to the public library and found that one of the three authors was living thirty miles away so they arranged to visit him on their bicycles to ask for his help. Others built huts in their gardens to work at their bicycles or radio sets. There was no end to the variety of the occupations; it seemed that for everyone and not just for those with telescopes that the sky was not the limit. It certainly was not for one boy, deprived though he was. Seeing what others had done with their bought meccano sets, he, at the age of ten, gathered up the tins which his mother threw away and hammered them and punched holes in them to make his own meccano.

In such schools vocational guidance has a much firmer base. This could be the argument which would influence the hard men and women who construct national curricula and know not what they do. Leisure activities form the golden triangle of parents, teachers and children.

Nicholas Gillett, Oakcroft, Cross o' th' Hill, Malpas, Cheshire SY14 8DH (tel 0948 860 213).

Children's courts for school bullies

Extracted from two pieces in the Times and from material from Kidscape.

Kidscape was founded in 1984 by Michele Elliott, a teacher and educational psychologist. Her survey of 4,000 children found that more than two thirds had been bullied at some time and 38 per cent were being regularly bullied. Elliott devised the 'bully court', a forum in which bullies are tried and sentenced by their peers. The idea has been tried already in 30 primary schools and will be extended to any secondary school that wants to try it.

> ### 'Her survey of 4,000 children found that 38 per cent were being regularly bullied'

Two of the court's four members are elected by classmates and the other two are appointed by teachers. A teacher sits as chairperson to ensure fair play. Punishments have included bans on school trips and on using playgrounds and tasks such as tidying classrooms.

Kidscape also issue a sheet of suggested ways of breaking up bully gangs and for dealing with gangs from outside the school – in the latter case, Kidscape advises 'take photographs – they tend to run away when they see a camera.'

Kidscape, 82 Brook St, London W1Y 1YG (tel 071 493 9845).

Children's Ombudsman

Information monitored for the Institute by Karen Pennike from an article by Michael Ryan in Parade magazine.

Since 1981 Norway has had an official called the 'Barneombudet', the Advocate for Children. This person's job is to ensure that 'children are seen as people, with their own needs and their own rights – rights equal, but not identical, to those of adults.' For instance, the Barneombudet has worked with the energy ministry to move high-tension wires from areas where children play; it won lower class-room temperatures for a particular Oslo classroom; and it successfully lobbied for a law to prohibit parental striking of children. The law specifically prohibits the Barneombudet from interfering in disputes with families. Children who phone with stories of abuse are asked for their permission and then the local child welfare authorities are asked to take up the matter.

Trond Viggo Torgensen, the physician who has been appointed as the Barneombudet, has set up a free phone number children can call with their messages about what they think is important, with a TV show once a week in which he will take up their topics. His staff, which includes a sociologist, a lawyer and a secretary, answer thousands of phone calls and letters each year; and their phone number is listed in every phone book in Norway.

'Children are people of equal value. They must be given a channel through which they can be heard'

A similar Children's Ombudsman office is being set up in Costa Rica. Says Torgensen: 'The important thing is the principle: Children are people of equal value. They must be given a channel through which they can be heard.'

A school with its own money, courts and taxation

A school that deserves to be a model for others – from an ancient but still relevant article in the American magazine 'Parade', by Mark and Dan Jury, monitored for the Institute by Roger Knights.

'Why should we have to work hard and pay more taxes, just to support a bunch of people who won't work?' demands Leo Bona, an 8th-grade 'lawyer.' A chorus of cheers, from students upset with the 30 percent income tax levied on them, greets his question. Finally a solution to the school's welfare system is found – the dole is replaced with government-subsidised jobs.

'Gilman School has its own economic and social system, complete with a currency called thalers'

Such discussions are typical at the Gilman Middle School of Vermont, a public school whose revolutionary 'Thaler System' represents an educational breakthrough. In addition to the usual classroom studies, Gilman has its own economic and social system, complete with a currency called 'thalers' that duplicates the outside world to a remarkably realistic degree.

The 85 students in grades 5 through 8 (ages from 11 to 14) hold jobs, pay taxes, spend their thalers on goods and services in the school, enforce their own laws, formulate school policy and grapple with the dilemmas of inflation, unemployment and economic slowdown.

'Thaler is not simulation,' says Gilman ex-principal Barry Grove, who developed the system. 'The thaler currency is backed, not by an educator's intentions and fantasies, but by

dollars. It's a massive plagiarism of life superimposed on a school, and it gives the students a consciousness of the workings of economics, capitalism and private enterprise – which they need to be successful in life.'

'To earn thalers, the students work – as library aides, cafeteria workers, maintenance crew, bus patrol, office aides'

The actual thaler resembles monopoly money and is worth a penny (thaler is the German equivalent of dollar, and at Gilman is pronounced 'thayler'). To earn thalers, the students work – as library aides, cafeteria workers, maintenance crew, bus patrol, office aides.

Students also work at jobs generated by the Thaler System: at the Gilman Bank and Trust, the Payroll Department (each student receives a weekly check, with taxes and Social Security deducted), the Employment Office, Licence and Patent, Legal System, Postal Service, Student Tutor Corporation, and two dozen other 'public jobs.'

Other students operate private businesses, ranging from Lynne's Homework Reminder Service to D & M Skateboard Repair. 'Thaler is fun,' says Shawn Maillet, 14, who spends recesses and lunch hours putting his classmate's skateboards in shape. 'Sure, you've got to work. But you can buy things and do things that you couldn't without Thaler.'

'At the Thaler Redemption Centre, students can purchase items from Sears' and Ward's catalogues'

Those 'things' include buying snacks and fruit at morning breaks, plus renting recreational equipment (pool table, air hockey, electronic video games, pinball). At the Thaler Redemption Centre, students can purchase items from Sears' and Ward's catalogues, plus merchandise from softballs to CB radios.

'A student may think that he or she is working to buy a hair dryer or to go on a trip,' says Norman Parent, Gilman's principal, 'but they're learning throughout the entire process. As soon as they start handling money and dealing with taxes, payments and interest, there's no way they don't learn maths.'

'These kids accept responsibility and thereby gain control over their environment', he says. 'Once they grasp the reality of that – they're hooked'

Barry Grove emphasises that Thaler isn't a game, but something that the students live with every day. 'These kids accept responsibility and thereby gain control over their environment,' he says. 'Once they grasp the reality of that – they're hooked.'

He tells of one Gilman student who couldn't do anything right and had a poor self-image. The youngster started off with the simplest job in the school – emptying garbage cans in the cafeteria. 'He did it well and won an Employee of the Month award,' says Grove, 'and for the first time his schoolmates noticed him. Now he's risen to foreman, is supervising others and is a new person.'

Grove began to formulate the Thaler System in 1971 while teaching in Maryland. In an attempt to break through the apathy of his 6th grade students, he began offering them challenges and incentives, and was amazed at the way they responded.

He continued improving upon the idea when he moved to a school in Rutland, Mass. However, he realised that he needed a principalship to experiment with his idea. At a Boston placement agency, Gilman, in the northeast corner of Vermont, was suggested.

'I thought I was in Appalachia,' says Grove, recalling the first time he crossed the Connecticut River and drove through the scattering of former company houses that make up Gilman.

'The Gilman Middle School had employed five principals in four years. Vandalism was rampant, and discipline required the bulk of each teacher's time'

The town's paper mill, which since has been replaced, had cut back its work force from 1700 to 200, devastating the local economy. The Gilman Middle School had employed five principals in four years. Vandalism was rampant, and discipline required the bulk of each teacher's time.

Even so, the school board wasn't excited about hiring an outsider who possessed a missionary zeal about a programme with a foreign-sounding name. But Grove received the job of principal at $9200 a year, and in 1976 he began the Thaler System.

Three years later the number of Gilman students on or above grade level in Metropolitan Achievement Tests has increased by almost 40 per cent. Vandalism is non-existent.

'The lack of disciplinary problems is attributed to the Thaler legal system. This relies on peer judgment to uphold a Bill of Rights and Code of Laws adopted by the student body'

The lack of disciplinary problems is attributed to the Thaler legal system. This relies on peer judgment to uphold a Bill of Rights and Code of Laws adopted by the student body.

Each year, the principal conducts a law course, culminating in a written and oral 'bar exam.' Three quarters of the applicants funk. The highest scoring student is appointed judge, next highest is bailiff, and the others become attorneys. Anyone going to court at Gilman must have a legal representative.

During a recent lunch break, the Thaler legal system was operating. 'All rise,' intoned the bailiff, age 11. 'Court is now in session. Honourable Terry J. Schmidt presiding.'

The junior high school students rose as 7th-grader Terry entered the room in a long, black choir robe. The charge was assault and battery – one student slugged another and broke his glasses – and the cost to replace the spectacles was $28.

The mothers of both the plaintiff and defendant appeared in 'court', after agreeing that the decision of the student jury

would be final. The junior high lawyers nervously shuffled papers, as Judge Schmidt banged his gavel for order and the trial began. The jury rejected the defendant's plea of self-defence, and both students were required to pay $14 each for the new glasses.

'The Bill of Rights states that everyone is to be treated with dignity and respect. And the teacher can be sued'

'In this school, kids have protection,' says Norman Parent, 'not only from each other, but from teachers as well. If a teacher says, "Sit down, stupid," that's wrong – the Bill of Rights states that everyone is to be treated with dignity and respect. And the teacher can be sued – especially if there were witnesses.' (If a teacher or principal loses a case, they must apologise in front of the student body and faculty members.)

'One teacher was sued this year for not giving a proper warning before issuing a group punishment,' says Judge Schmidt, 'and one student was sued by his 6th grade classmates for acting up in class – he kept shooting spitballs.'

Despite their new economic and legal responsibilities, the students remain normal adolescents. Paul Gilman is the teenage president of the bank (600 thalers a week). He worked his way up from pay-roll clerk, and now oversees a manager, two tellers and the operations of the bank.

'We had a run on the bank right before the auction,' he says, 'and we almost ran out of money – but we finally made it. Then one girl said she deposited money, but we never found the deposit slip. We gave her the 2000 thalers or we would have been sued.' He agrees that being president of the bank has taught him a lot, but when asked about his plans for the future, Paul replies, 'In some ways I want to be a stock car race driver.'

Perhaps the only frustrated person involved with the Thaler System is Barry Grove, now assistant superintendent at the Jacksonville, Vermont, School District. What's bothering him? It's simply that he can't understand why the programme has not been adopted by school districts throughout the land.

Schools as model states

Nicholas Gillett

Extracts from a proposal.

There is an evident need for people to understand the unwritten British Constitution and the conventions of fair play which make it work. It would be useful if schools, or failing them, classes, formed model states to carry out some of their business. At least an outing could be arranged. In the case of an outing, the Foreign Secretary would be responsible for making contacts with the institutions to be visited, the Chancellor of the Exchequer would raise the funds and supervise payments and one can easily envisage roles for the ministries of Food and Agriculture, the Environment and so on.

'It would be useful if schools formed model states to carry out some of their business'

The Cabinet would meet and ministers would have to obtain the approval of both the elected House of Commons and the House of Lords, the latter being appointed by the head teacher or the teacher. An opposition to improve the 'legislation' could easily be formed and a major issue might divide the pupils into parties.

Mr Heath once commented that of all the needs for inventions, the greatest was for ways of producing democratic citizens.

Nicholas Gillett, Oakcroft, Cross o' th' Hill, Malpas, Cheshire SY14 8DH (tel 0948 860 213).

UK Youth Parliament

The Institute for Social Inventions is working to help set up youth parliaments, to coincide with adult general elections, with MPs aged between 11 and 18. At best, such a parliament would debate and pass resolutions, rather like the House of Lords, on educational and youth issues, and on any other matters, such as environmental concerns, that it chose to consider. It might also have its own governing party and cabinet (and shadow cabinet) if it so decided.

> 'It would debate and pass resolutions, rather like the House of Lords, on educational and youth issues, and on any other matters, such as environmental concerns, that it chose to consider'

But its most important work would be at the school level, with secondary schools encouraged to form their own school parliaments, and with candidates following traditional or new or no party lines. These parliaments could get their teeth into real work in the sense of drawing up and carrying out plans for improving their schools.

If there were enough schools participating, there might be an intermediate level of parliament at the county level, as those elected at the school level could then be candidates for a county parliament, with county MPs able to stand as candidates for a national parliament.

The likely gains from such an exercise include:
• Giving young people, who are unrepresented in our democracies, a voice, in proportion to their backing from their peers;
• Giving young people a training in democracy and politics, and an interest in national issues;
• Giving young people and the public at large hands-on experience of possible improvements to our electoral systems, assuming that new forms of proportional representation were tried with the youth parliament elections;
• Encouraging school authorities to allow pupils more say in the improving of schools through the formation of councils or school parliaments;
• At the county level, helping coordination between schools, which is otherwise likely to suffer as opting-out continues;
• Giving the public advance warning of future voting trends.

The aim would be to announce the results of the youth national elections in advance of the adult national election results, to maximise the resulting publicity. Costs would be minimised by making the schools responsible for any local expense and for the travel costs of its MPs to county and national level meetings, which would be rare events.

If you know of a school that might like to take part, please encourage it to contact the Institute for Social Inventions, 20 Heber Road, London NW2 6AA (tel 081 208 2853; fax 081 452 6434). A similar exercise for the European level took place in Lisbon, organised by a European Youth Parliament (President Bettina Carr-Allinson), 19 rue du Parc, 7730 Fontainebleau, France (tel 60 72 36 70; 64 23 44 83).

Contract between teenager and parents

Martin Herbert

The following is extracted from Martin Herbert's book, 'Living with Teenagers' (published by Basil Blackwell, 108 Cowley Road, Oxford OX4 1JF, 1987, paperback).

It may seem odd or demeaning to negotiate an agreement – perhaps even to draw up a written contract – with a son or daughter. Yet such procedures can be extremely effective in easing interpersonal difficulties and disagreements. When making a contract, remember the following points:

> 'To negotiate an agreement, perhaps a written contract with a son or daughter, can be extremely effective in easing interpersonal difficulties and disagreements'

(1) Be very specific in spelling out the desired actions.

(2) Pay attention to the details of the privileges and conditions both parties to the agreement expect to gain from it. (Parents may want their son to complete his homework and attend school regularly; he, on the other hand, desires more free time with his friends, or more pocket money.)

(3) Those actions chosen for the youngster to fulfil must be readily observable. (If the parents or teachers are unable to discern whether an obligation has been met, they cannot grant a privilege.) This requirement applies also to parents.

(4) The contract should impose sanctions for a failure to fulfil the agreement. Each party should know precisely what the penalties are for breaking the contract. The sanctions are agreed in advance, are decided by both sides and are applied consistently.

(5) There can be no arbitrary, unilateral tinkering with the terms of the contract after signing. (Changes must be negotiated and agreed to by both sides.)

(6) A contract can provide a bonus clause so that extra privileges, special activities, etc are available to both parties, for consistent performance over a long time.

(7) There should be a built-in scheme for monitoring the amount of positive reinforcement given and received. (The records are kept – a chart or notebook – to inform each participant of the progress, or lack of it, of the agreement.)

Sample formal contract

Between Mr and Mrs Smith and Anne Smith
Mother and father would like Anne to:

(1) Let them know about her movements when she goes out at night; Anne will let them know about her movements when she goes out at night by: telling them where she is and with whom; letting them know when she'll be home.

(2) Be less moody; she won't go silent ('sulk') for hours on end when reprimanded or thwarted.

(3) Be more ready to say sorry; she will apologise when she's been in the wrong.

(4) Show more concern about her school work (eg homework); she will put in at least an hour per night.

(5) Stop being so rude to her father, eg walking out when he gives her advice.

Anne would like her mother and father to:

(1) Stop criticising her friends all the time; stop calling them names and saying they're no good, unless they are making a particular, constructive comment.

(2) Admit when they are in the wrong, ie they will apologise when they have been in the wrong in their confrontations with her.

(3) Give her more pocket money (a sum agreed) and to review the amount every six months in the light of the rising expense and changing nature of her commitments.

All agree:

(1) That the terms of the contract will not be changed except by mutual discussion and agreement.

(2) That disputes will be settled by the witness (grandmother), whom all accept to be objective and fair-minded.

(3) That successful execution of the contract for a month will be rewarded by a family treat (first month: an outing to a posh – named – restaurant).

(4) That failure to carry out individual terms of the contract will result in a fine on each occasion: an amount of X for Anne; and Y amount for Mr and Mrs Smith respectively. The money is to go in a 'penalty box' (kept by the grandmother), the proceeds of which will go to a charity of her choice.

Signed:
Anne
Mr Smith
Mrs Smith
Grandmother (Witness)

Sex education without fuss

Mrs Woollett

From a letter by Mrs Woollett in the Guardian.

Before we began school (during the war) our mother was called in, handed a very informative book on sex education, and asked to explain it and all aspects of the subject before we started the school that September. I do not know of anyone who objected.

> 'Our mother was handed a book on sex education, and asked to explain it and all aspects of the subject before we started school'

Children taking responsibility

Nicholas Saunders

In Denmark, any group of parents can get a standard sum of money per pupil from the state for organising their own school and employing their own teachers. At one such school, the Albertslunds Lilleskøle in the suburbs of Copenhagen, the older children do the school cleaning. The money saved is used to send the children on working holidays. Each classroom also has a kitchen, and the children buy food, prepare and cook it, and wash up. The children may grumble, but parents argue that the arrangement provides a useful discipline and training for them.

> 'The older children do the school cleaning. The money saved is used to send the children on working holidays'

Nicholas Saunders, top floor, 14 Neal's Yard, London, WC2H 9DP (tel 071 836 9404; fax 071 379 0135).

Pupil-run businesses at school

Adapted extract from the Examiner, USA, monitored for the Institute by Roger Knights.

At first glance it looks just like any other school, but beyond the doors it's a whole new world. You can hardly believe your eyes. There's a romantic-smelling flower shop; a Cordon Bleu restaurant complete with colonial decor and chandeliers; a bank with a vault, security cameras and two teller windows; a cheerful, free day care centre for children of students and a garage with eight bays and a noisy machine shop.

These 'businesses' are run by pupils at Brattleboro Union High School in Vermont, as part of an innovative vocational programme for those who are not going on to college. A total of 14 programmes teach practical skills including secretarial and computing that students can use when they leave. It is all non-profit and the students are not paid. A full-course meal in the restaurant (trout florentine etc) costs about $2.50. To get used to the working world, students punch in with a time clock and rotate jobs within their particular programme. Each business has an adult professional overseeing it, but the students handle day-to-day operations and make most of the important decisions.

Schoolchildren designing own curricula

Gregory Wright

This proposal from Gregory Wright in California sounds very similar to the actually existing College for Independent Study in the UK, but aimed at a younger age group.

School pupils in all publicly-supported schools should have the opportunity to spend a half-year at the primary level and a full year at the secondary level in an individually-tailored and largely self-constructed course of studies based on each pupil's personal abilities and interests. The process of designing this 'special studies' course, with the help of teachers, would be part of the preceding school year's curriculum.

Pupils in such courses would choose a few courses from the school's basic curriculum, particularly those subjects relevant to his or her main study areas, and for the rest would develop a timetable of self-chosen reading, and self-planned craft, artistic, shop, laboratory, computer, research, hobby, domestic, athletic, performance, entrepreneurial, community-service and other activities and pursuits.

Each pupil would select in advance – or be selected by – one (or two or three) of the school's teachers with skills in the appropriate areas to act as mentors. Community participation also would be essential, with pupils calling for assistance from experts in the community.

> 'Each child would be stimulated to think in advance about his or her own most distinct personal abilities, assets, interests and fascinations – and to plan ahead for a project or set of projects'

The advantages of such a development include:
• Each child would be stimulated to think in advance about his or her own most distinct personal abilities, assets, interests and fascinations – and to plan ahead for a project or set of projects.
• This would lead to a greater sense of personal responsibility for how their lives develop and, hopefully, to a sense of personal uniqueness and self-esteem.
• It provides more diverse opportunities for every child to succeed and an incentive to marginal or alienated pupils not to drop out; it might lead to a reduced youth crime rate. Secondary-level drop-outs would receive an invitation to return to school to plan and then pursue their 'special year.'
• It will help turn out new graduates who have a wider range of proven capabilities and interests.

Ed: Such courses could incorporate elements of group work so as to provide experience of working in a team, and for mutual support, particularly at the primary level. A gentle way to try the idea out is for more schools at slack points in the curriculum to encourage pupils to spend a mere week or fortnight on a project of their own devising.

• *Gregory Wright, 14161 Riverside Drive #3, Sherman Oaks, CA 91423, USA (tel 818 784 0325).*
• *Eunice Hinds, Director, The College for Independent Study, 20 West Street, Oxford OX2 OBQ (fax 0277 231838).*

Pupils pacing themselves

Hakan Jaerbur

Hakan Jaerbur was one of the prize winners in the Swedish Institute for Social Inventions' competition.

I teach at a secondary school. A few years ago I found my situation untenable. I prepared my lessons, tried hard. And built good relations with the pupils. But still they seemed to have no joy in learning. I was continually working to overcome resistance, gather attention, carry the class. It seemed the pupils were working for me rather than themselves, and using only a fraction of their capacity.

I began to realise that we have to sell our wares better, We have to help the pupils understand the joy and usefulness of each type of knowledge. If they still don't want it, we should take it off the curriculum.

> 'My first step was to distribute a questionnaire to all pupils asking "what should you be taught in school?" We arrived at a currriculum which the pupils agreed was important'

My first step was to distribute a questionnaire to all pupils (around 1000 in number). The major headings were: 'why do people want to learn?', and 'what should you be taught in school?' – 923 replied. The results were tabulated and distributed to all pupils.

With the help of this material, and many discussions, we arrived at a curriculum content which the pupils agreed was important. The next step was to organise the material in such a way that each pupil can succeed, over and over, in every subject.

Our regular school books contain an impossible amount of material in relation to the time available. Teachers feel under pressure to communicate all of it, and instead communicate their stress.

American research shows that, given sufficient time, most pupils (75%-85%) can achieve the results of the top 30%. So I decided to let each pupil pace him or herself. The material for each term and subject is divided into basic material and select material packages. A pupil can at any time ask to be tested on any package. He or she knows that full marks on the basic package will automatically give a pass mark in that subject. Anything higher than a pass mark requires one or more select packages.

I have a dream – a dream that every child shall long to go to school every day, viewing the school as the source of desirable and desired knowledge and skills; and feeling 'that's where I feel recognised, acknowledged. Where I succeed, experience self-confidence and the joy of work well done.'

> 'I can be tested in this right at the beginning of term, and spend the rest of the time with the stuff I choose for myself'

And I would wish for every teacher the special delight I experience when, at the beginning of the summer holidays, 80% of my pupils come and ask me for next term's basic materials 'because then I can be tested in this right at the beginning of term, and spend the rest of the time with the stuff I choose for myself.'

Hakan Jaerbur, Stopvägen 85, S-161 43 Bromma, Sweden (tel 46 825 2072).

Badge for social responsibility

Margaret Chisman

A way to involve children, at least in small communities, in looking after (and also being responsible for) those things that children were previously vandalising – could be by means of some publicly acknowledged promise, for example scouts or girl guides taking a badge for public responsibility, or a secular confirmation service (as in Norway), to include a promise of the acceptance of some social work. Items that might need social action of some sort could include dog droppings on pavements, litter, garden and park plants stolen or dug up and vandalised telephone boxes and automatic chocolate machines.

Margaret Chisman, The Bungalow, Near the Station, Tring, Hertfordshire HP23 5QX (tel 0442 823281).

School pupils earning used bikes

Adapted extract from Wisconsin State Journal (USA), by Denise Sanders, monitored for the Institute by Roger Knights.

An innovative 'Earn-a-Bike' programme at Marquette Elementary School in the Williamson-Marquette neighbourhood (Wisconsin State, USA) allowed primary school pupils to win used bikes, donated by the community. They 'earned' the bikes by gaining 100 points, based on completed tasks and good behaviour.

The idea came from a parent whose son's bike was stolen as part of a rash of bike thefts in the area, involving an increasing number of younger kids.

Parents had to sign contracts to say whether or not their child could participate. 65 kids signed up for the 10-week project. 62 received bikes at an awards ceremony.

Steve Meier, a co-ordinator with the police department, taught the pupils bicycle rules and safety procedures, and Trek Bicycles donated helmets. Carolyn Stanford, the head teacher, said she might consider repeating the programme in the future.

Earning points for adulthood

Dr John Hart

The peak age of offending for both males and females is below the school leaving age – 15 for males, 14 for females. Juvenile crime is a seemingly intractable problem. To tackle it, social commentators argue, education will have to be improved to bring out the personal worth of all pupils, social deprivation will have to be ameliorated, and the worst effects of family break-up, which is very much on the increase, will have to be countered in some way by greater social support from outside the family. A less acquisitive, self-orientated moral climate might be beneficial. Above all, though, the desire of individual boys and girls to behave well will have to be strengthened. It is with this in mind that a novel suggestion can be made relating to the transition from childhood to adulthood.

At present, you can legally have sex and marry with parental consent at 16, drive a car at 17, vote, consume alcohol in a pub, enter into hire purchase and other financial agreements at 18, and sit on a jury and get the traditional 'key to the door' at 21. The coming-of-age experience is thus distributed over half a decade. What I recommend is that we concentrate more of the changes at 18 in order to make more of the entry into adulthood. This leaves the way open for us to postpone conferment of adult status on those who do not behave in an adult way – which for our present purpose means in a law-abiding fashion.

'He or she would automatically suffer a three-year postponement of his or her age of majority to 21'

How would the system, which can be called the 'majority rule', work? The crimes and misbehaviour of young people would be punished in the usual ways but in addition a points score would be entered into the record book rather in the way that drivers earn points towards a ban when they offend on the road. For example, possession of cannabis or persistent severe indiscipline in school might be worth one point, vandalism two points, burglary three, mugging four and so on. Any individual who got five or more points, say, would fail to comply with the majority rule. As such he or she would automatically suffer a three-year postponement of his or her age of majority to 21. This could 'bite' as a punishment, and thus operate as a deterrent, if it hit the social life, mobility and wallet of a young man or woman. This it would do in the case of social life because the right to drink alcohol in pubs, presently triggered at 18, would be deferred to 21. Mobility is more difficult because the current legal age for driving a car or a motor-cycle over 49cc is 17. The simple expedient is to raise this to 18 – which would also reduce accidents. As to the wallet, the young person will not be able to hold credit cards or enter into hire purchase agreements of any kind. If we wanted to strengthen the financial incentive to good behaviour, the state could deposit a sum of money, eg £100, with an investing institution on behalf of each child at birth for collection at 18 only by those who do not misbehave. Regular financial statements to the individual would be a useful reminder of the growing size of the nest-egg and of what is at stake. Forfeit money could go to a crime victim's compensation 'pot.'

It is not recommended that the miscreant 18 year olds be prevented from marrying without parental consent as marriage tends to be a reforming institution.

An element of compulsory training for the 16-18 age group would help to establish 18 firmly as the age of majority. Another useful move in this direction would be to make the sale of cigarettes to under-18s illegal. Penalties for those selling alcohol to under-age drinkers could also be strengthened.

The majority rule system might seem negative. To balance this, a positive component could be incorporated which would enable those who have misbehaved to 'reduce their deficit.' The kind of activity that is relevant here would be community service or sporting endeavour. The key idea would be involvement in some socially useful project.

Training to comply with the majority rule could start as early as 11 or 12 and be continued to the end of a child's school career. Though conducted at school, the early sessions should involve parents so as to strengthen family commitment to keeping children on the straight and narrow. Health propaganda aimed at the young on alcohol, smoking and drugs has backfired in the past by perversely glamorising the undesirable. This might be avoided in the majority rule context by focusing on the rights and duties of citizenship and on the advantages of adulthood achieved early. At the age of 18 a youngster would receive a document confirming his or her adult status and describing the implications of this coming of age. This might go a small way to bringing it home to young people that they are now adults. At present, it is perfectly possible for some 'youths' on the dole to go on feeling not quite adult practically into their thirties.

This is an extract from the book 'Wealth and Well-Being: A National Strategy for the Nineties' by Dr John Hart, (published by Oxon/Harper and Row, 1988, at £8-95). This book won a Social Inventions Award. Dr John Hart's address is 16 Burleigh Court, Cavendish Place, Brighton, BN1 2HR (tel 0273 720879).

Forum Theatre – a new way to resolve children's fights

Michael Soth ran a Social Invention Workshop with a class of 22 seven and eight year olds at Earlsfield School in South West London. He showed them a creative way to resolve their fights – to re-enact these fights twice, the second time with elegant variations – as he describes in this article:

One morning, when the children came into the classroom, one girl had a bleeding lip. She had been involved in a fight on her way to school. The children were excited and talked among themselves: 'next time I'm really going to beat him up,' 'no, he's much stronger' and so on.

The teacher asked what had happened and was immediately flooded with six different versions of the event at the same time. She told all of them to be quiet and asked the injured girl. Whilst recounting what happened, she was interrupted by the other children, who were getting impatient and making comments, and then by the teacher, who asked the interesting question: 'Why is it always *you* who gets into fights?'

The girl got defensive. 'I'm sticking up for myself,' she responded. Raised eyebrows from the teacher, and another child saying 'this is boring' finally made the girl give up and subside into sulking. The teacher was not entirely satisfied with this conclusion, but she knew of no other way to deal with it, except to warn, 'If I were you, I would be more careful in future.'

This example, with an exceptionally patient and well-meaning teacher, is nevertheless quite typical. My feeling is that nothing has really been resolved and that the same thing will happen again tomorrow.

What is lacking is the belief that human beings can actually resolve conflicts to the satisfaction of everybody involved. Most children operate on the assumption that human beings are basically hostile to each other and are only held back by the guarding and policing forces of law, order and authority.

I understand this belief as the children's accurate perception of most adults they come into contact with. The children

mirror, in an unmediated and raw form, the largely unconscious underlying assumptions by which most of us shape our social reality (although a lot of well-intentioned adults would disagree vehemently that they are in fact operating on these assumptions). The violence and distress in the ordinary school yard is an elequent reminder that the slogan 'Don't do as I do – do as I say!' doesn't actually work very well in education.

This situation to my mind calls for urgent social invention. We need structures that make conflict resolution possible without violence.

The method I used with this class, and which worked astonishingly well, is called Forum Theatre. It was developed by the Brazilian, Augusto Boal, who was inspired by the writings of Paolo Freire, and worked in South America with those suffering from oppression.

The basic method is as follows:

The conflict is first discussed. When the situation, behaviour and feelings of those involved are clear and understood by everybody, they 'perform' this 'original' once from beginning to end without interuption.

'The whole audience is encouraged to say "stop" at a point where they feel that an alternative behaviour is possible'

Then they repeat it a second time, but this time the whole audience is encouraged to say 'stop' at a point where they feel that something is wrong or that an alternative behaviour is possible. They are then invited to take somebody's role in the original and to act it differently. Somebody acting differently changes the whole course of the interaction and so it is possible to observe whether a more satisfactory and less oppressive conclusion is reached. If not, the original is played a third time and is again open to changes and alternatives. In this way, different ways of behaving are tried and the possible results elucidated. This collective process of replaying and transforming the original oppressive situation into one that everybody is happy with, involves everybody's creativity and makes reaching a consensus possible.

With the children, we took up conflicts that happened in playtime and used all the emotional 'charge' that the children brought with them to keep them motivated in, for once, investing energy in actually resolving the conflict.

Usually we spent quite some time listening to everybody's version of what had happened before we could agree on what the sequence of events had been. It was very important to give everybody space in creating this 'original' (the reproduction of what had actually happened). If we did not do this, the children dropped out and gave up, feeling ignored or misrepresented, and were not interested in working out alternatives.

In the beginning they needed a great deal of guidance until they all understood the ground rules of Forum Theatre. Thereafter the process was quite smooth, and my main work was to hold them back from all shouting 'stop' and wanting to suggest alternatives at once.

It was important that we made it very clear that we were not on anybody's side. By the end of term, the groupings that used to form, threatening the other side with retribution – which seemed to me like a Lilliputian version of superpower politics – were no longer necessary. We had provided a structure for conflict resolution that they all accepted and felt safe with, for they were confident that they would be able to establish their needs and position through it.

The children got so involved that they wanted to demonstrate Forum Theatre to their school assembly, which they did. In the last session of term they discussed what they had learned: mainly, they said, 'how to avoid fights, how not to be greedy and hog things, how to listen to each other, and how to respond to name calling.' The feedback from parents and teachers was that they felt the children had learned something that would be useful for the whole of their lives.

Michael Soth, 16 Riverside Road, Oxford OX2 OHU (tel 0865 723613).

Studying peaceful societies and tribes

The following item is from 'Tranet' newsletter (USA).

'there have been societies, such as the Tahitians, the Kung! and the Eskimo which did not know war'

Which societies have been the most affectionate and lived in the most peace? This is the topic for a course on the history of human relationships proposed by Art Rosenblum in 'Aquarian Alternatives.' Present history courses deal primarily with wars and the competition for power. But there have been societies, such as the Tahitians, the Kung! and the Eskimo which did not know war and which lived in affectionate relationships with one another. The proposed course of study would give us insights for developing a culture of peace and human kindness.

• *'Tranet', Box 567, Rangeley, ME 04970, USA (tel 207 864 2252).*
• *'Aquarian Alternative', 5620 Morton St, Philadelphia, PA 19144, USA.*

Schools social audits

Alec Dickson

'Every college of further education, every polytechnic and every university could apply their skills and knowledge to human needs and the solution of community problems'

Every secondary school, every college of further education, every polytechnic and every university could encourage its students, as an integral part of their curriculum or course, to apply the skills and knowledge they are acquiring to human needs and the solution of community problems. Here and there one can point to individual lecturers who are doing this – but only one single institution – Coventry Polytechnic – is making a serious attempt to do so as an institution. In effect it would entail institutions of education developing an extra dimension as resource centres of help to their region, as the

Land Grant Colleges in the U.S.A., established under Lincoln's Presidency have striven to do.

One technique – so simple that it can be grasped by a senior class in any school (although it could be applied to a factory just as well) – is to demonstrate how to undertake a Social Audit. Were it to be a college of education, one would start by listing under 'Assets', the qualifications, backgrounds, hobbies and possessions of every staff member, starting with the Principal: his academic speciality, his National Service with the Royal Engineers in the Korean campaign, his particular interests, his car(s) ... and so on with every single member of staff. Bravo, it is better than Unesco! Then what the Americans would call the 'plant': the labs, workshops, transport, swimming pool, cafeteria, gymnasium, library, orchestral instruments, stage, etc. Astounding: a veritable Aladdin's Cave! Now the students – their linguistic capabilities, sporting and musical talents, academic specialisations, artistic gifts. Incroyable! Add all this together – and these are the institution's assets. As for the 'Debit' side of the column, a survey of human needs and social problems in a one mile or five mile radius will reveal what cries out to be tackled.

'One would start by listing under "Assets", the qualifications, backgrounds, hobbies and possessions of every staff member'

Can the books be balanced? A Social Audit will probably indicate that the institution possesses the skills, talents and equipment to make a contribution to 80% or more of the local needs. And the sad conclusion will be reached that most of our institutions are contributing only 5% of their social potential.

Alec Dickson, 19 Blenheim Road, London W4 IVB (tel 081 994 7437).

320 hours per year of community service

Adapted extract from an article entitled 'Why Schools Don't Educate', by John Gatto, published in the Sun, USA, and monitored for the Institute by Roger Knights.

What does a restructured school system need? It needs to stop being a parasite on the working community. I think we need to make community service a required part of schooling. It is the quickest way to give young children real responsibility.

'I had every kid, rich and poor, smart and dipsy, give three hundred and twenty hours a year of hard community service'

For five years I ran a guerrilla school programme where I had every kid, rich and poor, smart and dipsy, give three hundred and twenty hours a year of hard community service. Dozens of those kids came back to me years later, and told me that this one experience changed their lives, taught them to see in new ways, to rethink goals and values. It happened when they were thirteen, in my Lab School programme – only made possible because my rich school district was in chaos. When 'stability' returned, the Lab closed. It was too successful, at too small a cost, to be allowed to continue. We made the expensive, elite programmes look bad.

There is no shortage of real problems in this city. Kids can be asked to help solve them in exchange for the respect and attention of the adult world. Good for kids, good for the rest of us.

Community service, independent study, adventures in experience, large doses of privacy and solitude, a thousand different apprenticeships, family involvement in the curriculum – these are all powerful, cheap, and effective ways to start a real reform of schooling.

Tutoring – of students by students

Alec Dickson

Every teacher in the States is familiar with the concept and practice of tutoring, whereby an older or abler pupil acts as tutor or mentor to a younger or less advanced child. It can be done on a one-to-one basis or with a small group; it can be done between pupils in the same class or school, but sometimes more effectively between, say, a high school pupil and an elementary school youngster; it can concentrate on difficulty in reading or in maths.

'An older or abler pupil acts as tutor or mentor to a younger or less advanced child'

In 1989, a high-powered conference, the first ever, took place at Imperial College, London, on the whole concept of tutoring, with sessions showing the many different forms it can take. Its director was Dr Sinclair Goodlad, who has pioneered the involvement of students of electrical engineering in helping pupils in comprehensive schools in Brixton and Pimlico with their maths.

Alec Dickson, 19 Blenheim Road, London W4 IVB (tel 081 994 7437).

Homework TV Hotline

Adapted excerpt from an item in the Wisconsin State Journal (USA) by Marci DeWolf, monitored for the Institute by Roger Knight.

Homework Hotline in Broward County, Florida is a call-in cable live TV show, with nine people staffing two phone banks, where students can get help with their homework. The programme is run by Instructional Television Centre and is produced by the public schools for the county's 160,000 pupils. Real teachers are the stars, helping kids with maths and other subjects.

Students' voices are heard on air, but only first names are used. Up to 20,000 callers have tried to get through in a week. They also give away prizes, often donated by local retailers, through game-show-like segments called 'Challenge Quest' and 'Brainteasers.' The show's host is Mindy Frumkes, a popular DJ. One of the four school teachers who share on-air duties says that 'it's a great programme. Although you are working with one child, you are actually teaching hundreds.'

'People They Laughed At' book

Valerie Yule

In every library there should be a book entitled 'People They Laughed At.' We need to be more aware of how much the world has been improved by people whose ideas were at first laughed at, and how much time and effort and even lives have been wasted because other people's first impulse has always been to ridicule and say 'it can't be done' and 'impossible.'

'The world has been improved by people whose ideas were at first laughed at'

The book would show how when it comes to new ideas, about one in a hundred will be a winner. So people who have silly ideas may still come up with a good one that should not be dismissed – and people who have had good ones can still have silly ones.

There would be an appendix of good ideas that have been taken up without the inventor having to struggle, too, to show that this can happen as well.

The book would show the danger in going overboard in taking up a great expensive scheme without pilot studies, just because conmen and charismatic people can be plausible, and greed can be blind (eg South Sea Bubbles and groundnuts in Africa) and how easy it is to say 'no' to quite simple schemes, as a reflex. It would quote Northcote Parkinson. And it would show how easy and valuable pilot experiments often can be – instead of crying 'no, it can't be done' as a matter of course.

There could be one edition for 8 to 12 year olds, in every school, another for 15 years upwards, and a third edition, possibly in chronological volumes, for institutes of tertiary education – with all editions of course available for general sale.

Valerie Yule, 57 Waimarie Drive, Mount Waverley, Victoria, Australia 3149 (tel 807 4315).

School Social Invention Workshops

The Institute for Social Inventions has for over four years now been running social invention workshops in state schools. The formula is very simple: a class (of any ages from 7 to 18) is allocated a budget of up to £25 to spend on a project of their own devising that will benefit either the school or the local community, with the project to be completed within one term of weekly two-hour sessions.

In session 1 pupils look at problems in their school, neighbourhood and own personal lives, selecting one or two problems to focus on. In session 2, they are taught 'brainstorming' as a way of coming up with as imaginative as possible ways of tackling these problems. In session 3, they draw up an action and evaluation plan, so that they will know at the end of the term to what extent they have succeeded, according to their own criteria. Thereafter, the pupils carry out their plan, sometimes working hard between sessions, and often ending up with striking projects. The following items describe some of the workshops.

Pooper Scooper Action Squad

A class of 23 seven and eight year olds at Essendine Primary School, London W9 were asked to think up a list of neighbourhood problems. The one that they decided to 'brainstorm' about was dog's mess, since the streets around the school were particularly fouled.

They made colourful placards with pictures and messages such as 'I hate dog's mess' and they laboriously sent out a press release announcing the formation of a 'Children's Pooper Scooper Action Squad' – for it was the Parisian technological solution of Pooper Scooper motorbikes that appealed to them, motorbikes with hoovers on the back which go up on the pavement to hoover up the mess.

With the Daily Telegraph, Paddington Mercury and LBC radio in attendance, the children visited Richard Branson's barge near their school with a petition suggesting that he spend some of his clean-up millions – he was then in charge of the government's environmental programme, UK 2000 – on buying some of these pooper-scooper motorbikes. Branson was halfway across the Atlantic in his Virgin Challenger 2 at the time, but his staff kindly allowed the children to go all over the barge, and said that Branson would like to call in at their school on his return.

> 'The children also wrote to the Westminster Council, who responded by bringing over from Paris one of the Pooper Scooper motorbikes, the first to be tried in the UK'

To fulfil their Action Squad image, the children used plastic gloves and seaside spades to collect demonstration amounts of dog's mess for the newspaper photographers. The children also wrote to the Westminster Council, who responded by bringing over from Paris one of the Pooper Scooper motorbikes, the first to be tried in the UK.

The class teacher, Isla Robertson, was delighted with the workshop, as the Westminster Council subsequently made a special effort to clean up around the school. 'You can't imagine what a disaster it is,' she pointed out, 'when you have 20 young children out on an expedition and one of them falls in dog's mess, there's no way to get them clean.'

This project won a Social Inventions Award in the Youth category. There are presently some 120 'Pooper Scooters' motorbikes at work in Paris.

Video of trouble with the police
Karen Chessell

A report from schools workshop leader Karen Chessell.

Ten non-academic fourteen year olds in my social inventions workshop at Raines Foundation School, Bethnal Green, were encouraged to brainstorm on problems to do with school, the community and their personal lives. Two major problems areas were identified: experiencing school as a 'prison' and getting into trouble, especially with the police. Further brainstorming for solutions to these problems produced the idea of going out of the school and making a drama documentary film that could be used to teach younger children how not to get into trouble.

Under my guidance and that of their teacher Carolyn Hallohan, the pupils set about outlining a film script and enlisting information and help from relevant sources. A video camera was organised by one of the pupils. Welfare Education Officer, Mr Waters, gave valuable preliminary information on legal aspects of juvenile crime and also accepted an acting role as social worker. Sergeant Jackie Hunt and PC Russell Taylor from the Bethnal Green Police Station not only agreed to come to talk to the class but also to take part in the dramatised 'arrest' scene complete with police van and its flashing lights. Furthermore, they arranged for the use of the Arbours Street Magistrates Court so that scenes in the charge room, courts and cells could be shot.

> 'The dramatised "arrest" scene complete with police van and its flashing lights'

Five of the pupils proved themselves to be 'naturals' as actors, doing justice to the work the whole class put into ideas for plot, location-hunting, music and artwork. The film is scheduled to be screened to other classes, with money from donations going to a local detention centre.

Just an Excuse to Have a Good Time

Leslie Freed and Nicholas Albery ran a Social Invention Workshop at Acton High School where a dozen sixth formers raised £660 for Cancer Research by deciding to put on the first public event the school had had for two years, a multi-cultural event called 'Just an Excuse to Have a Good Time.' There was £1 back at the door for those who came 'snazzily' dressed. The hall was packed out, with a central stage, and the audience grouped round little tables, and there were fancy foods from many cultures served in the intervals between sexy and funny acts, Armenian dancing and other magical events. At one of their last public events someone was stabbed. Not this time.

• *This Acton High School project won a Social Invention Workshop Award in the Youth category.*

• *'Social Invention Workshops – A manual' designed for teachers or other group leaders, is available from the Institute for Social Inventions, 20 Heber Road, London NW2 6AA (tel 081 208 2853; fax 081 452 6434) for £2-50. The Institute pays for and provides Social Invention Workshop leaders for state schools, mainly in the London region.*

Innovations Counsellors for teachers and parents

It seems there is a need for Innovations Counsellors in UK schools whose role would be to help *teachers and parents* in schools to develop, obtain funding, implement and evaluate their own projects for improving local education – a logical counterpart to the Institute's Social Invention Workshops in schools, where *pupils* do just this.

Valerie Yule worked as an honorary Innovations Counsellor with the Australian Schools Commission Innovations Programme, 1974 to 1978 (when she left for Scotland). Among the projects she helped get going were:

• School gardens run by teachers and children in disadvantaged areas with no gardens.

• A children's farm in an inner suburb (Collingwood) to delight and teach children, which still continues, against all the odds.

• Book-making facilities for children to turn their own writing into books for libraries and classrooms, including making local histories from interviews.

• Classes of older children 'hearing' the reading of younger children and reading to them.

• Children sharing responsibility for the maintenance of their schools as 'young housekeepers', with specific privileges.

• Secondary school pupils sharing in creche care of small children.

• 'Engineering experience' in primary schools, on the lines of the German 'fischertechnik' approach to training practical problem-solving and mechanical reasoning in young children.

'The emphasis in these projects was that the ideas must come from the people who would be carrying them out'

'The emphasis in these projects was that the ideas must come from the people who would be carrying them out. I was the facilitator.'

Valerie Yule, 57 Waimarie Drive, Mount Waverley, Victoria, Australia 3149 (tel 807 4315).

'O Level' Social Inventions

Mrs P.A. Pitcher studied at the Shipley College in West Yorkshire for her 'O Level' exam in English language. Her tutor gave the class an assignment to create a social invention, having shown them various papers from the Institute for Social Inventions.

'Mrs P.A. Pitcher studied at college for her O Level exam in English language. Her tutor gave the class an assignment to create a social invention'

Mrs Pitcher and her eleven fellow students came up with socially inventive ideas that were of a surprisingly high standard, which suggests that this might make a suitable assignment for a variety of classes. Here are examples of their ideas:

Adopt a House

Mrs Pitcher suggests that old people who could no longer cope alone could ask to be carefully matched by the local council with young families living in bed and breakfast accommodation. The council would buy the old person's house at the current market value, the parties would sign an agreement, and the family would move in, with the old person retaining at least one room as their own, and having full access to bathroom and kitchen.

'Old people who could no longer cope alone could ask to be carefully matched by the local council with young families living in bed and breakfast accommodation'

The council would visit initially every month and then every three months to make sure everything was going according to plan. There would be no obligation for the young couple to look after the older person, unless of course they wished to do so. On the death of the old person, the young couple should be offered the house at a reduced price, taking into account monies paid by them in rates and rent, or be allowed to remain as tenants.

Mrs Pitcher, 24 Old Langley Lane, Baildon, W. Yorks, BD17 6SG (tel 0274 581906).

Park and Pet Protection Club
Lisa Robinson

My friends and I set up a Park and Pet Protection Club, housed in a large hut which used to be part of a youth club, and open to all from 7 upwards. Our aims are to clean up the town's parks and to help the RSPCA. To look after the parks, we go around in small groups picking up litter and cleaning up ponds by removing dumped items that might prove harmful to pond life. Last year we received council finance to plant fifteen new trees. The club helps show people that the young are not always a nuisance in society.

'I'm driving not drinking' badges
Jacki Metcalfe

As part of the government's Christmas campaign against drinking and driving, pubs could supply badges saying 'I'm Driving Not Drinking' to relevant customers, with one free soft drink to each wearer as an incentive, and bar staff alerted not to serve alcohol to badge wearers.

Driving Schools League Table
Adrian Kitching

To help eliminate cowboy driving schools, the examiner after the driving test should give the driver a form to fill in, to be sent to the Driver Licence Centre at Swansea. A League Table of the driving schools in each area could thus be assembled.

'To help eliminate cowboy driving schools, a League Table of the driving schools in each area could thus be assembled at the Driving Licence Centre'

Voluntary Service Computing

Worth School is relating computer studies to the production of software for pupils with severe learning difficulties.

'Pupils are writing software specifically for use by 67 handicapped youngsters at the local Catherington Special Needs School'

Mr Truman has organised at Worth School, (an independent school for boys) under the heading of Voluntary Service Computing, a group of 13 to 17 year old pupils who are writing software specifically for use by 67 handicapped youngsters at the local Catherington Special Needs School.

This software is now sold nationwide by the school under the name 'W.E.Soft', with any profits being used to provide computing facilities for the handicapped.

Programs such as 'Colour Me! and Build Me!' and 'Roll-Over' (for recognising geometric shapes) are played by several users at once, thus teaching social skills too such as disciplined turn-taking, tolerance and the ability to deal with disappointment. Several of these programs are being marketed in Norwegian to Special Schools in Norway. The school also produced a program called Makaton Match for training pupils to recognise Makaton Symbols. This program has reached Australia.

Worth School has attracted users in both infant schools and pre-school groups, and amongst speech therapists and occupational therapists. The English package is used in secondary school and in a school with moderate learning difficulties, although initially designed for Special Schools. 'We are finding our software has a much wider use than we had originally envisaged.'

J. Truman, Head of Computing, Worth School, Paddockhurst Road, Turners Hill, Crawley, Sussex RH10 4SD (tel 0342 715911).

Computerised maths exam centres

Alison Crawshaw

In a nutshell, my suggestion – which is totally realistic – is that there should be access to computer-based and computer-marked elementary arithmetic examinations at centres (schools themselves and other) all over the country. In essence the examination would be very easy and consequently only a high mark would carry any weight. The test would have the special advantage that it could be taken (say) every month, so that candidates could improve their performance by repeated attempts until they achieved full marks or near it.

From time to time we read of the sensationally disappointing results of arithmetical performance among young school-leavers. I am concerned here with the subject of arithmetic only, but it would be possible (and I personally think useful) to extend my scheme to algebra and perhaps other subjects as well. However arithmetic is the outstanding example as far as

feasibility is concerned. This system would make it possible to avoid the cumbersome process of our normal public examinations which for many is a single and disastrous experience.

Such a test should be open to all (children included), but I am thinking particularly of the young innumerate school-leaver. The existence of the examination would give the young (and indeed the older) unemployed person a structured goal and produce a real rise in performance.

When I say 'performance', I do mean just that, for I am convinced that many, sadly perhaps most, school-leavers are under-achievers, sometimes to an absurd or tragic degree.

I write as someone who has coached dozens of young people who have not been given good mathematics instruction in their formative years. The main fault that I have found with the teaching they have already received (apart from not knowing the tables) is that it has been at far too high a level for the baffled pupil, who quite naturally simply gives up. I have taught a child for instance who did not understand decimals, yet had been taught arithmetic 'to other bases.' She had no idea what the normal base was. Hence my emphasis on an elementary syllabus, assuredly related to 'real life', together with a very good performance.

The use of computers for setting papers would be a simple way of maintaining a constant standard of variable questions. The computer would be programmed to print questions on (say) fractions, decimals, simple interest, hire-purchase agreements, speed/distance and time, areas/volumes, unitary method, averages, percentages and ratio. Calculators would not be allowed, but 'heavy' arithmetic would be avoided.

'The computer would have (say) 100 questions in each category fed into its memory, and test papers would be produced (by randomisation) with a question of each type'

The computer would have (say) 100 questions in each category fed into its memory, and test papers would be produced (by randomisation) with a question of each type. The chances of two papers being identical would be so small that it could be ignored. In any case the questions themselves could be changed at suitable intervals. In theory only one central computer would be needed and papers could be delivered by fax machines when required. This might or might not be more economical.

Candidates would pay for this examination, even if only a non-economic fee, to discourage frivolous use.

Books of sample papers and worked examples should also be available.

May I emphasise the entirely practical advantages of my suggestion: the low cost once the computers and fax machines were installed; the fairness; the availability to all; and above all the rapidity with which the results could be produced and the frequency with which the test could be taken. Several groups of people could take the examination in the same room at different times in one day, with no difficulty in supplying different papers for each group – or even each candidate.

Incidentally at the modest level I am considering, there would be no shortage of teachers, though of course it would be possible to have more than one level of examination.

I will finish with the comment that while it is not necessary for a nurse to have passed GCSE mathematics, it may be positively dangerous for her not to understand decimals: indeed I understand that so-called 'metrication deaths' are not unknown.

Ed: Perhaps the computer program could also offer the examinee a chance to go back over mistakes in the examination, offering coaching on those particular points, using good graphics, humour and real life or science fiction examples, making it all as much like an exciting computer game as possible – to help make up for any deficiencies in their regular teacher.

Alison Crawshaw, 13a Porchester Terrace, London W2 3TH (tel 071 262 6012).

The Computer Whizz Kids Club

Nicholas Albery

My son Merlyn, when he was 11, wrote a booklet entitled 'Learning Computer Programming in One Day – A Guide to BBC Basic.' This booklet enlightened me, as a computer illiterate. The programs take about four to five hours to plough through, allowing for tea breaks, and they got me to the stage where I was able to write one simple but subtle computer game of my own. My program took me most of one day to compose but it was a wonderful experience, like having a fine scalpel opening up whole new areas of the brain. We are hoping that parents will obtain this booklet as presents for their offspring – indeed it might suit anyone between 9 and 90 who feels overawed by computers (and who has access to a BBC/Acorn computer, the sort used in most schools). We also hope that schools will use it in computer training classes.

> 'A child who is enthusiastic about computer programming is at the same time learning algebra, graphic design, creative writing and typing skills'

I much prefer my son doing programming than watching TV or playing computer games. Learning a computer programming language now seems to me just as vital as learning other 'foreign' languages such as French. A child who is enthusiastic about computer programming is at the same time learning maths, algebra, graphic design, creative writing (for adventure programs) and typing skills. But above all, the child gains a sense of 'mastery' and self-esteem from being able to get a computer to perform well enough to create entertaining or useful programs, and the child learns the perseverance necessary to 'debug' a program of its inevitable initial errors.

One parent commented about her son's comprehensive school that the only children in the whole school who went on to university were those who made the leap from playing computer games to computer programming, because these children's enthusiasm led to their learning outside school and to forming in effect their own learning network where they were continuously referring to each other for help with their programming problems.

It can be a lonely anti-social experience for youngsters to sit glued to computer screens at every available moment. So Merlyn's booklet introduces a Computer Whizz Kid Club, (again for all ages). The club is open to those who have done its basic programs, who would like a Programming Pal to exchange programs with, or 'Super Whizz Kids' they can phone for advice. Club members send in a photograph and details of their computer and peripherals, and are sent a club badge and the details of a suitable partner with whom they can begin to exchange their own programs and games.

'Learning Computer Programming in One Day', by Merlyn Albery-Speyer, is published by the Institute for Social Inventions, 20 Heber Road, London NW2 6AA (tel 081 208 2853; fax 081 452 6434), £2-50 incl. p&p. The Computer Whizz Kids Club is at the same address.

Computer programming holidays

Allen Carter and Peter Tilsley

Computer Park is a specialist computer holiday, with nine computer supervisors, for forty beginner or advanced participants of all ages from 10 to adults, although mostly patronised by teenage boys aged 13 to 17. Based in a splendid Queen Anne mansion in Northamptonshire, it is run by enthusiasts brought together from a wide range of computing backgrounds – education, industry, research and development, and we as the directors have a great deal of experience in education and training. Computer Park is for two weeks in August each year, costing about £325 per week, all in.

Unlike computer holidays which, when you read between the lines, only allow a couple of hours 'hands-on' experience per day, our computer rooms are open from 9am to 9pm every day and have more computers than people using them.

What makes Computer Park special to many people is the atmosphere. The staff are very friendly and helpful and there is never any regimentation – everything is optional, with you deciding what you are going to spend your time doing. Many participants come back for their fifth or sixth consecutive year.

Activities listed in the brochure include: numerous programming competitions, introductions to various programming languages, games techniques, graphics, computer games, group projects, a daily desktop-published newsletter, a barbecue, swimming in the pool and table tennis. Computer Park, 25 Bridge Street, Rothwell, Kettering, Northants NN14 2JW (tel 0536 712627).

Unisim

Peter Walker MP once suggested that pupils in the last year at school should be taught about National Savings, unit trusts, shareholding, mortgages and how to start up a business – all through a 150 page book. Mr Walker subsequently accepted the Institute for Social Invention's rider that computer games, like an extended version of Monopoly, could play an important part in the process of introducing pupils to all aspects of money, and would be more likely to hold pupils' attention than books.

It could also be a useful educational tool for Eastern Europeans wanting to learn the basics of the free market system.

'Pupils in the last year at school should be taught about National Savings, unit trusts, shareholding, mortgages and how to start up a business'

No such computer game exists at present. The nearest thing to it seems to be Unisim, produced by Unilever for schools at a subsidised price of £20. In this game, four companies set up factories to produce chocolate bars, and compete to see over the course of the term which can gain the dominant position, judged by percentage share of the market and accumulated profit.

Each period, the pupils have to decide how many crates to produce, the price in each market region, the number of sales staff and wages; how much advertising and market research to pay for; whether to set up new production lines; whether to borrow more money from the bank; and whether to pay dividends. The tutor can vary a number of elements, bringing on a Christmas rush, or altering the raw material price, warehousing costs and interest rates, or issuing union claims.

It sounds sophisticated, and is aimed at students aged 16 and over. The Institute tried out the basic game on a group of children aged 11 to 15, who took to it like mosquitoes to blood, absorbing profit and loss accounts and balance sheets. They went through six periods of trading, supposed to take half a term, in one evening. It has to be said, however, that none was less than £150,000 in debt by the end. As one teacher commented: 'They realise it's not as easy to make a profit as some people think.'

Unisim, Freepost, P.O. Box 10, Wetherby, West Yorks LS23 6YY (tel Alan George, Unilever Educational Liaison, 071 822 5804).

Comment by Valerie Yule

In Australia this has gone even further. One schools competition involved investing a small sum on the Stock Exchange, and the winning class made thousands of dollars' profit. (I do not know if I really like this training in greedy speculation.)

Valerie Yule, 57 Waimarie Drive, Mount Waverley, Victoria, Australia 3149 (tel 807 4315).

A database of students' best work

Jeff Mason

Adapted extract from a proposal submitted to the Institute.

The computerised course database, in my vision, uses technology to offset the alienation and intellectual isolation of student life in higher education. It holds out the opportunity for students to engage with something more than their own individual academic careers. It offers a chance to be acknowledged and remembered for good work.

Ideally, each student obtains a copy of the master disc at the start of the course. This, copied in turn, becomes the basis of an interaction between student and database. New work is added and then transferred to the master disc, where it is collected and collated. At the end of the year, a final edit becomes the master disc for the next year, and so a sustainable project comes into being. Before very long, each new student will start work standing on the shoulders of the ones who have gone before, if only two or three years before. Each will have the chance to lend their own shoulders for later students to stand on in their turn.

'the computerised course data base contains the best students' essays, research reports and course suggestions'

The database also holds easily accessible information relevant to specific courses: bibliographies tailored to specific needs, teaching schemes, course outlines old and new, course histories and the evolution of relevant syllabuses, lecture notes, old exam papers, essay questions and topics, pertinent excerpts from course texts; and the best students' essays, research reports, journal abstracts, student evaluations and course suggestions. It holds, in addition, an up-to-date handbook with the course dates, rules and assessment regulations. The database is open to each generation of students to investigate and enhance.

The research database promotes the growth of academic life. Just as philosophy, literature or history have their own major texts and authors, so a course-based database contains major student texts. The index will record their best work topic and name. In a few years the work of generations of students will be represented in the files, whose work will be part of the appeal of particular courses. A small-scale tradition forms around the data base. New students are invited to take it up and carry it into the future as a project to which they can make a contribution.

Jeff Mason, 67 Harvard Court, Honeybourne Road, London NW6.

Mouth organs for every child

'When young, what is more exciting than to make a noise, the beginning of music,' writes Beatrice Landale, with reference to the Harp Start School, which would like to place a mouth organ in the hands of every child in the kingdom and to teach them how to play. The project was started with three children in Caister-on-Sea in Norfolk by David Michelsen and Norman Ives and in its first few weeks grew to fifty, all by word of mouth.

'The Harp Start School would like to place a mouth organ in the hands of every child in the kingdom'

They now meet on Sundays from 2 to 4pm at St Mary's Church Hall, Regent Road, Great Yarmouth; and they have acquired the support of Sir Yehudi Menuhin and Larry Adler. The children are taught to play chord, bass, diatonic and chromatic harmonicas, learn to read and write music, and learn about stage craft and media craft. No charge is made, although donations and sponsorship are sought. Children without harmonicas are encouraged to buy one for £5 or under.

The Harp Start School, 1 Links Close, Caister-on-Sea, Norfolk NR3 5DD (tel 0493 728654 or 071 359 5168).

Pathfinder Club

Eileen Chandler

Many legal footpaths throughout the country have become blocked, overgrown and difficult to walk (or even find). Often people turn back as they do not wish to trespass on farming property. So the paths often disappear completely and there is no real access to many beautiful parts of the country.

Yet there are many unemployed young people on Community Service who would be available to clear these paths and erect the necessary signposts. Maps are available from local authorities or sometimes other sources (local bookshops, ramblers clubs, local history societies, etc).

> **'The class would walk this path each month and keep records of the changes noted for each season'**

Once the paths clearly exist, each school in the area should be asked to join the Pathfinder Club. This would mean that each class in the school would 'adopt' one particular local path. (The paths chosen would obviously depend on the age of the children and the distance, etc involved). The class would then walk this path each month (or as often as possible) and children would keep records of the changes noted for each season – budding of certain trees, different birds seen, crops planted, nests notes, and the different animal tracks in snow.

Children would be helped to understand the necessity for the Countryside Code and the need to conserve wildlife. Better access would create better understanding and treatment of plants and animals and hopefully less vandalism to trees.

I went ahead with the Institute for Social Inventions' suggestion and tested the reactions of all those people who might be affected if the Pathfinder Club were to go ahead in this district.

I wrote explaining the scheme to the local headmasters, heads of community education, heads of community service, National Farmers Union, Leicester Footpaths Association, Leicester Landowners Association, Ramblers Association, Uppingham Parish Council, Leicester Rural Community Council and the countryside and recreation officer for Leicester Council.

Mr Bob Gilson, the countryside and recreation officer and Miss Mills from the Manpower Services Commision did, in fact, come out from Leicester to meet me, and I was by then able to show them the very enthusiastic replies from the various organisations and local people I had contacted.

Leicester Council employed someone, using Community Programme funding, to take the Pathfinder Club into schools. Information packs were produced for teachers, and paths were cleared, initially by young people on government schemes.

The Uppingham parish councillors were very enthusiastic about the Pathfinder Club idea and a councillor volunteered to check all land ownership of local footpaths so that the Pathfinder scheme could go ahead in Uppingham as well as Leicester.

> **'Leicester Council took the Pathfinder Club into schools in the area. Information packs were produced for teachers, and paths were cleared, initially by young people on government schemes'**

Eileen Chandler, 67 Stockerston Crescent, Uppingham, Rutland, Leicestershire LE15 9UA. One of the Leicester Council officers responsible for helping launch the scheme was Rosemary Mills (tel 0533 323232), who says that it ran successfully for the duration of its Community Programme funding.

Yoga in schools

Rosemary Owen

All schoolchildren from the age of five onwards should have regular, timetabled sessions of yoga exercises.

> **'All schoolchildren from the age of five onwards should have regular, timetabled sessions of yoga exercises'**

Yoga is a good way of helping children to develop an awareness of their own bodies and feelings. It has an exhilarating and calming effect, and could lead in later life to a marked reduction of stress, postural and blood pressure problems and nervous disorders. New evidence also suggests that it may be helpful in preventing diabetes.

Yoga can be adapted for all children, including the physically impaired and the overweight. It does not need to be presented as a religious practice, nor does it conflict with any religion.

Rosemary Owen, 12 Vicarage Close, Billesdon, Leicestershire LE7 9AN (tel 0533 755 750).

Label-challenging games

Keith Kennedy has developed a range of over twenty games that challenge habits, cliches and labels and which he has used in his teaching in schools, colleges and hospitals since 1965. 'I can vouch, also,' Kennedy writes, 'that some are playable in "parlour" venues.' They are 'games in which human conditions and terms are re-examined and temporarily, during play, restructured and renamed. They are central to my working life.' Some examples include:

Camera Adventure

Camera Adventure. A group is despatched by bus or train to an unknown destination carrying sealed orders which can only be opened in transit. Thus a group of 25 school pupils, age 14 upwards, in sub-groups of five, found themselves in London's Dockland called upon to photograph and to tape-record 'manifestations', 'tokens' and 'symptoms' of love.

> 'A group of 25 school pupils found themselves in London's Dockland called upon to photograph and to tape-record "manifestations", "tokens" and "symptoms" of love'

Squeeze

Squeeze sessions where each person is given a blank book (a quantity of A4 paper in a spiral binder) and has to fill it with a story or memoir in one hour, using words and pictures, and with time checks at five-minute intervals.

> 'Each person is given a blank book and has to fill it with a story or memoir in one hour'

The Identi-Kit

The Identi-Kit where a group explores self-images through each person filling a booklet with drawings or photos to a number of pre-set captions – such as 'This picture of me is a lie', 'When I am sad I look like this', 'These are my images of heaven and hell', 'This picture irritates me', 'The movie-story of my life will include this compelling scene', 'I dream...', 'I love...'

Keith Kennedy, 55 St Anne's Crescent, Lewes, Sussex, ISD BN7 (tel 0273 478131).

Student loans repaid by National Insurance contributions

Dr Nicholas Barr and colleagues at the LSE have proposed an ingenious and compelling alternative to the government's bank-based student loans scheme. They suggest that student loans could be repaid via National Insurance contributions. To those who criticise this idea for ideological reasons as being too 'public sector', Dr Barr replies that National Insurance contributions are collected by employers, who simply send a cheque to the Department of Social Security once a month. These repayments would be earmarked at source and passed directly to the lending institutions, and need never become part of the National Insurance Fund. The following is adapted from Dr Barr's 102 page paper, 'Student Loans: The Next Steps' (Aberdeen University Press):

Though phasing out parental contributions is desirable, the student loan facility in the early days might best be used mainly to boost student incomes, and parental contributions phased out only when that has been achieved.

Our scheme allows substantial saving on student maintenance, and could be introduced in such a way that there are public expenditure savings from the first year onwards. The scheme thus offers resources for an immediate expansion of higher education.

The savings in public expenditure are very large – with savings of £300 million per year by 2005, and even more if the loan is allowed to exceed half the grant. The real resource savings are almost as large. Thus it is possible to have substantial expansion of higher education in the 1990s and also Treasury savings in the early 2000s, when the demographic crunch comes.

Because the additional National Insurance contribution is small, labour market distortions will be minimal. For those above the upper earnings limit, the repayment is equivalent to a lump-sum tax.

> 'The scheme is fair and will be seen to be so. No one repays more than they have borrowed; and with income-related repayments no one repays more than they can afford'

The scheme is fair and will be seen to be so. No one repays more than they have borrowed; and with income-related repayments no one repays more than they can afford.

The scheme is flexible: it allows early repayment by graduates (or their employers) who wish to do so; and it can accommodate a variety of social policy goals.

Avoiding repaying loans through black economy work will be rare. There is little incentive to evade National Insurance contributions, since one's future benefits are involved. And graduates whose loans have to be written off entirely because they do not earn 20 per cent of average earnings in any single week throughout their entire working life will be increasingly rare. The contract which a student signed upon taking out a loan could include a clause converting it into a mortgage-type loan upon emigration, with debt enforcement through the courts if the government so wished; or the previous contributions or future benefits of defaulting emigrants could be attached.

Since students borrow from private-sector sources and since banks receive a reliable return, the scheme is readily extensible to new classes of students (eg those studying part time, and those currently eligible only for non-mandatory grants) without the need for a battle between the Department of Education and the Treasury.

The scheme accords well with one of the key Beveridge principles. It reinforces the contributory principle and helps individuals to be self-supporting by enabling them to redistribute to themselves at different stages in their life cycle. This is what retirement pensions do. Student loans are an up-front pension. Since the private market does not readily supply long-term unsecured loans it is efficient that there should be some state involvement, at least in providing a mechanism for collecting repayments.

> 'The scheme is flexible, cheap to run, easy to understand, administratively simple, politically attractive, efficient, fair and easily extensible'

The scheme, in short, is flexible, cheap to run, easy to understand, administratively simple, politically attractive, efficient, fair and easily extensible.

The government's scheme, in contrast, has combined effects of defaults, write-offs and administrative costs that wholly outweigh any public expenditure savings. It would be cheaper simply to give the students the money. (A similar conclusion was reached by a Swedish Royal Commission on their private sector loan scheme.) The cumulative addition to public spending between 1990 and 2027 for the government scheme over the National Insurance scheme is £18.3 billion.

Dr Nicholas Barr, The London School of Economics and Political Science, Houghton Street, London WC2A 2AE (tel 071 955 7482). This scheme won a Social Inventions Award. The government's scheme, in its first year, spent almost £13m giving out a mere 180,000 loans worth a total of £70m; ie, on average, an administrative cost of £72 per £388 loan.

Education on a human scale

The Human Scale Education Movement has been formed to increase the general awareness that, for education to be truly effective, the whole physical and social environment must provide young learners with the feeling that they, as persons, are what matter most to the learning community.

It also promotes such structures and relationships by pointing to good practice and encouraging new initiatives, and supports parents and teachers working for change in the mainstream.

Human scale education can be achieved in large as much as in small schools. If the will to establish supportive relationships is there, the means can be found irrespective of the school's size.

Action for Change

The Movement's patrons include Lord Young of Dartington, Anita Roddick and Sir Yehudi Menuhin. The Movement has selected three initiatives for action and support:

'Allow large schools to restructure on a human scale'

Minischools and other schemes that allow large schools to restructure on a human scale. Examples of minischooling such as Stantonbury Campus in Milton Keynes show that it works well.

Small schools, especially where the intention is that they should be non-fee paying and have open access. The challenge is to provide a wide curriculum and high adult/pupil ratio without being 'uneconomical.'

Flexischooling, which encourages schools to combine school with home-based or community-based education.

How the Movement works

The Human Scale Education Movement, launched in 1987, operates at both a national and local level and provides conferences, a newsletter, a handbook 'Working Together: exploring values in education', a forum for dialogue between the maintained and alternative sectors and local branches which form for discussion, support and action.

Minischooling

Minischooling was discussed by Philip Toogood in a booklet published by the Movement ('Minischooling – The Answer for Overlarge and Falling Rolls Schools', 1987, £2-50). One part of the book charts the story of the minischools experiment between 1970 and 1983 at Madeley Court Comprehensive in Telford New Town. A striking transformation was achieved:

'Theft in the minischools was almost as absent as it is in a submarine. Attendance was well over 90% on average'

'Theft in the minischools was almost as absent as it is in a submarine. Attendance was well over 90% on average. Children could communicate with each other. The teachers related to each other as people and not as members of a subject discipline area. Parents got to know teachers, often holding committee meetings in pubs and homes.

'We could have introduced a school dinner parent cooperative and done our own maintenance and cleaning too, had this been permitted.'

'The vision is one of federations of minischools within old large school sites; above all, of children in a setting small and sane enough for them to be treated as human beings'

The vision is one of federations of minischools within old large school sites; associations of autonomous small schools; and networks of 'flexischools' for all ages. But above all, children in a setting small and sane enough for them to be treated as human beings.

Fiona Carnie, Human Scale Education Movement, 96 Carlingcott, near Bath BA2 8AW, Avon (tel 0761 433733). A subscription to their newsletter costs £12 (£8 for the low-waged).

Adopt-a-Planet £1,000 competition

Readers are urged to involve their local schools in this competition, sponsored by the Gulbenkian Foundation since the scheme's launch in 1991. It focuses on anti-vandalism and anti-graffiti projects:

'Any class of any age can enter. They must select an area in the neighbourhood to "adopt" that has been vandalised'

Any class of any age (or any youth club members) can enter. They must select an area in the neighbourhood to 'adopt' that has been vandalised and must draw up and carry out their own imaginative scheme to improve it. The final deadline for entries is October 9th each year. There is no entry form, but entries should ideally include before and after photos, and entries will be judged according to how imaginative the projects are, how persevering, how well written-up; and on the extent to which they have drawn in local support and funding.

The main overall winner for 1991 was:

George Farmer School in Holbeach, Lincolnshire. Here the Year 10 and 11 City and Guilds Land Based Studies Group decided to adopt a disused pond in Holbeach, one mile from the school, which had become, they say 'an eyesore, a dumping site and a general embarrassment.' They got a local contractor to excavate the pond, and the pupils cleared the area and planted shrubs, trees and wild flower seeds. Police and local farmers are helping keep watch over the area to prevent future dumping. The pupils spent the prize money on a bird table, nesting boxes, benches and another small pond.

The other winners were:

'the renovation of a neglected and vandalised area next to Sherwood Library'

Sherwood Park County Primary School in Tunbridge Wells, Kent. They chose to campaign for the renovation of a neglected and vandalised area next to Sherwood Library, and they persuaded the council to order three new seats and two new bins and to make other improvements. They also organised a 'Plant a Bulb for Sherwood Day', and spent their prize money on play equipment for their adopted area. They submitted a giant dossier of their ideas for the area - the project was carried out by pupils throughout the school, ranging in age from four to eleven, using their drawings, paintings, poems, letter writing, site sketching, design and technology skills and vivid imaginations.

Nicholas Albery, General Secretary, the Council for Posterity, 20 Heber Road, London NW2 6AA (tel 081 208 2853; fax 081 452 6434).

Children's Alliance for Protection of the Environment (CAPE)

Ingrid Kavanagh

I was the original coordinator of the Adopt a Beach programme in Texas. In that capacity, and as honorary consul to Costa Rica, I introduced the concept of volunteer beach clean-ups in Costa Rica through a cooperative agreement between schoolchildren.

'I introduced the concept of volunteer beach clean-ups in Costa Rica through a co-operative agreement between schoolchildren'

The beach clean-up spread rapidly as a children's programme throughout Costa Rica – and was soon copied in Honduras. Seeing the potential for an international children's conservation movement that could encompass numerous environmental action programmes in addition to the beach

clean-ups, I have formed an independent non-profit organisation called CAPE – the Children's Alliance for Protection of the Environment. We have established a partnership with the United Nations Environment Programme.

Children can join CAPE without charge, either individually or as part of a group, and a newsletter will be sent out. Other initial projects include:

• Expansion of the beach clean-up campaign

• Sponsorship of co-operative tree-planting programmes for children, to raise awareness of the global importance of rain forests

• Promotion of other community clean-up and beautification programmes by children.

'An International Beach Appreciation Day. On the date selected, children all around the world help clean beaches'

• Sponsorship of an International Beach Appreciation Day. On the date selected, children all around the world help clean beaches.

• Participation in a Global Clean-Up Party, in conjunction with World Environment Week. A manual describes how children can take part.

• Each national CAPE 'chapter' appoints an advisory board composed of children and is invited to send a delegate from this body to the annual meeting of the international board of directors.

Ingrid Kavanagh, CAPE, PO Box 307, Austin, Texas 78767, USA (tel 512 478 6728 day; 512 258 0557 residence).

Højskole High School

Nicholas Saunders

The UK would do well to imitate the Danish Højskole High School system. This was invented in 1820 by a man called Grundtvig, who was actually a vicar with rather radical ideas. Thanks to his connections with royalty, he was able to implement his scheme whereby every adult Dane has the right to spend three months at a residential course in order to study something for their own self-development, at any time in life.

'Every adult Dane has the right to spend three months at a residential course in order to study something for their own self-development, any time in life'

These high schools are privately set up and some are very loosely run. Some are just people wanting to have a good time, some are for serious study. Some schools are for the study of fashionable subjects like martial arts, peace studies or psychotherapy, some are for crafts and literature, and some are very political – the one thing that they have in common is that they are courses for self-development rather than training for work.

Nicholas Saunders, top floor, 14 Neal's Yard, London WC2H 9DP (tel 071 836 9404; fax 071 379 0135).

The world does not need successful people

Adapted extract from an article entitled 'What is Education for?' by David Orr, in 'In Context' 27 (USA).

There is a myth that the purpose of education is that of giving you the means for upward mobility and success. Thomas Merton once identified this as the 'mass production of people literally unfit for anything except to take part in an elaborate and completely artificial charade.' When asked to write about his own success, Merton responded by saying that 'if it so happened that I had once written a best seller, this was a pure accident, due to inattention and naiveté, and I would take very good care never to do the same again.' His advice to students was to 'be anything you like, be madmen, drunks, and bastards of every shape and form, but at all costs avoid one thing: success.'

'Be anything you like, be madmen, drunks, and bastards of every shape and form, but at all costs avoid one thing: success'

The plain fact is that the planet does not need more 'successful' people. But it does desperately need more peace-makers, healers, restorers, story-tellers, and lovers of every shape and form. It needs people who live well in their places. It needs people of moral courage willing to join the fight to make the world habitable and humane. And these needs have little to do with success as our culture has defined it.

Chapter three

RELATIONSHIPS

Relationships – the main research findings

What have social scientists found out about the relationships between men and women that is not either obvious common sense or by now already well known? Not a great deal, it seems, to judge from two of the best books on the topic. However, in case these research findings can inspire you to social inventions, here are some of the interesting tit-bits that these books contain. First, the more academic of the two books, 'Human Relationships', by Steve Duck, published by Sage Publications (28 Banner Street, London EC1Y 8QE), 1986, which lists references to over 400 books and papers:

• 'Men "fall in love" at an earlier point in a relationship than women do, but women fall out of love sooner than men do.' (Walster and Walster, 1978).

• 'Contrary to popular myth, men are more romantic in their views of love than women are, and over two-thirds of the women surveyed say that they would marry a man whom they did not love – if everything else about the person was acceptable.' (Kephart, 1967).

• 'We find it more appropriate to sit opposite people with whom we will have an argument and to sit next to people with whom we agree. (Sommer, 1969; Cook, 1968). Conversely, it is harder to disagree with someone sitting next to us.'

• 'Speakers often adapt their speech (rate, silences, accents, loudness) to be more similar to that of the partner, particularly when they wish to relax that person or to ingratiate themselves.' (Giles et al, 1973).

• 'One reason why "like is attracted to like" is because we dislike uncertainty. We feel surer about a partner and of our relationship's future the more like us they are. Research consistently shows that people choose partners who come from their own racial, religious, economic, intellectual and social background.' (Kerckhoff, 1974).

• 'Liking for a partner can be re-established or aided by means such as keeping a record, mental or physical, of the positive or pleasing behaviour of our partner rather than listing the negatives and dwelling on them in isolation (Bandura, 1977), ... (or by making) greater efforts to understand the reasons that our partner may give for what is happening in the relationship.'

• 'Couples with high conflict in courtship do not seem to learn to handle it any better and continue to be highly conflictive in later marriage.' (Kelly et al, 1985).

• 'Happy couples express agreement more often than they express disagreement with the spouse during problem solving or conflict.' (Gottman, 1979; Riskin and Faunce, 1972).

• 'What is the best premarital predictor of marital stability? It is the ability to deal with conflict in the time before marriage.' (Kelly et al, 1985).

> ### 'Liking for a partner can be re-established or aided by means such as keeping a record, mental or physical, of the positive or pleasing behaviour of our partner'

• 'The more premarital sexual partners that a person has, the less marital happiness he or she is likely to report.' (Athanasiou and Sarkin, 1974).

• 'There is a gradual decrease in happiness over the first 10 years of marriage (Rollins and Feldman, 1970) but it increases after the children leave home.' (Argyle and Henderson, 1984).

Candida Peterson's book, 'Keeping Love Alive', published by Dove Communications (60-64 Railway Road, Blackburn, Victoria 3130, Australia, £5-95), is more aimed at lovers, with charts for the reader to fill in that will tell you everything from how idolatrous your love is and whether your conflict strategy is satisfactory to how well you would cope with widowhood. The research findings Peterson reports include:

• 'For Maslow's exceptionally mature and well-adjusted "self-actualisers" the quality of the love satisfactions and the sex satisfactions both improve with the age of the relationship ... improved by familiarity with the partner rather than by novelty.' (Maslow, 1954).

• Evidence for heightened sexual arousal under conditions of high anxiety was provided by Donald Dutton and Arthur Aron (1974). 9 out of 33 men meeting an attractive young female on a dangerous bridge rang her subsequently to ask for a date, as against only 2 out of 33 men on a safe bridge.

• 'When asked to give general advice from the vantage point of their experience, most of the older couples told their interviewers that the single most important feature of a successful marriage was not sexual satisfaction, emotional closeness or even personality growth, but rather "sharing" and "effective expression of true feelings". ' (Stinnett et al, 1972).

> 'Evidence for heightened sexual arousal under conditions of high anxiety: 9 out of 33 men meeting an attractive young female on a dangerous bridge rang her subsequently to ask for a date, as against only 2 out of 33 men on a safe bridge'

• 'Marjorie Fiske (1979) found that the single best predictor of morale and mental health after the age of 60 was having an intimate "confidant".'

Ed: The only two social innovations I could find in Peterson's book were, firstly, the not-new idea of fixed-term marriage contracts:

• 'Brides and grooms refrain from ambitious promises of lifelong affection and simply agree to stay wedded until the contract expires (often after five years). At this point they are required to make a thorough assessment of the marriage's strengths and weaknesses. Only if they discover that it still suits them, and that their more mature natures are at least as compatible as their earlier personalities were, will a further fixed-term contract be drawn up.'

And secondly, a small idea for stimulating conversations between spouses:

• 'The Mehans (who share childcare and work) have made it a rule that the spouse who stays home cooks dinner, while the one remaining at work is responsible for seeing that conversation over the meal never flags. Once the rule came into effect, they both found themselves reading the newspaper more, and paying more attention to the car radio and the gossip at work, so as to be able to fulfil the conversational part of the bargain.'

Man-woman brainstorms

Nicholas Albery

One of the main ways in which the Institute for Social Inventions has explored new and imaginative ways for improving the relationships between women and men, has been to host a number of brainstorming groups. In case any reader would like to try running similar groups on this theme – the participants found the meetings very stimulating and refreshing – the format for these two-hour sessions is normally roughly as follows:

The brainstorming ground rules are explained: state ideas briefly like telegrams; no criticism of another's ideas; if you do not like someone's idea, improve it or go off on a tangent of your own; go for quantity of ideas, do not worry about the quality; weird, wild, outrageous ideas are welcome. All ideas are recorded (in our case on rolls of lining paper using felt tip pens).

First there is a ten-minute warm-up exercise such as: imagine it is the year 2020, you are the benevolent leader in a tiny country of Lichtensteinian proportions. You have managed to introduce laws, structures, customs and changes of lifestyle that have helped improve the way women and men get on out of all recognition. What measures did you take?

The remaining time is divided more or less equally between participants, and each in turn is invited to outline a personal problem in their relationship with the opposite sex. The others in response brainstorm ideas or projects for helping tackle that class of problem (not necessarily that person's personal problem, so there is less need for defensiveness on the proposer's part. It is more an assumption that other people probably have similar problems and that social inventions might help).

> 'Each in turn is invited to outline a personal problem in their relationship with the opposite sex. The others in response brainstorm ideas for helping tackle that class of problem'

The trial one-off groups that the Institute has experimented with have been too short to come up with very worthwhile or weighty projects, although a group committed to carrying out a project and meeting once a week for say ten weeks using the above formula in the initial meetings would no doubt be able to do so – just as our school groups routinely succeed in creating projects from brainstorming their own topics of concern. But these new groups have proved to be a superb and creative way to bring together men and women with very diverse views, ranging from unreformable macho men to radical feminists, where normally a discussion would have stood no chance of getting going. I would recommend this type of meeting to any group wanting to break the ice and discover more about each other's views and approaches to life.

Here are a just a few of the many hundreds of ideas the participants proposed:

• A group at the Association of Humanistic Psychotherapists' conference came up with the idea for popularising heterosexual Non-Pen-Friends (non-penetrative sex), (developed in an item below by Nicholas Saunders), as one response to the AIDS threat.

• There should be a menu of several hundred different legal marriage contracts that a couple could choose from, with varying conditions and lengths of contract, or they could have one designed à la carte.

• There could be a charity or housing co-op for single parents (or for parents who do not get on very well), with each adult having their own accommodation, but sharing a communal garden totally enclosed by the houses, so that the children can play safely, with access to a multitude of adults. In fact all new family housing in cities in these violent days should be designed with a communal garden totally enclosed by clusters of seven or eight houses.

> 'All new family housing in cities in these violent days should be designed with a communal garden totally enclosed by clusters of seven or eight houses'

• How to meet girlfriends or boyfriends if new to a city? Any permutation of sexes would work, but in this example it is two men who go to a tourist spot together, they wait until they spot two women they fancy, then buy four ice-creams, and offer two to the women, saying that their friends have gone off, and it would be a shame to waste them.

> 'Two thirds of the participants on a two-week course ended up pairing off and were still together a year later'

• Where is the best place in Europe for people in their thirties and forties to meet new mates? Answer: the Skyros Growth Centre on the Greek Island of Skyros, where two thirds of the participants on a two-week course ended up pairing off and were still together a year later. The combination of a romantic setting, massage and therapy in the morning, nude beach in the afternoon and home-made theatre and parties in the evening is very powerful. (The Skyros Centre, c/o 1 Fawley Road, London NW6, tel 071 431 0867. For those that prefer sport to therapy, the Atsitsa Centre, run by the same organisation, offers sporting holidays on the other side of the island.)

• Advertise a competition for the best design for a research programme into what are the significant factors for long-term compatibility, the prize being enough money to carry out the research, leading perhaps afterwards to a computer-based pairing service.

• The couple at the start of a relationship to put their ideas on life in order of importance (for example concerning having children or willingness to earn money conventionally), so that each partner is warned from the start.

• When arguing with your spouse, half way through the argument, agree between you to switch and play the other's part. It is easier to give up arguing if you are gleefully surrendering on the other's behalf.

> 'When arguing with your spouse, half way through the argument, agree between you to switch and play the other's part. It is easier to give up arguing if you are gleefully surrendering on the other's behalf'

• Boss time, where each partner in turn gets what they want from the other for half an hour.

• Teach co-counselling at schools, so that children learn to listen to their partner for half an hour without interruption and without constantly planning their own reply.

• Forum Theatre sessions for arguing couples, where they re-enact their argument to the audience of similar couples, and at the second re-enactment any spectator can call a halt and go in the middle and take over one of the parts, going on to demonstrate a more creative continuation or resolution. (For further details see the item on Forum Theatre in this book's chapter on Education.)

• A couple need to find other ways to get high together besides sex – chanting, dancing, yoga, church or whatever.

• 'The only social invention a couple needs is to relax and tell the truth.'

The man who found a wife through a large sign outside his house

Adapted from an article by Steve Plamann in the National Enquirer (USA).

Harley Cobb placed an estate-agency size notice in front of his house in Pasadena, California. It read, in large smart lettering: 'Widower 55 seeks attractive lady (40-60), friendship ... maybe more' and gave his phone number. His sign and his story appeared in newspapers and on TV, and he received more than 4,000 calls from marriage-minded women around the world. He interviewed 800 and dated 81 of them before meeting his wife, Helen, who lived in the neighbourhood.

Helen, 46, remembers: 'When I first saw Harley's sign, I thought to myself, "There's a fruitcase". But one day I happened to be walking by when he was outside, posing for a photographer. I thought to myself: "He looks normal".'

She phoned him. They met twice. They got married.

The Adventure and Romance Agency

Ken Campbell

Early in January last year I was approached in the Hampstead Pub which used to be called The Cruel Sea by an exceedingly charismatic gent who I'd say was in his thirties. I'd never met him before to my recall, but he knew my name and immediately gained a sympathetic hearing by his declaration that the Fringe was currently lifeless in comparison to my great experiments of days gone by.

He told me his name was Peter Northover and he ran the Adventure and Romance Agency. He showed me a brochure exciting us to the type of work undertaken by his outfit. He hadn't a spare one to give me, and nor could he give me the address of his Agency, since, he claimed, it didn't have one. But he allowed me to copy down what I wished to of the strange brochure. I have my notebook of the time to hand, and I quote from it for you now (apparently the copy was inspired by GK Chesterton, but so far I've been unable to locate the particular piece).

> 'Our customers are given a glimpse of that great morning world of Robin Hood or the knights errant, when one great game was played under the splendid sky'

'We believe we do a noble work. It has continually struck us that there is no element in modern life that is more lamentable than the fact that the late twentieth-century person has to seek all artistic existence in a sedentary state. If s/he wishes to float into fairyland, dash into battle, soar into heaven, or slide down the banisters, s/he buys a copy of Time Out. We give our clients these visions, but we give them exercise at the same time, the necessity of leaping from wall to wall, of fighting strange gentlemen, of running down long streets from pursuers – all healthy and pleasant exercise. Our customers are given a glimpse of that great morning world of Robin Hood or the knights errant, when one great game was played under the splendid sky. We give them back their childhood, that god-like time when we can act stories, be our own heroes and heroines, and at the same time dance and dream.'

I asked Peter the cost of his service. It was £1,000 for six months, £1,800 for the whole year. 'I've got what they call Writer's Block at the moment,' I told him.

'Our service has cured a number of cases of Writer's Block,' said Peter.

'What writers have you cured?' I asked.

'That I can't tell you,' said Peter. 'Due to the nature of our service, one client must never know of the existence of another. If they uncover it, fine, but you can appreciate that it's rarely helpful to the scenarists of the client's adventure. If a truly exponential excitement growth is to take place in our customer, he must never be clear whether he is in a natural situation or one we're laying on.'

'Has Howard Brenton ever done it?' I wanted to know.

'I'm not saying whether Howard has ever done it or not,' said Peter, 'but I'll permit myself to tell you at least one member of the "Romans in Britain" team was one of our clients at the time.' Michael Bogdanov? I thought to myself. Michael always seems so alive, enthusiastic, cooking ... and he rode through that 'Romans in Britain' scandal with such fine, swashbuckling style ...

A further quote from the brochure:

'Did you ever, as you walked alone through thronging streets upon some idle afternoon, feel the utter hunger for something to happen – something, in the splendid words of Walt Whitman: "Something pernicious and dread; something far removed from a puny and pious life; something loosed from its anchorage and driving free"?'.

> ## 'Something pernicious and dread, far removed from a puny and pious life; something loosed from its anchorage and driving free'

I wrote Peter Northover a cheque for the whole year.

When Tsai Chin rang me up out of the blue to ask if, were I to be invited to represent the Fringe at the Chinese Embassy Reception for British Theatre Persons, I would respond in the positive, I responded that were that to happen I would indeed respond in the positive. This phone call came less than a week after I'd written the cheque. When she next rang, suspecting that this unlikely invitation came in some way via the Adventure and Romance Agency, I attempted to call the bluff in this way: 'You do realise, Tsai,' I said, 'that the drama which infests me is the one far removed from the puny and the pious; I go for things unproved; things in a trance; things, Tsai, loosed from their anchorage and driving free.' She replied: 'Me too, dear. Great.' And 'See you there.'

I spent my first hour at the Chinese Embassy reception talking to Tom Courtenay, David Gothard and Arnold Wesker – pleasant enough chats, but none obviously leading towards romantic or adventurous conclusion. Then there was Tsai Chin hovering on my shoulder. There was by this time only about 50 minutes to go of the reception, so if I was to be steered towards adventure here, it had to happen soon. I said quietly to Tsai: 'I'm not making proper use of my time here. I'm keeping myself to kind faces of a time or two ago. Would you be so kind as to nudge me towards my future?' She silently indicated a certain person, alone, musing at the Grub Table. With no certainty that a play had begun, but nonetheless with an incredibly growing excitement, I moved to where I'd been bidden, and spoke my first line to she who might be the leading lady.

Postcript: I was reading this article to a member of the Institute for Social Inventions. He thought the inspiration for this splendid service, and much of the brochure copy, comes from G. K. Chesterton's 'The Club of Queer Trades.'

Postpostcript: He's rung back to say not only that but P. G. Northover is one of the characters in that book!

• *Ken Campbell, 74 Watermint Quay, Craven Walk, London N16 6DD (tel 081 800 1651). This piece first appeared in Time Out magazine. The Institute for Social Inventions has initiated an Agency inspired by this piece, enquiries and bookings 081 208 2853). Ken Campbell is the Agency's President.*

Polyfidelity

Eve Furchgott

Polyfidelity is a new multi-adult family structure in which clusters of best friends come together around shared values, interests, life goals and mutual attraction. Inside such a Best Friend Identity Cluster (B-FIC), family members are non-monogamous, relating to all their partners without a hierarchy of preference. Thus in a heterosexual polyfidelitous B-FIC, each of the women has a sexual relationship with each of the men, and no group member relates sexually to anyone outside the family group.

While different groups might work out different methods for determining who will sleep with whom every night, the method used successfully by actual polyfides in the United States is the 'balanced rotational sleeping schedule.' This arrangement has each person sleeping with a different partner each night, sequentially (using the chronological order of when people joined the group as the sequence), until at the end of the list, at which time she/he comes back around to the first person again.

Romantics might consider such a system too 'mechanical', but those who use it think it is a marvellous way to ensure that every twosome in a B-FIC has equal and ample time to build their own special, one-to-one intimacy. Being non-preferential does not imply that the relationship inside any dyad (set of two people) is identical. Every combination has its own unique qualities (called 'lovjoy' by practitioners of polyfidelity) which does not have to compete with any other dyadic relationship.

Polyfidelity offers a number of obvious advantages over more traditional family and intimacy styles. It caters to the desires of those who like sexual variety, yet allows this to occur in the context of lasting, deep, meaningful relationships. This blend of spice and stability is very refreshing to people who, in other situations, have had to forfeit a stable home life in order to experience variety, or vice versa. The problem of having unrealistic expectations of what one partner can provide that often occurs in two-adult families is solved; no one individual needs to be all things to anyone else. For single parents, or parents in general, a polyfidelitous household is a marvellous environment in which to raise children. The burden of responsibility and care that would otherwise fall on one or two individuals is spread out throughout the group, which allows the adults to be involved in many activities besides childcare, and gives the children a healthy assortment of good role models; adults with whom to build caring, trusting relationships.

'The intimacy of women or men sharing the same sexual partners and living space is unique to polyfidelity, and delightful'

Then there are the benefits of same sex camaraderie in the privacy of one's own home. The intimacy of women or men sharing the same sexual partners and living space is unique to polyfidelity, and delightful. The whole problem of jealousy is much more easily solved in this context than in others, because the pleasure and closeness one observes in the relationship of any two of her/his partners in no way threatens her/his own relationship with each of them. In fact, the opposite is true: the better the relationships are between all family members, the more secure the group is as a whole, and the stronger each individual's relations with any of her/his partners. In an age where social fragmentation and loneliness have reached epidemic proportions, polyfidelity offers its adherents a fantastic, built-in social and psychological support system, in an atmosphere conducive to individual growth and change. The support system is economic too, as the cost of living for many adults sharing space and other resources cooperatively is much lower than the cost of living for people in one or two-adult households.

Polyfidelity does require some profound changes in how one views relationships and the world in general. Certain conditioned premises must be rejected – for instance, that it is impossible to have more than one intense, emotional relationship at the same time, or that if you really care about someone, you will get jealous about his/her other involvements – and new ones accepted. Polyfidelity is not suited to everyone, but there are probably many millions of people who have a hard time finding satisfaction or fulfilment in marriages, couples or open-ended affairs for whom this new lifestyle will be a dream come true.

Polygamous families in various parts of the world have always been one-sided (one man and many wives, or, occasionally, one woman and several husbands). Polyfidelity is the first family structure to equalise that condition, and could never have existed in times or places where old-fashioned morality ruled people's lives. It is a product of the women's movement, as well as a branch of the communal living and kibbutz movement.

Currently, polyfidelity is being practised by two groups in San Francisco (one with nine members; one with eight) and scattered other, smaller clusters in various other places. In addition to those actually doing it, there is a growing network of hundreds of other people who are watching the people in the live-in 'test tubes', and studying the polyfidelity alternative with some notion that, in due course, they may want to try it for themselves. Discussion groups have formed in many places for people who are interested in learning more about polyfidelity

and meeting others of like mind. The original polyfides in San Francisco (this group has been together for 17 years) are active in encouraging people everywhere to study what they are doing as a prototype, which can be analysed and replicated (with or without modifications) all over the world.

'The problems polyfidelity solves: loneliness, jealousy, social fragmentation, housing shortages, single parenting, economic strain, emotional boredom'

The broader ramifications of this family structure are potentially quite significant, because of the problems it solves (loneliness, jealousy, social fragmentation, housing shortages, single parenting, economic strain, emotional boredom) and because of the new vistas of responsible hedonism it opens up.

Subscriptions to the quarterly book-length Kerista journals on 'Advanced Practical Scientific Utopian Theory' are available for $18 from Kerista, 543 Frederick St, San Francisco, CA 94117, USA (tel 415 4753 1314 or 415 665 2988).

88 guidelines for group behaviour

The Kerista Commune in California (described in the item above) have published a booklet with their 88 'behavioural and attitudinal guidelines' for members of their commune to follow – guidelines that were 'plainly agreed upon and clearly understood by us all,' and which allowed them to 'create a communal scene and a growth process that really work.'

'Clarity on these issues is fundamental to healthier, happier relationships'

They encourage others to examine each one of these guidelines and to decide which to include as a criterion in friendships, or to 'make up your own contract to suit your own private predilections.' Their premiss is that clarity on such issues is fundamental to healthier, happier relationships. Here is an adapted selection from some of the more intriguing guidelines:

• **Non-Interference in Art**: The project originator has the right to maintain control over the project as others join her/him and want to turn it into a different sort of thing than she/he had in mind. This applies to originating a social activity or outing, a household space, a best friend cluster, a discussion group, a special interest group, a theatrical activity and so forth.

• **Friendship Model**: This model involves recognition of distinct 'relationship rings', each representing a different level of intimacy and involvement. All relationships are defined and clearly articulated in terms of how and where they fit into this model, so that people do not try to be either closer to or more distant from each other than they really are in objective reality. If you are in a relationship ring which you find too intense, move back (meeting less often for instance). If you'd like to get closer to someone, bring it up for mutual evaluation.

• **No Unconditional Relationships**: The whole point of a social contract is to build conditional relationships! A breach of the conditions of any relationship is grounds for some type of reaction or re-evaluation of the relationship. Conditionality is basic to integrity and healthy emotions.

• **Overwhelming Evidence**: When a vote or opinion goes unanimously against the way you are voting, go along with the vote cheerfully, giving the overwhelming opinion of everybody else involved due respect, rather than remaining stodgy and stubborn.

See previous item for Kerista Commune's address. The booklet is free (US$1 postage) or there is a computer version on a Mac floppy disk (in HyperCard) for US$10.

Ending the state's marriage monopoly

Matthew O'Keeffe

The whole legal process of marriage and divorce would be better off in the free market. David Friedman in his Machinery of Freedom wrote as follows:

> 'There exists a government monopoly bigger and more inefficient than the Post Office. It is a service industry run so inefficiently that customers frequently wait in line for years before receiving any attention'

'There exists a government monopoly bigger and more inefficient than the Post Office. It is a service industry run so inefficiently that customers frequently wait in line for years before receiving any attention and spend years more waiting for the government to finish a job that should require a week or two.'

He was referring of course to the state court system in general but he could just as well have been speaking of its particular service of divorce. If marriages were dealt with as 'voluntarily entered contracts', then conditions for divorce and settlement could be worked out contractually, in advance, and the process of separation made far less tedious. Of course there would be nothing to stop conservatives entering into marriages which are considerably harder to break or lawyers devising marriages with the aim of maximising the welfare of children. I do not believe that state marriage laws are what keep the family together. The Mormons, historically the greatest defiers of such laws, are the most family-minded people I have ever met. I believe that marriage should endure, and as a Catholic I find the idea of homosexual and polygamous marriages distasteful. I do not, however, see this as a good reason for outlawing them. Wilhelm Von Humboldt summed up my case quite well almost 200 years ago:

'The results of marriage are as various as the characters of the persons concerned, and, as it is a union so closely related to the very nature of the respective individuals, it must have the most harmful consequences when the State attempts to regulate it by law, or through the force of its institutions to make it rest on anything except simple inclination.'

Adapted from a paper entitled 'Marriage and the State' written by Matthew O'Keeffe whilst a student at Oxford University, published as Political Notes No. 31, by the Libertarian Alliance, 1 Russell Chambers, The Piazza, Covent Garden, London WC2E 8AA (tel 071 821 5502).

The family as a corporate entity

Professor Sol Tax, who is now retired from the Department of Anthropology at the University of Chicago, once proposed that the extended family be given legal status as an entity. He developed the idea in a provocative paper which deserves renewed attention, and from which the following adapted extracts are taken:

'The extended family could be given legal status as an entity'

We have watched what many have thought was the disintegration of the family, as its traditional functions have been pre-empted by other social institutions in the industrialising world; as mobility has increased; and with increasingly single-standard sex freedom. Though we value families in political oratory, government does not recognise the existence of the family, with rare exceptions. Nothing except special interest groups now stand between the whole society on one side and our individual identification number on the other.

'To pool resources over some generations, perhaps including health and life insurance, pensions and social security'

My proposal is to give legal status to extended families who want it, and to make this advantageous. A new variant of corporate form, eg, partnerships, cooperatives, or small (non-profit?) corporations would be chartered for families which find it advantageous (under such a charter) to pool resources over some generations, perhaps including health and life insurance, pensions and social security.

'The family' as a voluntary corporate group might begin with the three generations but extend indefinitely horizontally and vertically, with new members enlisted by marriages (involving choice of family or a half-share in each) and subsequent births. The law would of course provide means for individuals to leave the corporate group, and for the corporate group to be dissolved.

The incorporation of the family would be functional to the degree that it could take advantage of other institutions in the private and public sectors of our society that provide advantages to groups, and which limit liability in co-operative endeavours. But the value of such a new institution would be greatly enhanced if the administration of social services now going to individuals would alternatively and advantageously be offered them to encourage the growth and spread of the new institution as a matter of public policy. This contrasts with a situation in which most social services tend to replace rather than to utilise family ties.

Some further points:

• Kinship can include adoption; and a chartered family as a whole can adopt a person.

• A single household of husband-wife-children is not chartered as a family, at least not until one or more of the children marry.

• Income tax liability, and such contracted benefits as for retirement and social security might be pooled for chartered families.

• In its subsequent evolution, a family might join larger family-type groups, so that members of an endogamous religious sect, or a community of American Indians, might make themselves legally a single family.

Professor Sol Tax, Apt 307, 1700 East 56th Street, Chicago 60637, USA (tel 312 363 0990).

Conversation deepening

For those who enjoy the new vistas revealed by occasional structured conversations, or for those brave enough to combat their own shyness: a paper, credited to Mr Hinely, but with no address or further details, found in the Institute's files, proposes that any group or any two persons wanting to deepen their knowledge of each other, could agree to a session where they select at random from the following 'conversation deepening' sentences, which they then complete and discuss.

> 'Any group or any two persons wanting to deepen their knowledge of each other, could agree to a session where they select at random from a menu of "conversation deepening" sentences'

(1) I like best the type of work which... (2) Most bosses... (3) Modern woman... (4) People usually think I... (5) The thing that makes me mad is... (6) The people I wonder about are... (7) The trouble with most marriages is... (8) I feel happiest when... (9) I could be a better worker if... (10) My proudest moment was... (11) During my school days... (12) Most men... (13) I believe... (14) My future... (15) I frequently... (16) I feel miserable... (17) If I could only... (18) My family... (19) People of my age... (20) I often suffer... (21) I've always envied... (22) During my childhood, my father... (23) To me, love... (24) I admire... (25) What I need most is... (26) I am greatly embarrassed... (27) Failure... (28) Being alone... (29) Mother... (30) I do well... (31) To me, money... (32) I am... (33) My home... (34) People laugh... (35) I worry... (36) If I were not... (37) My friends... (38) At times, I feel... (39) I can't understand... (40) To me, death... (41) Secretly, I... (42) I can hardly wait... (43) Why do I... (44) I always try... (45) My moral principles... (46) Most quarrels in marriage... (47) I'd like to forget... (48) My favourite type of person... (49) Heavy drinking... (50) My greatest trouble... (51) If I could choose anything I wished, I would choose to be ..... because... (52) If I could make any one change in people's behaviour, it would be ..... because... (53) I wonder... (54) The things I enjoy most are... (55) The happiest time I can remember was when... (56) The things I'm best at are... (57) The thing I fear most is... (58) When I look at myself, I see... (59) I feel that other people usually think of me as being... (60) To me, sex... (61) School... (62) Friends...

> 'People usually think I.....'

This Conversation Deepening could provide sentences for an adult version of the Magic Circle scheme for primary school-children (described in this book in the chapter on Education).

Lunch time launchers

Less personal than the above Conversation Deepeners, are 'Lunch Time Launchers', drawn up by the late Stan Chisman as a way of stirring up heated but thought-provoking conversations on ethical, philosophical, political and futuristic topics. Here are a few examples:

• What is the purpose of mankind?

• Down which paths should we take a conscious decision not to let or encourage our scientists to go?

• Are we at a stage that nothing should ever be created without arranging, in advance, for its disposal, eg. nuclear submarines, atomic power stations, car bodies, non-returnable bottles?

• If you were very rich what would you do with your time?

• What do you despise in others? Why? Are you justified?

• What questions could we use as a selection mechanism for a spouse?

• Is the world a better place than 1,000 years ago?

• What will be the addictions in 20 years' time?

• The ancient Egyptians had no concept of perspective – in what ways is our civilisation incapable of seeing what later generations will see as obvious?

> 'The ancient Egyptians had no concept of perspective – in what ways is our civilisation incapable of seeing what later generations will see as obvious?'

Neo-tantric yoga

David Miskin

Many couples who would otherwise split up, perhaps particularly those with children, could save their relationship and cement the bond between them if they adopted what I call 'neo-tantric yoga'. This consists of a ceremony or ritual of making love, with the male so far as possible avoiding orgasm, and with the ritual taking place at regular, pre-determined times, preferably on a daily basis before getting up – however busy the couple are, however many children they have, they can manage at least ten thrusts or 'strokes', and several hundred if not pressed for time, to set the tone for the day.

> 'However busy the couple are, they can manage at least ten thrusts or "strokes", to set the tone for the day'

It needs to be seen as not so much a matter of sex as a ceremony of commitment by both partners, a renewing of their pledge, for better or for worse, one that is undertaken whatever the state of the relationship (almost) however depressed or stressed or tired or sulky or rushed either feels; a ceremony that is beyond desire or even readiness (with the help of lubricating creams). It can be seen too as a chance to talk, and because the physical connection is maintained, the relationship tends not to feel under threat, whatever the theme being discussed; within that contact all sorts of problems dissolve more readily, arguments and hurts can be aired and heard, with less feeling of threat to the other; and even aggressions can be play-acted.

So many couples allow divisions to creep into their lives, bit by bit, with getting to the point of making love becoming a series of obstacle courses to be run, with the frequency diminishing as tensions build or as babies arrive. Whereas neo-tantric yoga helps rid the relationship of sexual frustration without focusing on sex as such – and without of course preventing other kinds of love-making at other times.

Couples who became adept at this neo-tantric ceremony might even begin to study the actual (far more subtle) Eastern rites as described in books such as 'Tantra – the Yoga of Sex' by Omar Garrison (published by Causeway Books, 92 Madison Avenue, New York, NY 10016, USA, $7-95, 1973). Similar approaches are described in 'The Tao of Love and Sex' by Jolan Chang (published by Wildwood House, 1977, £4-95), in 'Sexual Secrets' by Nik Douglas and Penny Slinger, (published by Hutchinson of London, 1979) and in 'Tantra, the Supreme Understanding' by Bhagwan Shree Rajneesh (published by the Rajneesh Foundation, 17 Koregaon Park, Poona 411 001, India, 1975).

A ritual without intercourse

At times when, for whatever reason, love-making is not appropriate, couples can fall back on other quick and simple rituals to start the day, such as one where they repeat together a shortened form of their marriage vows: lying in bed, looking into each other's eyes, and touching each other intimately, they can say together, for instance, 'I (name) love and cherish you (name), now and forever, for better, for worse, in sickness and in health, so help us God.'

Bedsits for arguing couples

Lynda Finn

Much more thought could and should be given to the fact that people split up on many occasions because they simply do not have their own space. Women find that what should be their leisure hours are spent mending or ironing until they fall into bed, when they are expected to indulge in all kinds of jollifications by the chap who has no doubt snoozed in front of the TV after eating the tea his wife prepared, cooked and cleared away! OK, so people get sick of the sight of each other and often say 'if I could just get away for a while' or 'I need to get away from the pressure for a time.' If this could be admitted early on in the deterioration of a relationship, a total breakdown could be avoided and the core of the plan is as follows:

> 'Where it is possible to allow the man to role-play the woman's typical day (and vice versa) it should be part of marriage guidance that such things should be tried'

That where it is possible to allow the man to role-play the woman's typical day (and vice versa) it should be part of marriage guidance that such things should be tried. Therapy could entail swapping roles for as long as it is practical to do so. Each would then get a good idea of the pressures on the other person which they may not have realised existed. Perhaps Dad could take a week off work and 'play Mother' whilst Mum went off each morning to do some form of community work which would give her pleasure – helping at school, reading to old people, painting, bumming around on a bike, anything at all just so long as she was out of the home environment and could not help or hinder Dad as he learned. Clearly it would be too difficult to ask her to do paid work like her husband's just for that short time, but if the wife already works then it is more necessary than ever that she should be relieved of the strain. Most sole dads say, too late, 'I never knew how hard my wife worked at home.' Few men see what difficulty women have in the home.

> 'I suggested that we might separate but not split up, that he should move into one of the nice bedsits in the area and continue to maintain daily contact with the children and give us both time to stop feeling resentful towards each other'

When my husband and I were going through a very bad patch in 1981, I suggested that we might separate but not split up, that he should move into one of the nice bedsits in the area and continue to maintain daily contact with the children and give us both time to stop feeling resentful towards each other. His macho image of himself would not allow this, although it did allow us eventually to break up and lose all contact! Eventually I could stand it no longer and walked out. My idea might have saved us for many years longer and it was only when we had been apart for six months that my husband said 'Let's try that idea you suggested years ago.' By that time I had had enough and did not want to go back to him.

Look how many people gaze back on their courting days with affection and wonder what went wrong. More often than not it's their own natures which changed due to not having the skills to stay married, not having the breathing space they had when they were courting – a bolt hole to run to when they had had a row and needed time to miss the partner again once the anger clouds had blown away. To reproduce, as far as possible, these courting days, in effect means giving each partner their own bolt hole again where the first resentment can be worked through before it is joined by another.

Lynda Finn, 71 Triangle Road, Massy, Auckland 8, New Zealand.

MDMA – a drug for healing relationships?

Nicholas Albery

The following article was published in the Guardian and looks at some of the implications of the drug Ecstasy.

'A good MDMA session is comparable to two years' traditional therapy;' 'it produces that vital and transforming factor in psychiatric sessions, honesty;' 'it invites self-disclosure and self-exploration' – these are quotes from some of the several hundred psychotherapists and psychiatrists in America who have made use in their practices of the psychedelic amphetamine drug MDMA. In the UK, MDMA has been illegal since 1977, and in the States since 1985. But under its street name of 'Ecstasy' or 'Adam', it continues to be consumed illegally by hundreds of thousands of users in the Western world.

The literature is beginning to accumulate as to its potential dangers and benefits – there are a handful of reports to date of deaths resulting directly or indirectly from MDMA use (one of a healthy woman in her early thirties taking only two to three times the 'average' dose); and one published report of a near-fatality concerning a healthy 33 year old female publishing editor whose second MDMA experience, with an average dose, led to hallucinations and delirium, and to treatment in a hospital critical care unit for hypothermia, regulatory distress and pulmonary oedema. There are also anecdotal reports of seizures and that MDMA may reduce resistance to infections. Rats given high doses of MDMA suffered degeneration of serotonergic nerve endings in the brain – in humans the serotonergic system helps regulate sleep, mood, sexual activity and sensitivity to stimuli. Monkeys have proved susceptible to MDMA damage at lower levels than rats, in fact at levels only two to three times higher than the average human dose (there is however evidence of subsequent recovery – serotonin levels that had fallen 80-90 per cent showed only a 30-40 per cent depletion ten weeks later); the preliminary findings from research on 34 long-term human users is that they too have 'persistent alteration in the serotonin system', although this study is now to be repeated with better controls.

Add to these warning signs, the fact that only two out of five street samples tested by Face magazine turned out to be MDMA, and the conclusion seems to be that it is not a suitable drug to take casually. But since many people will inevitably continue to use it, there is an urgent need to put MDMA through all the trials that any new drug would undergo – to gather further data, for instance, on its toxicity and carcinogenicity.

> 'Perhaps MDMA's greatest potential in therapy is non-verbal, in somatic therapy, to remove the blocks that prevent contact with the life force within the body, the blocks that hinder the "elan vital" from flowing'

Promosing research is now under way at Dr David Nichols' laboratory at Purdue University, Indiana. He is investigating how MDMA neurotoxicity is produced. 'It now seems likely,' writes his supporter Rick Dobin, 'that the therapeutic properties of MDMA can be separated from the toxic properties.' If this proves true, and once the contra-indications are more firmly established, it may be possible to recommend the drug or a variant of it for its therapeutic potential as a relatively mild psychedelic normally without the hallucinations and loss of ego that LSD can cause (although positive results using LSD in the treatment of prisoners, alcoholics and terminal cancer patients were reported in the days before LSD was made illegal). The overwhelming majority of MDMA users report good experiences, and do so more consistently than LSD users in the past, with only mild side effects such as nausea, jaw tension and tiredness afterwards. One of the attractions of the drug for recreational users is that it tends to make them feel more sensual and increases the pleasure of physical contact. In one study, for instance, 32% of users reported an increased desire for sex while under the drug's influence, although 84% reported a decreased ability to attain orgasm. This leads Robert Leverant of Sebastopol, California, to suggest that 'perhaps MDMA's greatest potential in therapy is non-verbal, in somatic therapy, to remove the blocks that prevent contact with the life force within the body, the blocks that hinder the "elan vital" from flowing.' Certainly people seem to fall in love more readily under its influence – it can promote inappropriate 'pair bonding.' In California they sell T-shirts which say 'Don't marry for six months after Ecstasy.'

San Francisco psychotherapist Dr Philip Wolfson argues that there is 'a volume of experience indicating that MDMA is effective in the treatment of depression, marital discord and couple therapy.' His work also leads him to believe that the drug offers 'unique possibilities in the treatment of psychosis.' Whereas the traditionally used neuroleptic drugs create a zombie-like effect and a profound loss of identity, with the possibility of Neuroleptic Malignant Syndrome, permanent brain damage and death, research into potentially less dangerous drugs of the MDMA variety is constrained 'by the spectre of abuse' and by the necessity for an 'absence of pleasurable or energy-giving properties' in psychiatric drugs. 'If a substance is desired by a human being,' writes Dr Wolfson, 'it is taboo to the psychiatric and governmental bureaucrats.'

Dr Wolfson believes that drugs such as MDMA could help maintain or increase a sense of non-psychotic identity, reduce aggression and paranoia and improve communication and empathy. He envisages such a drug being used on a voluntary basis for five-hour sessions once every five days, with daily psychotherapy in between. He is excited by the prospect: 'No new clinical agent of importance has been placed in psychiatry's hands since the introduction of haloperidol almost twenty years ago.'

Dr George Greer, a psychotherapist in Santa Fe, New Mexico, who has studied the effects of the drug on 69 patients, is equally enthusiastic: 'We have not heard of any long-lasting problems following MDMA sessions supervised by professional psychotherapists. Because of this fact, we have not been overly concerned by the reports of neurotoxicity in animals. We currently believe that, for all but extremely rare cases, there is a significant gap between the highest therapeutic doses and clinically significant toxic doses.' One of his clients was a terminal cancer patient in his early seventies. He had had four MDMA sessions in a nine-month period, and these were the first times he had been really pain-free in four years. In his first session, he experienced 'being inside his vertebrae, straightening out the nerves, and "gluing" fractured splinters back together.' In between sessions, he had 'greater success in controlling painful episodes by returning himself to an approximation of the MDMA state. He noted in particular that the feelings of "cosmic love" and especially forgiveness of himself and others, would usually precede the relief of physical pain.'

'It made me feel how all of us would like to feel we are anyway'

The Scottish psychiatrist and author, the late Dr R.D. Laing, has been quoted in a similar vein: 'It is a shame that MDMA has been criminalised, because it could take its place in the pharmacopoeia.' It is a drug that enhances feelings of self-esteem. 'It made me feel,' said Laing, 'how all of us would like to feel we are anyway.'

In Switzerland, with permission from the government – possibly out of deference to its powerful pharmaceutical companies, Switzerland is not a signatory to the 1971 International Convention on Psychotropic Drugs – six doctors are using MDMA and other psychedelics in the treatment of patients suffering from reactive depression, addictive disorders, character neuroses, phobias, obsessive-compulsions and anorexia nervosa. Their preliminary reports are encouraging.

• *Serious researchers can gain access to the literature on MDMA at the Institute for the Study of Drug Dependence's library in London. For details phone 071 430 1993. There is also a sizeable file in the Institute for Social Inventions' library (tel 081 208 2853).*

• *Rick Doblin, 23A Shaler Lane, Cambridge, Mass. 01238, USA (tel 617 547 7271). Doblin runs a centre for research into MDMA and the psychedelic drugs, and publishes a newsletter. He is the author and publisher of a paper entitled 'Regulation or Prohibition? MDMA Research in Switzerland and the United States'.*

• *An aubiographical book by the chemist who (legally) synthesised (and researched the effects of) a hundred or more drugs in the MDMA family has been published, entitled 'Pihkal (Phenethylamines I Have Known And Loved) – A Chemical Love Story' by Alexander and Ann Shulgin (published by Transform Press, Box 13675, Berkeley, CA 94701, USA, $18-95; also available from Rick Doblin, address above).*

Computer Divorce Agreements

Gillian Brown

I am struggling with the design of a PC computer program to help divorcing couples reach agreement on financial relief and arrangements for children, without the distortions, expense and complications introduced by using lawyers.

The program consists of detailed questions requiring simple answers, and enables the partners to record their circumstances (which are then displayed graphically side by side) and to resolve their problems, in their own time.

The advantages include:

• A computer is patient and is thus an ideal tool for making mistakes and a multitude of drafts.

• Seeing the situation graphically, as a picture, helps detach the antagonists from the problem so that it can be looked at from arm's length.

• It would replace the extraordinary lawyer's method – he writes to his solicitor, who writes to her solicitor, who writes to her – if the message becomes somewhat garbled it is hardly surprising. It is easier to talk to the man on the moon.

'A PC computer program to help divorcing couples reach agreement on financial relief, without the distortions, expense and complications introduced by using lawyers'

• It ought to be cheaper.

I learnt the hard way to detect the difference between Law, law and lore, and ecclesiastical law. The parties have to come to an agreement and make proposals and give a financial account to the court. This sort of thing is not easy at the best of times; suddenly in divorce when the lines of communication are irretrievably broken down, it somehow becomes many other people's business.

A service backing this scheme would receive feedback, enabling improvements to be made, and it would keep records of how people do come to amicable agreements. Even at present, there *must* be success stories, but why do they not go on record?

I now have a pair of guinea pigs (a couple undergoing divorce) who each recognise that the computer is not taking sides. I had almost forgotten how difficult even the simplest things become during divorce proceedings.

Gillian Brown, Eastern Town, Meeth, Okehampton, Devon EX20 3EP (tel 0837 810643). Brown might be willing to enrol further guinea pig couples in trying out her program; and could do with help in refining its graphics.

Unwedding

From an item by Phil Reeves in the Independent.

A ceremony called 'The Ending of Marriage' is being pioneered by Sheila Davis, a senior divorce courts welfare officer in Birmingham. She asks couples to stand in her office while she takes them by the hands, and tells them to bid farewell along the following lines:

'Goodbye. Thank you for the good times in our marriage. I wish you luck in your new life. Our relationship will continue as mother and father of our children, but not as husband and wife.'

'Goodbye. Thank you for the good times in our marriage. I wish you luck in your new life. Our relationship will continue as mother and father of our children, but not as husband and wife.'

Mrs Davis, herself divorced and remarried, believes that the ceremony helps reduce the tears and acrimony of separation and divorce. 'The idea is to help people to become unstuck emotionally. It enables them to say goodbye to each other as man and wife, and hello as mum and dad of their own children.'

About 50 couples have been 'unmarried' in Birmingham, and the idea appears to be catching on elsewhere. Mrs Davis has received enquiries from other welfare officers after including the ceremony in probation service courses she gives.

Women Welcome Women

Frances Alexander

Women Welcome Women, with some 500 members in 25 countries – including East Germany, China and Hungary – encourages women to visit others in their homes and their work. 'We suggest visits should last only a few days, unless some payment is made. There will be the occasional disastrous visit, but we expect the majority to be pleasant and happy.'

The organisation is constituted as a non-profit-making trust. It makes no charge, depending on donations. Founded in 1984 by Frances Alexander, as 'a little contribution to bringing about more friendship in a troubled world, with something for the housebound mother as much as the feminist or company executive', it is run from an Amstrad PCW computer in her spare bedroom. Each year, besides occasional newsletters, there are reunions for the members – planned in 1990 for England, Hungary, Sweden, Canada and Belgium.

Sample quotes from satisfied users of the network:

> 'When travelling abroad one misses so much if you have no chance of visiting homes as well as historic buildings'

'When travelling abroad one misses so much if you have no chance of visiting homes as well as historic buildings.' (Judith, Blackpool).

'Excellent, especially in times when people haven't got so much money to stay in a hotel.' (Christa, Bielefeld).

'I especially enjoyed going to Vicki's school for a couple of days.' (Susan Doxtator, Wisconsin).

Women Welcome Women, c/o Frances Alexander, 'Granta', 8a Chestnut Avenue, High Wycombe, Bucks HP11 1DJ (tel 0494 439481).

Running Sisters

Alison Turnbull

The Reebok/Running Magazine Sisters Network began in 1983, when a group of journalists at Running Magazine were looking into the reasons why women seemed slower than men to discover the benefits of running for fitness. We asked for volunteers to come forward – 'Big Sisters' who were experienced women runners; and 'Little Sisters' – complete beginners who wanted someone to help them start a regular running programme. The response, nearly 900 replies, was amazing in

view of the fact that we had placed the announcement at the back of the magazine – a magazine read mostly by men. With two 'Littles' to every 'Big' sister, 500 of these women, ages from 18-62, trained together for a 10 miles race.

> 'Big Sisters who were experienced women runners; and Little Sisters – complete beginners'

We tapped the Little Sisters while they were still glowing with pride after the race, and asked 'Would you now like to help someone else get started?' 98% ticked the 'yes' box. So began the Sisters Network which now has over 5,000 active members. We also pair up 'Twin' Sisters – women of the same standard who need each other's motivation to improve.

The Reebok Running Sisters Network, PO Box 3, Diss, Norfolk IP22 3HH.

Fostering communities

Alec Dickson

The old Children's Department of Glasgow City sent many of the children in its care to be fostered by farming families on the Isle of Tiree, in the Inner Hebrides – a marvellous upbringing amongst loving foster parents in a near-idyllic setting – and infinitely preferable, economically and psychologically, to their being consigned to children's homes on the institutional pattern.

> 'What Scottish farmwives in Tiree can give to children in care, and Belgian housewives can give to the mentally handicapped, housewives in colliery communities, where pits have been closed, could give to many of these people'

Some 25 miles to the east of Antwerp is Gheel, where since the Middle Ages Belgian farming families have taken in the adult mentally handicapped, accepting them as members of their families and keeping them for life.

The British government is now running down as many as possible of the old-style immense institutions for the mentally ill and discharging the patients into community care. But it is already apparent that neither local authorities nor existing voluntary agencies have the wherewithal to look after all those discharged – and that a proportion will always need support and care. But what Scottish farmwives in Tiree can give to children in care, and Belgian housewives can give to the mentally handicapped, housewives in colliery communities, where pits have been closed, could give to many of these people referred to above. Since the DHSS has funds for this purpose, it would mean an addition to their financial resources. We need to investigate what fostering communities could achieve in Britain – and be prepared to learn from the French 'L'Arche' approach.

Alec Dickson, 19 Blenheim Road, London W4 IVB (tel 081 994 7437).

AIDS – a different view

Branko Bokun

The following is a summary of some of the unorthodox views expressed in Bokun's pamphlet with the above title.

In the battle between the AIDS virus and the immune system maximum attention has been concentrated on one side of the problem: research for an antiviral therapy or vaccine has taken absolute priority.

Would it not be prudent to spend time and money on the research to improve the efficiency of our natural defences? After all, any disease develops when the balance between the body's natural defences and the disease agents has broken down. By ensuring the efficiency of our immune system within its optimal range, we could prevent not only AIDS but many other diseases.

> ### 'It is possible to catch AIDS and carry it until death from old age if our immune system is at its optimal efficiency'

It is possible to catch AIDS and carry it until death from old age if our immune system is at its optimal efficiency. Millions of people carry the herpes virus in a quiescent state. Herpes only produces blisters when our immune mechanisms descend to the level of its deficiency at which herpes becomes active. The herpes virus returns to its dormant state as soon as the reasons which lowered our immuno-efficiency disappear.

Some years ago, hysterical panic broke out in the USA over herpes. People would cross the street rather than risk contact with someone sporting a suspicious looking blister.

Scientific researchers insist that most carriers of AIDS will develop the disease and die in five to seven years. There is no proof of this, but as this kind of statement introduces panic and stress, the chances are it is true. The panic and stress will lower their immunity to fight the disease and they will die.

In general, male homosexuals seem to have a lower immunity than average, thus making them more susceptible than others to opportunistic infections, ARC, Kaposi's sarcoma or AIDS. It is not only individuals or groups of people who decide to put themselves into precarious or insecure states of existence of their own accord who incur immunodeficiency, but also individuals, groups and communities of people who have been placed into these states by law, prejudices, economic or social pressure.

According to the USA's Centre for Disease Control in Atlanta, black and Hispanic people are approximately three times more likely to develop AIDS than white people.

Likewise, drug addiction increases fear and anxieties and it is mainly these fears and anxieties which reduce the efficiency of the drug abuser's immune system. Most haemophiliacs are already in a lower than normal efficiency of their immunity, and this makes them more susceptible in the first place, not only to AIDS, but to many opportunistic infections. A mother infected by the AIDS virus can transmit it to her child in utero or through her milk. I think we should take into consideration the possibility that a mother could transmit her immunodeficiency to her unborn child, making the child susceptible to all kind of infections. In fact, children born with any deficiency in their immunity, easily develop frequent bacterial infections, coupled with chronic diarrhoea and weight problems. The high incidence of venereal infections among male and female prostitutes increases their immunodeficiency which makes them even more vulnerable to other infections, and to AIDS. In central Africa, the passage from a stabler and more serene tribal or village life to the urban bustle has brought anxiety and stress, and overactivity of the neuroendocrine system which damages people's susceptibility to all kind of diseases including AIDS. Another major group at risk in Africa are the five million displaced persons living in a permanent state of anxiety and stress.

Titles in the press such as: 'AIDS: the new Holocaust' might well make AIDS become a holocaust.

In order to prevent certain diseases of groups at risk, it would often be enough to reduce the tempo, rhythm or eagerness that individuals of that group put into their lifestyle. Male homosexuals do not need to become 'straight' in order to avoid being part of a group at risk. If they could establish their togetherness and relationships on a more mature and a more serene basis they might become less susceptible to infections.

Some people justify sexual liberation and sexual promiscuity, labelling them 'natural drives'. Obsessions or excesses are not, however, 'natural drives' or 'imperatives' but a creation of the human adolescent mind.

It is interesting to note that epidemics played a salubrious role as they often eliminated or reduced excesses. There is also historic evidence that morality, good taste and common sense improved after any epidemic. AIDS could do the same.

Doctors today no longer advise the best medicine for many disorders: a few days' rest from agitation and eagerness, as their patients cannot relax or rest without the aid of damaging tranquillisers. The overconsumption of medical drugs and immunisations might, at least partially, reduce the potential of our immune mechanisms.

The modern tendency to solidify individual autonomy has killed off large families and communities, destroying the sense of belonging. The rapid progress in science and technology could be another damaging factor. The progress is much too quick and too big for us to adapt adequately to it, and this creates instability and confusion, therefore a strain on both our brain and body.

By taking ourselves too seriously, we tend to dramatise everything. This tendency increases tension and strain. Self-ridicule can rid one of over-seriousness. By mocking our over-seriousness, by joking at our pretensions and self-importance, we acquire the joy of living, the best medicine for immunity to diseases.

Experiments carried out by the Common Cold Research Unit in Salisbury, showed that over-serious people were more susceptible to the ordinary cold than cheerful people. What is valid for a cold could be valid for AIDS, ARC and even cancers.

Branko Bokun's pamphlet is available free from him at Vita Books, 2 Chelsea Square, London SW3 (tel 071 352 6919).

AIDS treatment self-help

'New Realities' (available from Box 26289, San Francisco, CA 94126, USA) recorded the suggestions of San Franciscan William Calderon, a young AIDS sufferer who believes he is now cured,

having had a remission of all symptoms for the previous two years. Here is what Calderon advised fellow sufferers:

> ### 'For any cure, you need the support of other people. It can be a spouse, friend or relative, but you need someone who loves you'

• For any cure, you need the support of other people. It can be a spouse, friend or relative, but you need someone who loves you and believes you can get well. I could not do it alone. There were days when I was too tired. Then Henry, my partner, would make sure I'd meditate, eat more or take vitamins.

• Lead your life as normally as you can. Make the extra effort to dress, to work, to live each day and not give in to the disease.

• You can't get well unless you forgive everyone. You don't have to love them, but actively put in good thoughts for them.

• The fear of the disease is worse than the disease itself. In that fear is hopelessness which seems to make an illness worse.

• Take EST (Erhard Training Seminars) or some similar mind-training course to develop the conviction that it is possible to change your life and to look objectively at other people's programming.

• Learn what Carl Simonton says about changing negative attitudes and using visualisation techniques. Simonton is the author of 'Getting Well Again' and his cassettes, 'The Role of the Mind in Cancer' and 'Mental Imagery as applied to Cancer Therapy' are available through the Cancer Counselling Centre, Box 1055, Azle, Texas 76020, USA.

• Good nutrition and vitamins. I took massive doses of Vitamin C (16 to 24 grams per day), B12, calcium, Vitamin E and concentrated vegetable capsules, and followed an anti-cancer diet – eating large amounts of broccoli, bell peppers, tomatoes, cantaloupes and carrots. This approach is described in 'The Lifelong Anti-Cancer Diet' by Carmel Herman Reingold (Signet Books 1982).

• Lots of rest.
• Love.
• Humour.
• Love.

This article featured in the American Readers Digest of the alternative press, the Utne Reader, Box 1974, Marion, Ohio, 43305, USA, $4 for current issue, $18 subs.

Non-pen friends

Nicholas Carr

Nearly every disaster has its positive side, and the threat of AIDS has opened up the possibility of widespread acceptance for new codes of sexual behaviour. Already it has become acceptable to discuss in public the intimate details of the ways we relate to each other sexually.

The following suggestion is a viable alternative to celibacy or using condoms with extra-marital lovers – and has many positive virtues besides avoiding the risk of AIDS.

> ### 'A mutual agreement to draw the line at penetration with new or casual sexual partners'

There is really nothing new to the idea itself – simply a mutual agreement to draw the line at penetration with new or casual sexual partners. Although this cuts out the possibility of having a 'complete' sexual experience, I believe that it is a fair price to pay for avoiding the worries that so often spoil the fun: the fear of catching herpes, AIDS or venereal diseases; worries about pregnancy and contraceptives; anxiety about sexual performance; the surfacing of deep-seated guilt feelings; and concern that aroused emotions may result in one or other partner getting hurt.

I do not consider myself particularly promiscuous – in fact my sex life has consisted of a series of monogamous relationships. But between these there have been periods when I have had many lovers, either for the excitement, the warmth or in search of a new long-term partner. Most of these casual sexual experiences have been disappointing, and even when they have been good have sometimes downgraded a relaxed friendship into an awkward relationship. And there have been emotional tragedies afterwards, when I have had painful longings which my partner has not shared, or vice versa.

> ### 'A clean dirty weekend: we were able to relax and laugh a lot, it was continuously sexy, and it felt romantic and caring too'

Several years ago, after the ending of a serious relationship, I decided to avoid my usual pattern of casual sexual relationships. However, I discovered that celibacy was not the answer, it just made me tense. Then I got talking with a woman who was in the same situation, and we decided on fulfilling our needs (for warmth at least) by sleeping together but avoiding making love – which we carried on doing regularly until she found a new mate. Next I invited a woman (whom I had only met briefly when we had talked about this) to spend a clean dirty weekend with me, and we both had a wonderful time: we were able to relax and laugh a lot; it was continuously sexy because I avoided ejaculation, and it felt romantic and caring too. We both felt nurtured and warm inside after the weekend, yet the fact that we had not 'made love' spelt out that we were not committed to one another. On another occasion I slept with a woman who had had many casual affairs since breaking up with her man. I insisted (rather against her choice) on a non-penetration pact, and to her surprise she experienced the first orgasm of her promiscuous fling – due, she thought, to being relaxed enough to let go. So, even as a 'non-believer', she found that the restriction on penetration gave her more freedom to enjoy the experience.

> ### 'Withholding penetration and avoiding ejaculation actually heightens the experience, as is well established in many traditional practices including Tantra'

This might all sound like some sort of perversion which should not be applied to someone you regard as a potential spouse. In fact, it is a wonderful preparation for a good sexual relationship – to get relaxed together and enjoy the stimulation of one another's touch before going 'all the way'. Withholding penetration and avoiding ejaculation actually heighten the experience, as is well established in many traditional practices including Tantra.

There is, as I mentioned, nothing new or dramatic in having sex without penetration. What I am promoting here is the idea that it should be accepted as normal outside monogamous relationships. 'Non-pen' sex is sexy, it is safe and it is fun – and it will not leave you wishing you had never set eyes on each other.

Lack of touching leads to violence?

Part of this item is adapted from a controversial article by Howard Bloom in Omni magazine entitled 'The Importance of Hugging' (itself an excerpt from an unpublished book).

The societies that hugged their kids were relatively peaceful. The cultures that treated their children coldly produced brutal adults, according to a survey of 49 cultures conducted by James Prescott, founder of the National Institute of Child Health and Human Development's Developmental Biology Program in the States.

> 'The societies that hugged their kids were relatively peaceful. The cultures that treated their children coldly produced brutal adults'

Prescott's observations apply to Islamic and other cultures, which treat their children harshly. They despise open displays of affection. The result: violent adults.

Abu-Lughod, for instance, reports that Bedouin society outlaws close, warm relationships between men and women. Kissing or hugging openly is considered disgusting, almost inhuman. A couple who indulge in such a moment of warmth would be subject to contempt, fury and hatred.

> 'The Mundugumor, are brought up in stiff baskets as infants, and grow up as hostile warlike adults'

Ashley Montagu in his book 'Touching, the Human Significance of Skin' (published by Harper and Row 1977), gave a similar example. The Arapesh in New Guinea, who are carried around with a great deal of skin contact as infants, have as adults no competitive games and no organised warfare. Their southern neighbours, the Mundugumor, are brought up in stiff baskets as infants, and grow up as hostile warlike adults.

As various researchers have advocated, babies thrive best when nursed at the breast, when not placed in cots or nurseries, and when carried around not in prams or pushchairs, but on their mothers' and fathers' fronts and backs.

• *For a brief summary of the relevant research, see 'Touching, The Promotion of Touching in Casual Social Encounters' by Nicholas Albery and others (ISBN 0 9505244 3 3, published by Revelaction Press, c/o 20 Heber Road, London NW2 6AA, tel 081 208 2853; fax 081 452 6434, 1982, £5-95).*

• *Howard Bloom, 705 President Street, Brooklyn, NY 11211, USA (tel 718 622 2278).*

How to introduce a new kitten to an old cat

Adapted extract from an article about pet therapy in 'You' magazine by Adriane Pielou entitled '100 Ways to Cure a Cat', monitored for the Institute by Yvonne Ackroyd.

The problem that seems to concern most of the New York pet therapy class is how to introduce a new kitten to an existing pet. Carole Wilbourn clasps her hands: this is one of her favourite topics. The key, she says, is to pretend that the newcomer is your old cat's responsibility ('Get a neighbour to deliver the kitten and then go out and leave your cat to discover the kitten for itself') and to ignore the kitten for the first fortnight.

> 'The key is to pretend that the newcomer kitten is your old cat's responsibility and to ignore the kitten for the first fortnight'

'Your kitten should be 100 per cent invisible to you! At feeding time tell your old cat, "I'm putting down two bowls so your friend doesn't touch your food." Say, "I'm cleaning your friend's ears to save you the bother." The kitten will be fine because it's getting attention from the older cat, and the older cat will be fine because it'll realise the newcomer isn't going to usurp it.' (*Ed:* a similar approach is said to work with new babies being introduced to older brothers and sisters.)

'The key to cat therapy, of course,' Carole says, 'is treating the owner. A happy person has a happy cat.'

Practise random kindness and senseless acts of beauty

With our news media constantly reporting random cruelties and senseless acts of violence, it is a relief to turn to the following article spotted on an American computer network. It originated in Glamour magazine (USA) and was monitored for the Institute by Chris Welch.

It's a crisp winter day in San Francisco. A woman in a red Honda, Christmas presents piled in the back, drives up to the Bay Bridge tollbooth. 'I'm paying for myself, and for the six cars behind me,' she says with a smile, handing over seven commuter tickets.

One after another, the next six drivers arrive at the tollbooth, dollars in hand, only to be told, 'Some lady up ahead already paid your fare. Have a nice day.'

The woman in the Honda, it turned out, had read something on an index card taped to a friend's refrigerator: 'Practise random kindness and senseless acts of beauty.' The phrase seemed to leap out at her, and she copied it down.

Judy Foreman spotted the same phrase spray-painted on a warehouse wall a hundred miles from her home. When it stayed on her mind for days, she gave up and drove all the way back to copy it down. 'I thought it was incredibly beautiful,' she said, explaining why she's taken to writing it at the bottom of all her letters, 'like a message from above.'

Her husband Frank liked the phrase so much that he put it up on the wall for his seventh graders, one of whom was the daughter of a local columnist. The columnist put it in the paper, admitting that though she liked it, she didn't know where it came from or what it really meant.

Two days later, she heard from Anne Herbert. Tall, blonde and forty, Herbert lives in Marin, one of the country's ten richest counties, where she house-sits, takes odd jobs and gets by. It was in a Sausalito restaurant that Herbert jotted the phrase down on a paper place mat, after turning it around in her mind for days.

'That's wonderful!' a man sitting nearby said, and copied it down carefully on his own place mat.

'Here's the idea,' Herbert says. 'Anything you think there should be more of, do it randomly.'

Her own fantasies include: breaking into depressing-looking schools to paint the classrooms; leaving hot meals on kitchen tables in the poor parts of town; slipping money into a proud old woman's purse.

'Kindness can build on itself as much violence can.'

Says Herbert, 'kindness can build on itself as much violence can.'

Now the phrase is spreading, on bumper stickers, on walls, at the bottom of letters and business cards. And as it spreads, so does a vision of guerrilla goodness.

'The phrase is spreading, on bumper stickers, on walls, at the bottom of letters and business cards. And as it spreads, so does a vision of guerrilla goodness'

In Portland, Oregon, a man might plunk a coin into a stranger's meter just in time. In Patterson, New Jersey, a dozen people with pails and mops and tulip bulbs might descend on a rundown house and clean it from top to bottom while the frail elderly owners look on, dazed and smiling. In Chicago, a teenage boy may be shovelling off the driveway when the impulse strikes. What the hell, nobody's looking, he thinks, and shovels the neighbour's driveway too.

It's positive anarchy, disorder, a sweet disturbance. A woman in Boston writes 'Merry Christmas!' to the tellers on the back of her cheques. A man in St Louis, whose car has just been rear-ended by a young woman, waves her away, saying, 'It's a scratch. Don't worry.'

Senseless acts of beauty spread: a man plants daffodils along the roadway, his shirt billowing in the breeze from passing cars. In Seattle, a man appoints himself a one man vigilante sanitation service and roams the concrete hills collecting litter in a supermarket cart. In Atlanta, a man scrubs graffiti from a green park bench.

They say you can't smile without cheering yourself up a little – likewise, you can't commit a random act of kindness without feeling as if your own troubles have been lightened if only because the world has become a slightly better place.

'Like all revolutions, guerrilla goodness begins slowly, with a single act'

And you can't be a recipient without feeling a shock, a pleasant jolt. If you were one of those rush-hour drivers who found your bridge fare paid, who knows what you might have been inspired to do for someone else later? Wave someone on in the intersection? Smile at a tired clerk? Or something larger, greater? Like all revolutions, guerrilla goodness begins slowly, with a single act. Let it be yours.

Anne Herbert, PO Box 5408, Mill Valley, California 94942, USA.

Chapter four

HOUSING

A social invention that failed

Dr Alice Coleman

Original inventions need a free-ranging mind unhampered by doubts and self-criticism. but once an invention has been formulated, evaluation becomes essential. A new idea is not necessarily a good idea. It may bring great benefits, or have little effect, or create a social disaster, so an assessment is vital for deciding whether to proceed, amend or discard.

'Families have been forced to share corridors, staircases, lifts, lobbies and grounds'

One of the most widely applied social inventions of the last 50 years was never treated in this way, and as a result has brought about widespread social breakdown. It is the replanning of the residential environment to replace the traditional street of houses-with-gardens by estates of flats where families have been forced to share corridors, staircases, lifts, lobbies and grounds, in the belief that this layout would create instant communities. In practice, it created just the reverse – problem estates – but the government department which decreed it found the perfect excuse for escaping blame. They claimed that it was fatuous and reductionist to suggest a causal connection between design and social breakdown, and then proceeded to build more problem estates that have proved to be even worse.

The Land Use Research Unit at King's College, London, has tried to investigate housing design with an open mind. We surveyed over 4,000 houses built over the last hundred years and over 4,000 blocks of flats, noting a variety of design elements and also the distribution of vandal damage, and the presence in and around the entrances of litter, graffiti, urine and faeces. Later we were able to add data on children in care, juvenile arrests, burglary, robbery, theft, criminal damage, fires, bodily harm, sexual assaults, and two types of vehicle crime, with preliminary evidence for alcoholism, drug addiction and personality disorders.

We recognised that people are all different, and that any given design would not affect everyone equally, but were alert to the possibility that some features might affect fewer people than others. If this were systematically true, there might be a case for modifying the worst designs in the hope of alleviating the associated social breakdown.

'All blocks with a zero disadvantagement score were totally free from crime during the study year'

There proved to be clear trends relating all our test measures (litter etc) to 12 design variables in houses and 16 in blocks of flats. For each design there is a *threshold* value, below which there is less than average social breakdown. By counting the number of designs which breach their threshold value in each house or block, we can rate each one with a *disadvantagement score*, with zero as the optimum. All the zero-scoring blocks were totally free from crime during the study year, whereas those with scores of at least 13 averaged one crime per five dwellings.

We suggest, therefore, that design is a major factor in many aspects of social breakdown. This cannot be disproved by calling it reductionist. It needs to be tested in practice by changing the designs in a Design Improvement (DI) scheme, to see whether benefits actually ensue.

Statistically, the worst design for *spreading* crime to the maximum number of blocks is the presence of overhead walkways between buildings. Where these bridges have been removed, there has been a noticeable drop in crime, nocturnal disturbances and pollution by excrement. Designs which maximise the *volume* of crime are grounds shared among many blocks and multiple gates or gaps leading into the estate from the surrounding roads. These features can be changed by enclosing each block inside its own wall, with only one gateway, to prevent outsiders from taking shortcuts across its territory. This course of action has reduced the fear of crime and made it possible to eliminate litter and graffiti completely. Subdividing large blocks into smaller self-contained sections reduces the cost of maintenance and vandal-damage repairs, while giving traditional front gardens to ground-floor flats helps children to become polite and better integrated into the community.

> **'It has resulted in a complete cessation of crime. Tenants say they have thrown away their sleeping pills, and no longer need the psychiatrist'**

The best DI scheme to date has simultaneously improved five deleterious designs. It has resulted in a complete cessation of litter, graffiti, excrement, vandalism and crime for six years to date, and the tenants say they have thrown away their sleeping pills, and no longer need the psychiatrist. This evidence is particularly valuable because a similar estate nearby has been reconditioned at a similar cost, but has had no design changes, and continues to be beset by all the old social ills from litter to one crime per dwelling per year.

What we need most in this field is the social re-invention of housing freedom. It is no accident that problems seem fewest in 1930s dwellings, as these were the most advanced forms to evolve by natural selection. Residents were free to select good innovations and reject bad ones, and this process gave each household clear control over its own separate territory, with features which can now be recognised as effective aids to child rearing and community development. If we had not been denied a further half-century of housing evolution since 1939, there might well have been further stabilising benefits, instead of the present retrograde situation due to doctrinaire ideology.

> **'1930s dwellings, the most advanced forms to evolve by natural selection, gave each household clear control over its own separate territory'**

Social inventions are needed, but let us not assume that they are all automatically good. Modern Movement housing is one that has been disastrous.

Dr Alice Coleman, of the Department of Geography, King's College London, Strand, London WC2R 2LS (tel 071 836 5454). Dr Coleman's book, 'Utopia on Trial – Vision and Reality in Planned Housing', is published by Hilary Shipman at £7-95. Mrs Thatcher when in power took note of Coleman's housing research and seven estates are now undergoing systematic trials.

A fund for tenant improvements

Groups such as tenants and landlords (or employees and employers) should have some money for long-term improvements set aside for use by the tenant (or employee). The landlord could only refuse if it was for something silly, unsafe, etc.

The reason for this is that many tenants put little thought into long-term improvements to their property. They just complain. This approach might help considerably. The government could encourage it with tax relief or similar.

Mark Dunn, 96a Cowlishaw Road, Sheffield, S11 8XH.

Response by Nicholas Saunders

In Denmark something along the above lines does happen: landlords have to set aside 10% of the rent into a fund for internal decorations and repairs. This may be drawn on by tenants.

This money can be used either towards paying outside contractors; or for materials only if the tenants wish to do the work themselves. In practice it is only enough if the tenant does do the work.

Nicholas Saunders, top floor, 14 Neal's Yard, London WC2H 9DP (tel 071 836 9404; fax 081 379 0135).

Compulsory computerised house selling
Steven Burkeman

A perfect market depends on perfect knowledge, and this scheme would use computer technology and a measure of compulsion to produce perfect knowledge as follows:

> **'A perfect market depends on perfect knowledge, and this scheme would use computer technology and a measure of compulsion to produce perfect knowledge'**

When you wanted to sell a house, you would be obliged to fill in a form which would give details of your house and its location, the number of bedrooms, the garden, the garage, etc as well as a broad price range (e.g. £30,000-£40,000). You would also pay a small fee such as £5 to finance the system. All these details would go on to a computer.

When you wanted to buy a house, you would indicate your requirements on a similar form, and the computer, which would cover properties nationwide, would print out particulars for your selected neighbourhood. You would then view your shortlist, and the role of a third party would be limited to negotiating on price. This negotiation might reasonably be carried out by the agencies responsible for financing the purchase or sale – usually building societies.

Steven Burkeman, 8 Whitby Avenue, York, YO3 OET (tel 0904 425499 h; 0904 627810 w).

Libraries replacing estate agents
Michael Joseph

Michael Joseph, a former conveyancing solicitor, has suggested something similar to the previous item in the Guardian – his scheme uses libraries rather than computers, as the following extract explains.

Make it obligatory for the seller to supply the local librarian with four photographs of the house, front, back and outlooks - as well as details of the address, price, number and dimensions of the rooms, and size of gardens.

> 'Photographs and particulars would be displayed on boards in the public library; cheapest houses on the left, more expensive on the right'

These photographs and particulars would be displayed on boards in the public library; cheapest houses on the left, more expensive on the right. A detailed map of the area is also displayed.

With a bit of luck, the seller could save £500 to £2,500 in estate agent's fees while the purchaser avoids innumerable wild goose chases.

Alongside the house details on the board would be displayed the information normally obtained by a conveyancing solicitor through a 'preliminary enquiries' form to the seller's solicitor, and 'local search' questions to the local council.

This would provide the few items of fixed information about the property which a purchaser needs to know, plus a comprehensive map supplied by the council on which it marks those few houses and areas where it has issued a notice or has a proposal.

After agreeing the price of the house with the seller, the purchaser is given a copy of the land certificate.

He or she then simply checks on the council map that the local authority has no designs on the house.

Houses for sale with pre-arranged mortgages

Nicholas Saunders

Although there is much competition to offer mortgages to house purchasers, the various financial bodies seem to have overlooked the simple and effective system in Denmark, where houses are put on sale with mortgages already arranged for whoever buys the house, irrespective of financial status. In this way, for instance, groups of young people in Copenhagen with less than £1,000 capital each have been able to move to the country and to buy small farms.

> 'In Denmark, houses are put on sale with mortgages already arranged for whoever buys the house, irrespective of financial status'

In Denmark, the monthly repayment figure is always quoted in the sale price of a house, almost as if it were a rent, although there is also a small deposit of 5 to 10 per cent.

The advantage for buyers is that there is no expense and delay whilst their viability is being checked.

The advantage for sellers is that the sale is less likely to be held up or to fall through once it has been agreed.

There is no good reason why someone selling a house in this country should not be able to arrange a mortgage for it on the security of the house alone. The present UK mortgage system insists on the double security provided by both the house itself and the purchaser's financial status, but the recent competition from banks and others could mean that the first institution to

offer the Danish system would corner a healthy share of the market.

Nicholas Saunders, top floor, 14 Neal's Yard, London WC2H 9DP (tel 071 836 9404; fax 071 379 0135).

Mortgage interest tax relief on second homes

Clive Akerman

I propose a doubling of mortgage interest tax relief, subject to some simple restrictions.

If an individual has lived in a housing stress area (designated by ministerial decree and defined as one where there are more potential households than homes; basically the South East of the country) in an owner-occupied home for a minimum of, say, five years, then the tax concessions on that home should be retained and duplicate concessions made available for a second home in the provinces – *provided that* the second home became the prime residence and the original residence were rented via a recognised housing association.

This would encourage a job-seeker to move out of an area with the highest pressure on housing, would free a home for rental in the most stressed area, and more important, provide a safety net should the individual require to return to the South East in pursuance of his or her career. The cost to the community would be two sets of mortgage interest tax relief – which is not, in fact, a lot of money as the standard rate of tax is reduced. (The maximum is, I believe, 40% top tax rate x £30,000 limit on relief x 10% say, interest rate per annum = £1,200 a year.)

> 'The solution has three major benefits – it is simple, it is cheap and it could be put into effect very quickly and easily'

Such an approach does not call for many new houses, and those which are built will be in areas of low land and labour costs. We will reduce pressures on Green Belts; we will be making a valuable move towards homogenising the country and reducing the problems of success in the South East; a new town will no longer be needed in Stowmarket, Suffolk; we would free a great deal of housing in areas of greatest need; we would improve the quality of life of many people. And the 'solution' has three major benefits – it is simple, it is cheap and it could be put into effect very quickly and easily.

Clive Akerman, 92 Sandbrook Road, London N16 OSP (tel 071 241 0866).

Planning permission for second homes

The Institute for Social Inventions has promoted this proposal, originally put to the Institute in the following letter by Desmond Banks of London W10.

The use of houses that would otherwise be occupied by local

people as second homes can blight rural communities. Absent owners contribute nothing to community life. If local people have to compete with outsiders for property, prices must inevitably rise, perhaps putting them out of reach. If there is not enough housing to serve the local community, that inevitably leads to overcrowding, homelessness or migration.

> 'A second home could be defined as "a residential property that is occupied upon less than 91 days in any calendar year" '

If you want to use a residential property for business purposes, you have to obtain planning permission. You should have to obtain planning permission, too, if you want to use a house as a second home. A second home could be defined as 'a residential property that is occupied upon less than 91 days in any calendar year and that is not the occupier's only or main residence.' Permission should only be granted if the local council is satisfied that the house or flat is not needed to accommodate local people or is unsuitable.

The Labour Party's new approach to second homes

The Labour Party has recently made moves towards a similar approach to that outlined above, announcing that 'local authorities will be given the option of deciding whether second homes will in future require planning consent.' Existing second homes will be exempt.

Sleep in the street before house buying

Ken Campbell suggests that people before buying a house in rougher parts of cities should park a van in the street on a Saturday and sleep in the van overnight. How a neighbourhood behaves at its worst on a Saturday night could put you off buying and so save you much heartache later.

Ken Campbell, 74 Watermint Quay, Craven Walk, London N16 6BT (tel 081 800 1651).

Women's Building Forum

The Women's Building Forum (Kvinnors Byggforum) is a club for Swedish women of many different professions who are interested in seeing that women's ideas and experience are better used and catered for in building projects of all kinds. 'Careful planning of our communities can lead to greater social interaction, less stress, better conditions for children, and to greater equality between men and women.'

> 'Careful planning of our communities can lead to better conditions for children'

The club was formed in 1979 and has two hundred members all over Sweden. Quite a few of them are architects or building engineers or otherwise interested in housing and planning. Groups are formed to deal with specific questions, such as organising conferences, running study groups and making use of their planning checklist that covers every scale of development from a flat to whole regions. They also have a newsletter.

Kvinnors Byggforum, Box 8080, S-10720 Stockholm, Sweden. Its Chairwoman is Cecilia Jensfelt (tel 468 260 231 h; 468 790 8588 w).

Pattern Language for community architects
Nicholas Albery

The right tools for 'community architecture' are beginning to be recognised. 'Pattern Language' by architect Christopher Alexander (published by OUP, New York) allows any group of people to take an informed part in the design of their own houses or neighbourhood.

It is as simple as painting by numbers, with the book containing more than 250 patterns to choose from. The patterns put flesh on the bare bones of the principles for human scale architecture that the Prince of Wales has advocated.

> 'Pattern Language allows any group of people to take an informed part in the design of their own houses or neighbourhood. It is as simple as painting by numbers, with the book containing more than 250 patterns to choose from'

For instance the committee of the Bramleys Housing Coop in London W11, when planning their new housing, were circulated some 40 of the most relevant patterns, and could give each a grading as to its importance for them. After further debate, the result took shape as a small cluster of low houses, plus flats all with balconies, with overhanging roofs and decorated brickwork, surrounding a totally enclosed communal garden. As architects Pollard, Thomas, Edwards and Associates admitted (although one of their partners criticised 'Pattern Language' for its 'whimsicality'): 'We would not have built such a particular solution without a specific client. We tend to be tamer.'

'Pattern Language' tends to be in stock in the UK at the Town and Country Planning Association bookshop, 17 Carlton House Terrace, London SW1Y 5BD (tel 071 930 8903).

Ten design principles
The Prince of Wales

'A Vision of Britain' (Doubleday, £14·95) by the Prince of Wales has set out his ten principles that should govern good architecture. These principles are very much in tune with the Institute's own bias towards the human scale. If all housing developments for single mothers, for instance, had the conviviality and safety of

enclosed communal gardens or squares, as advocated by Prince Charles, then the lives of both mothers and their children would be transformed.

- New buildings should blend with the landscape;
- The size of buildings should be in relation to their public importance and key elements should be obvious;
- Buildings should respond to 'human scale';
- They should be in tune with neighbouring buildings;
- Architects need humility;
- The privacy and feeling of safety of squares, alms houses, universities and the Inns of Court should be studied;

'The privacy and feeling of safety of squares, alms houses, universities and the Inns of Court should be studied'

- Districts should compile inventories of local materials;
- Buildings without decoration give no pleasure;
- Traffic signs and lighting should be kept under control;
- The users of buildings should be consulted more closely.

Crypts and the homeless

Alec Dickson

It has been demonstrated by St Martin's in the Fields how help can be given to the homeless and others in all sorts of trouble, by conversion of the crypt for this purpose. The number of people in distress has greatly risen. Many City churches lack a role except for lunchtime services and special programmes. To convert a crypt for the homeless, to install the required equipment, protect access to the church proper (and property), cover all risks with insurance, and look after running costs – all this would cost money. But the City houses the richest corporations, banks, insurance companies, etc in Britain. St Mungo's, Centrepoint and similar bodies have shown what can be done – and that volunteers are forthcoming to help with the staffing. This would be a historic reversion to the time when the Church was the sole provider of welfare. It would coincide with a readiness amongst large, rich companies to project an image of corporate responsibility.

Alec Dickson, 19 Blenheim Road, London W4 IVB (tel 081 994 7437).

Cooperative Land Banks

Shann Turnbull

Cooperative Land Banks are a way to make all users of residential property the owners and controllers of their neighbourhoods, whether in an industrialised society or in squatter settlements of an underdeveloped economy. Each resident,

besides a perpetual lease on a dwelling, acquires shares in the neighbourhood.

Both dwelling and shares can be freely sold, but the price of the shares (reflecting improvements in the neighbourhood) are determined by the bank – enabling it to become self-financing and a provider of cheap or free land to low-income earners. It is a form of social capitalism.

'Both dwelling and shares can be freely sold, but the price of the shares (reflecting improvements in the neighbourhood) are determined by the bank'

The Cooperative Land Bank structure has been incorporated in a pilot programme initiated by the Land Commission of New South Wales in Australia to establish new self-help intentional communities to house people without assets or income; and a Ph.D thesis on the Cooperative Land Bank idea has been completed by Thomas Johnson in Boston, Massachusetts, USA.

Mr Johnson believes that it provides a means for upgrading the extensive run-down areas in North American cities without the use of public funds. In countries with extensive public housing estates, the Cooperative Land Bank's structure provides a technique for introducing self-management and privatisation of housing estates.

The ability of a Cooperative Land Bank to make housing sites and services self-financing would allow traditional banking organisations to participate in the upgrading of squatter settlements. Because such a bank creates a grass roots self-governing precinct, it can offer political as well as financial advantages to sponsoring governments.

Over 80% of housing in the world is constructed by the occupants and their families. The greatest problem in obtaining affordable housing, whether or not it is self-built, is to obtain access to suitable land. The more suitable the land in terms of access to income-producing activities, water and other services, then the more expensive it becomes. The effectiveness of a Cooperative Land Bank in making land self-financing increases as the value of land increases with its development.

As the value of land is typically around 30% of the cost of housing, this bank structure would provide a means for eliminating the deposit gap for housing everywhere. This benefit indicates how much more efficient it is compared with traditional land tenure systems; and more equitable too, as it eliminates the capture of 'unearnt' windfall gains in land values, a feature which substantially increases its economic efficiency.

Shann Turnbull, GPO Box 4359, Sydney, NSW, Australia (tel 612 233 5340). Shann Turnbull is the author of 'Democratising the Wealth of Nations', published by the Company Directors Association of Australia, 1975. His ideas are dealt with in depth in the book 'The Living Economy', edited by Paul Ekins, published by Routledge and Kegan Paul.

Chapter five

NEW MONEY SYSTEMS

Money as a social invention

Conrad Hopman

Conrad Hopman here describes the background to a computer-ised multi-barter system that he has created.

In a sense the whole universe is an exchange medium. Observable reality can only be observed because it is information. Information is meaning and meanings define each other in context. To be observed, reality must change so it can induce changes in the observer – activate nerve cells, affect information stored in the brain. Since meanings define each other, the spacetime-meaning continuum curves around to redefine itself in indefinitely many ways without beginning or end. Just as physical substances such as alcohol or drugs can affect the mind, so creative changes in the mind can affect the whole physical universe in a process which takes place outside of spacetime. This is the essence of magic. Humankind could thus perhaps take a more important part in the process of joyful creative exchange which surrounds it.

Subparticles are not just bits of stuff, but ripples of energy which combine to form the illusion of substance, just as wind forms ripples on a lake or sunshine in raindrops reveals a rainbow. Atoms, molecules, living cells are formed out of the ever more complex interchanging energy patterns. This interchange takes on more complex and wonderful forms in the plant and animal worlds. Plants breathe in what animals breathe out, animals consume plants and each other – so species keep each other healthy; herbivores do not overbreed and overgraze, carnivores develop keen senses. The interplay of evolution, eliminating the superfluous like a sculptor, creates humans – who continue the exchange process again on more complex, subtle levels.

Initially it is barter: exogamy – women are exchanged freely or taken in battle. Cattle, whence our words 'capital' (Latin 'caput' = head) serve as unit measures of value. But cattle and chattel (also from 'caput') are cumbersome. How to transport value over space and time? Or make big investments over long periods and ensure that each contributor will be reimbursed fairly? Females may not be constant measures of desirability and cows cannot be kept long or carried far. If they are eaten they cannot be exchanged – hence the useless accumulation of half-starved herds which represent tribal riches. More forests are cut down for pasture, more pasturelands turn into deserts. As central Asia gradually turned into the Gobi desert, nomads turned into warriors – so Europe was regularly invaded out of the East – which is also where the barbarians who sacked Rome came from.

With agriculture came the need to measure value through time more accurately. How can the farm hand who clears the land, irrigates and sows it, know he will get a fair share of the harvest? It has been shown (in 'From Reckoning to Writing', Scientific American, August 1978) that our numbers and alphabets descend from such needs to keep records. The dummy clay sack represents the real sack of wheat the hand will get. In the meantime he can exchange it for clothing or a gift for his girl-friend; it is the bearer of the dummy who exchanges it for the real thing.

But clay dummies are easily copied. What is needed is a system of tokens whose supply cannot be so easily manipulated. It is necessary to invent the value of gold and silver. Initially this is not obvious. Primitive man lives in nature surrounded by beauty and danger – why should he attribute great value to a soft, heavy, rather useless yellow substance? The problem was solved in Mesopotamia: Will Durant ('Our Oriental Heritage', Simon and Schuster, 1954, p.244) quotes Heroditus on the 'whores of Babylon':

> 'Every native woman is obliged once in her life to sit in the temple of Venus and have intercourse with some stranger...she must not return home until some stranger has thrown a piece of silver into her lap and lain with her'

' "Every native woman is obliged once in her life to sit in the temple of Venus and have intercourse with some stranger...she must not return home until some stranger has thrown a piece of silver into her lap and lain with her." Such temple prostitutes were common in western Asia, we find them in Israel, Phrygia, Phoenicia, Syria, etc.'

It was the most ancient practitioners of the oldest profession who, in effect, created the value of gold and silver by obliging men to associate what they really desired with something they had to be made to desire – so old is that advertising gimmick. A given weight of gold or silver was defined as having the value of one intercourse; the metal had backing and a unit of measure was established. We owe the women much – no longer was it necessary for a village to have a large herd of cattle, nor its chief to have a big harem to prove their worth. Riches could be counted in gold, cattle eaten and sexuality less monopolised.

But gold was not without problems. Trade was hampered by complex checks of weights and purity at each exchange. It was Croesus, king of Lydia, who, about 550 BC, invented coins by stamping the marks of his realm on lumps of metal and guaranteeing that all coins so produced had exactly the same weight and purity. The concept of price came into sharper focus and trade expanded enormously. Increasing volumes of trade required increasing volumes of money. This Croesus and others who copied his idea were happy to supply. But the newly created money was not, of course, given away for free. Croesus became one of the richest men of antiquity. He had discovered a trick perfected by others after him – while he mixed a little copper into his gold coins and found that they retained 'face value', we now have paper notes. His newly created money also served the needs of his state. It became possible to organise transport, communications, education on a large scale in a coordinated centralised way using the power of newly created money.

Progress was enormous – but it had its shadow side. Law-givers, tax-collectors, police and military also were organised 'to keep law and order for the benefit of the nation' and the state became a parasite of the people who had to keep on accepting debased coinage. Tensions arose between governors and governed which could be diverted outwards. This justified the acquisition of more weapons which, not incidentally, could also be used for internal repression. Since the government controlled money, organisation and weapons, whereas the rest of the population did not, it always played a winning hand.

If taking real value from a person against his will without giving anything in return is theft, then issuing intrinsically worthless tokens and using them to obtain real goods and services can enable some people to rob others on a very large scale indeed. Gold tokens, like paper money, can be attributed symbolic value because they are 'rare'. Unlike things with real intrinsic value, tokens have no value unless they can ultimately be exchanged for real value. If some people are able to issue tokens and use them to obtain a lot of real goods and services, the process is fundamentally dishonest. Over the centuries a variety of subtle swindles developed on Croesus' original trick. So tax money mixed with newly issued currency (international loan, budget deficit...) can be lent out at interest to banks ('bank rate') who lend it out at a higher rate. When borrowed money is spent, its receivers deposit it in banks where it is again lent out at interest – and so on, indefinitely. So it now seems that the entire world is in debt to its banks – and financial collapse may be imminent. In spite of official propaganda, such institutionalised injustice cannot be in the 'national interest' – it is extremely harmful to the population of the planet as a whole.

It is edifying in this context to read about the decline and fall of Rome – how tensions within society were diverted into war at its frontiers, how free men who went out as soldiers came back to find that their small farms could no longer compete with the latifundiae – great agricultural combines run with slave labour. The Romans had slaves, we have robots; they had Colosseums, we have television; they had breadlines, make-work projects, class wars between rich and poor, overstuffed bureaucracies, the stifling of initiative with taxation, inflation and interference, and so do we.

> ## 'The Romans had slaves, we have robots; they had Colosseums, we have television; they had breadlines, make-work projects, class wars between rich and poor, overstuffed bureaucracies, the stifling of initiative with taxation, inflation and interference, and so do we'

Rome collapsed, imploded. Barbarian mercenaries employed to defend its frontiers went to the capital to collect several years' back pay and, getting none, stayed on to sack it. In fact it was not those barbarians (from whom most of us are descended) who destroyed Rome, but the injustice of money. Its subjects had no recourse against the internal colonialism of the state, no means of fighting the functionaries, getting rid of the tax-collectors and the whole rotten, parasitical superstructure. As freedom, enterprise and goodwill gave way to dependency, apathy, hate, crime, drugs, hedonism and superstition, the collapse of Rome became inevitable.

If we do not want to follow that road again, we will have to devise an exchange system which is both fair and efficient. The Community Cooperation Coordinator system (CCC) is a step in that direction (and is explained more fully in the next entry). Briefly, it can be built on to provide public services in free cooperation and competition, rather than as rackets. Fundamentally, this is a special case of ensuring fair returns on investment – again a matter of fair exchanges. There is no need to have social systems in which politicians and bankers live in outrageous luxury in the capital while peasants starve in the countryside. We do not have to kill nature to provide more taxes for nation state protection rackets – we already have more than enough weapons to kill all life on earth several times over. We do not need tin pot dictators who use Croesus' technique to accrue enormous personal wealth nor public services which are sinecures for civil servants. There is no need for money in international trade – more than half of which is done through various forms of barter anyway. In fact, we have no need for money at all, nor need trade be national or international. All we need is fair, efficient exchanges. But it is upon the ability to issue and control money that the nation state system is founded.

Every minute several thousand hectares of forest are cut down; large parts of the earth are turning into deserts and the rest filled with junk and industrial wastes. Several animal and plant species become extinct every week. Specialists have predicted unpleasant climatic changes if we continue to pollute the atmosphere at the present rate. Since the beginning of the century, war and traffic accidents have taken hundreds of millions of lives – terrorists a few thousand. But do we see any serious effort on the part of governments of nation states to do away with polluting transportation and energy generation systems? Do they not encourage the production of automobiles, nuclear power stations, strip mining, and do they not raise taxes and so increase pressure on the people and the land?

The organisation of this planet into nation states has outlived its usefulness. No state can protect its citizens militarily – the old game of 'I can hit harder than you' no longer works now that it is possible to make weapons of any desired megatonnage. As events are proving, states cannot provide economic security either – the protection, public service and credit rackets they run are, in fact, the real causes of inflation, unemployment, depressions and many other forms of waste and unfairness. The 'justice' they dispense is founded on an old trick which enables some people to get something from others for nothing – a form of robbery. If we are serious in our desire for world peace, we can do more than trust in the efficacy of prayer. We can start moneyless exchanges which make redundant the whole system of military machines which justify internal oppression through tacit collusion. We will do away with nation states or they will do away with us. Time is running out.

Exchange systems other than those based on the 'good faith in the XXX nation state government' have been proposed elsewhere. So there are a variety of schemes out for privately issued coins or commodity-backed promissory notes. These actually pose problems similar to those solved by Croesus or the Babylon women. Commodities used for backing currencies are inevitably available in different qualities or locations and they cannot be sold or consumed. How are prices to be calculated if multiple coinages of more or less dubious worth or backing are in concurrent circulation? If some board of directors is to decide how long a line of credit is to be allocated to each member of the community, will that authority not be subject to much temptation? Is its 'guarantee' that each participant will, in fact, make good on any credit accorded him not similar to the Croesus trick? If insurance is demanded, who should decide its cost? And what if the insurers themselves default? A Funded Direct Exchange (FDE), where each participant makes a deposit in case he or she dies or defects, seems simpler and more efficient.

> 'A culmination of several thousand years of increased abstraction – cattle, metals, coins, paper, to price information used for the direct, fair, efficient exchange of any values over any expanses of space and time'

The new system I am proposing goes beyond the FDE idea. It uses prices without the concept of a value bearing exchange medium and is thus, in a way, a culmination of several thousand years of increased abstraction – cattle, metals, coins, paper, to price information used for the direct, fair, efficient exchange of any values over any expanses of space and time. In this system, measure is always given for measure. Hence there is none of the injustice which is inevitable when some people 'guarantee' for others the value of an essentially valueless exchange medium. There is also no unemployment, inflation or boom-bust instability, but it does make efficient investments possible as well as public services which really are responsive to the public's needs. The CCC is not intended merely as an improved system for increasing personal and collective well-being. It is the expression of a new vision of Divinity, a new way of relating to this fantastic universe of ours.

Conrad Hopman, BP 225, Noumea, New Caledonia, South Pacific, (tel 687 26 21 26. Hopman's ideas are detailed in his 180,000 word 'Book of Future Changes, Living in Balance in the Electronic Age', (published by the Institute for Social Inventions, 1988, ISBN 0 948826 10 X, but now out of print and available only through libraries or on microfiche from the author).

Abundance without money value

Conrad Hopman

Conrad Hopman here explains some of the technicalities of the scheme outlined above:

Abundance without money describes an economic system which has prices, but no money to be used as though it were a value substance. There is no double barter (rights to goods, properties and services bartered for money which is bartered for real value) and there is no double ownership (money *and* what it can buy). There are no legal fictions (companies, banks, states) which ever own real properties (factories, estates, rights to receive or perform any particular services); and real flesh and blood people never own fictitious value – tokens, numbers in accounts which are treated as though they themselves had value. How my proposal achieves this is by balancing accounts as completely and as continuously as possible.

Company earnings are entirely and continuously distributed to individual shareholders and employees as dividends and salaries. Such earnings are not 'money' but rights to real value, including shares in companies and other common properties. They are managed professionally by agreement just as employees' services are – and managers are themselves employees who earn salaries and dividends.

In the system, called 'Community Cooperation Coordinator' (CCC), numbers retained on computerised community bank accounts represent rights to obtain real value but have no intrinsic value of their own.

The CCC can start from within the present set-up, with small computerised exchange 'nodes' or networks, which can later be interlinked, like cells in a body, to form a single coherent whole.

The CCC helps to create socially and economically efficient and fair communities, without unemployment or inflation. As these multiply and expand, a new socio-economic structuring comes into being – simply, organically, and without a lot of ideological bitterness. As Blake remarked, 'good can really only be done in minute particulars.'

The CCC differs from simple barter in that exchanges are many for many (multi-lateral), rather than being one for one (bilateral, one thing for another at a given time).

In the present system, value is measured in terms of one 'thing' – money – which has little intrinsic value and is created arbitrarily out of nothing by select members of society. In the CCC, the value of each thing is measured in terms of all others by all members of the community. This is perhaps the hardest aspect to grasp: there is in the CCC no common measuring stick whose value is supposed to remain constant. Rather, the price of any given good, service or right serves as a measuring stick against which all the others can be measured. The lengths of all measuring sticks vary, but the length of any one stick at any time can be estimated in terms of the 'background' of all others. The CCC creates a debit-credit continuum whose structure is comparable to space-time.

'The value of each thing is measured in terms of all others by all members of the community. There is no common measuring stick whose value is supposed to remain constant'

The seller of a good simply does more or less what happens today – looks to the prices of other goods, and tries to guess how much buyers will pay in order to estimate a sales price.

The CCC has its own unit measure of value, represented by the symbol X. There are two requirements of prices expressed in X. One is that when a node is started up, prices expressed in normal currency units should be convertible into X in easy mental calculations. The other is that prices in X in nodes at different locations should be roughly equal. For this reason, the value of one X when a node starts up is defined as being roughly equal to the average hourly wage of an 18 to 20 year old employed person; the conversion factor being adjusted so that quick calculations are possible. When several nodes are interlinked, prices at some are automatically recalculated so that prices at all are expressed in identical X units.

Before giving a detailed example, here are some of the CCC's other advantages:

- It can be used by any group of people wishing to increase their internal cohesion.

- It requires no two-tiered social order separating those who regulate money and tax and govern from the beneficiaries of such services. In a CCC there is order but with no specific centres of control.

- The money system means that some people get something for nothing. Not so in the CCC.

- The system is not readily taxable, whilst at the same time encouraging people to cooperate voluntarily to care for the 'commons', which the present economic system is contriving to ruin.

- No services, including government services, are monopolised.

- The CCC does not encourage unnecessary production of goods.

- There can be no depressions or boom-bust cycles.

The CCC is as complicated as the money system, but could be learned through a Monopoly type game in the first instance. Just how complicated it appears, the following 'simple' example will demonstrate.

Let us assume that a certain young lady lives by making dresses during the day and selling her charms at night. She is interested in painting and astrology, and owns her dressmaking shop and the apartment she lives in.

When she registers at the CCC, she records for the computer her name and telephone number only, since that is all she wants. She enters her sewing ability, astrology and painting interests and requests the barter network to give her a list of other persons with similar interests so that they can contact each other.

She forms a 'composite person' (the CCC equivalent of a 'company') of which she is initially the only member and declares her shop to be managed by this composite person of which she is also sole shareholder. This shop is entered with what she considers a reasonable nominal price.

In the Agreements Register she enters payment arrangements in which she accords herself 10% of her earnings as only shareholder and 90% of her earnings as only working partner in her company. She also sets rates indicating under what conditions she is willing to part with a share of her 'base' (the shop) or to acquire other 'bases'. The value of her base immediately rises above its physical worth because she has committed herself to pay dividends on it.

The wisdom of this procedure becomes evident when other people wish to join her enterprise as associates or to invest in it. Then she will be ready to share increased earnings according to freely established agreements.

The apartment is registered as a property with no price since she does not intend to exchange it. Records are also entered for each of the main kind of dresses that she makes. Each of these gets the system code for dresses and her own user code for style, size, etc, a nominal price and any description she feels is pertinent. She also registers her dressmaking services at an hourly rate.

Now, when people ask the system for dresses and sewing services, her services will turn up and can be compared with others. Because dresses are not usually bought unseen, prospective customers will probably go to her shop to try them on. If a dress is sold, the customer can pay with a cheque in the usual way, or the transaction can be stored in a computer terminal.

'This young lady can also apply sales "coefficients" or "filters". Some customers have been loyal and courteous, others nasty or dishonest. She can associate a 'Sales Filter' on the computer with each dress model for each customer, so that the prices can vary for particular customers'

This young lady can also apply sales 'coefficients' or 'filters'. Some customers have been loyal and courteous, others nasty or dishonest. She can associate a 'Sales Filter' on the computer with each of her dress models for each customer, so that the prices can vary for particular customers.

One way or another, her earnings would enter the register. But this lady has expenses as well as earnings. She buys food, needs medical care and saves up to go travelling. At every accounting period her expenditures are balanced against her earnings. If she has earned more than she spent, she acquires rights to shares. If she has spent more than she earns, she loses some property rights – possibly to her shop if she had nothing else to cede before it.

How does all this differ from other barter clubs? Unlike these, the CCC has an internal measure of value, it has mechanisms for optimising investments and public services internally, it has arrangements for defining ownership and ensuring that agreements will be binding and it can operate without, or in spite of, official money systems.

The CCC is on IBM PC compatible computer programs, on 8

diskettes with accompanying manuals which are available for US$500 from Conrad Hopman, (address above).

Green Dollar LETSystem

A paper, edited from information supplied by Guy Dauncey and published by Ledis (The Planning Exchange, 186 Bath Street, Glasgow G2 4HG, tel 041 332 8541) gives a very good account of the Green Dollar Local Employment and Trading (LETS) System on Vancouver Island, Canada. The following are extracts, and many of the points are also relevant for those considering starting a Hopman Community Co-operation Co-ordinator system (described above).

Origins

The Green Dollar LETSystem was established in 1983 by Michael Linton, a self-employed business studies graduate who was concerned about the 18% unemployment rate on Vancouver Island. He observed that while many local people had skills and products to offer, their lack of money prevented them from trading with each other. The LETSystem is really only an information exchange, which uses a computer to keep track of account holders' green dollar trading transactions. Its objective is to stimulate trade, local economic activity, community relationships and personal self-confidence.

> 'The objective of LETSystem is to stimulate trade, local economic activity, community relationships and personal self-confidence'

Organisation

The account holders list what their wants are and what they have to offer in a regular monthly newsletter, eg:

068 - -	Simple Car Mechanics	Rosie	645 3773
069 - -	Lawn Mowing	Dave	339 4567
075 ++	Building Work	Andrew	776 4263
086 ++	Fresh Vegetables	Jenny	776 9375

'++' means 'to offer' and '- -' means 'wanted'. People get in touch with each other and negotiate a trade and a 'green dollar' price. No money is exchanged – a message is put on the LETSystem answering machine and the information is registered in the books and the computer. The sum total of 'credits' in the system always balances exactly the sum total of 'debits' or 'commitments', hence the use of '+' and '-' symbols. Account holders can take out 'loans' simply by spending green dollars, and running up a debit account. No interest is charged on 'overdrafts' and no interest is given on positive account balances.

Technical Questions

Personal income tax: The Canadian tax authorities have ruled that green dollar earnings in pursuit of your normal occupation are taxable, but that other green dollar earnings are not.

Sales Tax (VAT): Sales tax is collected in normal dollars on top of the green dollar price, if necessary.

Shops: Many shops offer goods for a mix of normal and green dollars, eg '10% green.' A dentist in Courtenay regularly offers his services at 50% green.

Difficulties

(a) In order for a system to flourish, considerable persistence is needed by individual people to get new people to join, and to publicise the system's existence.

> 'People get in touch with each other and negotiate a trade and a green dollar price. No money is exchanged'

(b) In British Columbia, the welfare authorities have ruled that green dollar earnings count as normal earnings, which hinders the LETSystem's usefulness to unemployed people. In Whangarei, New Zealand, a 'blind eye' arrangement has been made with the welfare authorities allowing a trial period during which time green dollar earnings will not be counted as income. A similar arrangement will be needed in the UK for the LETSystem to be of value to unemployed people, single parents, etc.

Starting a System

(a) A LETSystem can start with as few as 20 people. It can be based initially among a group of friends, or around a neighbourhood, community or church organisation.

(b) Write off for the LETSystem manual and programmes. These are available on IBM-compatible diskettes, from which you can print your own 250 page manual. This should be read and digested by key people in the group.

(c) LETSplay is a simulated version which allows people to become familiar with the system. The rules are in the manual.

(d) An answering machine and a personal computer are needed, and someone should be familiar with logging in entries and keeping records.

(e) A commitment is either needed from 5 to 6 key people who will work at getting it going for six months, or a grant is needed to fund a part-time organiser for six months. A LETSystem will not get going on its own without effort.

(f) Groups starting a LETSystem are asked to pay a one-off licence fee of £50 to Landsman Community Services Ltd to cover the costs of pioneering and developing the system. There are also start-up costs for printing the newsletter, office supplies, etc. A group of 40 could cover start-up costs of £300 by paying £10 each for lifetime membership, and a per transaction fee of around 15p should cover running costs. You may be able to pay suppliers in green currency.

(g) Once initial planning has been done, a group can start trading within 2 to 3 weeks. Future expansion should be taken slowly. Publicity tends to look after itself.

There are now some 50 LETSystems in Canada and the USA, 35 in Australia and 20 in New Zealand.

• *For further information contact: Michael Linton, Landsman Community Services Ltd, 375 Johnston Avenue, Courtenay, British Columbia, Canada V9N 2Y2 (tel 604 338 6877).*

• *Guy Dauncey's address is 2069 Kings Road, Victoria, BC V8R 2P6, Canada (tel 604 592 4472 h; 604 592 4473 w and fax).*

A Green Pound UK network

Some of the following information is from an article by Susannah Herbert in the Daily Telegraph and another by Margaret Dibben in the Independent.

A UK Network for the LETSystem, called LETSlink UK, was formed in 1991 with LETS representatives from around the country. It aims to encourage new start-ups and offers advice and training. There are at present at least eight such trading communities in the UK. For instance, in Totnes, Devon, more than 100 locals calculate their debits and credits in a currency called the Acorn. And in Blickling, Norfolk, the Rural Community Association (treasurer Ms Viv Horner) has encouraged the creation of a barter network – examples include a haircut in return for flowers; home-made curtains for a car service; and goats milk in exchange for child minding. In Stroud, the 143 LETS members include the local taxi firm, a cafe, printers and plumbers. Payment is in 'Stroud' currency by cheque from a special cheque book. It costs £7-50 plus 10 Strouds a year to belong to the scheme, and 2.5 per cent in Strouds is added to each transaction to cover the costs of administration.

Are such exchanges taxable in the UK? The Inland Revenue requires 'people who make a living out of exchanging services for goods to put a monetary value on the things they receive – but if you are just doing a favour for a friend, it is not taxable.'

• *Liz Shephard, LETSLink UK, 61 Woodcock Road, Warminster, Wilts BA12 9DH (tel 0985 217 871).*

• *A London LETS trading system, under the name 'The Networking Market' is being set up in London by Sabine Kurjo McNeill, with a £15 joining fee, and a further £3 if a copy of an IBM compatible disk about the system is required. Sabine Kurjo McNeill, 21a Goldhurst Terrace, London NW6 3HB (tel 071 625 8804).*

The Electric Pound

Nicholas Saunders

In about 1978 I had the idea that to stop inflation required basing money on a commodity that was essential to all economies, of intrinsic value in the production of goods, and yet which could not be stored, to avoid hoarding.

> 'I had the idea that to stop inflation required basing money on a commodity that was essential to all economies, of intrinsic value in the production of goods, and yet which could not be stored, to avoid hoarding'

The answer was electricity. As it is used in such vast quantities in industrial societies, governments could not afford to subsidise it for long, so its value in any society would be 'real'.

The value of, say, £1, would be locked to the present Kilowatt Hour of electricity at cost of production, excluding distribution.

Nicholas Saunders, top floor, 14 Neal's Yard, London WC2H 9DP (tel 071 836 9404; fax 071 379 0135).

Energy Dollars

Shann Turnbull

Shann Turnbull has a similar proposal to Nicholas Saunders' idea above, although in a more complex form.

The unit of electrical power output, the Kilowatt Hour (Kwhr) has much appeal as a universal unit of value for an autonomous community banking and monetary system.

> 'Money would be created by the owners of the power generator. It would be in the form of a voucher, or contract note to supply a specified number of Kwhrs at a specified time in the future'

Money would be created by the owners of the power generator. It would be in the form of a voucher, or contract note to supply a specified number of Kwhrs at a specified time in the future. These notes would be created and issued by the owners of the generator to pay for its purchase and installation. The value of notes which could be used for redemption in any given time period would be limited by the output of the generator. The notes which had a specified maturity date would represent the 'primary' currency. Such currency notes would be held mainly by investors, investment banks and banks. Commercial banks would hold the primary currency notes as a reserve currency in like manner to a bank holding gold or a merchant banker holding grain or other commodities.

Similarly, the commercial bank would issue its own notes which the holders could convert or cash-in to the primary notes or reserve currency, and which could be used to pay their power bills at the time specified. The secondary notes could be denominated in Kwhrs but without any specified redemption time. They could thus be used as hand-to-hand money in the community.

Some of the more important issues to be considered in comparing the suitability of Kwhrs or gold as a basis for a monetary system are set out in the table below:

Evaluation criteria	Kwhr $	Gold $
Unit of value	Kwhr	Ounces/grams
Quality testing	Not required	Density
Intrinsic consumerable value	100%	10%
Subjective value	Nil	90%
Changes in consumption	Related to total economic activity	Little related to to economic activity
Global availability	Universal	Haphazard
Changes in production	Related to consumption	Little related to consumption
Rate of change	Relatively stable	Less stable
Cost of production	Relatively stable by region and in time	Fluctuates with region and in time
Cost of storage	Not required	1% of value p.a.
Cost of insurance	Not required	1% of value p.a.
Cost of distribution	Increases with distance	Changes little with distance

Shann Turnbull, GPO Box 4359, Sydney, NSW 2001, Australia (tel 612 233 5340). The full pamphlet, Selecting a Local Currency, is available from Centre 2000, 2 O'Connell Street, Sydney, 2000, Australia, for Aus $1.50.

Interest and inflation free money

'Interest and inflation free money' by Margrit Kennedy (17DM prepaid from Permakultur Institut, address below).

Why do we have a money problem? Margrit Kennedy's answer in this booklet is that it is because 'of the payment of interest from those who have less money than they need to those who have more money than they need.' To summarise her arguments:

Interest acts like a cancer in our social structure, with money following an exponential growth pattern. Inflation through the printing of money is a way for the government to overcome its increasing interest-related indebtedness. Government income in West Germany rose only 300% between 1968 and 1982, whilst its interest payments rose by 1,160%.

'In contrast to interest, a money system in which people would pay a small fee if they kept money out of circulation'

Kennedy and others propose, in contrast to interest, a money system in which people would pay a small fee if they kept money out of circulation. Everyone would have two accounts, a current account losing 6% a year, and a savings account with no interest (but with the new money retaining its value). Borrowers would pay only a risk premium and bank charges (amounting to about 1.5%). Banks too would be subject to use fees if they were to sit on their money, so would be keen to give loans. Banknotes would be printed in different colours, with some recalled once or twice a year, without prior announcement.

'Land reform would be required. Owners of land would pay 3% of the value of their plot to the community each year and this would be used by the community to buy land which came on the market'

Land reform would also be required, or there would be a tendency for surplus money to be attracted to land speculation. Owners of land would pay 3% of the value of their plot to the community each year and this would be used by the community to buy land which came on the market. Alternatively, land owners would pay no fee for 33 years; after which the land would belong to the community, with the ex-owners and their descendants retaining the right to use the land – with payment of a 3% lease annually.

Tax reform would also be needed or otherwise the economic boom following the introduction of interest-free money would have serious environmental consequences. Income tax would be replaced by a product tax related to the environmental costs of the product.

'People invested in furniture, artwork and everything else that promised to keep or increase in its value'

Kennedy sketches several historical examples, such as the 1932 Worgl labour certificates in Austria (described in the next piece), to illuminate her monetary arguments. She tells how between the 12th and the 15th centuries in Europe a money system was used called 'Brakteaten'. Issued by the respective towns, bishops and sovereigns, it helped in the exchange of goods and services, whilst also, unfortunately in Kennedy's view, serving as a means of collecting taxes. For every year the thin coins made from gold and silver were 'recalled', one to three times re-minted, and devalued on average about 25% in the process. Since nobody wanted to keep this money, people instead invested in furniture, solidly built houses, artwork and everything else that promised to keep or increase in its value. Some of the most beautiful works of art and architecture came into existence. 'For while monied wealth could not accumulate, real wealth was created.'

Kennedy also quotes a prophetic letter by the economist Sylvio Gesell who in 1890 had propounded the use-fee as a replacement for interest. His letter to the editor of the newspaper 'Zeitung am Mittag' in Berlin was published in 1918, shortly after World War I, when everyone else was talking about peace and many international organisations were being created to secure that peace:

'In spite of the holy promise of all people to banish war, once and for all, in spite of the cry of millions "Never a war again", in spite of all the hopes for a better future, I have this to say: if the present monetary system, based on interest and compound interest, remains in operation, I dare to predict today, that it will take less than 25 years for us to have a new and even worse war. I can foresee the coming development clearly. The present degree of technological advancement will quickly result in a record performance by industry. The build-up of capital will be rapid in spite of the enormous losses during the war, and through its over-supply will ... (affect) ... the interest rate ... Economic activities will diminish and increasing numbers of unemployed persons will roam the streets ... within the discontented masses, wild, revolutionary ideas will arise and also the poisonous plant called "Super-Nationalism" will proliferate. No country will understand the other, and the end can only be war again.'

'We can predict a crash mathematically. But instead of learning the hard way, we may chose the soft evolutionary path'

We have been warned. 'We can predict a crash mathematically,' writes Kennedy. 'The question is just when and where it starts. But instead of learning the hard way – which means economic disaster and social chaos for millions of people – we may chose the soft evolutionary path of change.'

Dr Margrit Kennedy, Permakultur Institut, Ginsterweg 4-5, D-3074 Steyerberg, Germany (tel 49 5764 2158; fax 49 5764 2368).

Depreciating community-owned currencies

David Weston

The following piece is updated from one first published in New Economics No 11.

There was a time when people were so convinced that the earth was flat, that the idea that it was round was inconceivable.

Likewise today, the idea of a community or region issuing and using its own currency and running its own bank may seem just inconceivable.

But it has happened.

The Worgl Schillings

In the early 1930s the small town of Worgl in the Austrian Tyrol, suffering like every other town in Europe and America from the Great Depression, took the unlikely step of issuing its own currency.

Its burgomaster, Michael Unterguggenberger, faced an empty treasury, because the unemployed citizens could not pay their taxes; roads and bridges needed repair and parks needed maintenance, for which the town could not pay; and idle men and women earned no wages.

He recognised that all three problems could be solved if he could find the connecting link.

That link was *money*. The three problems coexisted because no one had any of it, and his simple solution was to create money locally.

He issued numbered 'labour certificates' to the value of 32,000 schillings, in denominations of 1, 5 and 10 schillings, respectively. These became valid only after being stamped at the town hall, and depreciated monthly by 1 per cent of their nominal value.

It was possible for the holders to 'revalue' them by the purchase, before the end of each month, of stamps from the town hall, in the process creating a relief fund.

> ### 'The small town of Worgl in the Austrian Tyrol, suffering like every other town in Europe and America from the Great Depression, took the unlikely step of issuing its own currency'

The depreciation not only encouraged rapid circulation, but also the payment of taxes, past, current and upcoming. These taxes were used to provide social and public services.

At the end of each year, it was required that the notes be turned in for new ones. No charge was made for the transaction if the required stamps had been affixed. Subject to a 2 per cent deduction, the town also undertook to convert the labour notes into Austrian schillings.

To facilitate this conversion at any time – and thereby provide a cover for the relief certificates – the trustees deposited at the local Raiffeisen Bank (credit union) an amount in Austrian currency equivalent to the issued local currency.

The money was loaned out to trustworthy wholesalers at 6 per cent interest. Interest thereby flowed back into the town treasury, yet further facilitating transactions with the 'outside' world.

Wages paid in the new money

The burgomaster put this money into circulation by paying 50 per cent – later raised to 75 per cent – of the wages of the town's clerical and manual workers in the new money.

The workers found that all businesses in Worgl accepted the currency in payment and at face value, and the notes returned to the parish treasury as dues and taxes. Economically, there was no inflation, and politically, the money was unanimously acceptable to all the municipal parties.

> ### 'Because it was a depreciating currency, it circulated with rapidity, boosting the local economy. Further, many paid their taxes in advance because it was financially advantageous'

Because it was a depreciating currency, it circulated with rapidity, boosting the local economy. Also, not only did people merely pay their current taxes in the currency, but also discharged their tax arrears. Further, many paid their taxes in advance because it was financially advantageous.

Apart from the obvious employment benefits, physical assets were created. These included improvements in the main street and its drainage system, street lighting, new road construction, manufacturing of kerb stones and drainage pipes, construction of a ski-jumping platform, and fencing and construction of a new water reservoir.

Although the Worgl money was unanimously accepted at the local level, there was great opposition from two centralist forces – the Tyrol Labour Party and the Austrian State Bank.

In both cases, there seemed to be the fear of the experiment spreading, for the idea was copied by the neighbouring town of Kirchbichel. The town monies were valid in both places. Other towns in the Tyrol also decided on issuing depreciating money, but did not proceed because of threats from the State Bank.

The experiment curtailed

Ultimately, the State Bank threatened legal proceedings and on September 1st 1933, the experiment was terminated.

In an analysis, Unterguggenberger concluded that depreciating currency fulfils the functions of money much better than unvarying nationalised currency. He noted that no difficulties or complaints had arisen in making payments in the new currency or in affixing stamps, and that the local currency was accepted by all businesses very shortly after starting the project.

He also suggested that, not only did it work at the town level, but it could also be applied in larger entities including regions, provinces and the state.

Although the experiment was terminated in Austria, it was noted and tried elsewhere. In Canada, for instance, the government of the Province of Alberta set up a provincial depreciating currency in the mid-1930s in the form of Prosperity Certificates.

The 'danger' of its success prompted the central government to ban it.

What lessons?

What lessons can be learnt? First and foremost, that there is nothing sacred about the 'national' money with which we grew up.

Money – as information technology, metal chips, paper slips and electronic blips – is what people will accept in payment for goods and services and taxes.

> 'It was the fact that the community or regional money could be used to pay taxes, and also exchanged for familiar national currency, that made it acceptable and successful'

If they will accept community or regional money, then it is as good as £s or $s or Dms. It was the fact that the community or regional money could be used to pay taxes, and also exchanged for familiar national currency, that made it acceptable and successful.

> 'A depressed community in an apparently hopeless situation found a way of ending the seemingly insoluble problems of unemployment'

The most important lesson, however, is that a depressed community in an apparently hopeless situation found a way of ending the seemingly insoluble problems of unemployment, local decline and lack of a reliable tax base, symbiotically through the use of community-owned currency.

The prime candidate for the cause of community and regional decline is the centralised banking and money system. By definition, 'national' money is political.

The banks are also political in as much as they make policies to siphon off local wealth and value into their central financial vortex.

> 'The centralised banks collect money from the regions in a nation and invest in a booming area'

This vortex is well described by Myrdal's 'cumulative causation effect.' The centralised banks collect money from the regions in a nation and invest in a booming area, creating a further boom, which demands more national money from the regions, which creates...

Conversely and concurrently, the communities and regions are deprived of their wealth – via the national money – to feed the voracious appetite of the centre. Even if some of that money is re-imported into the community or region, it is as externally controlled capital.

In the process the communities or regions lose control of their economy, and also their political systems, becoming dispensable 'Regions of Sacrifice'. Scotland is a prime example.

A duplication of the process is now evolving in the push for a European central bank and a single European currency.

From observation and experience, there is no doubt that the European Monetary System will be used to enhance a corridor of centralised financial power running from London to Zurich and connected to the other major financial centres of Europe, including possibly Moscow. The centralisation of power has always created problems, and its abuse comes as no surprise.

The appropriate decentralisation of power, known as the Principle of Subsidiarity, can and should take place. This principle states that the priority for decision-making and action-taking should be at the most decentralised level possible. Only when those decisions and actions impinge upon the well-being of the next larger communities or regions, should those too have an influence.

> 'It will require authorisation to be given to local and regional governments to create their own currency in the form of non-interest bearing local bonds to be used as money'

In practical terms, it will require authorisation to be given to local and regional governments to create their own currency in the form of non-interest-bearing local bonds to be used as money.

Community barter

In discussing these ideas, it is also important to understand the difference between community currency and community barter systems.

A community barter system – like the LETSystem, which is *not* a community currency – is usually based on voluntary organisational sharing of information about goods and services available from individuals in an area. The accounting is usually based either on time or the nationalised currency (pounds, dollars, etc).

Such a system has three basic weaknesses:

• It tends to be limited in scope to a handful of dedicated practitioners, usually in largely rural or semi-rural areas.

• It does not cater for transactions outside the community.

• It encourages hoarding, rather than the circulation of wealth and energy, and can only expand by recruiting new producers – there are no 'built-in' inducements to encourage the circulation of goods and services.

A community currency, on the other hand, can be used by *anyone* in the community as a 'means of payment' for *any* commodity or service.

The only limit to the expansion of its circulation is its acceptability, so it encourages all forms of economic activity. If suitable provision is made for 'convertibility', it can facilitate transactions with people and organisations outside the community, and indeed encourage community 'import replacement'.

Also, of course, communities may agree – as they did in the Tyrol – to accept each other's currency at par.

Workable now?

The example of Worgl suggests several prerequisites for success:

• The currency be *accepted* by local government and other 'official' organisations in payment for taxes, rents, licences, etc, and be *used* by them for their own local payments.

• It must be exchangable into national currency, though some deterrents to conversion – a discount on face value, perhaps – may be needed to prevent the whole issue from disappearing from circulation.

• It is essential to encourage the circulation of community money and to discourage 'hoarding', through automatic depreciation.

The demise of the Worgl experiment has its lessons, too. It will be necessary to amend the present situation under which only the state – English or European – can issue money – pounds or ECUs – as legal tender. Otherwise the issuers of community currency, and perhaps even its users, will face state sanctions.

It will also be necessary to persuade workers that they are not being cheated if part or all of their pay is in community currency.

The experiment is surely worth trying, and the growing strength of the regional movement in Britain and Europe suggests that there would be political support in many places for such initiatives.

David Weston, 24 Howe Close, Wheatley, Oxford OX9 1SS (tel 08677 2832; fax 08677 3351).

The need for regional currencies

The arguments above and in this item – adapted from an article in 'New Catalyst' (Canada) sent to the Institute by the American Schumacher Society – are perhaps equally relevant to Eastern Europe and to the debate on a common currency for the EC.

We have all become so accustomed to assuming that national currencies are the norm and preferable. In her book, 'Cities and the Wealth of Nations' (Random House, 1984) Jane Jacobs illustrates 'how national currencies stifle the economies of regions.'

She views the economy of a region as a living entity in the process of expanding and contracting. She understands the role of a regional currency as the appropriate regulator of this ebbing, flowing life. If a region does not produce enough of its own goods, relying heavily on imports, its currency is devalued. As a result, import costs increase, discouraging trade. At the same time, because the currency is less in demand, interest rates will decrease, thereby encouraging local borrowing for the production of 'import replacing' goods. Conversely, if the region is adequately supplying its own needs, then its currency 'hardens', that is, holds its real value relative to other currencies. As a result, imports are cheaper, encouraging trade, and interest rates higher.

> 'Can small businesses in rural areas compete with international corporations and the federal government for access to national currency?'

Currencies are powerful carriers of feedback information, then, and potent triggers of adjustments, but on their own terms. Should the Industrial Great Lakes Region or the Farmbelt States, both in a condition of severe economic depression, adjust their local economies in the same manner as the thriving Sunbelt or the booming Silicon Valley of the West

coast? Can small businesses in rural areas compete with international corporations and the federal government for access to national currency, especially when interest rates are kept artificially high by the federal government?

The dependency on national currencies actually deprives regions of a very useful self-regulating tool and results in the paradoxical creation of stagnant economic pockets in a seemingly properous nation.

Zoo-Zoo Vouchers

A 'local currency' scheme reported by the American Schumacher Society concerns Zoo-Zoo, a 'natural foods' restaurant in Oregon, USA, now defunct, but which flourished for many years as a workers' cooperative. On one occasion they decided to expand and move to larger premises. To finance the move they held benefits and persuaded friends to lend them money, but this still left them $10,000 short. They raised this amount by pre-selling future meals, issuing $10 food vouchers, stamped 'Help the Zoo now' and with varied 'Valid after' dates – to prevent people redeeming them in one rush.

> 'They raised $10,000 by pre-selling future meals, issuing $10 food vouchers'

Even the carpenters working on the new premises accepted part payment in Zoo-Zoo food vouchers, and customers bought more than they would need to give to friends. Zoo-Zoo food voucher customers were their best advertisers, bringing friends who paid in dollars.

Five businesses in Great Barrington, Massachusetts, have since copied Zoo-Zoo's example, with help from the Schumacher Society. One restaurant owner – spurned by the banks for a loan to be able to move across the road when his lease expired – issued 500 of his own Deli Dollars. Each note sold for $9 and could buy $10 worth of food, as long as customers waited at least six months to redeem it.

Susan Witt, E. F. Schumacher Society, Box 76, RD 3, Great Barrington MA 01230, USA (tel 413 528 1737).

Loans that can only be spent at local stores

Guy Dauncey

An example of community banking comes from North Dakota, USA. During the Christmas period of 1987, banks in 16 small towns offered interest-free loans of up to $1,000, not in cash but in scrip, which could only be spent in local stores. The stores collected the scrip and were reimbursed in cash by the banks. This helped to keep local money in town, and helped to offset the usual haemorrhage of money away from the local economy into the huge shopping malls.

Guy Dauncey, 2069 Kings Road, Victoria, BC V8R 2P6, Canada (tel 604 592 4472 h; 604 592 4473 w and fax). Extracted from his book 'After the Crash – the Emergence of the Rainbow Economy' (Green Print/Merlin Press, 1988).

The Commodity Pound

Ivor Pearce

The proposal is for a new currency called the Commodity Pound Sterling – with the bundle of commodities making up the base of the retail price index becoming the standard of value.

It is absurd to try to store value in units of money the value of which changes erratically. The standard objection to all plans to eliminate inflation has always been that they are 'politically impossible' to implement. It must therefore be important to preserve, wherever possible, all that is familiar. With the Commodity Pound, the public are already accustomed to the retail price index, and would have nothing else to get used to except the absence of inflation as measured by the index.

Commodity Pound notes would be guaranteed redeemable so as to enable the purchasing in the market of the bundle of goods defined to be the fixed value of the notes given up.

Notes bought by the authorities when the index is above one would have to be taken out of circulation; when the index is below one they would have to be be returned to circulation through relief of taxation or by the purchase from the public of bonds. Although this system would have nothing at all to do with gold, the analogy with the gold standard is exact.

Exchange rates between national currencies all based upon different commodity standards would be no more and no less stable than relative costs of production of the different commodity standards, that is to say, infinitely more stable than at present.

> 'There must also be something wrong with a banking system which is able to rent, at a price which is automatically hedged against inflation, money which it produces in uncontrolled quantities at near zero cost'

The abuse of money by politicians will vanish, sooner or later. But there must also be something wrong with a banking system which is able to rent, at a price which is automatically hedged against inflation, money which it produces in uncontrolled quantities at near zero cost.

Ivor Pearce, Professor of Economics, University of Southampton, University Rd, Southampton SO9 5NH (tel 0703 595000).

Private monetary systems and no Bank of England

> 'The Bank of England should be abolished, private banks should be allowed to issue their own currency, and money should be backed by a basket of commodities – thus a typical consumer's weekly "shopping basket" would make up the new pound sterling'

Kevin Dowd in a booklet entitled 'Private Money' (details below) suggests that the Bank of England should be abolished, that private banks should be allowed to issue their own currency, and that money should be backed by a basket of commodities – thus a typical consumer's weekly 'shopping basket' would make up the new pound sterling, chosen in such a way that the value of the pound would not alter as the new definition took effect. The historical evidence indicates that private monetary systems, as in Scotland from 1728 to 1844, have been stable and successful. Whereas the Bank of England, claims Dowd, 'has a record of losses which is comparable to those of the worst managed nationalised trading companies.' He concludes that:

'The lessons of history are very clear. We will never attain monetary stability while we maintain a heavily regulated banking system and entrust its safety and the value of the currency to a central bank. The record of government money is a record of disaster. We must entrust the safety of the banking system instead to those who have a self-interest in protecting it, and we must re-establish a commodity basis for the currency to ensure that prices remain stable'.

• *'Private Money' by Kevin Dowd, published by the Institute of Economic Affairs, 2 Lord North Street, Westminster, London SW1P 3LB (tel 071 799 3745), 1988, £4-50, 71 pages. Readers interested in this theme are also referred to the Libertarian Microfiche Publishing ideas archive maintained by John Zube in Australia. For a £5 cash note he will send a selection of microfiche books and papers on this and related topics – John Zube, 7 Oxley Street, Berrima, NSW 2577, Australia (tel 048 771 436).*

• *Kevin Dowd, Department of Economics, University of Nottingham, Nottingham NG7 2RD.*

Chapter six

TAXATION

No local tax without a say in the allocation

Nicholas Albery

One way for people to become more involved in developing their neighbourhoods would be if allocation of at least a proportion of local tax money (for non-basic services?) could be decided not by the council but by each resident. An occasional newsletter would list which projects needed money and how much they needed – community centre, playground and so on – and your tax money would be earmarked according to your order of preferences – if these were over-subscribed (or if you did not bother to select your preferences), the money would go towards the councillors' own preferences amongst under-subscribed projects.

> 'Your tax money would be earmarked according to your order of preferences'

Citizens would also be allowed to put projects needing money into the poll tax newsletter, if supported by the signatures of a certain number of local residents.

The main underlying principle would be: no taxation without a say in the allocation.

Nicholas Albery, 20 Heber Road, London NW2 6AA (tel 081 208 2853; fax 081 452 6434).

Acknowledging public benefactors

An adaptation by Nicholas Albery of a suggestion from Valerie Yule for popularising tax-paying amongst the wealthy.

There could be a voluntary wealth tax for anyone with an income in any one year of over £OAP 300 (ie over three hundred times that of an average state-aided old age pensioner). This tax could be paid to the registered charities of the taxpayers' choice, or to non-charitable projects of their choice for which they could get approval from a local authority or from central government. To encourage the benevolent tax-payer (and to put social pressure on non-payers) the list of projects and benefactors (alongside the list of non-payers) would be released to the media, and plaques or other indications would be put on whatever the money paid for, as a public acknowledgement – eg a Liverpool bus might carry the name and badge of Ringo Starr, a subsidised book or magazine could carry a logo near its masthead or frontispiece with the name of the benevolent taxpayer, and a road would be signposted as 'mended as a public benefit 1993 by ....'

> 'The list of projects and benefactors (alongside the list of non-payers) would be released to the media, and plaques or other indications would be put on whatever the money paid for'

Valerie Yule, 57 Waimarie Drive, Mount Waverley, Victoria, Australia (tel 807 4315).

Returning taxes to the neighbourhood

David Wallechinsky

Adapted extract from 'The People's Almanac No. 2', edited by David Wallechinsky and Irving Wallace, published by Bantam Books, New York, 1978.

We often hear it said that a major problem today is that the people don't trust their leaders. But I believe that the opposite is true. The real hindrance to democracy is that the leaders don't trust the people. In the interest of purifying our democracy and restoring its egalitarian ideals, I propose a $25 billion tax rebate. And I further propose that this large sum be returned in the following manner:

(1) The entire nation shall be divided into districts of 1,000 people each, the divisions being made by an impartial computer.

'Each district of 1,000 people shall receive $100,000 to do with as it sees fit'

(2) Each district shall receive $100,000 to do with as it sees fit.

(3) A period of time shall be designated for free discussion of any and all proposals for using the money.

(4) On a specified date, an open meeting shall be held in each district to discuss and vote on what to do with the $100,000.

Here is a list of some of the possibilities:

(1) Fund a small business, employing local people and bringing continuing money into the community.

(2) Put the money in banks and use the interest to have an annual party.

(3) Join with other districts for larger projects.

(4) Buy a retreat in the country, community centre, park, orchard and garden, or library.

(5) Create scholarships to send local students to college.

I have spent many, many hours thinking about this proposal and would be glad to talk about it with anybody who is interested.

David Wallechinsky, 310-25th St, Santa Monica, California 90402, USA.

Unitax

Farel Bradbury

Farel Bradbury has been promoting Unitax for many years, and this version of an energy tax seems to have several advantages over other more recently proposed Green taxes and Carbon taxes.

'The Unitax alternative to VAT is absurdly simple: you just measure the net input of energy in units such as gigajoules into any geographical area and divide it into the public sector budget for that same area. This yields a Unitax of so many pounds sterling per gigajoule'

The Unitax alternative to VAT or other taxes, national or local, is absurdly simple: you just measure the net input of energy in units such as gigajoules (eg 15,000,000 GJ per year) into any geographical area and divide it into the public sector budget for that same area (eg £40m per year). This yields a Unitax of so many pounds sterling per gigajoule (eg £2-67 per GJ, that is about 39 pence on a gallon of petrol, for an average UK rating district; and all domestic and commercial rates are abolished). Unlike sales, income or local council taxes, the Unitax is administered at the very few initial energy-supply points (and at points of import or export). Energy is already measured at the points of import and export, so there is little new bureaucracy and we are dealing with a bulk commodity which it is difficult to hide – so evasion is difficult while economies are to be welcomed. The Unitax works its own way through the systems of distribution and consumption without further paperwork, yet the amount paid is inescapably linked with the standard of living. That is the gist of it.

Two further points arise. First, this is *not* just an 'energy policy'. It is true that we will 'save it', cut waste (and pollution), recycle, find alternatives, revolutionise transport, and the heat-pump will become economically viable. Because Unitax is raised at source – where the prime energy first has a price placed on it – it becomes a constituent of *all* other material resources: plastics, steel, fertilisers, paper, electric light – hence the term 'Resource Economics'. Nor is it a system of rationing for scarce commodities, although it may do that – I think it will moderate some of our more intensive and artificial uses of materials and the way we use capital intensive methods to oust labour. But energy *must* continue to flow where there is life; likewise we must raise taxes. Even if energy were abundant and free, therefore, Unitax provides an essential social valuation of resources linked at all times to the quality of life.

Secondly, this is *not* just a welfare policy. It is true that the proposal includes a provision of a non-selective Basic Income for all citizens – at least in the developed stages of Resource Economics. This is because a certain amount of energy consumption is required to support life. Consumption above this 'threshold' will then vary with the quality of life: the higher the lifestyle, the more Unitax that is paid in that consumption. This threshold is the point at which the 'regressive' nature of so-called energy taxes becomes 'progressive' and the Basic Income is calculated as its energy equivalent (about £55 per week for all adults if *all* other taxes – including the funding of the Basic Income itself – were today replaced by a Unitax of about £15 per GJ). The Basic Income does away with much painful bureaucracy: replacing pensions, the dole, child allowances, student grants, etc. Such a distributive mechanism also holds out the solution to many modern problems – not least 'unemployment' – gives 'wages to housewives', minimum income, and paves the way to 'no-fault' compensation for loss and, important in this technological age, a copyright income. The 'poverty trap' disappears because you keep all you earn without forfeit and, of course, there are neither 'Black Economy' nor Social Security fiddles. Readers may also see the solution to the EC CAP problem: a Basic Income to farmers would allow free-market food price and distribution without intervention.

'It is quite wrong that revenue is raised on price or earnings or wealth; it should be derived from consumption which is prolific, not from the enterprise of labour and investment which is limiting'

The Resource Economics Proposition has been designed as a comprehensive economics system. Indeed, it has yielded the proof of where classic economics have become screwed up and shows how national budgets may be balanced and world imbalances corrected. This age is characterised by 'consumerism' and needs this new set of rules. In context, it is quite wrong that revenue is raised on price or earnings or wealth; it should be derived from consumption which is prolific, not from the enterprise of labour and investment which is limiting. The one common constituent in all consumption is energy. It is not labour-added value that should be taxed (as by VAT), but energy-added value (by Unitax) if you want a happy economy.

Incidentally, some people think that if you live in a cold climate you would pay more Unitax. Not so. Because more energy is used (for heating), the tax is distributed more thinly. For example, if you double the consumption, the Unitax rate is halved yet yields the same revenue. So, broadly, everyone pays the same Unitax. Unitax is not like an old-fashioned energy tax and this dynamic mechanism also adjusts for changing efficiency of consumption as time goes on.

Farel Bradbury, Hydatum, PO Box 4, Ross-on-Wye, HR9 6EB (tel 0600 890599; fax 0600 4514).

Replacing VAT with Unitax

Adapted from a booklet entitled 'Unitax, a new environmentally sensitive concept in taxation' by Malcolm Slesser (published by Hydatum, address above, ISBN 0 905682 47 5).

Unitax could be phased in, leaving much of the tax structure intact for the moment. The obvious candidate for replacement is VAT. This is so for several reasons:

• Unitax operates like VAT in its effects – adding costs only as each processing step uses additional energy. The effect of VAT is to tax labour, whereas Unitax does not.

• Value-added taxes place an enormous administrative burden on the operation of industry and commerce. Unitax places no such burden.

• Unitax can be slowly increased as taxes on earnings are reduced.

• VAT is a mandatory tax in the EC. If Unitax is to be introduced it should be at the EC level, though there is a case for having a trial in one country first.

• Unitax gets round the internal European arguments as to what should and should not be value-added taxed (eg children's clothing, houses etc).

If Unitax were initially only required to replace VAT and similar taxes on expenditure (other than duty on wines, beers and spirits) then the amount to be raised by Unitax (again taking the UK as an example) would be some £50 billion per annum. To replace this, Unitax would have required to be £7.7 per Gigajoule. At this rate, petrol would be much the same price as now, though electricity could cost about 2.2 times as much with present methods of generation.

> ## 'Unitax would have required to be £7.7 per Gigajoule. At this rate, petrol would be much the same price as now, though electricity could cost about 2.2 times as much'

Unitax is an idea whose time may have come, but nonetheless getting it implemented will be a slow process. Because many people will lose their livelihood if Unitax comes in (accountants, taxmen and some civil servants) there is bound to be an opposition quite unrelated to the merits of the concept.

Professor Malcolm Slesser, Centre for Human Ecology, 15 Buccleuch Place, Edinburgh EH8 9LN (tel 031 650 3470; fax 031 650 6520).

Global strategy on resource taxes

Adapted from 'Caring for the Earth – A Strategy for Sustainable Living'.

Resource taxes are useful for limiting demand when it is not important to establish a maximum level of aggregate resource use. Such taxes could replace existing taxes; or the money they raise could be returned to the taxpayer for investment in better pollution control equipment and other subsidies.

Resource taxes should be introduced gradually to avoid economic disruption. A pre-announced schedule of increasing the taxes over a period of 10 or more years would give the private sector time to adapt. Matching declines in the rates of other taxes would make resource taxes more acceptable. It is more important that resource taxes are equitable, easy to modify and able to steer the economy in directions that are in society's interest, than that they are based on unattainably exact measures of social cost. The aim is to raise taxes on behaviour we want less of, such as depletion and pollution; and reduce them on what we want more of, such as employment of labour.

'Caring for the Earth' is published by World Wide Fund for Nature and others, and is available by post for £11-95 incl. p&p from Earthscan Publications, 3 Endsleigh Street, London WC1H 0DS (tel 071 388 9541).

Environmental taxes year 2010

Ernst von Weizsacker

From a paper 'Regulatory Reform and the Environment, the Cause for Environmental Taxes', published by the Institute for European Environmental Policy, 53 Endsleigh St, London WC1H 0DD (tel 071 388 2117; fax 071 388 2826).

The following criteria should be observed for all environment taxes:

(1) Taxes should be charged on factors for which there is a broad consensus that they are damaging the environment.

(2) Environmental taxes should be just in terms of distribution. In case of need, social policy compensation should be given.

(3) The administrative cost of collecting environmental taxes should be small.

(4) Environmental taxes should be introduced slowly and in steps to give the economy and technology time to adjust.

(5) Environmental taxes should be introduced throughout the EC, if possible.

Following these criteria, I could imagine the following European taxes within twenty or thirty years (1988 prices):

(1) *Energy:* ECU 7 per gigajoule of fossil and nuclear energy.

> ## 'A tax of ECU 100 per square metre of ground newly covered by buildings, concrete or macadam'

(2) *Ground coverage:* ECU 100 per square metre of ground newly covered by buildings, concrete or macadam; ECU 2 annually per square metre already covered – as a steady incentive to restore unused ground.

(3) *Water:* ECU 10 per cubic metre of polluted waste water

or ECU 3 per cubic metre of water used.

(4) *Waste:* ECU 50 per ton of unsorted solid waste, ECU 500 per ton of hazardous waste.

(5) *Air:* ECU 1,000 per ton of SO^2, NO^x, CO or hydrocarbons, ECU 100 per ton of methane, ECU 50 per ton of CO^2.

EC proposals for an energy tax

Adapted from articles by Tom Walker, Nicholas Schoon and David Usborne in the Times.

Although hotly opposed by industrial lobby groups, the scheme of Carlo Ripa di Meana, the European Community environment commissioner, to levy $10 on a barrel of oil by the year 2000 has been welcomed by environment ministers. The European Commission wants to put $3 on a barrel in 1993, and then add another dollar per year until 2000 – this would raise in the region of £38 billion. It has been calculated that if the full tax were introduced now, it would cost the average UK household about £130 a year.

The tax has credibility because Holland, Germany and Denmark, the more ecologically conscious Northern EC states, are all threatening to impose their own energy taxes. The UK government is cautiously supportive of the general idea, as long as there are to be balancing tax cuts elsewhere, with any revenue staying in national exchequers. However it is concerned about Europe going it alone, leaving American and Japanese industries with cheaper energy (and thus greater use of energy, with no overall global reduction).

Pollution charges

'Pricing for Pollution', by Wilfred Beckerman (second edition published as Hobart Paper 66, by the Institute of Economic Affairs, 2 Lord North Street, London SW1P 3LB, tel 071 799 3745; fax 071 799 2137, £4-95 plus 50p p&p).

Dr Wilfred Beckerman of Balliol College, Oxford, has argued in print since 1956 that pollution is better controlled by charging for it through pollution taxes or marketable 'rights to pollute' than by regulating it. He notes that the world's politicians are beginning to catch up with him, giving the example of Sweden, where the use of pollution charges is most advanced, and the States, where Bush introduced a programme of 'emission reduction credits', with a market in such rights, to combat air pollution.

'Pollution is better controlled by charging for it through pollution taxes or marketable "rights to pollute" than by regulating it'

To those who condemn pollution charges as a licence to pollute, Beckerman replies scornfully: 'As if regulations specifying maximum amounts of pollution that firms could carry out without paying a fine were not also a "licence to pollute" and free at that!' The desirable features of pollution charges include:

• They are less dirigiste and politically authoritarian than quantitative controls.

• They are less dependent on fashionable outcry than

regulations, as taxes tend to stay in place once the machinery has been established, and this would be so for pollution taxes, even if the number of votes to be won from being seen to be Green were to diminish for a few years.

• They ensure that pollution is reduced most in firms that can reduce it at least cost.

'They provide firms with a continuing incentive to reduce pollution'

• They provide firms with a continuing incentive to reduce pollution.

A key objection is that it is impossible to measure the pollution sufficiently for pollution to be charged for, but Beckerman responds that 'whatever can be controlled must be measurable; and if it is measurable it can be taxed or priced.' The analogous instance Beckerman gives is of a restaurant annoying neighbours by frying smelly onions. It may not be easy to measure the smell, but just as it would be theoretically possible to control the number of onions used per day, so it would be equally feasible to tax their use.

'Un-owned or communal environmental resources could be privatised. If someone has an interest in husbanding elephants, eagles, the sea and the atmosphere, then, like any other valuable commodity, they will ensure that it is optimally utilised and conserved'

Dr Cento Veljanovski goes further in his introduction, making the more radical suggestion that un-owned or communal environmental resources could be privatised, simply seeking 'to provide a legal framework and an initial assignment of property rights, leaving it to the market to decide how best the resources are used. If someone has an interest in husbanding elephants, eagles, the sea and the atmosphere, then, like any other valuable commodity, they will ensure that it is optimally utilised and conserved. Poaching, the dumping of waste – using scarce resources as if they had no value – would simply not occur. But defining and enforcing property rights in the environment is often impossible, either for technical reasons or because the costs are simply much too high. In such cases other devices (such as tradeable pollution permits) can be used.'

'The best way forward probably lies in a combination of methods: Unitax energy tax as the main background tool, with "pollution reduction incentives" where Unitax was proving ineffective, and with regulations as a last resort'

The best way forward probably lies in a combination of methods: perhaps Unitax energy tax as the main background tool to encourage energy conservation, with 'pollution reduction incentives' where Unitax was proving ineffective (and as a way of giving advantages to the developing world), and with regulations as a last resort where these methods of choice failed, or where an absolute ban was required. But all these techniques need to be placed in a wider framework – a philosophy that recognises that present trends of consumption cannot logically be other than unsustainable, and that consciousness-raising is required to usher in an age of 'living more simply so that others may simply live.'

Emission reduction credits in the States

Adapted extract from an article in the Times by Paul Griffin, a partner with the solicitors Denton, Hall, Burgin and Warrens.

In the States the creation and trading in emission reduction credits is regulated by the Environmental Protection Agency.

Originally, the creation of a 'bubble' under which credits could be offset against higher pollution levels elsewhere was limited to sites in common ownership.

If a company owned several sites emitting excess levels of waste, one site could be adapted to create a large enough reduction in emissions to offset against the others, saving the expenditure needed to reduce the levels of pollution from all sites.

The bubble principle has been extended so that it now applies to sites throughout the US, regardless of ownership, and a market for the trading of credits has developed.

Credits can be used, sold, stored or even banked depending on the owner's economic needs and future prospects. Market brokers match companies that have credits to sell with those that need to buy.

Despite being viewed as a way of achieving environmental controls more rapidly and cost-effectively than the traditional 'command and control' approach, this method of enforcement is, not surprisingly, controversial.

Although its advantages include lowering the cost of pollution controls, some environmentalists have attacked the scheme on the grounds that it condones continued pollution by permitting the purchase of the right to pollute.

> **'Some environmentalists have attacked the scheme on the grounds that it condones continued pollution by permitting the purchase of the right to pollute'**

Some environmentalists also argue that an ability to reduce pollution should not become the subject of speculation, but instead should always be utilised in the fight against the destruction of the environment.

Supporters, however, insist that the credit trading system benefits both industry and the environment. Although it seems most unlikely that a similar system will be adopted in Britain in the near future, the pace of environmental change indicates that the prospect may not be ruled out in the long run.

The UK's Environmental Protection Bill contemplates overall limits to emissions and reserves the government's right to make national quotas for total releases.

If pollution controls were created in Britain and a US-style market developed, it is possible that the scheme for regulation of emissions would require a regulatory scheme if these 'rights to pollute' were regarded as investments under the Financial Services Act.

A tax on transport pollution

Adapted extract from an article in the Times by Ross Tieman.

Sir Alastair Morton, the Eurotunnel chief executive, has proposed a tax on transport based on its environmental impact. Emissions, noise, casualties and land-take would be the key components of an index system which would favour modes of transport that caused least harm to non-users. This pollution levy, partly in place of existing taxes, on all forms of transport, would raise £25 billion within five years. This money would go into a transport investment fund, making 50 year loans with low initial interest rates and the fund taking a share of profits.

> **'Emissions, noise, casualties and land-take would be the key components of a tax index system'**

Tax perks for the company minibus

Margaret Buckley

Taxation should discriminate in favour of the company minibus (up to 25 seats) rather than the company car. Employees agreeing to take part should be given some financial inducement. Computerised routes and pick-up points would be linked in some cases to 'Park and Ride' schemes.

> **'Taxation should discriminate in favour of the company minibus (up to 25 seats) rather than the company car'**

Members of all grades and departments would mingle, and the working ride might partly replace the working lunch.

Employees might get a taste for being relieved of the driving in and out, to and from work, and discover that they had more energy for their tasks.

Margaret Buckley, Old School House, Vicarage Road, Meole Brace, Shrewsbury SY3 9EZ (tel 0743 352076).

A voluntary Green Tax

An item monitored for the Institute by Gregory Wright.

The Green Tax is a completely voluntary donation that you collect from your customers to help offset the environmental costs of doing business. Simply collect the voluntary tax (a suggested 9% of sale) and, twice a year, give one half to local environmental restoration projects (tree planting, gardens, parks, river clean-ups, etc) and one half to environmental activist projects (opposing clear cutting, discouraging pollution, changing production processes, supporting alternative energy use, etc). One mail-order book business (Books to Build a New Society) have collected and distributed over $5,000 from their customers in this way.

• *The Green Tax, Fingerlakes Green Fund, PO Box 6578, Ithaca, NY 14851, USA.*

• *Books to Build a New Society, New Society Publishers, 4527 Springfield Avenue, Philadelphia, PA 19143, USA (tel 215 382 6543).*

Transitional Basic Income scheme with an optional 'workfare' element

David Chapman

The idea of the government using taxation to provide everyone with a Basic Income (BI) is usually thought of as a very radical measure, a drastic, and very expensive, change from the present system, which therefore is unlikely to be adopted for many years yet. But I make here a new proposal for a less radical BI, not all that different from the present system, but in fact a great improvement on it, which could be put into operation in a year once there is support for it. Once adopted, it could, if people demanded this, be improved by stages into a conventional BI. This new transitional BI scheme is as follows:

> 'A less radical Basic Income scheme, not all that different from the present system, but in fact a great improvement on it, could be put into operation in a year'

For the sake of brevity, let us use the term 'maximum benefit' to refer to the total of whatever benefits a household would receive under the present system, if they had nil income and nil savings. Each household is paid BI greater (but in most cases only slightly greater) than its maximum benefit. In the case of a couple, any BI in respect of children is given to the caring partner, and the rest of the household's BI is equally divided between the two of them. A person's BI is paid as a cashable welfare cheque, or directly into the person's bank account.

To pay for this, three tax increases are made. Firstly, National Insurance (ie social security tax) of 9 per cent is extended to income above £350 per week. Secondly, National Insurance is in effect extended to investment income, by charging on it an extra 19 per cent tax, but only on income above the average income. Thirdly, a 'special tax' of an extra 7 per cent is levied on all income, ie the tax gives no allowances.

A household is then taxed according to one of the two following schedules, the 'primary' or the 'secondary', whichever one results in the lower amount of tax.

Primary tax: 75 per cent of income (ie earnings plus investment income, both before tax). Or *Secondary tax:* consisting of income tax as at present (plus any increase re investment), plus NI (extended to higher incomes), plus a special tax of 7 per cent of all income (ie no allowances), minus a 'special credit' (= about £9 per week at present), or two credits in the case of a couple, plus a lump sum equal to the total BI received by the household.

(The special credit is equal to 7 per cent of average income – the same percentage as the special tax. Average income is defined as the national total of personal incomes, divided by the number of adults, including in this number the non-taxpayers.)

Clearly, the result of this will be that low-income households will pay primary tax. Their disposable income (ie income plus BI minus tax) will be their BI (equal to at least their 'maximum benefit'), plus 25 per cent of their pre-tax income.

Higher incomes than this will pay secondary tax. The disposable income which any household will get will thus be:

Either its present disposable income plus £9 (or £18 in the case of a couple), minus 7 per cent of its pre-tax income.

Or (if it would be more) its BI (equal to at least its 'maximum benefit'), plus 25 per cent of its pre-tax income.

Thus any household with below-average income (or below twice average income in the case of a couple) will be better off under this scheme than they are now. There might also be some above-average-income households which will be better off, ie those for which their BI plus 25 per cent of their pre-tax income would be more than their present disposable income.

Would Basic Income destroy the incentive to work?

An objection often put against Basic Income schemes in general is that many people would just live off their BI and do no paid work, so that the tax base from which the BI is paid would be seriously reduced. I see no way of predicting for certain whether or not this would happen. But if we introduced the above scheme and found out that this did in fact happen, it would be possible to correct the situation, and bring more people into work, by modifying the scheme as follows.

Any person of working age who was not sick, handicapped, a carer with some minimum of responsibilities, or a full-time student would be paid part of his/her BI (let us say £25 per week) not in cash but in the form of a reduction in the tax he/she had to pay. The rest of his/her BI would be paid as before.

If a person could not find paid work of the ordinary kind, the state would offer to pay for sufficient hours of low-paid work to earn at least £25 per week plus a sum enough to pay the expenses of working (travel to work etc). The work would usually be done for organisations at present using voluntary labour, such as Oxfam, Age Concern, pressure groups, political parties, etc. The state would reimburse the organisations for paying the wages of these workers.

> 'The state would offer to pay for sufficient hours of low-paid work to earn at least £25 per week'

Note that anyone who earned more than £33-33 per week – the amount which, under the first scheme, would have been paid, at 75 per cent, £25 of tax – would be exactly as well off under this BI scheme as under the first one. But someone who earned nothing would be £25 worse off.

Conclusions

• This BI scheme would redistribute income from (most of) those above average income, to those below the average income.

• A large majority of persons (70 per cent or more) have income below the average, so even this preliminary and transitional BI scheme might expect to get majority political support.

'This preliminary and transitional Basic Income scheme might expect to get majority political support'

• It will reduce or remove the unemployment and poverty traps (especially if a lower primary tax rate than 75 per cent proves to be affordable with the yield from the above tax increases).

• This BI could easily be put into operation. All it needs is (a) an extension of the present arrangements for paying old age pensions to the rest of the population, and (b) a simple change in the formula for calculating income tax. (No new assessment is required, additional to the determination of a person's income which is already being done.)

Dr David Chapman, Democracy Design Forum, Coles Centre, Buxhall, Stowmarket, Suffolk, IP14 3EB (tel 0449 736 223).

A labour tax

Fred Allen

A labour tax that you could either fulfil or pay someone else to do is a good idea. It solves the problem of getting nothing from the unemployed. The form that labour should take must be left to the taxpayer.

Fred Allen, 13 Shelly Row, Cambridge, CB3 OBP.

Response from Nicholas Albery

I ran a pilot project along these lines several years ago for the hundred residents of a housing co-op in Shepherds Bush. Residents could either pay a £2 'tax' each week or sign up on the circulated worksheet for an average of 20 minutes work on a community project (although unpopular jobs such as fixing the sewers were worth a quicker rate, such as 10 minutes – so residents could work off weeks of tax with one job – with the job coordinator accepting the least 'expensive' bid; conversely, popular jobs such as watering the flowers might be worth a much slower rate – a full 30 minutes might be required to pay off the week's requirement. Residents could also propose jobs needing doing for adding to the worksheet).

'Residents could either pay a £2 "tax" each week or sign up on the circulated worksheet'

The scheme worked well for a time, but needed an element of compulsion (such as eventual loss of one's place on the co-op rehousing list) to prevent residents gradually dropping out as the initial spirit faded.

Obviously such a scheme could be expanded to cover a whole neighbourhood, with the 'labour tax' being a small allocated part of your tax payment to the council, which you could recoup through labour. It would be a way for unemployed people to top up their dole money, whilst at the same time improving the local environment. It would need to be supervised by a neighbourhood committee, working through a jobs coordinator. But the formation of such neighbourhood committees, with a real task to get their teeth into, would be a major positive step forward anyway.

Nicholas Albery, 20 Heber Road, London NW2 6AA (tel 081 208 2853; fax 081 452 6434).

Comment by Vivienne Marks

'Knitting together the community'

I salute the idea of allowing volunteers to 'work off' a proportion of the local tax due from them. Active citizenship means more than an economic contribution to the community. The above proposal applied to local council taxation would lead to: a lowering of local government expenditure; a large number of volunteers; an increasing awareness amongst those volunteers of the satisfaction to be gained from a worthwhile, caring activity, and a consequent knitting together of the community; a decrease in the crime rate; an improvement in the health and well-being of the very old, the very young and many other vulnerable people; an increase in the amount of goods and materials repaired or recycled; and a cleaner, tidier environment.

Vivienne Marks, Little Grove Cottage, Waldron, Heathfield, East Sussex TN21 ORE (tel 043 53 2840).

£50 less tax per new worker

Dr David Chapman

Adapted from a detailed paper.

It is proposed that the present taxes on income – income tax, and other employees' and employers' national insurance contributions – should be abolished, and be replaced by a payroll tax paid by the employers, at a rate which would yield the same revenue as before. The employer would receive, for each worker, a tax-free allowance on the first £50 of wages per week.

The employer would therefore have a strong incentive to spread the available work among more workers, which would save him or her tax by bringing in more allowances.

Employers would have an incentive to provide more jobs for the unemployed. Instead of giving overtime to existing workers, they would seek to take on new workers, if possible part-timers. They would first engage any unemployed workers who already had the appropriate skills, and later perhaps take on new workers to train. If workers left or retired, or if production could be expanded, part-timers would be appointed to fill the vacancies. For if the same amount of work could be spread between more workers, every extra worker who could be engaged would reduce the employer's taxes. Likewise, when pay rises were being negotiated, employers would seek to include a reduction in the hours of the working week as part of the bargain, so as to be able to take on more workers, even if there were no opportunities to increase the total number of hours worked.

Dr David Chapman, Democracy Design Forum, Coles Centre, Buxhall, Stowmarket, Suffolk IP14 3EB (tel 0449 736 223).

How best to redistribute wealth between regions

Frances Kendall

Adapted extract from 'The Heart of the Nation – Regional and Community Government in the New South Africa', by Frances Kendall (published by Amagi Books, PO Box 92385, Norwood 2117, South Africa, tel 011 442 8898; fax 011 442 7247).

Problems with redistribution

The more governments rely on their own sources of revenue, the greater incentive they have to make sensible fiscal decisions, balance budgets and strive for efficiency. When they have access to grants, their incentives change to maximising the amount of their subsidies, rather than seeking ways to improve local economies. For example, if the subsidies are based on local government costs, as they often are, the incentive is to maximise costs. And if grants are based on poverty, the interest of the authorities is served by maximising local poverty.

> 'If the subsidies are based on local government costs, the interest of the authorities is served by maximising local costs'

Another problem caused by subsidies is that recipients tend to develop a dependent mentality instead of striving for self-sufficiency. This problem is compounded if subsidies are conditional on meeting certain criteria. Furthermore, when local governments are told how their money should be used, they cannot remain accountable to their constituents.

Intergovernmental grants that aim to remove all inequality between communities protect bad governments from the consequences of their actions, and interfere with the useful demonstration of the relative strengths and weaknesses of policies and programmes which result from local control.

How to minimise the problems of redistribution

Intergovernmental grants are sometimes linked to particular programmes. Alternatively, they may be unconditional and distributed by formula.

The second alternative is far preferable to the first. Studies in the USA show that when poor areas receive transfers over which they have control, they make better spending decisions than when a big jurisdiction dictates the use of subsidies to them. The fact that they are unable to raise sufficient revenues locally should not be used as an excuse to deprive poorer areas of the political right to determine their own needs. They should receive grants according to a formula, with no provisos, so that they can spend the money according to local priorities.

Some governments may wish to introduce a tax credit system whereby any citizen who contributes to a neighbourhood non-profit development trust or corporation receives a credit against national, regional or local taxes of, for example, between 10% for high-income earners and 80% for low-income earners. This would mean that development programmes compete for citizen support rather than government support.

The Canadian system

The Canadians have developed a way of calculating intergovernmental transfers that minimises the ill-effects of redistribution. This system has been in effect since 1957.

The federal government works out a Representative Tax System (RTS) based on a weighted average of provincial taxes including 39 separate types of taxes, rents and user fees. This is arrived at by dividing the total revenues from each tax by the total tax base. For example, the total property tax receipts divided by the total property tax base of the country comes to 1.65%. To determine the RTS the same calculation (revenues divided by tax base) is applied to every tax on an annual basis.

The RTS is a fictional system and none of the provinces use it, but if it were applied to the tax bases of all ten provinces it would yield the same total as that which they collect from their own diverse systems.

The government's accountants average out the amount the five middle provinces would raise per capita if they charged taxes at RTS rates. They then apply the RTS to each province's taxable resources and make up the difference between the potential RTS revenues of an average province and the potential RTS revenues of any province that falls short of the average, with a single, no-strings-attached, annual grant.

Federal equalisation grants are not related to the way in which the provinces raise their own taxes, and those that receive grants are not told how to spend them. But the system does ensure that each province could, if it wanted, raise sufficient resources to meet public needs at a level which is average for the entire country by applying the RTS and adding on the grant. Even though four of the ten provinces (Ontario, Alberta, Saskatchewan and British Columbia) do not receive any RTS payments, the system is well accepted in Canada.

This kind of system can be applied between first- and second-tier, and between second- and third-tier, levels of government. In other words, national governments can provide equalisation grants to poorer regions based on RTS assessments, whilst regions use a similar system for redistribution among local communities. At the regional level, equalisation grants should be paid annually, but within regions, subsidies might be paid bi-annually or quarterly.

If such a system were introduced in South Africa, the Central Witwatersrand metropolitan region and the Western Cape would probably receive nothing, whereas Zululand and the Eastern Cape would be in line for equalisation grants. Within the Central Witwatersrand metropolitan region, Johannesburg's Northern suburbs and CBD would not be entitled to subsidies from the metropolitan government, whereas community governments in Soweto and Alexandria would.

> 'In South Africa it would help meet the oft-repeated demands for government to close the gap between the rich and poor'

A system of this nature does not avoid all the negative consequences of wealth redistribution, but it escapes the worst of them, and in South Africa it would go a long way towards meeting the oft-repeated demands for government to close the gap between the rich and poor.

Frances Kendall, 57 Glenrose Road, Melrose 2196, Johannesburg, South Africa (tel 27 11 442 8898; fax 27 11 442 7247).

Chapter seven

UNEMPLOYMENT

Workstart Overseas

Cairns Campbell

The basic concept

Train a group of young people (18-25 year olds) in useful skills which they could use overseas in a Third World country. When they have completed their training, send them overseas along with their instructors to help local people with a worthwhile, pre-identified project. This would be done in conjunction with an agency already working in this field, such as VSO, Oxfam, etc.

> 'Many training and employment projects lack the stimulus of a clearly identifiable aim or product which the trainees can accept and adopt. As a result the work is often classified as "funny work", with the resultant lack of trainee motivation'

Many training and employment projects lack the stimulus of a clearly identifiable aim or product which the trainees can accept and adopt. As a result the work is often classified as 'funny work', with the resultant lack of trainee motivation. 'Workstart Overseas' overcomes this problem and could prove a powerful vehicle for the training and development of young people.

The advantages

(1) It widens the horizons of a group of young people who otherwise would not aspire to such a character-broadening experience.

(2) It provides real meaning to the work and training undertaken.

(3) It develops teamwork and self-reliance among the trainees.

(4) Young people, with the practical skills, and with the confidence and experience gained from working overseas, would have a greater ability to find employment after the assignment.

(5) In addition to supplying skills, whole turnkey packages could be developed using redundant equipment, renovated by the trainees and re-assembled overseas. This is important, as semi-skilled trainees would not necessarily be welcome without the hardware.

(6) The whole process could help develop an outward-looking attitude among young people and the community they come from.

(7) It provides worthwhile work with no danger of 'competing' with local industry.

(8) It is an excellent opportunity to introduce other training: team building, the history and geography of the country to be visited, self-sufficiency catering and project management.

(9) It is an easily repeatable project with almost no limit to the useful work needing doing. A number of projects could be initiated one after the other at three-month intervals and the experience gained on the first few would help to develop the others.

An example based in Dundee

The need is established through a voluntary organisation for good quality but basic mechanical engineering workshops to be attached to schools in certain areas of Africa. Workstart, an organisation in Dundee that trains the unemployed, obtains donations of appropriate equipment from businesses etc in the Dundee area. Under instruction the equipment is renovated, catalogued and brought up to satisfactory condition by the trainees who also learn how to use it. The equipment, along with all ancillary equipment, is packed for shipment. The trainees along with their instructors spend three months in Africa helping the local school assemble the equipment, including basic building alterations. They would also help with skills transfer.

Cairns Campbell, Rowen Consultancy, 12 Stonefield Crescent, Thornly Park, Paisley PA2 7RU (tel 041 884 5901). Further details about Workstart from Stuart Lindsay on 0382 450345. This scheme won a Social Inventions Award and was successfully tried out in Dundee for the duration of its funding. A 16 page brochure about it is available from the Institute for Social Inventions for £1, postage and packing paid.

Housing for the unwaged

Determined groups of unemployed people could set up their own educational and other networks, buying themselves places to live in the process, as a Birmingham group of three men and women, ex-students in their early twenties, have demonstrated. They established the 'New University' based in a house in Hockley (although they have since changed the name from 'New University' to 'Radical Routes' as part of a network of nine housing co-ops). This house they bought for £35,000, by forming a 'New Education Housing Co-operative Ltd' and by obtaining a mortgage, with loans from supporters for the deposit. The 25 year mortgage is being paid off through charging themselves rent of £25 a week each, which housing benefit covers.

> **'The 25 year mortgage is being paid off through charging themselves rent of £25 a week each, which housing benefit covers'**

They decorated the house and began to host events, such as a weekend on 'Radical Education' and a 'Skills and Knowledge Sharing Festival'. Roger Hallam, one of the six, who dropped out from his course at LSE to help launch the New University, from the outset hoped to bring together a number of similar houses to form a network. The idea was to sell loan stock to well-wishers (who can state what interest rate they require) and to put this money down as deposit for mortgages on further houses. As Hallam says, 'with a lot of radical projects, the biggest problem is usually lack of finance. Here we have the beginnings of a financial alternative for the homeless and the unwaged, particularly for those in areas outside London where house prices are not too high and the registered rents not too low.'

Their Radical Routes network now includes Giroscope, a workers' co-operative in Hull, which has renovated fourteen houses for local homeless young people. Giroscope has set up a creche, and are helping to get a printing co-op going.

The newsletter 'Radical Routes' is available for £6 subs (£3 unwaged) from the 'Radical Routes' (the name for cheques), 24 South Road, Hockley, Birmingham B18 (tel 021 551 1679). They have produced a booklet (price £1 incl. p&p) on how to set up a project such as theirs. There are also Radical Routes co-ops in Northampton, two rural ones, and one for lesbians and gays in Nottingham. The scheme won a Social Inventions Award.

A bell rung for job-winners

Ronnie Seagren

The performance statistics place Training Inc among the best employment-training programmes in the USA. Its Indianapolis site was the first job training programme to rely on performance-based funding. Of candidates who start in the Boston programme, for example, 90% complete the demanding 14 week schedule and 85% of those get jobs soon after graduation. A year later, 80% are still on the job and almost all have won a rase or promotion.

The key factor is having the trainees act the part. Their activities mirror the real world six hours a day, five days a week. They are expected to dress for work, to arrive on time and to interact professionally with the staff and fellow trainees. The office has departments, not classrooms. Every day one of the trainees rotates into the role of receptionist for the entire office. Simulated work projects provide the feel of the professional world. In a typical site, 36 people work on typing, word processing, data entry, filing or book-keeping in learning groups of 12 or 13, using materials that simulate business content.

Rather than training people in a union hall, church or community centre in the trainees' neighbourhoods, the programme purposely highlights the potential work environment. The professional office with beautiful rooms for the various departments tells the trainees clearly from the start that they are worth the investment.

On a field visit, they may go to an insurance company to tour the departments, to meet with personnel, see the flow of work, hear about the experience of a Training Inc graduate, and eat lunch in the corporate dining room.

> **'All kinds of mock interviews: by pairs, before a panel of peers, on videotape, with outside interviewers, with professional human resource people, at a job fair, and in other offices'**

The preparation for job search involves individual work through a manual and seminars on wardrobe and first impressions, followed by all kinds of mock interviews: by pairs, before a panel of peers, on videotape, with outside interviewers, with professional human resource people, at a job fair, and in other offices.

> **'Whenever someone gets a job, their placement is added to the "job board", a bell is rung, and work stops so that everyone can hear about what happened'**

When it comes actually to looking for a job, however, the trainees do it on their own. A job developer may help with leads, but the trainees set their own appointments, and get the job (or not) themselves. They debrief after every interview, with a staff person and sometimes with a team of other trainees. Whenever someone gets a job, their placement is added to the 'job board', a bell is rung, and work stops so that everyone can hear about what happened.

Early in the cycle, trainees organise an Open House at which they host usually over a hundred family and friends. This has helped build family respect and support for the training effort, often easing personal pressure on the trainees.

Training Inc has a strong follow-up component. Graduates feel free to come back, rejoice over their victories, discuss their failures, and seek advice for further career steps. The initiators of Training Inc are the Institute of Cultural Affairs who have added a peer mentor programme in Indianapolis. Graduates who have been employed at least a year volunteer their time to work with current trainees during the programme and during their first three months on the job. A Life Methods Training Programme is also available for graduates who have worked for one to six years. The programme focuses on developing life management skills for upward mobility – economic planning, supervisory skills, meeting facilitation, public speaking, presentation skills, parenting and family conflict management.

This is a brief extract from 'Imaginal Education' by Ronnie Seagren (of ICA Canada, 577 Kingston Road, Suite 1, Toronto, ONM4E 1R3, Canada, tel 416 691 2316); which appeared in a special 'Transforming Education' issue of 'In Context' journal, available for $25 per year (from PO Box 11470, Bainbridge Island, WA 98110, USA, tel 206 842 0216; fax 206 842 5208). Training Inc won a Social Inventions Award. Their address is: Sheila Maguire and Carol Walters, Training Inc, 730 Broad Street, Newark, New Jersey 07102, USA (tel 201 642 2622).

'Create', encouraging enterprise through community projects

Linda Brookes

'Create' is a non-profit-making organisation which believes that people are the most important resource of Cleveland. Through its staff it helps individuals and organisations to foster an enterprising environment which encourages new ideas and creative responses to change.

> 'Create provides a consultant facilitator and working capital to self-managed groups working on projects of community benefit'

Create provides a consultant facilitator and working capital to self-managed groups working on projects of community benefit. But Create works across and with all sectors: with unwaged and community groups; in government training schemes both with trainees and supervisors and managers; in education with governors, teachers and pupils; and in the public, private, commercial, statutory and voluntary sectors. Create is setting up a training course to accredit other facilitators in the Create model of enterprise facilitation and it offers training courses to industry and others. It also organises conferences about training. Create has a staff of 15, including seven facilitators and consultants.

It receives a cocktail of funding from the Training Agency (for whom it runs a national pilot), local industry and the county council.

Its underlying principles can be encapsulated as follows:

• Everyone can be enterprising given proper encouragement and the right environment.

• Through its work, Create inspires others to meet change in positive, proactive and powerful ways.

• Create has a responsibility to be a pioneer in its field on behalf of the community.

• Work with Create should be fun for staff and participants, and should have positive outcomes for participants, leading to positive outcomes for the community.

• All the people Create works with deserve respect and our best professional standards. Create strives to be honest in its work and to create a bond of mutual trust between itself and the individuals and organisations with whom it comes into contact.

Create Development Trust Ltd (enterprise skills development through community benefit projects), 7/9 Eastbourne Road, Linthorpe, Middlesbrough, Cleveland (tel 0642 850229).

The Apprentice Alliance

An Apprentice Alliance is needed in the UK. In San Francisco, the Apprentice Alliance is a non-profit organisation, which publishes 5,000 copies of its directory annually, matching would-be apprentices with over 200 'masters', people who have 'achieved excellence in their chosen fields' – craftsmen, cooks, gardeners, photographers, computer programmers, book designers, guitar makers, etc.

Masters are evaluated by the Apprentice Alliance for the quality of their work, their willingness to share their skills and for the conditions of their work place. The directory gives a biographical sketch of the master, a description of their work, and the master's conditions for apprentices – length of service, minimum and maximum hours per week and special aptitudes required.

> 'Matching would-be apprentices with over 200 "masters", people who have "achieved excellence in their chosen fields" – craftsmen, cooks, gardeners, photographers, computer programmers'

Normally no payments or only small payments are made to the apprentices – labour is exchanged for education. Apprentices pay a total of $125 and masters pay $150 to the Alliance once satisfactorily matched, and the placement is monitored by Lu Phillips, the one Alliance staff member, who operates from a small office at the back of an artist's studio. She reports that 'when you match up someone who really wants to teach with someone who really wants to know, it is one of the finest one-to-one relationships.'

Apprentice Alliance, 151 Potrero Avenue, San Francisco, California 94103, USA (tel 415 863 8661). This scheme was highly commended by the judges in the Social Inventions competition.

Job Telegrams
Nicholas Saunders

In San Francisco, I examined noticeboards in a cafe and bookshop. Some people looking for jobs make a 'telegram' listing all of their skills, from plumbing to listening to problems.

Nicholas Saunders, top floor, 14 Neal's Yard, London WC2 (tel 071 836 9404; fax 071 379 0135).

Green employment agency

The Institute for Social Inventions believes that there is a need for an environmental organisation to set up a Green Employment Bureau, for those seeking work, whether paid or unpaid, in ecologically-minded organisations and businesses.

Business students to help unemployed

Alec Dickson

Scores of courses in Business and Management Studies are organised in institutions of higher education around the country, generally on the 'sandwich' model, i.e. with a period where the students are attached to a company or firm. However, it is becoming increasingly difficult to find companies and firms ready to accept them. Since the ability to identify unmet needs, inadequate facilities or goods or services beyond the public's resources – and to organise an appropriate response – is surely the essence of success in commerce, business and management, why not attach these students of Business and Management Studies instead to groups of the young unemployed (or not-so-young jobless) to seek out or devise opportunities? To the best of my knowledge this has not yet been fully explored either by the MSC or schools of business studies.

> 'Why not attach these students of Business and Management Studies to groups of the young unemployed (or not-so-young jobless) to seek out or devise opportunities?'

Alec Dickson, 19 Blenheim Road, London W4 1VB (tel 081 944 7437).

The unemployed as language ambassadors

Eustace Wait proposed that selected unemployed youth could be sent overseas to give practice in speaking English to foreign nationals:

> 'Selected unemployed youth could be sent overseas to give practice in speaking English to foreign nationals'

'I have travelled extensively as an English teacher in the Middle and Far East and I am convinced that such "language ambassadors" would be greatly appreciated. They do not need much training, since their ability to speak their mother tongue is all they need. They would be welcomed by university students and young business people, who constitute the great majority of English-learners in Asia.

'Possible solutions to the problems of work permits, travel costs and accommodation have been worked out but other finance would also be required. Perhaps the Manpower Services Commission would be open to the argument that this scheme is helpful to the community.'

Eustace Wait, c/o 10 Wootton Gardens, Bournemouth, Dorset, BH1 1PW.

Allotments for the unemployed

Deda Francis

In the good old days, citizens had to go on a waiting list to get an allotment. Not any more. Now that so many women are going out to work, frozen vegetables have come into their own, with the result that there are many vacant allotments. Some of these are threatened with development. These green oases are lungs in our cities and we must keep them.

> 'Frozen vegetables have come into their own, with the result that there are many vacant allotments'

With the help of a friend who is my sleeping partner (we each put in £50 at the outset), I have started 'Allotments for the Unemployed'. We help with rents, tools and seeds. The latter I buy at a discount from a friendly garden centre. Tools come from army surplus, sales and friends. All the project needs is a little spare cash and a contact with the unemployed. The local press and Friends of the Earth have helped with publicity.

> 'I have started "Allotments for the Unemployed". We help with rents, tools and seeds'

How it works: an unemployed person calls at the Norwich Claimants Union, for instance, to have his DHSS problems sorted out, and sees our poster. I send him to the appropriate City Hall Dept to get an allotment near his home. Then he sends me the bill, which I pay to City Hall. In the first season two allotments were rented, and in the second season four allotments.

A productive allotment can greatly reduce a family's food bill and provides fresh organically grown vegetables. It can also be the source of much pleasure and social life (allotments are friendly places). In addition to all that allotments make excellent picnic sites. In fact every urban family needs one!

So let's save our allotments and at the same time help the unemployed.

Deda Francis, 11 Mill Road, Reedham, Norwich NR13 3TL (tel 0493 700 408).

Compulsory sabbaticals

Margot Kogut

If, say, there is a 10% level of unemployment, this can be absorbed, in theory at least, by a 1-in-10-years compulsory 'sabbatical' leave.

Such a sabbatical is relatively easily envisaged for professions such as teachers, civil servants and even office workers, as well as manual workers, especially on automated production lines – any situation where work is not too specialised, and where different individuals can stand in for each other.

> **'A 10% level of unemployment can be absorbed, in theory at least, by a 1-in-10-years compulsory "sabbatical" leave'**

The financial aspect would have to include receipt of the dole – which would not involve increased expenditure on the social services account – but also provision for additional income from a savings scheme contributed to by employer and employee as part of their normal working conditions; enough to allow them on sabbatical about half their salary, and no restrictions on earnings outside their usual employment (such as private coaching for teachers).

The idea is based on the observation that to be free of the usual routine for a period of months, or even a year, is quite a blessing if financially it is not catastrophic and can be foreseen and prepared for.

> **'To be free of the usual routine for a period of months, or even a year, is quite a blessing if financially it is not catastrophic and can be foreseen and prepared for'**

In so far as the unemployment of recent years is due to technological advances and to 'automation' in all its guises, the problem is to avoid creating 'two nations' – a well-off population in work, and an impoverished section of the long-term unemployed. At least in some trades and professions, the available work must be shared.

Dr Margot Kogut, 19b Fitzjohn's Avenue, London NW3 5JY (tel 071 794 6278).

Thirteen weeks extra paid holiday a year

Cairns Campbell

The idea is that four people should share the work at present done by three. Each person would thus work for three weeks, followed by one week's leisure. This would enormously increase employment: but it would require wages, if left unsubsidised, to be reduced by 25%. However, each unemployed person costs the government at least £8,000 a year, therefore the government would tend to save enough to make up the wages of four people by 25%. Schemes for all lower paid

workers, who make up the bulk of the unemployed, could thus be financed at no cost to the government.

The increase in paid holidays would provide the strongest incentive for employees to initiate action. Employers too would have little to lose and might benefit from fresher labour.

> **'The idea is that four people should share the work at present done by three. Each person would thus work for three weeks, followed by one week's leisure'**

Other advantages include: there would be scope for higher paid workers to take a little less money (95% of their previous salary) for a lot more leisure; there would be a more equal society, for leisure is only of value when combined with work; leisure activities would evolve; there would be opportunities for voluntary service; and young people would benefit.

A pilot scheme in one area such as nursing (with its shift patterns and heavy work loads) might be a good way to begin.

Cairns Campbell, the Rowen Consultancy, 12 Stonefield Crescent, Thornly Park, Paisley, PA2 7RU (tel 041 884 5901).

Compound National Insurance on overtime

Mark Goyder

A very simple innovation would be for the Chancellor to introduce compound national insurance on all overtime hours worked. No employer would be forced to stop using overtime, but all employers would be forced to think hard about it, and I am sure as a result that we would see a reduction in overtime working. Alongside this, steps need to be taken to open up and make easier the possibilities of part-time work to replace overtime.

> **'A very simple innovation would be for the Chancellor to introduce compound national insurance on all overtime hours worked. No employer would be forced to stop using overtime, but all employers would be forced to think hard about it'**

I am horrified at the extent to which we are two nations when it comes to paid work. Some of us have too much of it, and some of us have none at all. Mechanisms can and must be found to make it possible for paid work to be better shared.

Mark Goyder, The Clearing, High Street, Hawkhurst, Kent TN18 4AQ (tel 0580 753485).

Chapter eight

ECONOMICS AND BUSINESS

How to tame the stock market

Professor Leopold Kohr

Professor Kohr, economist and winner of the Right Livelihood Award, also known as 'the Alternative Nobel Prize', is the author of several classics. The best known is his witty, elegant and prophetic 'The Breakdown of Nations' – written in 1951 (and published by Routledge and Kegan Paul in 1957, and in paperback in 1986; also published by Dutton Paperbacks, New York, 1978, and Methuen, New York, 1988, $4.95). His most recent book is 'The Inner City' (published by Y Lolfa, Wales, 1989), which was highly commended by the judges in the Social Inventions Awards.

Knowing something of economics is, as Professor John Kenneth Galbraith once said, not always a good thing. Often it is no more than echoing 'the word of the year,' as Stephen Potter would put it, without anyone knowing the sound of which he or she is the echo. Or as my old friend Professor Anatol Murad once told me when returning from a colloquium sponsored by the Board managing the US Federal Reserve System: 'Their strength is the unanimity of their error.' They are right as the African rainmakers are right who conjure rain so long that in the end it is bound to come, not because of their command over the elements but because of statistical law – the only law that, according to the Nobel prize-winning physicist Erwin Shrödinger, exists in the universe. It governs the earthquakes of California, the occurrence of wars, of traffic accidents, of child abuse, of the seven to twelve year periodicity of business cycles as well as of the sunspot activities with which they were linked by such observant visionaries as Joseph of Egypt and Jevons (1835-1882) of Manchester. And it governs the frequency of stockmarket crashes.

What can be done?

Only four things can be done about such crashes if one wants to avoid their consequences. The first is: to do what Anatol Murad (whom I quote as often as Boswell quotes Samuel Johnson) does with lottery tickets: at the cost of $1.00 per week, his winnings amount to an assured $52.00 per year – by not playing. Similarly, if you want to play safe on the stockmarket, don't buy any shares. That does not mean you cannot lose your money – but you cannot on the stockmarket.

The second is: to do with a stockmarket crash the same thing that Hitler – who, as Galbraith pointed out, fortunately understood nothing of economics – did with inflation: forbid it. This can be achieved by abolishing the free enterprise system in favour of a socialist security system as in the Soviet Union, where stockmarkets do not crash because they do not exist and hence offer no room for the appropriate statistical law to enact itself. Nor, however, does it offer room for the tremendous profit-stimulated productivity during the inter-crash period which leaves infinitely more behind in material assets than any crash can ever destroy. Nor, on the other hand, does it prevent the cyclical destruction in non-economic areas, which offer no obstacle to the relentless operation of statistical laws in cases such as drought and sunspot-conditioned famine, passion-induced AIDS, technology-caused pollution, or jealousy-stimulated warfare – all of which, unlike stockmarket crashes, destroy assets for good.

The third possibility lies not in the abolition of the free enterprise system, but in its limitation through Keynsian government controls and an enlargement of the public sector of the economy in the area of public utilities and natural monopolies, that is: enterprises which by their very nature require a scale that does not lend itself to competitive fragmentisation. However, in a world so globally integrated as ours, more and more enterprises assume a scale so enormous that, whether they started out under private or under public ownership, they will end as an Orwellian Big Brother and Sisterhood that will crash not economically but physically, for sheer lack of balance, just as a boat will sink if all passengers rush from its right side to the left or when they take flight from the left side to the right.

The scale of the problem

The fourth possibility – the only one that could work in this age of giantism – lies in approaching the whole problem not economically or ideologically but dimensionally. What is wrong with a modern crash is not the crash but the size of a modern crash, just as what is wrong with today's unemployment is not unemployment but its *enormity;* and with war, not war but the *scale* of modern war. And the scale of an evil has nothing to do with religion, ideology, economic system, or inept leadership, but with the size of society which it afflicts. What we confront is therefore no longer old-fashioned *business* cycles inherent in every free-enterprise system but *size* cycles affecting every overgrown community, and becoming the more severe the larger such a community grows, producing, as Flora Lewis wrote of the 1987 crash (Herald Tribune, October 24-25), 'a chain reaction that swept through every financial centre around the world in less than 24 hours.'

> **'What is wrong with the current crash is not the crash but the size of the crash, just as what is wrong with today's unemployment is not unemployment but the enormity of its numbers; and with war, not war but the scale of modern war'**

Territorial reform

This being the case, the answer to the scale-induced problem of financial devastation is not economic, political, or ideological but territorial reform. Not bind the world still tighter together in united action, but, as I have advocated for 45 years, reduce the scale of human societies and associations to dimensions where they cannot only be controlled if and when controls are needed; but where the problems, along with the associations, are so reduced in scale, that most of the time they can once again be resolved by multi-centred regional, local, cooperative and individual action. Hence the solution lies in the direction towards regional devolution, not global hand holding which offers the world aid but infects it with AIDS.

> **'The answer to the problem of financial devastation is not economic, political, or ideological but territorial reform. Not bind the world still tighter together in united action, but, as I have advocated for 45 years, reduce the scale of human societies and associations'**

Galbraith, delightfully as always, speaks of the 'financial memory from one period of sophisticated stupidity to another' as amounting to about ten to fifteen years – a span of time not much different from what Jevons' sunspot theory suggests for business cycles. I would rather speak of the period *between* sophistication – when everyone is right in his stock market actions and predictions because everything is still fresh and new and small and beautiful – and stupidity – when everyone becomes panicky and wrong because everything has grown old and too big, and is subject no longer to human grasp but to the insensitive working of statistical inevitability. This can be checked only by reducing the size and numbers of nations, populations and markets to magnitudes in which human

intervention rather than statistical law is the factor determining historic events.

Until this happens, crashes can be predicted but not prevented, even if the governments would be in the hands of the prophets who say they have foreseen them all along. If they want to do something about preventing them, they must first of all recognise the phenomenon of the as yet uncharted course of *size cycles*, and advocate not unified action but devolution, not common but regional markets within whose reduced dimensions fluctuations cannot reach crash proportions in the first place. What one needs in stormy weather is harbours, not the open seas whose uncheckable giant swells are statistically bound to lead periodically to disaster. But this, with the exception of Welsh, Cornish and Scottish nationalists and some Liberals, no one wants – certainly not Mrs Thatcher or Neil Kinnock.

Professor Leopold Kohr, 170 Reservoir Road, Gloucester, GL4 9SB (tel 0452 23815).

Long-term shares

Jamie Carnie

A major structural problem with capitalism as it exists in Britain today is that businesses, driven ultimately by the short-term interests of their share-holders, do not invest adequately in their long-term future. It is not easy for a director to justify substantial expenditure on research and capital investment designed to produce a profit in perhaps five to ten years time to his shareholders – if they are more concerned about getting a good dividend this year or about being able to sell their shares next year for a profit.

Even long-term investors such as the major building societies, insurance companies and pension funds rarely look more than one or two years ahead, and if anything the weight of their substantial presence reinforces the short-termist pressures of the investment marketplace. As a result we are losing out to countries such as Japan where a government ministry (MITI) has been responsible for encouraging and coordinating long-term research and development in industry.

This situation could be rectified relatively easily, by means of a new instrument in the stockmarket, the heart of the capitalist system, which would provide a counter-balance in favour of long-term industrial vision. This instrument would take the form of 'long-term shares' whose issue and purchase would be a legal requirement.

> **'A counter-balance in favour of long-term industrial vision would take the form of "long-term shares" whose issue and purchase would be a legal requirement'**

A law would be introduced requiring companies to issue a certain minimum percentage of 'long-term' shares whenever they issued new ordinary shares. Perhaps 10 per cent of the total value of the issue would need to be made in the long-term form. (A formula would be devised to require companies with existing shares to replace a proportion of these by long-term shares over time, perhaps with some support from government.)

The long-term shares would be traded in a special parallel long-term stockmarket. The new type of shares would be like any other shares except that when bought by someone they could not then be resold until a further five years had elapsed; they would then have to be sold by the owner during the subsequent year, or held for a further five years. and so on. Long-term shares would be identical to any other type of share. Owners of them would count as owners of the company in the normal way, and would have normal voting rights at shareholder meetings and during takeover bids.

> **'A requirement for all individuals and companies who own more than a certain total floor value of shares to hold at least 10 per cent of them in long-term shares'**

Obviously these shares, with their restriction on when they could be sold, would not be popular, so the same law would phase in a requirement for all individuals and companies who own more than a certain total floor value of shares to hold at least 10 per cent of them in long-term shares of their choice. (This floor value would perhaps be somewhere around 20,000 in order to exclude the small individual investor who might otherwise be frightened off from investing at all, but to include the very wealthy and the major institutional investors.)

> **'The new shares would compel boards of directors to plan and invest for the future in an unprecedented way'**

What would be the effect of this be? Obviously those people who held the long-term shares of a company (and who could not get rid of them until five years had passed) would be very interested in ensuring the long-term health of the company, a message which would come through forcefully at shareholder meetings. The existence of the new shares would enable, and indeed compel, boards of directors to plan and invest for the future in an unprecedented way.

Some other points of detail: it may be necessary to allow the sale of long-term shares before their five-year term in exceptional but well-defined circumstances – eg bankruptcy of the owner. Clearly UK investors purchasing shares on foreign markets would have to remain subject to the law. If they were not required to purchase 10 per cent of the value as long-term shares on the UK market there would be a stampede of money out of the country. The situation for foreign investors purchasing into the UK market is less clear and would have to be thought out carefully. This requires more technical knowledge of the detailed workings of the global investment market than I possess, but there seems to be no reason in principle why foreign investors should not be allowed to carry on as now, without being subject to any requirement to buy long-term UK shares.

There would almost certainly be an adjustment period where overall UK share prices would probably change considerably upon the introduction of such changes, but the market would soon restabilise and should then carry on as normal. The adjustment period would have to be planned carefully and may require some financial support from the government, but the long-term benefits to the UK economy of the changes would potentially be considerable.

James Carnie, 96 Carlingcott, Bath BA2 8AW (tel 0761 436945).

Zero inflation through credit permits for lenders

Dr David Chapman

I propose that the total amount of credit in the UK should be controlled directly. This would be done by providing that any lending by a bank, building society, hire-purchase firm or any other institution should require a government-issued permit.

> **'Any lending by a bank, building society, hire-purchase firm or any other institution should require a government-issued permit'**

The method of controlling inflation which the present government has chosen, is that of adjusting the interest rate. This has been far from completely successful, and has had undesirable side-effects. The object of the adjustments is to limit and stabilise the total amount of lending. The theory behind it is presumably that there must be, at any time, some rate of interest which would hold the total lent at the target figure. But there seems to be no way of knowing what this 'ideal' rate of interest actually is, and in any case it may well change over time, which would increase the difficulty of finding what it was.

The permits I propose would be issued only up to a certain amount – the total amount of credit the government decided on as the target. A 'rent' would be charged for a permit, a charge per year of x per cent of the amount it gave permission to lend. The price would be continually adjusted (for all permits, not only just the ones being issued) so that the total amount which banks etc took up was not significantly below the target, and so that there was no significant unsatisfied demand for further permits when the target had been reached. A bank of course could at any time give back to the government part of its holding of permits, in which case it would cease to pay the rental charges on those given up. And at any time it could take on extra permits at the current rent.

In effect, the limited number of permits would go to those prepared to offer the highest rent, ie there would be a market in these permits. Permits would be allocated not bureaucratically, but by this market. Thus the scheme would provide credit control, but would achieve it by a market mechanism. Note however that there would be no point in starting a private market in permits, because if bank A bought a permit from bank B, the permit would still give only B permission to lend, not A. Note also that very little extra bureaucracy would be required by the scheme, as the government already needs to know the amount being lent, for taxation and other purposes.

In respect of lending between private individuals, a permit would be required if the sum lent was above a certain amount. But even below this amount, if the creditor had no permit, he/

she would lose all legal claim to repayment of capital and interest, thus risking default. Thus it is seems likely that few loans would be made without permit – only those between persons able to trust each other, such as friends and relatives.

Any borrowing in the UK financed by overseas money would also require the same permits, and the amount borrowed would count towards the target total national amount.

But how would this target amount be determined? The simplest way would be to start the scheme by issuing permits at zero price for all existing loans. This would determine the initial target *(Ed:* without giving a pecuniary advantage to the existing lenders, as the price they will later pay for these permits adjusts continuously, remaining an equal percentage charge for all permit holders, old or new). The target would then be continually increased (or decreased) at the rate at which the real national income increased or decreased. This could be expected to maintain stable prices, ie zero inflation, provided that the velocity of money remained stable.

The scheme's advantages

How then would the result of this proposal differ from that of past government attempts to control inflation by varying the interest rate?

'The total amount of credit would be stable, growing slowly in line with real national income'

(1) The total amount of credit would be stable, growing slowly in line with real national income.

(2) Prices would be stable – ie zero inflation.

(3) The interest rate would be more stable than it is at present, though it would probably be higher than the average of the present highly unstable rates.

(4) The above three factors would contribute to the general stability of the economy, providing a more stable business environment in which downturns in business activity and in employment would be less likely.

(5) The banks etc would pass on most if not all of the rent of the permits, charging the borrowers a rate of interest higher than now. However, the rate paid to lenders would if anything tend to be less than now. Hence, if demand for credit rose, pushing up the rent of permits and the rate of interest to borrowers, this would not in general attract into the country the money of foreign lenders, as it tends to do under the present system.

(6) The scheme would provide a new and substantial source of government revenue – the income from the 'rent' charged for permits to lend. This would come mainly from borrowers in the form of higher interest charged, but perhaps also from banks in lower profits, and from lenders in lower interest received.

Dr David Chapman, Democracy Design Forum, Coles Centre, Buxhall, Stowmarket, Suffolk IP14 3EB (tel 0449 736 223).

Editorial comment

Gordon Pepper of the Institute of Economic Affairs has also criticised the Chancellor's reliance on interest rates to control inflation and monetary growth. He proposes that the Bank of England adjust its assets and liabilities to control the growth of its own balance sheet, as necessary buying or selling bills of exchange or foreign currency. The control of this high-powered money would in turn restrict the ability of the banks to supply bank deposits.

'A Firm Foundation for Monetary Policy' by Gordon Pepper (published by IEA, 2 Lord North St, Westminster, London SW1P 3LB, tel 071 799 3745; fax 071 799 2137; £2-50).

Community Economics

'For the Common Good – Redirecting the economy towards community, the environment and a sustainable future' by Herman Daly and John Cobb (published by Green Print, 10 Malden Road, London NW5 3HR, 1990, £9-99).

This book is very much in tune with the Institute for Social Inventions' philosophy of the need to recapture a human scale in our societies. Consider, for instance, the following excerpts:

• The authors quote Thomas Jefferson: 'The article nearest to my heart is the division of counties into wards. These will be pure and elementary republics, the aim of all of which taken together composes the State, and will make of the whole a true democracy as to the business of the wards, which is that nearest and dearest concern, ... admitting personal transactions by the people.'

• 'We call for rethinking economics on the basis of a new concept of *Homo economicus* as person-in-community. ... The goal of an economics for community is as much to provide meaningful and personally satisfying work as to provide adequate goods and services.'

'If India had adopted Gandhian (village-based) economics, there would be far less heavy industry there, but there would also be far fewer urban slums and far healthier rural life'

• 'If India had adopted Gandhian (village-based) economics, there would be far less heavy industry there, but there would also be far fewer urban slums and far healthier rural life. The prosperous middle class would be smaller, but the desperately poor would also be far less numerous.'

• 'A national economy for community will be a relatively self-sufficient economy. This does not preclude trade, but it does preclude *dependence* on trade, especially where the nation cannot participate in determining the terms of trade.'

• About free trade they write: 'US workers are invited by US capitalists to share their wages with the hungry of the world in the name of "world community". The majority of the nation is invited to lower its standard of living so "we" can be more "efficient". But who is "we", and efficient at what? Certainly not efficient at providing a decent living standard for the majority of our citizens! And while we are about the business of lowering wages in the interests of efficiency, let us not forget to lengthen the working day, lower the minimum legal age to work, cut back retirement and sick leave, and so on. Equilibrium with the world labour market will not permit such benefits.

'In sum, we believe it is folly to sacrifice existing institutions of community at the national level in the supposed service of non-existent institutions of community at the world level.'

• 'The very concept of an optimal scale for the entire economy, relative to the supporting ecosystem, just does not exist in current economic theory: ... how many persons simultaneously living at what level of per capita resource use is best for community, where community includes concern for the future and non-human species as well as presently living humans?'

'The United States of America could again become a federation of states with each state bearing some responsibility for its own defence'

• The authors take up the Institute's argument that the superpowers need to talk as much in terms of multi-lateral dismemberment of their centralised empires as in terms of multi-lateral disarmament. 'The future danger that the Ukraine might launch a war against the United States is much less than the past danger of the Soviet Union attacking the United States. Similarly the Ukraine would have little to fear from an independent New York.' The United States of America could again become a federation of states (*Ed:* better still a loose commonwealth) 'with each state bearing some responsibility for its own defence, although it would be protected in part by its federation with the others.'

'The average food item travels 1,300 miles from where it is grown to where it is consumed'

• They report various projects in the States for reducing reliance on distant trade: 'Buying locally grown agricultural products makes sense. The average food item travels 1,300 miles from where it is grown to where it is consumed ... Yet Hendrix College in Arkansas managed to increase its purchases of food within the state from 9% to 40% within one year.'

• 'We reaffirm community with all peoples, with other animals, with all living things and with the whole earth.'

The Bigness Complex

Walter Adams and James Brock

The Institute for Social Inventions approves of the Fourth World Review's slogan 'for small nations, small communities and the human scale.' Walter Adams and James Brock, two American professors of economics, argue the 'small is beautiful' line in their book 'The Bigness Complex – Industry, Labour and the Government in the American Economy' (published by Pantheon Books, New York, 426 pages, $22·95). Their agenda for action is admirable, so far as it goes, although the Fourth World movement would take it further, with the breakdown of the United States into its constituent parts and with the dismantling of large firms, even those with under '$1 billion in assets.'

Power and the control of power pose the greatest challenge to a free society. Through monopolisation, mergers and sheer bigness, power tends to subvert the competitive market. It does so in a variety of ways: obtaining, or striving to retain,

government cartelisation of inherently competitive fields, pleading for government protection from foreign competition and forcing government bail-outs of collapsing corporate giants to avert the threat of massive shut-downs, lay-offs and plant closings.

The current American 'isms' – neo-liberalism on the left and neo-Darwinism on the right – are not the answer. The neo-liberals would trust a coalition of Big Business, Big Labour and Big Government. The neo-Darwinists would put their faith in the select few anointed by an untrammelled laissez-faire marketplace. Yet neither 'ism' offers a persuasive answer to Lord Acton's warning that power tends to corrupt and absolute power corrupts absolutely. Neither provides a reliable social control mechanism.

An agenda for action

• The current merger mania is clearly out of control. Billion-dollar mega-corporations are roaming the Darwinian jungle, making helter-skelter acquisitions or merging with one another. Our own preference would be to bar all corporate mergers involving corporations with assets of more than $1 billion.

'Billion-dollar mega-corporations are roaming the Darwinian jungle, making helter-skelter acquisitions. Our own preference would be to bar all corporate mergers involving corporations with assets of more than $1 billion'

• The lodestar of public policy should be comprehensive deregulation – the dissolution of a government-industry-labour power complex. In trucking and airlines, for example, regulation was not an instrument for protecting consumers from exploitation, but a means of protecting vested interests from competition. But economic deregulation must be carefully distinguished from social deregulation. There are some regulatory tasks – the assurance of pure foods and drugs, clean air and water, automobile safety and protection from toxic or otherwise hazardous waste – which must, for better or worse, be entrusted to government.

• Public bail-outs of collapsing business complexes seem to have become the order of the day, rendering the Bigness Complex even more powerful and even less accountable to society. Bankruptcy is a competitive market society's ingenious resolution of the problem of preserving physical assets and keeping them intact, while at the same time realigning the financing of those assets, the management of them, and the uses to which they are put.

Unfortunately for the nation, the hold of the Bigness Complex remains as powerful as ever among some prominent economic policy-makers – witness the astonishing suggestion that 'the thing that prevents the American automobile industry from competing effectively with Japan is that General Motors is too small.' These public perorations now emanating from Washington are most depressing, because they attest to the durability of mythological belief and the addiction to ideological dogma, even at the highest levels of government. A cynic once said that establishments reward the lies that sustain them and punish the truths that embarrass them. More unfortunate, perhaps, they also believe the myths that undermine them.

James Brock is Professor of Economics at Miami University (Ohio). Walter Adams is Distinguished Professor of Economics at Michigan State University (Department of Economics, Marshall Hall, East Lansing, Michigan 48824, USA, tel 517 355 4465).

Humanising corporations

Shann Turnbull

The formation of time-limited 'Ownership Transfer Corporations' would allow increased profits to those multinational companies which chose to give up two to five per cent of their equity each year to the employees or national superannuation funds – providing a means to reduce foreign ownership whilst still attracting foreign investment.

> 'The formation of time-limited "Ownership Transfer Corporations" would allow increased profits to those multinational companies which chose to give up two to five per cent of their equity each year to the employees'

It is a way of making corporations compatible with nature and humans, with Ownership Transfer Corporations (OTCs) emulating nature by developing through cycles of death and birth.

An OTC is created when the constitution of a corporation transfers the rights of all the initial shareholders to others without cost at a set rate of say five per cent per year after the first dividend. The rights of the initial shareholders would then terminate twenty years later. The initial shareholders of an OTC would typically obtain greater profits if the tax rate for OTCs were reduced by around ten percentage points. Such a tax incentive would provide a basis for the voluntary introduction of the OTC concept.

Gold mining corporations have limited life but many have nurtured new corporations in other activities. A well-known example with its origin in Australia is British Petroleum Limited.

Naturally occurring limited life corporations illustrate the practicality of the OTC concept. Many developing countries require foreign enterprises to be constituted on a limited life basis. The French and German forms of corporation evolved with limited life to meet commercial needs.

However, in England, corporations such as the East India Company and the Hudson Bay Company were created with unlimited life as an instrument for colonising foreign lands. It was for this political reason that other imperial powers gave their corporations unlimited life in the 19th century. This political attribute is no longer appropriate or required in corporations.

If humans are to colonise this planet on a sustainable basis, enterprises will need to be sensitised to preserving nature – an outcome which will require corporations to develop on a human scale and be owned and controlled by their stakeholders.

Stakeholders are those people whose lives are affected by the corporation. They would include shareholders, employees, suppliers, customers and host communities.

OTCs create a mechanism to localise the ownership and control of corporations and so a means to decentralise wealth and power.

OTCs provide a technique for introducing: employee ownership, corporate self-governance, greater efficiency in the capital markets, more foreign investment with foreign ownership fade-out, and a highly efficient means for technology transfer. They would substantially reduce the need and motivation for corporate take-overs, asset stripping, 'greenmail' and so the need to regulate the securities industry closely.

OTCs would create a boom in the securities industry as all profits would be distributed and corporate growth would be financed by the capital markets. The substantial cashflows distributed by mature OTCs would be redirected by both its initial and new shareholders into its corporate offspring and other new businesses. OTCs create a means to programme change and progress on a sustainable basis into the corporate engines of society.

Shann Turnbull, GPO Box 4359, Sydney, NSW 2001, Australia (tel 612 233 5340). This suggestion won a Social Inventions Award.

Pendulum arbitration in monopoly services

David Davis, the Conservative MP for Boothferry, in 'The Power of the Pendulum', a pamphlet published by the Centre for Policy Studies, proposes that all public and private industries and services where a particular supplier enjoys a market share of more than 75 per cent (eg ambulancemen, teachers, railwaymen, etc), should have their disputes resolved by compulsory pendulum arbitration. In this system, an independent arbiter must choose between pay claim and offer, rather than deciding partly in favour of one side, partly of the other; thus encouraging more moderate behaviour by both parties.

> 'Ambulancemen, teachers, railwaymen, etc, should have their disputes resolved by compulsory pendulum arbitration. In this system, an independent arbiter must choose between pay claim and offer'

There would be two optional variations on the pendulum process (each of which would require agreement on both sides in the negotiation).

The first variation would be a pause for conciliation.

The second variation would allow issue-by-issue pendulum arbitration. Both sides would need not just to agree to use this procedure, but would also have to agree which issues to separate. This would enable them both to minimise their risks in issues where their difference of view was slight.

A critical aspect of such arbitration is the criteria by which the arbitrator makes his judgement. These should favour proposals which would:

(1) Improve the level of service given by the monopoly.

(2) Give the best value for money for the taxpayer.

(3) Enhance the joint interests of the employees and the enterprise.

(4) Reflect local market values and 'going rates' for the enterprise and ensure the proper availability of these skills for the monopoly.

(5) Enhance career prospects and motivation of the employees.

Thus a union's claim based on proposals for improved productivity would have a much better chance of success than a bald demand. On the other hand, the employer who could justify his proposals in terms of better motivation and career prospects, and demonstrate that his pay rates are competitive, would enhance his chances.

'The Power of the Pendulum', £4-95 from the Centre for Policy Studies, 8 Wilfred Street, London SW1E 6PL.

The Foundation for Appropriate Economic Solutions

A Foundation in Salzburg, Austria, has been established by Helmut von Loebell. The Foundation for Appropriate Economic Solutions (Dialogzentrum für angemessene Wirtschaftsweisen) is aiming for international and interdisciplinary dialogue on more just economic forms for humanity and the planet. It will act as a centre for disseminating appropriate and innovative economic solutions, with a bias towards those that have a 'human scale'. It will enter into dialogue with socially relevant groups in society, whether churches, workers' unions, political parties, people's initiatives, self-governed enterprises – indeed with anybody who has ideas as to economic solutions for society tomorrow. It hopes to become a major 'crossroads' for future-oriented networks.

Its first project is the study 'Alternative and Appropriate Economic Models – in theory and practice'. The Foundation will have a board of three people and a steering committee consisting of Nicholas Albery, Frank Bracho, Erszébel Gidai, Gerald Häfner, Hazel Henderson, Rolf Homann, Robert Jungk, Robert Muller, Ziauddin Sardar, Jakob von Üexkull, Michaela Walsh and James Robertson.

> **'A centre for disseminating appropriate and innovative economic solutions, with a bias towards those that have a human scale'**

Helmut von Loebell, The Foundation for Appropriate Economic Solutions, Nonntaler Haupstr. 58a, A-5020 Salzburg, Austria (tel 43 662 84 46 19, fax 43 662 84 81 53).

A British Mondragon

There have been several attempts made in the UK (by Jo Grimond among others) to copy the success of the Mondragon co-ops in Spain, where a Spanish priest after the Civil War initiated a series of linked firms which now employ over 20,000 people and have their own bank. The latest UK attempt is New Enterprise Development Ltd (NED) in Glenrothes, Fife, whose founder director Cairns Campbell aims to create at least two new large-scale businesses each year. Among the many unusual features of this local enterprise agency are that they are on the look-out for successful entrepreneurs to whom they can pay a salary for researching and developing a business idea for up to a year before the first employees are taken on; and all employees on joining will be required to take a £1,000 to £2,000 stake in the company 'so as to encourage a feeling of commitment.' Campbell himself was director of the Scottish Co-operative Development Committee until 1985 and his primary motivation in starting NED is to 'help unlock the potential in employee ownership.'

> **'All employees on joining will be required to take a £1,000 to £2,000 stake in the company so as to encourage a feeling of commitment'**

Their first firm will be manufacturing raised access flooring for offices, taking on 15 workers in year one, and aiming for 25 to 50 within three years. Besides head-hunting entrepreneurs, Campbell would also welcome worthwhile business ideas – he expects that the most fruitful approach will be to set up partnerships with foreign companies, manufacturing under licence.

NED, Saltire Centre, Glenrothes, Fife, KY6 2DA, Scotland (tel 0592 775000).

Financing urban creativity
Jane Jacobs

Jane Jacobs in her notable book 'Cities and the Wealth of Nations' (published by Random House, New York, 1984, ISBN 0 394 48047 3) has shown how nations are the economic dependents of their cities, subsiding into poverty as cities lose economic vitality. Here is an adapted extract from her book instancing how the city of Boston, stagnant economically after the war, bounced back.

Ralph Flanders (who later became a US senator from Vermont) reasoned that Boston's trouble was what he called its low birth rate of enterprises. He persuaded a handful of moneyed colleagues to accept his point of view, and in 1946 they formed a small venture capital firm to do what used to be called merchant banking. The object was specifically to invest in small new enterprises, and specifically in Boston. For this purpose they had a capital of almost $4 million, which, owing to inflation in the meantime, would be the equivalent of about $28 million today.

It so happened that the first applicants for capital were three young scientists who had started a tiny high-technology enterprise, using their own and their families' savings. They could not continue without additional investment and were about to close up because investors in Boston and New York would not advance them capital. The new Flanders group, their last hope, agreed to invest in the fledgling business, and then rapidly in several other small innovative technological enterprises that became the next applicants.

> 'The enterprises they financed – because these were what offered themselves, and their proprietors seemed realistic in their devotion to what they were trying – began to multiply by division. The Boston regional economy was rejuvenated'

The enterprises they financed – because these were what offered themselves, and their proprietors seemed realistic in their devotion to what they were trying – began to multiply by division: employees broke away and started new enterprises of their own, many of which Flanders and his colleagues also financed. Upon this base, upon its many subsequent ramifications and breakaways, and upon the multiplying suppliers of materials, instruments, tools and services that served the new enterprises and thus were supported by them and by one another, the Boston regional economy was stunningly rejuvenated. Today Boston has one of the few vigorously extending and intensifying city regional economies in the United States.

Germane economic correction depends on fostering creativity in whatever forms it happens to appear in a given city at a given time. It is impossible to know in advance what may turn up, except that – especially if it is to prove important – it is apt to be unexpected.

Mercury – loans to small alternative businesses

Mercury, the ethical banking institution with Rudolph Steiner leanings, is, with ICOF (the fund for cooperatives), the only ethical investment body in the UK that provides loans to small alternative and green businesses (rather than to big companies on the stock exchange). It is an authorised institution under the Banking Act and was founded in 1974. But until recently you needed to be rich enough not to mind your money losing value to be able to bank with Mercury, as they offered only a fixed rate interest of between zero and seven per cent. Nowadays they are also offering variable rates of interest equivalent to those at building societies for minimum balances of £500 (with one month's notice needed for withdrawals).

> 'The only ethical investment body in the UK that provides loans to small alternative and green businesses'

This must be one of the greenest and safest ways to bank one's savings. The money deposited will be used 'as part of Mercury's liquidity, thus maximising the use of lower-interest bearing money to be lent to our ever-growing list of projects. Mercury will also lend out of this pool to projects that can afford higher rates.'

Those, however, who are still prepared to lend under the old fixed rate system can specify which of the projects they want their money allocated to.

• *Mercury Provident, Orlingbury House, Lewes Road, Forest Row, East Sussex RH18 5AA (tel 034282 3739; fax 034282 5711).*

• *A free 'Independent Guide to Ethical and Green Investment Funds' is available from Holden Meehan, top floor, 40 Park St, Bristol BS1 5JG (tel 0272 252874; fax 0272 291535).*

The Network for Social Change

The Network for Social Change is a British self-help group for rich people who aspire to use their resources to make the world a better place. It was founded in 1985 and now has about 60 members so far, but is on the look-out for more. The membership requirements are, first, to have assets of over £250,000, either earned or inherited (excluding the main residence), and, second, to be willing to put a minimum of £2,000 a year into socially or environmentally beneficial causes, not necessarily through the Network for Social Change. The projects which the Network members fund collectively are all sought out by members themselves. Unsolicited applications are not considered.

> 'To be willing to put a minimum of £2,000 a year into socially or environmentally beneficial causes'

One member says: 'it is a deeply unfair society in which we live, and if you have money in a world where it is unequally distributed you are in a powerful position. However, the responsibility can become too much, and you can get really paralysed by the guilt.'

The twice annual conferences of the whole membership encourage a sharing at many levels and challenge directly the isolation of those with money.

One recently joined member commented: 'My husband and I got involved in Network about seven months after we got the money from the sale of our business, and it helped us to get things into perspective.' She also asks, 'Where else can you talk about your money and not worry about people looking at you sideways?'

Projects that they have funded range from an education centre set up by miners' wives in Yorkshire to a tree nursery in the Cape Verde Islands developing species suitable for drought-stricken Africa, to an Indian project producing artificial limbs that are suited to local cultural conditions.

The Network was inspired by the examples of two United States-based organisations, both of which channel funds from the rich to 'change agents', 'transformational' projects or community-based organisations. They are now giving away millions of dollars compared to the British organisation's £300-350,000, but then as Network Chair, Patrick Boase, comments, 'The scale of the problem is not so large over here!'

Patrick Boase, The Network for Social Change, PO Box 2030, London NW10 5AW.

The Business Network

The Business Network aims to foster a new holistic approach to business and to bring ecological and spiritual values into business life. Its co-founder, Edward Posey, quotes Einstein on the need to 'widen our circle of compassion to embrace all living creatures and the whole of Nature in all her beauty.' The Business Network, which has a membership of 350, draws in people from a wide range of business ventures.

> **'The need to widen our circle of compassion to embrace all living creatures and the whole of Nature in all her beauty'**

There are newsletters twice a year and stimulating monthly meetings and meals in Central London to discuss 'holistic business' ideas. Guest speakers have included Paul Ekins, author of 'The Living Economy', Jose Lutzenberger, a Right Livelihood Award winner, and Willis Harman, founder of the World Business Academy.

Since the Network's launch in 1982, several special interest groups and projects have formed from it, the latest being the Computing Group, exploring the possibility of setting up projects in computing and information technology. The Gaia Foundation, which works internationally to develop mutual relations with projects and people in the South, leading to partnership with people in the North, arose out of a Business Network special interest group.

The Business Network, Room 1126, Trafalgar House, Grenville Place, Mill Hill, London NW7 3SA (tel 081 959 3611 Tues/Thurs; fax 081 906 1700). Membership costs £35 a year, although 'nobody is turned away for lack of funds.' For information and the current programme, send an SAE.

Negotiating the difference for charity

Frederick Mulder

Business Network member Frederick Mulder, a dealer in old master and modern prints, describes an unusual approach to negotiating.

> **'I asked $140,000. My client offered $120,000. After a certain amount of toing and froing we were at an impasse. Suddenly I had a brainwave; why not ask if he would be willing to give the $20,000 difference away if I accepted his offer'**

I had bought a very beautiful Munch colour mezzotint. I offered it to a good client whom I knew collected Munch and who was planning to give his collection to the Fogg Art Museum at Harvard University. I asked $140,000. My client offered $120,000. After a certain amount of toing and froing we were at an impasse. I thought I had asked the market price for the print and did not want to accept less; my client was not prepared to pay more. Suddenly I had a brainwave; why not ask if he would be willing to give the $20,000 difference away if I accepted his offer. Plucking up courage, I asked; it was not

something I had ever done or heard of being done before, although I dimly remembered the story of the art dealer, who, faced with an irreconcilable difference between what he wanted and what a famous pianist wished to pay for a painting, asked the pianist what his concert fee was. The amount was that of the irreconcilable difference, and the dealer proposed that the pianist give him a private concert; both parties went away happy. My client quickly accepted and in fact generously offered to give away $25,000 instead of $20,000. I even told him my cost, and we both agreed that the remaining profit was a fair one. I had been mostly involved in funding Third World and environmental projects, and we agreed to split the $25,000 between Oxfam and Greenpeace, both organisations I knew well.

What struck me afterwards was how my suggestion changed our whole attitude to the transaction and to each other's role in it. Whereas before we were in a traditional commercial confrontation, with each of us trying to secure the best price for ourself, the idea that we might together give away all or part of my profit turned us into allies with a common purpose. I realised also that I had not been so concerned about what my client actually paid as about ensuring that I was not unreasonably beaten down; likewise my client was not so concerned about what he actually paid as about ensuring that he had gotten the lowest price. Introducing the 'gift' element changed the tone of the discussion and made us both less sensitive about the question of who would win.

> **'The idea that we might together give away all or part of my profit turned us into allies with a common purpose'**

This was another step in helping me to look at commercial transactions in a new way. I began by seeing a transaction as a way of turning a profit, and thus earning a living. When I began to give a substantial part of my profits away, each transaction became a way of realising funds for another purpose. Now I have gone a stage further and try to involve some of my clients in the action of giving money away. Hopefully this has a ripple effect; the client may become further involved in the particular cause to which he has given, and may also himself begin to see transactions in a new way.

Frederick Mulder, 83 Belsize Park Gardens, London NW3 4NJ (tel 071 722 2105; fax 071 483 4228).

Bets to back jobs

Marjorie Virgo

The objectives are to encourage punters to gamble on investment in local businesses – instead of horses, dogs and football – and to channel a good proportion of the gambling money into investment in those businesses.

> **'Encourage punters to gamble on investment in local businesses'**

To carry this out, prospectuses give information on a selection of local companies printed in local newspapers. Access is via self-service terminals in High Street premises. After deduction of administrative expenses, 50% of the total sum wagered is invested in the most popular choice of business and awarded as an investment to the punter who wins a weekly lottery. 50% is invested in a portfolio of shares in *all* the companies, awarded twelve months later to the punter who most accurately predicts the performance of those companies in the year ahead.

Marjorie Virgo, 2 Eastbourne Avenue, Acton, London, W3 6JN.

Comment by Valerie Yule

A simpler approach might be to have shares in local industries (with safeguards against fraud) available for sale in betting shops.

Valerie Yule, 57 Waimarie Drive, Mount Waverley, Victoria, Australia 3149 (tel 807 4315).

Low level Tenure

Denis Midgley

It would be a useful innovation to allow tenured job security to apply only in the career grade itself, such as that of lecturer or scientific officer. Each promotion would then involve a healthy competition, with the successful rewarded by at most five years of higher status. To say that tenure should not apply to this new status would not mean that all right to tenure is forfeited – which is the diabolical situation in some instances known to me. Tenure in the lower career grade would be retained. In the same way, the Dean of Faculty is typically not tenured as a dean in this country; he reverts to a lower status on completion of a few years of office.

'Allow tenure job security to apply only in the career grade itself'

There is no disgrace in wishing to have limited tenure of this type; some young men, after seeing a father cast aside just before the completion of a career in private employment, feel rightly justified in placing security before cash reward, when seeking employment.

Also it is generally agreed that judges should have tenure, with the job security leading them to act without fear or favour. Similarly academics' search for truth should be as unimpeded as possible by fears that their discoveries may displease those in authority.

Denis Midgley, 20 Elvaston Avenue, Hornsea, East Yorkshire HU18 1HA (tel 0964 533435).

OwnBase for home-based workers

Extracted from 'Executive Post'.

OwnBase newsletter is the brainchild of Chris Oliver. She has worked out of home for most of the last twenty years, and started the newsletter, which has 260+ members, to provide mutual support and information for those working from home. Occupations range from accountancy and astrology to tapestry designing and weaving. The newsletter covers topics such as: How to be 'out' to callers when you're obviously in and working? How to extract money owed by customers who are also friends?

Members network together via a contact list and informal get-togethers. In July 1989, a Members' Association took over responsibility for developing the concept.

'How to be "out" to callers when you're obviously in and working? How to extract money owed by customers who are also friends?'

OwnBase, Chris Oliver, 56 London Road, Milborne Port, Sherborne, Dorset DT9 5DW (tel 0963 250764).

Interest on late payment of bills

Nicholas Saunders writes: 'Lattice Structures, a small firm in mid-Wales making Islamic screens, were promised payment within 28 days of delivery of a large order, and in fact were not paid for four months. Many small businesses and self-employed tradesmen are exploited for credit in this way. Their cash flow problems stem from having to pay up quickly on their bills, whilst large firms tend to push for longer credit.'

'The cash flow problems of small firms stem from having to pay up quickly on their bills, whilst large firms tend to push for longer credit'

The Institute advocates that the UK government introduce the Danish system whereby small firms are protected from big firms' late payments by a statute charging interest on late payment – it seems that the system in Denmark works very satisfactorily.

Danish law provides that in the absence of any other agreement, interest is charged once payment becomes due (if such a date is found in the contract); in other cases, interest is charged if a letter is sent requesting payment of the principal and indicating that interest will be charged a month from the date of the letter. The interest rate allowed for is 6% above the Danish Central Bank's 'discount rate' (making a total of approximately 13% per annum at present).

Many Danish firms charge a higher rate of 2% or 1.5% per month, payable 30 days from the end of the month found on the invoice. But legal cases have established that it is not sufficient for this higher interest requirement to appear on invoices. It must be in the conditions of sale.

There have been very few problems since this system became general from 1986. In the early days a few companies would try to avoid paying the interest, and sometimes good customers would be let off 'this once', but now firms pay up quite readily. The rate charged varies from about 1.2% per month to 2.5%. Currently 1.5% per month seems to be the average. The introduction of this new business climate was facilitated originally by the government bringing together all the various business associations, who agreed that getting cheap credit from small firms through late payment was unfair, and that this new system should be introduced.

A recent CBI survey showed that nearly one in five small firms in the UK was under threat because of late payment of bills, and a large majority of small and medium-sized businesses backed a statutory right to interest on outstanding debts.

The Institute for Social Inventions sympathises with the government's desire to avoid legislation and its desire to simplify the conditions under which businesses operate. Statutory interest would, surprisingly, help achieve this. At present there is a right to interest, but one has to get a county court judgement in one's favour to acquire it (in the county court interest of 15% from the due date is awarded on debts). How much simpler it would be and how much less recourse to legal processes would be involved, if statutory interest were in place and were part of the business climate.

There is such a statutory right to interest not only in Denmark but in West Germany, the Netherlands, France, the United States and Norway. In one or two of these countries the legislation is not widely known about, but where it has been introduced or publicised fairly recently, it appears to be effective – in Norway, for instance, there is little incidence of late payment of debts.

> 'There is a statutory right to interest for late payment not only in Denmark but in West Germany, the Netherlands, France, the United States and Norway'

Perhaps a statutory right to interest may eventually become the EC norm.

The above information came partly from the Danish Industry Ministry (tel 45 1 923350); a Danish lawyer in London, Christian Emeluth (tel 071 497 9389); Ole Christensen at the British Embassy in Copenhagen (tel 45 126 4600); Andy Scott at the CBI (tel 071 379 7400) and Colin Gray, Deputy Director-General at the Small Business Research Trust (tel 071 828 5327).

A work credit system for use in businesses

Nicholas Saunders

Summary

The Institute for Social Inventions is looking for a business that is still at the planning stage which might like to take advantage of the work-credit system, for such a system could have an extremely beneficial effect on the standard employer-employee relationship.

In this system (adapted from the American 'Walden 2' commune experiments), each task within the day's work is awarded credits, with the value of the credits being decided by the workers themselves, so that the most unpopular jobs receive the highest credits. Among the many advantages are that people can then work nearer to their own preferred individual pace, at work of their own choosing, and be paid according to the real value of their work, with the element of self-assessment resulting in less interference by the employer.

Free consultancy advice is offered to the first business prepared to take up this work-credit system.

Introduction

This is a system for paying staff more fairly, and one which can be extended to everyone concerned in a business including the customers. The assessment is made by those doing each job in such a way that it is automatically revised at regular intervals. As the assessment comes from the workers, it is unnecessary for a 'boss' to evaluate their worth, thus eliminating a cause of tension. As payment is by credits, staff are more free to work at their own pace and to choose which jobs they do.

Principle of operation

The work involved in the business is divided into specific jobs; or where it is impractical to distinguish some jobs, these may be combined in a category – for instance, book-keeping and ordering stock may be included in 'office work'.

> 'A list of the day's jobs is posted along with their credit ratings. The staff choose their jobs (from those that they are qualified to do)'

Specific jobs are allotted a number of credit points each – for instance 12 points for cleaning the work area; 10 points for banking the day's takings and so on. Non-specific jobs are allotted points by time – say office work 20 points an hour; driving a van 15 points per hour. In practice, most of the jobs would be specific but examples depend on the type of business. Where several people work together, they of course share the credits for the work they do.

The operation in practice

A list of the day's jobs is posted along with their credit ratings. The staff choose their jobs (from those that they are qualified to do), and cross them off the list, taking a note of how many credit points they have earned.

Re-assessing the credit rating

The jobs that are not chosen (ie those that are taken when no choice is left) are automatically upgraded in credit rating – by having their number of credit points increased by, say, five per cent. Of course common sense would prevent this happening if there were a particular reason applying that day. There would also be an opportunity for workers to alter the credit points – either at a regular meeting or by each person having a 'ration' of points they could change each week.

The total wages allocated per week would be divided by the total number of credit points – so, for instance, each point might be worth 13p – and each person's wages calculated accordingly.

Extensions of the principle

It would be necessary to establish some form of agreement with staff, at the outset, about how the total wages are to be calculated. For many businesses – such as a shop – this can conveniently be a proportion of turnover. It would then be necessary to have an agreement with the staff that all work (within set parameters) was to be completed each day, however long (or briefly) they had to work. There would, of course, be no 'overtime' as such, but long hours would normally be linked to high turnover. This device of linking total wages to turnover is generally seen to be fair by everyone and is a great advantage when it comes to costing.

> 'Say that the business is expanding, all the staff will work more and more (and earn more and more) until they decide that they had rather earn less and work less'

A further extension is for the staff to decide whether to take on more people. Say that the business is expanding, all the staff will work more and more (and earn more and more) until they decide that they had rather earn less and work less. On contraction, the staff could decide if, when and whom to lay off.

The third – and most fundamental – extension is to include those in the 'boss' position. Obviously, fewer people would be qualified to manage than to do basic jobs, but it seems to me that responsibility could be assessed and rewarded by credit points. And, to complete the set-up, why not those risking and investing their capital too?

Optional extension – combined workers'/consumers' co-op

Imagine this system in operation in a shop that catered for regular customers. It would then be possible for those who own the business to sell it to the customers so that it became a co-op. Or the same result could come from a group of prospective customers putting in money to set up the business.

The structure appears to incorporate a conflict, on the intellectual level at least – that of the customers' interests versus the workers'. But, in practice and with goodwill, I think that this is no real obstacle.

I visualise a committee of owner/customers who would lay down overall principles, employing a group of workers on the work-credit principle. The workers and customers would have joint meetings to agree on a manager and important changes – but apart from that, the staff would have control of all day-to-day and week-to-week running of the business.

Is your business at the planning stage?

I had hoped to use this system in a retail business employing some twelve people which had already been going for some years. However, in this instance there were particular difficulties, perhaps compounded by the fact that the conventional structure was already well established.

The Institute is therefore looking for a business that is still at the planning stage that might be interested in using this work-credit system and in evaluating its usefulness – so that the system can, if proved helpful in practice, be then publicised more widely, with the aim of creating an improved structure for the employer-employee relationship.

The Institute will endeavour to help the first business to take up this system, not only with advice on the work credit front, but also with business advice generally, if required.

The types of business that might be most suitable include shopkeeping, distribution and many light industries and farming.

Nicholas Saunders, top floor, 14 Neal's Yard, London WC2H 9DP (tel 071 836 9404; fax 071 379 0135).

The Direct Charge Co-op Supermarket
Nicholas Saunders

In Nanaimo, Canada, there is a novel structure for a consumers' co-op – which could probably do much to revitalise the moribund Co-op Society shops in this country, or could be set up independently.

The system is that members pay a high subscription which is sufficient to pay the overheads of the shop or supermarket, and non-members are excluded. Members may then buy goods at little above wholesale price, as the major costs have already been covered by their subscription. This encourages member loyalty.

> 'Instead of competing with other supermarkets, trying to sell more by "special offers" and other come-ons, the Direct Charge Co-op does best if it sells *less* – providing it keeps its members satisfied'

The result is profound – instead of competing with other supermarkets, trying to sell more by 'special offers' and other come-ons, the co-op does best if it sells *less* – providing it keeps its members satisfied. The co-op thus becomes a true agent of its members, aiming to satisfy their needs rather than sell them more than they want.

The system also involves many other sophistications, such as compulsory investment in the co-op by means of a check-out levy. This generates capital for expansion, and provides an essential stabilising effect – if a rival supplier tries to seduce away members, their subscriptions would be paid out of the levy until the required six months' notice elapsed.

Nicholas Saunders, top floor, 14 Neal's Yard, London WC2H 9DP (tel 071 836 9404; fax 071 379 0135).

Neal's Yard principles

Nicholas Saunders has initiated many of the businesses in Neal's Yard, Covent Garden, which have all survived to date – the first, a wholefood shop, was started more than ten years ago. Others followed in quick succession, the bakery, the dairy, the coffee shop, the apothecary, the soup and salad bar, the therapy rooms, the desk top publishing studio and the Agency for Personal Development. In the following he outlines his approach:

My ideas about work were influenced by Gurdjieff – that fulfilment does not come from making everything easy, but by doing a variety of things which stretch your abilities, including physical work. So jobs were rotated, from cleaning to dealing with the money, and I used to encourage responsibility by giving workers turns at managing the business with authority to sign cheques – often without even knowing their surnames, which shocked the bank manager.

> **'My ideas about work were influenced by Gurdjieff – that fulfilment does not come from making everything easy, but by doing a variety of things which stretch your abilities, including physical work'**

The atmosphere was one of high energy, with no nonsense, and attracted an enthusiastic lot of workers. The wholefood business was making a lot of money too, so I divided up the profits among the workers and reduced the prices still further.

After helping set up the wholefood shop and the bakery, I had ideas of starting more shops. I was not convinced that worker co-ops or any other set-up was ideal, but wanted to lay down some principles. Clare from the bakery helped me draft these 'Neal's Yard Trading Principles' (although not all have subsequently been adhered to by all the now independent businesses):

(1) All food must be prepared or at least packed on the premises.

(2) The ingredients must be 'wholefood', ie pure, without additives such as flavourings, colourings or preservatives. Highly refined ingredients must be avoided.

(3) Prices must be reasonable.

> **'Descriptions (both verbal and written) must be straightforward, down-to-earth and objective. Persuasive, enticing or glamorising descriptions must not be used'**

(4) Descriptions (both verbal and written) must be straightforward, down-to-earth and objective. Persuasive, enticing or glamorising descriptions must not be used.

(5) The size and style of notices must be simple – not attention-seeking, enticing, image building or making use of any advertising or merchandising techniques.

(6) 'Point of sale aids' must not be used.

(7) Information about recipes, ingredients, quality and suppliers must be freely available.

(8) The neighbours must be given consideration and cooperation.

(9) All staff must be free to see accounts and attend meetings where they may freely express their views.

(10) Jobs should be rotated as far as possible, and in particular no one should be left with the unpopular jobs.

(11) Outside contractors should be avoided if the work can be done by the regular staff.

(12) In the event of the business growing, it should not expand or set up branches, but instead should assist and encourage some of its staff to split off and start another independent business.

What was behind these principles was my belief in direct feedback between the customer and the person producing the goods. Instead of separate experts doing each part of the process of manufacturing, packing, transporting and selling, the same person could do all those jobs with more satisfaction

– for simple but important reasons such as feeling the customers' appreciation.

Although productivity was bound to be lower as measured by output in each individual job, this could be made up for by savings in packaging, transport and in far lower overheads, as administration often accounts for half the cost of production. Additionally, there were often advantages in being able to sell fresher products – and this was particularly relevant for wholefoods where no preservatives are used.

At the time particularly, I was against businesses expanding beyond about a dozen workers or setting up branches, because a small scale allows direct communication between people, without need for internal memos or a personnel department. In a small business people also feel more contact with the boss – it tends to be fairer whatever the business structure.

Nicholas Saunders, top floor, 14 Neal's Yard, London WC2H 9DP (tel 071 836 9404; fax 071 379 0135). A 60 page booklet 'The Neal's Yard Story' is available from the Institute for Social Inventions, 20 Heber Road, London NW2 6AA (tel 081 208 2853; fax 081 452 6434) for £1·95p incl. p&p.

Dean Clough Mills

Ernest Hall came from a very poor family of 13 children and wanted to be a piano player. He treated business almost as a hobby, but became rich. He used the money he made to save the old derelict Dean Clough Mills in Halifax – three quarters of a mile of empty buildings, which in 1982 had seemed to everyone an almost insoluble problem. Hall sees his purpose in life as being to help people achieve their own inner genius, and he helped in the revival of Halifax by creating 1.2m sq ft of workshop space in these old mills for artists, craftsmen, small and big firms: everything from photographers, graphic designers, printers and architects to a wholefood co-op employing 60 people, a home for the Northern Ballet, and (in the more recent stages) some blue chip companies.

> **'Hall sees his purpose in life as being to help people achieve their own inner genius'**

To quote from 'Dean Clough' by Eric Webster:
'In a major act of faith he set out to create an environment which would deliberately stimulate and encourage enterprise, and thereby form a model for long-term success in a much broader arena. With an astonishing swiftness Dean Clough took on a new lease of life as a wholly integrated industrial, educational and cultural community.

'Dean Clough is now the home of around 180 businesses, with upwards of 1,800 people working on site. Many of these are first time ventures.'

'The development of a solid commercial base,' comments Ernest Hall, 'has enabled us to graft on increasingly ambitious elements. We established an art gallery through which we act as patrons and which has resulted in the collection of over 150 works of art; we appointed an artist in residence and an arts curator, both of whom receive substantial financial support, a creative working environment, and of course, the gallery space itself.

'We are demonstrating that the arts and education play a

vital part in economic regeneration, and also that artistic integrity need not be compromised by moving "art into enterprise and enterprise into art".

'The prestigious Slade School of Art opened in 1988 as an extension of Dean Clough, providing a major focus for the people of Calderdale in particular, and the North of England in general.'

In 1988, the first Enterprise Campus was launched at Dean Clough, based on a partnership between the private sector and the Local Education Authority.

Its aims are to enrich the educational experience of young people currently involved in education and training programmes, in schools and colleges, with the thriving craft and artistic life of Dean Clough – the Slade School, the Open College of the Arts, theatre and environmental initiatives – also contributing to the rich mix.

The same possibilities for learning and enrichment are offered to adults in Calderdale, particularly the unemployed and other disadvantaged groups.

'We believe individuals are potentially powerful beyond limit, and with motivation can make progress towards any goals they set themselves,' Ernest Hall concludes.

> 'To satisfy the need for individual achievement against a backcloth of pride in the local community'

'We see these recent developments as a virtual renaissance in Calderdale. It is a re-statement of our commitment to local regeneration but not of a narrow economic kind alone. It is a commitment to provide the broadest range of experiences for as many of the people of Calderdale as possible and to satisfy the need for individual achievement against a backcloth of civic culture and pride in the local community.'

Dean Clough Industrial Park, Halifax (tel 0422 344555). 'Dean Clough and the Crossley Inheritance' by Eric Webster is a Dean Clough Publication. Ernest Hall has a very fine slide show about Dean Clough and would be a good person to invite to address any group planning inner urban regeneration.

Displaying bills to shame overchargers

Any organisations or establishments open to the public or with a newsletter of some sort might be interested in the following amusing way of combatting overcharging by plumbers, solicitors or other such service-providers:

> 'Whenever the owners receive an excessive bill for services rendered, they display the bill and, if possible, the accompanying explanation'

Traquair House in Peeblesshire in Scotland is a stately home open to public, with a museum displaying ancient documents such as recipes and accounts. It now has a new section: whenever the owners receive an excessive bill for services rendered, they display the bill and, if possible, the accompanying explanation from the professional concerned. Solicitors,

accountants and others are put to shame when their hourly rates are disclosed.

Traquair House, Innerleithen, Peeblesshire EH44 6PW, Scotland (tel 0896 830 323).

Portfolio Life

Professor Charles Handy explained his Portfolio Life concept at an Institute meeting: 'What I am trying to do is evolve a lifestyle for myself. I looked into my concerns and activities, and one thing I did was to resign my full-time, tenured professorship. I created what I call "a portfolio life", setting aside 100 days a year for making money, 100 days for writing, 50 days for what I consider good works, and 100 days for spending time with my wife.

> 'I created what I call "a portfolio life", setting aside 100 days a year for making money, 100 days for writing, 50 days for what I consider good works, and 100 days for spending time with my wife'

'I mark these days out in my diary. When people phone and ask me to do something, I can then say, "I'm terribly sorry, that's my day with my wife". It is a freeing way of life. A 100 days a year for me is enough for making money, there is no point in making more; and I find I do as much work in 100 days as I used to in a year.

> 'If somebody asks what you do, and you can reply in one sentence, you're a failure. You should need half an hour'

'I go to a lot of management courses and try to turn these managers into portfolio people – "don't just be a systems manager for IBM, don't be a one-dimensional character, become a portfolio person now". I am trying to make such a lifestyle respectable for career people. If somebody asks what you do, and you can reply in one sentence, you're a failure. You should need half an hour.'

Jobs are continually going to get shorter in years, smaller in hours. More people will be self-employed or will be offered bits of jobs rather than full-time, lifetime jobs. Most of us, at some time in our lives, are going to find that our jobs no longer dominate our lives. We shall need to find a new organising principle.

If, rather than think of life as work and leisure, we think of it as a portfolio of activities – some of which we do for money, some for interest, some for pleasure, some for a cause – that way, we do not have to look for the occupation that miraculously combines job satisfaction, financial reward and pleasant friends all in one package. As with any portfolio we get different returns from different parts and if one fails the whole is not ruined.

Professor Charles Handy, 1 Fairhaven, 73 Putney Hill, London SW15 3NT (tel 081 788 1610).

Chapter nine

WELFARE

Brokerage and Direct Payment for those with disabilities

Nancy Marlett

Independent Service Brokerage, winner of a Social Inventions Award, is a scheme developed by Heather MacLean, Nancy Marlett and others of the Calgary Association for Independent Living. It provides the help of a 'broker' intermediary and a small committee of family, friends and professionals, to enable those with disabilities to identify their own financial and other needs, which are then funded by the state. The disabled person is thus in charge, interviewing and selecting would-be helpers.

> 'The innovation consists of providing community support in the form of an independent agent – ie not paid by the government or the service providers – to help persons with exceptional needs secure and manage their own funds'

This article deals with the progress made in Alberta, Canada, in redressing the lack of power experienced by persons with disabilities and continuing health needs. The innovation consists of providing community support in the form of an independent agent – ie not paid by the government or the service providers – to help persons with exceptional needs secure and manage their own funds.

This concept marks the final step in the recognition of the rights of persons with continuing needs that started with the processes of de-institutionalisation and community care. It turns the user of services into a purchaser of services. It makes the service providers accountable to the person, not to an agency or to the government. It removes many of the barriers that make it impossible to become full citizens.

Many groups and sectors have been involved in making the innovation a reality. Yet, although it is being used by over 15,000 persons, there is no official policy in existence. The central impetus of the invention has been the working relationship of consumers (persons with disabilities) and government officials and the University of Calgary rehabilitation studies programme.

Such grass roots innovation may be easier in a country like Canada which has ten provinces able to experiment with concepts on a small scale. Although small scale innovation may be more difficult in Britain, there are an increasing number of instances where the funds needed to prevent unnecessary institutionalisation are given directly to the person or family to purchase the services needed. In the UK such direct payment exists as a well-kept secret. In the past four years, however, persons in Alberta have had access to a broker who can act as an independent agent able to work for the consumer in the process of securing and implementing direct payment.

The broker

The broker is the instrumental link between the person with a continuing exceptional need, the funding sources and the resources and services in the community. The broker advises and assists the person and his family or friends to identify the supports needed, secure the funding resources and to negotiate and set up customised services to the person's specifications.

This does not mean that the current method of providing services, where agencies are funded to provide services to a target group, will or should disappear. For those lucky enough to fit into group programmes or preferring to have agencies design and provide services, this alternative will continue. It does mean that there is an alternative for those who are not currently being adequately served by agencies and for those who are willing to assume the responsibility of managing their own services or supports.

The term 'broker' conveys a business connotation that makes some uneasy, and in reality the broker does encourage a small business approach to providing customised services for persons with disabilities and their families. A broker may be an increasingly important person as privatisation continues in Britain. With direct grants to seniors who require institutionalisation, the individual and the family can easily be lost in the

Shirley's Story

I was just an ordinary woman – a mother, a wife, a hockey fan. Then I gradually lost control of my legs, my arms, and my physical strength, of my rights as a woman apart from my husband.

He and I would have had to separate in order for me to qualify financially for the help I needed to stay at home. We wouldn't get a divorce, so I had to go to an institution, where I lost control of all the little things that make life human – when and what to eat, shopping, someone to talk to in the early morning light.

Behind the walls that shut out my world I found others who shared my quiet anger and together we put our hopes into beliefs of independent living, of taking charge, of supporting each other and anyone else who shared our dreams.

Each one of us brings our strength. My outward stubbornness comes from an inner quiet and trust – that there is someone up there. He is a sculptor – when he takes away a little bit here he adds a little bit there, moulding and trying to make a better person. I just have to keep looking for the chances that his changes bring.

Now I'm taking charge and living on my own, in spite of your ideas that 'people like me' should be in institutions because it is 'efficient' – even though I can hire my own staff to live on my own for much less; in spite of your need to protect me, to see me as sick, to look after me when I want to look after myself; and my own feelings of guilt that I am causing those who love me pain and anxiety because of my need to risk, to be on my own, to be in control of my life.

'Now I'm taking charge and living on my own. I can hire my own staff to live on my own for much less'

I know about your fear that no one will be there to rescue me if something goes wrong. I know you want me to be safe and secure – to accept my disability.

I may need someone to do the things I can't. I may need to use machines more nowadays, but I've got it together, I've taken charge, done what I had to do. I'm still just an ordinary woman, living each day as it comes. I just wish I could physically reach out and touch someone.

Shirley Garth

rush to the market place.

There are two versions (with many variations within each) of personalised funding (funding allocated to the individual based on specific needs) that could work in the UK.

Individualised funding

(1) Individualised funding, where the funding is 'attached' to the person, but managed and monitored by a third party. Given the current system of grants through the DHSS and the need for local authorities to top up allocations to voluntary agencies to meet some clients' exceptional needs, it is conceivable that a brokerage model might be seen as a means of negotiating these extra funds so that the existing voluntary agencies or new services could provide the services.

It is also possible, given the Kent experience with community alternatives for persons with serious behavioural problems, and a number of private, non-profit-making schemes run by parents, that a model similar to the popular Community Living model in Canada may be feasible in Britain. In this the agency broker prepares funding estimates with the person or family and assists them to secure the funding from a central government source. The agency then works to provide services to the client as requested.

'The agency is accountable: if the person is not satisfied with the service provided, she can pull her money out and find another more satisfactory arrangement'

This model has the advantage of dual accountability – the agency is accountable to the government and the person for the quality of services. In theory if the person is not satisfied with the service provided, she can pull her money out and find another more satisfactory arrangement.

It is imperative within this community living model to establish an independent board of parents and hopefully consumers to monitor the services and be advocates on behalf of the person and families where they cannot do this for themselves.

Direct funding

(2) Direct Funding. In the other version, once the funding is negotiated, it is given directly to the person, family or person willing to assist. If individuals are able to manage on their own, they do so in the same manner that those with independent wealth have always done.

If individuals are not able or prepared to manage their services on their own, they have a number of options – they could hire an agency to provide the services for them (as is the case in privately funded special care), or they could have the broker (or volunteer committee of people they select) assist in setting up and monitoring services for them.

In Canada the role of supporting persons in their quest to establish their own lifestyle seems best suited to the emerging Independent Living Centres. The Calgary Association for Independent Living pioneered an exciting set of services to help disabled persons manage their own lives; including a computerised information bank of practical support that people may be looking for – from attendants, to people able to alter clothing. This data bank is run for their peers by persons with disabilities and provides the essential safety net for those willing to try to make a go of it on their own.

Joshua committees

The heart of the organisation is the peer support programme that puts people in touch with others that they can share ideas and time with. This support is essential for those who might otherwise be too timid to try living on their own. Joshua committees – so named because they are a means of people coming together to bring down the walls of oppression –

consist of people that the person chooses to help them in their dreams. These committees have meant that even those with very complex medical or behavioural needs and those who are very handicapped in making decisions or making their needs known can have access to direct payment. The committees can take a lot of time to develop if the person has lost all contact with family and friends through being in an institution, but the results have been well worth the effort.

27 persons whose needs were considered too difficult to handle in the community made such dramatic improvements that many of us are now reconsidering whether agencies and institutions inadvertently create many of the problems that disappear when the person is listened to.

Centres for independent living

Britain also has centres run by disabled people that are there to help individuals take control over their lives. They are called Centres for Integrated Living (CIL) and two, one in Hampshire and the other in Derbyshire, are already offering a service similar in some ways to that of the Calgary Association for Independent Living. A broker could work for the CIL and would assist the person and his family to secure funds through the local authority. The Centres are the ideal community resource to assist the person to manage his own services. Hampshire has produced an excellent resource for managing services including securing funds, hiring staff, personnel management and accountability of funds.

> 'A broker could work to assist the person and his family to secure funds'

The British CILs face the same funding restrictions that similar Centres do in Canada. Because they do not offer hard services – eg housing and vocational services – they do not qualify for service dollars. Indeed in Canada, Centres avoid offering direct services because they would create conflicts of interest – not only assisting people to manage their own lives but providing the services.

These Centres support any person with a disability and therefore do not easily fit into the charity game that seems to prefer to fund simple causes – eg learning difficulties, the blind etc – they do not fit easily in the competition between specific disability groups for the most worthy of charity dollars. Most independent or integrated living Centres prefer to remain small, use volunteer effort, earn money or find new funding sources to make sure that they can act as advocates on behalf of the people they are supporting.

Given the current climate in Britain, it is quite conceivable that freelance service brokers could emerge who would act with or on behalf of the person to assist the family to secure funding, to locate or develop services, and could be available to help negotiate contracts or to assist the person or family to monitor services. In Canada there are freelance brokerage services emerging for persons with disabilities and for aged persons. To date, we have not solved the questions related to payments for freelance brokers, but nevertheless a committed group are pioneering the options.

Nancy Marlett, 4th Floor, Education Tower, University of Calgary, 2500 University Drive, Calgary T2N 2N4, Canada (tel 403 284 7511). In the UK: c/o School of Education, Open University, Milton Keynes, MK7 6AA, Bucks (tel 0908 652649).

By and for those with disabilities
Edis Bevan

The Open University in Milton Keynes, in conjunction with the organisation Disabled Persons International, has set up a research centre run by and for disabled people. The aim of the centre is to encourage and support research by the disabled into topics that they themselves feel to be of importance, and particularly into the many difficulties placed on people with disabilities in relating to a world designed exclusively for the able-bodied.

> 'The aim of the centre is to encourage and support research by the disabled into topics that they themselves feel to be of importance, particularly into the difficulties in relating to a world designed for the able-bodied'

The hope is that a major part of their work will be to direct research towards social inventions as opposed to technical fixes through hardware aids. Disabled people too often live in information ghettos. They are in contact with immediate family and with diverse experts on their 'conditions' but they are peripheral to the information cores that sustain power and influence in society and help determine the distribution of resources. They suffer from 'Information Disability'. It is important that new patterns of information exchange be built up to break the walls of the ghettos.

The Centre is seeking information for its database on existing research efforts by disabled people and on organisations controlled by the disabled around the world.

Edis Bevan, Disabled Persons International Research Centre, Gardner Building, Open University, Walton Hall, Milton Keynes MK7 6AA (tel 0908 653231).

Creativity for those with mental handicaps

'Parcels' is a co-operative with a dozen members, providing services to the Exeter Health Authority and City Council. It has designed a resource library of various visual, dramatic and sound media 'parcels' for stimulating those with mental or other handicaps, helping them to develop life skills needed to live in the community.

Fifteen foot puppets, giant tortoises, shadow theatre, a gigantic walk-in apple and a giant board game for wheelchairs covering an entire floor, are among the 'parcels' the organisation's minibus can deliver.

Parcels workers are artists, musicians, model makers, a carpenter and drama assistants. Their aim is to help those with mental handicaps to learn to grow, open up to their surroundings and have fun.

'Parcels', Mickelwright Centre, Whipton, Exeter, EX1 3RB (tel 0392 64497).

Musical soundbeams for the handicapped

'A way to introduce very young children in school to the delights of making music through movement – a child just running towards the machine, for instance, produces complete scales of notes as the child approaches'

Edward Williams, Richard Monkhouse and Robin Wood at Electronic Music Studios in Truro, Cornwall, have produced a simple machine enabling handicapped people with minimal movements to control big majestic sounds. Up to four linked ultrasonic echo-sounders, connected to a music synthesiser, detect the presence and range of any part of the body entering the beams, so that minute movements up to six metres away can be used to create dramatic musical effects. Their machine also has potential for dancers and other performing artists, and could be a way to introduce very young children in school to the delights of making music through movement – a child just running towards the machine, for instance, produces complete scales of notes as the child approaches.

Over 60 systems are now in use in special schools in the UK.
Robin Wood, EMS, Trendeal Vean Barn, Ladock, Truro, Cornwall TR2 4NW (tel 0726 883265). Prices start at £775 per unit. The potential of this scheme for children and the handicapped was highly commended in the Social Inventions Awards.

Blind receive Guardian newspaper via home computer

Adapted extract from an item in the Guardian by Peter Large.
The Guardian newspaper's computers are now disgorging the full news text of the paper every night over British Telecom data lines to AirCall Teletext, which then uses the same technology that produces teletext pages of news on the home TV screen to broadcast the Guardian to blind users' home computers.

'Computer software enables the blind customer to search the whole paper, using key words, in less than four minutes'

The RNIB's new technical development department, in a project led by Cathy Rundle, has written computer software that enables the customer to search the whole paper, using key words, in less than four minutes.

There is a braille version available as well as the microchip-generated voice version. The whole package costs at least £1,500, with six local authority libraries – at Ashton-under

Lyne, Exeter, Gateshead, Leicester, Paisley and Sheffield – providing a trial service.

The Guardian sees the trials as the initial route to instant delivery of newspapers to customers' home computers for screen reading or print-out.

Textured paving stones for the blind

Throughout Japanese cities, specially textured paving stones embedded in pavements guide blind pedestrians along a safe route. A change in texture – to lateral bars, lengthwise bars, knobs etc – indicates a change in direction, stairs or obstructions ahead. They also mark the edge of platforms, helping sighted people too.

From '283 Useful Ideas from Japan', by Leonard Koren (published by Chronicle Books, San Francisco, 1988, and available for £5·95 from Neal Street East shop, 5 Neal St, London WC2, tel 071 240 0135).

'Barefoot' Social Skills course

The People to People Social Skills course, started in 1985, has been the first voluntary, community-based social skills training group in this country. The course runs for eight weeks in Stevenage and each class lasts roughly one and a half hours. The course fee is £10, although this is waived in cases of hardship.

People to People offers training in social skills to people who suffer shyness or a lack of confidence. It covers relaxation, territoriality, body language and the use of voice and spoken language in the context of everyday social and work situations. It does not attempt to cover subjects for which expert guidance or therapy is necessary.

'It is not necessary for the organisers of training courses in social skills to have formal qualifications'

It is the brainchild of Dr Keith Stoll, a consultant clinical psychologist with considerable experience in the field of interpersonal skills, who believes that it is not necessary for the organisers of training courses in social skills to have formal qualifications.

During the course, the leaders ensure that nobody is feeling excluded or threatened by the group and it is emphasised that it is natural to feel nervous (one of the aims of the course is to point out the positive aspects of being shy and to give people permission to feel as they do).

After each class, the leaders discuss individual progress and will, if necessary, telephone members of the class to talk about any difficulties they may be having with the course.

Training sessions for leaders are organised locally from time to time, using the experience of volunteers who have already led courses. This training is freely available to people from other areas who would like to start their own groups. The detailed notes for course leaders are also available at cost, on condition that the notes are *not* used in connection with private or commercial classes.

Future plans include the strengthening of contacts with the medical profession and the creation of new groups elsewhere, perhaps working under their central guidance.

Alec Roscoe, People to People, 25 Temple Court, Bengeo, Hertford.

Lambeth Caring Houses Trust

Lambeth Caring Houses Trust was established by Linda Vellacott in 1978 to provide a homely rather than hostel atmosphere, where the residents live together as much as possible like a family group. There are three homes each housing ten single men with a variety of problems, who have formerly led either unsettled or institutionalised lives, and who need some degree of support in order to live in the community. A team of six workers looks after the three households, and the small 'human scale' of the organisation is reckoned as a vital factor in its success.

Creative development for the residents is encouraged through individual programmes for their journey towards health and wholeness. Small group activities, one-to-one therapy, body work, the relationship to the natural world, to animals, to trees and the countryside, are all explored.

The work is innovatory and cost effective in comparison to NHS psychiatric hospitals where drug therapy is the norm.

Lambeth Caring Houses Trust, 184 Stockwell Road, London SW9 9TF (tel 071 274 5736).

A newspaper sold by the homeless

Information extracted from The Big Issue No. 2, from an article in the Times by Melinda Wittstock, and from an article in the Independent by Imogen Edwards-Jones.

The Big Issue is a monthly 28 page colour tabloid, initiated by the Body Shop, and modelled on Street News, an equivalent publication in New York with a circulation of 150,000. 'The Big Issue is sold by homeless people as an alternative to the humiliation of begging. About 1000 of London's 75,000 homeless sell the paper, working in trained teams of five or ten, and keeping 40p of the 50p cover price of each paper sold. The remaining 10p goes to housing and training organisations to cover administrative expenses.

The cost of producing the newspaper is due to be covered by advertising revenue.

'It's no different from begging, except that now I feel that I have some dignity and self-respect'

Tracy Banstead, who sleeps on the Strand and has been on the streets for four and a half years, is a team leader selling the papers at Charing Cross station. She says 'It's no different from begging, except that now I feel that I have some dignity and

self-respect.' She has noticed that her team mates are now buying trainers, socks, clothing, etc.

The paper itself is a mixture of stylish articles not aimed at the homeless and material that is, such as a page of photos of missing persons. It even includes a number of social improvement suggestions, such as a proposal for a Find-out-who-your-neighbours-are day; and for a government recommendation, as in Sweden, that motorists, when their cars are stationary for more than one minute, should turn off the engines.

Editorial comment

Perhaps The Big Issue could research and serialise a 1990s version of the 'Project London Free' booklet of information, which in the 1970s was distributed free to 14,000 poor Londoners, telling them everything that was available for free in London: from change for photocopied pound notes at Hammersmith tube station to test driving Rolls Royces, plus more vital information in between, such as where to get free food, accommodation and entertainment.

The Big Issue, 25 The Green, Richmond, Surrey TW9 1LY (tel 081 332 6700; fax 081 332 0954).

Giving meal coupons to beggars

Adapted from the Weekly World News and the National Enquirer (USA), both monitored for the Institute by Roger Knights; and from the Independent.

'The whole idea was to separate the hungry from the hustler'

An alternative to giving beggars in the streets cash could be to give them food vouchers or Luncheon Vouchers. The American equivalents include a project run by the Emergency Aid Resource Center for the Homeless in Houston, Texas. This sells coupons for a free meal – in $10 booklets of 10 coupons, which are purchased by 'good samaritans'. 'The whole idea was to separate the hungry from the hustler, the needy from the greedy,' said Maxene Johnston, president of a Los Angeles organisation which has operated a coupon programme since 1989.

Berkeley, California, has a similar programme which has successfully discouraged people from begging for money to spend on alcohol and drugs. Beggars can redeem vouchers, which are sold for 25 cents each at a dozen stores, at any of 30 businesses offering food, laundry services, bus fares and even hot showers. Of 20,000 vouchers printed so far, about 10,000 have been sold and 2,700 have been redeemed.

Charity coupons

A letter writer to the Times, Robin Williamson, has suggested a slight variant of the above – that UK charities working with the homeless get together to offer 'charity vouchers'. People would buy a book (£1 vouchers in books of five or ten). Each voucher could then be exchanged for food or practical help at any of the charities taking part, with addresses and perhaps a free helpline telephone number printed on the ticket. The further advantage would be that when a voucher is exchanged the charities can offer counselling as well as sustenance.

Robin Williamson, Greenaway, London Road, Balcombe, Haywards Heath, West Sussex.

Editorial comment

The snag in practice (compared with a food coupon or Luncheon Voucher idea, which gives access to a wide variety of businesses) might be the understandable unwillingness of charitable organisations to turn away those without vouchers.

Flix Club for young girls

This was one of the prize winners in the Swedish Institute for Social Inventions' competition.

> '13-20 year olds in Stockholm who got into bad company and habits, in 1989 formed a club to keep themselves and others out of danger'

13-20 year olds in Stockholm who got into bad company and habits, in 1989 formed a club to keep themselves and others out of danger. They've organised make-up evenings, ski trips, and rafting; and they've cooked, sewn, ridden, body-built and video-viewed together. They meet twice a week and also patrol the streets with social workers, and visit schools. They have inspired several other such clubs in Sweden.

Flix, Olof Palmes gata 27, S-111 22 Stockholm, Sweden (tel 46 8796 9699).

Community Caring Fund

Moray Chalmers

In our local community at present, small functions are held periodically to provide a fund in the event of a person needing expensive or special medical treatment. The fund is known as 'Community Caring Fund'.

Almost £8,000 was raised in 18 months to provide an electric wheelchair for a person crippled in a road accident and who had only the use of his left hand. Another patient had kidney stones which required laser treatment that had to be performed in a London hospital and was not available on the National Health Service.

Moray Chalmers, Migdale Mill, Bonar Bridge, Sutherland, IV24 3AR (tel 08632 521).

Missing people's photos on taxis and shopping bags

Item from a Sydney magazine (Australia), monitored for the Institute by Valerie Yule.

Photographs of missing people will be printed on tens of millions of plastic supermarket shopping bags under a plan by police and retailers to find the people.

Several major supermarket chains, including retail giant Woolworths, have already expressed interest in the scheme, which follows the highly successful Operation Taxi set up last month.

Already one Sydney teenage runaway has been found by the project which features photographs of missing people on the back of taxis in capital cities.

In the latest scheme, planned by Mr Charlie Yip of Adantos Pty Ltd, a Sydney-based consulting firm, at least one photograph of a missing person will be featured on one side of white plastic shopping bags.

Charrier bags

Charles Smith

'Charrier Bags' are similar to plastic carrier bags which are at present sold in shops and stores for 5p. Ten major charities will be asked to join the scheme by lending their names and logos for the Charrier Bags. The bags would be wholesaled to the shops by the manufacturer in packs of 50 (five for each charity), and would then be retailed at 1p more than ordinary bags. This additional 1p would be paid by the shopper in the knowledge that it would be passed on to the charity whose logo the bag bears. Shoppers would also be encouraged by a poster and media campaign to ask for a Charrier Bag by name. Stores which have their name on their bag at present would have it included on the Charrier Bags they order.

The scheme would be operated by the bag manufacturer who would divide the money raised equally between the ten charities selected. The selection of the charities would be carried out by the bag manufacturer and the Charrier Bag designers Smith and Strom. Shoppers would not be able to select specific Charrier Bags but would have to take the first one offered.

Charles Smith, 60 Ommaney Road, London SE14 5NT.

Bed and breakfast money for Oxfam

Rosemary Schlee

My husband and I started this Bed and Breakfast scheme in about 1984 with one hostess; a third of the charge is given to Oxfam. We try to raise over £10,000 clear for Oxfam each year, and have managed to enrol 40 households in Woodbridge, Ipswich, Felixstowe and other local towns and villages (also Cambridge, Norfolk and Hampshire). We badly need people to come forward who live in attractive small or medium-sized towns, and who would be ready to run the scheme (with all our know-how and assistance) in their own areas. It has to be an attractive town, otherwise you would not get enough people wanting to stay there, and we do not think big cities suitable.

That spare room could be working for you and for Oxfam. Local regulations do not apply on this scale. Guests appear about 6pm, go out to eat and are gone by 9am. So far no one has bounced cheques or asked to sit downstairs or to watch TV. A married woman earns over £2,800 before tax is due. The notional costs of guests, with a proportion of your house overheads and rates, will make tax unlikely. When a third of the proceeds is going to Oxfam, tax is all the more unlikely. If guests look uncongenial at the door, keep them talking, then remember that last night's guests had asked to return. A couple for one night in summer could bring in £28, less a third to Oxfam, leaves £18-70, less £2-50 summer costs, means £16-20 clear profit to you. And Oxfam has cleared £50,000 so far.

Rosemary Schlee, Deben Lodge, Melton Road, Woodbridge, Suffolk IP12 1NH (tel 0394 382740).

Auction of Promises: how to raise £16,000 in one evening

Kara Conti

The following concerns an auction of services which on two occasions has raised over £16,000 for King Alfred School, London NW11, and which could be copied by other schools, by churches or by any community groups with a strong local following.

Well it worked a treat! Just like they said it would. When Maria Fforde, King Alfred School parent of many years, left the school, she bequeathed to us a large brown envelope of correspondence on the subject of school auctions in America – on how they were run and how phenomenally successful they were. The material sat about on our files. 1987 was the year it bore fruit.

> 'An auction of services and goods promised by parents – each one a literally price-less item not normally available to be purchased. The idea captured everyone's imagination'

The result was an auction of services and goods promised by parents – each one a literally price-less item not normally available to be purchased. To our delight, we found that an enthusiastic auction committee and a hard-working parent-staff network were able to whip up 222 lots to auction in a couple of months.

'In-house solicitation' our American friends called it. The response from parents was amazing. The idea captured everyone's imagination. Parents were able to offer what came easy to them and cost virtually nothing, giving others the opportunity to make unique purchases, with the school getting all the cash.

A chance lift resulted in our finding our very own parent auctioneer, Roger Keverne, and quite wonderful he was. Four and a quarter hours he sat there and never lost his voice or temper and never went to the loo!

By the end of the first quarter hour we had made over £1,000, by one hour £3,000, by two hours £7,000 and so it went on. We could not believe our eyes and ears. Committee members stood around with inane smiles all over their faces. So all right, it went on a long time, but there were still over two hundred people there at midnight. Towards the end, huge sums were still being reached, for example £660 for a week in a French farmhouse, £400 for a box for six at Tottenham Football Club with lunch.

Our final sums show that, after costs are deducted, we have made £16,000. Not bad, eh?

Kara Conti, c/o King Alfred School, North End Road, London NW11 (tel 081 455 9601).

In-House Solicitation

Ed: Here is some information from the large brown envelope from America mentioned above.

In-House Solicitation: Call up every parent. Make some specific and imaginative suggestions as to possible offers. Some of the best sellers are holiday homes, sports tickets, autographed equipment, dinners at luxury restaurants, meals made by parents, party entertainment (clowns, magicians), and things like bikes, handmade clothes and doll's houses.

For the King Alfred School Auction they produced a Receipt Form noting the donated item and the donor's name, address and telephone number; and a Purchase Slip confirming to the purchaser what had been got and how to contact the donor. With hindsight, they wish they had produced a third form to tell the donor about the purchase (or that the item remained unsold).

222 lots for auction

King Alfred School printed a 44 page A5 booklet describing the 222 lots for auction. Here, to stir your imagination in case you should contemplate holding a similar auction, are some examples.

- Lot 23, a tea party for twenty in a large garden complete with musical interlude by professional classical guitarist.
- 33, a gourmet continental breakfast with a selection of coffees and/or tea and continental papers on a Sunday, served at your home.
- 36, novelty birthday cake made to buyer's specification.
- 67, a day in an artist's studio, materials and model supplied.
- 95, seamstress will make any article of clothing for you if you provide the material and pattern.
- 103, bathing and grooming of your dog, large or small.
- 107, a valuation of your antique furniture by an expert.
- 109, the use of a word processor to type thesis or small manuscript.
- 110, textile repair for up to four hours (textiles, tapestries, embroideries, etc).
- 113, three hours' gardening.
- 115, solicitors will convey your property (sale or purchase).
- 121, a logo/letterhead design for a small business, ideas, designs, artwork and typesetting.
- 123, four hours of biodynamic massage.
- 128, two year course of psychoanalysis.
- 137, a day's micro-computer consultancy.
- 138, eight Latin lessons.
- 139, five hours' pottery tuition.
- 142, one hour's skating instruction.
- 159, a day out in a Rolls Royce with a chauffeur.
- 161, tea for two at the House of Lords.
- 164, a visit for two around a newspaper office.
- 183, a holiday farmhouse near Montelimar, France.
- 196, a weekend for up to eight in a Peak District cottage.
- 199, a fortnight's daily house visiting to care for your plants or pets whilst you are away on holiday.
- 201, a weekend sailing on a 33 foot yacht with a qualified skipper.

- 207, a half hour flying lesson.
- 209, one day's fly fishing.
- 213, acting audition or interview coaching.
- 214, a speech written for any occasion by a comedy scriptwriter.

Other useful titbits of information from the booklet's introduction:

- Entrance £2-50, viewing from 6 to 8pm, live auction 8pm, buffet and bar throughout. Sealed bids from those unable to attend will be received at the school offices up until (two days before).
- *From the General Rules:* The school makes no warrants or representation of any kind with respect to any items or service sold. Please inspect where possible.
- All items must be paid for in full before the buyer's departure for the evening.
- Unless otherwise specified, all auctioned services must be used within one year after the auction and dates and times are to be arranged between the buyer and donor at their mutual convenience.

A detailed booklet, 'Auction of Promises', on how to run these auctions, is available for £1-95 (incl. p&p) from the Institute for Social Inventions, 20 Heber Road, London NW2 6AA (tel 081 208 2853; fax 081 208 2853).

Mandatory A4 introductory appeals

Nicholas Albery

To alleviate the fund-raising burden for small charities applying to the hundreds of foundations that give money to charities, my proposal is as follows:

> 'In future these foundations only consider an appeal that is on one single-sided sheet of A4 paper'

As many of the major or minor trusts that can be persuaded would get together and announce that in future their letter-openers will not pass on to them any appeal (even from a body seeking a further grant) that is not in a simple standard format – one single-sided sheet of A4 paper. Any more bulky applicants will simply, if they are lucky and if it is the trust's practice to reply to all applications, get a postcard informing them of this single-sheet policy (the word would soon get around anyway). Then the trusts would decide which applications they wanted more details about, and would send these select few a small amount, say about £10, as an initial donation to help cover the cost of preparing these further details. (This suggested payment is not an essential part of my proposal, but does seems fair. The cost of making these small donations might well be covered by the saving in the trust's staff time, compared with having to plough through the old bulkier applications.)

Any cost to the trusts would also be slight compared to the massive saving of time and resources for small voluntary organisations throughout the UK, who could then get by on a couple of days' fund-raising a year. There are of course a number of snags to this proposal that need ironing out:

successful applicants would perhaps need to be given a special code to put on their envelopes to ensure that their evaluation reports, publications, journals and progress reports were not dumped by the letter opener. And being able to get this follow-up information through to the trusts would give them something of an inside track, especially as it would hardly be feasible to prevent information about future projects seeking funding from appearing in such mailings. Nor do I think my proposal would lead to widespread redundancies for fundraising staff, as no doubt the big organisations would redeploy their fundraising effort to evade the A4 limitation by lobbying in other more subtle ways. But the saving for the smaller voluntary organisations would remain.

Steven Burkeman of the Joseph Rowntree Charitable Trust believes that such a scheme would have two main disadvantages: in summary, how can there be a 'funding relationship' if general, non-personalised appeals are accepted? And, secondly, an A4 page would be too uniform a restriction to tell you enough about an organisation.

But what I am proposing is merely an introductory (mandatory) stage, an A4 sheet sent to any and every trust that the applicant, by going through a trusts directory, thinks may be able to help. That is only the first stage: then the trust can respond if it wishes and build up the 'funding relationship' Steven Burkeman speaks of and can request a more detailed picture of the applicant.

Large trusts such as the various Rowntrees Trusts have to reject a thousand or more applications each year. For the vast majority of these rejections, surely an A4 page would be enough to tell the trust that they were not right for it? Yet some trusts want things like copies of audited accounts even for the initial approach or, worse still, four copies of everything. Or they expect you to write off first for their guidelines, or to fill in their own forms (which can only be one using an obsolete typewriter, not a word processor) – all terribly resource and time consuming.

> 'Regular mailings to the large trusts, and any voluntary organisation could, for a price, get an insert application in the mailing'

Taking this a stage further: if my proposal were widely accepted by trusts, a body such as the Directory of Social Change or the Charities Aid Foundation could make available address labels of trusts in off-the-shelf or computer-tailor-made categories (for instance, trusts over £100,000 p.a, peace and disarmament trusts, etc) which voluntary organisations could obtain. Or this coordinating body could announce regular mailings to say 1,000 large trusts, and any voluntary organisation could, for a price, get an insert application in the mailing by sending in its A4 page (which could be reprinted for it). Thus, at best, total time spent sending out one's annual appeal could be reduced to the time it takes to send one A4 page to the coordinating body.

Lukes Fitzherbert at Directory for Social Change seems to like my proposal, and is contemplating asking trusts next time he circularises them to tick a box if they want to specify this method of approach in their directory entries.

Nicholas Albery, 20 Heber Road, London NW2 6AA (tel 081 208 2853; fax 081 452 6434).

Chapter ten

CRIME

Terrorists with neutron bombs?

Conrad Hopman

The following article discusses how to deal with the likelihood that terrorists will gain access to chemical and nuclear weapons.

These comments may be of interest to those who are concerned with security. Several processes which have been going on quietly for some time are now combining to produce an unstable situation. Great and rapid changes may be expected; those who fail to read the omens could be hurt.

Frontiers are losing their significance as nations become increasingly interdependent, forming trade associations and common markets. The global communications network not only makes the world seem smaller; societies are opening up, revealing themselves, becoming more vulnerable to each other. Weapons are smaller, deadlier, preciser; information on their fabrication and use is more readily available. So more nations and organisations are acquiring access to nuclear, chemical, force field or other arms and more hobbyists and chemists are able to assemble or synthesise very nasty things in their garages.

'The essential components of a neutron bomb can be carried in a back pack'

It is not to be expected that urban guerrillas will use explosives forever, nor that their activities will continue to be as muted as they are now. The essential components of a neutron bomb can be carried in a back pack, the rest obtained from local electronics and hardware stores, the whole thing assembled in a rented apartment and set off in anonymity from half a world away. Poison gas is no harder to smuggle or make in clandestine labs than drugs.

Consider the following scenario:

Ten kg of a very poisonous gas are released in a subway ventilator during a rush hour. There are several thousand casualties. More or less at the same time data diskettes, video cassettes and letters are thrown into mail boxes and over garden walls, addressed to newsmedia organisations. They are in different languages – and apparently come from different Attacker Organisations. When pieced together the message to the Victim Government is roughly as follows:

'Many other deadly devices have been hidden in many places (ready to poison water mains, blast nuclear or chemical plants, etc). They will be used if our demands below are not met to the letter.

'We regret the loss of innocent lives deeply. The Government must give X million to the family of each person killed or injured. The necessary funds must be taken proportionately from the 5% wealthiest people in the country. This must be done within one month.

'No attempt whatsoever must be made to find us or our weapons. No rewards may be offered, no pictures posted, no house searches made for any such purpose. All customs and police are to be removed from all sea and airports. All walls, mines, watch towers and officials are to be removed from all frontiers. All police and customs data files and computers must be destroyed.

'Three quarters of the military and police budgets are to be redistributed as follows: X millions to families with yearly incomes of less than ..., Y millions to charities A, B, ... Z [some of which are abroad].

'All land confiscated from farmers during the last five years is to be returned to them at no cost by the confiscating institutions.

'All prisons are to be opened and their inmates freed.

'The following are to be destroyed completely: all nuclear weapons, test sites, launch pads, these types of warships, tanks and planes: ... The destruction is to be televised and the wreckage left accessible for public inspection at the following locations... by ../../.. All other depots of weapons and munitions must be left totally unguarded and people invited to help themselves. Everyone is invited to report any incidences of non-compliance to these orders via CB radio or the official newsmedia which must broadcast them. Anonymous checks will be made to ensure that this is done.'

The Government refuses to deal with the terrorists. There are riots – many people demand, some get, gas masks and guns (making them impervious to police tear gas and able to shoot back). The army is put on alert and a nationwide search turns up some more gas – which may have been left as a warning. There are false alarms, some people are caught and confess. The Government maintains it has the situation under control. Six weeks later power lines are cut and another two devices go off at night in neighbourhoods where many high officials live. In a while letters and cartoon cassettes are found in Athens, Berlin, Calcutta which make headlines around the world. The demands are repeated. Additionally, the Government is ordered to have all overseas bases closed and troops brought home. Several prominent politicians and generals must be shot in front of TV cameras. Their corpses are to be left on Main Square. This time, compliance is more or less complete. Once frontiers are open, anyone can bring anything in and escape with impunity. The flow of more or less organised illegal immigrants swells to a flood.

Conventional overt tactics of warfare – standing armies, star wars gear, battleships – are useless against such terrorist or covert tactics. As nuclear and other arms proliferate, conventional tactics are increasingly useless against each other too. There is no telling how high local warlets could escalate – several billion dead, nuclear winter, the biosphere poisoned for millennia. So military establishments tend to keep each other stalemated in postures of heavily armed non-intervention. Having nothing else to do, their arms tend to turn inwards where they meet with less resistance. Hence the dreary scene of military coups and dictatorships with a 'delicate balance of terror' background. Conventional tactics are very expensive. At present about one sixth of the earth's produce – about 1 to 2 million $ a minute – is spent on arms. This enormous burden is everywhere crushing the life it is supposed to protect. The dreary scene is also one of enormous protection rackets which appear to justify each other in mutual tacit collusion. But they are, in fact, becoming worse than useless. We would obviously all be much better off if we could be rid of such rackets altogether.

'Conventional overt tactics of warfare are useless against terrorist or covert tactics'

In the above example it was assumed that covert tactics were used to kill many thousands of people. This was probably unnecessarily harsh. A society does not have to be totally disarmed and disorganised in order to be taken; crippling or replacing its pinnacle of power may suffice. A lot can be done with economic take-over, media or union control... The Attacker Organisations' identities and motives were not revealed. Perhaps the Attacker Organisations were in fact several groups which had various aims. But these could probably have been achieved with fewer or no deaths and more use of clever psychology. There are advantages to using covert tactics humanely: it is easier to enlist the population to help Attacker Organisations or, as in the example, to ensure that demands are obeyed. The more a society's distribution of wealth and power is skewed, the more unemployment, discontent, hate there is within it, the easier it can be got at internally with covert tactics.

The basic difference between covert and conventional tactics is that in conventional tactics protagonists know who and where they are. Secrets and surprise are essential to both – in this sense conventional tactics are covert also. Acquiring a country which has been reduced to radioactive rubble or poisoned by Agent Orange is not as rewarding as taking it over with most homes, factories and people intact. But, since they risk revealing themselves, any Attacker Organisations with such intentions must be careful how they do this. Other organisations might well be inclined to combine against them – especially if the Attacker Organisations are perceived as being brutal. But covert tactics can be used beneficially in ways that overt tactics cannot. There is a potential here to give new hope to oppressed, wasted lives, re-green countrysides which have been exhausted by taxation and erosion. If Attacker Organisations demand ransom, they must ask it for many besides themselves. They may be able to force their victims to self-destruct – but do not stand to gain much from doing so. So there may be an element of altruism here; perhaps a hint of chivalrous ideals. In any case, covert tactics require bravery, loyalty and initiative in ways that the recent wars did not.

'It would not be surprising to see covert tactics used increasingly by religious, ecological and pacifist organisations'

Covert tactics are not new. Nations which indulge in covert tactics themselves are easy targets for retaliation. But they can, and do, employ others for such purposes. Covert tactics instigated by foreigners will probably be made to seem locally inspired and vice versa. Arms dealers are beginning to add chemical and nuclear weapons and production facilities to their catalogues and could offer after-sales services as well. Multinational organisations have been involved in covert tactics (as in the fall of the Allende government in Chile). Parallels with the mercenary fighting of the 18th and 19th centuries (eg British forces in the American Revolution) are not hard to find. We are accustomed to associating religiously motivated terrorism with the Middle East. But European history provides honourable precedents: the Templars, Knights of St John, Rhodes and other religious warrior orders. It would not be surprising to see covert tactics used increasingly by religious, ecological and pacifist organisations, as well as by the more conventional liberation fronts.

Traditional forms of warfare are limited to 'outbreaks' – singularities in space and time of violence which could now be so extreme as to be suicidal for all. But opportunities for covert tactics and the needs and means to use them are developing continually. Covert tactics can be precise, effective, rewarding, cheap. Good use can be made of surprise, bluff, timing and the adversaries' weakest points. They can be used to pre-empt situations in which overt aggressive interaction might seem justified. They could, perhaps, help relieve the planet of its dangerous, expensive overburden of useless military personnel and material, diverting resources to more beneficial ends – education, cleaning up the environment, exploring inner and outer space ...

But it is wise not to be naive. The earth's population, which was just over one billion at the beginning of this century is expected to pass six when it ends, and to continue to grow exponentially. Generalised economic collapse may be imminent. Very nasty combinations of covert and conventional tactics continue to be possible – particularly against those who are unwise enough not to prepare potential adversaries with suitable covert tactics. The best way of doing this is not with secret agents. In order to deal with such tactics effectively, a government must have the full cooperation of its people. Harsh controls, and the taxes required to enforce them, can be counterproductive.

'Covert tactics are like microbes; they can only be checked by strengthening the social body internally'

When firearms made cutlery and castle walls obsolete, the solution was to reorganise society into nation states. Hanging onto old solutions, building thicker walls, was suicidal. The same is true now. Those who continue to pour their lives into protected perimeter weaponry may well find that they are not the strongest, best defended winners, but the worst losers. There is another solution: society can be restructured so that it is much more cohesive and loving. Covert tactics are like microbes; they can only be checked by strengthening the social body internally. A truly cohesive society is not only able to resist all forms of covert and conventional tactics (or to make better, possibly beneficial, use of them on others); it also has less need for aggressive interaction of all kinds.

Any change from conventional to covert tactics is pointless unless the need to kill is itself reduced. A wider spread of covert tactics without more justice could lead to the generalised and inconclusive sort of gang feuding which characterised parts of the Renaissance. In order to be cohesive, society must be fairer. The first requirement for survival in this age is that the exchange system should be honest. A little thought will show that this is not possible as long as our economies run on tokens whose supply is controlled by some for the benefit of others. We must get rid of money which, though intrinsically worthless, continues to be treated as though it had value.

The approach I propose for a free and fair society, the Community Co-operation Co-ordinator, received the Institute's 'Best Economic Social Invention' award. Computer programs are available to run this system on compatible micro-computers. When linked together, such mini-economic systems give society the new nervous system it requires to deal effectively with all kinds of disruption and subversion. Not incidentally such a network is also an exchange system based on agreements rather than money in which there is no inflation or unemployment; all exchanges can be transparently fair and efficient.

The Community Co-operation Co-ordinator is described in the chapter on New Money Systems. Conrad Hopman's address is BP 225, Noumea, New Caledonia, South Pacific (tel 687 26 21 26).

Prison incentives in the 18th century

Nicholas Albery

The commercially-run prison convict ships in 1790 might give the present government food for thought when drawing up its plans to privatise prisons here. 'The Fatal Shore' by Robert Hughes (published by Collins, 1987), tells the story.

The convict ship Surprize, bound for Australia, was on contract from Camden, Calvert and King, whose agent on board was Thomas Shapcote. It undertook to transport, clothe and feed the convicts for a flat inclusive fee of £17 7s 6d per head, whether they landed alive or not.

'In this privatised hell, the starving prisoners lay chilled to the bone on soaked bedding, unexercised, crusted with salt, shit and vomit, festering in scurvy and boils'

In this privatised hell, the starving prisoners lay chilled to the bone on soaked bedding, unexercised, crusted with salt, shit and vomit, festering in scurvy and boils. 36 out of 254 convicts died at sea. One convict, Thomas Milburn, would later describe the voyage in a letter to his parents:

'When any of our comrades that were chained to us died, we kept it a secret as long as we could for the smell of the dead body, in order to get their allowance of provision, and many a time have I been glad to eat the poultice that was put to my leg for perfect hunger. I was chained to Humphrey Davies who died when we were about half way, and I lay beside his corpse about a week and got his allowance.'

It is worth noting that conditions only improved when there was a financial incentive for delivering prisoners to Australia in a healthy condition and when an ex-convict who had experienced one of these ships drew up guidelines for how they should be run.

Similarly, Dr David Chapman (in a scheme described in the chapter on Old Age), proposes that residents in old people's homes should provide an incentive for the management by giving a regular rating which would determine what bonus the management is to receive from government funds. Prisoners could also make the same assessments, he believes, provided that there were safeguards such as fines for prisons that allowed escapes, or that let drugs in.

'The Fatal Shore' is engrossing in its description of the convict system in Australia and of the multitude of incentives (to supplement flogging and hanging) that its first governors were forced to come up with in an effort to cope. Governor Macquarie, for instance, paid the convicts some 45,000 gallons of rum to build the Sydney hospital, and offered 60 convicts their freedom if they could build a road through the Blue Mountains within six months instead of the estimated three years (they succeeded). Is it possible that prisoners today might respond to similar if less arduous ways of winning their freedom? Indeed the whole experiment of transportation, had it not been deformed by its unnecessary and truly appalling cruelties, would doubtless have beeen judged a success in prison reform terms. As Robert Hughes, the author of 'The Fatal Shore' writes:

'It did give a fresh start to many thousands of people who would have been crushed in spirit or confirmed in crime by long stretches in an English prison. And the post-colonial history of Australia exploded the theory of genetic criminal inheritance. Here was a community of people, handpicked over decades for their "criminal propensities" and for no other reason, whose offspring turned out to form one of the most law-abiding societies in the world.'

Nicholas Albery, 20 Heber Road, London NW2 6AA (tel 081 208 2853; fax 081 452 6434).

Prisons as ashrams

In 1969 Bo Lozoff and his wife Sita were living a Utopian hippy lifestyle on a trimaran sailboat in the Caribbean, when their boat became involved in a drug smuggling saga which ended with a close relative being sent to jail for 40 years. Bo Lozoff's eventual response was to seek a job as a prison guard. He was turned down, and instead set up the Prison Ashram Project, which now encourages meditation in American jails throughout the world and sends free, to any prisoner anywhere in the world, a compendium of wisdom entitled 'We're All Doing Time – A Guide to Getting Free'. In this book Lozoff outlines the philosophy of karma and reincarnation and suggests a simple set of meditation, yoga and breathing exercises.

'The Prison Ashram Project sends free, to any prisoner anywhere in the world, a compendium of wisdom entitled *We're All Doing Time – A Guide to Getting Free'*

He is not just proselytising a philosophy but sharing personal insights with individual prisoners, and he includes in the book a series of very moving letters from prisoners, with his replies. One chapter, for instance, is devoted to the inner development of Maury Logue at the Oklahoma State Penitentiary, who had stabbed a number of other inmates and was locked up for almost 24 hours a day. In an early letter to Lozoff, Logue writes how eight guards beat him up with clubs when he was handcuffed, scarring him for life, and how he intends one day to exterminate society's leaders: 'no mercy offered and none shall be given. My record speaks for itself.' The breakthrough in their correspondence began when Lozoff sent Logue an illustrated fable about a mean, tough convict befriended against his will by a prison cat. Ironically, Logue was writing: 'I'm making an honest attempt to readjust my conduct, I'm trying to clean up my act,' shortly before being stabbed to death by two other inmates as he stood handcuffed in the showers.

Prison Ashram Project (UK)
Nicholas Colloff

Through one of those amazing synchronicities which so often happen when an idea is rife, Ann Wetherall started her work with prisoners in the UK a few years ago in much the same way as Bo Lozoff. Originally motivated by her interest in the spiritual experiences of those held in confinement, she began corresponding with an increasing number of prisoners, becoming aware as she did so of how deeply they needed to question life's most fundamental premises. When she came to name her work, she chose, for almost the same reasons, though completely independently as she had never heard of Lozoff, the same name as he had chosen: The Prison Ashram Project.

A few months later she was given 'We're all Doing Time' and found that it contained so much of the material she was having to collect from various sources, that it formed an admirable and time saving substitute, followed later by Lozoff's 'Lineage' and 'Just Another Spiritual Book', thus freeing her to expand the project further.

The aim of the project is to turn the negative situation of a prisoner into something more positive by enabling him or her to make use of their cell as a house of retreat or ashram, and to form a new picture of themselves as people able to use their time to spiritual purpose, rather than merely serving time.

'Enabling prisoners to make use of their cell as a house of retreat or ashram'

The project corresponds with prisoners, thereby deepening the links between inmates and outmates; sends, free of charge to any prisoner who requests them, Lozoff's books, mentioned above; runs a cassette library for loan to prisoners; and has produced a video, featuring an interview and workshop with Bo Lozoff, available for sale. It has established a number of regular workshops in self-awareness and relaxation for young offenders; and is piloting a prison community project at one youth custody centre with the aim of meeting the need of people who have committed crimes against other people to become kinder, more caring human beings, to be given the opportunity to learn new skills and exercise responsibility in a context of service, discovering within their new acts of kindness a freedom which gives them hope and self-respect – in the belief that education and training on its own are only a partial answer. Both in and out of prison, we need opportunities to integrate our personal and spiritual growth with our social activity. The project also supports the establishment of groups for spiritual practice in prisons; and, when invited, gives occasional workshops and talks in prisons. A twice-yearly newsletter is also produced.

Since 1987 the Project has grown, mainly by word of mouth, from an initial three prisoners to, at the last count, over a thousand prisoners scattered in a hundred prisons and youth custody centres in the UK and the Republic of Ireland, the initiative of contacting the project coming from the prisoners themselves.

'As for me, the past year has been the most meaningful, most real of my life. Who could ever imagine a man's freedom being found in prison?'

At heart the project is based on the understanding that a place of confinement can be a space for growth, and a negative situation can be an opportunity. 'As for me, the past year has been the most meaningful, most real of my life. Who could ever imagine a man's freedom being found in prison?' (a prisoner). At the least this project can give somebody confined for long periods something positive to do. At the most it can transform lives.

• *The Prison Ashram Project, P.O.Box 328, Oxford OX2 8RJ (tel 0865 57907). Bo Lozoff's books are available free to prisoners in the UK and the Republic of Ireland from this address or can be ordered through Element Books, The Old School House, The Courtyard, Bell Street, Shaftesbury, Dorset SP7 8BP (tel 0747 51448; fax 0747 51394).*

• *Bo Lozoff's address is the Human Kindness Foundation, Route 1, Box 201-n, Durham, NC 27705, USA (tel 919 942 2138).*

The Human Kindness Foundation

Bo Lozoff

Extracts from a recent talk by Bo Lozoff about the work and philosophy of the Human Kindness Foundation (see also the previous item).

People who defend the prison system, or who want to build even more prisons and sentence more people, they are the idealists, not me. They're 'negative idealists', because they have a punitive ideal which reality continues to disprove. It simply doesn't work. Hurting people who hurt us just perpetuates a lot of hurting.

> 'The vast majority of prisoners hate their lives, and they begin to shine when someone comes along and shows them they can be of value'

I would say that over 90% of prisoners would love to straighten their lives out if given a decent chance. Very few people are dead-set on doing wrong. The vast majority of prisoners hate their lives, they feel like worthless losers, and they begin to shine when someone comes along and shows them they can be of value.

That's why I'm so passionate about prisoners doing some kind of 'good works' instead of just getting an education and job skills. As somebody named Susie Gomez once said, 'It is an honour to be asked to help.' It's an amazing experience to introduce a prisoner to that honour, and to watch the profound changes which take place.

I don't say to set everyone free. There may always be twisted people who need to be removed from society to protect the public. And sometimes somebody may even forfeit his right to ever again be trusted with his freedom – perhaps like David 'Son of Sam' or Charles Manson. Why should the public be guinea pigs?

But there are very few people like that, and we already have *more* than enough prisons to hold them. And even so, we can create optimum conditions for their redemption so that even if they're behind bars for the rest of their lives, they have an opportunity to become respected writers, inventors, thinkers, artists, or humanitarians, contributing to the world through their unique restrictions and humility for their past.

> 'That's why I'm so passionate about prisoners doing some kind of "good works" instead of just getting an education and job skills'

But those are the few. The *many* are prisoners who would be better served through imaginative combinations of house arrest, community service, electronic monitoring, family counselling, restitution, drug and alcohol rehabilitation and so forth. Prisons should be the last recourse. And prisons offer *no* solution to problems which are primarily social and medical, such as drug abuse.

The Human Kindness Foundation rely on free-will donations rather than grant applications. Their address is above.

Prisons with menus of 'kindness projects'

Bo Lozoff goes into more detail about his ideas for service to the community by prisoners.

Human beings – including prisoners – have a fundamental need to contribute something to the world around them, a need to focus their attention sometimes on the problems of others instead of solely on themselves.

There are prison inmates who translate books into braille, raise vegetables for nearby nursing homes, operate a children's radio station, build and repair toys for needy children, build playground equipment for day-care centres, raise money for charities, correspond with terminally ill children, run a wide variety of delinquency-prevention and substance-abuse programmes – all without leaving the prison.

> 'At most prisons, empathy and altruism are virtually impossible to express, because conservatives and liberals alike have unwittingly designed prisons as narcissistic environments'

But such programmes are rare. At most prisons, empathy and altruism are virtually impossible to express, because conservatives and liberals alike have unwittingly designed prisons as narcissistic environments. An inmate's attention is focused intensely on himself, whether in negative pursuits (physical survival, power struggles, con games) or positive ones (education, vocational training, parole plans). How can we be surprised when an offender gets out and seems to be a 'taker', entirely self-concerned, with no giving skills of his own? He's had no practice at all.

In our pluralistic culture, all the elements of the conservative and liberal myths seem to have amalgamated into one monstrously counter-productive prison system: 'Lock 'em up, punish, educate and release.' It almost guarantees an unending stalemate, because conservatives can go on blaming the system's failures on its liberal tenets, and liberals on its conservative ones.

But what if the problem doesn't lie in the battle between conservative and liberal values, but in their underlying narcissism instead? Nearly every code of ethics, philosophy, or religion points out the unsatisfactoriness of intense self-concern. Even outside of prison, people who are obsessed with themselves do not live very happy lives. We see tragic figures like Christina Onassis, Howard Hughes, and Elvis Presley, and we shake our heads in wonder. We read about the crimes of greed committed by Boesky or DeLorean and we think, 'My God, how many millions do they *need*?' We should realise by now that education, training and privilege do not guarantee happy or constructive lifestyles. Our current prison system is reminiscent of former California governor Jerry Brown's observation, 'When there's a problem, conservatives deny it exists, while liberals throw money at it.'

I've heard from a number of prisoners who claim that neither punishment nor rehabilitation programmes had much effect on them until they stumbled onto an opportunity to be of value to others. And suddenly, the education and training programmes, and even the fact of their punishment, finally found a context which enabled them to turn their lives around.

They discovered within their acts of kindness a freedom which gave them hope and self-respect and, often for the first time, a connection with the rest of humanity.

'The vast majority of prisoners would love to become kinder, more trustworthy people'

Our crime-and-punishment dilemma is not the simplistic Willie Horton morality play politicians shove down our throats at election time. The truth is, because we eventually release 99% of them, we have to hope that criminals become more decent human beings. A very small percentage of prison inmates may not want this decency, but I know from fifteen years' experience of dealing with tens of thousands of prisoners that the vast majority would love to become kinder, more trustworthy people. To be successful, a prison system needs to allow opportunities towards that end.

'Each prison could have a menu of "kindness projects" in which inmates are invited to participate'

Each community has so many needs, it's hard to imagine that some of them couldn't be met by volunteers from the nearest prison – and I don't mean highway beautification crews, but rather projects with direct beneficiaries, projects with a heart-to-heart quality. Each prison could have a menu of 'kindness projects' in which inmates are invited to participate. Such programmes as the examples mentioned above have gone on in prisons for many years, but for the most part they're not supported administratively or respected as a serious component of rehabilitation; they're regarded mostly as 'fluff'. All I'm suggesting is to shift our rehabilitative focus to the obvious: the cultivation of empathy and altruism is paramount, not fluff.

Many prisoners have left deep scars in their victims' lives and have been deeply scarred themselves – before, during and after their crimes. The milk of human kindness is a time-tested balm which heals such wounds and scars. With more recognition, planning and institutional support, 'kindness projects' could become a staple in our prison systems and affect millions of lives for the better, on both sides of the bars. The following, for instance, are two suggestions I can make for such projects.

The Great Convict Smoke-Out

Here's one of these great ideas where everybody wins: how about starting a project in your prisons for inmates and staff to quit smoking, and donate all the money that would have been spent on cigarettes into a charity pool?

At a women's prison recently, I looked around and did some calculations, $600 a day was being spent on cigarettes, going towards nothing except poor health. $600 a day equals $219,000 a year – which could fund an entire shelter for battered women, abused children or homeless people.

Recycling in the joint

In the prison visiting area alone, on a weekend, there are probably several whole barrels of drink cans that are trucked out with all the other garbage to a local landfill. And think about how many pounds of newspapers, books, mail and magazines get tossed out every day in your prison. Persuade the administration to allow a recycling crew of inmates who are willing to help out. A recycling agency may pay for all those cans and papers and the money could go into a special 'human kindness' account, for you to send donations to those in need.

Bo Lozoff is preparing a book entitled 'The Freedom of Kindness' demonstrating the variety of compassionate services that are or could be provided by inmates. It will be available free of charge to prison staff and to prisoners themselves. The latter can also receive free Lozoff's book 'Lineage and Other Stories' – which are wise and witty tales of prisoners and others facing up to challenges and developing courage, self-honesty, humour and a sense of awe and wonder in the process ($9 incl. p&p overseas to non-prisoners).

Prisoners as firemen

Extracted from a report by Philip Smith in the National Enquirer (USA), monitored for the Institute by Roger Knights.

The local fire department in Alte, Georgia, in the States, is made up of 10 prison inmates, headed by a non-inmate fire chief. The prisoners, sentenced for crimes from murder, to drug dealing and armed robbery, are from the Lee Arrendale Correctional Institution, one of Georgia's toughest maximum security prisons. They have four fire trucks, 120 hours of training 'and so much pride in their work that not one has ever tried to escape. The only inmates we don't allow in the department,' says Fire Chief Dan Pitts, a prison staffer who runs the department, 'are those who've committed sex crimes, arson or crimes against law enforcement officers. We only use inmates who are minimum security risks.'

'The prisoners have four fire trucks, 120 hours of training and so much pride in their work that not one has ever tried to escape'

The 10 fire fighters, who sleep in a separate dormitory from the other prisoners, handle fires within the prison and about a dozen blazes a month in the small towns surrounding the prison.

Prisoners training dogs for the disabled

Extracted from a document sent by Michaela Edridge.

In the USA, the introduction of pets into a couple of state prisons has proved to be a remarkably successful venture. The most noteworthy is the scheme set up at the Purdy Treatment Centre for Women, Gig Harbour, Washington. It was established with the help of an ex-offender, Kathy Quinn, and the object was for inmates to train dogs to aid disabled people. Warders and governors were wary at first, but the scheme has been successful in every way. The self-esteem of prisoners has increased dramatically and they now feel that they have a link with the outside world, as well as being able to do something worthwhile with their time; many of those involved go on to work with animals on leaving the prison, and the relationships between inmates and staff has improved greatly.

• *Michaela Edridge, 267 Hillbury Road, Warlingham, Surrey CR3 9TL.*

• *Lesley Scott-Ordish, PRO Dogs, Rocky Bank, 4 New Road, Ditton, Maidstone, Kent ME20 7AD (tel 0732 848499).*

• *Society for Companion Animal Studies, c/o Anne Docherty, The Mews Cottage, 7 Botanic Crescent Lane, Glasgow G20 8AA (tel 041 9452088).*

Helping prisoners escape

Martin Marsh

It might be a good idea to help people to 'escape' from prison. One assumes that a person in prison is imprisoned not only in a physical sense but also by their attitudes. In this new system there would be, in each prison, an 'escape officer' who would act as a consultant, advising prisoners how to escape in the shortest possible time and giving them support and encouragement as needed. The escape officer would offer prisoners a series of choices of escape routes (long ones, short ones, difficult ones, easy ones, ones involving social activity, or without) at each stage.

'The shortest escape routes would depend on an active choice of difficult tasks'

In order to protect society and to satisfy society's demand for stiffer penalties, the shortest escape routes would depend on an active choice of difficult tasks, social commitment and commitment of leisure time to learning social inventiveness. The advantages include:

• Any change in attitude would be more profound because it would be based on their own motivation, and demonstrated actively by their series of choices.

• Completion of an escape route could be a source of pride and redemption to an ex-prisoner. They could present future employers or critical neighbours with a certificate showing that they had escaped from prison in a short period of time compared with their original sentence and detailing some of the choices which they had made on the way.

• It would be difficult to fake reform – a person would be altered by their own choices.

• It would be a humane way of introducing tougher influences upon prisoners – because they would choose these options themselves in the full knowledge of their implications.

Martin Marsh, 32 Midhurst Avenue, Muswell Hill, London N10 3EN (tel 081 444 5685).

Prisoners translating books

Nicholas Albery

Part of my book on 'Breathing Therapies' was translated for a publisher in Germany by a prisoner on a ten year sentence in a German jail. Official work is done in some German jails, mostly time-killing, mindless jobs paying very little money. So

any work doing something creative is a real alternative – in this particular case, the prisoner was apparently pleased to have helped translate a book about a therapy he could practise in his cell.

The publishing enterprise is a shoestring alternative venture run by Werner Pieper of Löhrbach. 'I fairly often get requests from prisoners or mental patients for free books,' Pieper says. 'I always send some in return, since I know that every copy will be eagerly devoured by several people. But with each book I enclose a note to say, "I'm not the Roman Catholic church or a charity, if there is anything you could do in return I would be very grateful".'

As a result, Pieper has received usable illustrations for books, as well as translations. He pays the prisoners not only in money, but also in books and little things that they need in jail and could not otherwise get. Translators are also supplied with paper and dictionary. 'Sometimes the translation has to be worked over later,' Pieper acknowledges, 'but even basic translations are a big help.'

Would such a scheme work in this country? Stephen Shaw, director of the Prison Reform Trust, says that the nearest parallels at present are the UK prisons which operate Braille units, but he believes that translation, illustration and repair of books would be a 'logical progression.'

Work in British prisons, as in German ones, is 'often purposeless and even demeaning, with prisoners' earnings averaging £2 a week,' Shaw comments, and given the declining emphasis on industrial work throughout the prison system, and the Home Office commitment to developing worthwhile alternatives, ideas on this West German model 'could and should play an expanding role.'

• *Nicholas Albery, 20 Heber Road, London NW2 6AA (tel 081 208 2853; fax 081 452 6434).*

• *Publisher Werner Pieper, Alte Schmiede. D-6941 Löhrbach, West Germany (tel 06201 21278).*

Delinquents into donors

Alec Dickson

No other category of young people receives so much intensive physical excercise, under the supervision of professional specialists in Physical Training (PT), as do those serving sentences in youth custody institutions (formerly borstals), detention centres, etc. Although this may help to build up those with flabby physique and reinforce discipline generally, it is not training for the performance of any useful role on release.

Suppose that a part of this regime were devoted to instruction in the organisation and leadership of games and leisure activities for younger children – bearing in mind that 7-11 year olds can – out of school – cause very great mischief (for example with the lift system in high rise blocks) and absorb hundreds of police man-hours in investigation. Suppose, then, that a portion of the time spent on the current, conventional PT programmes were devoted to training 16-18 year olds, say, in how to organise legitimate activities, particularly in back streets, waste ground and where there may be an absence of football pitches, but not excluding the possibility of using public parks.

Some heads of primary schools might be ready to allow a small group of lads from these institutions, under supervision or escort, to visit their schools and discover what activities their children respond to. The idea would be that they would undertake this responsibility on their release. Having accepted and placed hundreds of borstal youths in situations where they have been entrusted with the care of others, the basic notion fills me with no dismay at all. But this kind of undertaking would be non-residential – and some kind of sympathetic supervision would be desirable from the YMCA, after-care officers, the Sports Council, parks and recreation staff, younger police or cadets.

Other considerations apart, this venture (a) might lead to encouraging old games (as portrayed by Breughel centuries ago) and new ones, not requiring expensive equipment or expansive playing fields; and (b) might represent one very small step in more young people actually playing rather than watching others play.

Alec Dickson, 19 Blenheim Road, London W4 1VB (tel 081 944 7437).

The Guardian Angels

The Guardian Angels aim to help protect the traveller on the London underground. Whatever the government's reservations about this group may be, they have had a salutary effect on the authorities, who have been shamed into placing more police on the underground system as a result – and the government is rumoured to be considering a Guardian Angels type scheme of its own. Dr Alec Dickson, the founder of Community Service Volunteers, comments that 'it does us no credit if we "rubbish" the Guardian Angels. Rigorously self-disciplined, unpaid and imaginatively trained, they are visibly succeeding not only in New York, but in other cities, often being invited into areas by the mayor. What the Guardian Angels offer is a role, responsibility and, possibly, risk.'

> 'It does us no credit if we "rubbish" the Guardian Angels. Rigorously self-disciplined, unpaid and imaginatively trained, what they offer is a role, responsibility and, possibly, risk'

The Guardian Angels, Colin 'Gabriel' Hatcher, Chapter Leader, c/o Tom Hibberd, The Tonbridge Club, 120 Cromer Street, London WC1 (tel 081 694 2797); American founders are Curtis and Lisa Sliwa, Guardian Angels, 982 East 89th St, Brooklyn, NY 11236, USA (tel 010 1 212 420 1324). The London Guardian Angels won a 1989 Social Inventions Award.

Tube Guardians given half-price season tickets

Nigel Bradley

My suggestion is to screen season ticket holders who are tube travellers and to invite suitable ones to an evening event. They would be offered half-price season tickets to become 'special policemen' on the tube when they travelled.

Vigilance training would be given and each year a percentage

discount would be allowed.

The Commuter Guardians would be a cross between policemen, Guardian Angels and caring fellow travellers.

Nigel Bradley, 91 Hawsley Avenue, Chesterfield, Derbyshire S40 4TJ (tel 0246 208473).

No riots in small prisons

John Papworth

Adapted extract from a letter in the Times

The Times reported that 24 prisoners in the cells of a Doncaster police station were serving their sentences 'in an atmosphere free of the tension and the harsh conditions of a conventional prison', prisoners and officers were on first name terms and officials visiting the unit were 'astonished by the transformation of attitude and the peaceful mixing of what would normally (sic!) become a critical mass.' The Times report concludes that it would have been impossible to apply these conditions to the 1,600 locked in Strangeways prison when the place exploded in violence.

> 'They were quickly able to restore conditions not by appealing to the goodwill of the prisoners but by cutting their groups into smaller and more manageable units'

Well, of course. But why then is Strangeways being rebuilt? Do we really learn from history that we learn nothing from history? More than 30 years ago Professor Leopold Kohr, in his book 'The Breakdown of Nations', pointed out that after years of trouble in the overcrowded Korean prison camps it began to dawn on the authorities that 'the cause of difficulty was not the incorrigible nature of the communists but the *size* (my emphasis) of the compounds containing them. Once this was recognised, they were quickly able to restore conditions, not by appealing to the goodwill of the prisoners but by cutting their groups into smaller and more manageable units.'

Of course small units cost more to run, but we surely need to ask ourselves whether we want prisoners released back into society after serving a sentence during which they have been treated with humanity, or after years of brutalisation in such hell-holes as Strangeways? It is surely rather late in the day to discover that far from serving the purpose for which our prisons exist they are defeating it.

John Papworth, 24 Abercorn Place, London NW8 9XP (tel 071 286 4366).

Small-scale borstal

Nicholas Saunders

An interesting social experiment in Denmark that could be adapted for the UK is the household-sized communal borstal. In Denmark this has been tried for ten years now and is called Miljoerne.

It consists normally of some four inmates and three staff (and any staff children). There are about ten such borstals, mostly based in farms. The farming provides a sense of responsibility, with looking after animals and routine work; and everything is decided communally at table by the inmates and staff.

These mini-borstals are considered a success, and are able to run on the same per capita costs as the big institutions.

Nicholas Saunders, top floor, 14 Neal's Yard, London WC2H 9DP (tel 071 836 9404; fax 071 0135).

Ha-Has round jails

Nicholas Saunders

A modern high security jail in Denmark (near Ringe in Fun) has a ha-ha sunken wall (further protected electronically), allowing the prisoners to see out into open countryside and so not to feel enclosed. The prisoners are divided into small mixed households (although there are ten times as many men as women). Each household does its own cooking and washing up, and does its shopping from its own budget in the prison supermarket. The prison has its own factory.

> 'A modern high security jail in Denmark has a ha-ha sunken wall, allowing the prisoners to see out into open countryside'

Is it not time for the UK prison service to move into the twentieth century?

Nicholas Saunders, top floor, 14 Neal's Yard, London WC2H 9DP (tel 071 836 9404; fax 071 379 0135).

Getting help from police stations

Alec Dickson

Trouble occurs in families, for obvious reasons, in the evenings and at weekends – precisely when departments of social services are closed and their duty officers extraordinarily difficult to contact. On the other hand, the police, whose stations are virtually the only government offices open day and night, are sometimes still rather reluctant to get involved in domestic quarrels.

> 'The police, whose stations are virtually the only government offices open day and night, are sometimes still reluctant to get involved in domestic quarrels'

Suppose a police station in a deprived area were to make available a small interviewing room to be staffed by third year students of social work (who would be able to contact the social services duty officers) and to whom distraught people could be referred by the desk officers initially. If the 'trouble' appeared to be serious and urgent, eg abuse of a child, the social work student could then request the station sergeant to send a car

around to the house.

The results might be:

(a) Distressed citizens would receive assistance; (b) The police themselves would be relieved to a large extent of domestic problems, to concentrate on crime; (c) Social workers in training would receive a baptism of fire and acquire experience of sharing problems with the police; (d) People in the neighbourhood would come to view the police station as a place from which help could be sought – which is surely one aim of police policy today.

Alec Dickson, 19 Blenheim Road, London W4 1VB (tel 081 944 7437).

Police in wheelchairs

From an item in the Examiner (USA), monitored for the Institute by Roger Knights.

> 'Half the members of the Californian Capitola police department are in wheelchairs, acting as parking enforcement officers'

Half the members of the Californian Capitola police department are in wheelchairs, acting as 'parking enforcement officers'. 'We've been hiring the handicapped for parking enforcement for ten years, and it's worked well for us,' says police captain Tom Hanna. 'They're very hard workers, and grateful for the opportunity to be of service and to earn an income. They wear police uniforms and work right alongside the rest of us.'

Danny, whose legs were paralysed four years ago when he fell from a bridge, says that 'placing tickets on cars is no problem. But if it's a big truck and I can't reach the windshield, I call one of the other parking enforcement officers who are mobile and they take care of it. We do get hassled occasionally, but we point out that if they disagree, they can take it to court. Once in a while we encounter someone who's had too much to drink and we have to call another officer, but that's a rarity.'

Captain Hanna says that his seaside city's policy of hiring the handicapped would work well in other communities. 'They've proven to us that they can get the job done.'

Cardboard police

Adapted from pieces in the Star (USA) monitored for the Institute by Roger Knights, from pieces in the Guardian by John Ezard and in the Times by Quentin Cowdry and in the Economist; and from an item submitted by Michael Mc Sweeney.

In Japan, as a warning to motorists, there are concrete policemen at some accident black spots. Likewise, the introduction of cardboard cut-out policemen has reduced speeding offences by 33% around Copenhagen, and the experiment may be extended to other police work.

The cut-outs have been placed beside notorious speeding blackspots near the Danish capital. Now they are to be erected at crossings where drivers often jump lights. From time to time they will be replaced by real officers.

In Bradford, West Yorkshire, some shops and garages have erected plywood police officers in an attempt to reduce shop-lifting – despite protests from the local police, who think that their plywood representatives will be widely mocked and will further reduce public confidence in the police. In Tyne and Wear, shoplifting plummeted by 70% in a year-long trial, when retailers installed cardboard cut-out policemen. And in Skokie, Illinois, USA, Anatomical Chart Co. are selling a full-size police mannequin for $375 – 'the urban scarecrow, the latest weapon in the war on crime' – which police place in otherwise empty patrol cars to deter lawbreakers, such as drivers intent on breaking the speed limit.

> 'A full-size police mannequin for $375 – the urban scarecrow'

Language is as individual as fingerprints

Adapted extracted from an article by Nigel Hawkes in the Times.

Andrew Morton and Professor Sidney Michaelson of the computer science department at the University of Edinburgh have shown that transcripts of speech or written text are as individual as fingerprints and can be used to judge whether a confession was a true one or not, through examining the length of sentences and the frequency of occurrence of nouns and short words.

> 'To judge whether a confession was true through examining the length of sentences and the frequency of occurrence of nouns and short words'

The first stage is to prepare a chart of sentence length. This is done by calculating the average length in the sample of prose, then counting the number of words by which every successive sentence is either greater or less than the average. These differences are then added together in succession to form a cumulative sum and are plotted on a graph.

The next stage is to analyse in the same way the occurrence of words within the sentences. Suppose, for example, that an individual's use of two- or three-letter words is absolutely consistent. The chart measuring the frequency of such words will have exactly the same shape as the chart of sentence length. Printed on transparent paper and appropriately scaled, the two charts will lie more or less on top of each other.

Using this method, Morton has examined the confessions in the Carl Bridgewater and the Birmingham Six cases, none of which appear to be in one individual consistent style. He has also investigated the American claims of having discovered a 'new' Shakespeare sonnet – and he doubts them. In response to the argument by Iris Murdoch that she consciously uses a different style in her philosophical writings than in her novels, he shows that it is less different than she supposes.

This new method requires no statistical knowledge. 'Judgements can be made by eye, laying one chart on top of another.' An interesting test will be to see whether the courts are willing to accept this evidence, and what credence they accord it.

Libel in county courts

The following proposal, publicised as a letter to the Times, was highly commended in the 1991 Social Inventions Awards. The judge who is responsible for this suggestion does not want his name published in connection with the award. Additional information comes from a news item in the Times by Frances Gibb.

Defamation cases should be commenced in the county court and tried by county court judges. The cases are not worth high court time and they do not demand high court skills.

Divorce was once strictly reserved to the high court. Now divorce proceedings must be commenced in the county court. So should defamation cases.

At a stroke the worst blemish on the administration of justice would be removed, and the outrageous damages, costs and delay would be reduced.

There would still be twofold protection against, for instance, a newspaper that decided it could libel with impunity, believing that the damages would be less than the benefit of the increased circulation: (a) damages that can be awarded in the county court will have a substantial £50,000 ceiling and (b) the case is *commenced* in the county court, but can be referred to a higher court if necessary.

> 'The case is *commenced* in the county court, but can be referred to a higher court if necessary'

This proposal was also presented by libel lawyer Brian Raymond at the 1991 Law Society conference. Lord Justice Neill's committee has gone further and recommended the idea of an arbitration scheme to settle small libel cases out of court, with power to award damages of up to about £1,000.

Glowing disc to cut car theft

Adapted extract from an item by Kevin Eason in the Times.

Bright high-adhesive stickers costing a few pence could help reduce crime, which is costing Britain almost £1 billion a year.

While car makers spend millions of pounds installing locking systems to try to deter thieves, police forces believe a scheme requiring motorists' co-operation and a couple of securely stuck fluorescent discs may cut substantially the number of cars stolen.

> 'Gives the police authority to check a car displaying the stickers if it is being driven after midnight'

South Yorkshire police will ask motorists to register their cars with the force under its vehicle watch scheme. It gives police authority to check a car displaying the stickers in the front and rear windscreens if it is being driven between midnight and 5am.

About one in five of the 9,443 vehicles stolen in South Yorkshire last year were taken in the five hours after midnight. Patrol car officers will know that they are likely to be tracking thieves when they see a moving car displaying fluorescent discs during the agreed 'curfew' hours.

The idea, originally from the United States, has been tried

successfully for nine months in Cumbria, and a Metropolitan police pilot scheme is running in north London.

Of 5,000 cars registered under the scheme in Cumbria, only three have been stolen. Two were recovered and the third was stopped by police. No thefts have been recorded from cars displaying the fluorescent discs.

This has convinced South Yorkshire police that the scheme could work in a region with more crime than rural Cumbria. They have an initial target of 10,000 vehicles but believe thousands more motorists will join.

Chief Inspector John Heritage, of the force's crime prevention department, said: 'it is a very simple idea. If we spot a car on the road in the hours when the motorist has said it will not be driven, it can be checked unhindered immediately. The bonus is that the thieves also know that the car will be stopped on sight and checked.'

The anti-bike thief box

Fred Allen

Here is a neat little idea – the agent provocateur bicycle. If professional bicycle thieves are working in a town, as they were in Cambridge, you take your bicycle to a centre where the agent provocateur box is welded to it. In this box you have something or nothing. Something is costly, nothing is cheap. The bicycle thief does not know which, so the service is cheap and effective, the casual thief gets away with it, the professional is certain to get caught, for he is certain to steal an active one. Radio, pheromones or ultrasound can be used to trace the bike. The local press, radio and television get interested, and any sane thief packs it in – the rest get caught.

Fred Allen, 13 Shelly Row, Cambridge, CB3 OBP.

Legalising trade in marijuana seeds only

Nicholas Albery

I disagree with those such as Judge Pickles who say that cannabis should be legalised and taxed, doubtless then to become an industry to rival the present tobacco empires. Cannabis can have harmful effects, especially when mixed with tobacco and breathed in more deeply than tobacco normally is, and one study at least has shown that it can promote schizophrenic episodes.

> **'It should be illegal to promote the use of marijuana through advertising or to trade in other than the seeds'**

Marijuana leaves, drunk as tea, or smoked on their own without tobacco, as tends to happen more in the States than here, might be less harmful. My proposal is that it should be legal both to grow marijuana for personal consumption or to obtain a cannabis syrup on prescription; but that it would be illegal to promote their use through advertising or to trade in other than the seeds.

Nicholas Albery, 20 Heber Road, London NW2 6AA (tel 081 208 2853; fax 081 452 6434).

Community or Penitence Stamps

Mr W.D. Harrison proposes that Community Stamps valued at £5, £10 and £20 be issued by the courts, the police, traffic wardens, railway and bus inspectors, car park attendants, public servants or sports officials for compulsory purchase by minor offenders – those for instance who drop litter, let their dogs foul the pavement, abuse the police or vandalise. These would be for cases where a court appearance or a normal fine would be inappropriate or where the offender preferred an on-the-spot reckoning. The funds realised would be used to support local community facilities.

Stamps would have to be produced for inspection within a defined period, or the amount would be doubled at intervals until the sum was large enough to warrant court proceedings.

People could also voluntarily buy these stamps if concerned to improve their community, either as a form of penance for something they know they have done wrong, or more simply as part of some social fund-raising event, or to replace the office or factory 'swear box'. Harrison believes that the purchaser should be given a choice of which local amenities – hospital, library, schools, parks, etc – his stamp money would go to.

> **'People could also voluntarily buy these stamps if concerned to improve their community, as a form of penance for something they know they have done wrong'**

Penitence Stamps

Children could be introduced to a junior variant, with small Penitence Stamps stuck into a folder at each misdemeanour. When a page was full, the child might have do do a minor task during break, or see the head, or have the parents purchase the page. In secondary schools only, the pupils would have to pay between £1 and £10 for their stamps.

A Snakes and Ladders-type game introducing the whole concept has also been designed and successfully tried out at the Basildon Primary School, with three more schools about to try it.

Harrison has written to a very large number of influential people and organisations, campaigning for this proposal. Any school or other organisation willing to give these stamps or the game a try please contact W.D. Harrison, Casita, 12 St David's Road, Langdon Hills, Basildon, Essex SS16 6HA (tel 0268 412462).

Chapter eleven

HEALTH

Health Quotients

Dr John Hart

The following is an extract from the book 'Wealth and Well-Being – A National Strategy for the Nineties' (Oxon Publishing, £8-95), winner of a Social Inventions Award.

'HQ is a measure of a person's health and well-being on the lines of the IQ measure of intelligence'

One thing people lack is a memorable, quantitative assessment of their health. The 'HQ' concept meets this need. First mooted in Social Inventions Journal (No. 4), HQ stands for Health Quotient. It is a measure of a person's health and well-being on the lines of the IQ measure of intelligence. By definition, average health is 100. The advantage of the idea is that an individual gains a precise view of his health and could establish a clear objective for improvement. The HQ would need to measure objective indicators of health such as blood pressure, but also behavioural elements such as drinking and smoking, and 'well-being' elements such as stress and even the difficult-to-define 'contentment'. Sir Douglas Black, of inequalities of health fame, said in a Christie Gordon Lecture:

'Of their nature, "health statistics" relate to morbidity and mortality, not to "positive health", which in a euphoric passage we define as a "positive expression of vigour, well-being and engagement in one's environment or community".'

The HQ concept could be an integral part of a preventive screening programme. Screening specific groups for cervical and breast cancer is already justified, by smear and X-ray mammography respectively, as is measuring blood pressure to detect hypertension (a Black Report recommendation) and assessing blood cholesterol for predisposition to coronary heart disease. Furthermore, a battery of tests is becoming available from biotechnology companies that enables identification of those who are most likely to succumb to common conditions such as diabetes, emphysema, heart disease, several cancers and even, it is said, alcoholism, long before they actually do so. New pregnancy tests have been developed enabling the identification of genetic disorders such as cystic fibrosis and Huntingdon's Chorea. A new generation of 'physician office' diagnostic tests are arriving. Among these is a kit allowing plasma cholesterol to be determined in two minutes using a pinprick blood sample. Screening is an idea whose time has come – particularly combined with an HQ component which leads to the adoption of healthier lifestyles.

The HQ part of the screening process might well comprise three stages: a preliminary questionnaire, the test itself, and a follow-up interview. The pre-test questionnaire would seek to establish dietary pattern, behaviour, social circumstances, typical levels of psychological stress, information on vaccinations previously received, present and previous illnesses and disabilities, and use of health service facilities in the recent past. Also obtained would be information relating to disease and death among the subject's parents, grandparents and blood relatives to establish the genetic background.

The HQ test itself would be a comprehensive 'medical'. Conventional height, weight and other measurements would be made together with hearing and eye tests, and so on. Blood and urine samples would be analysed. The hapless punter would also be subject to 'treadmill' exercise stress tests with computer assisted monitoring to assess cardiovascular and lung function. Other screening assessments would be made in what would clearly be an extensive test schedule.

The follow-up interview would inform the individual of the HQ findings and identify the potential for improvements, focusing on key risk factors relevant to that person. The 'sub-100' subjects would be given particular attention in this regard. The intention would be to develop a Personal Programme for Risk Reduction, covering diet, exercise, etc. The opportunity could also be taken to give information, where appropriate, on family planning, sexual diseases including AIDS, dental hygiene, availability of NHS and personal social services, sickness support groups (of which there are almost 9,000, including one for people with diseases so rare they thought no one else had it), local sporting activities, counselling services, welfare benefits (eg heating grants), accident prevention and so on. The HQ follow-up could also be used to improve immunisation take-up relating to polio, measles, rubella and whooping cough.

Who to screen? A representative sample of the entire population, and members of high risk groups. The representative sample would enable a 'national HQ' to be determined. This would provide the basis for determining progress against a target of a 10 per cent improvement in Britain's health by the year 2000. It would also facilitate broad-based international comparisons in the health sphere in the way that GDP figures permit in the economic sphere. It will have a further advantage: it will enable us to determine 'productivity' in the health business in terms of the HQ score added by a certain measure, health team or hospital.

Dr John Hart, 16 Burleigh Court, Cavendish Place, Brighton BN1 2HR (tel 0273 720879).

Consumer audits in the NHS

Adapted extract from the 'Report on Activities' published by the College of Health.

'To look at the service provided from the patient's point of view, rather than that of the clinician or manager, and to give full emphasis to emotional well-being'

The College of Health, a charity, has developed 'consumer audits' in the NHS to complement other more familiar forms of value-for-money or clinical assessments. In essence, the idea of consumer audit is to look at the service provided from the patient's point of view, rather than that of the clinician or manager, and to give full emphasis to emotional as well as physical well-being, to humanity, dignity and courtesy, and to the quality and clarity of communication between staff and patients.

For instance, the College of Health was invited to undertake a study of patient satisfaction in the maternity unit of a large district hospital in an inner city district in London. In-depth interviews were carried out in the women's homes six weeks after discharge. In addition discussions were held with a group of Muslim women and members of the local National Childbirth Trust.

The main findings included:
• Lack of information about the choices and services available for ante-natal care and delivery;
• An appointments system that was too inflexible for mothers with other young children;
• Lack of help and information for women who could not speak English;
• Poor continuity of care for some women during their delivery;
• Inadequate staffing levels sometimes led to women in labour being treated in an unacceptable manner;
• Women on the post-natal ward were given inadequate help with breast feeding to the extent that some switched to bottle-feeding;
• The early discharge policy was not flexible enough for women with special needs.

The College of Health's report has 32 recommendations for action or change, all of which were agreed between management and staff and approved by the Health Authority and a timetable for implementation drawn up.

It is particularly interesting to note that only five of the 35 proposals entailed new cash expenditure, the total sum being £3,100. The vast majority involved changes in practice or attitude.

As a result of this study a Consumer Audit Checklist is being developed for the providers of ante-natal and maternity services.

College of Health, St Margaret's House, 21 Old Ford Road, London E2 9PL (tel 081 983 1225; fax 081 983 1553).

Improving casualty departments

The Institute for Social Inventions has initiated a campaign for the improvement of hospital casualty departments. Several of the Institute's contacts have had to wait many hours in casualty, turning green with broken bones, to get attention.

'They had to wait many hours in casualty, turning green with broken bones, to get attention'

They report not being kept up to date with what was happening or when they were likely to be seen; and no one helping to sort out childminding or transport-home problems, etc.

The government has announced a Patient's Charter, which includes an understanding that 'authorities will increasingly set and publicise clear Local Charter Standards, including waiting times in accident and emergency departments, after initial assessment.' This is all to the good as far as it goes. But many other improvements are urgently needed:
• Increasing the number of doctors in casualty departments up to levels recommended by the British Association for Accident & Emergency Medicine;
• Reducing the proportion of junior, inexperienced doctors working in casualty departments, given that they are attempting to deal with many of the hospital's most seriously ill and injured patients;
• Independent consumer bodies such as 'Which Way to Health?' or the College of Health publicising details of the best and worst casualty departments and their own comparative listings of waiting times (a) for those with serious disorders (b) for those with minor self-limiting injuries;
• Financial incentives to hospitals to lessen waiting times. At present hospitals receive a 'block grant' to run their accident and emergency service, a grant which is not dependent on the number of patients seen. They therefore at present may be tempted to conserve their grant by rationing use of the system through increased waiting times. There could be new scaled incentives based partly on any increases in the number of patients seen in categories (a) and (b) above, and partly on any lessening in waiting times in these categories;
• Assigning volunteers or counsellors to talk with people waiting in casualty, to help sort out non-medical problems, to make phone calls for the patient, to liaise with the nurse in charge, etc;

• Airport-type TV monitors to let people know likely waiting times for non-urgent cases or other developments;

• Transport to take patients to neighbouring hospitals if they are not so over-stretched;

• Prominently advertised suggestion schemes so that patients can add their ideas.

A model hospital

A floor of San Francisco's Pacific Medical Center has become the USA's first 'consumer-oriented hospital unit.' Its features include a non-institutional, home-like decor, free nutritional guidance, nurses who give massages, tapes and films, uninterrupted sleep schedules and a low noise level.

• *Planetree, California Pacific Medical Center, 2333 Buchanan, San Francisco, CA 94115, USA.*

• *Adapted from New Sense Bulletin, $3 ($50 per annum) from P.O.Box 42211, Los Angeles, Calif. 90042, USA.*

Hospital earplugs not sleeping pills

The NHS could offer patients the choice of safe earplugs or sleeping pills, instead of merely sleeping pills, as at present. It might also be a good idea if they could offer masks for the eyes.

Claire Lachowicz, 40 Aycliffe Road, Shepherds Bush, London W12 0LL (tel 081 743 6685).

Life-saving videos

Details from the 'San Francisco Chronicle' monitored for the Institute by R.D. Sheridan.

With the help of a $15,000 video laser, viewers watching a video on 'Shotgun Wounds to the Abdomen' can guide a staff of nurses and technicians through a simulation of emergency procedures to save a boy's life. If the viewer fails to administer the proper care, the patient dies on screen.

This film was one of over 400 entries in a medical film festival put on by the John Muir Memorial Hospital in Walnut Creek, California.

'For some surgical procedures, there is no better way to teach than on film,' says festival director Chip Bissell.

The four main cot death risks

A campaigning 'This Week' programme on ITV persuaded the NHS to notify all health professionals in the UK of some of the main situations likely to lead to cot deaths, as discovered in New Zealand research. New Zealand has greatly reduced the cot death rate there – it used to be as exceptionally high as it is in the UK (four deaths per 1000 babies).

The controlled New Zealand research revealed that:

• 73% of all cot deaths were of babies lying on their stomachs;

• 63% were of babies whose mothers smoked;

• Those babies sleeping in the parents' bed (as opposed to merely being fed there) were three times more likely to die than those who slept in a cot;

• 33.6% were not being breastfed.

The New Zealand research indicates that the UK rate of 2000 cot deaths a year could be reduced to 500 a year, if a sufficiently widespread and persuasive campaign were conducted to inform parents and health professionals of these risk factors.

The UK government's leaflet does not mention the last of the four New Zealand factors, about the importance of breastfeeding, but adds that babies must not be allowed to get too warm (through use of duvets or too heavy blankets).

Literature is available from the Foundation for the Study of Infant Deaths, 35 Belgrave Square, London SW1X 8QB (tel 071 388 8282); or the Department of Health leaflet 'Reducing the Risk of Cot Death' is available from Health Publications Unit, No 2 Site, Heywood Stores, Manchester Road, Heywood, Lancashire OL10 2PZ.

Self-directed health education for kids

A suggestion by an American doctor, Tom Ferguson in his journal Medical Self-Care, reprinted in the Utne Reader (Lens Publishing Co, 1624 Harmon Place, Suite 330, Minneapolis MN55403, USA; subs $28).

'Our dependency on the medical profession is largely a product of training by the culture,' says Ferguson. 'So if you want to make the biggest impact in a 20 to 40 year period, probably the most cost-effective thing you could do would be to arrange for kids at school to be in charge of a "health programme" that would allow them to study whatever they wanted, and that would put people who knew something about health – nurses, doctors, health educators – at their disposal. They would learn that they could initiate and control and be in charge of health care – which is just the opposite of what we learn now.'

> 'Arrange for kids at school to be in charge of a health programme'

A Currie scale for health warnings

Nicholas Albery

This is a slightly tongue-in-cheek analogy to the Richter scale for earthquakes. Why not a similar scale for health warnings, named, I suggest, in honour of Edwina Currie and her ministerial salmonella warnings, and administered by a reputable independent health organisation? Health warnings would then range in seriousness from 10 Curries, for an epidemic with millions dying, to 1 Currie, for an infection causing death or severe handicap in very exceptional circumstances. Such a scale would be an instant way for the public to know how seriously to take each new health scare, and the warnings could be upgraded or downgraded as necessary.

> 'Health warnings would then range in seriousness from 10 Curries, for an epidemic with millions dying, to 1 Currie, for an infection causing death or severe handicap in very exceptional circumstances'

Nicholas Albery, 20 Heber Road, London NW2 6AA (tel 081 208 2853; fax 081 452 6434).

Personal logbooks for patients

Item excerpted from the 'Journal of Alternative and Complementary Medicine'.

A personal 'logbook' scheme, in which patients can keep a record of the medical treatment they have received, has been started by Dr Harry Howell at the Candida and Colon Clinic in Sherborne, Dorset, as part of his campaign to take the mystique out of medicine.

> 'Patients can keep a record of the medical treatment they have received'

The logbooks contain details of each patient's medical history along with a comprehensive outline of treatment being undertaken. There is also a page devoted to good dietary advice.

Dr Howell explained: 'Patients have a right to know the truth about their condition and having a logbook to keep with them certainly helps them to feel more relaxed and involved with their treatment.'

Dr Howell fills in the patient's logbook himself, and despite the extra time this takes he is convinced the benefits to the patient far outweigh the disadvantages to him.

Dr Howell, Principal, Candida and Colon Clinic, 93 Cheap Street, Sherborne, Dorset DT9 3LS (tel 0935 813257). This scheme was highly commended in the Social Inventions Awards.

Patient's advance request for full information

M.E. Wright

Adapted extract from a letter by M.E. Wright of Cambridge in 'Which? Way to Health'.

I have drafted the following letter to my new GP to establish an understanding between us from the start. I would be interested to know how far others might find this a pattern for their own wishes – a sort of patients' charter:

'I am keen to remain independent of others and in control of my life as long as possible, and to that end to co-operate in my health care as fully as possible. I would like to have early diagnosis on any complaints, and full information about what symptoms may mean, of alternative treatments, and of risks taken in having or refusing them.'

> 'I would like to have full information about what symptoms may mean, of alternative treatments, and of risks taken in having or refusing them'

Art in the doctor's surgery

Adapted extract from the West Midlands Arts Newsletter, monitored for the Institute by Kim Taplin.

Malcolm Rigler, GP at Withymoor Village Surgery in Brierly Hill, said recently: 'The arts are essential to my work as a doctor.'

> 'Visual artists were employed to work with local people both towards a set of health education posters and on a celebratory lantern procession'

His surgery serves mainly a large housing estate. One of his projects was 'A Breath of Fresh Air' for which visual artists Alison Jones and John Angus were employed to work with local people both towards a set of health education posters and on a celebratory lantern procession. The posters are bright, witty and accessible, innovative both aesthetically and in health promotion. They are now in demand across the country.

The lantern procession was warming and spectacular, and lantern-making skills were passed on to the local people, who are now teaching others, towards further celebrations.

And the work continues. Dave Reeves, a poet who lives in Dudley, has started work in the surgery, offering writing advice on anything from letter writing to poetry, from reminiscence to fiction-making. A particular focus of his work will bring together local school pupils and elderly people to exchange, share and begin to articulate in writing their experience of being ill, being cared for, of caring, and of being well.

> 'The crucial connection is being made between well-being and self-empowerment, between community health and shared artistic endeavour'

Underlying all this work, the crucial connection is being made between well-being and self-empowerment, between community health and shared artistic endeavour.

The longer term aim is to strengthen the curative and information links between the local surgery, other doctors locally, the wider health service, education, the libraries and churches in order to move towards a situation where individuals, families, other groupings and the wider community feel they are, as far as is humanly possible, in control of their own lives, and can promote the health and well-being of their own community.

Promoting Self-Esteem

From an article by Ivor Davis in the Times.

The California Task Force to Promote Self-Esteem, created in 1987 by Assemblyman John Vasconcellos, received a $245,000 allocation from the state budget and Californian counties set up their own committees on self-esteem.

'Virtually every social problem can be traced to people's lack of self-love'

'Virtually every social problem we have,' says anthropologist Andrew Mecca, the group's chairman, 'can be traced to people's lack of self-love: alcohol and drug abuse, teenage pregnancy, crime, child abuse, chronic welfare, dependency and poor educational performance.'

Eight professors at the University of California have each written a chapter for the Task Force's first book. 'What started as a huge joke,' says Mecca, 'has become an international subject for serious study. I have spoken to more than 40,000 people on the subject in just one year. Even the most hardened cynics are being won over.'

California Task Force to Promote Self-Esteem, and Personal and Social Responsibility, Executive Director Robert Ball, 1130 K Street, Suite 300, Sacramento, CA 95814, USA (tel 916 322 0236).

Aluminium Precaution Notice

Nicholas Albery

Aluminium poisoning, with loss of memory, tremors and jerking, was first reported in 1921, and there is evidence that aluminium can be a neurotoxin. It has been implicated as a factor in patients with senile and presenile dementia of the Alzheimer type and in parkinsonism-dementia. It is widely accepted as the major toxic factor in renal dialysis encephalogy, leading to speech disorders, dementia and convulsions.

The majority view is that, outside an industrial setting, aluminium normally presents no health hazard, but it is nevertheless disturbing that many manufacturers continue routinely and unnecessarily to add aluminium to their products (for instance to some indigestion medicines) and that some water boards outside London add aluminium during the purification process.

My fear is that, as in the case of lead in petrol, it could be at least a decade before the minority scientific warnings are generally accepted, and before the powers that be take adequate precautions, whilst manufacturers and the scientists in their pay or under their sway, will fight a strong rearguard action.

Aluminium is just one example. In our high technology society, there will inevitably be an increasing number of instances of this nature, and the response of government will characteristically be one of years of delay whilst they ponder the issue through commissions of investigation.

My proposal is that some non-governmental organisation of repute should take upon itself to publicise 'Precaution Notices' early on in such cases. These notices would summarise the research results to date, would name the products on the market which contained the suspect compound and equivalent products which did not, and would advise what other precautions concerned members of the public should take. It might also be possible to publicise a 'Reliability Quotient' which would indicate what percentage of the relevant independent scientific community felt that the research findings were sufficiently cogent to justify taking precautions (in the case of aluminium, the Reliability Quotient would still be low at this point, probably under 35%).

'A Reliability Quotient which would indicate what percentage of the relevant independent scientific community felt that the research findings were sufficiently cogent to justify taking precautions'

Postcripts

• The water companies should treat water with ferric sulphate rather than aluminium sulphate. The Lancet (14/1/89) and research published in Norway in 1986 show that aluminium sulphate in the water treatment process – and in the UK high levels were found in Northumberland, Tyne and Wear, Durham, Devon and Cornwall – is linked at such levels to a 50 per cent greater risk of Alzheimer's disease. Yet South West Water for several years successfully used ferric sulphate as a substitute for the main Plymouth water supply and other test sites, and only discontinued doing so because its use required greater supervision than aluminium sulphate to prevent discoloration of the water occurring.

'The water companies should treat water with ferric sulphate rather than aluminium sulphate'

• Thames Water are one of the authorities that do not treat their water with aluminium sulphate, because they use a land-intensive process. But with privatisation they intend to sell off some of their land. This could mean that Thames Water (and other similar authorities) will need to use more additives in their water treatment works.

• The water privatisation bill should be amended to ensure that a water company cannot sell bottled water. Thames Water, for instance, have said publicly that they may one day sell bottled water. The danger is that it would then be in the commercial interest of such companies to allow the tap water to become as murky as they can legally get away with, so as to increase sales of their bottled water.

'It would then be in the commercial interest of water companies to allow the tap water to become as murky as they can get away with, so as to increase sales of their bottled water'

Nicholas Albery, 20 Heber Road, London NW2 6AA (tel 081 208 2853; fax 081 452 6434).

Treatment tips

Nicholas Albery

There needs to be an organisation to which anyone suffering from a particular disease can write in with tips for fellow sufferers as to what has helped him or her, apart from the normal drugs.

'You would be sent all the suggestions for your disease'

We need to take advantage of 'ordinary' people's experience. They live with a disease day-to-day and are quite likely to develop little initiatives that help. Self-help groups can spread this kind of information too, but I imagine a situation where you would be sent a computer print-out of all the best positive suggestions for your particular complaint, which would also record the number of respondents who claimed to have (or to have not) been helped by each suggestion – with perhaps formalised questionnaires for particular suggestions. You would pay for this service, although perhaps less if sending in suggestions of your own at the same time. The organisation would edit the suggestions, adding comments, excluding those that were known to be harmful, keeping a watchful eye on manufacturers' publicity attempts, and keeping in close contact with the main organisations dealing with each disease. At the bottom of each print-out would be a list of relevant reading material and the names and addresses of self-help groups.

This could be a more useful experience for some than attending a self-help group. In the print-out a sufferer would only be exposed to positive suggestions, whereas in a self-help group the suggestible may find themselves adopting the symptoms of fellow sufferers.

A more orthodox version of this Treatment Tips proposal would be a computer network for doctors' surgeries, where a patient who has just been given a particular diagnosis, could be given an up-to-the-minute print-out of a clear explanation of the disease and of useful treatments, detailed warnings connected with any prescribed medicines or with infectiousness, any good self-help tips, and the addresses of self-help groups. Often these are matters that a new sufferer would like to know and to explore, but which a doctor might be unlikely to have the time to talk about fully.

Computer diagnosis in the waiting room

There could also be very user-friendly computers in waiting rooms with expert diagnosis software. Patients would respond to the computer's questions about their symptoms, and the doctor seeing them subsequently would have fuller information than he or she could extract in the normal brief encounter.

Nicholas Albery, 20 Heber Road, London NW2 6AA (tel 081 208 2853; fax 081 452 6434).

Medical advice by phone

From an article in Newsweek by Annetta Miller and Lourdes Rosado, monitored for the Institute by Roger Knights.

A recent development in health care in the States is for high-tech methods of connecting patients with health information:

• The Doctors By Phone service in New York offers medical advice for $3 a minute. It is staffed by 80 physicians, who are paid £40 an hour to advise callers on everything from Lyme disease to chapped lips. Most callers are not experiencing medical emergencies but want general information.

• Ask the Pharmacists, in Chapel Hill, North Carolina, charges $1.95 a minute for a phone-operated pharmaceutical advice service.

'Connect by modem over the phone to access d.i.y. diagnostic computer programs'

• The San-Francisco-based InterPractice Systems is restricted to patients of its health maintenance organisation, but allows them to connect by modem over the phone to get answers to medical questions and to access d.i.y. diagnostic computer programs. InterPractice's chief executive officer, Dr Albert Martin, believes that by eliminating unnecessary office visits, the program could cut operating costs by 20%.

Exercising against backache

From the Independent.

A new treatment for backache which uses intensive exercises during actual bouts of pain has been developed in Denmark. The new approach flies in the face of orthodox medical advice that rest is the best thing for backache. But practitioners say that it can relieve virtually 100 per cent of acute cases and 80 per cent of chronic cases, even in patients who have suffered for years.

'Doctors have always told their back pain patients to keep quiet and warm and not to move – to avoid the things that cause them pain,' says Professor Preben Plum, one of the method's keenest advocates. 'What we do is the exact opposite.' Their exercises are repeated 60 to 100 times during an hour's session. People with acute back pain can only perform these exercises, however, with the help of an assistant – any intelligent, fairly strong adult will do – whose job it is to carry the weight of the sufferer while the movements are made – until he or she feels able to perform them unaided. Most sufferers will feel sufficiently pain-free to start doing the exercises themselves after about an hour, Professor Plum maintains, because by then their back muscles will have started to function normally.

'Back pain is prevalent in our society because machines have taken over most of the work which was formerly carried out by people'

The treatment, developed by Professor Plum and former bodybuilder Teedy Ofeldt, is based on the theory that back pain is prevalent in our society because machines have taken over most of the work which was formerly carried out by people. This means that many of our muscles, especially those in our backs and shoulders, have become weak and unable to function normally.

The exercises are reproduced on a poster available for £2·50 including postage from Back Pain Poster, the Independent, 40 City Road, London EC1Y 2DB, with cheques made payable to 'Newspaper Publishing plc'.

First Aider stickers

Steven Burkeman of York was slightly shocked when he realised that he had no idea who were the nearest 'first aiders' in his neighbourhood, able to help in an emergency. He and Ian Care propose that the first aid organisations should issue to those completing courses not only the certificates, but also a few stickers with a white cross on a green background, saying 'First Aider' – which could then be stuck on work desks, vehicles or front windows.

'First Aider stickers on work desks, vehicles or front windows'

'We use these symbols at work, even on our overalls,' says Ian Care, 'with a fire symbol for members of the fire crew and those trained in fire fighting' – London Underground should use these symbols on their unifoms.

The St Johns Ambulance already provide pin-on badges for both children and adults; but Pamela Mounter at the Red Cross warns that members of the public with first aid stickers in the window could be taken advantage of by muggers gaining access by pretending to be injured.

Steven Burkeman, 8 Whitby Avenue, York YO3 OET (tel 0904 425499 h; 0904 627810 w). Ian Care, 8 Kings Drive, Littleover, Derby DE3 6EU (tel 0332 46089).

Black triangles for new medicines

Dr Andrew Herxheimer

A black triangle should be put on the label of all dispensed medicines that are new enough for the Committee on Safety of Medicines to want all unexpected effects reported to them. Then patients can tell their doctors and the doctors can report the effects to the Committee. I want the Committee to propose this labelling officially to pharmacists, doctors and industry.

Dr Andrew Herxheimer, 9 Park Crescent, London N3 2NL (tel 081 346 5470; fax 081 346 0407). The idea is expanded in Self-Health issue 18 (published by the Consumers Association, 2 Marylebone Road, London NW1 4DX).

Nurses responsible for individual patients

From the Daily Telegraph, monitored for the Institute by Nigel Bradley.

Miss Rebecca Malby, 25, a project officer from Waltham Forest Health Authority, received the Cosmopolitan Woman of Tomorrow award. She has devised a new approach to hospital care in which patients are assigned to nurses who are individually responsible for them from admission to discharge.

Wildlife areas around hospitals

Pat Hartridge

This idea was born during two grey weeks in November 1984 in the isolation unit of the Churchill Hospital Oxford, awaiting diagnosis of Legionnaires' Disease. My stay was enlivened by a robin who perched on a wall outside my window. A string of nuts would probably have produced a bluetit or two, and a birdtable would have been better than TV. My home convalescence was enlivened by recording wildlife from my window.

'To encourage birds, bees and butterflies to come closer to the wards, to be seen by the patients'

So this plan for wildlife areas around hospitals is to encourage birds, bees and butterflies to come closer to the wards, to be seen by the patients; and by using birdbaths, feeding stations, nestboxes and plants specially chosen to be attractive to them:

• To encourage those patients who are keen to record sightings of various species for their own interest and to add to their local nature conservancy records;

• To help create an interest outside the daily routine of the ward, and encourage visitors to bring gifts of birdseed rather than flowers when visiting.

For the long-term disabled, there would be visiting speakers on wildlife topics to increase knowledge and to add enjoyment to observation, with, perhaps, the help of volunteers from nearby schools to help with the maintenance of the sites once established.

After putting this idea to the Institute for Social Inventions, I was encouraged to enter it in their annual competition *(Ed: it won the Ecology prize in 1986)*. In order to do this, I had to show that the scheme was viable and I therefore approached local hospitals for their reaction. The Churchill Hospital was particularly enthusiastic and with the active help of the Assistant Nursing Officer, Mrs Petursson, the areas to be planted were planned.

My original idea – for two or three gardens to be planted and maintained by volunteers from the hospital and local schools – was defeated by its own success. The site proved so rich in likely sites that a more organised workforce was obviously needed and I got the Berks, Bucks and Oxon Naturalists' Trust to act as agents for me through their MSC Community Programme. This programme ended in 1988, and the scheme has since depended on myself and one or two volunteers.

The Royal Society for Nature Conservation have since put together a research report and project pack on how to get such hospital wildlife gardens off the ground (we convinced them that it was with great difficulty!). There are now a large number of Hospital Wildlife Gardens in progress or under consideration in the UK.

Pat Hartridge, 49 Old Road, Wheatley, Oxford, OX9 1NX (tel 08677 4487). The research report (£3) and project pack (£2) are available from The Royal Society for Nature Conservation, the Green, Witham Park, Waterside South, Lincoln, LN5 7JR (tel 0522 544400).

Sensorium

Yvonne Malik

Tape sounds – of the dawn chorus, lambs, swallows, the sea, wind in the trees, waterfalls, milk bottles, handbells; bunches of – hawthorn, bluebells, mints and herbs, cut hay; the feel of – pussy willow, feathers, autumn leaves, chestnuts still in their spiky jackets, candied peel, etc. A 'sensorium' with these components could bring a reminder of the seasons to those confined to the sameness of long-stay hospitals and retirement homes and could be of help in a hospice. The idea could be adapted by individual families or small groups, who would make their own choices with particular persons or circumstances in mind. The senses, particularly those of sound and smell, and to a lesser extent those of touch and taste, would help bring the flavour of the changing seasons. Perhaps a local museum could join in and add things from past hobbies and pastimes, objects which could be borrowed and hand-held.

'The flavour of the changing seasons'

Yvonne Malik, 145 Walker Street, Rhodes, Near Middleton, Manchester M24 4QF (tel 061 643 1461).

Stroke Language

Valerie Yule

The idea of 'Stroke Language' is a simple system of signs that everyone should know, so that if they are ever in the situation of being paralysed or unable to communicate in the normal ways, they can still transmit messages by whatever movement remains possible to them.

It could be designed by a medical and speech-therapy team in close collaboration with Stroke Associations and other representatives of patients and families, and copies could be available in Post Offices, Libraries, schools, etc as well as in hospitals for patient-staff-visitor use.

One of the worst things for patients who cannot speak or write is the inability to communicate even urgent messages about their needs and wants, even though they still have the mental ability to think, learn, and remember. Sometimes in a hospital or emergency situation, people are faced with others who speak a completely different language. If there were a public system of signs, then in an emergency, communication could remain possible.

There would be alternative means of communicating the major needs, based on the behaviour that is most commonly remaining to paralysed and badly hurt people – eg communicating through the eyes, or gross motor movements of mouth or limb, or fine movements of one hand.

For example, suppose there was international agreement about eye movements:

Eye movements

Shut in response to a question = no;
Open wide = yes;
Moving round = don't know, not sure;
Blink quickly = food need;

'Eyes shut in response to a question = no. Open wide = yes'

Turned to nearest wall = toilet need;
Turned up = pain or discomfort;
Turned to nearest window or furthest wall = need for company;
Blink slowly = need for sleep;
Screwed up = want TV, book, radio, or other entertainment.

Once the major need has been communicated, other people can find out the exact need by asking questions that can be answered 'yes/no'.

Patients could be shown a large chart giving these signs and their meanings (in both print and symbol) so that they could use the sign they wished. Patients who could point in any way, eg finger, or stick between the teeth could also point to the message they wished to make.

Alternative means for the same messages could use tongue, fingers or toes, or head turning.

It is often too late to learn a 'Stroke Language' after communication has been cut off. Better for everyone to have some idea of it beforehand.

Valerie Yule, 57 Waimarie Drive, Mount Waverley, Vic. Australia 3149 (tel 807 4315).

Editorial comment

There is a device called an E-tram frame which is used for communicating through eye movements. The frame consists of transparent perspex on a base, with letters of the alphabet on the perspex in various colours and these colours repeated on each corner. The patient looks at a corner to indicate a particular colour, such as red, and the 'listener' can then elucidate through 'yes/no' questions which of the red letters (A, B, C or D) the patient is referring to. It is a laborious method of communication, but at least can be used for complicated thoughts.

There could be a role for Yule's Stroke Language, as a quick and simple language to complement the E-tram frame, and particularly for use in emergencies (although, as with the E-tram frame, it would be harder for stroke victims with damage to the left hemisphere of the brain to master). One of Yule's eye movements should indicate 'get me the E-tram frame, I have something complex to say.' Yule suggests involving schools; children could be taught ten or so basic eye movements at school as a kind of game – the movements might then have become second nature by the time they came to need them.

'The patient looks at a corner to indicate a particular colour, such as red, and the "listener" can then elucidate through "yes/no" questions which of the red letters (A, B, C or D) the patient is referring to'

Mirror Image Therapy

Richard Frenkel

The mirror is anti-hallucinogenic. When a therapy patient is actively hallucinating, he is asked to look at his image in the mirror and to focus constantly on his image. Invariably the voices disappear from the patient for a period of twenty-one to twenty-six seconds. Ambulatory patients are taught to carry pocket mirrors with them so that they can control the 'voices' any time they wish.

> 'Patients carry pocket mirrors with them so that they can control the "voices" any time they wish'

More generally, Mirror Image Projective Technique (MIPT) is a diagnostic-therapeutic instrument that is within easy reach of any psychotherapist.

The patient is asked to focus on his mirror image. When the patient becomes inducted into a 'mirror trance', he is then asked to free associate to his image. Defences are unblocked and the unconscious mind is permitted to flow, bringing forth vital feelings and thoughts of recent and past experiences. Intermittently, the patient focuses and unfocuses his eyes upon the image, as he ventures from reality to the unconscious and back. He is a participant observer while using the mirror. In some cases, immediate interpretations can be made from the data gathered. Occasionally, primary instantaneous insight is gained by the patient.

Child Mirror Therapy was employed with five child stutterers. The seven-year-old children all took turns using the mirror in the classroom. They free associated to their mirror image rather easily as if it were play therapy. They exposed their problems to their fellow students and teacher. Many simple problems were solved rather quickly for the children.

Depression. The MIPT is most useful in decreasing depression. The mirror is an antidepressant instrument. At times it will provoke the patient to cry, and thus relieve anger. This reduces the depression in the individual.

Suicide prevention. Since the MIPT decompresses depression, this reduces considerably the chance of the patient acting in a suicidal manner.

Reducing anxiety. The mirror precipitously reduces a patient's anxiety. Mirror responses 'gush out' from the patient and anxiety disappears. I term this the 'gushing phenomenon'. Panic states are thus obviated. Phobic patients are helped by this mirror manoeuvre.

Extracted from the extraordinary volume of 724 pages, 'The Psychotherapy Handbook, the A to Z Guide to more than 250 Therapies in Use Today' (New England Library, US$ 9-95).

Schizophrenic helped by 'flow' happiness theory

Adapted extract from an article by Mark Honigsbaum in the Independent.

Mihaly Czikszentmihalyi, a professor of psychology at the University of Chicago, believes that he has identified the source of human happiness. It comes from what he calls 'flow', a state of deep concentration or concentrated activity. It is a universal experience that occurs whenever individuals set themselves a goal and seek to overcome the obstacles in their way to enjoying it. People typically then report feeling strong, alert, in effortless control and at the peak of their abilities. Emotional problems and the sense of time seem to disappear.

> 'He has identified the source of human happiness. It comes from concentrated activity'

Czikszentmihalyi cites the case of a female schizophrenic in Holland who had failed to respond to conventional psychiatric treatment. Using an electronic beeper, psychiatrists interrupted the woman at different points in the day and asked her how she felt. After doing this a number of times, they discovered that she was invariably happiest when cutting her nails. Concluding that this was for her an optimal experience, they found her a job as a manicurist and successfully returned her to the community.

Czikszentmihalyi's book 'Flow: The Psychology of Optimal Experience' has sold more than 300,000 copies in the States.

Vegetarian diet eases arthritis

Adapted from an article in the Lancet (12/10/91) by Dr Jens Kjeldsen-Kragh and colleagues of the Department of General Practice, University of Oslo, and from a report in the Independent by Celia Hall.

Fasting is known to be an effective treatment for rheumatoid arthritis, but most patients relapse on reintroduction of food. The effect of fasting followed by one year of a vegetarian diet was assessed in this randomised, single-blind controlled trial.

> 'They began with a seven to ten day subtotal fast. After the fast the patients re-introduced a 'new' food item every second day'

27 patients were allocated to a four-week stay at a health farm. They began with a seven to ten day subtotal fast – taking only herbal teas, garlic, vegetable broth, decoction of potatoes and parsley, and juice extracts from carrots, beets and celery. After the fast the patients reintroduced a 'new' food item every second day. If they noticed an increase in pain, stiffness or joint swelling within two to 48 hours this item was omitted from the diet for at least seven days. If symptoms were exacerbated on reintroduction of this food item, it was excluded from the diet for the rest of the study period. During the first 3.5 months, the patients were asked not to eat food that contained gluten, meat, fish, eggs, dairy products, refined sugar or citrus fruits. Salt, strong spices, and preservatives were avoided – likewise alcoholic beverages, tea and coffee. After this period, the patients were allowed to reintroduce milk, other dairy products and gluten-containing foods in the way described above. The patients who did not use cod liver oil supplemented their diet with vitamin D during the first four months.

A control group of 26 patients stayed for four weeks at a

convalescent home, but ate an ordinary diet throughout the whole study period.

After four weeks at the health farm the diet group showed a significant improvement in the number of tender joints, Ritchie's articular index, the number of swollen joints, pain scores, the duration of morning stiffness, grip strength, erythrocyte sedimentation rate, C-reactive protein, white blood cell count and a health assessment questionnaire score.

In the control group, only pain score improved significantly. The benefits in the diet group were still present after one year, and evaluation of the whole course showed significant advantages for the diet group in all measured indices.

Food allergy or intolerance is unlikely to explain the improvement in all the patients who changed their diet. Interest has been drawn to dietary fatty acids and their ability to modulate the inflammatory process (Kremer JM, Lawrence DA, Jubix W, et al. 'Dietary fish oil and olive oil supplementation in patients with rheumatoid arthritis. Clinical and immunological effects.' *Arthritis Rheum* 1990; 33: 810-20). A switch to vegetarian diet causes an extensive change in the profile of the fatty acids of the serum phospholipids. These changes may favour production of prostaglandins and leukotrienes with less inflammatory activity.

This dietary regimen seems to be a useful supplement to conventional medical treatment of rheumatoid arthritis.

- *'Controlled trial of fasting and one-year vegetarian diet in rheumatoid arthritis' by Jens Kjeldsen-Kragh, Margaretha Haugen, Christian F. Borchgrevink, Even Laerum, Morten Eek, Petter Mowinkel, Knut Hovi, Øystein Førre.*
- *Dr J. Kjeldsen-Kragh is at present at the Institute of Immunology and Rheumatology, National Hospital, Olso, Norway (tel 47 2 867010; fax 47 2 207287).*

Ibogaine as a possible cure for drug addiction?

From MAPS Vol II Number 1, from an item in Green Action (USA), Vol. 7, No. 1, monitored for the Institute by Roger Knights, and from a communication from Howard Lotsof.

Promising research with the drug Ibogaine – derived from the African Iboga plant – gives hope that addiction can be cured.

'Early tests show Ibogaine to be 70% effective in curing heroin and cocaine addiction'

In 1956 CIBA-Geigy (a major drug company) found Ibogaine potentiates morphine analgesia, but did not pursue it. In '61-'62, Howard Lotsof and a group of spin-off researchers found that of seven drug users (3 heroin, 4 cocaine and heroin) trying Ibogaine, five spontaneously cleaned up, without intending to. In 1966, the FDA banned all further research into about 25 indole compounds, including Ibogaine.

In the eighties, Lotsof founded a small, private company called NDA International, run out of Staten Island, NY. NDA is developing Ibogaine as a treatment to block the physical symptoms of withdrawal from heroin and cocaine. United States patents have been awarded to him as the inventor of the ENDABUSE (Ibogaine) procedure.

Early tests show Ibogaine, claims Lotsof, 'to be 70% effective in curing the craving for heroin and cocaine and 100% successful in enabling physical withdrawal.' Most attempted cures for heroin addiction fail 90% of the time.

ENDABUSE is non-narcotic, and not a replacement drug; is non-addicting; is administered orally without injections; is rapid – beginning to work within 35 minutes, and the treatment is completed and the patient sent home within 48 hours; is clinically administered and long lasting – a booster is required in a few cases after 5 or 6 months; and is natural, in that the active ingredient is extracted from the Tabernanthe Iboga plant, found in West Africa (where it is used in rituals related to the Bwiti religion for rites of passage to adult life).

In 1988 doctors in the Netherlands at Erasmus University, Rotterdam, published confirmatory evidence that Ibogaine attenuated withdrawal symptoms in rats made morphine dependent. Further work in the States has been done at the Albany Medical College and the City University of New York Medical School.

- *Howard Lotsof, NDA International, 46 Oxford Place, Statten Island, NY 10301, USA (tel 718 442 2754; fax 201 487 2117).*
- *MAPS, the Multidisciplinary Association for Psychedelic Studies, 1801 Tippah Avenue, Charlotte, NC 28205, USA (tel 704 358 9830; fax 704 358 1650).*

Concession-rate therapy

'The Holistic Health Concessions Register' is an informal telephone service detailing private therapists or alternative medicine practitioners who are prepared to make 'realistic' concessions to the unemployed or people on low incomes.

It was started by Sarah Mole, a single parent living in Poplar on social security. 'I went looking for therapy myself,' she says, 'and I was put off by the exorbitant fees. It made me cringe to go round asking for a cheaper rate.'

The register, run by David Burke, is free to those seeking information. There are over 250 practitioners on the books (covering acupuncture, reflexology, psychotherapy, homeopathy, counselling, osteopathy, massage, hypnotherapy, dietary therapy, assertion training, aromatherapy, metamorphic technique, alexander technique, spiritual healing, rebirthing and iridology). More practitioners, prepared to offer concessions to the low wages or unemployed, are welcomed. They are asked to pay a £10 subscription fee to fund the Register.

Holistic Health Concessions Register, 55a Longbridge Rpad, Earls Court, London SW5 9SF (tel 071 244 7578).

Counsellors not GPs

Tim Pears

I suggest that the person a patient meets at their health centre should be not a GP but an agent, a counsellor. This person would listen to the patient describing themselves and their symptoms, and be able to inform the patient of the various treatments available – the whole range of medical practices.

The patient – or client – would be able to choose the medical approach suited to their condition, as well as one that felt suitable for their own personality. It is, after all, one of the insights of holistic medicine that different approaches represent different metaphors for our ideas of health and illness, and that belief in the efficacy of a treatment may be as relevant to recovery as the material basis of that treatment.

An increasing number of people are turning away from orthodox medicine towards a wide range of alternative medicine: acupuncture, analysis, osteopathy, massage, herbalism and so on, that have in common both a holistic and a preventive approach to health.

If this is what people want, one might ask why it should not be made freely available within the Health Service for which they pay through income tax.

Tim Pears, 116a Walton Street, Oxford OX2 6AJ (tel 0865 52605).

Complementary medicine on the NHS

Adapted extract from an article by Cassandra Marks in 'I-to-I' magazine (92 Prince of Wales Road, London NW5 2NE, tel 071 267 7094; fax 071 284 3063).

A unique health project has managed to gain funding without doing it under the auspices of a doctor: the Hoxton Health Project was set up in 1987 as an NHS pilot project, funded by the Inner City Partnership and the local health authority. A group practice of alternative therapists, including acupuncture, homoeopathy and shiatsu massage, they provide treatment to local people over the age of 55. Conducting a clinical audit assessing variables such as pain relief, joint movement, drug intake and the quality of life to demonstrate their effectiveness, they are now applying for permanent funding from the NHS. They look set to become the first such clinic made up of lay practitioners to be part of the establishment.

> 'An NHS pilot project providing acupuncture, homoeopathy and shiatsu massage to local people over the age of 55'

Cassandra Marks, 8A Burghley Road, London NW5 (tel 071 485 9362).

The Neal's Yard Agency for Personal Development

Extracted from a press release for one the most recent additions to the alternative businesses in Neal's Yard, Covent Garden, started by Institute director Nicholas Saunders and his colleagues.

Everyone needs an agent. Even rich and famous novelists like Jeffrey Archer have agents to help them on their way. But everyone, not just writers, would benefit from an agent to help them develop their own personal untapped potential in life. So far there have been literary agencies, job agencies, marriage agencies, travel agencies, all sorts of specific agencies – but now, for the first time, an agency for the development of the whole person, situated in that mecca for alternative lifestyles: Neal's Yard.

> 'Everyone, not just writers, would benefit from an agent to help them develop their own personal untapped potential in life'

The Agency opened in 1991, run by psychotherapist and self-defence teacher Ulrike Speyer, adventure holiday specialist Mike Carnill and by Nicholas Saunders, the founder of the 'Alternative London' guides and the man who started most of the businesses in Neal's Yard.

> 'A whole person is a group of sub-personalities, most of which often get very little chance for exercise'

So, do you want to remodel your whole life? Or do you just want some fine tuning? The Agency can help. A whole person is a group of sub-personalities, most of which often get very little chance for exercise and development, lost in the routine habits of life. The Agency can help you select a set of courses that draw out this unused potential.

The Neal's Yard Agency for Personal Development can start you off, if you wish, with an in-depth consultation, a kind of personal audit, where you look at the way your life has been, is now and could be in the future. The consultant helps you with this audit and helps you select the first steps on the paths you would like to explore – whether workshops, courses, activities, therapies or whatever it may be.

For instance, at present people often jump impulsively into unsuitable personal therapies that can last for years and cost them thousands of pounds, without first consulting someone who knows the range of therapies available, and what might suit that particular person.

Or you may be dissatisfied with the way your life is going and want help in exploring your purpose in life; or you may want a complete change or new adventures.

> 'The Agency acts without charge to the client to provide leaflets and other information on a huge variety of courses a alternative possibilities on offer'

For those that don't feel they need an in-depth consultation, the Agency simply acts without charge to the client to provide leaflets and other information on a huge variety of courses and alternative possibilities on offer. So whether you want two weeks of sand, sea, nude bathing and mild therapy on a Mediterranean island; a Rebirthing course in Spain; a five week opportunity to live and learn alongside famous alternative gurus and teachers in Devon; or evenings of shamanistic rituals and dancing in London – then this Agency has the details. There are hundreds of such courses on offer, with the information now gathered together in one place, enabling you to redesign your life with your own tailor-made course of study, workshops and activities; and to fulfil your untapped potential

– physical, emotional, spiritual, political and creative.

The Neal's Yard Agency for Personal Development, 14 Neal's Yard, London WC2H 9DP (tel 071 379 0141; fax 071 379 0135).

Stress Addiction

Branko Bokun

Extracted from a summary of a book by Branko Bokun, 'Stress Addiction – A new theory on evolution' (published by Vita Books, 1989, £6). Bokun is also the author of 'Humour Therapy' (see next item for this).

We are slowly becoming a species of stress addicts. Stress helps the secretion of our brain's opiates, drugging us often to the point of excitement or euphoria. Our obsession with individuality and individual freedom, accompanied by loneliness, is nothing but a major source of stress-related brain opiates.

Our evolution seems to provide a constant increase in the complexity of our minds. If the increase in complexity carries an increase in instability and vulnerability, as it appears to do, then the evolution of the human mind can only increase its precariousness and its insanity. Evidence of this trend can be seen in the constant increase in restlessness and agitation, crime and cruelty, drug addiction, individual indifference and selfishness.

Adapted short extracts from the book follow, to give a taste of its unusual perspectives, which are interesting theories, even where not backed by solid factual evidence:

• Each existence craves for the lesser instability of the previous existence. The general feeling of everything in the universe is that of nostalgia, of a desire to return to the lost paradise of the previous existence. The basic drive of the universe is the drive towards a lesser instability.

'The basic drive of the universe is the drive towards a lesser instability'

• If the first molecule of living matter had been able to express itself in human terms, it would have stressed that it was in an agitated state, that life was fear. In biblical terms, it could be said: 'At the beginning there was fear, and fear begat life.'

• Presumably the fittest are those who are successful in life. In order to be successful, one needs more energy, more aggressiveness, more competitiveness, more ruthlessness and more callousness. This can only be provided by an above-average instability and vulnerability. In fact, evolution seems to produce ever increasing complexities which implies ever increasing instability and vulnerability.

• My theory is that a new species mainly evolves from the more unstable group of individuals of the species.

'Pygmies grow at a lesser rate than other human groups. I think that this is probably due to the fact that pygmies are the happiest people in the world'

• In prepubertal growth there is no significant difference between pygmies and their non-pygmy neighbours. It is during their adolescence that pygmies grow at a lesser rate than other human groups. I think that this is probably due to the fact that pygmies are the happiest people in the world. They spend their adolescent and adult lives playing, dancing and giggling in a happy environment.

• Being more lonely and more role performing, individuals belonging to the middle classes are more susceptible to senile dementia than individuals belonging to working classes.

'When our limbic brain's efficiency is thrown by stress opiates, our mental activity and behaviour become dominated by our oldest brain, the brain we inherited from our reptilian ancestors. The main characteristics are instant gratification, cruelty and extreme selfishness'

• When our limbic brain's efficiency is thrown by stress opiates, our mental activity and behaviour become dominated by our oldest brain, the brain we inherited from our reptilian ancestors. The main characteristics are impulsiveness, automatism, instant gratification, violence, cruelty, nastiness, deviousness, extreme selfishness and self-centredness, here and now reasoning and unscrupulous self-preservation.

'Humanity risks new epidemics due to the progressive increase in stress-induced immuno-deficiency'

• Lessons on anxiety and stress should be introduced in schools and universities and on the shop floors of factories. These courses should explain that humanity risks new epidemics due to the progressive increase in stress-induced immuno-deficiency; and that it is only through humbleness that we can reduce stress addiction, because humbleness reduces pretentiousness. This is the only way to slow down the evolution of humanity towards mental insanity.

Branko Bokun, Vita Books, 26 Chelsea Square, London SW3 6LF (tel 071 352 6919).

Humour Therapy

Branko Bokun (see also above item) advocates the need for humour therapy in 'cancer, psychosomatic diseases, mental disorders, crime, interpersonal and sexual relationships.'

'The brain is also a gland, and that its glandular activity can be manipulated by thoughts or ideas created by the brain's mental activity'

Bokun argues in his book 'Humour Therapy' (published by Vita Books) that the brain is also a gland, and that its glandular activity can be manipulated by thoughts or ideas created by the brain's mental activity. The author blames the mentality of the adolescent male that pervades our society for resulting in high emotional arousal, 'inquietude, uncertainty and the fears of isolated and lonely individuals.'

Humour therapy helps us to realise that both unhappiness and gloom are infectious. 'That is why the pursuit of personal happiness only acquires a realistic meaning if it becomes the pursuit of other people's happiness.'

Bokun proposes humour courses, to help restore our inborn disposition towards playfulness, joy of living, curiosity, exploration and flexibility. His suggestions include:

• Develop a sense of self-ridicule, for instance by talking to oneself in the mirror;

• See amusing and happy films and plays, and read humorous books and magazines;

• Dedicate a corner of one's home to toys, as the mere sight and feel of them lessen tension. Hang pictures of children and animals on the walls rather than staid or gloomy ancestors;

• Find a hobby, but change it the moment it is taken over-seriously. Preferably choose a hobby that cannot go against nature's harmonies, such as sailing or gardening;

• Have a pet and talk to it;

• See life through a haze of analogies to memorised jokes and anecdotes;

• Repeat three times every morning 'I am not the centre of the universe';

• Remember the eleventh commandment 'thou shalt not take thyself too seriously.'

Branko Bokun, Vita Books, 26 Chelsea Square, London SW3 6LF (tel 071 352 6919). The Humour Therapy book (221 pages) is available from this address by mail order for £5 incl. p&p.

The 'Wellness' show

Extracted from the Guardian.

Dr Patch Adams of Arlington, Virginia, charges no money, carries no malpractice insurance and lives with patients in a country farm setting.

'His "products" include nutrition, exercise, wonder, curiosity and love'

Joy, he says, is more important than any other drug. Dr Adams promotes his philosophy of health care through a stage show in which he plays a 19th century snake-oil salesman. His 'products' include nutrition, exercise, wonder, curiosity and love.

Dr Adams lectures regularly at medical schools throughout the US and has begun building a hospital and health care centre on a 310-acre farm in West Virginia. His income is based on donations and fees from his 'Wellness' show.

'The best therapy is being happy. All the other things doctors can do are at best aids,' he says.

'Health is typically defined as the absence of disease. To me, health is a happy, vibrant, exuberant life every single day of your life. Anything less is a certain amount of disease.

'We will never think in terms of cure rates. It gives a false sense of security. People are always "in process" until they die. You don't cure depression. You help a person find happiness, according to their own definition, and hopefully you help them to perpetuate that.

Additional extracts from an interview with Dr Patch Adams in the Washington Post Magazine:

'When a person comes to me, unless the problem is an arterial bleed, which has to be addressed that second, the first goal is to have a friendship happen out of that relationship. So we spend three to four hours in the first meeting. We might go for a walk. If you like to fish, maybe we will go fishing. If you like to run, we run together, and I'll interview you while we are running. By the end of that time, I hope we have a trust, a friendship starting to develop, and from there we can proceed.

'From the start, it was obvious to me that we had to have fun in what we were doing. Forget the patient, it had to be fun for us. Life has to be fun! I saw what life was like when I was serious. I had ulcers and I wanted to kill myself. That was me as a serious person. That failed.

'When you say "That doctor has a good bedside manner", what are you really talking about? The element of love and humour that they bring into the room.

'But the fact is, until we build our place with beds for our patients and the technology required of a modern medical facility, a model, we will have no impact on the health care delivery system in this country, and that's what we're about.'

Dr Adams writes in a letter to the Institute:

For 18+ years we have tried to challenge the problems of health care delivery in the US in a single model:

• By not charging any money – addressing the issue of the power that greed has in our society.

• By carrying no malpractice insurance.

• By living together. Staff and patient can feel a home environment that is not only hospital but also home – farm, theatre, crafts centre, recreational facility, in a beautiful material setting – all to address the issues of boredom, loneliness and fear that also are hurting most patients.

• We will be a place to study health in relationship to community and how one can learn skills of cooperation and compromise. The whole community is an 18 year example of joyful inter-dependence.

• We find humour so important that we will substitute a silly, playful hospital in place of serious ones.

• It will be the first inter-disciplinary hospital in the US – having respect for and working in cooperation with all healers.

• It will be a hospital whose underlying ethic is that of living healthy lives and not just conquering sickness.

Dr Patch Adams, the Gesundheit Institute, 2630 Robert Walker Place, Arlington, Virginia 22207, USA (tel 703 525 8169). He is trying to raise up to four million dollars for his hospital project. The Gesundheit Institute puts out an occasional newsletter called 'Achoo!' ('Good health is a laughing matter – and that's nothing to sneeze at!').

A Mood-Menstrual Diary

Dr Norma Williams

In order to know our place in nature we need knowledge about ourselves. The menstrual cycle in adult female humans is a mixed blessing and women themselves view motherhood with ambivalence. The hormonal changes throughout the menstrual cycle echo this ambivalence and provide opportunity for self-help and self-understanding.

Each woman experiences mood swings and physical exhilaration or depression in response to these hormonal changes.

'How to Keep a Mood Menstrual Diary' is a little book that

includes a year's supply of diary charts with explicit instructions for recording human female responses. Charting responses is a simple, easy way which will give individual women insight into their own bodies and will enhance gender identity.

I have been a gynaecologist for nearly thirty years and I created these charts at the end of the seventies. I have found them very useful in my own practice among women of over thirty different nationalities.

The charts have been used by women of all ages from educationally sub-normal teenagers to happy housewives, international scientists and multinational bankers.

'How to Keep a Mood-Menstrual Diary', by Dr Norma Williams, published by the American Women's Health Centre, 25 Weymouth St, London W1N 3 FJ (tel 071 935 4853) (£4·95 + 50p p&p).

Editorial comment

John Illman reported in the Guardian some research by Dr Donna Stewart, associate professor of psychiatry at Toronto University. Two thirds of the women she questioned reported at least one positive change associated with the pre-menstrual week. Dr Stewart asks: 'what effect does the current emphasis on negative changes have on the expectations of women?'

> '31% feeling increased sexual enjoyment; 18% reporting more attractive breasts; 18% having more energy; 11%, more creative ideas'

The positive pre-menstrual changes reported to her included 32% of the women having a tendency to clean or tidy; 31% feeling increased sexual enjoyment; 18% reporting more attractive breasts; 18% having more energy; 11%, more creative ideas; 8%, performing better at work; 6%, increased confidence; 4%, more calm and relaxed; 4%, increased interest; 3% more sense of well-being; 2% more attractive facial features; 2% performing better socially.

A Pre-Menstrual Tension Centre

Malena Griffiths

A large proportion of women suffer from pre-menstrual tension – P.M.T.

Society too is suffering as a result. Yet under the right circumstances, this difficult week every month can be turned to good effect – there needs to be a 'pre-menstrual centre' where women suffering from P.M.T. can go to have their heightened sensitivity and creativity nourished.

The Women's Centre in Wesley House, Covent Garden, are interested. A PMT Centre there would be a place with a library, a space for relaxing, advice and exchange of experiences and counselling.

Malena Griffiths, Flat 19, 17 Broad Court, London WC2B 5QN (tel 071 240 0556).

Birth trauma and social dynamics

'Every institution is a womb, every boundary is a potential cervix and every change is a little birth,' says David Wasdell, founder director of the Unit for Research into Changing Institutions (URCHIN), a Docklands-based charity. 'Groups react to threat with psychotic levels of anxiety. It is these underlying, primal fantasies at the international level which help explain the arms race. The group's boundaries carry the terror of the cervix. Out-groups threaten these boundaries.'

> 'Every institution is a womb, every boundary is a potential cervix and every change is a little birth'

Our memories reach back before birth, Wasdell claims, and our stress at birth, with cranial pressure and oxygen deprivation, is a shattering and traumatic event for most of us. At a social level, whenever the circumstances unconsciously remind us of birth, for instance as at present, with high stress, low resources and rapid change, this primal trauma is reactivated: 'behaviour regresses, and is characterised by inter-group oppression, scapegoating, paranoid boundary controls and outbursts of anarchic system-destructive activity.'

David Wasdell dealt with his own early traumas through a process of regression and integration. Releasing these has led, he says, to a 'phenomenal increase in my creativity' – and to the publishing of a wide variety of URCHIN research papers. He works internationally as a 'process consultant' and lecturer with business organisations, churches, universities and other institutions, investigating the psychodynamics of large social systems under stress.

David Wasdell, URCHIN, Meridian House, 115 Poplar High Street, London E14 0AE (tel 071 987 3600; fax 071 515 8627).

Chapter twelve

NEIGHBOURHOOD

The only real wealth is cultural wealth

'Bolo Bolo' is a visionary booklet (published by Paranoia City Verlag, Zürich) The main questions it addresses are as follows:
- 'How would I really like to live?'
- 'In what kind of society (or non-society) would I feel most comfortable?'
- 'What do I really want to do with myself?'
- 'Regardless of their practicality, what are my true wishes and desires?'
- 'And let's try to picture all this not in a remote future (reformists always like to talk about the "next generation") but in our own lifetimes, while we're still in pretty good shape, let's say within the next five years...'

> 'How would I really like to live?' 'In what kind of society (or non-society) would I feel most comfortable?' 'What do I really want to do with myself?' 'Regardless of their practicality, what are my true wishes and desires?'

The book's author, styled only as 'p.m.', discusses the constituent elements of his human-scale utopia. The stress is on cultural diversity and on a network of autonomous neighbourhoods, which work together in regional assemblies and whose inhabitants have freedom to 'vote with their feet.' The important point is made that the real wealth of the 'bolos' ('bolo' very roughly = 'neighbourhood' in the author's new international core vocabulary) is not financial but lies in their cultural wealth, their diverse spiritual and material potential or 'nima' as the author terms it – 'their habits, philosophy, values, interests, clothing styles, cuisine, manners, sexual behaviour, education, religion, architecture, crafts, arts, colours, rituals, music, dance, mythology, body-painting: everything that belongs to a cultural identity or tradition.' What follows is extracted from the book's footnotes.

> 'The real wealth of the 'bolos' is not financial but lies in their cultural wealth, their diverse spiritual and material potential'

The Bolo – a context for living

A 'bolo' is the basic agreement (between individuals), a direct personal context for living, producing and dying. It isn't just a traditional neighbourhood, nor a self-help network, nor a tribe. It's true that the number of its inhabitants (500) corresponds to the minimal number of members of the traditional tribe. About 500 individuals form the smallest possible genetic pool of the species Homo sapiens. It seems that this social unit has been typical for all societies of gatherers/ hunters for millions of years – (ie well before Homo sapiens came into being. See Richard E. Leakey and Roger Lewin, 'People of the Lake: Mankind and its Beginnings', Avon, 1979, p. 111). So it's probable that we could feel comfortable in communities of this size. Yet a bolo has many other advantages in the fields of agriculture, energy, medicine and cultural identity.

> 'About 500 individuals form the smallest possible genetic pool of the species Homo sapiens. It seems that this social unit has been typical for all societies of gatherers/hunters for millions of years'

The number of 500 persons seems to be a kind of upper level limit for 'spontaneously' functioning larger social organisms. It corresponds to the inhabitants of typical older urban neighbourhoods in a lot of countries, to an infantry battalion, to the capacity of a larger hall, to the size of a medium enterprise, to a medium-sized school, etc. The reasons are not purely genetic or traditional. The number of 500 persons permits a minimal diversity of age, sex, interests, a basic division of work. At the same time, self-organisation is still possible without special

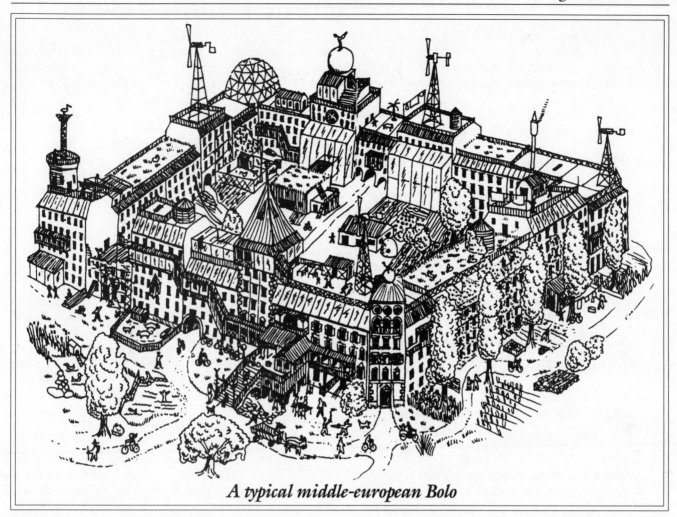

A typical middle-european Bolo

organisms, anonymity is not a necessary consequence (you can still know personally all members of the community, but without necessarily being close friends). Age groups are large enough for social interaction and even endogamy is possible. In an advanced industrialised country there would be about 200 young persons (1-30 years), 200 persons in the middle (30-60), and 100 elderly persons. Age groups (1-9, 10-19, etc) would comprise between 20 and 40 persons (except above 80 years, of course). In Third World areas, these numbers would be different at first (300 young, 150 middle, 50 old), but later on would adapt to the figures above.

'500 persons seems to be a kind of upper level limit for "spontaneously" functioning larger social organisms'

It's typical for most of the alternative and utopian theorists that they conceive their basic communities from an administrative or purely ecological or technical point of view. This is also the case for anarchist or syndicalist theories and for most utopias.

'The Hopi say that a man cannot be a man when he lives in a community that counts more than 3,000 persons'

Thomas More, in 1516, combines 30 large households into units of about 500 persons ('Thirty households, fifteen from either side, are assigned to each hall and take their meals there.' 'Utopia', Washington Square Press, 1971, p. 59). The basic communities of the 19th-century utopians (Fourier, Saint-Simon, Weitling, Cabet, Owen etc) are mostly larger, because they're oriented towards pure autarchy. Fourier's 'phalansteres' are little universes containing all human passions and occupations. Most modern utopias are in fact totalitarian, mono-cultural models organised around work and education. Ironically, some utopian elements have been used for the conception of prisons, hospitals and in totalitarian regimes (fascism, socialism, etc).

'Most modern utopias are in fact totalitarian, mono-cultural models organised around work and education. Ironically, some utopian elements have been used for the conception of prisons, hospitals and in totalitarian regimes'

In 'A Blueprint for Survival' (The Ecologist, Volume 2, No. 1), the basic units are 'neighbourhoods' of about 500 persons that form 'communities' of 5,000 persons and 'regions' of 500,000 persons, which in turn are the basis for 'nations'. Callenbach ('Ecotopia', Bantam New Age Books, 1975) proposed 'mini-cities' of about 10,000 people and communities of 20-30 persons. In a Swiss study (Binswanger, Geissberger,

Ginsburg, 'Wege aus der Wohlstandsfalle', Fischer Alternativ, 1979, p. 233), social units of more than 100 persons are considered to be 'non-transparent', while the Hopi say that 'a man cannot be a man when he lives in a community that counts more than 3,000 persons.' Skinner's 'Walden Two' (Macmillan, 1948) is populated by 2,000 persons, and the largest crowd in his system is 200 persons. See also Galtung's self-reliance communities: 10 squared, 10 cubed, etc.

Most utopias are full of general prescriptions that are compulsory in all their basic dimensions (clothing, work timetables, education, sexuality, etc), and they postulate certain principles of internal organisation (democracy, syphogrants, etc). Reason, practicability, harmony, non-violence, ecology, economic efficiency, morality, all are central motivations. But in a bolo culturally defined people live together and their motivations are not determined by a compulsory set of moral laws. Each bolo is different. Not even a perfectly democratic structure can guarantee the expression and realisation of the desires of the participating persons. This is also a basic flaw of many proposals for self-administration (block councils, neighbourhood-defence committees, soviets, grassroots democracy, etc), especially if such grassroot organisations are initiated and controlled by state or party organisms. Only cultural identity and diversity can guarantee a certain degree of independence and 'democracy'. This is not a question of politics.

> 'Not even a perfectly democratic structure can guarantee the expression and realisation of the desires of the participating persons. Only cultural identity and diversity can guarantee a certain degree of independence and "democracy" '

As the bolos are relatively large, there will be subdivisions and supplementary structures and organisms in most of them. Such problems as having (or not having) children, education (or better: no education at all), polygamy, exogamy, relations, etc cannot be dealt with in such a large frame. These structures will be different in every bolo (*kanas*, families, large households, gangs, single cells, dormitories or not, totems, etc).

> 'Most properties of an "ideal tribe" can be applied to the bolo (cultural identity + self-sufficiency + size + hospitality), but the "real" tribes have left us in the mess we have now. The tribes (that's all of us!) haven't been able to stop the emergence of the planetary work-machine'

For many reasons, the bolos aren't simply tribes – their time has irrevocably gone. The slogan 'Only tribes will survive' sounds beautiful and romantic, but our unfortunate history shows us that tribes haven't survived in most parts of the world, and those that remain are still disappearing. What we know today as tribes are mostly patriarchal, crippled, isolated, defensive and weakened structures, and can serve no longer as practical models. It is true that most properties of an 'ideal tribe' can be applied to the bolo (cultural identity + self-sufficiency + size + hospitality), but the 'real' tribes have left us in the mess we have now. The tribes (that's all of us!) haven't been able to stop the emergence of the planetary work-machine. Once upon a time we were all good savages, yet here's this monster civilisation. There's no reason to assume that the actually surviving tribal societies would have done better – they've just been spared by the circumstances. Only today we can take care of preventing the same 'mistake' (every mistake has got to be made once in history…maybe twice…) happening again. The industrial work-society was not a pure hazard; we've got to face it, learn from it, and no flight into the tribal myth will help us. The real 'Tribal Age' starts just now.

> 'For many of us, society will never be supportable and a "good society" is the name of our nightmare'

Social organisation always means social control – even in the case of the flexible, loosely defined bolos. When money disappears as a means of anonymous social control, this control will reappear in the form of personal, direct supervision, interference, constraint. In fact, any form of solidarity or help can also be considered as a form of social constraint. Every bolo will have to deal with the inevitable dialectics of constraint and help in a different way. Personal social control is the 'price' we pay for the abolition of money. Almost nobody will be able to isolate him or herself and to disappear in the anonymous interstices of a mass society like the present, except in those bolos based on conscious anonymity. Society always means police, politics, repression, intimidation, opportunism, hypocrisy. For many of us, society will never be supportable and a 'good society' is the name of our nightmare. For this reason bolo'bolo cannot be a homogenous system for everybody – there will be left-over spaces for small groups, singles, bums, hermits, etc. Not everybody can live in society. (This aspect is also missing in most utopias or political ideologies – except in good old liberal philosophy, bolo'bolo is closer to liberalism than to socialism … but liberalism alone is as totalitarian as socialism: the ideology of the dominant)…

Cultural identity

The bolos are not primarily ecological survival systems, for if you *only* want to survive it's hardly worth it. The bolos are a framework for the living-up of all kinds of life-styles, philosophies, traditions and passions. Bolo'bolo is not a life-style in itself, but only a flexible system of limits (biological, technical, energetical, etc). As for the knowledge of such limits, ecological and alternativist materials can be quite helpful, but they should never serve to determine the content of the different life-styles. (Fascism had its biological elements…). At the core of bolo'bolo there's 'nima' (cultural identity) and not survival. For this same reason, nima cannot be defined by bolo'bolo, it can only be lived practically. No particular 'alternativist' identity (health foods, earth shoes, woollen clothes, Mother Earth mythology, etc) is proposed.

The crucial function of cultural identity is illustrated best by the fate of the colonised peoples. Their actual misery didn't start with material exploitation, but with the more or less planned destruction of their traditions and religions by the Christian missionaries. Even under present conditions many of these nations could be better off – but they just don't know any more *why* they should be, or what for. Demoralisation goes deeper than economic exploitation. (Of course, the industrialised nations have been demoralised in the same way – it just happened longer ago and has become part of their standard cultures.)

> ' "Culture" is more important than "material survival". People who are about to starve struggle for their religion, their pride, their language and other "superstructural fancies" before they demand a guaranteed minimum wage'

On Western Samoa there is no hunger and almost no disease, and the work intensity is very low. (This is due mainly to the climate and to the rather monotonous diet of taro, fruits and pork.) Western Samoa is one of the 33 poorest countries in the world. It has one of the highest suicide rates in the world. Mostly those killing themselves are young people. These suicides are not due to pure misery (even if it cannot be denied that there is misery), but to demoralisation and the lack of perspectives. The Christian missionaries have destroyed the old religions, traditions, dances, festivals, etc. The islands are full of churches and alcoholics. The paradise had been destroyed long before the arrival of Margaret Mead. In spite of some vulgar-Marxist conceptions, 'culture' is more important than 'material survival', and the hierarchy of basic or other needs is not as obvious as it might seem, but rather 'ethnocentric'. Food is not just calories, cooking styles are not luxuries, houses aren't just shelters, clothes are much more than body insulation. There's no reason why anybody should be puzzled if people who are about to starve struggle for their religion, their pride, their language and other 'superstructural fancies' before they demand a guaranteed minimum wage. It is true that these motivations have been manipulated by political cliques, but this is also the case with 'reasonable' economic struggles. The point is, they exist.

> 'Since the 1960s a period of cultural invention has begun in many – especially industrialised – countries. Having been disappointed by the material riches of the industrial societies, a lot of people have turned to cultural wealth'

Where should the nima come from? It is certainly wrong to look for cultural identities *exclusively* in old ethnic traditions. The knowledge and rediscovery of such traditions is very useful and can be very inspiring, but a 'tradition' can also be born today. Why not invent new myths, languages, new forms of community life, of housing, clothing, etc? One person's traditions can become another's utopia. The invention of cultural identities has been commercialised and neutralised in the forms of fashion, cults, sects, 'waves' and styles. The spreading of cults shows that a lot of people feel the need for a life governed by a well-defined ideological background. The desire that is perverted in the cults is the one of unity of idea and life – a new 'totalitarianism' ('ora et labora'). If bolo'bolo is called a kind of pluralist 'totalitarianism', that's not a bad definition. It can be said that since the 1960s a period of cultural invention has begun in many – especially industrialised – countries: oriental, Egyptian, folk, magical, alchemical and other traditions have been revived. Experimentation with traditional and utopian life-styles has begun. Having been disappointed by the material riches of the industrial societies, a lot of people have turned to cultural wealth.

Since the nima is at the core of a bolo, there can't be any laws, rules or controls over it. For the same reasons, general regulation on work conditions inside the bolos is impossible. Regulated working time has always been the central show-piece of utopian planners. Thomas More in 1516 guarantees a six-hour day, Callenbach a 20-hour week, Andre Gorz ('Les chemins du Paradis – l'agonie du Capital', Galilee, 1983) proposes a 20,000 hour work life. After Marshall Sahlins' research on 'Stone Age Economics' (1972), the two or three hour day is about to win the race. The problem is, who should enforce this minimal working time, and why? Such regulations imply a central state or a similar organism for reward or punishment.

Since there is no state in bolo'bolo, there can't be any (even very favourable) regulations in this field. It is the respective cultural context that defines what is considered as 'work' (= pain) in a certain bolo and what is perceived as 'leisure' (= pleasure), or if such distinction makes any sense at all. Cooking can be a very important ritual in one bolo, a passion, while in another bolo it's a tedious necessity. Maybe music is more important in the latter, whereas in another bolo it would be considered noise. Nobody can know whether there will be a 70 hour work week or a 15 hour work week in a bolo. There is no obligatory life-style, no general budget of work and leisure, just a more or less free flow of passions, perversions and aberrations.

Paranoia City Verlag, Postfach 406, 8026 Zürich, tel 010 411 241 3705 – Anwandstr. 28, 8004 Zürich; 1985; ISBN 0-936756-08-X; 12 Swiss Francs for the English edition, 15 for the Russian, DM 9.80 for the German. There are also editions in Italian, Portuguese and Dutch. The English edition can also be ordered directly from Semiotext, 522 Philosophy Hall, Columbia University, New York, NY, 10027, USA.

Local Distinctiveness

The organisation Common Ground have published a leaflet advocating a 'campaign for locality and distinctiveness.' Its suggestions include:

• Ask 'What makes this place different from another?' Which are the natural, man-made and cultural elements which combine to tell you that you are in your place and not another community two, 20 or 200 miles away? Are there local details and regional touchstones you can identify? Incorporate your findings on a parish map and put it up in a public place for all to see, discuss and act upon.

• Take parish walks by yourself and with friends to look for and discuss the features which make your place distinctive.

• Organise walks with local planning officers and councillors so you can discuss how change, if necessary, should be made.

• Become a 'local correspondent'; express your knowledge

and concerns about locality to the editors of your local newspapers and local radio programmes.

• If you have distinctive buildings, shops, woods in your area, tell the owners how much you appreciate them.

• Take photographs, make drawings, incorporate them into your parish map or put up an exhibition in your community centre, library or village hall which shows the mixture of things which you feel it is important to hang on to.

• Produce postcards which capture the essence of your place.

• Poems, books, photographs, plays, paintings, music, songs, films and festivals can reflect the character of your area and its people. Can you encourage new work which enhances place?

• Explore local sources of stone, brick and wood, and how they might be used today.

• Ask for local produce in local shops, in season.

The Local Distinctiveness Project is seeking alternatives to the spread of uniformity throughout Britain. It is exploring how people recognise the distinctive character of their surroundings, and why this is important to them. Using examples, we hope to encourage the creation of newly distinctive features as well as sensitive responses to existing ones.

Common Ground, 45 Shelton Street, London WC2H 9HJ (tel 071 379 3109; fax 071 836 5741).

Editorial comment

More effective than just walking around with local planning officers and councillors, at least for areas under threat, is to have a Future Workshop where local people brainstorm their own ideas as to how the area's distinctiveness and character can be retained and enhanced, leading to their own future master plan, which they can then require politicians to abide by.

> 'A Future Workshop where local people brainstorm their own ideas as to how the area's distinctiveness and character can be retained and enhanced'

These Future Workshops are described further in the chapter on Promoting Social Inventions.

Creating urban parishes

The health of the body politic depends on the health of its basic cell, which is the parish or neighbourhood, the only level of local government that people can readily identify with, and one which largely transcends party politics. One of the surest ways to bring about urban renewal would be to create parish councils in the cities – local people are the best experts on the needs of their areas; and it is no accident that one of the biggest and most successful unemployment schemes in Britain (with 150 workers) was run by a parish-scale council, Llanelli Rural Community Council in Dyfed, with projects for church and chapel restoration, a watchdog anti-vandalism patrol, pamphlets about local history and a garden clearance scheme for elderly people.

The Association for Neighbourhood Councils very much

hopes that the Secretary of State for the Environment will reconsider the Local Government Boundary Commission's depressing recommendation against urban parish councils for Birmingham.

> 'One of the surest ways to bring about urban renewal would be to create parish councils in the cities'

But what more can be done to promote parish identity and development in the cities?

Parish mapping

One proposal is to extend the 'Parish Mapping' project to the cities. Parish mapping involves identifying the boundaries of your parish or neighbourhood; celebrating these boundaries by walking around them, 'beating the boundaries' as you go – copying old rituals such as upending children at significant boundary points; then involving local schoolchildren and others in drawing up a map of what people most value in their local area, and fixing this map in as prominent a place as possible, for instance by painting it on the wall of the community hall. A further possible extension of parish mapping is for local people to draw up a 'future map' of what they would like to see developed in their area. But for the basic scheme, see the booklets 'Parish Maps' and 'Parish Boundaries' (each £1·75 incl. p&p), from Common Ground.

Parish rates

At present, part of the Boundary Commission's reluctance to recommend urban parish councils is that there is no legal upper limit to the rates such a council can set. A new maximum 3p urban parish council rate would be fair, allowing the average-size council to collect about £100,000, or one and a half per cent of the total rates bill. The Institute for Social Inventions proposes as a further safeguard the principle that there should be no parish rates without the voter having a say in the allocation. The parish council could produce a regular leaflet in which local projects needing funding would describe themselves, and voters would then select which projects to support (see the chapter on Taxation for more on this).

• *The Association for Neighbourhood Councils, Baskerville House, Broad Street, Birmingham 1 (tel 021 200 1027).*

• *Common Ground, 45 Shelton Street, London WC2H 9HJ (tel 071 379 3109; fax 071 836 5741).*

Semi-autonomous parish zones

The report, 'Breaking the Deadlock – Releasing the Energy', published by the Neighbourhood Initiatives Foundation (Suite 23-25, Horsehay House, Horsehay, Telford, Shropshire TF4 3PY, tel 0952 503628) recommends, amongst other ideas for community development, the formation of Community Planning Zones:

The idea of a Community Planning Zone is a modified version of the Simplified Planning Zone that has been introduced by the government for large-scale commercial developers. A Community Planning Zone would have as its purpose that of allowing a local parish council to undertake its own planning in accordance with criteria to be agreed beforehand with the local Planning Authority.

> 'A Parish Trust would be able to develop land and could make part of it available on terms within the reach of those in housing need'

The district council would pass a policy resolution to take development control decisions according to requests made to it by the parish council. The latter would set up a Parish Trust, a registered charity with membership limited to parish councillors. It would be able to develop land and buy and sell land. It could buy land at any price (unencumbered by the district valuer's valuations) and could make part of it available, for instance, on terms within the reach of those in housing need.

The community itself could take the initiative both in preparing plans and making them happen. Instead of reacting, usually negatively, to development proposals made by outsiders, it would face the challenge, and have the advantage, of working out a locally acceptable scheme for itself. The increase in value that development usually brings might not be as great as that which accrues to an outside interest erecting an office block or laying out a theme park, with all the enormous profits going to the outsider; but it might still be substantial and would be properly shared out for the benefit of the community as a whole (with the parish eligible for not less than 50% of the local authority's share of the betterment generated in the area).

Community audits

Freer Spreckley

A community co-op is a way of developing economic self-management in definable communities. We have to move away from job creation – there are no jobs – to wealth creation. One way is to carry out social audits to evaluate the social wealth in a community. Then, look at the entire income of a housing estate – £50,000 to £100,000 per week – and where it goes. £40,000 can be retained within the estate if it acts on a survey of its own needs. Next, look at ways a community can retain its wealth, perhaps by setting up entire service networks.

> '£25 per week spent on groceries by a family on social security means £15,000 on the estate as a whole'

The major problem on estates is not vandalism but total hopelessness. However, within that hopelessness there is nevertheless wealth passing through. £25 per week spent on groceries by a family on social security means £15,000 on the estate as a whole. One can open a small grocery shop, owned by the community, with any profit staying within the community.

The first commercial plan debated by a community co-op on one large estate was for opening a community betting office. The Ladbroke's betting office on that estate made more money than any other shop they have in the U.K. By running their own betting office, the money would stay within the estate. Although I do not agree with betting, one cannot be too moralising. Most voluntary agencies in Hong Kong are provided for from money from the race courses.

Tackling conflicts within communities

Chris Elphick worked for many years with local communities such as Easterhouse, a Glasgow housing estate with high unemployment, helping people release their creative energies through theatre, celebrations and festivals – in the belief that once the enthusiasm and self-confidence were there, employment schemes and other self-help projects would follow. A major achievement saw the creation of the Easterhouse Mosaic Mural – the largest modern hand-built mosaic in Europe – which years later still stands in the middle of the estate untouched by graffiti, a tribute to the skill and vision of local residents. Having left Easterhouse, Chris Elphick was involved with one final achievement on the estate when he helped the Body Shop establish a soap manufacturing plant employing only local labour chosen for their commitment rather than their skills ('skills are easy to learn') and giving a percentage of the profits to the local community.

He experienced at first hand the contrast between the real practical achievements in such communities and destructive internal group tensions exacerbated by external pressures. As he puts it: 'Passion and anger, charisma, commitment, vision, inspiration and unorthodox leadership go hand in hand with a commitment to participative democracy. Such groups usually learn through doing, often in a very painful way.'

Elphick has established a new organisational development consultancy, Kirkham & Elphick, with his partner Hazel Kirkham. This aims to help groups reach their 'underlying well of creativity,' and to discover ways of transforming disempowering aspects of community life such as insecurity, scapegoating, conflict and jealousy so that the transmuted energies benefit the community. 'It's a question,' says Elphick, 'of how it is possible to be creative within the context of poverty, dependency and disadvantage that characterises many communities. How can I be creative, in other words, with neighbours I don't always like, in a work situation I find tense and with constant worries about money?'

Working in close partnership with their clients in the public, private and non-profit sectors, Kirkham & Elphick thus try to help people and organisations to increase their effectiveness.

Chris Elphick, Kirkham & Elphick, 63A High Street, Bangor, Gwynedd LL57 1NR, Wales (tel 0248 372036; fax 0248 372035).

Fighting the council with DTP posters

Michael Moon

Adapted extract from 'Pamphleteering in the 1990s or the Copeland Clog Wars', published by ABMR.

Four weeks ago, chunks of cast-iron guttering fell off a Georgian building in the street where we have our old bookshop in Whitehaven, a small town on the West Cumbrian coast.

'I decided to start a small war'

I decided to start a small war.

I thought I would put up posters and name names. I would state who owned the rotten buildings, what his address was, what his telephone number was and I asked people to ring him up and to ask why he was almost single-handedly ruining the streetscape. Friends breathing in noisily through their teeth said I'd get sued. He's better off than you – he has more clout – what's more, his married daughter is a councillor! So much for her civic pride! I wrote several scripts on my computer, printed them on our laser printer in 30pt Helvetica – big and bold, and with a bucket of Solvite and a six-inch paste brush, went down the street, wearing my black apron, and put up posters on the doors and windows of the offending shops. I went back and forth all day, writing more as the Muse took over, and pasting more – unabashed – in broad daylight, on a market day. I coined some quite good phrases, or so I thought, like:

'Apathy has caused more dereliction in Whitehaven than dry-rot ever could.'

'What I was doing was an electronic form of pamphleteering – just as Swift and Defoe had done centuries before'

As I put up the signs, and made them more readable, it crossed my mind that what I was doing was an electronic form of pamphleteering – just as Swift and Defoe had done centuries before. How mine differed, was that I was more direct, more immediate and I was my own typesetter. I decided that an element of humour would go a long way to prick the bubbles and came up with phrases like these:

'If it takes a set of jump leads to make our Council act over building dereliction – Gear Box on Lowther Street have plenty in stock!'

'If it takes a set of jump leads to make our Council act over building dereliction – Gear Box on Lowther Street have plenty in stock!'

Gear Box loved the passing fame and put copies up in their windows. Another one read:

'If you are tearing your hair out trying to get this Council to act over building disrepair in Roper Street, Ian Kyle will cut it straight again – and his charges are very reasonable.'

With the computer on, it took but a few minutes to bob and weave to the changes, and I was out again with the Solvite bucket and brush as the climate changed. I was better prepared than the Council, unpredictable and quick. The fact that I said I would be prepared to go to jail seemed to filter back to the Council and it put them in a pickle.

Ed: The article ends with suspense: 'What happened next, I'll tell you next month.'

Michael Moon, The Second-Hand Bookshop, 41/2 Roper Street, Whitehaven, West Cumbria (tel 0946 62936).

Neighbourhood corporations

Joseph Rosen

Adapted extracts from a letter. Joseph Rosen writes in his introduction: 'I came across a note in the Fourth World Review concerning your Institute. Like the man in the play who was very much surprised to find he had been speaking prose all his life, I find I am a social inventor without realising it.'

A new type of neighbourhood corporation would encourage its membership to be independent producers and distributors of goods and services. In this respect, it would be different from the traditional corporation in which the organisation is the productive instrument and the personnel are considered no more than another resource. This new type of corporation would reverse the arrangement and become a source of support for its membership. The board of directors of the organisation would be elected by the membership on the true democratic principle of one person one vote. They might extend this idea of democracy a bit further by having some of the board appointed much as jurors are selected for court duty.

'The neighbourhood corporation would depend on the interest and inclination of its members: eg child care, teaching and tutoring, carpentry, radio broadcasting or banking'

The productivity of this type of corporation would depend on the interest and inclination of its members. A few such possibilities are gardening, aquaculture, cooking, baking, child care, teaching and tutoring, carpentry, furniture making, weaving, aid for the elderly, transport services, clothes making, tailoring and food preserving. There might eventually be ventures into journalism, radio broadcasting, theatre, concerts, university courses or banking. The only limitation is the imagination and abilities of the membership. It is with such prosaic activities that people will avoid total dependence on the unstable bureaucratic economy. In so doing, they will find true freedom and self-realisation.

The board of directors would oversee the functioning of the local economy by calling and conducting general meetings, appointing committees, and correcting problems that might arise. Their primary function would be to help the membership become efficient producers of goods and services, both for home consumption and for trade. They would see that the producers obtained proper instruction and guidance; help in the sourcing of material, equipment and facilities; make arrangements for mutual aid; and develop a purchasing agency or help in the selling of goods and services.

Much like a customary corporation, they could also make arrangements for group medical insurance, financial aid, and outside consultants such as lawyers, travel agencies or accountants.

The membership of the corporation would be open to those who have an interest and are willing to work for its success. Its natural participants would be those who do not have a niche in the traditional economy, such as a homebound parent with children, the marginally employed, retirees, students, the handicapped, and people who are disinclined to participate in an authoritarian system.

Those who are fully employed in the traditional economy would also be included in the new corporation. This could be of mutual benefit in that the fully employed would bring official money and expertise into the independent local economy. They could extend their income by also using the alternative exchange for local goods and services when possible.

It is this coming together on a consistent basis that is a prerequisite for building democracy. They will find that political steps will be necessary to safeguard and extend their own endeavours. In such circumstances, democracies will differ from those built up under bureaucratic conditions, in that they will have democratic content and not just its form.

Joseph Rosen, 5 Partridgeberry Lane, South Hamilton, MA 01982, USA (tel 508 468 4140).

Neighbourhood Initiatives Foundation

The Neighbourhood Initiatives Foundation was set up in 1988 by the Housing Associations Charitable Trust and the Town and Country Planning Association and is directed by Tony Gibson whose Lightmoor New Community self-build project, received a 1987 community architecture award. The Foundation has helped residents to launch neighbourhood development schemes on Tyneside, in Birmingham and the Rhondda; and in the Community Forest projects in Essex and the North East. The work centres on locating the wasted resources within each neighbourhood – derelict land, under-used premises and above all, people – youngsters needing a chance to show their mettle and make their mark, middle aged people redundant before their time and elderly people with a wealth of experience to pass on.

The Foundation provides:
• Decision-making packs, manuals and Fact Banks for schools, communities and professional bodies;
• Introductory workshops and advanced courses in the use of 'hands on' techniques;
• Links with projects that have achieved results and can pass on their experience;
• Practical proposals on dislodging bureaucratic log-jams and encouraging working relationships between Us and Them.

The Foundation also asks:
Do you know of derelict land or empty buildings that could be brought back into use?

Dr Tony Gibson, Neighbourhood Initiatives Foundation, Suite 23-25, Horsehay House, Horsehay, Telford, Shropshire TF4 3PY (tel 0952 503628).

Neighbourhood Innovations Programme

Bill Berkowitz

I helped create this Neighbourhood Innovations Programme in my home town of Arlington, Massachussetts.

Run from Arlington's Department of Planning and Community Development, the programme advertises 'Got an idea for your neighbourhood?' and makes small awards of up to $1,000 to neighbourhood groups for starting activities to improve neighbourhood life. Their current budget is $5,000 a year.

Examples include: neighbourhood fairs, tool lending libraries, skills exchanges, job clearing houses and computer co-ops.

> **'The Department will look for originality, feasibility, concrete neighbourhood support, specific neighbourhood benefit, and potential lasting value'**

The leaflet distributed explains that in the letters of application, people have to 'try to include a list of names and addresses of people in your neighbourhood who support your idea. The Department will look for originality, feasibility, concrete neighbourhood support, specific neighbourhood benefit, and potential lasting value. Some preference will be given to applications from low and moderate income groups.'

'Think about what you would like to see in your neighbourhood,' the leaflet urges, 'your imagination is the only limit. Maybe we can help make your idea come true.'

> **'Your imagination is the only limit'**

Bill Berkowitz, 12 Pelham Terrace, Arlington, MA 02174, USA (tel 617 646 6319).

One thousand pound awards for 'local heroes'

Nominate an 'unsung hero or heroine of community work' by mid-September each year and they may receive one of the £1,000 Whitbread Community Care Awards. The emphasis is on voluntary work and personal sacrifice that involved young people, helped those with disadvantages of age or handicap, or improved the community or the environment. A previous year's winners, for instance, included Mavis Rivers from Darlington who, after losing her husband, set up a bereavement centre as a day centre and visited those too shy to come to the centre. Questions to answer about the nominees are: is the work carried out on a voluntary basis; how long has the work been undertaken; how many people are involved; how much time is given; how are funds raised; how many people benefit; describe the community work carried out; why do you think this individual or group deserves recognition?

> **'Mavis Rivers from Darlington, after losing her husband, set up a bereavement centre, as a day centre and visited those too shy to come to the centre'**

Nomination forms are available from Whitbread Community Care Awards, 1 Central Street, Manchester M2 5WR (tel 061 832 1638).

Auctioning honours to community benefactors

Based on a conflation of ideas from Professor Leopold Kohr, Nicholas Albery and Valerie Yule:

Innovation in cities tends to be stifled by red tape, lack of patronage and lack of community identity, with the average rich company or individual feeling no particular loyalty to the local neighbourhood, or responsibility for improving it. One slightly eccentric idea would be to auction a particular lifetime honour, such as a new type of knighthood, one per rural or urban parish, to the highest bid over a reserve amount – the winning bidder would then have to put the money into a neighbourhood fund.

> 'To auction a particular lifetime honour, such as a new type of knighthood, one per rural or urban parish, to the highest bid. The winning bidder would then have to put the money into a neighbourhood fund'

This fund would invite new and imaginative proposals for improving the area; a committee with local authority appointees on it would put those proposals which met basic criteria on a short list, leaving the final choices to the benefactor, who would also be able to suggest projects. Entries thus selected would be given a fast track by the local authority through planning and other obstacles. So to become Sir David of Seven Dials or Lady Marilyn of Easterhouse, veritable 20th century mini-Medicis, able to build follies and Albert-type Memorials almost at whim, would require a substantial financial commitment. It is the sort of honour that the Prince of Wales should delight in creating.

For a wilder version of this idea, see Leopold Kohr's book, 'The Inner City', £4-95 from Y Lolfa Press, Talybont, Aberystwyth, Dyfed SY24 5HE, Wales (tel 097086 304).

Parish secondments

Jan Morland

Why couldn't each Parish Council in the country with an unemployment level above say ten per cent be seconded one or more people who will be on a two or three year commitment, paid full time, whose job it is to get to know the local inhabitants and to implement a scheme decided on by the councillors? There could even be lists of schemes suggested from the community which could be voted on by town poll (or when the next local council elections are held).

> 'People who will be on a two or three year commitment, whose job it is to get to know the local inhabitants and to implement a scheme decided on by the councillors'

I am thinking of projects for swimming pools, housing cooperatives, gardens, playgrounds, perhaps clubs for the youngsters who are out of work where they may go to play snooker and so forth.

The whole idea is to galvanise people to help themselves, instead of feeding it in from above and wasting such a lot of time and resources on bureaucracy. Large-scale government schemes can be inappropriate.

Mrs Jan Morland, 10 High Street, Glastonbury, Somerset (tel 0458 32420).

Compulsory community service

The Prince of Wales

The Prince of Wales believes that all young people should take part in a compulsory period of national community service. In his view, it would make positive use of unused energy that could otherwise turn into anti-social behaviour. The following is adapted from a piece in the Times.

The idea should not be swept under the carpet each time it is raised because there is criticism from a vociferous minority.

Ever since I became involved in the problems faced by young people I have tried very hard to put myself in their position, or at least to operate from the basis of what I felt when I was young.

I have been guided by a firm belief in the value of being challenged, at some point of your life, as an individual who is part of a team. I have seen in so many cases (not just my own) the effect of such challenges on the development of the individual and the subsequent increase in self-confidence.

> 'Basically, all of us at some stage or other – especially when we are young – need to be encouraged to do things that we initially don't like the idea of'

Basically, all of us at some stage or other – especially when we are young – need to be encouraged to do things that we initially don't like the idea of, but which, on doing them, we find to be not nearly as bad as we originally feared.

Neighbourhood Aid

Nicholas Albery

Charity begins at home and also ends up overseas in this Neighbourhood Aid scheme, inspired by Live Aid: each neighbourhood of 500 to 5,000 people in this country would be encouraged to get together and form its own mini-council. The councils would be charged with developing their areas and particularly with supporting the music and arts – running street parties, encouraging the formation of local bands, working in the schools, providing venues and rehearsal rooms, perhaps even setting up community music centres with rooms and instruments for hire.

> 'Unemployed people applying to their neighbourhood council would be able to obtain help in tackling any creative project, in return for a supplement to their benefit'

Unemployed people applying to their neighbourhood council would be able to obtain help in tackling any artistic or creative project that appealed to them, or could obtain any other work locally that needed doing, in return for a supplement to their benefit. A scheme like this might appeal to right-wingers, as it would be like a non-compulsory community form of National Service. Some Training Commission and EC funds could be rechannelled in its direction, also Arts Council money, and money from local businesses, foundations and patrons.

Neigbourhood Aid would help solve several problems at the same time: unemployment would be reduced with the creation of many worthwhile jobs; and we could even begin to regenerate our inner cities. The Easterhouse Festival Society found that celebration and festivities are the best ways to begin the revival of morale in run-down urban areas. Once people begin to join together to eat and drink and sing and laugh and dance, social problems which might have looked hopeless before, begin to be seen as challenges needing to be tackled.

Neighbourhood Aid would have an effect on that curse of modern urban life – loneliness. People would have the opportunity to begin to get to know their neighbours. The act of forming the mini-councils would also help define, like a second Domesday Book, the boundaries of each neighbourhood, revitalising these well-nigh obliterated but vital foundation blocks of the wider society .

Finally, Neighbourhood Aid could grow as a 'human scale' supplement to the mass scale work of the aid organisations. At best I can envisage a future in which every neighbourhood in Europe is allocated a twin village in Africa, India or elsewhere in the Third World, with Neighbourhood Aid projects raising money for the twin, but also arranging the training and sending of skilled volunteers. In the process First Worlders would get an invaluable education in the long-term problems of the Third World. Such twinnings already exist – Bishopston, a neighbourhood in Bristol, has for many years done valuable work in its twin area of Kuppham in India, so there is experience on which to build.

Nicholas Albery, 20 Heber Road, London NW2 6AA (tel 081 208 2853; fax 081 452 6434).

Neighbourhood wardens

Nicholas Saunders

As far as social services are concerned, specialisation in people would be far more appropriate than in a particular task.

Consider the present system: for each locality, the people are serviced by a postman, a milkman, a social worker, a policeman, a dustman, a street sweeper, a meter reader and others. They do only their job; they are specialists in their work. However, they cover a relatively large area and serve many more people than they can get to know.

Consider an alternative: combine all these jobs, but make the areas much smaller. The 'general social serviceman' (male or female) will serve only a small number of people, perhaps a hundred, and so their area may be only a single block of flats or a hundred yards of a city street.

> 'The "general social serviceman" (male or female) will serve only a small number of people, perhaps a hundred, and so their area may be only a single block of flats or a hundred yards of a city street'

Their work is no longer anonymous; they are doing things for people they know and the people know them too. They are appreciated for doing their job well – so it becomes more rewarding. Situations such as old people dying without anyone realising it, just could not happen. Crime would not go unnoticed either.

Similarly, they would look after their patch with pride. They would be in touch with the appropriate department if the street lights were faulty or a paving stone were loose. They would in fact be the missing link between the authorities and the public that they exist to serve.

Of course they would replace the services they act for only at the most local level. For example, they would gather the rubbish and put it out in one pile for collection; the mail for their territory would be dropped off to them by the Post Office. So they would have the back-up of all of the services with their specialist training and resources.

They would need a mini-depot, just a room to use as an office and as a store, for instance to keep parcels until people come home. People would come there with their problems, and it would be a centre for that small community.

Nicholas Saunders, top floor, 14 Neal's Yard, London WC2H 9DP (tel 071 836 9404; fax 071 379 0135).

Street wardens for local policing

Extracted from an item in the Times by Stewart Tendler.

Chief Superintendent Susan Davies from Dorset Police proposed at the annual conference of the Police Superintendents' Association in September 1989 that street wardens could replace police officers on patrol in providing local information, dealing with minor offences and providing a reassuring police presence – thus releasing police constables for more important duties.

> 'Street wardens could replace police officers on patrol in providing local information, dealing with minor offences and providing a reassuring police presence'

Wardens would be subject to the same kind of regulations as regular police – including a no-strike provision. After gaining experience and further qualifications, those who wanted to could go on to become fully fledged constables.

The Police Federation vice-chairman spoke out against the proposal: 'The Public is not going to settle for second-rate powerless auxiliaries as a substitute for the real thing.'

In London, Scotland Yard is considering a system of volunteer patrols or 'Blue Angels', based on the Guardian Angel patrols.

Postcript from Susan Davies

Susan Davies writes to the Institute:

I understand that the Norfolk Constabulary is engaging in an experiment with 'peace wardens' along the lines of the street warden idea. If the experiment is successful I imagine we shall see other initiatives being introduced in other parts of the country.

Chief Superintendent Susan Davies, Headquarters, Dorset Police, Winfrith, Dorchester, DT2 8DZ (tel 0929 462727).

Elected neighbourhood representatives

In the booklet 'How to make Democracy Work', Leonard Orr in California describes a scheme whereby, he believes, a nationwide network of elected neighbourhood representatives could come about without waiting for changes in the way local government is run. Leonard Orr tried out his method successfully back in 1968: it simply involved asking the hundred people on his block to sign his petition for election as neighbourhood representative – a petition which made clear that other people could also stand for nomination – and then declaring himself elected once the majority had signed without a rival appearing. The duties of such grass roots leaders include a weekly support group, a monthly meeting, a monthly newsletter, interviews in person or on the phone with those who cannot come to the meetings, and regular communication with elected representatives at council and national level. They can ask for tithes and financial support from the people they represent, if needing to earn money from their work.

'It simply involved asking the hundred people on his block to sign his petition for election as neighbourhood representative'

Leonard Orr writes: 'Elections are now meaningless and apathy abounds. Only elected representatives can change this by keeping everyone in the voting area informed. Your representative can solve your problems with bureaucracy, can prevent crime, can expand community prosperity, can be a friend to teenagers and senior citizens, and can help you "sell" all your good ideas and represent all your human and political concerns.

'Sticking your neck out to organise neighbourhood meetings is scary. You are daring to risk failure, criticism, ridicule, not to mention success. However, as Napoleon Hill said, "Fear, the worst of all enemies, can be effectively cured by forced repetition of acts of courage".

'Fear, the worst of all enemies, can be effectively cured by forced repetition of acts of courage'

'Another emotional obstacle to organising your neighbourhood is the uncomfortable feelings which arise from dealing with so many different people. As a result of our increased mobility, and the fact that it is no longer economically necessary to cooperate with the people in our community, we have gotten used to only associating with people with whom we feel comfortable. Our cities are criss-crossed with networks of like-minded people, while being devoid of communities. This is a great loss to all of us. Not only do we miss out on the rich diversity of knowledge, culture, and experience which we could gain by having relationships with people who are different from us, but it is precisely from these people, with whom we feel the most uncomfortable, that we have the most to learn about ourselves.'

'How to Make Democracy Work – Neighbourhood Representation, the Grass Roots Dream', by Leonard Orr, published by the author, Box 5320, Chico, CA 95927, USA (tel 916 893 8643 or 916 994 3737), 1987. $15, 119 A4 pages. A VHS tape ($50) is also available.

Community dreams

The book 'Community Dreams' by American Bill Berkowitz (published by Impact Publishers) contains a surfeit of 'ideas for enriching neighbourhood and community life.'

It is written from the perspective of the future, as if these utopian neighbourhoods were already in existence and life were one long community festival. It was hard to imagine whilst reading it how any unemployed person could survive with apathy intact the hundreds of schemes for economic development, or how anyone would have time to slump in front of the TV with all the good works expected of them, or where somebody who was even temporarily fed up with neighbourliness could hide their head. But that is more the penalty paid for writing the book imaginatively, as if all the schemes were taking place in one region, rather than simply providing an encyclopaedia of ideas, as in the present volume.

There are some 800 schemes for improving the quality of life in the book. Here are two of the more striking ideas:

• I have always thought that there should be parts of tube platforms and other public places where it would not be considered eccentric to do one's exercises whilst waiting. Similarly, Bill Berkowitz writes:

'One walker asks her partner, "Would you mind if I take a stretch?". She leaps for the exercise bars overhead'

'One walker asks her partner, "Would you mind if I take a stretch?". She leaps for the exercise bars overhead. A Lifecourse winds in and out of the downtown area. Fifteen exercise stands, each with equipment stretching different muscles of the body. Each numbered, with pictographs and instructions, and charts listing skill levels by degree of competence. Morning and evening commuters pause at each station.'

• 'Scorecard is a watchdog group chosen by the neighbourhood associations. Scorecard holders walk the streets, and record police responses, cleanliness levels, code violations, fire waiting times. They grade on pre-set criteria, worked out in advance with the department in question.

'They put out a quarterly report card with numbers. Their grades mean money. They are bribed and threatened, which is a good sign. They are tough and controversial, and meant to be. A lot of people don't like them, and partly for that reason they are going to be around for a while.'

> ### 'It is hard, rock-bottom hard, to leave a lasting mark on one's community, much less society'

To non-dreamers who object 'it won't work' Berkowitz replies 'maybe you could modify the idea for your own setting'; and to those who say 'it's a band-aid for a society crumbling at the centre,' Berkowitz counters, 'you are cut and bleeding.'

Berkowitz is the best sort of visionary, one with his feet on the ground, busy earthing his visions, and he is realistic as to limitations: 'tear-stained limits bound any intervention. Reformers will meet their wailing wall. Most interventions fail, or fade away fast. Only a handful yield enduring and desired change; only a thimbleful change which is also widespread. It is hard, rock-bottom hard, to leave a lasting mark on one's community, much less society. And so it may be wise to honour any actor, simply for acting.'

Bill Berkowitz, 12 Pelham Terrace, Arlington, MA 02174, USA (tel 617 646 6319). 'Community Dreams – ideas for enriching neighbourhood and community life' is published by Impact Publishers, Post Office Box 1094, San Luis Obispo, Calif. 93406, ISBN 0-915166-29-1, price $8-95.

The Village Alive Campaign in Finland

Paul Ekins

Adapted from an article by Paul Ekins in Resurgence magazine (No 12, Resurgence, Ford House, Hartland, North Devon).

In 1976, Lauri Hautamaki, then an Assistant Professor of Geography at the University of Helsinki, was 'familiar with the theories of Participatory Action Research, with their emphasis on self-initiated rural revival.' With colleagues he identified fifty-one villages in Finland which had mobilised through Village Committees in defence of their way of life.

As a result of the researchers travelling through the countryside spreading the story of these activist villages – the services they had saved, the new local government resources they had won, the multiple activities they had engendered – more and more villages followed suit.

1978 saw the start of the Village Alive Campaign, in which a relay baton was taken from village to village, symbolising revitalisation. The project emphasised the practical role of the school in village life and the Adult Education Institutes organised events at both village and municipal level. The researchers compiled a guide, 'Village Alive', which sold 3,000

copies. They talked of 'real-life utopias' and the mass media started to take an interest in the villages' achievements. An eight-part radio course entitled 'A Village Develops' was listened to by an estimated 22 per cent of the country's farmers. Now there are over 2,200 Village Committees, democratically elected each year at well-attended meetings of the whole village, and covering practically every rural community in the country. One village, for instance, built a village hall with voluntary contributions of materials and labour, established a music school and organised many social, artistic and craft events. Two others have produced their own village master plan for future development, which they sent to their municipal council. These plans have ensured that their respective municipalities did not foist unwanted projects on the villages.

> ### 'A relay baton was taken from village to village, symbolising revitalisation'

Many of Finland's villages are demographically stable for the first time in thirty years, and, although threats and challenges remain, these are now met with an absolutely palpable spirit of commitment to community.

Paul Ekins, 42 Warriner Gardens, London SW11 4DU (tel 071 498 8180).

Village tool share

Ian Care

In my parents' village, the church and horticultural society hold a store of infrequently used tools which are available to 'shareholders'. These include such things as roof ladders, long reach rollers for painting ceilings, A-frame and engine hoist and chainsaw. Maximum loan time is a week unless no one else requires the item. Labour is also shared and paid back on a points system (as in babysitting circles).

Ian Care, 8 Kings Drive, Littleover, Derby DE3 6EU (tel 0332 46089).

> ### 'In the village, a store of infrequently used tools which are available to "shareholders"'

Comment by Valerie Yule

Village tool share is like the way some Australian public libraries, in the inner suburbs of Melbourne especially, will lend out tools in the same way that they lend out books.

Valerie Yule, 57 Waimarie Drive, Mount Waverley, Victoria, Australia 3149 (tel 807 4315).

Buy a village green

'Village Greens for England' will sell you a piece of village green for £25, freehold and complete with legal title and all fees. Your Deed of Conveyance is 'a masterpiece of the calligrapher's art,' and refers on the front to ownership of part of the Village Green of Strumpshaw in the County of Norfolk. All the references to size of plot and conditions are on the reverse side.

Your purchase will help make possible the creating of a village green with trees, shrubs and wildflowers, thus protecting a piece of England from development for ever. Adjacent to the medieval church on the brow of the hill in Strumpshaw, offering panoramic views, a few acres have the planning approval of Broadland District Council to form a Village Green. The longer term prospect is of Village Greens being created all over the UK.

Village Greens for England, Strumpshaw, Norwich, NR13 4NP (tel 0603 714610). This scheme won a Social Inventions Award.

Sholver Rangers

Sholver Rangers was founded in 1985 by an unemployed ambulanceman, Martyn Atkinson. Situated on a run-down council housing estate on the windswept Pennine hills above Oldham in Lancashire, the Sholver Rangers began as a group of young people intent on improving their environment, cutting vandalism and relieving boredom. The youngsters set about creating a nature reserve on 9 acres of land on the western edge of the estate – land provided, along with two adjoining council houses, on a peppercorn rent from the council.

The land was badly tipped and an estimated 30 tons of rubbish was removed. To date, 60,000 indigenous trees and shrubs have been planted, along with an abundance of wild flowers. A path has been laid, designed for use by disabled members of the community, the Royal Engineers have dug a pond and built a sports pitch, and others have helped to create sculptures, a boardwalk and a bird hide. Other activities enjoyed by the youngsters include archery, canoeing, orienteering and travel as far afield as Bostwana.

A number of similar projects have been set up in Oldham, Leeds and Merseyside, and, under the aegis of the Rangers Foundation for Youth and Community in the Environment, it is intended to spread across the UK and into Europe by the year 2000.

Martyn Atkinson, Rangers Foundation for Youth and Community in the Environment, The Fulwood Centre, Rembrandt Walk, Oldham OL1 4PH, Lancashire (tel 0706 840289).

Neighbourly eating

Nicholas Saunders

A small-scale innovative Danish practice which I liked and thought could act as a model elsewhere, was that of a group of independent families who bought neighbouring houses for sale. They also bought a workshop building, an old smithy. They decided to knock down the walls between the gardens – except for one family which wanted to keep its wall. With their own labour they converted the smithy into a communal dining hall. A communal meal was cooked each evening by the eight families on a rota basis. Once every eight days, a family had to buy all the food and cook it – it was hard luck if there were a large number of people that day, but it tended to work out evenly in the long run. You had to say if you were going out.

You could do swaps with other people if you did not want to cook that day. There was a charge for guests.

> 'A kitchen and dining room which was open for membership for anyone who lived nearby – there were about 30 members. There was a rota for who did the cooking, and the person cooking bought the food'

Somewhat similar was a scheme for mostly single people living in the same area of Copenhagen. They had got together a kitchen and dining room which was open for membership for anyone who lived nearby – there were about 30 members. Again there was a rota for who did the cooking, and the person cooking bought the food. If someone did not have much money, he or she prepared something simple.

Such a scheme could appeal to people in Britain living alone, who do not like to cook elaborate meals for themselves, but would not mind a lot of effort once a month. It would probably depend on finding a neighbourhood of like-minded people living fairly close to each other.

Nicholas Saunders, top floor, 14 Neals Yard, London WC2H 9DP (tel 071 836 9404; fax 071 379 0135).

The Unofficial Community Cafe

This project won a Best Neighbourhood Social Inventions Award.

Patrick Graham, a professional sound recordist, knew very few of his neighbours living in Numbers 1 to 244 Inverness Place, Cardiff. So he converted an estate agent's For Sale sign to read 'Unofficial Community Cafe. Open and free to all local residents as long as the sign is up'; and persuaded a local firm to let him run off a hundred copies of a newsletter about it.

Graham has had a trickle of visitors ever since, almost all women, coming in for a cup of tea. 'Now nearly everyone on the block says hello to me,' says Graham, and a young mother up the road has even borrowed the sign to host the cafe for a time.

'There are no official opening times,' he adds, 'just up with the sign and kettle full when you want visitors, take it in or pass it on when you don't.' He vets people at the door and has had no trouble so far. And his experiment in neighbourliness has cost him nothing, with visitors bringing gifts of tea and coffee.

Patrick Graham, 217 Mackintosh Place, Roath Park, Cardiff CF2 4RP (tel 0222 491127). The project is dormant now that he no longer lives in Inverness Place.

Cohousing

In 'Cohousing: a Contemporary Approach to Housing Ourselves' by Kathryn McCamant and Charles Durrett, the authors write that there are over 125 such Cohousing ('bofaellesskaber') communities in Denmark, ranging in size from 6 to 80 households. The authors have helped set up similar schemes in the States: 80 groups are at some stage of the Cohousing planning and design process, quite a few with sites in Davis, California; the first group of 26 households has moved in. Here is an adapted extract from the authors' description of the Trudeslund Community where they spent six months:

'I know I live in a community because on a Friday night it takes me 45 minutes and two beers to get from the parking lot to my front door'

Situated in the town of Birkerød, just north of Copenhagen, Trudeslund's 33 residences and a large common house were completed in 1981. The residences line two pedestrian streets, with the common house located at the highest point where the streets meet. With cars kept at the edge of the site and houses clustered together, much of the lower end is left wooded, making it a favourite place for the children to play.

A cooperative store in the common house is stocked with household goods, from toothpaste to cornflakes. Each household has a key, so that residents can pick up goods at any hour. They write down what they take in the account book and receive a bill at the end of the month. The store is run by one of nine 'interest groups'. Every adult is a member of one such group. Other interest groups are responsible for the outdoor areas, special children's activities, the monthly newsletter and minutes of meetings, the heating system, the laundry room, general maintenance, social events and overall coordination of community activities.

When residents take the laundry out of one of the two communal washing machines, they put the next load in, so no one has to wait for an empty machine. Detergents are bought in bulk. Also located in the common house are a workshop, a darkroom for photography, a television room, a walk-in freezer, a guest room, a music room for teenagers and a central computer connected to a personal computer in each home.

Many residents eat in the common house dining room three or four times a week, and have more intimate family dinners at home the other evenings. On any evening, 50 per cent of the residents, and often more, eat together. Two adults, assisted by one child, plan, shop, prepare, serve and wash up after dinner. Each resident has to cook only once a month. Residents sign up for dinners at least two days in advance and pay for the meal after dinner, when the cooks have divided the cost by the number eating.

'Many residents eat in the common house dining room three or four times a week'

Two families share a car, five others own a sailboat together. There is only one lawn mower. Older kids keep an eye on the younger ones. Babysitters are never lacking. Afternoon tea after school provides a meeting place for both children and adults. As one Trudeslund resident put it: 'I know I live in a community because on a Friday night it takes me 45 minutes and two beers to get from the parking lot to my front door.'

The development process

At the outset, the group invited four firms to submit design proposals. Completion of construction came two and a half years after the first planning meeting. Half of the original

members had dropped out. Now each resident owns a house and a portion of the common areas. Prices worked out as comparable to those for single-family residences in the surrounding area that have no common facilities. Resale value of Trudeslund houses has steadily climbed.

'Cohousing: a Contemporary Approach to Housing Ourselves' by Kathryn McCamant and Charles Durrett (published by Ten Speed Press, PO Box 7123, Berkeley, CA 94707, USA, tel 510 845 8414; fax 510 524 1052. $19.95, 208 pages). The authors can be contacted at 1250 Addison St #113, Berkeley, CA 94702, USA (tel 510 549 9980). 'Cohousing' is trademarked to them.

Sunday Salon

Every Sunday evening for many years now, Jim Haynes' Atelier A2, a former painter's workshop, has becomes a 'salon restaurant', with a different volunteer chef preparing a meal each time. It is 'a unique event, circled on the calendars of many members of the foreign writers' community as the social highlight of the week.' To quote from an interview for 'She' magazine:

If any readers are planning a trip to Paris, and would like to come to dinner, all they have to do is call on a Sunday morning, not too early, and if they're among the first 45 to telephone, they'll be welcome.

Everyone is expected to put 70 francs in an envelope with their names on the outside. This helps to pay the costs of producing the evening. All profits go to Poland and elsewhere.

'People are often amazed that I open my door to the world and wonder if I'm ever taken advantage of. I can say unequivocally that it's 98% a joyful experience'

'For over 8 years, we have been sending food, clothes and medicine to Poland,' says Jim. 'People are often amazed that I open my door to the world and wonder if I'm ever taken advantage of. I can say unequivocally that it's 98% a joyful experience. It is always an interesting mix of people, who exchange telephone numbers, addresses, become friends, lovers, create projects, etc. I still enjoy producing the dinners after some 14 years. Sometimes I think I am crazy – but I continue because it brings me and so many others so much joy.'

Jim Haynes, Atelier A2, 83 rue de la Tombe-Issoire, 75014 Paris, France (tel 331 4327 1767 or 331 4327 1909).

Post-industrial villages around schools

Clive Akerman

The fabric of community organisation that needs to be woven might be roughly described as a 'return to the village.' My concept of a post-industrial society, where unemployment is seen as an opportunity rather than as a threat, includes this reinvention of the village.

There needs to be a capital fund that can be used to provide (by lease or purchase) equipment which 'skill-sharers' are unable to provide themselves. Thus the 'village carpenter' might be adequately provided with hand tools, but require capital fund assistance when it comes to a lathe. Painters and decorators might need the occasional use of scaffolding, and so on.

Such capital goods held in common for the 'village' need storage space, and in some cases – such as the lathe – working space. This already exists in the ownership of the community.

Why are our schools so underused?

Industrialists make best use of expensive assets by working them around the clock. Our schools should be open as community resources for every hour for which there is a demand.

> **'Industrialists make best use of expensive assets by working them around the clock. Our schools should be open as community resources for every hour for which there is a demand'**

This will lead to considerable savings as well as benefits. Local authorities provide accommodation for all manner of groups in buildings designated for the purpose. Thus pensioners' luncheon clubs often inhabit space used for nothing else. School canteens could be used to provide breakfast facilities (late) lunch and dinner facilities, and so on, whilst releasing the special purpose buildings for more productive purposes.

School workshops should be available to the community at all times they are not in use within the educational environment. Their art studios, music rooms and cookery classrooms should be available around the clock to persons who wish to use them. Charge those who can afford to pay, for the facilities plus materials, charge the rest for materials. Our schools are our most underused resource.

Clive Akerman, 92 Sandbrook Road, London N16 OSP (tel 071 241 0866).

Campaign for After-School Clubs

Social inventor Michael Young (Lord Young of Dartington) is spearheading a campaign to ensure fuller use of schools after hours by the children themselves. With Matthew Owen of the Institute of Community Studies, Young has written a pamphlet for the campaign and hopes to launch a Foundation for After School Activities which would give pump-priming grants to good local schemes. The money for this Foundation will come, they hope, from the new Sports and Arts Trust, from charities and from the government.

They point out that most schools open only during normal school hours (57% in their survey) and are thus not being used for 70% of the year, a very unproductive use of valuable resources. Only 8% of their sample were open till 6pm or later on five days a week. One such that did impress them however was Seymour Park Primary School in Trafford.

This school has had an after-school playscheme for the last ten years, with enough pupils each day for at least two football teams. This scheme has relied on the dedication of its coach Harry Singleton, who turns up five afternoons a week, whatever the weather. 'It's been wonderful for me,' says Harry, 'I've made so many friends. I know kids from the school who are having their own children now. My own son comes and the father of one of my four grandchildren.' Harry and three other workers are paid by the Local Education Authority who took over financial responsibility when Urban Aid funding ran out.

The campaign's proposal is that every school's governors should decide what after-school activities to encourage, ranging from sports and games, to computer practice, dancing and photography. And that these clubs should be staffed by part timers, such as students on educational courses, and by volunteers, who will often be retired people.

• *Michael Young and Matthew Owen, Institute of Community Studies, 18 Victoria Park Square, Bethnal Green, London E2 9PF (tel 081 980 6263).*

Portobello Road Treasure Hunt

11-year-old girls from the Moroccan immigrant community at Bevington School raised £60 for the local Moroccan poverty fund by publishing a Portobello Road Treasure Hunt for Tourists, designed with help from Yvonne Ackroyd and the Institute for Social Inventions, and published with help from local shops who paid for display advertisements in the guide. It proved a good way for the girls to get to know their own neighbourhood better. Tourists taking their children with them to the Portobello Road market were able to prevent them becoming restive during adult stall-gazing by obtaining a copy of the guide for their kids and leaving them to solve the 39 clues. Solving the final clue led to a Moroccan cafe which offered sweetmeats to all who came to claim their reward.

Other schools with interesting neighbourhoods could produce similar treasure hunt booklets for the tourists.

> **'Tourists were able to prevent their children becoming restive by obtaining a copy of the Portobello Road Treasure Hunt'**

Animated trails

The Company of Imagination has a pool of artists and teachers specialising in sculpture, creative writing, masks, music, painting, costumes, puppets, performance, photography, movement and video. During the summer months they work with groups of adults and children to create Animated Trails – guided walks through the countryside or part of town, which incorporate a number of short presentations along the way. These presentations, static or mobile, amusing, challenging or mysterious, are created by the participants over a three to four week period and then shown to the public as an animated trail. They are designed to stimulate audience and participants into seeing familiar places with fresh eyes. Participants' reactions include: 'the most wonderful creative experience of my teaching career;' and audience reaction: 'it was magical.'

The Company of Imagination, PO Box 328, Ethersett, Norfolk NR9 3PU (tel 0603 507197).

Pavement furniture recycling

Carola Zentner and others have proposed the following idea.

In Germany and Austria on a regular basis everybody puts outside their front door any bulky items for which they no longer have any use, ranging from beds and tables to lampstands and boxes of china.

Before the dustmen arrive, students, young and hard-up newly marrieds, bargain hunters and people who simply enjoy browsing, are allowed to help themselves to anything that takes their fancy.

'I think it's a great way to recycle goods,' writes Zentner. Another correspondent adds: 'I seem to remember that a lot of the "viewing" went on after dark so perhaps people were a bit embarrassed, but I'm sure the idea would catch on, although it would be a good idea to try to keep out dealers.'

Ed: The Islington Council's reaction to this idea was that it might cause an illegal obstruction of the pavement.

Carola Zentner, 38 Woodland Gardens, London N10 3UA (tel 081 883 0535).

Dog's mess bags

A neighbourhood survey in Plaistow, London revealed that the local problem which most agitated local people was dog's mess. Alison Church of Hertford proposes that dog owners follow her simple example – keeping a rolled-up plastic bag attached with a rubber band to the dog lead. Then if your dog fouls the pavement or park, you put your hand inside the bag, to make it like a glove, pick up the mess, draw the bag back over your hand turning it inside out, tie it up and drop it in a litter bin.

'Unlike a pooper scooper,' she says, ' a plastic bag can be easily carried and costs nothing. If this were to be widely advertised, as in Sweden, concerned dog owners would be delighted to know of it and local authorities could feel free to apply stringent bye laws to the complacent.'

> **'A neighbourhood survey in Plaistow, London revealed that the local problem which most agitated local people was dog's mess'**

In the UK, MGB Waste Systems Ltd have a Robidog System which dispenses plastic bags and provides a bin to dump the bags in. It has been tried out by Kensington Council amongst others.

Alison Church, 115 Queens Road, Hertford, Herts SG13 8BJ (tel 0992 583079).

Compulsory dog insurance

Patrick Graham

Adapted from a suggestion submitted to the Institute – a suggestion that has since been discussed in a Times leader and elsewhere.

I propose compulsory insurance for dogs as for cars. Third party insurance would be compulsory although many owners might opt for a fully comprehensive option. All dog owners would need only one licence (as for TVs) but all dogs would have to wear copies on their collars with the owner's name and address printed, and the breed and colour registered.

The benefits of this system are many:

• The cost might deter light-hearted Christmas presents of unwanted puppies.

• Responsible owners would not suffer from others' bad habits.

• Recurrent offenders would automatically be punished (in the pocket) or lose their licence.

• Dangerous breeds would be expensive or impossible to insure.

The further addition of pooper-scoopers as compulsory accompaniments to the urban dog walker would mean that within a short period of time the streets, avenues and parks would be clean and safe, and dog owners would no longer be the curse of the cat-loving classes.

Stray dogs would be traceable fairly accurately through the breed and colour registry – something similar and more is done with cars, those other great polluters of the streets. The only arguments I can see against it are all connected with cost – which I believe to be a fair price to pay for the pleasure of 'owning' a dog. If a national insurance scheme were to be established, there could even be lower premiums for pensioners and exemptions for farmers; but the principle holds good and the costs of leaving things as they are are much too high. Ask the dogs waiting to be put down by the RSPCA.

• *Patrick Graham, 217 Mackintosh Place, Roath Park, Cardiff CF2 4RP (tel 0222 491127).*

• *Pet Plan (tel 0800 282250), the UK's biggest animal health insurers, has launched a third party legal liability policy. It provides up to £2 million insurance cover, and costs £10 for one dog or £15 for three. (From a news item in the Times.)*

Chapter thirteen

ENVIRONMENT AND ECOLOGY

The Council for Posterity

Professor Richard Scorer

The future is essentially unpredictable. Unforeseen discoveries, declarations of new objectives, boredom with old promises, and the emergence of new genius sway the unstable surges of history with alarming irregularity.

Yet some trends are clear. The rate of change appears to have increased throughout the world's existence. While several hundred million years at least seems a safe bet for the possibility of life on earth, we nevertheless find ourselves:

- Using up in at most a very few centuries the world's store of mineral fuel for the purpose of daily living;
- Destroying large capital reserves of forest, fish and genetic variety, and seriously damaging the habitat of most other life forms;
- Multiplying our own species beyond all reasonable bounds, making the sustenance of this excess possible only by the destruction of anything in the biosphere which does not contribute to that greedy process, and consuming anything that does.

'This makes us a plague on earth, lacking the dignity of the lion and without the tolerance of the fauna of the field'

This makes us a plague on earth, lacking the dignity of the lion and without the tolerance of the fauna of the field.

We have become like this because we fostered images of ourselves which are not only disastrously arrogant but fundamentally in error.

We are escaping slowly from the fear that we may destroy ourselves collectively by unrestrained war, or individually by the depressing limitations of our psyche. The pessimism of the recent past is demonstrably curable; but it requires the widespread acceptance of a more loving picture of ourselves, our environment and of human purposes. The acceleration of change has so reduced our perspectives in our worries about our own persons and the uncontrollability of human conflict

that we have forgotten the world, as if its state were of secondary importance to ourselves. The evident power of today has made us lose sight of the billion years ahead.

To extend our feeling of community with all of life, which has been lost from those human societies who wondered at the incomprehensibility of space and time and the mystery of life, to extend the sense of responsibility which we undoubtedly feel towards our own young children, to the multitude of generations ahead, and to keep their environment beautiful, we need a new priesthood who will tell us the story of humanity as we have only recently (in the last 200 years) come to know it through science. I would call this a Council for Posterity.

To establish this we would naturally draw on our experience in the past of setting up learned bodies to inform and guide us into truer perceptions of our own reality. But we may prefer to make it more personally anonymous than assembling a collection of grey eminences. We cannot presume at first to specify any limiting terms of reference, but can require it to teach us to love the world we scarcely yet know. It will be necessary to specify new concepts of greatness beyond the individual. At the moment of history when we have at last learnt about our own evolution we have to halt our destruction of the very foundation of that marvellously creative process.

Above all we have to learn that the greatest benefit and opportunity we can give our descendants is that there be fewer of them. Even if we can divert our impatient energies into games, philosophies and space 'toys', we still need to understand individually the exciting and absorbing story of life, of which we are but one manifested form among many whose silent genetic wisdom surrounds us.

'We are one of the atmosphere's children'

The story of the ocean has still to be explored. What is already known about its origin, its evolution and its wealth is enough to indicate that it will be framed in allegories that will humble us. Already the story of the atmosphere glows with drama that can be Part One of the story in which we will tell our children how they came to be what they are.

We are one of the atmosphere's children, and if we may call

ourselves the most glowing of the brood, we must remember that it participated in the evolution of all mammals and was not designed or made for for us, but we evolved in it. It may yet produce in the eras stretching a million times a human generation forward a species which, when telling its offspring of their origins will speak of us with admiration or contempt. Which shall it be?

The Council for Posterity must also take on the role of Counsel for Posterity. It must consist of people who can devote their deepest thoughts to the theme and muster all the arguments to call the present generation away from its myopic trends.

It will need:

• Scientists who can speak with authority about the believed facts of global evolution;

• Ecologists, in particular, who can gather together a responsible statement of the danger in the present trends;

• People with experience in politics, economics and historical interpretation who can imagine the themes which will make people want to act in a way so that when future generations describe us we would be proud to hear what they say;

• Writers who can present a picture of humanity which young people can absorb, and be stimulated to want more of, and to develop a hope that they can be part of the road into the future – rather than become the refuse of the present.

The Council will need young and old, people from various traditions, but not anyone who believes his own tradition (eg Islam or Christianity) has authority of a superior kind not possessed by others. Each is merely one of the experimental traditions of history (which itself is a very new thing in the world). The Council must merge science with morality. It must destroy the dichotomy which sets the individual on a pedestal while sending conscripts to death in defence of individualism. It must recognise the limitations of all human issues, for time dissolves them. Thus human rights, animal rights, sacredness of human life, sacredness of all life, territorial property and ownership concepts, limits to personal wealth and poverty, legitimacy of political authority – all these require new definition in the light of scientific knowledge and the ecology of nature.

If the Council is sponsored by Government it must be free from any threat or pressure, and must have no national or racial commitment. Thus it needs a promise of about a decade of support, which would give it time to demonstrate its value as a force in formulating human self-images, and visions of the community of life on earth, which are intelligible to ordinary school children. It must generate a humility together with a sturdy commitment among the young. This means understanding the motivations of the present self-oriented generation; and by capturing its imagination to draw it into new objectives without overtly criticising the viewpoints from which they are to be weaned.

In order not to be invidious a list of names from the past who are not available but who typify the qualities required could be:

H.G. Wells, Julian Huxley, John Boyd Orr, Tom Paine, Francis of Assisi, Peter Medawar, Isambard Brunel, Albert Schweitzer, Albert Einstein, Mahatma Gandhi, Erasmus, Chief Seattle, Martin Luther King, Aesop.

To gather the nucleus requires about £1m capital or £100,000 a year, or a rich publisher or industrialist's foundation to sponsor the experimental stage. I do not favour a UN or EEC base because much would be wasted that way in bureaucracy and in generating political acceptance.

There already exist many texts which will provide the basis for most of the educational documents required. In an era of less urgent change and growth they would probably suffice by gradual permeation of the educational systems. But that progress is slow, and the recrudescence of dogmatic religious and political beliefs requires a counter force.

The Council must be competent continually to examine the behaviour of governments and to re-examine the assumptions on which their policies are based. For this reason, a broader than scientific authority is required, and verbal power will be useful.

The Council would formulate political and social objectives consonant with Earth System Science. It would not concern itself with the promotion of scientific research, but with its political and economic impact and the legitimacy of technological exploitation. It must concern itself with the prospect of widespread dearth of resources, starvation, and the present uncontrollable growth of human numbers and its incompatibility with the hope of future freedom.

And it must inspire with words of pride the objectives of the young.

The following names are some of the people who have provided thematic texts on which some of the Council's work could be based: David Attenborough, David Bellamy, Jean Medawar, Richard Dawkins, Paul Ehrlich, Donald Mann (Negative Population Growth), the Chinese government's one child policy, Eric Deakins, James Lovelock, NASA – Earth System Science. A much fuller bibliography is possible.

Academic Inn speech

Professor Scorer returned to the theme of a Council for Posterity at an Academic Inn dinner. Here are extracts from his paper for this occasion.

Today, the biggest task is probably to bring the interests of posterity as a force into the marketplace where finite resources are sold, where the use of territory is determined, and political ideals are scrutinised and put to the test. I am not advocating any new ideal, but for the introduction of a new factor in decision making. One can readily imagine how the interests of posterity might have been affected, for instance, by differently planned consumption of North Sea oil. Those who would oppose requiring the interest of posterity to influence decisions might have a good case on the grounds that the future cannot be predicted. Those who think that their profession does already take posterity into account will probably find that their time scale is far shorter than I am saying is needed. But those of us who think posterity should have a presence with power in the marketplace need to show by examples where it would have been beneficial in the past. The opposition will, no doubt, easily invent cases where the influence, as they imagine it, might have been bad because of new discoveries and inventions. Moralists will be extensively employed sorting out how much we in the present ought to sacrifice so that posterity may benefit.

> 'The biggest task is probably to bring the interests of posterity as a force into the marketplace where finite resources are sold'

We are concerned to protect posterity from harm rather than to think in any detail about any benefits it may get. In particular we seek to keep its options open and not circumscribe them with inadequate fundamental resource limits.

'The voice of posterity, like the voice of a child, can be a source of moral leadership, creative of wise intentions, of delicate beauty in a clumsy and ugly society'

The voice of posterity, like the voice of a child, can be a source of moral leadership, creative of wise intentions, of delicate beauty in a clumsy and ugly society. It must stop us from stealing from our children.

The purpose of Councils for Posterity is to introduce a more perceptive note about what we are doing inadvertently, as well as intentionally, in the world. It is, however, not simply an attempt to gather together the good intentions of the numerous existing activists in environmental protection. A main aim is to make a moral approach acceptable in a world where it is considered foolish not to be selfish and opportunist. Morality is about abstinence and sacrifice; it is about self-discipline; being intelligent as well as clever (which means examining and criticising objectives as well as pursuing them); it is about the beauty of relationships with all of life, about the experience of love which transcends indulgence.

The Council is the involvement of ourselves in the passage of time. We are created by the past, and are creating the future not only as we can see it around our home, but also through participating in the great adventure of creative evolution where our effort is meaningless by itself. It entails being humble and bold.

Professor Richard Scorer (of the Department of Mathematics, Imperial College); home address, 2 Stanton Road, London SW20 8RL (tel 081 946 1313 h; 071 589 5111 w). This scheme won a main Social Inventions Award.

Council for Posterity's progress

A UK Council for Posterity, based on a scaled-down version of Professor Scorer's ideas, was launched in 1990. The initial core group include Scorer himself, Herbie Girardet, Fern Morgan-Grenville, Professor Thring, Tanya Schwarz, Guy Dauncey, Liz Hosken, Brian Aldiss, Lord Young of Dartington, Doris Lessing, Sir William Golding, Anita Roddick, Maxwell Bruce QC, Brain Aldiss, John Seymour, Dr Alice Coleman, Teddy Goldsmith and Diana Schumacher, with Nicholas Albery of the Institute for Social Inventions as General Secretary. The Council is the 'UK National Liaison Unit' for the UNESCO-related Global Network on Responsibilities Towards Future Generations (in Malta) and the Council's plans include:

• To provide legal representation for the interests of future generations at any inquiry or assembly looking into developments with potentially very harmful long-term effects.

• To stimulate the development of Declarations of the Rights of Posterity and to publicise their contents. (See the Council's own draft in the box to the right.)

• To involve young people through a £1,000 Adopt-A-Planet competition in schools, where classes caretake local areas that have been vandalised and carry out imaginative plans

for environmental improvements. (See the chapter on Education for more details on this.)

• To present awards for the best published articles or books about future generations. The authors will be invited to present their themes at dinner-discussion award ceremonies.

• To encourage the formation of similar Councils in other countries.

'Posterity offers you an altruistic aim, a life with added meaning'

To those whose first scornful reaction is 'What has posterity ever done for me?' the Council answers: 'It offers you an altruistic aim independent of age, sex, family, creed or nationality; that is, a life with added meaning.'

• *The Council for Posterity, 20 Heber Road, London NW2 6AA (tel 081 208 2853; fax 081 452 6434).*

• *Hilary Caruana, International Liaison, Global Network on Responsibilities Towards Future Generations, International Environment Institute, c/o Foundation for International Studies, University of Malta, Valletta, Malta (tel 010 356 224067 / 234121 / 234122; fax 356 230551; Greennet 'FutureGen' or 'Dialcom 75:cmi025').*

A Declaration of the Rights of Posterity

Those who live after us have no voice amongst us
We therefore declare and determine their right
to inherit a planet which has been treated by us
with respect for its richness, its beauty and its diversity

a planet
whose atmosphere is life-giving and good, and can
remain so for aeons to come

a planet
whose resources have been carefully maintained and
whose forms of life retain their diversity

a planet
whose soil has been preserved from erosion
with both soil and water unpoisoned
by the waste of our living

a planet
whose people apply their technologies cautiously
with consideration for the long-term consequences

a planet
whose people live in human-scale societies
unravaged by population excess

a planet
whose future generations have interests
which are represented and protected
in the decision-making councils of those alive today.

This Declaration was published on April 22nd 1990 by the Council for Posterity, 20 Heber Road, London NW2 6AA (tel 208 2853; fax 081 452 6434). Please send in your suggested improvements or alternative versions.

The Rights of Nature

Robert McParland

From Robert McParland's review of 'The Rights of Nature' by Roderick Frazier Nash (University of Wisconsin Press, $ 27-50). The review appeared in Breakthrough magazine (published by Global Education Associates, Suite 456, 475 Riverside Drive, New York, NY 10115, USA, tel 212 870 3290. $7 or $27 membership).

> 'When Thomas Jefferson wrote that all men are created equal, he was not thinking of women or racial minorities, nor the idea of extending ethical treatment to animals, plants and rivers'

As environmentalism evolves as a social movement, the idea of liberating nature from human persecution emerges more frequently and forcefully. When Thomas Jefferson wrote that all men are created equal, he and his colleagues (and his country) apparently were not thinking of women or racial minorities, nor the idea of extending ethical treatment to animals, plants and rivers. But today, US Federal law provides legal protection for endangered species and habitats.

Today, the field is prepared for 'mass participation in ethically impelled environmentalism.' The Rights of Nature now concern lawmakers, theologians, scientists, and the many individuals who seek to secure the inviolable worth of the natural world for future generations. Nash believes that serious confrontations could arise between advocates of the Rights of Nature and those now profiting from nature's exploitation.

A Declaration of the Rights of Nature

(1) Nature – animate or inanimate – has a right to existence; that is, to preservation and development.

> 'Nature has a right to the protection of its eco-systems, species and populations, in all their inter-connectedness'

(2) Nature has a right to the protection of its eco-systems, species and populations, in all their inter-connectedness.

(3) Animate nature has a right to the preservation and development of its genetic inheritance.

(4) Organisms have a right to a life fit for their species, including procreation within their appropriate eco-systems.

(5) Disturbances of nature require a justification. They are only permissible, firstly, when the presuppositions of the disturbance are determined in a democratically legitimate process and with respect for the rights of nature; secondly, when the interests of the disturbance outweigh the interests of a complete protection of the rights of nature; and thirdly, when the disturbance is not inordinate.

Damaged nature is to be restored wherever possible.

(6) Rare eco-systems, and above all those with an abundance of species, are to be placed under absolute protection. The driving of species to extinction is forbidden.

From 'Rights of Future Generations, Rights of Nature', edited by Lukas Vischer, published by the World Alliance of Reformed Churches (1990, Geneva). Sent in by one of the booklet's contributors, Professor Peter Saladin, Forrerstr. 26, CH-3006, Bern, Switzerland (tel 31 44 8006).

The Natural Step – A National Plan for sustainability

Dr Karl-Henrik Robert is one of Sweden's leading cancer researchers, who has developed 'The Natural Way' as a method of reaching consensus about sustainable futures within the scientific community in Sweden. With persistence he reached an agreed 22nd draft of a report on environmental problems and on the most critical avenues for action. He persuaded the king, schools, and industrial sponsors to back the report, and arranged for the sending of an educational package to every household in the country, outlining the steps needed to make Swedish civilisation environmentally sustainable for the long-term future. This project was backed by artists and celebrities on TV, it has led to seminars for MPs; study circles; and an environmental youth parliament – and it promises in the long run to reorganise completely the nation's way of life, bringing it 'into alignment with the laws of nature'.

> 'The steps needed to make Swedish civilisation environmentally sustainable for the long-term future'

The £1,500 Award

'The Natural Step' project has since been adapted for Poland and Hungary. In the UK, the Institute for Social Inventions has recognising it with the special £1,500 Body Shop Award for the 'Best Social Invention 1991'; and the Council for Posterity, the organisation (described above) working for the interests of future generations is attempting to initiate a Natural Step network in the UK. A big meeting to launch the idea in the UK was held at the Royal Society for Arts in March 1992, in association with the Schumacher College and the Gaia Foundation.

> 'The Council for Posterity will attempt to initiate a Natural Step network in the UK'

Consensus-building

Marilyn Mehlman of the Swedish Institute for Social Inventions writes:

In my view, Dr Karl-Henrik Robert's most significant social invention is his method for achieving consensus on tricky, complicated, often highly scientific matters in a way that does not reduce agreement to the lowest common denominator but that actually produces rather radical position statements. His work has for example developed a position statement on energy (production and use) endorsed by virtually all leading scientists in Sweden, regardless of opinions on topics like nuclear power, and which has been presented to the House of Parliament. He describes his method as leading discussion back to the 'trunk' of the problem tree rather than chattering about peripheral twigs and leaves.

PCB pollution

Dr Robert gives an example of this consensus-building:

If a politician were to ask a random selection of scientists whether or not the reproductive organs of seals are destroyed by the chemical PCB, it is very unlikely that he would get the kinds of answers that would be helpful in arriving at a decision. He might hear, for instance: 'That has not been definitely established yet.' 'Yes, *that* has now been clearly established.' 'Our laboratory has identified a toxin that plays a far more destructive role,' and so on.

That's the sort of thing that happens with questions about the leaves of the environmental tree. But, if one begins with the trunk or branches, the answers become clearer and more consistent. For instance:

Is PCB a naturally occurring substance? No, it is artificially manufactured by man. All scientists agree on that.

Is it chemically stable, or does it quickly degrade into harmless substances? It is stable and persistent. On that they all agree, as well.

Does it accumulate in organs? Yes it does.

Is it possible to predict the tolerance limits of such a stable, unnatural substance? No, since the complexity of eco-systems is essentially limitless. Nevertheless, it is known that all such substances have limits, often very low, which cannot be exceeded.

Can we continue to introduce such substances into the ecosystem? Not if we want to survive.

> ## 'I went to the king, and asked him if he would endorse the project. He agreed'

The final answer is what the politician actually wanted to know from the beginning, since he is probably not particularly interested in the reproductive organs of seals. Yet, most public environmental debate is preoccupied with such relatively minor details. This happens whenever we fail to proceed from a basic frame of reference, or overview, which makes it possible to focus on the fundamental issues, without getting lost in a confusion of isolated details.

Networking

Dr Robert explains the organisational structure:

The Natural Step is not a new organisation. This is a network of people. We have a lot of good people involved from the Swedish Federation for the Preservation of Nature, the World Wildlife Fund and so forth, but we are not getting any money from membership as those organisations do. Just the opposite – we are begging for money from industry, and finding other

sources, and our message is, 'Please join these organisations.' And that has a very big effect on their membership.

Sponsorship

I built networks wherever I went. When I went to Swedish TV and said that I and all the artists and scientists and this big government office wanted to educate the whole Swedish people, and we would like to have a party on TV celebrating it, they said, 'Certainly. How could we refuse if you succeed with all these other things.' From there I went to the king, and asked him if he would endorse the project. He agreed. You can understand that I slept worse and worse the longer I did this, because I was building a tremendous programme without any money at all. I was *really* nervous by the time I approached the industrial sponsors. But on the other hand, by the time they saw it, it was like a parcel with a ribbon on it. It was so concrete, with dates and everything, that they understood that if they didn't buy it now, this crazy chap would take it to someone else!

> ## 'Tomorrow's market and tomorrow's technology. In ten years, the market will be about *nothing else* but sustainability'

So industries must move from defending themselves to being heroes, ahead of everyone else, fighting for tomorrow's market and tomorrow's technology. In ten years, the market will be about *nothing else* but sustainability.

Antagonism

As soon as we see an enemy, we ask him for advice. We say, 'Would you please help us to sort out this problem?' When you get the answer, very rarely is it a threat to what you want to do. And by following his advice, two things happen: first, he has part of the responsibility for it now, because it's his advice you are following; and secondly, the project generally improves – because most people have rather good ideas!

Next Steps

Future plans include:

• Emphasis on the Natural Step Institute and on intensified co-operative problem-solving by dynamic business leaders, public officials and natural scientists.

• Papers on energy policy, agriculture and the national economy to be distributed to members of parliament and others.

• An environmental youth parliament, featuring a closed-circuit TV symposium uniting 100,000 youths from schools across Sweden.

• Six 'environmental quiz programmes' on TV.

• Six humorous public service messages for cinema and TV, with a celebrity demonstrating how he or she has learned to act with greater environmental responsibility in everyday life.

• Eight TV variety programmes, organised by Anni-Frid Lyngstad of ABBA.

• *The Natural Step, Box 70335, 10723 Stockholm, Sweden (tel 010 46 8 210935; fax 208229). (Information initially from 'In Context' magazine, PO Box 11470, Bainbridge Island, WA 98110, USA, tel 2067 842 0216; fax 206 842 5208. Subs $25.)*

A Global Strategy for Sustainability

*'Caring for the Earth – A Strategy for Sustainable Living',
published by World Wide Fund for Nature (Panda House,
Weyside Park, Godalming, Surrey GU7 1XR, tel 0483 426444;
fax 426409), and by the United Nations Environment Programme & the World Conservation Union, ISBN 2 8317 0074
4; 228 pages, available by post for £9-95 (£2 p&p) from Earthscan
Publications (3 Endsleigh St, London WC1H 0DS, tel 071 388
9541).*

'Mauritius, Antigua, Barbados and Portugal are the only four truly praiseworthy countries in the world – with both low energy use and low total fertility rates'

'Caring for the Earth' is a magnificent report – government
ministers of the environment in countries around the world
would be well advised to ensure that as many as possible of its
120 well-argued action proposals are carried out without
delay. It forms a good basis for a UK national plan for
sustainability that the UK Natural Step project (see above) is
calling for. It is also wise in its advocacy of the vital role for local
communities in making the necessary changes. It highlights
too the rights of future generations and explores the detailed
indices that will be required for measuring sustainability and
quality of life, proposing a new measure of True Sustainable
National Income to replace GNP. It is practical in its detailing
of the taxes and economic incentives that can goad us in the
right direction, and in its five-yearly targets to the year 2010 for
assessing progress. It also contains many inspiring examples
and unexpected statistics – for instance, its tables show that
there are only four truly praiseworthy countries in the world –
ie with both low energy use and low total fertility rates: the
world's appreciation is owed to Mauritius, Antigua, Barbados
and Portugal. The following are a few other adapted highlights
from the report:

• If an activity is sustainable, for all practical purposes it can
continue for ever. 'Sustainable development' is used in this
strategy to mean: improving the quality of human life while
living within the carrying capacity of supporting eco-systems.

• Two things will need to be done: population growth must
stop everywhere, and the rich must stabilise, and in some cases,
reduce, their consumption of resources.

• Local communities must be enabled to manage the
resources on which they depend and to have an effective voice
in the decisions that affect them.

• The range of actions should include: parents teaching
their children to act with respect for other people and other
species; educators incorporating the world ethic into their
teaching; children helping their parents by explaining new
ideas they have learned at school; artists in all media using their
creative skills to inspire people with a new respect for nature;
scientists improving the public's understanding of eco-
systems; lawyers evaluating the legal implications of the world
ethic; technologists, economists and industrialists establishing
new technologies and business approaches to implement the
world ethic; politicians and administrators putting the needed

changes in public policy into effect.

• Taxes on the cleanest sources of energy should be low –
low for natural gas, moderate for oil, high for coal.

• The five economic instruments to promote sustainable
development are: resource taxes, charges, subsidies, performance
bonds and tradable permits.

'True Sustainable National Income = Net National Product minus depreciation of natural assets'

• A new statement of true national income is needed. It
might be:

True Sustainable National Income = Net National Product
(Gross National Product minus depreciation of human-made
capital) plus increases in natural assets minus depreciation of
natural assets minus defensive expenditures against environmental damage minus the costs of unmitigated environmental
damage.

• The best timber companies are capable of combining
profitability and sustainability. One Swedish company has a
nature conservation policy under which it conducts forestry
operations on its lands in such a way as to avoid permanent
adverse effects on soil and water; to preserve a rich variety of
plant and animal life; to protect all plant and animal species that
occur where it operates; to protect all archaeological and
historic sites; and to make reasonable allowance for the wishes
of the public regarding access to and use of company woodlands.

• National Conservation Strategies are to be prepared by
nationals of the countries concerned, usually by governments
in collaboration with citizens' groups, universities and research
institutions, the private sector and a wide array of other interest
groups.

• The estimated costs of implementing the major aspects of
this strategy, to the year 2000, total US$1,288 billion. This
breaks down in order of expense to:

Retiring third world debt $300 billion; increasing energy
efficiency $275 billion; protecting topsoil on cropland $189
billion; developing renewable energies $142 billion; financial
incentives $110 billion; education and health improvements
$101 billion; forest and tree planting $60 billion; family
planning services $59 billion; reducing deforestation and
conserving biodiversity $52 billion.

A National Trust for the future, run by Third Agers

*Adapted extract from a paper presented by Peter Laslett to the
Royal Society for the Encouragement of the Arts. Laslett was one
of the founders of the University of the Third Age.*

'Those now in the Third Age of their lives should regard themselves as trustees for time to come'

The future requires representation in the present if the duty
which we all owe to posterity is to be properly fulfilled. Those
now in the Third Age of their lives are best suited to fulfil that

representative function, and they should accordingly regard themselves as trustees for time to come. The crown of life comes in the Third Age after the workplace is left behind, when there is sufficient freedom from family obligations, economic, social or political compulsion, freedom in fact from the trammels of the Second Age, that of middle age. Such investigation as has so far been made of the attitudes of peoples in the various Ages yields surprising results: neither those in the Second Age nor the First have as great an interest in the future as those in the Third. For only with the Third Age can come that consciousness of freedom in the time dimension which alone can give rise to a duty to represent the future as a trustee. They are closer to the future for the reason that they live much more than do their juniors in the subjective mode of age and ageing. And they identify themselves with those who are to come, with their grandchildren for example, and increasingly with their great-grandchildren. But even those without offspring are well aware of what time to come is likely to be like, because they have seen so much of time already.

Much could be gained and much could be learnt, by extending the theory of the existing National Trust for this new and much wider purpose.

In the grandiose phrases of Edmund Burke, the National Trust represents 'a partnership not only between those who are living, but between those who are living, those who are dead and those who are to be born.' It is a partnership requiring from everyone a vigilance even more constant than John Stuart Mill required for the retention of our liberty:

Never to use too much water, too much heat, too many materials; never to pollute anything anywhere; never to discard anything which will not disappear instantly and of itself; never to join in any activity which will tend to depopulate the earth of any of its species, defoliate the landscape, upset the global atmosphere, desolate our habitat and so the habitat of all our successors.

It is for members of the Third Age, seeing themselves as the nominated trustees of those who are to come, to prompt, inform, and support the administrators, curators, keepers and librarians.

Every sensitive, informed, conscientious member of the Third Age should do everything possible to be aware and informed of the needs of posterity, of the rights of posterity, of things which posterity would most wish to inherit from us and of the things which menace those rights, of the habits and outlooks which have to be transformed if posterity is to be given its due.

'We do for those who follow us what has been done for us by those who preceded us'

If it is to be asked on what principle we are compelled to fulfil this debt to our successors in the world, the answer can be summarised as follows. We are obliged to hand over to them what we have inherited from the past in the condition in which that inheritance was received. We do for those who follow us what has been done for us by those who preceded us.

It has been the aristocracies which until recently have had the means, the leisure, the cultivation and the taste to act as trustees of the cultural and national societies and for such entities as the society of Europe at large. You only have to contemplate the elderly eighteenth century aristocrat who supervises the planting of a great avenue before his splendid house, knowing that he himself would never live to see the trees grow as tall as his own shrunken height, to recognise that these past patrons of the arts must have been conscious that they were representing the future.

It is the leisured members of the Third Age who should recognise that it is for them to take over where the dukes, the earls, baronets and plain esquires have had to relinquish their responsibilities.

Peter Laslett, Director, Ageing Unit, Cambridge History of Population and Social Structure, Trinity College, Cambridge.

Software for saving the planet

Chris Crawford has mortgaged his house to produce a computer game entitled 'Balance of the Planet', which helps educate the user about the complexity and inter-relatedness of the world's environmental problems. To play the game, you have to imagine you are the High Commissioner of the Environment at the United Nations, and that you have until the year 2035 to enact your policies for improvement.

'You have to imagine you are the UN High Commissioner and that you have until the year 2035'

At your control are the rates of tax on beef, CFCs, coal, fertilisers, heavy metals, logging, natural gas, oil, pesticides and the nuclear industry. These produce your income which you can then spend on research into coal, dam use, oil, nuclear power, solar power or basic research; or you can subsidise debt for nature swaps, family planning, recycling centres, solar energy or the use of wood stoves. There are 150 screen-fuls of background information as to causes and effects, although the strong temptation is to skip these and get on with 'policy execution' which leads to your 'results' for each five year period (your aim being to win points).

Thus, say you decide on 'business as usual' and make no changes of policy at all, for 1995 you receive the following feedback:

Problems:
Starvation points worsened by 549; Inundation points worsened by 164; Land abuse points worsened by 108; Lung disease points worsened by 82; Radiation waste points worsened by 43.

Successes:
Quality points improved by 19; Sustainability points improved by 15.

With the result that:
Overall, your score went down by 1020 points.

Business as usual

Repeating this no-changes policy, by the year 2035 your final score is -12,165 and the computer reports:

Your attempts to solve the problems of starvation were a miserable failure; your administration has led to great economic hardship around the globe; global warming became much worse, inundating large areas of coastal land; continuing air pollution took its toll in the form of lung disease; destruction of precious forests continued under your administration; you failed to stem the destruction of biodiversity; you did little to solve the problems of radioactive waste; land abuse grew slightly worse during your years in charge; now skin cancer deaths are on the increase; and as far as floods go, things got worse.

Institute members testing the software, using a wise caution, and carefully balancing the need for environmental taxes against the need to preserve the global economy, have been unable to score better than -8,860 by the year 2035 – which is all the more worrying, given that as a species we cannot replay the next decades until we get them right, nor do we have a superfluity of ecologically informed leaders.

The game is a triumph of design, and allows the player to change the underlying biases, to pro-nuclear, pro-environmentalist, pro-industrialist or pro-third world. As the author writes: 'This lets the player come backstage in the simulation and take control of many of the critical factors. Not only does this empower the player, but it also challenges him to examine closely his own beliefs.'

> 'In a sane world, the politician would be encouraged to practise his or her theories on a computer model of the world, before being unleashed on the real thing'

As a game it makes a good educational tool for any group of teenagers; and in a sane world, just as a pilot in training has to undergo arcade-style simulations, so the politician would be encouraged to practise his or her theories on a computer model of the world, before being unleashed on the real thing.

It is a political flaw in the game to concentrate all power on a potentially tyrannical and inaccessible United Nations High Commissioner. Perhaps one day there could be a multi-user version with different players representing the various countries.

'Balance of the Planet' is available in an IBM or Mac version, for £34-99 from the Cache Collection, 105 Gaunt St, London SE1 6DP (tel 071 407 3463; fax 407 3563).

The Chapman imperative: act as if you were going to live to be five billion years old

Dr David Chapman

David Chapman has come up with a Kantian-style ethical imperative for the late twentieth century, as detailed in the following extracts from his comments on the Pearce Report ('Blueprint for a Green Economy' by David Pearce, Anil Markanya and Edward Barbier, published by Earthscan Publications Ltd, 1989, £6-95).

Pearce favours taxes on non-renewable resources, and gives a formula for deciding what these taxes should be. The formula implicitly accepts that we should use up all of a given resource, and then move on to use up some substitute which is less convenient to use or more expensive to extract. Therefore the only questions to be answered are: how slowly should we use up the resource, so as to delay the eventual cost of having to change over to the worse substitute, and what level of tax would get it used up at this rate?

> 'We should therefore use up resources as we would if each of us were expecting individually to live (in averagely good health, etc) for 5 billion years'

However, I think that a different approach needs considering – that of fair shares between the generations. We should decide what would be a fair share of the reserves of each resource for us to use, and what should be the share for future generations, and levy a tax high enough to get our consumption down to this amount. In deciding what our share should be, we should bear in mind that it will be possible for human beings to exist on this planet (providing we do not destroy it) for about another five billion years. We should therefore use up resources as we would if each of us were expecting individually to live (in averagely good health, etc) for five billion years.

However, this does not mean that we should use up only one five-billionth of the reserves each year, for several reasons: much greater reserves might be discovered in future; substitutes might be discovered, or new production methods or styles of life which do not need the resource at all; also, much more efficient ways of recycling the resource might be discovered, so that less is needed. But it is clear that with this approach:

(a) We should use up resources much more slowly than we do now, or than we would with Pearce's formula;

(b) We should have a much higher resource tax, one sufficient to get our consumption down to this desired level; and

(c) It would be most effective to tackle this problem on an international basis, seeking global agreement on minimum resource taxes of the appropriate level.

David Chapman, Democracy Design Forum, Coles Centre, Buxhall, Stowmarket, Suffolk IP14 3EB (tel 0449 736 223).

The Laws of Vested Interest
Professor Meredith Thring

I feel that no Council for Posterity (see above) can do much good unless enough people are terrified about the future to 'have a change of heart'; and so are prepared to sacrifice quite a lot of short term advantages to the long term. Examples of such sacrifices are to reduce energy consumption in the rich countries to about one tenth of its present value; and for people to give up careers in 'defence' and to apply their brains to helping the poor countries to reach a state of education and security such that they voluntarily reduce family sizes.

Unfortunately, the aims of governments are:
• To stay in power and help their friends.
• To apply their classical dogma, as if it were absolute truth.

- To help their own group in the short term, regardless of other groups or the long term.

The economic laws under which we live are equally unfortunate:

- *The Law of Irresponsibility.* Whatever is right for our grandchildren is always uneconomic and almost always impolitic.

'The Law of Irreversible Luxury. Once a group of people have become accustomed to an unnecessary luxury, it cannot be withdrawn except by violence, eg by war or by revolution'

- *The Law of Irreversible Luxury.* Once a group of people has become accustomed to an unnecessary luxury, it cannot be withdrawn except by violence, eg by war or by revolution. Remorse is not sufficient, unless it leads to a complete change of heart.
- *The Law of Vested Interest.* When a large scale activity has developed giving a good livelihood to a group of people, they will use all kinds of propaganda to prove it is in the public interest and morally right. Examples: the slave trade; tobacco; tranquillisers; nuclear power.
- *The Law of Conquest.* If you lose a war against a gentlemanly opponent, you are better off in the long run than he is, because he does not allow you to waste your resources on excessive armaments.

Professor Meredith Thring, Bell Farm, The Street, Brundish, Suffolk IP13 8BL (tel 037 9384 296).

A sunshine limit to growth

William Rees

The following is a brief extract from a much longer article, entitled 'The Ecology of Sustainable Development' by William Rees, which appeared in Volume 20, No 1, of the Ecologist (£3, or £18 subscription, from Worthyvale Manor, Camelford, Cornwall, PL32 9TT, tel 0840 212711).

The Second Law of Thermodynamics states that in any closed isolated system, available energy and matter are continuously and irrevocably degraded to the unavailable state. Since the global economy operates within an essentially closed system, the Second Law (the entropy law) is actually the ultimate regulator of economic activity.

'Any form of economic activity dependent on material resources therefore contributes to a constant increase in global net entropy'

All modern economies are dependent on fixed stocks of non-renewable material and energy resources. The Second Law therefore declares that they necessarily consume and degrade the very resource base which sustains them. Our material economies treat other components of the biosphere as resources, and all the products of economic activity (that is

both the by-products of manufacturing and the final consumer goods) are eventually returned to the biosphere as waste. Thus, while we like to think of our economies as dynamic, productive systems, the Second Law states that in thermodynamic terms, all material economic 'production' is in fact 'consumption'. Any form of economic activity dependent on material resources therefore contributes to a constant increase in global net entropy (disorder), through the continuous dissipation of available energy and matter. It follows that contrary to the assumptions of neo-classical theory:

- There is no equilibrium in the energy and material relationships between industrial economies and the biosphere;
- Sustainable development based on prevailing patterns of resource use is not even theoretically conceivable.

The thermodynamic interpretation of the economic process therefore suggests a new definition of sustainable development which contrasts radically with present practice: sustainable development is development that minimises resource use and the increase in global entropy.

Eco-systems, unlike economic systems, are driven by an external source of energy – the sun. The steady stream of solar energy sustains essentially all biological diversity and makes possible the diversity of life on earth. Through photosynthesis, living systems concentrate simple dispersed chemicals and use them to synthesise the most complex substances known. Thus, in contrast to economic systems, eco-systems steadily contribute to the accumulation of concentrated energy, matter and order within the biosphere. In thermodynamic terms, photosynthesis is the most important materially productive process on the planet and it is the ultimate source of all renewable resources used by the human economy. Moreover, since the flow of solar radiation is constant, steady and reliable, resource production in the ecological sector is potentially sustainable over any time scale relevant to humanity. Ecological productivity is limited, however, by the availability of nutrients, photosynthetic efficiency, and ultimately the rate of energy input (the 'solar flux') itself. Eco-systems therefore do not grow indefinitely. Unlike the economy, which expands through resource conversion and positive feedback, eco-systems are held in 'steady-state' or dynamic equilibrium by limiting factors and negative feedback.

'Eco-systems, unlike economic systems, are driven by an external source of energy – the sun'

The consumption of ecological resources everywhere has begun to exceed sustainable rates of biological production. Nearly 40 per cent of terrestrial net primary productivity (photosynthesis) is already being used or co-opted by humans, one species among millions, and the fraction is steadily increasing.

'Biosphere resources are becoming increasingly scarce and *there are no substitutes*'

At present, markets do not even recognise such factors as nutrient recycling, soil building, atmosphere maintenance and climate stabilisation as resources. Thus, while market economics can usually price the scarce material inputs to manufacturing, it is virtually silent on the value of biosphere processes. Not surprisingly, it is these more critical resources that are becoming increasingly scarce *and there are no substitutes.*

'Any human activity cannot be sustained indefinitely if it uses not only the annual production of the biosphere (the "interest") but also cuts into the standing stock (the "capital")'

Clearly, any human activity dependent on the consumptive use of ecological resources (forestry, fisheries, agriculture, waste disposal, urban sprawl onto agricultural land) cannot be sustained indefinitely if it uses not only the annual production of the biosphere (the 'interest') but also cuts into the standing stock (the 'capital'). Herein lies the essence of our environmental crisis. Persistent trends in key ecological variables indicate that we have not only been living off the interest but also consuming our ecological capital. This is the inevitable consequence of exponential material growth in a finite environment. In short, the global economy is cannibalising the biosphere.

This means that much of our wealth is illusion. We have simply drawn down one account (the biosphere) to add to another (material wealth). It might even be argued that we have been collectively impoverished in the process. Much potentially renewable ecological capital has been permanently converted into machinery, plant and possessions that will eventually wear out and have to be replaced at the cost of additional resources.

Heilbroner has noted that the origin of surplus in the era of industrial capitalism 'has gradually moved from trade through direct wage labour exploitation toward technological rents, and that modern-day profits consist of combinations of all three.' We can now add a fourth profit source to Heilbroner's list; the irreversible conversion of biological resources.

For human society, carrying capacity can be defined as the maximum rate of resource consumption and waste discharge that can be sustained indefinitely without progressively impairing ecological productivity and integrity. The corresponding maximum human population is therefore a function of per capita rates of resource consumption and waste production.

'Hence we are within one population doubling of the "sunshine limit" to growth and at present rates will reach that limit in 35 years'

Through a thermodynamic analysis of food production, Bryson has estimated that about 900 square metres of cropland are required to produce the average per capita food energy requirements assuming year round cropping. With an average growing season of only 180 days, each hectare of agricultural land will theoretically support about 5.5 people. The present world population density is about 3 persons per arable hectare. Hence we are within one population doubling of the 'sunshine limit' to growth and at present rates will reach that limit in 35 years.

It should be understood that while human society depends on many ecological resources and functions for survival, carrying capacity is ultimately determined by the single vital resource or function in least supply. (On the global scale, loss of the ozone layer alone could conceivably lead to the extinction of the human species.)

Such considerations call seriously to question the Brundtland Commission's route to sustainable development through a five-to-ten-fold increase in industrial activity. Indeed, it forces a reconsideration of the entire material growth ethic, the central pillar of industrial society.

William E. Rees, Ph.D., Associate Professor of Planning and Resource Ecology, University of British Columbia, School of Community and Regional Planning, 6333 Memorial Road, Vancouver, BC, Canada V6T 1W5.

Property rights in air and water

Adapted extract from 'Libertarian Pollution Control' by Max O'Connor (published by Libertarian Alliance, 1 Russell Chambers, The Piazza, Covent Garden, London WC2E 8AA, tel 071 821 5502).

The existence of non-optimal amounts of pollution is due to the failure of the state to create or enforce property rights in the environment. The solution is to apply the principle of property rights to the air, to seas and to rivers.

'Property rights in the air around one's home did exist before the Industrial Revolution'

Property rights in the air around one's home did exist before the Industrial Revolution but then the courts began systematically to allow violations of these rights as long as the air pollution produced was not unusually greater than that from any similar manufacturing firm.

Private nuisance (such as the neighbour's bonfire) is usually dealt with effectively under common law, but in the area of public nuisance the system functions badly. If you are building a steel mill and are causing damage not only to your neighbour but to all the inhabitants within a forty-mile radius, the threat of a suit and the imposition of damages is in fact far less, since only an agency of the government is empowered to sue for public nuisance. Effective public nuisance suits would, in practice, mean the creation and enforcement of property rights in the air and water.

It may be objected that there is a difficulty in this solution to the pollution problem in that there are a large amount of damages to be claimed, but each one is a small amount, so that it is not worth anyone's while to sue. To solve the problem, it has been suggested that the law be modified to allow an individual to bring a 'class suit', a suit requiring payment of damages to himself and all others similarly damaged, however many thousands there may be. Says Robert Nozick, 'lawyers would go into business as "public's agents", charging a yearly fee to collect and turn over to their clients all the pollution payments to which they were entitled.'

Note: 'Anarchy, State and Utopia' by Robert Nozick (published by Basil Blackwell, Oxford, 1975).

From Consumers' to Users' Association

Valerie Yule

We live in the Age of Waste and so we have a Consumers' Association. But if we can wake up quickly enough to what is ahead the name will soon be changed to the Users' Association.

The aim of the redefined Association will be for buyers to get the best that we can without ruining the future – without taking all the irreplaceable natural resources, ruining the arable land and spreading the deserts.

> **'The Users' Association will include in its evaluations of a product: how durable it is; how repairable; and how recyclable'**

The Users' Association will include in its evaluations of a product some or all of the following:

- *How durable it is;*
- *How repairable*, and whether DIY, local repairer or back to the manufacturer;
- *How recyclable.*

Tables for product comparison will be extended to include the following:

- *Pollution Index.* A rating of how much pollution is involved in the making, in the using, and in the disposing.

> **'Rating how much a product will be laying a cost on future generations'**

- *Future Cost Index.* One Future Cost rating is how much a product will be laying a cost on future generations by taking up irreplaceable natural resources, such as oil or mercury, in its making or operation. A lesser Future Cost rating is how much it takes up renewable resources that are not being renewed properly – like rain-forest timber.
- *Energy Index.* Units of fuel required for operation.

Valerie Yule, 57 Waimarie Drive, Mount Waverley, Victoria, Australia 3149 (tel 807 4315).

New Consumer

New Consumer, the stylish magazine and movement launched in 1989, aims to mobilise consumer spending to achieve fundamental social and economic change. New Consumer acts like a kind of Green Which? magazine, rating companies on their environmental impact, respect for people, community involvement and many other factors.

New Consumer, Director Richard Adams, 52 Elswick Road, Newcastle upon Tyne NE4 6JH (tel 091 272 1148; fax 091 272 1615). New Consumer was the winner of a main Social Inventions Award. Subscriptions cost £10.

Shopping for a Better World

The New Consumer organisation (see previous item) has compiled a UK version of the American 'Shopping for a Better World' book, subtitled 'A Quick and Easy Guide to Socially Responsible Shopping.' It rates 2,500 major consumer brands for their:

Degree of disclosure of information; promotion of women; testing of animals; Third World policies; South African involvement; political donations; manufacturing of alcohol, tobacco, military products, or involvement in gambling.

So, for instance, a shopper considering buying Birds Eye frozen fish can see at a glance that it is manufactured by Unilever, who are displayed as being reasonably socially responsible in all the above categories, except that they test new products on animals, they have heavy involvement in South Africa and they have a brewery operation in Nigeria and minor involvement in tobacco sales in West Africa.

Steven Burkeman of York writes: 'This radical approach could work in the UK, where there are signs that more and more consumers do care about such things as the environmental impact of the products they buy, or the political and economic conditions in the country of origin. There is every prospect that effectively organised socially responsible purchasing will affect the behaviour of companies.'

'Shopping for a Better World' published by Kogan Page, £4-99, ISBN 0 7494 0483 3.

Postcards to ungreen companies

Clive Akerman

Pre-printed postcards might be produced to give feedback to the 'baddie' ungreen companies – so that we Green sympathisers who are spurning the 'baddies' and patronising the 'goodies' can tell the baddies what we have done and why.

For instance:

To the Marketing Director, _____ plc

Dear Sir,

I have this day spent £ _____ buying _____ from your competitor _____ . While I accept that your equivalent product is of similar performance at a similar price, I chose to purchase from your competitor because

_____

Yours faithfully,

_____

Address _____

_____

Loss of market share will cause a company to change – telling them WHY they have lost market share, and implicitly or explicitly telling them that they will be forgiven (we shall return to buying their products) if they mend their ways, will help us to move towards a society more sensitive to future generations.

The other two aspects of such a campaign should be:

1. Identify a list of the current 'Top Ten' most undesirable consumer products, with the reasons for their undesirability and a short list of 'OK' easily obtained alternatives.

2. Publicise the list, with the reasons and the alternatives. This can be by television consumer or current affairs programmes or newsletters. The mechanism must be legal, but otherwise anything within the reach and taste of the pressure group concerned is acceptable.

> 'Identify a list of the Top Ten most undesirable consumer products, with the reasons for their undesirability and a short list of "OK" easily obtained alternatives'

Clive Akerman, 92 Sandbrook Road, London N16 OSP (tel 071 241 0866). This simple idea won a prize in the Social Inventions Awards.

The Valdez Principles, a Green code of conduct for companies

The following introduction is extracted from an article by Leonard Doyle in the Independent.

The US Green lobby has joined forces with a broad coalition of 'socially responsible' investors to launch a new campaign, known as the Valdez Principles, focused on domestic and international companies which are chronic polluters of the environment.

Named after the Exxon Valdez tanker oil-spill disaster in Alaska, the Valdez Principles consist of a voluntary code of conduct for the environment, based on the Sullivan Principles campaign for US companies operating in South Africa, and the US campaign against discrimination in Northern Ireland, known as the MacBride Principles.

The coalition of environmentalists and investors, which controls more than £300 billion in investments, includes 14 US environmental groups, numerous religious groups, hundreds of fund managers and the entire pension funds of California and New York City.

A sign of their strength came when the Exxon Corporation agreed to appoint an environmentalist to its board of directors in the wake of the Exxon Valdez oil spill. Environmentalists persuaded institutional investors holding 22 million shares in the company (about 1.7 per cent of the shares) to press for the appointment.

> 'We will take responsibility for any harm we cause to the environment'

Because of the high public profile in the environment, politicians are lining up to endorse draft legislation in several states, and shareholder resolutions are being presented to corporations, requesting that they comply with the new principles.

'Any company that ignores environmental precautions or fails to act responsibly as a steward of our biosphere will be the focus of shareholder action,' said Joan Bavaria, the head of the Coalition for Environmentally Responsible Economies (Ceres) which helped draft the principles.

Text of the Valdez Principles

By adopting these principles, we publicly affirm our belief that corporations and their shareholders have a direct responsibility for the environment. We believe that corporations must conduct their business as responsible stewards of the environment and seek profits only in a manner that leaves the Earth healthy and safe. We believe that corporations must not compromise the ability of future generations to sustain their needs.

> 'We believe that corporations must not compromise the ability of future generations to sustain their needs'

We recognise this to be a long term commitment to update our practices continually in light of advances in technology and new understandings in health and environmental science. We intend to make consistent, measurable progress in implementing these principles and to apply them wherever we operate throughout the world.

(1) Protection of the biosphere

We will minimise and strive to eliminate the release of any pollutant that may cause environmental damage to the air, water, or earth or its inhabitants. We will safeguard habitats in rivers, lakes, wetlands, coastal zones and oceans and will minimise acid rain or smog, contributions to the greenhouse effect and depletion of the ozone layer, .

(2) Sustainable use of natural resources

We will make sustainable use of renewable natural resources, such as water, soil and forest. We will conserve non-renewable natural resources through efficient use and careful planning. We will protect wildlife habitat, open spaces and wilderness, while preserving biodiversity.

(3) Reduction and disposal of waste

We will minimise the creation of waste, especially hazardous waste, and wherever possible recycle materials. We will dispose of all wastes through safe and responsible methods.

(4) Wise use of energy

We will make every effort to use environmentally safe and sustainable energy sources to meet our needs. We will invest in improved energy efficiency and conservation in our operations. We will maximise the energy efficiency of products we produce or sell.

(5) Risk reduction

We will minimise the environmental, health and safety risks to our employees and the communities in which we operate by employing safe technologies and operating procedures and by being constantly prepared for emergencies.

(6) Marketing of safe products and services

We will sell products or services that minimise adverse environmental impacts and that are safe as consumers commonly use them. We will inform consumers of the environmental impacts of our products or services.

(7) Damage compensation

We will take responsibility for any harm we cause to the environment by making every effort to fully restore the environment and to compensate those persons who are adversely affected.

(8) Disclosure

We will disclose to our employees and to the public incidents relating to our operations that cause environmental harm or pose health or safety hazards. We will disclose potential environmental, health or safety hazards posed by our operations, and we will not take any action against employees who report any condition that creates a danger to the environment or poses health and safety hazards.

(9) Environmental directors and managers

At least one member of the board of directors will be a person qualified to represent environmental interests. We will commit management resources to implement these Principles, including the funding of an office of vice president for environmental affairs or an equivalent executive position, reporting directly to the chief executive officer, to monitor and report upon our implementation efforts.

(10) Assessment and annual audit

We will conduct and make public an annual self-evaluation of our progress in implementing these Principles and in complying with all applicable laws and regulations throughout our worldwide operations. We will work toward the timely creation of independent environmental audit procedures which we will complete annually and make available to the public.

> 'The creation of independent environmental audit procedures which we will complete annually and make available to the public'

Launch of Valdez Principles in the UK

Institute director Guy Dauncey chaired a Green Alliance meeting at BP's conference centre at which Gordon Davidson, director of the Social Investment Forum in the States, introduced the Principles to the UK ethical investment community and to UK environmental groups.

The Confederation of British Industry (CBI)'s Environ-

mental Business Forum in 1992 launched a six point programme, whereby its member companies agree to give a main board director responsibility for environmental matters, publish a policy statement, set clear targets for achieving the strategy, report progress publicly, ensure that employees understand the company's policy and help small businesses that cannot afford heavy overheads to improve their environmental performance. 'Without a clean record,' say the CBI, 'customers will not buy, bankers will not lend, insurers will not insure and people will not even apply for jobs.'

The European Commission also have a draft directive on civil liability for damage to the environment which would make companies *and* their banks jointly liable for clean-up costs. This is already frightening banks into directing their loans towards environmentally safe projects, in case they are left with heavy clean-up costs once a company has gone out of business.

- *Gordon Davidson, Director, Social Investment Forum, Coalition for Environmentally Responsible Economies (CERES), 711 Atlantic Avenue, Boston, MA 02111, USA (tel 617 451 3252).*
- *Green Alliance (Julie Hill), 60 Chandos Place, London WC2N 4HG (tel 071 836 0341).*
- *The last two paragraphs of the above story are adapted from two news items in the Times.*

Wanted: Enemies of the Earth and Greenwar International

Anthony Judge

An adapted extract from a letter to the Institute.

I propose the creation of two new organisations: Enemies of the Earth and Greenwar International. These bodies would function as 'counterparts' to Friends of the Earth and Greenpeace International. Their purpose would be to focus attention on the efforts of those who are endeavouring to degrade or destroy the Earth in one way or another. If the Earth is to be the scene of an archetypal battle between its Friends and its Enemies, then it is only fair that the heroes on both sides should be appropriately honoured.

> 'If the Earth is to be the scene of an archetypal battle between its Friends and its Enemies, then it is only fair that the heroes on both sides should be appropriately honoured'

Needless to say it is to be expected that people may be somewhat shy about declaring their membership in either body. They will need assistance. So we need a small trust of 'well-wishers' to set up the legal structures and to administer the secretariats. The trust could then invite nominations for membership – those who have demonstrated outstanding commitment to the degradation of the Earth.

As in any serious organisation, profiles of members will be carefully built up to indicate the domains in which they have demonstrated degrading capacity or in which they are anxious to do so. These profiles, with addresses, can be published in directory form. They should provide a source of income to cover general expenses.

A panel, modelled on the Nobel Prize Committee, could be appointed to select annually – on the basis of nominations – laureates in different domains such as: war, eco-destruction, disinformation, cultural degradation, health depletion, deprivation, weapons research, conspicuous consumption, betrayal of hope and human misery.

So that is the proposal. I trust that it tickles your imagination. Of course it would need to be done right. Maybe it would be better to do it rather than talk about doing it. One has no trouble in recognising ideal members.

Anthony Judge, Union of International Associations, rue Washington 40, 1050 Brussels, Belgium (tel 32 2 640 18 08; fax 32 2 649 32 69).

Ecology Begins At Home

'Ecology Begins At Home', by Archie Duncanson, a 64 page booklet obtainable from the author at Örnstigen 9, 183 50 Täby, Sweden (tel 08 768 63 20). ISBN 91 7328 737 7. Price £6 incl. p&p.

In a letter to the Institute the author writes that 'this booklet is about what we can do as individuals to clean up our world and make it beautiful again – now.

'I published it myself, 500 copies, at the Writers' Book Machine, a printing co-op for self-publishing authors in Stockholm, where I did the mounting, layout, sorting, binding and trimming.'

> **'Making his own bubbly drinks – chop a grapefruit, pour boiling water over it; when cool, strain and add sugar to taste and a pinch of yeast; bottle with tight caps and the drink will be bubbly in four to five days'**

Archie Duncanson tells the tale in this book of how he gradually cut down on his contribution to pollution and how we can all begin to make similar choices. He has been fairly radical: a self-confessed 'car junkie' he now restricts his car use to special occasions; a lover of fizzy drinks, he now avoids buying drinks in aluminium cans by purchasing them in returnable bottles or by making his own bubbly drinks – 'chop a grapefruit, pour boiling water over it; when cool, strain and add sugar to taste and a pinch of yeast; bottle with tight caps and the drink will be bubbly in four to five days'; he used olive oil with added vinegar to polish his furniture; vinegar and lemon juice for cleaning the toilet; strong camomile tea and hanging clothes in the sun for bleaching; he lets his hands dry naturally rather than use hot air blowers in public toilets; he makes do with radio instead of newspapers (except on Sundays!); he keeps a diary instead of taking photos; he takes the train instead of flying; he eats frozen bananas on sticks instead of manufactured ice cream; by trial and error he has discovered that a clothes washing machine only requires a single tablespoon of washing powder and thus only one rinse cycle; he tries to eat food that has been grown within thirty miles of his home;

all his vegetable peelings, eggs shells, coffee grounds, tea leaves, etc, go under his sink for a week to begin fermenting, then into the compost box on his flat's balcony.

> **'He eats frozen bananas on sticks instead of manufactured ice cream'**

Go thou and do thou likewise!

As Duncanson points out: 'We can look at the enormity of the whole world's pollution problem, and think "what difference can I make?" – and do nothing.

'Or we can look at our own share which we have control over, take responsibility and say: "I am going to do something about it!".'

> **'A class competition to see who can most cut down on their own or their family's garbage and pollution that term'**

This would be a very good book for schools to use in their science classes. The pupils could make some of the alternative foods, drinks and household chemicals and composts he describes, and could have a class competition to see who can most cut down on their own or their family's garbage and pollution that term; or an inter-school competition to cut down pollution and resource wastage by schools.

In Sweden the book is in use at day care centres, schools of all types, universities and adult evening classes – thus encouraging people to look at their own lives, to set an example and truly to make a difference in the world. More than 10,000 books have been printed to date.

Note: The Writers' Book Machine printshop co-op is c/o Arne Jakobsson (the founder), Författares Bokmaskin, Box 12071, 10222 Stockholm, Sweden (tel 08 6535880).

How Green are YOU?

Norah McGrath

Perhaps readers might like to try this test. Beat your editor, Nicholas Albery, who scored 99 (a Green Rating score of 82% if the top score possible is 120). It is adapted from Chat magazine (195 Knightsbridge, London SW7 1RE, half million circulation) and is devised by its features editor Norah McGrath, based on the Green Consumer Guide by John Elkington and Julia Hailes (Gollancz, £3-95). Guy Dauncey suggests that local media could run competitions using this test to find the greenest local household.

1. What happens to most of the plastic supermarket carrier bags you stagger back home with?

(a) They are reused for other shopping trips.

(b) They're put in a drawer – you intend to reuse them but generally forget.

(c) They go in the bin.

2. Do you usually buy vegetables:

(a) Loose?

(b) Pre-packed?

3. Do you buy your milk:

(a) In bottles?

(b) In cartons?

4. In what sort of boxes do you generally buy eggs?

(a) Polystyrene foam.

(b) Clear plastic.

(c) Paper.

5. What is the colour of the loo rolls you have in your bathroom?

(a) White.

(b) Coloured.

(c) Colourless recycled.

'You're buying a new dining table. It's available in a choice of three woods. You choose:
(a) Oak?
(b) Ash?
(c) Teak?'

6. You're buying a new dining table. It's available in a choice of three woods. You choose:

(a) Oak?

(b) Ash?

(c) Teak?

7. You're having a new kitchen fitted. You have a choice of three units. Do you go for:

(a) Solid mahogany?

(b) Chipboard?

(c) Solid pine?

8. The batteries run out in your radio/shaver etc. Do you:

(a) Replace them?

(b) Recharge them?

(c) You only have mains-operated appliances in your home.

9. What form of deodorant do you use?

(a) Aerosol.

(b) Roll-on or a solid stick.

(c) None.

10. Would the words 'CFC-free' on a household or toiletry aerosol:

(a) Make you more likely to buy it than a similar product.

(b) Make you less likely to buy it than a similar product?

(c) Have no effect on whether you buy it or not?

11. Would the words 'new' or 'improved' on a cosmetic or toiletry item:

(a) Make you more likely to buy it than another similar product?

(b) Make you less likely to buy it than another similar product?

(c) Have no effect on whether you buy it or not.

12. How do you get rid of flies in the home?

(a) Swat them.

(b) Spray them.

(c) Hang up a sticky fly paper.

13. How do you get rid of greenfly and other pests in the garden?

(a) Without chemicals.

(b) With chemicals.

14. How do you get rid of surplus DIY chemicals, like turps, strippers etc?

(a) In the dustbin.

(b) Down the loo.

(c) Down the sink.

15. How do you get rid of garden refuse?

(a) Compost heap.

(b) Bonfire.

(c) Dustbin.

16. Do you often walk or cycle rather than take transport?

(a) No.

(b) Yes.

17. Do you own a car?

(a) Yes.

(b) No.

18. If you are a car owner, do you:

(a) Use unleaded petrol.

(b) Know whether your car could be converted to run on unleaded?

(c) Not know whether your car could be converted to use unleaded petrol?

'Tick which of the following apply to you. Be honest. Do you:
(a) Smoke?
(b) Drop litter in the street?
(c) Leave the tap running when you are brushing your teeth?
(d) Always use a tumble dryer rather than a clothes line?'

19. Tick which of the following apply to you. Be honest. Do you:

(a) Smoke?

(b) Drop litter in the street?

(c) Leave the tap running when you are brushing your teeth?

(d) Always use a tumble dryer rather than a clothes line?

20. Do you have a jacket on your hot-water tank?

(a) Yes.

(b) No.

21. Is your loft insulated?

(a) Yes.

(b) No.

22. Is the inside of your kettle:

(a) Furred up?

(b) Clear?

23. Tick which of the following items you sort for collection or disposal at a recyling bank.

(a) Glass bottles.

(b) Tin cans.

(c) Paper.

24. Tick any of the following foods you buy or eat regularly:

(a) Takeaway burgers.

(b) Big portions of meat.

(c) Brazil nuts.

(d) Locally grown fruit and vegetables.

(e) Organically grown fruit and vegetables.

25. Where do your old clothes end up?

(a) In the bin.

(b) On family or friends.

(c) In charity shops or jumble sales.

Scores: 1. (a) 5 (b) 2 (c) 0 / **2.** (a) 5 (b) 0 / **3.** (a) 5 (b) 0 / **4.** (a) 0 (b) 0 (c) 5 / **5.** (a) 2 (b) 0 (c) 5 / **6.** (a) 5 (b) 5 (c) 0 / **7.** (a) 0 (b) 0 (c) 5 / **8.** (a) 0 (b) 5 (c) 5 / **9.** (a) 0 (b) 5 (c) 5 / **10.** (a) 5 (b) 0 (c) 0 / **11.** (a) 0 (b) 5 (c) 2 / **12.** (a) 5 (b) 0 (c) 5 / **13.** (a) 5. (b) 0 / **14.** (a) 5 (b) 0 (c) 0 / **15.** (a) 5 (b) 0 (c) 2 / **16.** (a) 0 (b) 5 / **17.** (a) 0 (b) 5 / **18.** (a) 5 (b) 2 (c) 0 / **19.** Lose 5 for ticks next to (a) or (b). Lose 1 each for ticking (c) or (d) / **20.** (a) 5 (b) 0 / **21.** (a) 5 (b) 0 / **22.** (a) 0 (b) 5 / **23.** Score 5 for every tick / **24.** Lose 1 for ticking (a) or (b), gain 5 each for ticking (c) (d) or (e) / **25.** (a) 0 (b) 5 (c) 5.

What your score means: Bright green (95 or over); **Pale Green** (60-94); **Hint of Green** (25-59); **Greenless** (0 or less to 24).

Avoiding Armageddon by redirecting space debris

Expanded from an article in the Times by Nick Nuttall.

In 1989, a cosmic boulder bigger than an aircraft carrier, passed within 400,000 miles of Earth, a mere whisker in astronomical terms.

The chilling scenario feared by astronomers is that of a collision between Earth and one of the 46,000 mph objects in the Taurid stream (cosmic rubble and dust that swings through Earth's orbit on biannual crossings).

'A collision between Earth and one of the 46,000 mph objects in the Taurid stream is analogous to a nuclear war'

Dr Victor Clube of the Department of Astrophysics at Oxford University says 'the matter requires urgent attention. It is crucial that everyone is woken up to the danger. It is analogous to a nuclear war with a megatonnage of the same order and all the effects of nuclear war with debris from the impact causing sunlight to be blocked, causing a Dark Age or Ice Age.'

'Power units that could attach and divert celestial boulders away from Earth'

The Institute of Aeronautics and Astronautics is calling for studies into power units that could attach and divert celestial boulders away from Earth. Dr Clube and others are concerned at suggestions of shattering incoming asteroids with nuclear weapons. They believe that there is the danger that by solving one large threat, it may create scores of smaller ones.

Keeping track of potentially dangerous asteroids would require at least six $12m telescopes distributed throughout North and South America, according to David Morrison, head of the Space Science Division at NASA Ames Research Center in Mountain View, California. 'With proper tracking techniques, astronomers could spot a potentially catastrophic one decades before it hit the Earth,' says Morrison.

'Cosmic Winter', a book on this subject by Dr Clube and Dr Napier, is published by Basil Blackwell (June 1990, £16-95).

Meteor stream key to earth's climate

Dr Victor Clube

I would now bet my bottom dollar that the core body of the Taurid-Arietid (meteor) stream (see previous item) is the ultimate key to everything that is going on in the atmosphere, affecting climate, ozone, etc. Yet the big guns of modern science are not trained in this direction at all.

'I would now bet my bottom dollar that the core body of the Taurid-Arietid (meteor) stream is the ultimate key to everything that is going on in the atmosphere, affecting climate, ozone, etc'

The Taurid-Arietid stream in history

Adapted extracts from 'Giant Comets and their Role in History' by Dr Clube (in 'The Universe and its Origins', edited by S. Fred Singer, published by ICUS, Paragon House, New York, 1990).

The largest if not the brightest meteor stream in the sky is the Taurid-Arietid stream. It approaches the earth by night from the asolar direction during the months of November/December and by day from the solar direction during May/June. Since the earth's crossing time for most other meteor streams is just a few hours, volume for volume and mass for mass, the source of this stream may not be far short of a million times larger than a typical one. And since a typical comet is a few kilometres in diameter, the ultimate source in this case may easily be a giant comet a few hundred kilometres in size.

There is a growing impression that giant comets progressively disintegrate into a variety of asteroidal debris. The Tunguska body of 100,000 tons is a case in point: it struck the earth on the morning of June 30, 1908, and was almost certainly a member of the Taurid-Arietid stream.

'The Taurid-Arietid stream may have produced the last ice age'

Whipple and Hamid accurately retrocalculated the orbits of a number of meteors to indicate that several major fragmentations have taken place during the last five thousand years. The most significant of these events took place around 3000 BC due to an encounter in the asteroid belt; another was deemed to have occurred around AD 500, with possibly yet another in the second half of the second millennium BC. The epochs around 3000 and 1300 BC in particular correspond to significant deteriorations in the global climate for two or three centuries or more. It is known from other studies that a correlation exists between global rainfall and the incidence of meteor dust on the earth; so the indications now are for a considerable degree of climatic control by the Taurid-Arietid stream. Indeed, its giant comet is likely to have produced the last ice age whilst modulating the climate during the subsequent interglacial through the intermediary of stratospheric dust veils.

Around 3000 BC a major fragmentation of the primary body would have produced a battery of comets; it would not be surprising if onlookers thought that they were witnessing a battle for mastery over the sky, and that this was in some way associated with the assaults on the earth that inevitably followed. Such global bombardments by Tunguska and super-Tunguska bodies would leave an indelible memory for the surviving humans and a lasting fear of the gods in the sky.

> 'We might even envisage destruction so great, and dark ages so effective, that only the dimmest memories will later exist of giants that once walked the earth'

Memories would be of local floods and widespread destruction by fire over areas the size of a nation. We might even envisage destruction so great, and dark ages so effective, that only the dimmest memories will later exist of giants that once walked the earth, of heavenly clouds that a creator once built in the sky, of prophets and messiahs who warned of doom and salvation, and of floods and cataracts of fire that were used to cleanse the earth. We might anticipate that the intellectual confusion would reach new heights when the comet-asteroid deities known to be responsible for all the mayhem finally disappear from sight – which they apparently did during the first millennium BC. We might anticipate the worship of new invisible gods or the diversion to new planetary gods. We might even learn to agree with an Aristotle, a Ptolemy or a Newton, as they seek to dismiss the thunderbolts of a previous generation and restore a sense of order in heaven and on earth. Each time, however, we ignore the Taurid-Arietid stream.

> 'A future confrontation with a barrage of Tunguskas is a very reasonable projection'

There is a swarm of boulders out there and a future confrontation with a barrage of Tunguskas is a very reasonable projection from the state of current knowledge. At least one form of star wars can be virtually guaranteed, and only time will tell whether we face a nuclear winter or a cometary winter.

Dr Victor Clube, Department of Astrophysics, Nuclear Physics Laboratory, Keble Road, Oxford OX1 3RH (tel 0865 273303; fax 0865 273418).

Satellite-verified incentives to help save the rainforests

Foster Brown and Tom Stone have shown (in 'Cultural Survival' magazine, 13/1/89, p. 35) that one way to keep abreast with the fine details of tropical rainforest clearance is through satellite photographs, which are relatively inexpensive (from $3 to $50 plus per photo) and which often offer the only up-to-date visual evidence of the dramatic changes in land use in Amazonia. They have distributed satellite images widely in Rondonia, providing them to rural extension agents, state environmental officials and local community organisers. But the Institute for Social Inventions is exploring whether such photos could have preventative and verification roles in stopping the annual burning (which now threatens the rainforests' role as the planet's air conditioner). For instance:

> 'Corruption would be largely avoided if annual satellite photos were used to decide the payments. Both the government and the governors would then have an incentive to police their areas, and to invest in firefighting and other measures'

(1) Could both the central Brazilian government and the governors of the relevant provinces be promised (by the West) money each year, the sum total being reduced in proportion to the amount of forest felling or burning in the previous year – with the proportions verified by satellite photos? According to the Ecologist magazine, the financier Sir James Goldsmith has suggested something similar – the payment of a sizeable annual rent by the industrialised world in return for protected forests; but to rely solely on the central Brazilian government to stop the burning of the rainforests is likely to prove inadequate. Amongst those others who need to be pressured are the provincial governors. Corruption would be largely avoided if annual satellite photos were used to decide the payments. Both the government and the governors would then have an incentive to police their areas, and to invest in firefighting and other measures.

(2) Could the individual owners of the rainforest enter into ecological farming agreements whereby they are paid an amount each year for say the next 25 years; the agreement to include a minimum 10% annual reforestation of any already cleared area, and a reduction in payment proportional to any further felling or burning? This would be very complex to administer, but again the proportions could be verified by satellite photos – which with the manoeuvrable satellites could readily produce comparable images each year. Such agreements with landowners would need backing up by agricultural extension services and support so as to enable settlers to stabilise their agricultural practices through agroforestry schemes for partial reforestation.

> 'The Union of Indian Nations needs to be supplied with the help of an international lawyer to draw up an application to the United Nations and the International Court for recognition as a nation'

(3) Similar ecological agreements could be made with the 180 Amazon tribes forming the Union of Indian Nations. A further proposal here is that the Union of Indian Nations be supplied with the help of an international lawyer to draw up an application to the United Nations and the International Court for recognition as a nation or nations, perhaps to form part of a wider Brazilian confederation. In international law they would have a very reasonable cause of action, if a referendum

were to show a majority in favour of independence, as they have a historical claim to the territory and they have not been recognised as Brazilians in the past. Brazil might conceivably acquiesce in return for debt relief.

Their chances of being recognised as an autonomous state are slight, it must be admitted, at least for the near future. But just the moves towards seeking independence, with Indian leaders in person presenting applications to the United Nations and with lawyers approaching the International Courts, and with requests for a UN peace-keeping observer force, etc, would provide continuous opportunities for the world media to grasp. It would help reduce the maltreatment of the Indians and the encroachment on their lands by making it that much more difficult for the Brazilian government or others, constantly under the spotlight of the world media and under pressure from world financial bodies, to act against the Indians or not to be seen to be defending their interests. (The less they defend them, the more the Indians have justification for seeking their own machinery of government.)

Such a claim for independence might at least help promote a compromise, whereby the Brazilian government gives more autonomy to the Indians and enforces more land rights for them than it had previously intended. And it would help change the image of the Indians from that of noble but primitive savages in the forest to that of international statesmen and diplomats. It could also help develop their own feelings of unity and self-esteem.

• *Foster Brown and Tom Stone are researchers at the Woods Hole Research Centre, PO Box 296, Woods Hole, Massachusetts 024543, USA (tel 508 540 9900).*

• *Satellite photos are available from EOSAT (4300 Forbes Boulevard, Lanham, MD 29796, USA, telex 277685 LSAT UR); from SPOT (1897 Preston Drive, Reston, VA 22901, USA, telex 4993073 SICORP); from INPE (Rodovia Presidente Dutra, Km 210, Cachoeira Paulista, SP 12.630 Brazil, telex 391125523 INPE BR); the Russians' Sigma Project military satellites produce much higher resolution images than Spot or Landsat, through Sigma Projects (Independent newspaper report by Mary Fagan, technology correspondent).*

• *Union of Indian Nations, Sao Paulo (tel and fax combined: 5511 624 246).*

The Forest Peoples' Fund

The Forest Peoples' Fund was set up by the Gaia Foundation to fund and support projects initiated by the Forest People themselves, particularly the Indians in the Amazon rainforest.

> 'Global Forest Peoples' Pledge, aimed at collecting pledges of support and money from five million people'

In 1989, the Fund, coordinated by Tanya Schwarz and others, contributed to funding and publicising the first Gathering of Amazonian Indian tribes at Altamira and helped the Union of Indian Nations in Sao Paulo both to develop its communication systems (providing fax machines and so on), and also to launch its Global Forest Peoples' Pledge, aimed at collecting pledges of support and money from five million

people around the word. This money will be channelled directly to the Forest People, for help in their determination to protect their rainforest homes.

Forest Peoples' Fund, 18 Well Walk, London NW3 1LD (tel 071 435 5000). This project won a Social Inventions Award.

Show Brazilians value of forest

Adapted from the Economist.

The best way the rest of mankind could help to save the Amazon would be to show Brazil that it could make a better living from keeping its forest and exploiting it sensibly than from destroying it. Up to now, commercial companies from the rich world have done virtually nothing to support research into the marketable products of the rainforest. The job of identifying new medicines, aromatic oils and timber, and of showing how they might be sustainably exploited, has been left almost entirely to an underfinanced handful of Brazilian research institutes. By strengthening these institutes, and by turning the Amazon into a vast research laboratory, willing governments could help to internationalise the rainforest by the back door. Pack it with botanists, climatologists, hydrologists and pharmacists who will bring in spending power and bring out new ideas: scientists are likely to be more successful conservationists than innocent Indians or under-equipped forest guards.

> 'Internationalise the rainforest by the back door. Pack it with botanists, climatologists, hydrologists and pharmacists'

Cultural Survival, a charity in Massachusetts, has set up a firm to buy and market rainforest products: as a result, Ben and Jerry's in the States has just launched 'rainforest crunch', made with brazil nuts (only from the wild forest) and cashews (used for reforesting degraded areas). The Body Shop is persuading the University of Belem, at the mouth of the Amazon, to look at seeds and plants for pot pourris and aromatic oils, and are getting an Indian tribe to harvest brazil nuts.

> 'Ben and Jerry's in the States has just launched "rainforest crunch", made with brazil nuts (only from the wild forest) and cashews (used for reforesting degraded areas)'

One small British firm, the Ecological Trading Company, was set up to buy teak and mahogany from Peru and Ecuador and has been inundated with orders.

Sometimes rainforest products in western shops could be sustainably managed but are not: chicle, the latex that makes chewing gum stretchy, is occasionally extracted by tapping trees, but more often, especially in Brazil, by cutting them down. Companies could make sure that such products are grown in a way that helps preserve the rainforest, and then advertise the fact.

A Botanical Peace Corps

Whole Earth Review in California announced the formation of a Botanical Peace Corps, a decentralised and leaderless network for amateur ethnobotanists willing to take direct action to save valuable plants. A 'wish list' of needed plants has been published and a field guide for those tourists willing to help collect specific seeds and plants. 'Most people don't enjoy the idea of being tourists,' they write. 'They want to respect and contact some authentic experience of forest or jungle environments. With a short period of training in the identification of endangered useful plants along the path of their itinerary, the right reference materials, a good illustrated guidebook and a list of local contacts, a traveller can become an explorer and contributor to the effort to save the most important parts of our dying botanical heritage.'

> ### 'A traveller can become an explorer and contributor to the effort to save the most important parts of our dying botanical heritage'

• *Botanical Peace Corps, PO Box 1368, Sebastopol, CA 95473, USA. Send a self-addressed envelope with international reply coupons from the post office with details of your journey.*

• *See also 8 pages of details in the Whole Earth Review No 60 (back issues $7, subs $24 in US bank cheque only), PO Box 38, Sausalito, CA 94966-9932, USA (tel 415 332 1716).*

School seeds study for Kew database

Forest Gate Community School in the London Borough of Newham have researched 500 seeds of the arid land plant Cassia obtusifolia, the leaves of which are fermented to produce a food product, kawal, used by Sudanese tribes as a meat substitute. Results from the school's research are stored on Kew Gardens' international database, SEPASAL (Survey of Economic Plants of Arid and Semi-Arid Lands).

The pupils' investigations ranged from simple weighing and measuring of the seeds to investigation of seed germination and growth under varying conditions of humidity, light and temperature. The Blue Peter TV programme have followed the work and there has been joint work with a twinned Kenyan school.

This was a pilot project leading to more such seeds research by schools. It was organised by the London Centre for International Peacebuilding and the Living Earth consultancy.

Niall Marriott and Roger Hammond, Living Earth, 37 Bedford Square, London WC1B 3EG (tel 071 436 0641).

Buy an acre of tropical forest

Programme for Belize is the coordinator of a coalition of environmental organisations and people taking personal action to end global warming. 110,000 acres of tropical forest in Belize are for 'sale' at £25 per acre, to be known as the Rio Bravo Conservation Area. (Individuals are given certificates of appreciation in return.) An educational programme will help local people to maintain the forest and improve their own standard of living from it.

• *Programme for Belize, PO Box 1088, Vineyard Haven, MA 02568, USA.*

• *In the UK: Programme for Belize, PO Box 99, Saxmundham, Suffolk, IP17 2LB.*

The erosion of civilisations

John Seymour

From notes prepared by John Seymour (author of 'The Ultimate Heresy' and books on self-sufficient farming), for an Academic Inn speech in London.

The philosophy of agriculture that I was taught at agricultural college in the early nineteen thirties, that Bigger is Better (the Economy of Scale) and that we must all become monoculturalists (the Economy of Specialisation), has led us to the brink of global disaster.

> ### 'The soil of our planet cannot bear the weight of over-large cities'

Travels and observations in over forty countries have convinced me that the soil of our planet cannot bear the weight of over-large cities. Soil may seem of little importance to city people but remember – without that twelve or so inches of brown powder round the earth this planet would be as barren as the moon.

Pre-city civilisation followed the law of return. The fertility which was taken from the soil in the form of food was returned to it in the form of dung. Huge cities cannot follow this law. We are at present mining the last remnants of rock phosphates and of potassium on this planet to dump on our soil – harvest and eat – and then dump into the ocean from which they can never be recovered. A little child could realise, if she thought about it, that this is not sustainable.

I shall speak only of the phenomena that I have myself witnessed:

Firstly, the *Cradle of Civilisation*. The country, often called by archaeologists the 'Garden of Eden', where agriculture, and therefore civilisation, first began. This is the stretch of perhaps a quarter of a million square miles of country to the north of Mesopotamia, once wonderfully fertile, still with a good climate for agriculture, but which is now a howling wilderness.

Secondly, I went south from there to the *Cradle of City Civilisation*. The first cities in the world were built by the Sumerians in the flat alluvial plain of the Tigris and Euphrates rivers in the south of what is now Iraq. That vast area – once the greatest irrigation scheme that has ever existed – is a salt desert. As for the cities themselves – their ruins are clearly that – not only did those cities ruin the land around them, but they also caused the destruction of the 'Garden of Eden', the rain-fed agricultural village culture of the north.

> ### 'That Cradle of City Civilisation - once the greatest irrigation scheme that has ever existed – is a salt desert'

Thirdly, I went and looked at the sites of other large city civilisations. The Minoan culture in *Crete*, starting about two and half thousand years before Christ, fell into ruin and totally disappeared after less than two thousand years for the simple reason that the soil went. Cretan farmers now farm their subsoil, with the olive and grape. Mainland *Greece* built its cities much later – and suffered the same fate. The reason why the Greeks had to turn to trade and industry was because their topsoil failed. *Rome* followed: the topsoil of Italy went into the sea because of the *latifundia* – the huge slave-worked estates – the agribusiness of their day. After this, the Romans provided the *panem* part of their *panem et circenses* from North Africa. If you want to see the huge granaries that they built to contain the grain mountains that they produced there you have to dig them out of the sand dunes.

Fourthly, *Africa*. The topsoil of Africa is being washed down into the sea. I saw sheet erosion and gulley erosion there such as I had never imagined could possibly have happened in such a short space of time. It is cash crop farming for the city people of the developed world that has destroyed the soil.

'In the Soviet Union, each year between 500,000 and 1,500,000 hectares of cropland are abandoned, so severely eroded by wind as to be no longer worth farming'

Fifthly, I decided to go and look at the Sumeria of today. The Great Plains of *North America* are the modern bread-basket of the world. The Black Soils of Russia , once the largest unbroken wheat-growing area on the planet, have been virtually destroyed by bad farming, and Russia is now dependent – the CIA, in its 'USSR Agricultural Atlas', noted that in the then Soviet Union 'each year between 500,000 and 1,500,000 hectares of cropland are abandoned, so severely eroded by wind as to be no longer worth farming'. India, China and Indonesia all have to import North American grain in times of shortage. We in Europe are heavily dependent upon North American soya for the protein part of our stock rations. So the soil of the American Great Plains is probably the most important thing in this world.

'By 2020 most of the topsoil of the eastern Great Plains of North America will have gone'

I went to Kansas. To put it briefly, the topsoil of the eastern Great Plains of North America is eroding down the great rivers so fast that nobody knows what to do about it. In the western Great Plains the topsoil all blew away in the dust-bowl period in the early nineteen thirties. But it is now in the East, with its better rainfall, that there is most concern. The high price of maize, wheat and soya, and also cotton, led to continuous cropping, with no legumes grown to provide nitrate, because the nitrate all comes out of the bag, with no animals because the animals have all gone to the dry West, and so no manure to stabilise the soil. And the soil is just going. Most experts I spoke to agreed that by 2020 most of the topsoil of the eastern Great Plains would have gone.

What can we do about it? The Chief Officer of the Soil Conservation Service of Kansas said to me: 'There is no soil erosion on organically rich soils.' There is no soil erosion, for example, on the farms of the Amish community who use neither heavy machinery nor chemical fertilisers. There was no soil erosion on one farm I visited where the farmer had *not* got rid of his cattle and so a third of his land was always down to alfalfa.

'There is no soil erosion on the farms of the Amish community'

The vast conurbations – I dare not use this beautiful word *city* to describe them – have got to go. The people have got to move out into the country again. And we have got to split up the huge agribusinesses and vast estates and estancias all over the world. We have got to get *people* back on the land again.

'The magic of ownership turns sand into gold'

And people will not return to their birthright – the land – as landless labourers or hinds again. They will have to get their fair share of it themselves. Arthur Young wrote: 'The magic of ownership turns sand into gold.'

The people who will leave the conurbations in the future, either because they want to or because they are forced, will demand their fair share of the Earth's surface.

And we must see that they get it.

John Seymour, Killowen, New Ross, Co. Wexford, Ireland (tel 353 51 88156).

Saving the planet with gravel dust

Gravel dust, often available free from the silt ponds at gravel pits, and rich in minerals and trace elements, should be added to your garden, according to the Soil Remineralisation movement. This movement is most active to date in Austria, Germany and the USA. Robert Schindele, for instance, writes: 'I discovered the phenomenon of gravel dust by accident. While building a 1.5 mile long road through my forest property near Melk, Austria, a lot of gravel dust developed. In areas where this dust settled, within a few months all the sick fir trees became healthy again and have grown very strongly since.'

'In areas where this gravel dust settled, within a few months all the sick fir trees got healthy again'

Don Weaver in his book with John Hamaker on the subject of gravel and rock dust ('The Survival of Civilisation', Hamaker-Weaver publications, California) writes: 'By adding gravel screenings from industry gravel pits east of San Francisco bay to my average organic garden at rates of 2 to 4 lbs per square foot, crop yields increased two to four times in quantity with unmistakable flavour enrichment. Pole beans climbing out of prolific zucchini and tomato beds went to 18 feet before being turned back by the weight of heavy beans at the top.' Hamaker's mineralised corn crop turned out to have 57% more phosphorus, 90% more potassium, 47% more calcium and 60% more magnesium than chemically grown crops from the same seed. On Lanzerotte in the Canary Islands, vines have flourished in soil rich in volcanic rock. And now in the UK, interesting results are beginning to show from the experiments at Springhill Farm near Aylesbury, where they are working in conjunction with the Department of Chemistry at Surrey University – growing wheat in soil to which granite dust from a nearby quarry has been added.

'During an ice age, as glaciers grind rock to a fine dust over millennia, a fertile soil is created'

The movement in the States has an almost messianic note. Joanna Campe, editor of 'Soil Remineralisation', believes that 'the ultimate poverty is poverty of soil. The fate of the earth hangs in the balance.' Remineralisation will help avert a new ice age: 'During an ice age, as glaciers grind rock to a fine dust over millennia, a fertile soil is created. Adding finely ground gravel dust nourishes the micro-organisms in the soil, whose proto-plasm is the basis of all life. Remineralisation can save the dying forests in the temperate latitudes. Otherwise, as forests begin to die off worldwide, giving off carbon dioxide, the climate of the earth is altered, triggering the transition from the warm interglacial to an ice age.' (*Ed:* An item in the Times also tells how increased amounts of greenhouse gases could also help cause a new ice age. Higher temperatures at the poles could cause more snow to fall, and cloudier summers will reduce the melting rate.)

Robert Schindele is even more extreme. He eats gravel dust, two teaspoons a day, and markets it in parts of Europe as a 'mineral dietary supplement' under the name 'Superbiomin' – despite heavy opposition from the German and Austrian pharmaceutical industry. 'For years my hair was as white as snow,' he says, 'but since I have been taking gravel dust, it is almost black again. Chronic diseases, especially gout, disappeared.'

He further claims that Superbiomin acts against radioactivity, 'breaking down the high oscillation rates of ionised particles, as confirmed by the Institute for atomic physics in the Ukraine.' Apparently after the Chernobyl accident, the Russians picked up 2000kg of Superbiomin with a military truck. 'I think this (gravel dust) discovery,' says Schindele, 'will be the biggest sensation of the century.'

Sources of information on this topic include:

• *A video entitled 'Stopping the Coming Ice Age' is available for $45 (UK VHS version) from People for a Future, 2140 Shattuck Avenue, Berkeley, CA 94704, USA (tel 415 524 2700). For the UK, specify the VHS version in your order.*

• *Mrs Betsan Coats, PO Box 77, Cotton Treet, Qld 4588, Australia (tel 071 444 361).*

• *Cameron Thomson, Hamaker Co-ordination, Scotaton Farm, Auchterhouse, Dundee, DD3 OQT, Scotland. He writes: 'My idea is for mobile rock grinders to go from farm to farm crushing stones, which are gathered anyway every year from our cultivated fields, and to incorporate the dust back into the soil.'*

• *Mrs Eirwen Harbottle, the London Centre for International Peacebuilding, Wickham House, 10 Cleveland Way, London E1 4TR (tel 071 790 2424) who is seeking schools prepared to help carry out long-term remineralisation experiments.*

• *'Remineralise The Earth' Newsletter, edited by Joanna Campe, 152 South Street, Northampton, MA 01060, USA (tel 413 586 4429), $18 subs. Research packet also available, $20.*

• *Don Weaver and John Hamaker's book 'The Survival of Civilisation', $12 from Hamaker-Weaver Publishers, PO Box 1961, Burlingame, CA 94010, USA (tel 415 347 9693).*

• *Robert Schindele, A-3122 Gansbach-Kicking, Austria (tel 02753 289), who sells the rock dust as a dietary supplement, despite widespread doubts as to its efficacy.*

• *Springhall Farm (which is carrying out remineralisation experiments), Hugh Coates and Dr Nadia Coates, Dinton, near Aylesbury (tel 0296 748432).*

• *Harry Alderslade, 9 Walter's Row, Morrell Avenue, Oxford, OX4 1NT (tel 0865 240545), with an international network of remineralisation contacts.*

• *David Langley, Redlands Aggregate, Crosby, Leicestershire, LE6 OSA (tel 0530 242151). Redlands run a number of gravel pits, and have in the past supplied gravel dust free for remineralisation experiments.*

• *Re. a new ice age from the greenhouse gases, contact Ann de Vernal of the University of Quebec and Gifford Miller of the University of Colorado.*

The planet fertile for 10,000 years every 100,000 years?

Cameron Thomson

An adapted extract from a letter by Cameron Thomson to various public figures

Twenty interglacials each lasting 10 or 11 thousand years during the last two million years is more than coincidence. Twenty glaciations each lasting around 90,000 years is more than coincidence. Have these not been Gaia's cycles during the Quaternary Period of her development – just as female Homo sapiens function in different ways during their development? Is glaciation not similar to menstruation in that it is a necessary part of a cycle which enables the organism to support life?

'Woman is fertile for 36 hours every 28 days. Is it inconceivable that Gaia is fertile for 10 or 11 thousand years every 100,000 years?'

Woman is fertile for 36 hours every 28 days; is it inconceivable that Gaia is fertile for 10 or 11 thousand years (or, more specifically, for only two or three thousand years – mesocratic or postglacial climatic optimum phase of interglacials) every 100,000 years?

The last three interglacials ended in 20 year transitions into glaciation with the violence and chaos caused by the differential greenhouse effect. Is it not true to say that the climate shift is no more than premenstrual (glaciation) tension? Is it inconceivable that Gaia has fertility cycles and symptoms that can be diagnosed and treated?

For Gaia, pollution is a natural phenomenon. The excess carbon and other gases at present in the atmosphere cannot remain there. Gaia will recycle them – with earthquakes and cooling higher latitude oceans acting as 'sinks' for atmospheric carbon. So does global biomass of course. Is it not glaringly obvious that we can remove excess carbon from the atmosphere and stabilise it at postglacial climatic optimum levels of 270-280 ppm by returning the carbon to earth as trees where it is stored during interglacials?

> 'The slight global warming there may have been for eight or nine years is occurring within the context of overheating tropical regions, advancing deserts and cooling higher latitude oceans and increasing incidence of earthquakes'

The general trend for a thousand years has been a cooling of the planet. During this time deserts have been advancing. carbon has been returning to the atmosphere, some of which has been removed by increasing earthquakes and cooling higher latitude oceans. The slight global warming there may have been for eight or nine years is occurring within the context of overheating tropical regions (greenhouse effect), advancing deserts and cooling higher latitude oceans (albedo effect) and increasing incidence of earthquakes. When the albedo effect – of sand and rocks in the tropics, snow and ice at the caps, and increasing cloud in the higher latitudes – is great enough, the earth will cool.

Ozone depletion is caused by gases interacting with moisture in the atmosphere. It is true that nitrous oxides, CFCs etc are increasing. But it is also true to say that there is more moisture (cloud cover) in the atmosphere, evaporating from the overheating tropical regions and travelling poleward.

Is it not time to begin remineralising the earth with crushed rock dust, simulating glaciation, to enable the earth's soils to grow and support the biomass necessary to stabilise atmospheric carbon at mesocratic phase levels?

In similar circumstances a gynaecologist would not let nature take its course. It is just as natural for a gaiaecologist to intervene.

Cameron Thomson, Hamaker Coordination, No. 3 Cottage, Scotson Farm, Auchterhouse, Dundee DD3 0QT, Scotland.

52 million trees = 1 factory

Monitored and developed by Kathleen Jannaway from an item in New Scientist.

In an innovative agreement which could be more widely copied, an American power company in Virginia has agreed to plant 52 million trees in Guatemala to absorb the amount of carbon dioxide that will enter the atmosphere from a new power station that it is building.

> 'An American power company has agreed to plant 52 million trees in Guatemala to absorb the carbon dioxide from a new power station that it is building'

The US Department of Energy have recently published a report on the work of Gregg Marland, a research worker at Oak Ridge National Laboratory which includes the statement that 'new forests covering 7 million square kilometres could absorb all the release of carbon dioxide from the burning of fossil fuels.' This area, as big as the US minus Alaska, may seem impossibly large to appropriate for new forests until it is realised that 30 million square kilometres world wide are at present used for deliberately bred livestock who also eat a large proportion of the crops from the 15 million square kilometres of crop land. Trees of the right species could yield maximum food per acre without the disturbance of soil required by arable farming. Energy forests could yield gas, electricity and liquid fuel, giving out no more carbon dioxide than they had already taken in.

Send stamps for trees leaflet, petition forms and ideas to Kathleen Jannaway, 47 Highlands, Leatherhead, Surrey KT22 8NQ.

Free trees from Tree Bank

The Dendrologist's Tree Bank Register records details of trees that are available free if they are for planting by amenity or conservation groups. The Register is run by the Dendrologist – a quarterly bulletin (costing £4 p.a.) of tree news and information for amateur enthusiasts and others who care about Britain's trees and woodlands. Details of trees offered, whether native, conifer or exotic, together with your name and address should be sent on a postcard to the Dendrologist. Requests for free trees should always be accompanied by an SAE as the scheme is run entirely by volunteers.

> 'The Tree Bank Register records details of trees that are available free if they are for planting by amenity or conservation groups'

The Dendrologist's Tree Register, The Dendrologist, PO Box 341, Chesham, Bucks HP5 2RD.

Mulching better than fertiliser for tree planting

From an item by Alistair Ayres in the Weekend Guardian, via its reprint in Permaculture News.

Over the last ten years the Forestry Commission, which plant around 12,000 hectares of trees a year, have been doing some interesting research. They found that preventing competition from other plants in the first couple of years is the most important factor in getting trees and shrubs off to a good start. Improving the soil and adding fertiliser was shown at best to be of secondary importance and in many cases provided no benefits at all.

> 'Fertilisers can scorch roots'

Gardening Which? tried this out and found that mulching along with either black polythene or bark chippings, produced much better results than traditional planting methods. Indeed, fertilisers can scorch roots and stunt growth if not properly mixed with the soil.

Gardening Which? is published by the Consumers' Association, 2 Marylebone Road, London NW1 4DX.

Trees and hippopotami

'It is fine to be a woman of my age – with grown-up children – with grandchildren for added joy – with responsibility only for myself – and to be healthy and full of crazy ideas' writes Anna Horn. Her market stall selling bread, jam and handicrafts in a small Swedish town has developed into a project called 'Future Forests' which has planted 700,000 trees in Kenya. In the early years Anna Horn gave the profits from her stall to a tree planting project in Mauritania. But then she and her friends decided it would be a greater challenge to have a project of their own, where they could help ensure the money went into the right pockets. At which point, a Swedish organisation called the Future In Our Hands decided to back their venture.

The results are that since 1984 some sixty villages in Western Kenya have been part of the Future Forest project, with the money given directly to women's organisations in the villages. Beside the village tree nurseries, the women's groups have used their increased self-confidence to start small-scale businesses, such as poultry farms, bakeries, child nurseries, dispensaries and vegetable gardens.

> 'Tree planting does start a development process going, which embraces women, families, villages and whole societies'

'Naturally everything has not been sunshine and light,' says Horn. 'The drought has killed many trees, and sometimes the goats, cows or hippopotami have damaged the plantations, but tree planting does start a development process going, which embraces women, families, villages and whole societies. And the project gives me joy, new experiences and wonderful friends.'

Anna Horn, Lilla Fredsberg, 171 71 Solna, Sweden (tel 08 85 88 70).

An Agroforestry vision

Robert Hart

Robert Hart is one of the initiators of the international Agroforestry movement with his books 'The Inviolable Hills' (1968), 'Ecosociety' (1984), 'Forest Farming' (1976, with James Sholto Douglas). Here is his vision of Agroforestry's full potential.

One of the first aims of anyone who cares about the future of humanity must be to ensure that every woman, man and child is adequately supplied with the basic necessities for self-fulfilment. This is possible.

Agroforestry, a system of intensive land-use in which economically valuable trees are grown in association with other crops, is being developed in many countries, especially in Asia, Africa and Australia.

It is applicable to almost every inhabitable part of the world. There are trees and hardy perennial shrubs that will grow in the most unpromising terrains, such as deserts, rocky hillsides and marshes. These provide 'nurse conditions' for more tender crops, such as fruit and vegetables.

By means of Agroforestry, a world population far higher than the present could be supplied with balanced diets, fuel, energy, fibres, building materials, medicines and the vital soul-food of beautiful environments.

Full employment for all could be ensured in the work of managing Agroforestry plantations and processing their products.

The resources involved would be renewable – therefore virtually infinite – and would not pollute the environment. Ugly cities and industrial wastelands could be made beautiful and healthy and the world's climate would be improved. Trees, by attracting rain and controlling the movement of groundwater through their roots, would prevent both droughts and floods. The stabilising effect of trees would prevent erosion and landslides.

Millions of families and small communities could become largely self-sufficient in the basic necessities of life.

Members of different ethnic groups could transcend their rivalries by working together to improve their environments and to supply their needs.

Great programmes of tree-planting and irrigation should replace military campaigns, their aims being, not to cause destruction, but to overcome poverty, hunger and disease throughout the world.

Robert Hart, Highwood Hill, Rushbury, near Church Stretton, Shropshire SY6 7DE (tel 06943 342).

The Forest Garden

After thirty years of study, research and practical experience in Agroforestry (see previous item), Robert Hart has established a small model forest garden on his farm on Wenlock Edge, a model that could be repeated many thousands of times even by those who possess only small town gardens.

> 'The Forest Garden can enable a family to enjoy a considerable degree of self-sufficiency, with minimal labour'

The Forest Garden can enable a family to enjoy a considerable degree of self-sufficiency, with minimal labour, for some seven months of the year, providing the very best foods for building up positive health. It is a miniature reproduction of the self-maintaining eco-system of the natural forest, consisting entirely of fruit and nut trees and bushes, perennial and self-seeding vegetables and culinary and medicinal herbs.

Robert Hart writes: 'It is no good waiting for the Powers-That-Be to take decisive action in the infinitely serious crisis caused by wholesale forest destruction, curbed and restricted as they are by blind prejudice and vested interests. Those who care, the ordinary people, should take action themselves to restore the earth's depleted forest cover, even though they may live in cities.'

Once established after about two years, the Forest Garden

is self-perpetuating, self-fertilising, self-watering, self-mulching, self-weed-suppressing, self-pollinating, self-healing and highly resistant to pests and diseases. The only work required is pruning, controlling plants that seek to encroach on each other, and mulching with compost once a year, after the herbaceous plants die down in the late autumn. It is:

• Self-perpetuating, because all plants are perennial or active seed-seekers, such as borage and cress; self-fertilising, because deep-rooting trees, bushes and herbs draw upon minerals in the subsoil and make them available to their neighbours, and because the complex should include edible legumes such as lucerne, which inject nitrogen into the soil.

'Self-watering, because deep-rooting plants tap the spring-veins in the subsoil'

• Self-watering, because deep-rooting plants tap the spring-veins in the subsoil, even at times of drought, and pump up water for the benefit of the whole eco-system.

• Self-mulching and self-weed-suppressing, because the scheme includes rapidly spreading herbs, such as the mints, and perennial vegetables, such as Good King Henry, which soon cover all the ground between the trees and bushes and thus create a permanent mulch. In fact, one main problem is to check their pervasiveness in the interests of less dominating plants.

• Self-pollinating, because all the fruit and nut trees are chosen to be mutually compatible for pollinating purposes – unless self-fertile – and also because the scheme includes many aromatic herbs and vegetables such as tree-onions and wild garlic, which undoubtedly exert curative influences on their neighbours.

• Resistant to pests and diseases, not only on account of the aromatic plants but also because any complex consisting of a wide spectrum of different plants does not allow the build up of epidemics such as is formed in monocultures.

The scheme is very highly intensive, making use of all seven 'storeys' found in the natural forest for the production of economic plants. These 'storeys' are:

• The 'canopy' formed by the tops of the higher trees;
• The planes of low-growing trees such as dwarf fruits;
• The 'shrub layer' comprising bush fruits;
• The herbaceous layer of herbs and vegetables;
• The ground layer of plants which spread horizontally rather than vertically, such as creeping thyme;
• The vertical layer occupied by climbing berries and vines;
• The 'rhizosphere', shade-tolerant root-plants.

In order to achieve maximum economy of space, these devices are employed:

(1) Some of the vegetables and herbs are grown on mounds, erected in accordance with the German Hugelkultur system.
(2) Full advantage is taken of fences for training climbing berries, such as the Japanese wineberry, and fan-trained plums.
(3) An apple hedge has been created according to the French Bouche-Thomas system, in which the trees (Allington Pippins) are planted diagonally so that they grow into each other.
(4) A hardy Canadian Brant vine is trained over the tool shed and another is to be trained up an old damson tree.

There is a 'family tree', comprising three compatible varieties of English eating apples, Sunset, Discovery and Laxton's Fortune, grafted on to a single root stock.

Conventional horticulturalists will object that food plants cannot achieve full productivity when planted in such close proximity to each other. But, as the natural forest and even the herbaceous flower border demonstrate, many plants thrive best when grown close to plants of other species. The reasons for this are contained in the science of plant symbiosis, about which very little research has been undertaken, since Ehrenfried Pfeiffer invented his system of 'sensitive crystallisation'. This is a study which must be extensively developed if Agroforestry is to attain its full potential.

'Conventional horticulturalists will object that food plants cannot achieve full productivity when planted in such close proximity to each other'

The Forest Garden's produce is health-promoting: just as in the 16th and 17th centuries, when England produced an amazing number of men of exceptional hardihood and genius, a standard article of diet was a salad, called 'sallet' or 'salgamundy', comprising a wide variety of cultivated and wild vegetables, fruits and herbs.

As for the Forest Garden helping restore the earth's forest cover, if ten trees were planted in a hundred thousand gardens, that would amount to a million trees. Quite a forest!

Robert Hart, Highwood Hill, Rushbury, near Church Stretton, Shropshire, SY6 7DE (tel 06943 342). A booklet entitled 'The Forest Garden' by Robert Hart is available from the Institute for Social Inventions (£2-95p incl. p&p), and a full-length book with colour photos, 'Forest Gardening' is published by Green Books (£7-95, ISBN 1 870098 44 7). There are now at least four Forest Gardens modelled on his.

Non-poisonous slug control

Robert Hart

It was after an entire generation of seedlings had been wiped out that I decided to make a comprehensive study of the likes, dislikes and habits of my slimy friends. I was determined to get even with them at all costs – except by the use of poisons. In this conservation project, poisons of any kind are taboo, even poisonous plants. Poisoned slugs can lead to poisoned birds, moles and hedgehogs.

'Poisons of any kind are taboo, even poisonous plants. Poisoned slugs can lead to poisoned birds'

Sir Albert Howard, one of the pioneers of the organic movement, regarded pests and disease germs as 'censors' of less-than-perfect health in plants, animals and soils. Any organism in a state of positive health has the ability to resist pests and diseases. At Howard's Indian agricultural research station, his cattle rubbed noses over the fence with cattle suffering from foot-and-mouth disease, and remained unharmed. It is said that a positively healthy appletree can even resist bullfinches. The reason for this is in the immune system, which nature provides to all living organisms, including mankind. Pests, disease germs and viruses are not the basic cause of disease; they are nature's method of destroying unhealthy tissues. They are attracted to acid substances; all organisms in a state of positive health, including soils, are predominantly alkaline.

'All organisms in a state of positive health, including soils, are predominantly alkaline'

There is little doubt that slugs are a symptom of acidity in the soil. Soil on which uncomposted farmyard manure has been spread is a breeding-ground for slugs. Therefore the first line of defence against them is a covering of lime. This not only sweetens the soil but also tickles their sensitive tummies, which they don't like. Wood-ash and soot perform similar functions. Watering the soil with liquid seaweed also has an alkalising effect. Calcified seaweed meal has the additional bonus of tiny shells, which also deter slugs.

Slugs also dislike strong smells. Many aromatic herbs, such as the various mints, tansy and balm, deter slugs and other pests and disease germs from attacking not only themselves but also their plant neighbours. The trouble with planting them between vegetables is that they are extremely invasive; they are as vigorous as the worst weeds.

'A herbal mulch, consisting of sprigs of aromatic plants and conifer twigs, deters slugs and other pests'

The best way to protect vegetable seedlings and transplants, I have discovered, is a herbal mulch, consisting of sprigs of aromatic plants and conifer twigs, which I spread between the rows. This not only deters slugs and other pests, but also screens the young plants from the wind, shades them from excessive sunlight and breaks the force of heavy rain. It also suppresses weeds and improves the soil, keeping it damp and preventing compaction. As it decays it feeds the young plants.

The herbal mulch also has a camouflaging effect. A bed of tender, young greenery can be irresistibly attractive to mischievous birds and mice, but, when surrounded by a many-coloured 'barbed-wire screen', the young plants are less conspicuous.

The final weapon in the campaign against slugs and other pests is constant hoeing. This not only breaks up lumps of earth, under which slugs love to hide, but also, by aerating the soil and removing obstacles to growth including weeds, hastens the young plants' growth. 'Keep them moving' is the watchword. The young plants soon acquire the vigour needed to enable them to resist pests and diseases themselves.

The final tip is, as far as possible, to choose plants with a natural immunity. Greedy slugs love brassicas which are greedy feeders, requiring lots of manure. But more and more members of the chicory-endive family are appearing in seedsmen's catalogues. These are attractive hardy plants with a wide variety of shapes and colours – some even develop red and variegated spears in the autumn – which originate from France and Italy. They are excellent substitutes for brassicas and lettuces throughout the year – and, from my experience, they are almost completely immune to slugs.

Robert Hart, Highwood Hill, Rushbury, near Church Stretton, Shropshire SY6 7DE (tel 06943 342).

Garlic-absorbing trees for protection from rabbits

From the Sun (USA) monitored for the Institute by Roger Knights.

Researchers at the University of Washington in Seattle have saved thousands of trees from destruction by deer and rabbits by planting pellets beside them that give off the smell of garlic. The pellets are gradually dissolved by rainwater, absorbed by the roots and then spread throughout the entire tree.

The tree then eliminates the compound as dimethyl selenide (the smell of garlic breath). The deer and the rabbits find the smell offensive.

Giving gardens to the needy

Dan Barker

Adapted extract from the Sun (USA), monitored for the Institute by Roger Knights.

'Barker builds gardens in the back yards of recipients – at no cost to them'

Dan Barker, a poet and novelist, has been giving away vegetable gardens in Portland, Oregon, for seven years. Funded by private foundations and trusts, Barker builds gardens in the back yards of recipients – at no cost to them. He constructs soil frames, brings in a trellis, seeds, fertiliser, tomato cages, pest controls, instructions, advice and cooking tips. Barker does his work in the needier neighbourhoods, where the proceeds – material, psychological and spiritual – can make the greatest difference. To date, Barker has built more than 525 gardens. Barker writes:

'when you plant, use three seeds – one for you, one for your neighbour, one for God'

The charitable trusts and foundations want to know if the gardens work. Do they dissolve the current anguish ripping the dignity from the impoverished? I can't say with certainty that one gang kid has been deflected from his run toward a violent end or prison, or that I've passed out sandwiches to people who have no reason to vote, or given shelter to homeless families. But I've saved thousands of people considerable money, time, and trouble, trips to the doctor, despair, sessions with their therapists, longing for death. I tell the gardeners that this is the store you don't have to go to. You get hungry, come on out and pick yourself a meal. When you plant, use three seeds – one for you, one for your neighbour, one for God. They always laugh when I mention God, or silently let the word slide on by. I go home knowing that I've planted the possibility of self-caring. But the donors want a figure; I tell them each garden is capable of producing at least $500 worth of food a summer, if you don't count gas, time, etc, and that 95 per cent of the gardens are productive the first year, 85 per cent the second –

I don't keep track after that, though often I run across a garden still producing after five or six years. Some people even load their gardens onto trucks when they move.

What is more difficult to convey is the health and joy alive in a seventy-year-old woman showing me her beans and tomatoes, or the pride of accomplishment beaming from the face of the twelve-year-old son of an ex-prostitute who put him in charge of the garden. Or the envy of neighbours – I put down a garden and the next year two or three neighbours will call for theirs. We're strictly word of mouth. I wouldn't know how well it was working otherwise. There's never been a shortage of recipients, only a shortage of money, time and energy.

The original idea was the diaspora of the perpetual garden, a way to reverse what is so celebrated now, the deprivation of the many for the gain of the few. Too ambitious a thought. The free market/welfare system victimises those unprepared for its complexities; it's too large, too pervasive to be countered by something so small as a garden, extended metaphor or no. Still, the notion contains the whole cycle of life, incorporating use of local materials (dairy and racetrack manures, construction subsoil, compost, surplus seed), reducing use of fossil fuels, reconnecting people with life – thus serving all.

Everything necessary is already in place: parks departments have tractors, trucks, working space, and greenhouses, much of the time underused; thousands of people desire to be of service to their neighbours, workers could be recruited from extension agents and agricultural programmes. All we have to do is put it together and get it paid for. One announcement on TV and there would be no end to the requests for gardens. People in need want all the help they can get. They will be the ones, and are the ones, who quiet the neighbourhood. They will endure and will invite peace from others.

It's taken me seven years to get the project into the black, and it couldn't have happened without the goodwill and generous hearts of my wife and friends. We lift ourselves. Accolades go to the foundations and trusts that have sponsored and believed in the work. They call it charity, but it is simply service, a providence that can even be employed by the recipients, as shown by several older women who wanted – and got – double or triple gardens so they could provide vegetables for the entire neighbourhood.

'Don't you think trying to lift the weight of suffering by one micron is real?'

They ask me why I do this, and I say it needs to be done. Don't you need a vegetable garden, one you can get to, one you can use without too much physical effort to maintain? There, now you've got one, good luck, happy to do it. Or, once, when I was tired and being interviewed, the young reporter asked 'Why?' and I said 'I'm out to change the world.' And when she asked, 'what do you do in real life?' my tact left me, and I replied, 'Don't you think giving away gardens is real life? Don't you think trying to lift the weight of suffering by one micron is real?' To affirm the good in you, in life; the Tao speaks of neighbours who do not tread on each other, but live their lives in quiet wonder, grow old and die. And the way to affirm the good life is to deliver it. If such an act challenges the men on the corner, good; shovels are easy to come by.

What is bothersome is not that giving away gardens is so wonderful, but that it is so rare.

Six pounds a week to save woodland

The Dandelion Trust has set up up an imaginative scheme to save an ancient woodland. The wood costs £58,000, of which Mercury Provident are lending the Trust £50,000, against the guarantee of people covenanting money over four years. Many people are covenanting or donating around £6 pw or more or less. This is a way for people without capital to donate money to save the deciduous woods in South Devon, and is an idea that could be carried out further into other areas of conservation.

More help is needed and all donations are very welcome.
The Dandelion Trust, 17 Rookfield Avenue, London N10 3TS (tel 071 833 2124).

Rights for Swedish animals

This scheme was highly commended in the Social Inventions Awards. The certificate went to Astrid Lindgren, author of the Pippi Longstocking children's books. The new Swedish Animal Protection Act, passed by the Swedish parliament, was an 80th birthday present for Astrid Lindgren from the Swedish Prime Minister, and is popularly known as 'Lex Lindgren'.

'Chickens are to be let out of cramped battery cages, cows are to be entitled to grazing space, and sows are no longer to be tethered'

It goes further than anything yet proposed by the UK government: with a ten year time limit for full implementation, chickens are to be let out of cramped battery cages, cows are to be entitled to grazing space, and sows are no longer to be tethered, but must have sufficient room to move, with separate places for eating, sleeping and excreting.

As the Swedish Ministry of Agriculture puts it: 'Hens for egg production are currently battery caged. Four hens are cramped together in a cage which allows each hen a floorspace of roughly the size of a school exercise book. The cages fail to meet even the most basic requirements of the hens – for moving, scratching, flapping, bathing and preening – and for laying. Such a system is unacceptable and must therefore be finally phased out. In future no form of animal husbandry which is so insensitive to the needs of the animals will be permitted'; but then the document concludes rather lamely: 'At present no viable alternative system has been developed, although research in this area is currently under way, notably in Switzerland.'

Astrid Lindgren complains that the new law is not as 'distinct and clear' as she would like, and intends to keep up the pressure with an annual symposium at the Swedish University of Agriculture in Uppsala, to review implementation of the Act. Lindgren was brought up on a farm and says that 'during my childhood cows, horses and pigs were our friends.' Now however she is 'filled with despair at their most appalling living conditions.' She rages against animals being treated not as living creatures but as 'production units' – 'living creatures cannot be weighed, priced and treated in the same manner as other industrialised products, without morally unacceptable results.'

> 'The campaign grew out of a newspaper article that Lindgren wrote about a cow that had to run more than six miles to find a bull'

The campaign grew out of a newspaper article that Lindgren wrote about a cow that had to run more than six miles to find a bull. Lindgren then joined forces with Christina Forslund, a vet, to prepare a detailed series of articles in the newspaper 'Expressen'. The tremendous public response forced the Ministry of Agriculture to capitulate, despite the assertions of farmers' organisations that food would become too expensive if animals had to be treated decently. But as Lindgren says: 'There is something in life that cannot be accounted for in monetary terms and that is respect for the living, and you can always feel in your heart what is right and what is wrong.'

• *Astrid Lindgren, Dalag 46, 113 24 Stockholm, Sweden (tel 46 8308085).*

• *Further details of the law are in English Press Release No 109, Swedish Ministry of Agriculture, S-103 33 Stockholm, Sweden (tel 8 763 1000).*

Getting free range chickens to go outside

Graham Knight

Extract from a letter to the Institute.

I understood that large free range systems unavoidably discourage hens from roaming.

But we have all been duped.

With my own eyes, I have seen thousands of hens roaming hundreds of yards from the house with no inducement besides grass and fresh air.

Not only that but they have no restriction on movement apart from the boundary fence. They are free to go outside at all times – night and day, summer and winter.

> 'Most large free range poultry houses have the feed trough as far as possible from the exits to discourage roaming'

The 'secret' of true free range is in the design of the poultry house which must deliberately discourage them from staying long inside. Most large poultry houses have litter underfoot and the feed trough as far as possible from the exits. Some managers have admitted to me that they don't want the hens to roam as it increases feed consumption. My new information suggests that the real difference in food consumption is in fact very small with the system I have seen. The extra energy for exercise seems to come from the increased grass consumption.

It seems to me that such is the wish to believe that genuine free range is vastly more expensive than battery, that many leading lights in the poultry industry have convinced themselves that this is so, and in the process have convinced many working for the industry with all sorts of dubious 'facts'.

Graham Knight, 15 Sandyhurst Lane, Ashford, Kent TN25 4NS (tel 02336 26677).

An ideal life for 5 hens mowing your lawn

Graham Knight has developed and sells a new type of garden hen unit for up to 5 hens. It looks like a lightweight circular playpen made of plastic tubing and netting, with a small hen house made of ply and timber. 'The hens are like mowers and can be moved in less than a minute to a fresh patch of lawn, without forming the usual smelly quagmire. In addition,' Knight adds, 'the hens eat grubs and dig over and manure the vegetable patch. Maybe this is one answer to factory farming of hens.'

A new order of knighthood, the Knights of Gaia

Sir John Seymour KOG

Knights of Gaia: Gaia was a Greek Goddess who was Goddess of the Earth. Her name has come to stand for the biosphere of planet Earth – the mantle of living creatures which surrounds this planet and makes it different from the others that we know. Gaia is now under savage attack – and from one of her own creatures. One species, which has immodestly and very incorrectly named itself *Homo sapiens*, has got completely out of control. It has got out of balance and – by discovering how to release the stored energy in hydrocarbon fuel – is raiding and destroying the rest of Life on this planet and, if unchecked, will destroy, or at the best severely degrade, the living mantle of the Earth and almost certainly destroy itself. Gaia will then, after a few million years, heal herself, and the miracle of Life will survive after all.

For those of us who do not wish this to happen (because we feel we have a vested interest in the survival of our species) and who take the matter seriously enough to be willing to devote our lives to it, there should be a new order of Knighthood, and I suggest that we call this the Order of the Knights of Gaia.

The word 'knight' still has a gallant, romantic and chivalrous ring to it, even though for the last couple of hundred years the knights we know of have been pot-bellied, sedentary, treble-chinned businessmen who have contributed liberally to the party funds. The Knights of Gaia will change this image. We will not contribute a penny to the party funds. We will not be pot-bellied or treble chinned. We will keep ourselves fit and tough for the job that we have to do.

> 'Our job will be to *fight dragons*, the dragons of Greed – Exploitation – Pollution – War-for-the-wrong-reasons – Obscene Size'

Our job will be to *fight dragons*. Now actual dragons may be amiable and even cuddly animals, who save their breath to warm the porridge of poor children. But the dragons we will fight are the other sort. The dragons of Greed – Exploitation – Pollution – War-for-the-wrong-reasons – any assault, in fact, on the living mantle around the Earth which, although we do not worship it, we consider sacred. Every Knight will no doubt make his own list of dragons. The creature at the head of my own list might well be – the Dragon of Obscene Size. Companies that are too big – countries that are too big – men or women who wield too much power – these are the dragons that I wish to sink my spiritual spear into.

A Knight of Gaia can be either man or woman, or anything in between. The only qualification to become a Knight will be:

The willingness to take a vow, out loud and with sufficient conviction to convince the listeners, to a quorum of six Knights of Gaia. The vow will be something like the following, although when there are more Knights than there are now the form of it might be modified:

'I vow that I will devote my energies, during the whole of my life on Earth, to protecting the integrity, variety, and beauty of Earthly Life, and to vanquishing the forces of evil that threaten to destroy it.'

If the listening Six are convinced of the sincerity of the postulant, she/he will be admitted into the Order. It will then be the new Knight's duty to: study, in depth, the issues involved, to take any action possible to conserve and aid the Life on our planet, to avoid any action that damages it, to try to convince other people of the seriousness of the situation and of the need to take action about it.

The Order is already founded. There are at present five Knights (male and female) and as they are too few and dispersed to make a quorum, they are to have the power of creating other Knights until the Order is larger. It is then hoped that there will be local Chapels, where Knights can meet and encourage each other.

But do not become a postulant unless you are deadly serious. The dragons that we must fight are serious – very.

Sir John Seymour KOG, Killowen, New Ross, Co. Wexford, Eire (tel 353 51 88156).

Parishes competing to be ecological guinea pigs

Extracted from BladSUSet No. 10, newsletter of the Swedish Institute for Social Inventions.

In 1986 Uppsala borough council passed a decision to declare a parish within the borough a 'special ecological area'. It would act as a pilot and research area for more environmentally conscious activities.

Several parishes competed for the honour, and in the end two were selected. Their biggest single investment so far has been 5.5 million Swedish kronor (over £550,000) for a large composting plant.

SISU, Svenska Institutet för Sociala Uppfinningar, the Now House, Peter Myndes Backe 12, 5 tr, S-118 46, Stockholm, Sweden (tel 46 8 772 4587; fax 46 8 422 641).

Ecological Village Association

Marilyn Mehlmann

Our association was formed at the end of 1986 with two aims: to act as a forum for people throughout Sweden who are interested in ecological building and living; and to see that at least one ecological village is built within easy commuting distance of Stockholm.

We have published an 80-page report on ecological building, we organise quarterly meetings and conferences, collaborate with various institutions, and are in touch with around 70 eco-village groups around the country.

We have not yet seen the birth of an ecological village in Stockholm. But we have around 15 active groups conducting discussions with various local authorities and regular regional meetings in both Stockholm and Gothenburg.

Ekoboföreningen Njord, c/o Marilyn Mehlmann, SISU – see address above.

Tuggelite, a Swedish eco-village

Extracted from BladSUSet No. 6, newsletter of the Swedish Institute for Social Inventions (SISU).

> 'Composting toilets are installed. Bath water etc is used for watering plants. Greenhouses lean-to on every house'

Tuggelite was completed in 1984. The 16 dwellings are built as terrace houses with a community house which has a child care centre. There are underground larders for storing eg root vegetables. Composting toilets are installed. Bath water etc is used for watering plants. Greenhouses lean-to on every house, so that incoming air is preheated in the greenhouses. The house external walls are built as two shells with 38 cm of unbroken insulation in between. There is 65 cm of roof insulation. Resource use has been cut by about two thirds. The capital costs are slightly higher, but the running costs are thus substantially lower.

The residents share many activities: weaving, photo lab, gymnastics, sauna, carpentry, song group, purchase of fruit and vegetables. Some group tasks such as caretaker are rotated, with adults on the rota every fifth week.

SISU – see address above.

Welsh solar village

David Stephens, a consultant building scientist, has acquired 9 acres of land with permission to build 90 dwellings (for some 300 people) for the establishment of a solar village (to be called 'Tir Gaia' – 'land of Gaia') near Rhayader, 'a very nice stone-built town with a medium size shopping centre and a high proportion of English residents' in Mid-Wales.

> '9 acres of land with permission to build 90 dwellings (for some 300 people) for the establishment of a solar village'

The site itself is on the sloping side of a hill, an unspoilt south-facing spot with a good view. The first four-bedroomed house is now built, and is, Stephens claims, the most advanced low-energy house in the world, 'calculated to save about 90%

of heating fuel.' Crops are to be grown under a greenhouse on the roof and 2,000 water bottles sandwiched between the floors will store solar energy.

'Crops are to be grown on the roof'

Each single person unit in the village is likely to cost about £30,000 and will probably attract 'semi-retired' people. Stephens hopes there will also be a housing association for people who cannot afford to buy.

'I am trying to set it up as a model for the future,' says Stephens. High quality, durable, solar-heated housing will be built. 'The first phase will be four bedroomed houses which can divide into flats or bedsits. One unit could be enough for one or two persons; families could buy two or three adjacent units, and sell one or two when space requirements reduce as children leave home etc.

'Although the garden areas will not be large enough for self-sufficiency in food, the greenhouse roofs will help greatly, especially in producing high-value early crops.'

Stephens is very much a social inventor and proposes a number of possible opportunities for people to earn a living at Rhayader, including: setting up an Institute to foster the research and practice of Green ideas; coordinating further trials of the Eco Lavatory (featured below) in Third World countries and running a Green Pounds and Green Fund scheme.

Stephens describes these initiatives and the village in his magazine, Practical Alternatives, available for £1 from the address below. (Serious enquiries from potential residents only for further details of the village. 'The aim is to attract environmentally aware people with organisational skills.')

Inflation + 6% from investing in solar housing

The Solar Housing Society has been formed to issue loan stock to help fund this Tir Gaia village, and later to fund solar villages throughout Britain. As Stephens puts it:

> 'Stocks can be linked to the General Index of Retail Prices, ensuring that the capital retains its real value despite inflation, plus up to 6% interest'

'The Society pays good interest and repays stock as agreed. It does not grant loans. Stocks can be linked if you wish to the General Index of Retail Prices, ensuring that the capital retains its real value despite inflation, plus up to 6% interest. The Inland Revenue has advised the Society that the inflation component is free of tax. Only the interest of up to 6% is taxable.

'The Society provides high security. Your savings will be invested in durable solar houses which should be more valuable than ordinary houses as fuel prices rise.

'Building solar homes will create real and meaningful jobs in practical conservation.'

David Stephens, Tir Gaia Solar Village, Rhayader, Powys LD6 5AG (tel 0597 810 929). His booklet 'The Survivor House' is available from this address for £4-95 incl. p&p. The plans for the village won a Social Inventions Award

The Green town of Davis

An article by Richard St George in Resurgence (No 134, £2-40 from Ford House, Hartland, Bideford, Devon EX39 6EE) describes how the town of Davis, near Sacramento in California, has been 'greened'. In the sixties, students working with local people produced an alternative local plan. Riding on this 'Green Ticket' three students were elected to seats on the local council. One of those original students, Bill Carter, is now the mayor. Changes made include:

• The planting of 17,000 trees, one in front of every house and parking lot, to give shade and natural cool.

• Houses are restricted to two storeys and business premises to four. New building regulations demand better standards of insulation, double glazing and require solar water heating. New housing developments concentrate on passive solar design.

• Allotments are available for flat owners with no gardens of their own.

> 'In the sixties, students working with local people produced an alternative local plan. Riding on this 'Green Ticket' three students were elected to seats on the local council. One of those original students, Bill Carter, is now the mayor'

• Material for recycling, pre-sorted, is collected from the streets by specially designed dustcarts.

• Cyclists have the right of way everywhere, with 42 km of bike lanes in the town and 28 km in the suburbs. There is even a unit of cycle police to regulate the bicycle traffic.

• No council decisions are made without a public hearing. The council members sit in a semi-circle facing the public galleries from which comments and suggestions can be considered.

Richard St George, 22a West Mall, Clifton, Bristol BS8 4BQ (tel 0272 743111). 'I have since been warned,' Richard St George writes, 'that my article presents a somewhat too-rosy picture of what is happening in Davis.'

A Green town for 12,000

Guy Dauncey

From a letter to the Institute from one of its directors, Guy Dauncey, who lives in British Columbia, Canada.

The main thing I'm up to is SO BIG that I hardly know where to begin!

> 'I'm involved in a project out here to build a whole new town, from scratch, for 12,000 people, as a model of community participation and ecological sustainability'

I'm involved in a project out here to build a whole new town, from scratch, for 12,000 people, as a model of community participation, community architecture and neighbourhood design, ecological sustainability and economic self-reliance.

The $15m investment cash comes from four trade union pension funds; and we are hopefully just months away from obtaining zoning (planning permission).

It won't be a car-free town; the investors are not convinced that 12,000 people will willingly sacrifice their cars, especially in a part of the world where public transport is still fairly rudimentary. We will be incorporating a car-free area within an early neighbourhood, as a way of testing the market's response. The investors feel that they are putting up $15m of their union members' money, and they want to be sure that the investment is safe.

The site of the town is quite remarkable: it's not only the site of a huge abandoned old cement works, but it's also an astonishing, steep, east-facing hillside, with three miles of waterfront, and stunning views.

Additional information from material sent by Dauncey:

• The co-operative for this new town of Bamberton plans to build between 200 and 500 housing units a year for 20 years on the 1,560 acre site 32 kilometres north of Victoria.

• With the new town springing up on the wooded hillsides, 'it should be a way to absorb the pressures of growth in the nearby communities, so they won't feel their rural lifestyle is being threatened.'

• The lower quarry will probably be flooded to become a lake. The higher quarry may become a natural park or something similar. The town centre on the waterfront will provide shops, restaurants, homes, a resort hotel and a marina, designed to be a vibrant, colourful centre for the town as a whole.

'The town is planned as a series of small, friendly neighbourhoods, focused around village greens'

• The town is planned as a series of small, friendly neighbourhoods, focused around village greens. In fact the whole of Bamberton is based on Christopher Alexander's book 'The Pattern Language' (OUP, New York) – this is the main architectural framework being used, plus a town planning context called 'Traditional Neighbourhood Development', which is basically the 'Pattern Language' applied to town development as a whole.

• There will be space for CoHousing, which involves a cluster of homes with shared ownership of a common house.

• Purchasers will have to live with land-use covenants imposing tight restrictions on topsoil removal, tree-cutting and use of chemicals and herbicides.

• The town will be wired with fibre-optics for advanced telecommunications.

• The emphasis will be on the use of community minibuses for local transport and car-pooling and community transit for longer journeys.

• A tertiary sewage treatment plant similar to that in Penticton, British Columbia, will be installed, producing compost, water for irrigation in summer and fish-quality water outflow in the winter months.

What I'd really like to do is to find a way to tap the creativity of the wider public, given that the chance to design a new town from scratch doesn't come up that often.

Guy Dauncey, 2069 Kings Road, Victoria, British Columbia, Canada V8R 2P6 (tel 604 592 4472 h; 592 4473 w, tel and fax).

Against a free market in agriculture

Sir James Goldsmith

The following is a brief adapted extract from the Caroline Walker Lecture given by Sir James Goldsmith at the Royal Society.

'All my life I have campaigned as vigorously as I know for the consumer's right to choose. Now I find that in the debate about intensive agriculture, freedom of choice is used in a way which I believe to be misleading'

All my life I have campaigned as vigorously as I know for the consumer's right to choose. Now I find that in the debate about intensive agriculture, freedom of choice is used in a way which I believe to be misleading.

Not long ago, I was discussing BST (the bovine growth hormone) with a Minister of Agriculture of a European government. His response was – print it on the label and let the public choose freely. That sounded like a good free market sentiment but, in fact, it is deeply flawed. How can a consumer know the truth about BST or about other genetically engineered new products or indeed about most of the marvels of modern science? Sometimes the true facts are not disclosed. Much more often the true facts are not known.

I started my business career by founding a pharmaceutical company which today is a good sized European company. I went on to form a food manufacturing and retailing company which ranked among Europe's largest. Of course I am not a scientist, but I have employed many. I have listened to them and participated with them in the excitement of developing new products. We can all get caught up in the thrill. I can assure you of one thing. None of us can know for sure the full extent of the long term effects of a completely new drug. The scientists who developed Thalidomide were not men of evil intent. They just did not know the truth.

I can state categorically that the idea that the consumer on his own, by referring to a label, can assess all the possible after-effects of a new chemical, pharmaceutical or biotechnological product, is nonsense and must be rejected.

Intensive agriculture destroys genetic diversity not only in seeds, but also, of course, in all forms of animal and vegetable life affected by cloning, embryo transfer, gene selection, creation of monocultures, tissue culture, genetic engineering and the other processes of intensive agriculture. The granting of patents for new life forms will accelerate this trend because the law requires that the new patented varieties be internally consistent, that is to say uniform.

Unfortunately, farmers will be forced to adopt all these new processes because, at least temporarily, yields will be greater. As farmers must survive in a competitive world, they will farm intensively or be driven out of business.

With thousands of researchers experimenting throughout the world and using their imagination to create instantaneous new life forms unknown to nature and therefore untested by the trials and errors of millions of years of natural evolution, is it possible to avoid mistakes and accidents which could have unimaginable consequences?

But there are deeper questions. Man is very clever but is his wisdom commensurate with his cleverness? Has man the moral right to create new microbes, new animals, new life forms? Are we wise to transform artificially the course of evolution and to do so at unimaginable speed? Do we realise that much of the change is irreversible? Can we convert animals and fields and forests and all things living into unnatural high performing machines whose only purpose is to serve human beings? Is changing fundamental genetic information in living things, which will remain part of their inherited characteristics, the ultimate form of pollution?

> ## 'Are we wise to transform artificially the course of evolution and to do so at unimaginable speed?'

I will return to easier questions – what should be done with the Common Agricultural Policy or CAP and with the current GATT negotiations as they affect agriculture?

The CAP must be reformed. A fundamental shift of objectives is required. The CAP should aim at bringing production into balance with demand by moving away from intensive methods and encouraging extensive farming. This would reduce surpluses, maintain a stable rural population, encourage family farmers and reverse some of the damage done by intensive methods. Also it would ensure that healthy food is available to consumers.

Over half the CAP agricultural budget would be economised by eliminating surpluses and this could be redirected to facilitating the move from intensive to extensive methods. We should not seek to reduce the overall budget.

> ## 'The GATT proposals for agriculture would do enormous harm. Take Vietnam as an example. The result there would be an exodus from the land to the towns of about 1.9 billion people'

The current GATT negotiations are very dangerous as they propose prohibiting nations from limiting the volume of imported agricultural products. In other words, they seek to create what they call a free and competitive world market in agriculture.

Competition is a form of controlled warfare. In such a contest, communities, in which small or medium-sized farms still predominate, would be washed away as if by a catastrophic flood; whole populations would be uprooted and swept into urban slums. Those who remained to try to compete against industrialised and subsidised agricultural imports, by necessity would be pressed into adopting the short-term solutions of intensive methods.

> ## 'A well-documented disease – agency capture – whereby the regulators are under the influence of the regulated'

According to current proposals, standards of safety and quality would be achieved by vesting the exclusive right to define world standards in the Codex Alimentarius, a Committee of the Food and Agricultural Organisation. Professor Philip James, Director of the Rowett Research Institute and a member of the World Health Organisation's Director General's advisory committee, is quoted as saying: 'Codex is dominated by the food industry.' And drawing on all my past experience, I can assure you that Professor James is right. The Codex Alimentarius suffers from a well-documented disease – agency capture – whereby the regulators are under the influence of the regulated.

The GATT proposals for agriculture, if adopted, would do enormous harm. Take Vietnam as an example of many countries making the first faltering steps towards rejoining the free world. It has a population of 67 million of whom 78% live on farms. Driving them from fields into urban slums would create deeper and longer-lasting devastation than the horrors of communism or the war. In the world as a whole, the rural population is 2.9 billion. Let us suppose that as a percentage of total population, it were to be reduced to the levels that exist in the 'new' countries like Canada or Australia. The result would be an exodus from the land to the towns of about 1.9 billion people. All in the name of efficiency and free markets.

Sixty years ago, the world's population was approximately 2 billion. Today it is 5.3 billion. The absolute numbers of those living in squalor has exploded. And during that same period, we have threatened the stability of the very fundamentals of life – water, soil, air, forests, the climate.

It is time to reassess the path that we have chosen. We must consider more profoundly the criteria which we employ to assess prosperity and contentment. We must select and use the extraordinary new tools of the technological revolution, in ways which are compatible with those criteria. And we must recognise that, at this moment, we might be riding an accelerating merry-go-round to hell.

A longer (but still incomplete) version of this talk features in the 'Fourth World Review' No. 49, £1-50 from FWR, 24 Abercorn Place, London NW8 9XP.

State support for Organic Agriculture (outside UK)

How it works in Denmark

The situation in Denmark, where the government is now spending 40 million kroners a year to support organic farming, is instructive. The late Christian Christensen, when he was Danish Minister of the Environment, gave a speech to an international bankers' conference, which was summarised in Mercury Newsletter 16:

The government is now spending 40 million kroners a year to support organic farming.

The Minister opened his talk by highlighting the two main problems facing agriculture today in Denmark:

(1) The pollution of the rivers and groundwater, and thus drinking water, resulting from the use of artificial fertilisers which leach through the sandy soil; and

(2) The cutbacks by the EC of farm production.

The Danish Ministries of the Environment and Agriculture have commissioned a joint enquiry into the place of organic and biodynamic agriculture in dealing with these twin problems.

The main problem in converting to alternative systems of agriculture is the resulting drop in farmers' income. Although five years ago this was estimated at 30%, today, with the increased demand for organic produce, this might be as little as 10%.

Results of the research show that three-quarters of Danish agriculture could be conducted organically. It would cost the economy a total of 3 billion kroner per year and would result in a rise of 15% in the price of homegrown food. The Danes spend 16% of their income on food. If the consumers were to pay the full price rise it would result in this proportion rising to 18%. What would they get as a result?

(1) 50,000 more people would be employed in agriculture.

(2) The balance of trade would improve even if prices of imports remained static.

(3) Energy costs would be halved.

(4) The use of nitrates would be reduced by between 10% and 40%.

(5) Food consumed would be purer.

(6) The health of both people and animals would be improved.

The conversion from chemical to organic and biodynamic farming methods would be best effected in dairy and wheat production. It would be difficult to apply to the Danish pig population which numbers 10 million, and will rise by the end of the century to 20 million.

Cooperation between farmers will be essential, particularly in the transport of slurry from the dairy to the wheat farmers (this does not apply to biodynamic cultivation). This cooperation may be difficult to achieve, particularly where there are farmers employing bad methods.

The transition to organic farming will be funded by the State. A new law in Denmark authorised grants for conversion, research and the provision of advice. A group of farmers in South Jutland has been the first to benefit from the new law. They started production of organic milk, which quickly sold out in the local shops. People want organic produce, they are frightened of the poisons modern chemical farming introduces into their food, and are looking for 'clean food'.

'The transition to organic farming will be funded by the State. '

Milk is the first step, but the Minister is confident that meat will follow quickly, together with vegetables. He recently enquired of a market stallholder whether he could sell his organic produce. The answer came back, 'No problem to sell, but we can't obtain enough.' With the government's annual budget of 40 million kroner for organic conversions, the main barrier will be fear of the unknown.

Published by Mercury Provident, Orlingbury House, Lewes Road, Forest Row, Sussex RH18 5AA (tel 0342 82 3739).

The Danish Act on Organic Farm Production (No. 363) established a Council for Organic Agriculture, with each of the following contributing one representative: the Ministry of Agriculture, the Ministry of the Environment, the Association of Biodynamic Farmers, the National Association of Organic Farmers, the Joint Committee for Organic/Biodynamic

Farming, the Association of Danish Farmers, the National Federation of Smallholders and the Consumers' Council.

The Danish conversion grants administered by this Council for Organic Agriculture amount to 1500 kroners per converted hectare in the first year, 800 in the second and 300 in the third. The conversion must cover the entire farm and be implemented within four years, with a commitment to continue as an organic farm for at least two years subsequently.

The Danish Ministry of Agriculture, Copenhagen (tel 010 451 923301).

The USA, Germany and Austria

• The State of Texas has changed to promoting low-chemical pest management.

Information from Pacific News Service/Utne Reader, USA.

'In Iowa, in a major policy turn-round, a $64.5m groundwater protection programme is funded partly by fees on chemical manufacturers and taxes on nitrogen fertilisers'

• In Iowa, in a major policy turn-round, a $64.5m ground-water protection programme funded partly by fees on chemical manufacturers and taxes on nitrogen fertilisers, is supporting research into alternatives to chemical dependency, and the development of practices that require lower inputs and protect the soil. A similar clause to put a tax on pesticides was defeated. *Information from the Centre for Rural Affairs Newsletter/ Utne Reader, USA.*

• In Germany, the government of Nordheim-Westfallen, a populous region with 100,000 farmers, has committed itself to enact a policy of soil protection and ecologically acceptable agriculture, emphasising the need to protect the soil from toxic emissions, and for research into ways of applying sewage and animal wastes to farmland, for the prevention of soil erosion and the use of integrated biological pest control methods in place of pesticides.

Information from 'Far From Paradise' by John Seymour and Herbert Girardet, published by Green Print, an imprint of the Merlin Press.

'In Austria, the government has brought in a package of measures for the whole country, assisting organic farmers to increase the quality of food'

• In Austria, the government has brought in a package of measures for the whole country, assisting organic farmers to increase the quality of food, create new jobs on the land, help towards conservation and reduce the country's import bill for fertilisers. In the Alpine National Park, farmers and villagers in the region of Neukirchen am Grossvenediger have formulated an ecologically benign development plan, including low input farming, traditional crafts and waste recycling.

Information extracted from the book 'After the Crash' by Guy Dauncey (Green Print, an imprint of the Merlin Press, £6-99).

A charter for agriculture

The Soil Association

The current crisis of over-production is a threat, not just to the EC but to the stability of British Agriculture, both now and in the future. The livelihood and, indeed, survival of British farmers and through them the whole fabric of agriculture and of rural society are now seriously threatened.

Unless there is a series of fundamental reforms, the crisis will only get worse. We, therefore, call upon all who are involved in determining the future of agriculture, food quality and the environment to incorporate the principles of this Charter.

PLEDGE TO:

(1) Ensure that all production and the management of farm resources are in harmony rather than in conflict with the natural system.

(2) Use and develop technology appropriate to an understanding of biological systems.

(3) Rely primarily on renewable energy and rotations to achieve and maintain soil fertility for optimum production.

(4) Aim for optimum nutritional value of all staple foods.

(5) Encourage decentralised systems for processing, distribution and marketing of farm products.

(6) Strive for an equitable relationship between those who work and live on the land, and, by maintaining wildlife and its habitats, create a countryside which is aesthetically pleasing for all.

The Soil Association, 86 Colston Street, Bristol, BS1 5BB (tel 0272 290661).

The Land Heritage Trust

The Land Heritage Trust in Somerset own four farms. The Trust's aim is that they should be managed ecologically in perpetuity. All four farms are out as agricultural tenancies on normal conditions plus some added organic ones. The Trust visit and walk around each farm at least once a year. The Trust says that there is very little income left after their spending on the upkeep of buildings and other expenses. They also charge rents 20% below the market level in the first few years to help the farmer become ecological (or for longer periods if there is no premium for sales of organic produce in their area). The Trust writes:

Land Heritage is a registered charity launched in 1984. It shares with other environmental organisations a concern for the conservation of the countryside and the furtherance of research into, and public education about, organic husbandry. What is unique about Land Heritage is that it is pursuing these objectives through the direct ownership of agricultural land, farmed by tenant farmers.

> 'It is pursuing these organic husbandry objectives through the direct ownership of agricultural land, farmed by tenant farmers'

The advantage of permanent land ownership by a charitable trust is obvious. The work put in to achieve high organic fertility may rapidly be dissipated if the land is sold and returned to chemical farming and the restoration to organic status may take years of not very profitable struggle. Land Heritage proposes both to preserve organic land, and to help in the restoration process by charging appropriately reduced rents for the necessary period.

Land Heritage seeks to obtain farmland by gift or legacy or purchase and to build up a network of supporters whose contributions will initially fund the publicity and appeals on which expansion must depend.

Land Heritage Trust is at Wellington, Somerset – this is a complete and sufficient address – (tel 082347 7764), contact David Ursall or Hugh Flatt. An annual supporter's subscription costs £10 and includes newsletters twice a year.

Vetiver grass – a new Green Revolution?

'As important to world agriculture as the Green Revolution – in fact the Green Revolution should not have happened without it,' announced a Voice of America broadcast, referring to comments by World Bank experts on a remarkably hardy plant called Khus or Vetiver grass, and its role in conserving moisture and preventing soil erosion. In the Southern Indian state of Andhra Pradesh, Vetiver grass led to increases in crop yields of up to 700%.

> 'Vetiver grass led to increases in crop yields of up to 700%'

The grass is planted about 20 centimetres apart in a single furrow along the contour lines of a slope, or along the edge of a terrace, or the top of a paddy field, or the side of a river or dam. It grows bush high, with roots up to three metres deep.

A Vetiver hedge slows down and spreads out rainfall, allowing it to filter through gently, without taking soil and silt with it. The deep, dense, spongy root system acts like reinforcing steel in concrete, protecting the soil under the plant and preventing terraces from collapsing. The roots also have a strong aromatic oil and are repellent to rats and other pests. The leaves are unpalatable to livestock and the hedge grows impenetrable for trespassers and even snakes. Or it can be cut back each year to prevent shading, with the leaves used as a mulch for trees to help retain moisture and deter insects. It is also practically sterile so it does not spread like a weed in farmers' fields.

Vetiver grass can grow almost anywhere. Although it is a subtropical plant, indigenous to parts of Asia, it has been grown successfully under snow in the Himalayas and in the African Sahel. The Masdar Group agricultural consultancy in Wokingham have Vetiver nurseries under way in Zimbabwe, Zambia and the Sudan. The grass can withstand fires, floods and droughts. Richard Grimshaw, World Bank Chief of the New Delhi Agriculture Division, says that it has 'survived under very, very dry, nearly drought conditions. It is the only grass which has survived, where everything else has died or been eaten flat.'

A Vetiver hedge is permanent, and after the third year requires no maintenance. Farmers can do all the work involved themselves, so it is between ten and a hundred times cheaper than the traditional soil erosion measure of building earthbanks – the latter can involve mechanical diggers, can burst in heavy rainstorms, erode and melt away in time and take a wide strip of land out of production.

> 'Vetiver grass is between ten and a hundred times cheaper than the traditional soil erosion measure of building earthbanks'

Vetiver grass is not a new solution or 'miracle plant'. Its effects have been proven over time. Over thirty years ago a road engineer in Tanzania used it to protect the wing-wall of a bridge on one side of the river. It is still there, holding the bank in perfect shape, although the concrete wall he built on the other side has long since fallen into the river and the bank it was protecting has partially eroded. And Richard Grimshaw describes a steep-sloped sugar plantation in Fiji where Vetiver was planted, again some thirty years ago: 'The results have been quite staggering. Over an area of three hundred thousand acres, soil erosion has been stopped and crop yields improved quite significantly.'

The World Bank is hardly renowned for its ecological awareness, but the promotion of Vetiver grass seems to be a step in a more positive direction.

Their field workers' booklet about it is available for 50p in stamps from the World Bank, New Zealand House, Haymarket, London SW1.

Phosphates will mean the end of cities

Folke Guenther

Adapted extract from BladSUSet 12-13, the newsletter of the Swedish Institute for Social Inventions.

Our coastal waters are heavily over-fertilised. The nutrients are not poisonous but they disturb the balance between different organisms. The most important nutrients in this connection are nitrogen and phosphorus.

> 'Any city imports phosphates with its food, and will sooner or later reach a state where leakage from dumps etc is as big as the total import'

Phosphorus is a vital nutrient for plants. A lot of it (but not all) can be removed from waste water. Any city imports phosphates (and other non-gaseous) elements with the food. Such elements will either follow waste water effluent from the town, or accumulate. The latter will lead to increased 'export' by leakage from dumps, landfills and other storage places. This will continue until the sum of leakages equals the total import.

At this point sewage treatment etc become meaningless and stands revealed as a gigantically expensive device for postponing leakage by a few years or decades. This could be called the bathtub syndrome: a bath with a plug in (the ideally efficient water treatment plant), but with the tap (phosphate import) turned on full.

The only sustainable solution requires a different structure to society, so that phosphates and other nutrients imported into conurbations are returned to the food-growing process. But this will be extremely difficult and expensive to achieve with the current size of cities. In the long run it seems we will have to restructure society into small towns and villages, with most of our food being produced locally – a development which will have other advantages too. Research into the necessary social structures is being carried out in Sweden.

Folke Guenther, Department of Systems Ecology, University of Stockholm. Home: Gödelövsvägen 5, S-240 13 Genarp, Sweden (tel 46 40480059).

Otters to test river purity

Fred Allen

An Otter Society could be formed to build a series of artificial holts for otters wherever a river seems unpolluted (natural holt sites often cause flooding and have been removed). Otters would then become the guardians of the water's purity. Otters, for instance, are excessively sensitive to PCBs in the water. If one in five of the holts were supplied with pet otters and these failed to breed and spread, then this would suggest that the water is PCB polluted. Apart from preventing otters breeding successfully, PCB does not seem to hurt them (although a female otter giving birth may die from the PCB suddenly liberated by fat mobilisation). With water due to be sold off, 'otter bioassay' as outlined here may be a helpful way of monitoring the private companies' claims. In the North Sea, 'seal bioassay' appears to be occurring willy nilly. Distemper never killed seals before, and it may well prove to be a PCB-driven immune deficiency.

> 'Build a series of artificial holts for otters wherever a river seems unpolluted. Otters would then become the guardians of the water's purity'

Fred Allen, 13 Shelly Row, Cambridge, CB3 0BP. A team at Essex University has now pioneered a method of analysing otter droppings for PCBs, aldrin, lindane and other pollutants.

Solving the slurry problem

John Seymour

John Seymour, the author of a number of books on self-sufficient farming, here confronts the irony that one of the banes of the environmentalist nowadays is manure slurry – yet dung is the prototypical fertiliser.

Slurry is a raw, stinking liquid which poisons waterways and does a lot of other nasty things besides (one of which is to spread and encourage parasites and other diseases). Grazing animals will not touch grass that has been contaminated with it for up to a year or more, and who can blame them? It almost always gets heavily diluted with rainwater, and the farmer has got to get rid of it – particularly in deep mid-winter when his land is too waterlogged to absorb it and it all runs down into the nearest stream.

Farmyard manure is straw, stover, bean haulms, bracken or any other dried vegetation that has been used for bedding for grazing animals, pigs, or poultry, dunged on by them, then stacked in a muck heap for several months, then spread out on the land. Far more of the valuable elements (N, P, K and certain trace elements) that were in the dung originally are fixed and retained and can be used by the crops on which it is spread. It does not contaminate water courses, nor does any of it sink down to contaminate the water supply. Above all it adds *humus* to the soil and it is the presence of this latter substance that makes organic agriculture (ie agriculture that was *traditional* until sixty years ago) quite different from non-organic.

'By divorcing the grazing animals from the land on which their food is grown, agribusinessmen have taken a solution and cut it neatly down the middle into two problems!'

As Wendell Berry so elegantly says, by divorcing the grazing animals from the land on which their food is grown, agribusinessmen have taken a solution and cut it neatly down the middle into two problems!

The problems are: what to do with the manure produced by the animals and how to fertilise the land which produced their food? The solution, which worked for thousands of years and will work again when the world gets sane again, is to keep the animals on the land which grows their food, and put their manure (suitably composted) back on the land. I would claim that a third problem has been produced by destroying that solution and that is – what to do with the *straw* inevitably produced by the crops that feed the animals and also that feed us. The agribusinessman burns it if he is allowed to, thus destroying what should be a most valuable addition to the fertility of his land. If he is not allowed to burn it, he chops it up small (with an enormous expenditure of scarce oil) and ploughs it into his land. If he does this, the bacteria that rot the straw rob the soil of all its available fixed nitrogen and so the agribusinessman has to dump ever more artificial nitrates onto his land (most of which eventually find their way down to the water table – or into the nearest river).

'Work on a mixed farm, with a great variety of crops and animals, is the most delightful thing in the world'

Critics argue that people are not going to be persuaded to leave the busy and exciting environment of a big city for the loneliness and isolation of a farming community. Therefore, because of a shortage of willing hands, we cannot go back to organic farming. They speak, rightly, of the utter boredom of life on the farm. But they are thinking of the large-scale agribusiness holding. Sitting in the cab of a vibrating tractor with ear-pads on for day after day is absolutely soul-destroying. But work on a mixed farm, with a great variety of crops and animals, is the most delightful thing in the world. I know – I have done both. There are *plenty* of people who would be only too glad to leave the ugly and polluted conurbations for that sort of life.

As for the ones who *don't* want to – who knows – when the oil runs out (remember the feedstock for all those lovely chemicals) they may have to. After all – we country people don't *have* to feed them, do we?

John Seymour, Killowen, New Ross, Co. Wexford, Ireland (tel 010 353 51 88156).

Need for a dual sewage system

John Seymour

Two subjects that are very close to my heart: muck and money.

'To extract all the soluble nutrients out of the effluent from our present drainage system will never be possible'

Of course human sewage should be returned to the land. Anyone can see that is impossible to go on feeding the billions on this planet by the process of extracting phosphate and potash from rapidly diminishing deposits, turning them into food crops, eating the latter and then dumping the P and K down the sewers into the sea. But we have given our sewage engineers the wrong brief. We have said: 'Get rid of it!' We should have said: 'Recycle it!' It is true that it is possible to withdraw a small proportion of the solid matter of sewage and make fertiliser of it – but to extract all the soluble nutrients out of the effluent from our present drainage system (which are the things that really matter) will never be possible. For all the rain that falls on the roof – all the billions of tons that falls on the streets – goes down the same pipe! The only thing that can possibly happen to it is that it gets dumped into the rivers and the sea.

We must one day, before all the potash and phosphate get used up, install a dual sewage system – and return all human sewage back to the land, thus instituting a cyclical system instead of the present linear one. The survival of our species depends on our doing this.

John Seymour, address above.

Sewage marshes as nature sanctuaries

Adapted extract from an article by Doug Stewart in the Smithsonian (USA), monitored for the Institute by Roger Knights.

'Sewage has been meandering through the park's chain of man-made marshes'

The Arcata Marsh and Wildlife Sanctuary is a 154 acre wetlands park about 280 miles up the coast from San Francisco. This quiet and perfectly pleasant-smelling park has turned Arcata into a tourist stop and bird-watching mecca. It also enables the town to meet California's strict sewage-discharge standards. Since 1986, partially treated sewage from the town's conventional primary treatment plant has been meandering through the park's chain of man-made marshes. After a two-month odyssey, it's piped into Humboldt Bay. The discharged marsh water is generally clearer and cleaner than the water already in the bay.

The system's low-key simplicity won the city a $100,000 grant from the Ford Foundation's Innovations in Government programme, and has set off a flood of enquiries from mayors and town engineers throughout the States.

Bob Gearheart, a professor of environmental engineering at the local college, Humboldt State University, had helped set up crop-irrigation systems using wastewater in several Third World communities. In developing countries, he found, high-quality fresh water was often unavailable and chlorine unaffordable.

The design he helped produce for Arcata involved digging out ponds from 32 acres of desolate waterfront land where a series of abandoned and decrepit lumber mills stood, dominated by an old county dump. Each marsh has a balance of open water and marsh plants. The shapes of the marshes are pleasantly irregular, and small man-made islands punctuate their surfaces. 'What really does the work here are the micro-organisms that grow around the roots and stems of these cattails.' The stem of the cattail is slippery, evidence of under-water bacteria and fungi that have latched onto it to feed on the organic nutrients in the water flowing past – tiny biological filters, in effect.

'The wetlands flora attract astounding numbers of waterfowl, herons, hawks'

Duckweed, cattails, pennywort and hard-stem bullrushes flourish in this nutrient-rich swamp water. The wetlands flora, in turn, attract astounding numbers of waterfowl: ducks, coots, egrets, herons, hawks, avocates, pelicans, peregrine falcons. And joggers huff down the redwood-chip trails, and office workers on their lunch breaks sit reading in parked cars. A visitors' centre is being planned for the park, and there's talk of posting signs inside the toilet stalls that will read: 'Thank you for your contribution.'

Bob Gearheart, Professor of Environmental Engineering, Humboldt State University, Arcata, Northern California, USA.

Converting human sewage into quality fertiliser

Adapted from Institute research; and from Business Week and RCRA Review (USA), monitored for the Institute by Roger Knights.

As fertiliser, human sewage has grave deficiencies. Even after treatment, the sludge that comes out of sewage plants is loaded with hazardous micro-organisms and laced with heavy metals, That rules out using it on soil intended for cultivation or even pasturage. In addition, the human waste lacks potassium, an essential element in fertiliser.

But disposing of sludge has become a serious environmental problem for many communities, so the incentive to find new

uses for it is growing. N-Viro Energy Systems Ltd, a private Toledo company, has found a way to convert the waste into fertiliser – by mixing three parts sludge with one part cement-kiln dust, another waste product. The highly alkaline dust kills off lingering micro-organisms, binds up the heavy metal, and is loaded with potassium, says N-Viro Chief Executive J. Patrick Nicholson. The result is an odourless, granular powder. At $100 per dry ton of sludge processed, N-Viro says its method costs about half as much as incineration and about 60% as much as composting.

'A way to convert the human sewage into fertiliser – by mixing three parts sludge with one part cement-kiln dust, another waste product'

The City of Toledo, Ohio, produces approximately 160 tons of sewage sludge daily. In the past, Toledo had trucked its sludge to landfill at a cost of approximately $8,000 a day. This was high cost and the problem of the smell induced Toledo to look for a better solution.

Now its Bayview Reclamation Plant recycles sludge into a fertiliser supplement to be used in agriculture, forestry and land reclamation. The Bayview Reclamation Plant was built in six months and can handle 15,000 dry tons of sludge annually. The facility cost less than $3 million to construct, and operation and maintenance cost will run at approximately $100 per dry tonne. The Toledo facility is built adjacent to a public golf course and two private marinas so it had to be smell-free. 'Neighbourhood support was critical in the development of this project,' says Pat Nicholson, president of N-Viro Energy Systems.

'The processing time for this technique is only three to seven days, compared to seven to 90 days for composting'

The process utilises kiln dust to pasteurise, stabilise, disin-fect, deodorise, dry and granulate municipal waste water sludge. The processing time for this technique is only three to seven days, compared to seven to 90 days for composting.

By combining two waste products, the result is a product which will be a benefit to society.

Earth Day Certificate of Merit
From an Earth Day report.

A Certificate of Special Merit was awarded to N-Viro Energy Systems for 'outstanding achievement in the area of solid waste reduction and recycling.' N-Viro was selected from more than 1,000 entries nationally in a 'Searching for Success' Programme sponsored by Renew America.

The first UK plant

The first UK soil from a sewage sludge plant is being provided for Southern Water by Simon-N-Viro, who are the UK agents for N-Viro Energy Systems Ltd. The plant at the Horsham Sewage Treatment Works in West Sussex is operating on a trial basis. 750 dry tonnes of sewage sludge cake will be processed into the pasteurised final product, N-Viro Soil. Their technical release concludes that 'using the proper dosage and mixture of alkaline admixtures is the key to the process. There are a combination of factors which produce the pasteurisation and drying of the product such as: high pH for 72 hours creates an anti-microbial environment; the correct volume of admixture for absorption of moisture will accelerate drying; at 52 degrees C pathogens, including parasites and ascaris, will not survive; ammonia released in the pile is also a disinfectant and the sludge product will have soil type organisms, but will resist microbial recontamination.'

N-Viro Energy Systems Ltd (Sally Robinson), 3450 West Central Avenue, Suite 250, Toledo, Ohio 43606, USA (tel 419 535 6374; fax 419 535 7008). Their agent in the UK is Dr Neville Hampton, Simon-Hartley Ltd, Stoke-on-Trent, Staffordshire ST4 7BH (tel 0782 202300; fax 0782 261494).

The Eco Lavatory

The Eco Lavatory, developed by David Stephens, a consultant building scientist, is an 'earth closet in a polythene grow-bag.' It is currently being piloted by Agribo, an agricultural cooperative in Kinshasa, Zaire, and Oxfam are sending the details to all their field officers, who, they believe, 'will be stimulated and informed by this excellent idea.'

The system is intended as an alternative to the village latrines promoted by the World Bank and the UN for use in the developing world, which not only cause embarrassment and tend to create a nauseating environment, but also completely lose the fertility value of faeces and risk contaminating the ground water.

> 'Faeces are excreted into a black polythene bag and covered with earth after each use. These bags are then used to nurture vegetables and trees'

It is a very simple waste-recycling scheme: with the Eco Lavatory system, faeces are excreted into a black polythene bag and covered with earth after each use. These bags are then used to nurture vegetables and trees.

For instance, the bag (half full of faeces) is tied at the neck and sunk 10 cms below the surface; ten holes in the bag are made with a pointed stick; tree seedlings or seeds are planted and watered each week with waste water and urine (in the Eco Lavatory system, urine is collected separately, and waste water from washing and cooking is added, and the mixture is used to water crops); after two years, the sides of the bag are pierced to allow shallow tree roots to spread. Meanwhile, the bag has retained water around the roots, allowing maximum use of available water. Trees planted in bags are protected from salinity.

The Eco Lavatory 'could transform Third World prospects, reducing water pollution, fly borne disease and bilharzia, and enabling food and trees to be grown in infertile and arid regions. People would also have more energy to tend their fields, output from small family farms would be greatly increased, and people would no longer have to seek work in cities or large farms to earn money to buy food. The men could stay at home, increasing the available labour, giving further production gains.'

For those in the UK whose septic tank is leaking and causing pollution, 'it will be far cheaper to start using an Eco lavatory and thus to get free organic fertiliser.'

Stephens has had an Eco Lavatory (based on a converted Elsan) in his inside bathroom since 1984. 'There is no fly or smell problem in the bathroom or garden, and the garden is abundantly fertile with no artificial fertilisers, animal manure or pesticides. Good crops of tomatoes, cucumbers, etc have been eaten raw.'

Stephens is seeking £50,000 funding to set up an institute to promote pilot trials of the Eco Lavatory and other resource-saving ideas; and meanwhile he is trying to persuade aid volunteer bodies to get their volunteers to set up such systems in the developing world.

David Stephens, Tir Gaia Solar Village, Rhayader, Powys LD6 5AG (tel 0597 810 929).

Sweet-smelling food for pigs

Adapted from items in the Independent.

The slurry being spread on Richard Adkins' pig farm at Tatenhill in Staffordshire has become more acceptable to neighbours since he has started giving his 120 pigs deodorised food, treated with a solution containing a violet-smelling yucca base. 'The slurry now has a nice violet smell which everyone seems to like – even the pigs.'

> 'He has started giving his 120 pigs deodorised food, treated with a solution containing a violet-smelling yucca base. The slurry now has a nice violet smell which everyone seems to like – even the pigs'

Professor Denis Headon, a biochemist at Galway University in Ireland, says that yucca plant extracts, added either to the animal feed or to manure storage tanks, reduces the smell by combining with the ammonia. And now a Derbyshire-based nutrition company, Colbron-Dawes, has developed a product based on the yucca plant called De-Odorase, marketed by BOCM Silcock.

Hawthorn hedges on estates

Margaret Buckley

My thesis is that the planting of hawthorn hedges would foster social harmony, in particular on large housing estates, to the benefit of large numbers of people.

> 'The planting of hawthorn hedges would foster social harmony'

Testing out my thesis, I wrote to Mr James Beardall, Parks Superintendent of Shrewsbury and Atcham Borough Council, to point out an area bordering a large council estate which I felt merited the treatment. He replied that it was a good idea which he would take up in the next planting season. He has done so and the hawthorn slips have caught! I have every hope that in a very few years they will add to the safety and amenity of an ugly route, crossing a dangerous stream, in my area.

Experts approaching the problem of vandalism from many different perspectives agree that tangible, easily recognisable boundaries provide physical and emotional security. The younger, more vulnerable or more disturbed the population, the greater the need for such security. Small children will panic in large, unfeatured areas; older children will vandalise what Alice Coleman calls 'confused space'. Territorial boundaries are felt to be so important to adults that families will bring law suits and nations will fight wars to establish or extend them; the parallels with the need for internal, psychological boundaries and constraints are obvious.

I advance the following thoughts in support of my contention:

'Hawthorn "slips" are very easily obtainable. They grow well and require very little maintenance'

(1) Hawthorn 'slips' are very easily obtainable. They grow well and require very little maintenance; (2) They increase in effectiveness over time, rather than depreciating, and are cost-effective; (3) They are indigenous to all parts of the British Isles, providing beauty of sight and scent particularly in early summer; (4) They are 'home' to many varieties of songbird and small mammal; (5) Compared with the unlovely concrete pillars and barbed wire, which invite attack, they are more neutrally, perhaps even positively, enclosing; (6) They are effectively child- and vandal-proof; (7) They provide some degree of baffle on the verges of noisy roads; (8) They require no great capital outlay nor sophisticated technology and there would probably be direct and indirect savings to the budgets of those local authorities which planted them; (9) They would, if they were planted, protected and replaced with sufficient determination, induce low-level contentment; (10) Play areas would become pleasanter.

The solution is not 'instant' and would only suit selected sites; it would not appeal to those who believe that the proper response to physical aggression towards property is an escalated counter attack. It should, however, appeal to schools, parents, conservationists, budget-conscious councils, local residents, playscheme leaders and motorists.

Margaret Buckley, the Old School House, Vicarage Road, Meole Brace, Shrewsbury, SY3 9EZ (tel 0743 352076). Her idea was highly commended in the Social Inventions Awards.

Quiet Zones

This proposal comes from Cheryl De Friez in Benicia, California:

Modern life has become so noisy that we are losing our hearing due to the constant bombardment of high decibel sounds. As I write, I am forced to listen to road construction outside my window.

Even our young children are showing signs of hearing loss, some in infancy, due to the loudness of available toys and stereo headphones.

'The establishment of Quiet Zones, where noise levels are strictly regulated'

My suggestion, as a person inundated daily by noise all around me, is the establishment of 'Quiet Zones', where noise levels are strictly regulated.

Initially, I would establish parks and nature areas where cars and motorcycles, portable radios, lawn mowers, airplanes, etc are prohibited.

This concept could be expanded to encompass living areas, where noise levels were strictly limited by consensus of the population.

My dream is of a once again noise-free world.

Cheryl De Friez, 207 West J Street, Benicia, California 94510, USA (tel 707 747 0105).

Deposits on newspapers

P.M. Bailey

Just as manufacturers in Canada are forced by law to offer a deposit on soft drink cans (which incidentally might be desirable in Britain too), so publishers of newspapers could be forced to offer a deposit on newspapers returned to the newsagents. The scheme would need to be enforced by law as it would be resisted by both publishers and newsagents, and would give an advantage to competitors if one publisher tried to introduce it on his own, putting up prices to cover costs.

'Publishers of newspapers could be forced to offer a deposit on newspapers returned to the newsagents'

Maybe this idea's time has not yet come, but I do not feel too disheartened. The best ideas I have ever had have always lain around ripening for a few years before they come out and get themselves achieved. When it is due, it will pop out.

P. M. Bailey, 44 Sparrowmire Lane, Hallgarth, Kendal, Cumbria (tel 0539 733204).

Editorial comment

The deposits might have to be too high to make economic sense. Roger Knights suggests instead that lottery tickets be offered, which could be financed by a very small increase in the price of the papers. This system could work in a number of ways. Nicholas Saunders, Josefine Speyer and I, for instance, have discussed three possibilities:

(1) You parcel up your old newspapers in string, put your name and address on the parcel and deposit it in the recycling bin. When the bin is unloaded at the recycling centre you are allocated lottery tickets in proportion to the weight of your contribution.

(2) As above, except that you take your parcel to the larger

newsagent or recycling centre locally, your contribution is weighed, and you are given lottery tickets on the spot. The newsagent, say, would then dump your papers in the nearest recycling bin and would also win lottery tickets per bin load (and the bin loads, to prevent fraud, would need approximately to match the number of tickets given out to the public by the newsagent).

(3) As with number (1) above, except that each tiny neighbourhood would have its own volunteer collector, who would use a hand weighing device to weigh contributions left out on a particular day each week by local people, would post the relevant number of lottery tickets through their letterboxes, and would then either leave them ready for the dustmen's special collection or would take them to the recycling bin. The volunteer coordinator would also be rewarded with proportionate numbers of lottery tickets.

'A national target for use of recycled fibre, and then allowing papers that beat it to sell their spare share'

(4) The simplest way for all this recycled paper to find a guaranteed market might be to establish rising target percentages of recycled paper that each newspaper must contain by particular years, through a system of tax incentives and penalties, or tradable permits, leaving it to the newspapers to devise their own preferred ways of ensuring that there are adequate supplies of recycled paper.

The tradable permits were suggested by Project 88, an American public-policy study – they work by setting newspapers a national target for use of recycled fibre, and then allowing papers that beat it to sell their spare 'share' to others that failed to meet it.

This last paragaph is adapted from an editorial in the Economist, monitored for the Institute by Roger Knights.

Financial incentives to be 'good'

The intriguing general principle that emerged from our discussion was that evil and greed have their financial rewards in society, but that there are few financial incentives at present to be 'good'. Lottery tickets could become a main currency for training the public in socially desirable behaviour, or for any activities for which it would be too costly to offer individual pay, as a reward for everything from recycling to car sharing.

'There are few financial incentives at present to be "good". Ideally, goodness would be financed from penalties for evil'

Ideally, goodness would be financed from penalties for evil, with court and other fines going into financing lotteries or into funds for non-offenders or into projects of community benefit. H. Macdonald, for instance, writes to the Institute proposing that people would receive a cheque each year accompanying their local government tax bill, as an equal share of the year's fines in that area – with the advantage that this would help console those living in areas with many offenders.

H. Macdonald, 8 Wilton Street, Brook Foot, Brighouse, Yorks. See also the item on Community Penitence Stamps in the chapter on Crime.

Cow to eat 4.5kg of newsprint daily

Adapted from Warmer Bulletin (available free from 83 Mount Ephraim, Tunbridge Wells, Kent TN4 8BS, tel 0892 524626; fax 0892 525287) and from an item by Billy Allstetter in Omni.

An Illinois scientist is feeding newsprint to cows. He believes that the paper can be transformed into feed that would comprise over 30% of the cow's diet; a large cow could thus eat 4.5 kilograms of newsprint each day.

Larry Berger, a professor of animal nutrition at the University of Illinois, shreds the newspapers (using only those with soybean oil-based ink, known to be safe for human consumption), treats them with water and two per cent hydrochloric acid and then boils the mixture for up to two hours. The heat and acid break apart the cellulose fibres enough for bacteria inside ruminants' stomachs to finish the job.

'The 30 million cattle in the States,' says Berger, 'could easily consume all the newspapers that are recycled.'

Hemp – 'a plant to save the world'?

Jack Herer

An adapted extract from High Times (USA), monitored for the Institute by Roger Knights.

'The good news is we've found a plant that can save the world. The bad news is ... it's illegal!'

The good news is we've found a plant that can save the world. The bad news is ... it's illegal!

Our challenge to the world: try to prove us wrong – if all fossil fuels and their derivatives (coal, oil, natural gas, synthetic fibres and petrochemicals) as well as the deforestation of trees for paper and agriculture (eg Brazilian and Indonesian rainforests), were banned from use in order to save the planet, to preserve the ozone layer and to reverse the greenhouse effect with its global warming trend:

Then there would be only one known renewable natural resource able to provide *all* of the following goods and essentials such as paper and textiles; meet all of the world's transportation, home and industrial energy needs, and clean the atmosphere – all at the same time: Cannabis Hemp.

'Some cannabis plant strains regularly reach treelike heights of 20 feet or more in one growing season'

• Some cannabis plant strains regularly reach tree-like heights of 20 feet or more in one growing season. In 1916, the US Department of Agriculture wrote in special bulletin No. 404 that one acre of cannabis hemp in annual rotation over a 20 year period, would produce as much pulp for paper as 4.1 acres of trees. Lignin must be broken down to make pulp paper. Hemp is only 4% lignin, while trees are 18-30% lignin.

Thus hemp provides four times as much pulp with five to seven times less pollution.

• Hemp is the most energy efficient annually renewable plant. Hemp biomass can replace every type of fossil fuel product. Biomass conversion, utilising the same 'cracking' technology employed by the petroleum industry will make charcoal to replace coal. Charcoal contains no sulphur, so when it is burned for industry no sulphur is emitted from the process. Sulphur is the primary cause of acid rain. The 'cracking' process also produces non-sulphur fuel oil to replace fossil fuels – methanol, as well as the basic chemicals of industry: acetone, ethyl acetate, tar, pitch and creosote.

'Hemp seed oil makes high grade diesel fuel oil and aircraft engine and precision machine oil'

• Hemp seed contains 30% (by volume) oil. This oil makes high grade diesel fuel oil and aircraft engine and precision machine oil.

• Hemp is 77% cellulose, a basic chemical feed stock used in the production of chemicals, plastics and fibres, with many times the cellulose found in cornstalks, kenaf or sugar cane.

• In most places, hemp can be harvested twice a year. It has a short growing season and can be planted after food crops have been harvested.

• Hemp is easy on the soil and an ideal crop for the semi-arid West and open range land of the States.

• The hemp seed is the second most complete vegetable protein source – soybeans alone have a bit more protein; however hemp seed is many times cheaper and its protein potential can be utilised better than soybean by the human body.

'With hemp seed in their diet, birds will live 10-20% longer'

• All domesticated animals, farm animals and poultry could be fed a nearly complete diet with just hemp seed extract protein and fat. Hemp seed cake was one of the world's principal animal feeds until this century. With hemp seed in their diet, birds will live 10-20% longer.

• Hemp cellulose and oils can be used for literally tens of thousands of other uses, from paints to dynamite.

• Hemp seed sown free from airplanes flying over eroding soil could reclaim land the world over. Hemp seeds put down a 10 to 12 inch root in only thirty days. The root breaks up compacted, over-worked soil.

'why not establish a Natural Guard of environmental soldiers to be our front line of survival?'

Instead of a National Guard, why not establish a Natural Guard of environmental soldiers to be our front line of survival – planting trees, harvesting biomass from marginal farm lands and rebuilding the infrastructure of America: our roads, bridges, dams, canals and railroad tracks?

This High Times article was itself excerpted from a book entitled 'The Emperor Wears No Clothes', by Jack Herer, published by Access Unlimited, PO Box 1900, Frazier Park, CA 932225, USA, US$12·95.

All containers recycled by law

Info from Tranet newsletter No 60 (subs $30 from Tranet, PO Box 567, Rangeley, ME 04970, USA, tel 207 864 2252).

Maine in the United States has a new recycling law which requires that juice, alcohol and water containers, as well as soft drinks, should be recycled, and that paper should be recycled by industry, and that plastics harmful to wildlife should be eliminated. The goal of the new law is 50% solid waste reduction by 1994.

Recycling with worms

Info from Tranet newsletter No 60 (address details above).

The small rural town (population 1,100) of Morton, Washington, USA, has instituted a vermiculture composting system, fuelled by specially-bred worms, which changes food, sludge and yard-waste into high quality top soil. Besides saving the town $10,000 annually, the recycling programme removes approximately 35 per cent of the volume going to the landfill.

A video, guidebook and user's guide is available for purchase or rental from the National Association of Towns and Townships (1522 K Street, Suite 730, Washington, DC 20005, USA, tel 202 737 5200).

Curitiba – reycling as a popular and heroic activity

Adapted from an article by Thomas Kamm of the Wall Street Journal (USA), monitored for the Institute by Mrs Cook.

Jaime Lerner, the mayor of Curitiba, a Brazilian city of 1.6 million inhabitants, is trying to invent the city of the future, with efficient bus systems, mobile schools for the poor from converted old buses and two thirds of the city's wastes being recycled.

Lerner favours small-scale, cheap and practical solutions to urban problems. Instead of building costly new recycling plants, for instance, he set out to 'turn each home into a factory', with a determined effort to get households to sort their garbage before putting it out.

'He distributed pictures of children's heroes in return for rubbish'

Instead of a costly advertising drive to promote the plan, Lerner launched the campaign in schools. He sent out people dressed up as trees to make the point that recycling paper could save forests. He distributed pictures of children's heroes in return for the children's turning in non-degradable rubbish like batteries and toothpaste tubes. The efforts turned children into 'secret agents inside each home.'

In slums that dustcarts could not enter, Lerner gave away bags of vegetables, fruits and dairy products or bus vouchers to slum-dwellers in return for their rubbish. In this way he made the city cleaner while also improving nutrition and boosting public transportation.

The city's recycling plant for non-organic rubbish is on the grounds of a foundation for indigents. 'We don't just recycle garbage, we recycle people here,' says Enrique Goldenstein, the foundation's head.

By stressing to the public that the recycling of paper goods saves an estimated 1,200 trees a day, 'we transformed the garbage man into an environmental hero,' says the mayor, who went to work as a dustman to launch the programme.

Extra waste bins for recyclables for Sheffield households

Up to 7,500 households in Sheffield are being given an extra waste bin – the Blue Box – into which they can put paper, glass, cans, plastics and batteries for recycling. The Blue Boxes will be collected weekly and loaded separately onto a specially designed collection lorry.

'Up to 7,500 households in Sheffield are being given an extra waste bin – the Blue Box – into which they can put paper, glass, cans, plastics and batteries for recycling'

The Blue Box collections are part of Recycling City, a project initiated by Friends of the Earth, with the aim of developing model recycling facilities in four cities. The project operates as a partnership between industry, government and the voluntary sector, with sponsorship provided by British Telecom and funding for a full evaluation to assess the practical and economic viability of the new recycling operations in Sheffield.

Rebecca Gwynn-Jones, Friends of the Earth, 26-28 Underwood Street, London N1 7JQ (tel 071 490 1555).

Mandatory deposits on containers

Adapted from an article by Andreas von Schoenberg in Warmer Bulletin (available free from 83 Mount Ephraim, Tunbridge Wells, Kent TN4 8BS, tel 0892 524626; fax 0892 525287); from an article by Ian Murray in the Times; and from the Economist, the European, the Guardian and the Independent.

The German government has brought in a controversial packaging ordinance which their Environment Minister described as the 'final departure from the throw-away society.'

The most important provisions require that:

• Producers and retailers have to accept for recycling and disposal all returned transport packaging.

• The consumer can leave all used packaging material at the point-of-sale.

• From 1993, retailers must accept all used packaging material returned by the consumer. To encourage the consumer a mandatory deposit of DM 0.50 will be levied on all drinks, detergent and dispersion paint containers. To date, deposits have only been charged on refillable glass bottles and plastics drinks bottles, the latter levy hitting French mineral water producers hardest.

• By July 1st 1995, 80% of packaging waste must be collected; and of this collected material, 90% of glass and metals must be recycled, and 80% of the remainder. Incineration, even if used to generate power, is ruled out.

400 German companies have set up the Duales System Deutschland (DSD) which runs its own waste-collection system, with companies' products carrying a green dot if they have paid between 1 and 0 pfennigs per item. The green dot indicates that their packaging can be recycled by the DSD.

Potsdam and Endenich, a suburb of Bonn, have been chosen as guinea-pig areas, but the group's ultimate intention is to provide every household in Germany with a separate bright yellow dustbin for recyclable packaging. Until that can be organised, the plan is to provide at least one huge bright yellow dustbin for every 500 homes in the city or 200 homes in the country.

British exporters to Germany say that the cost of complying with this new law will run into millions of pounds, and that such unilaterally imposed rules represent a barrier to trade and to the EC single market.

Incentives to reduce rubbish

Adapted extract from Warmer Bulletin (address above).

The authorities in Seattle (USA) are experimenting with volume-based garbage rates. Customers are asked to decide on their 'subscription' level according to the amount of garbage they need to dispose of each week. Rates increase significantly with higher levels. It is proving to be an extremely effective methods of waste reduction. It is seen as a fair system, with customers having control over the waste they put out for collection and therefore the amount they pay for the service.

'Customers are asked to decide on their "subscription" level according to the amount of garbage they need to dispose of each week'

In Florida they have introduced a bar code system on collection boxes: householders receive credit for recyclable material, and this is automatically deducted from their annual service bill.

For the UK it has been suggested that weighing and recording every bin and sack might be a fair solution, but it would be expensive to operate, not least by slowing down the collection rate. It could also encourage people to dump their rubbish in a neighbour's bin, or to flytip.

Only six per cent of waste is household waste. A proposal worth investigating is that of allocating companies quotas (sometimes called 'credits') for the amount of waste they generate; and then encouraging those companies who reduce most cheaply their share of rubbish to sell off spare credits to those who find it more costly to cut back.

The last paragraph is adapted from an editorial in the Economist, monitored for the Institute by Roger Knights.

Underground street litter containers

C. Gentles

One problem which local authorities seem to face is the frequency with which they have to empty their bins – especially at weekends a number are overflowing. They should sink a large container below pavement level over which could be placed a conventional-looking hinged bin. Then, weekly or whenever the situation demanded, a vacuum van could come along, turn back the bin, and draw out the contents in a 30 second operation.

C. Gentles, 41 Thames Mead, Crowmarsh Gifford, Wallingford, Oxon OX10 8HA (tel 0491 37778).

Sponsored recyclers

Maisie Redhead and Robert Stephenson

As members of a project concerned with recycling and waste reduction, it disheartens us to know that old telephone directories are not accepted by waste paper merchants because of their glued spines. It is not economically viable for the merchants to remove the spines, but as a fund-raising sponsored activity it would certainly be more valuable than walking around a cycle track, for instance.

> 'It is not economically viable for the merchants to remove the spines of telephone directories, but as a fund-raising sponsored activity it would certainly be more valuable than walking around a cycle track'

Many current recycling schemes are used by only a fraction of the population, whilst other possible schemes remain un-economic. But sponsored events such as the above would overcome the economic problem; would raise funds for a worthy cause; would obtain publicity for the great need for waste reduction schemes; and would help ensure the regular supply of materials and thus encourage capital investment in recycling initiatives.

Maisie Redhead and Robert Stephenson, 9 King's Drive, Hassocks, W. Sussex BN6 8DZ.

Editorial comment

I am favour of all sponsored activity being of a socially useful variety. But the French approach of subsidising the public to acquire home computer access to directory enquiries (and a large range of other Prestel-like services) would in the long run use less resources than printing and distributing directories, however much they are recycled. In the meantime, British Telecom should have a box on their bills that the customer can tick if no telephone directories are required for that number. Houses or businesses with several lines often simply throw away the extra new directories left on the doorstep for them.

Deposit on car batteries

From a notice sent to the Institute by Roger Knights.

Outlets selling car batteries in the state of Washington (USA) are required by state law to include a 'core charge of five dollars or more if you do not return your old battery for exchange.' It is illegal to put a vehicle battery in the garbage.

Energy used to clean old bottles 15 time more than for new

From two news items in Warmer Bulletin (address above).

The city of Munich requires that all mineral water, beer and milk be sold only in returnable bottles.

Meanwhile, the Australian Government's permanent Industry Commission has found that the energy and water expended in the collection and cleaning of returned bottles could be up to 15 times higher than that required to make new bottles.

Recycled paper means less trees

Adapted extract from 'The Global Consumer' by Phil Wells and Mandy Jetter, published as a Gollancz Paperback Original, £5-99, ISBN 0 575 05000 4.

> 'Recycled paper is a good thing to buy, but not to save trees; rather to prevent them being planted'

Tropical hardwood in the form of paper pulp finds its way into the UK in tiny amounts, if at all. Increasing demand for paper and for softwoods has led to more land in the UK and other temperate countries being turned into forestry planta-tions. In some cases, a valuable native eco-system has been destroyed. So recycled paper is a good thing to buy, but not to save trees; rather to prevent them being planted. As has been well put, buying recycled paper to save trees is like cutting down on sandwiches to save wheat.

Recycle four times then burn the waste paper for fuel

From the Warmer Bulletin (address above.)

Recycling paper does have other advantages compared with virgin paper: cutting import bills, reducing water use by nearly 60%, energy consumption by 40%, air pollution by 74% and water pollution by 35%

The Nordic countries provide a very high percentage of the world's paper – and their forests are increasing. An admirable forestry practice of planting two trees for every one harvested has produced a huge increase in afforested areas, albeit often of single tree types rather than the mixed woodland we all feel a warm glow about. Unless cut down, trees die and decay naturally, releasing the carbon dioxide – the major greenhouse gas – which they had trapped during their lives. Cutting them down doesn't increase overall the carbon dioxide release. Conversely, planting more trees has created more carbon dioxide absorbers. Turning the wood into paper fixes some of that carbon dioxide. If the paper is recycled, which can be done a maximum of four times to maintain fibre strength, and is then landfilled, the paper slowly degrades and releases the same carbon dioxide as the naturally dying tree, but with the addition of methane, a far more potent greenhouse gas. Burning waste paper for fuel once its useful life is over similarly releases that trapped carbon dioxide, but without the methane. There is no net carbon dioxide increase. But using waste paper to produce energy has another important side benefit as far as the greenhouse effect is concerned – the energy produced displaces energy that would otherwise have been generated from fossil fuels, which do produce a net carbon dioxide increase.

> '**An expanding packaging industry could – tongue in cheek – be said to be reducing the greenhouse effect!**'

Could the increase in paper use which must correspond to the increased quantities of paper in the waste stream, actually provide an environmental benefit by tying up more carbon dioxide? Since packaging, amongst others, provides a steady market for paper production, then an expanding packaging industry could – tongue in cheek – be said to be reducing the greenhouse effect! Nothing is simple, is it?

Imaginative environmental events

Gerard Darby

Environment Week '91 was managed by Institute member Gerard Darby, from whose report these adapted extracts are taken.

Environment Week in the summer of '91 was a great success with over 3,000 projects and events around the country. Many of these were extremely inventive and enterprising and could be copied by other groups in other parts of Britain. Some of the best were:

• A **Bike Mate** scheme which covers the whole of London and which was launched during the week by the London Cycling Campaign. The scheme will match a nervous novice with a more experienced cyclist who will teach their 'Mate' how to cope with the hazards of London traffic.

> '**300 children from ten schools beat the clock in their project to clear up a ten mile footpath by the River Wear Trail in one day**'

• **Environmental Challenges** which had to be completed against the clock: in Saltley, Birmingham, there was a five day programme of linked challenges such as tackling a wall of graffiti in half a day, making 50 hanging baskets for installing in a tower block in one day, making bird boxes – ten different activities all against the clock. In Sunderland, 300 children from ten schools beat the clock in their project to clear up a ten mile footpath by the River Wear Trail in one day.

• Young people had the chance to be a world leader for a day in a simulation of a **United Nations General Assembly** on the environment held at Camden Town Hall and organised by the United Nations Association for Youth and Students. Almost a hundred young people from different London schools represented over fifty countries and debated key international environmental issues.

• The **Barn Owl Re-Introduction Scheme** in Norfolk worked with inmates in the Britannia Training Wing of Norwich Prison to make barn owl nest boxes using timber donated by a local firm.

• Birmingham City Council launched Britain's first **full-time litter wardens** armed with spy cameras.

• Members of the **Llandaff Rowing Club** in Cardiff scoured the banks of the River Taff as part of a major clean-up exercise. Using their boating skills the oarsmen and women were able to reach piles of unsightly litter and debris.

> '**The best siting of a satellite dish, one that would reduce its visual impact on the environment**'

• North Tyneside Borough Council held an environmental competition. This included an award for the **best siting of a satellite dish**, one that would reduce its visual impact on the environment.

Gerard Darby, 10 Caversham Avenue, Cheam, Surrey SM3 9AH (tel 081 643 3798).

Global ecological alliance

Guy Dauncey

We need a new global alliance of ecologically-minded countries – a Global Ecological Alliance. Canada, the Scandinavian countries, Holland, Austria, Australia and New Zealand could take the lead.

> '**We need a new global alliance of ecologically-minded countries – Canada, the Scandinavian countries, Holland, Austria, Australia and New Zealand could take the lead**'

Member countries could develop bold joint initiatives to address the destruction of the tropical rainforests, the greenhouse effect, the ozone hole, Third World debt, oceanic pollution, soil erosion, etc and could work on positive measures such as ecological development initiatives, world youth-link initiatives, planetary celebrations of nature, etc.

Extracted from 'Building a Green Future – Ten practical ideas for environmental organisers and activists' by Guy Dauncey (intended for Canadian readers), Canadian $2·50 from Guy Dauncey, 2069 Kings Road, Victoria, British Columbia, Canada V8R 2P6 (tel 604 592 4472 h; 592 4473 w, tel and fax).

Environmental Legislation Ideas Bank

Guy Dauncey

We need an Environmental Legislation Ideas Bank, to gather together actual and proposed laws and regulations from all over the world, and to list them by category. Then if you wanted to find out what kinds of laws have been enacted to encourage recycling, for instance, you could simply look up 'recycling', take your pick, and shape it for local circumstances. With an Ideas Bank on computer network, regular user feedback could be included from people living under the new laws. Once established, legislators would also presumably be keen to file any new legislation, so as to gain credit for their work. The Bank might become self-supporting, on a subscription basis.

> 'We need an Environmental Legislation Ideas Bank, to gather together actual and proposed laws and regulations from all over the world'

Extracted from 'Building a Green Future – Ten practical ideas for environmental organisers and activists' by Guy Dauncey (details above).

Save the World Club

Des Kay

From Des Kay's Save The World Club Newsletter.

Things are really hotting up at Save The World Club (STWC) at the moment – and boy, don't they need to! People are joining at an unprecedented rate – getting involved with all sorts of affiliated organisations – Greenpeace, Friends of the Earth, CND etc – very encouraging. Remember you can still take advantage of free membership – the only requirement being a pledge to say 'I am a member of STWC, and today I will do all I can to help save the world' every day when you wake up.

> 'The only requirement being a pledge to say "I am a member of STWC, and today I will do all I can to help save the world" every day when you wake up'

Down here at the Kingston branch the pace quickens as preparations for the Kingston Green Fair reach an exciting stage. Billed as an Environmental Extravaganza, with stalls, clowns, jugglers, food, cabaret, inflatables, music, games, face painting, workshops and competitions, it takes place on the Monday Spring Bank Holiday.

When it is over, Kingston STWC are organising a directory of all we have gleaned – plus listings of all the relevant and sympathetic groups, equipment and entertainers – for STWC members throughout the country to start a network of annual Green Fairs, the village fetes of the future.

Des Kay, Cadbury Gardens, Kingston-Upon-Thames, Surrey (tel 081 546 1827).

A Calendar with 28 day months

Adapted extract from an item in 'The People's Almanac No. 3' (published by Bantam Books, USA, ISBN 0 553 01352 1).

Various plans for an improvement of the calendar have been suggested; but on January 1, 1917, Joseph U. Barnes of Minneapolis, USA, evolved a plan which is conceded to be by far the best yet proposed. Under this plan, our present complicated and inconvenient arrangement can easily be made so simple and convenient that printed calendars would soon be unknown. Only three simple changes are required. They are as follows:

• First, make New Year's Day an independent legal holiday. Have it fall between the last day of December and the first day of January. Do not include it in any week or month.

• Second, provide another independent legal holiday for Leap Year. Have it fall between the last day of one month and the first day of the next. Do not include it in any week or month.

> '13 months of exactly four weeks each, making Monday the first day of every month. The days of the week would then be permanently fixed'

• Third, divide the remaining 364 days into 13 months of exactly four weeks each, making Monday the first day of every month and Saturday the last work-day of every month. The days of the week would then be permanently fixed.

While making the change, Good Friday and Easter Sunday should be placed on certain fixed dates. According to history, the placing of these on fixed dates was seriously considered at the time that our present calendar was adopted. This change would secure a much-desired regularity and would be especially appreciated by members of the mercantile profession.

This simplified calendar could be adopted to take effect on Sunday, the first day of the next year, and the change would cause scarcely a ripple in our business or social life. Six months' experience under this simplified form would make us wonder why we put up with the inconvenience of our present form for so long.

The name chosen for the new month is Liberty. Barnes had, early in 1917, chosen the word Gregory, but the stirring events of 1917 and 1918 made the word Liberty so prominent that, when the president of a Minneapolis bank suggested it as a name for the new month, the suggestion was immediately adopted.

The new month is placed immediately after February, so in the new plan the months read: January, February, Liberty, March, etc. The independent legal holiday provided for Leap Year will be called Correction Day.

The advantages of this simplified calendar cannot be over-estimated. The savings of time and mental effort in making calculations for the future would be beyond all comprehension. These advantages would arise from the fact that all the months in the entire year would be just alike. Every month would have exactly four weeks and every month would commence with Monday and end with Sunday. All holidays and anniversaries would always fall on the same day of the week. Every day in all the months would receive an absolutely fixed place in the four weeks. Our present exasperating system of four and a fraction weeks to the month would be done away with, and there would be no more five Sundays in a month to upset all our calculations.

People are called upon every day of the year to set dates for future occurrences. Dates for meetings, payments, commencement of employment, quitting employment, occupancy or vacancy of property, legislation, etc would be consistent. This simplified calendar would enable anyone to tell at once on what day of the week any future day of the month would fall.

'Exactly the same length of time would elapse between all regular paydays, which is not now the case when paydays are monthly or semi-monthly'

Under this equal-month calendar, exactly the same length of time would elapse between all regular paydays, which is not now the case when paydays are monthly or semi-monthly. This would very greatly simplify terms of employment and be a great convenience to both employers and employees.

As another simple illustration of the inconvenience of our present calendar, it might be stated that millions of people ask every year on what day of the week Christmas will fall. Under this new form of calendar, everyone would know that as Christmas comes on the 25th day of the month, it would always fall on Thursday.

Source: Joseph U. Barnes, The Liberty Calendar and the First Year under the New Calendar, Minneapolis, Minn., USA, 1918.

Changing the clocks for more daylight

The Policy Studies Institute (PSI) issued a report on the costs and benefits of moving the clock one hour ahead of its current setting throughout the year. That would mean British Standard Time (BST) in the winter and Double British Summer Time (DBST) in the summer.

'Moving the clock one hour ahead of its current setting throughout the year'

There is now a likelihood of the government taking action to implement this change. The suggested smooth transition would be, after the necessary legislation, to maintain BST through the winter. In the spring of the following year, clocks would be put forward by a further hour to DBST, and in the autumn they would be put back by one hour to BST and so on, with thereafter the two clock changes each year, as at present.

The advantages

• There would be an extra hour of evening daylight on every day of the year, whereas for most people there would effectively be an extra hour of morning darkness in only the depths of winter.

'There would be a reduction of about 850 fatalities and serious injuries in road accidents'

• There would be a reduction of about 850 fatalities and serious injuries in road accidents.

• More daylight journeys for social and recreational purposes could be made, benefiting the old and children particularly.

• There would be an increase of over a quarter in the number of hours for outdoor leisure activities after school or work. As the Times diary put it: 'Cricket under the midnight sun – who could resist such a prospect?'

• An improvement in general health and well-being is predicted from the increase in exercise in daylight and sunlight.

• Earnings in tourism would rise by about £600 million annually covering those activities governed by the availability of daylight.

• Additional annual earnings of about £150 million for the leisure industries.

• An increase of jobs in the leisure and tourism industries.

• An annual saving of about £100 million in fuel costs and improved efficiency in electricity generation.

• Clock times between the UK and 93% of the EC would be identical for all twelve months of the year. This would be welcomed by the UK's EC partners.

• Businessmen would be able to make round trips to the continent within a day. Increased revenue for British airlines of £30 to £50 million would be generated.

• A large majority of organisations surveyed during the PSI study were in favour of the change.

The disadvantages

• It would exacerbate the already depressing start to the day in winter, especially for those whose work has to begin early irrespective of the availability of daylight, such as the postmen, milkmen, others in public services, and some farmers.

• It would be especially depressing for those living in Scotland, where daylight in mid-winter would not begin until 9.30 – although there would be the compensation of the extra hour of daylight in the afternoon.

• People may psychologically prefer to have daylight on rising than later in the day, if they have to choose between them.

• Unions in the agricultural and construction industries are likely to be strongly opposed, without equally powerful countervailing bodies.

• There will be adverse political repercussions in Scotland, although there are some who argue that Scotland could have its own time zone.

The conclusion

Bill Daniel, the Director of the Policy Studies Institute, comments: 'The government is inclined to believe that there is no such thing as a free lunch. The Policy Studies Institute judges that the advantages of reform relative to the low costs of making the change add up to a free and regular banquet.'

Progress

Michael Young (Lord Young of Dartington) chaired a conference on this theme and praised Dr Mayer Hillman's booklet, 'Making the Most of Daylight Hours' (published by Policy Studies Institute). 'It is a remarkable job,' he said. 'If Britain enters into a new relationship with the sun, it will be due to the work of one person who had an idea ahead of his time. It will be thanks to his dedication and research. The book is very solid, with the issues well delineated. It means the public debate will not be carried one way or the other by emotion and prejudice to the extent that it would otherwise have been. His proposal is a social invention, which is as important as a technological one, though rarer. In fact his case is almost too good to be true. It is a researcher's dream that all the points in favour should come out like this. A referendum on the issue might well produce a vote in favour even in Scotland.'

'If Britain enters into a new relationship with the sun, it will be due to the work of one person who had an idea ahead of his time'

At the conference, representatives of the Transport and Road Research Laboratory, Age Concern, the Rural Development Commission, Butlins Holiday Camps, the British Tourist Authority, the Sports Council and the CBI all spoke in favour, with the Building Employers' Federation, the Post Office and the National Farmers Union against (the three latter do not like early starts in the dark).

'It is an issue which ordinary people have not thought about,' Michael Young commented, 'and so public opinion polls may not produce meaningful results. But I do believe that the chances of the change occurring will be greater just because there is some opposition, otherwise the proponents might have sat back and not fought for it. Now it will be a lively debate, with small minorities showing strength of feeling on both sides.

'The strength of feeling against change is normally the greater, so the result is by no means an open and shut case'

'The strength of feeling against change is normally the greater, so the result is by no means an open and shut case.'

Following publication of a government Green Paper on the subject of the PSI proposal, two pressure groups were formed, one called Keep Summer Time British fighting against the change, and one called Daylight Extra, which is in favour. A government survey showed 55% of interest groups were in favour of the change and 34% were against. But most of the 4,000 letters and petitions have been against, particularly those from Scotland. Two public opinion surveys have recorded a 3 to 1 majority in favour of the change.

'The MPs were persuaded by the public outcry over horror stories in the press about children run over going to school in the dark on icy roads. The media had been unable to make a story about the larger number of unknown pedestrians saved by the extra afternoon daylight'

Interestingly, the previous similar experiment on these lines was ended by parliament on a free vote in 1970 by 336 votes to 81. The MPs then were largely persuaded by the public outcry over horror stories in the press about children run over going to school in the dark on icy roads. The media had been unable to make a story about the larger number of unknown pedestrians saved by the extra afternoon daylight.

'Making the Most of Daylight Hours' by Dr Mayer Hillman, is available at £4-95 incl. p&p from PSI, 100 Park Village East, London NW1 3SR (tel 071 794 9661 h; 071 387 2171 w; fax 071 388 0914). Dr Mayer Hillman won a 1989 Social Inventions Award for this proposal.

Chapter fourteen

QUALITY OF LIFE

Best ways of measuring quality of life

This chapter explores the best ways of measuring quality of life, and publishes some of the entries received by the Institute for Social Inventions in response to its competition on this theme.

The standard of living is improving, at least in the developed countries. But the quality of life does not necessarily improve at the same time. Are people happier, more fulfilled, more creative, more able to develop their potential? Are their relationships, work and leisure as satisfying? Do they find their neighbourhood and environment as pleasant to live in? Is there a supportive network of family, friends and neighbours to help in old age or with childcare?

Social Indicators Research and other journals have detailed the work on this theme since the early '70s, but how would you set about measuring quality of life, as opposed to the standard of living?

These were the main questions posed by the Institute's competition, which accepted entries in any one or more of the following five categories (and the Institute intends to continue publicising material received in these categories):

(1) **Idiosyncratic Personal Quality of Life Index** – if you had to design a questionnaire that you could fill in once a year, to ascertain from the resulting score to what extent your own personal quality of life had gone up or down, what would it consist of? The aim here is to broaden the perspective of social scientists who consider these issues. For instance, some people might want to assess how close they have been to nature, others to what extent their spiritual needs have been met or how much they have laughed of late – the questions can be ones that are fitted to you alone.

(2) **Individual Quality of Life Index**. As above, but the questionnaire should be applicable to anyone – for instance, a country's cultural differences could be allowed for by getting respondents to indicate what importance they attach to each question.

(3) **Quality of Relationships Index**. There may be overlap here with the Individual Index, but the only factor this would measure is the quality of relationships with family, lovers, neighbours, work colleagues and friends.

(4) **Neighbourhood Quality of Life Index**. This could either be one where inhabitants are asked to give their subjective assessments, or could be based on more 'objective' exterior assessment, or it could contain both these elements. The neighbourhood is defined here as any area that local people would tend to refer to as their immediate neighbourhood, in many areas not exceeding 1,000 inhabitants. Again the Index should be usable anywhere in the world. Most such Indexes to date have been from a Western perspective. The hope here is to draw up an Index that, if widely adopted, might encourage the developing world to avoid harmful imitation of the worst excesses of the lifestyle of affluent regions. A particularly satisfactory lifestyle in the third world (assuming basic needs for food, shelter and security are met) – such as that of a hill tribe in Thailand or a village in Kashmir's Ladakh – might then be able to score at least as high on a Quality of Life Index as a materially richer area such as Brixton in London or Easterhouse in Glasgow. The Index can measure negative or positive factors or both. Ideally it should be one that neighbourhoods would find useful in defending or developing their areas, and that they could even perhaps administer for themselves.

(5) **International Quality of Life Index**. There have been several attempts at this – Richard Estes' Index of Social Progress being probably the most advanced. But most attempts to date have been biased towards economic rather than ecological considerations, and have omitted people's own assessments of their well-being.

Besides those aims outlined above, the aims of this work are: to encourage people to consider and evaluate factors making for overall quality of life; to encourage leaders and others to take into account the effects of their actions on quality of life; to encourage the creation of human scale societies and aspiration towards non-material values; and to publicise the best work in this field.

Criteria

When considering the feasibility of proposals, the Institute bears in mind the following criteria, where relevant:

(1) Would the Index proposed be applicable worldwide, without an inbuilt bias towards higher ratings for 'First World' countries? (2) Would the Index be reducible to a number, with a resulting league table, even if supplemented by fuller 'small'

print? (3) Would it be largely independent of the economic standard of living? (4) Would it be relatively cheap and simple to administer? (5) Is it likely to prove credible, useful, and feasible (politically and in terms of funding)? Can it be implemented privately without relying on a United Nations agency or similar?

This chapter describes some of the ingredients said to make up this quality of life, and some of the attempts to measure it that have been made to date, in the hope of inspiring readers to create their own versions (and to submit them to the Institute).

Assess your own personal quality of life

Diana Chaudhuri

The Personal Quality of Life category in the Institute's competition was won by Diana Chaudhuri's Individual Quality of Life Index; Chaudhuri lives in Lowestoft in Suffolk, and has made an imaginative and idiosyncratic attempt, as an amateur, to formulate a series of questions (giving a possible final score of 100) which rate all aspects of life including inner life, outer practical considerations like health and income, relationships with other people in the home and community, relationships with the nation and world scene, and sense of overall perspective and purpose. And Chaudhuri has tried to make her Index universally applicable by keeping in mind people from widely different cultures – from tribal hunters to Third World village dwellers, from high income Westerners to slum dwellers and beggars. The following section gives her questionnaire in full, followed by her scorings (some of which need improvements). Chaudhuri would welcome suggested adjustments or changes, and would be prepared to help conduct a trial of her index. Perhaps readers would like to score themselves (Ed: I scored 75%) and send the Institute their scores and their comments and suggested improvements.

This questionnaire is designed for self-testing or for completely confidential use by non-government bodies.

1. Inner spiritual or aesthetic values

'Do you have a personal philosophy or religion which is a source of strength and comfort to you?'

(a) Do you have a personal philosophy or religion which is a source of strength and comfort to you?

(b) If yes, does this give you a clear sense of direction and purpose for living?

(c) Does the natural pattern of the seasons and of the needs and behaviour of other creatures help to shape your lifestyle?

(d) Is the environment of your home and work well ordered and beautiful?

(e) Do you share your day with other people whose company you value and enjoy?

(f) Do you have some time each day to yourself?

(g) Do you enjoy your own company?

(h) Do you feel a sense of peace, happiness and well-being at times during the day? This may be connected with working or religion, with love and intimacy, with family and parenthood, with closeness to nature, etc.

(i) Do you have a really close friend or relative with whom you can share your most intimate thoughts and feelings, whom you can frequently meet or speak with by phone or letter?

(j) If you live with other people, is your household a happy community where individuals relate well together and care for one another in an atmosphere of peace, security, affection and laughter?

(k) Are the relationships between members of your household secure and enduring?

(l) Do children in your household or in the neighbouring area enjoy abundant adult company, encouragement, time, love and approval?

(m) If you live alone, is this by choice?

(n) Whether you live alone or with others, do you meet people each day whom you like and who like you, and with whom there is mutual assistance and companionship?

(o) If you do not meet other people often, is your isolation a cause of sadness and loneliness, or is it a peaceful self-chosen isolation?

(p) Does your day include activities which are creative, where you feel interested and involved in the activity, and gain satisfaction from it?

(q) Does your day include some physical activity which stimulates you and gives you a healthy sense of effort and tiredness?

(r) Does your day include too much strong physical activity, leaving you feeling strained and exhausted?

(s) Does your year include some variety, some periods of complete change, such as festivals, pilgrimages, holidays, weekends, etc?

'Do youngsters growing up in your household or community feel a sense of purpose and optimism as they approach adulthood?'

(t) Do youngsters growing up in your household or community feel a sense of purpose and optimism as they approach adulthood?

(u) Are relevant education, suitable housing and employment readily available for young people in your community?

(v) Do you ever feel hopeless and helpless, depressed or despairing, because of issues which face your family, household, community, nation or the world?

(w) Have you a personal philosophy or religion which can help in a practical way to overcome such feelings as in (v) above, or the setbacks which you may face due to failures of income, illness or death of those close to you?

2. Outer practical considerations

(a) Does your household have a regular source of reliable income – either in money or in the basic necessities – sufficient for everyday needs of food, shelter, basic education, health care, transport and social needs?

(b) If income is below this level, is it erratic and often insufficient to cover even the most basic needs of survival?

(c) Do material needs cause you worry?

(d) Is your household income well above that required for the basic necessities listed in (a) above?

(e) Do you have worries and anxieties caused by surplus income, for example, concerning investment, rentings, second houses, employment of staff, etc?

(f) Do all the members of your household and close friends and relatives enjoy good health?

(g) Would ill health in (f) above create serious financial problems, as well as the worry and concern it would naturally create?

(h) Do you or your community have provision in the event of ill health or death of close members?

(i) Do health matters cause you or your immediate family or household serious worry?

(j) If any member of your family or close community has died over the last five years, do you feel that they received good medical treatment and all that could be done for them was done?

(k) Does your community have customs which embrace death, giving support to the bereaved and allowing them to grieve?

(l) Is the health care in your community comparable with the health care available in other parts of your nation?

(m1) Is the income of your community, the standard of living it enjoys and the opportunities available for the young people comparable with those enjoyed by the rest of your nation?

(m2) Is the life expectancy in your community well above average for the world? above average for your nation?

(n) Is your community fairly stable with few people moving in or out each year?

(o) Are the laws which govern your community generally regarded as just?

(p) Are grievances dealt with fairly, without corruption, high financial cost or oppression?

(q) Does the political climate seriously restrict your freedom of movement, worship, income or speech?

(r) Have any members of your community been involved in protest or confrontation with forces of 'law and order' over issues relating to the community?

(s) If so, did you feel the issue was dealt with wisely and fairly by the authorities?

(t) Have any members of your community been involved in petitioning, demonstrating or canvassing for issues of a wider nature which affect the nation or the international situation (this would include political, religious, environmental issues etc)?

(u) If so, did you feel the issues were dealt with wisely and fairly by the authorities?

(v) Do issues such as may be involved in (r) or (t) above cause you much worry or anxiety?

(w) Does the handling of protest etc in your nation cause you worry or anxiety?

(x) Do you know of individuals in your community who have suffered or are suffering at the hands of your government, because of their views or protest etc?

(y) Are you basically happy with the government of your country and the way its laws are administered?

3. More practical considerations

(a) Do you have easy access (in your home or neighbourhood – within quarter of a mile say) to an adequate, reliable supply of clean drinking water all year round?

(b) Do you have access to sufficient water to bathe in regularly?

(c) If your climate has hot seasons, do you have a source of cooling, such as fans, fridges, shade, etc?

(d) If your climate has cold seasons, do you have access to a source of heating in your home which you can afford to use as necessary?

(e) If insects are a problem in your locality, do you have effective protection, such as mosquito netting?

(f) If worms or insects are a local health problem, are there health schemes in your area which educate your community about the dangers and means of protection, and which offer good quality treatment to anyone affected?

(g) Is there a doctor, health worker, clinic or hospital open to anyone needing their services within five miles of your home?

(h) Is your diet varied and nutritious and sufficient at all times of the year to keep you and your community strong and healthy?

4. Relationships with other people, community, nation, etc

(Many points which might fall under this heading have already been considered.)

(a) Do you consider yourself to be a happy person?

'Would other members of your household or neighbourhood speak and think well of you?'

(b) Would other members of your household or neighbourhood speak and think well of you?

(c) Do you try to be honest, sincere and humble; and to listen to the opinions of other people?

(d) Do you try to work hard and take your share of community responsibilities, while remaining firm and not allowing others to push you around or demand too much of you?

(e) Have you or other members of your family been in any serious trouble during the last five years, with drug taking, dishonesty, violence, divorce, etc?

'Do you join in your community with artistic events such as dancing, singing or playing together?'

(f) Do you join in your community with artistic events such as music, dancing, singing, acting or playing together – this could be in family celebrations, religious celebrations, social events like parties, discos, fetes, festivals, etc?

(g) Does your household own a source of music or entertainment, such as a radio, record player, cassette player or television?

(h) Does any member of your household own and play an instrument or sing well and often?

(i) Can you think of any events which you are really looking forward to at the moment?

(j) Are you able to relax and to enjoy certain moments each day?

(k) How does the suicide rate of your community compare with that of your nation?

(l) How does the national human rights and suicide statistics compare with other nations in the world?

(m) Is there any item which you really very much need, but have not got?

(n) If so, is there any realistic chance of you obtaining this item in the next few years?

(o) If so are you working towards it?

(p) Would acquiring this item give you enduring satisfaction, or would other desires soon take its place?

'Would you rather be somewhere else?'

(q) Do you enjoy living as you do, or would you rather be somewhere else doing something else? Or would you even rather be someone else?

Scoring

1. Inner spiritual or aesthetic values. (a) Yes +2, Not really 0, Definitely not -1; **(b)** Yes +2, No +1; (c) A lot +2, A little +1, Not at all -1; **(d)** Certainly +2, Sometimes/some aspects +1, Rarely or never -1; **(e)** Very much +2, Some parts of the day +1, Some days 0, Now and then-1, Very rarely -2; **(f)** Yes +1, Somedays 0, Rarely or never -1; **(g)** Most of the time +1, Not much -1; **(h)** Yes, everyday +2, Sometimes +1, Rarely -1; **(i)** Yes every day +3, Yes every week +2, Yes several times a year +1, Quite close every day +2, Quite close every week +1, Quite close several times a year 0, No, not that kind of close -2; **(j)** (if live alone go to l) Yes, nearly all the time +3, Most of the time +2, Sometimes +1, Very rarely -1, Never -3; **(k)** Yes +3, Some of the time +2, Erratically +1, Rarely -1, Never -2; **(l)** Yes +3, Sometimes +2, Rarely -1, Very rarely -2; **(m)** Yes (or living with others) +1, No -2; **(n)** Yes +3, Sometimes +2, Very rarely -1; **(o)** Sadness and loneliness -2, Peace and happiness +2; **(p)** Every day +3, Every week +2, Several times a year +1, Very rarely -1, Never -2; (q) Yes every day +2, Yes every week +1, Several times a year 0, No -2; **(r)** Yes every day -3, Yes every week -2, Yes several times a year -1, Never 0; **(s)** Yes at least once a month +3, Yes several times a year +2, Very rarely 0, Not in the last five years -2; Never -3; **(t)** Very strong +3, Sometimes +1, No youngsters 0, Rarely -1, Very rare -2; **(u)** Good provision +2, Some provision +1, Very little provision -1, No provision -2; **(v)** Often -3, Sometimes -2, Very rarely 0, Never +1; **(w)** Very strong +4, Some strength +2, None -1.

2. Outer practical considerations. (a) Yes, sufficient +2, Usually sufficient +1, Rarely sufficient -2; **(b)** Yes very erratic -3, Yes never enough even for basic survival -4; (c) Yes, usually worried -3, Sometimes worried -3, Never worried +1; **(d)** Yes, well above +1, No – sufficient or less 0; **(e)** Yes, worried from excess -3, No worries from excess +1; **(f)** Good health +2, fair health +1, Some in poor health -1, **(g)** Yes, ill health would cause serious problems -2, No, financial problems would be few -1, There would be no financial problems from ill health +2; **(h)** Yes +2, Some +1, None -2; **(i)** Yes, we do feel worry -2, No, we never think of it 0, No, we know we would be OK +2; **(j)** Yes, all that could be was done +2, They did get some treatment +1, No one died 0, No treatment was available -2; **(k)** Yes, good support +2, Some support +1, Very little support -2; **(l)** Yes compares well +1, No, very poor in comparison -2; **(m1)** Comparable +2, Above average +1, Below average -2; **(m2)** Life expectancy well above world average +3, Above national average +1, About average 0, Below average -1, Well below average -3; **(n)** Stable +2, Quite mobile 0, Very mobile -2; **(o)** Most people accept them +2, Most people do not regard them as just -2; **(p)** Yes, grievances are dealt with quite quickly and fairly +2, Justice is there but takes a long time/costs a lot +1, There is very little justice available -2; **(q)** (The next

three as experienced by my immediate household and community:) Very restrictive -3, Some restriction -1, No restriction +1; **(r)** Yes +1, No 0; **(s)** No involvement or wisely +2, Unwisely 0, Very unjust -2; **(t)** Yes +1, No 0; **(u)** Wisely +2, Unwisely 0, Very unjustly -2; **(v)** Worry -2, Little worry +1, No worry -1; **(w)** Worry +1, No worry 0; (x) Yes -1, No 0; (y) Yes +1, Not really 0, Definitely not -1.

3. More practical considerations. (a) Yes +2, No -2; **(b)** Yes +2, No -1; **(c)** No hot seasons or yes +2, Sometimes +1, None -1; **(d)** No cold seasons or yes +2, Sometimes +1, None -1; **(e)** No problem or yes +1, No -1; **(f)** No problem or good health schemes +2, Few or poor health schemes +1, No health schemes -2; **(g)** Good within 5 miles +2, Poor within 5 miles 0, None within 5 miles -2; **(h)** Good diet +2, Fair diet +1, Poor diet -2.

4. Relationships. (a) Yes +2, Usually +1, Not really -1, No -2; **(b)** Yes +2, Probably +1, Not really -1, No -2; **(c)** Yes I try +3, Most of the time +1, Not really -1, No -3; **(d)** Yes +2, Most of the time +1, Not really -1, No -2; **(e)** Yes, serious trouble -3, Not really serious/not so recent -1, No +1; **(f)** Yes often +3, Sometimes +1, Now and then 0, Never -2; **(g)** Yes +2, No -1; **(h)** Yes +4, No -2; **(i)** Yes +2, Not really 0, No -2; **(j)** Yes +4, Usually +2, Rarely -2; **(k)** Below average +1, Average -1, Above average -3; **(l)** Below average +1, Average -1, Above average -3; **(m)** Yes -2, Not really 0, No +1; **(n)** Nothing needed or yes +1, Not really 0, No -1; **(o)** Nothing needed or yes, wholeheartedly +3, In a fashion +1, Not really -1; **(p)** Satisfied already or yes it would give lasting satisfaction +3, It would give some satisfaction +1, Other desires would replace it -1; **(q)** Enjoy being me and living as I do +3, Prefer to be in different circumstances +1, Prefer to be someone else -2.

Totals. 76 questions giving a possible total of 136 (not quite accurate as some questions are mutually exclusive, but it is close). Individual score divided by 136, with this total multiplied by 100, gives score index as a percentage.

Diana Chaudhuri, 66 Nowell Road, Barnes, London SW13 (tel 081 748 4821).

The Psychology of Happiness

Which kinds of people are likely to be happiest? And what are the best ways to become happier? Much of the research produces results which are unsurprising, but here are a few of the more interesting conclusions from a book called 'Psychology of Happiness' by Michael Argyle (Methuen, 1987) which gives references to over 400 studies:

'A good prediction of marital satisfaction was achieved from frequency of intercourse minus number of rows'

• In one study, a good prediction of marital satisfaction was achieved from frequency of intercourse minus number of rows.

• It has recently been discovered that lonely people do not have sufficiently intimate conversations with their friends and do not make enough self-disclosure.

• A recent British national survey found that only about 32 per cent would carry on at their present job if it were financially unnecessary.

• Examples of happy 'unemployed' people can be found among those middle and upper-class people of an earlier era who did not need to work, and did not do so. As far as we can see they were perfectly happy, in part perhaps because they had never heard of the Protestant ethic. Perhaps it was also because they had a fairly ordered way of life, with extensive duties and country pursuits.

• Anonymous saying: 'If you want to be happy for a few hours, get drunk. If you want to be happy for a few years, get a wife. If you want to happy for ever, get a garden.'

• An American study of 22 winners of large lotteries found no clear diference between their happiness and that of controls.

'Extroverts are happier: extroversion, (particularly its sociability component), can predict happiness 17 years later'

• Extroverts are happier: extraversion (particularly its sociability component) can predict happiness 17 years later.

• Subjects who were asked to inhibit their facial expression found electric shocks less painful (and had less physiological reaction to them).

• People in good moods tackle problems in a different way from those in neutral or sad moods. They move more quickly, adopt the simplest strategy, and accept the first solution they find. With one test problem, 75% of those who had seen a comedy film found the solution, compared with 13% who had seen no film.

• On sunny days people tip waitresses more.

• If people are met in a beautiful or comfortable room, they are liked more.

• The rate of contracting arthritis was much reduced among those with strong social support.

• Cynical people are more prone to heart disease.

• An experiment found that if householders were given a free sample of stationery at the door, and then telephoned with a request to help pass a message, they were more likely to do so, but the effect lasted only about 15 minutes.

• The evidence shows that to enhance happiness, one should get married, stay married, have children, keep up with relatives, have plenty of friends and keep on good terms with the neighbours.

• A treatment for depressed patients consisting of getting people to read positive self-statements at a number of points during the day has been found to be more effective than drug therapy and insight therapy; although the most successful treatments for depression have also included behavioural methods such as rewarding the pursuit of pleasant events with more therapy time, and social skills training.

Eccentrics are healthier

Adapted from the Examiner (USA) monitored for the Institute by Roger Knights; and from an article by Victoria McKee in the Times.

Not only do eccentrics live five to ten years longer than the norm, they are also, on average, healthier (visiting the doctor only once every eight years compared to about three times a year for the general public), happier and more intelligent than

the rest of the population. Dr David Weeks, author of 'Eccentrics: The Scientific Investigation' (published by Stirling University Press, 1988, £27-50), came to admire the sense of humour, creative imagination, and strong will which he discovered are common characteristics of the 1,100 eccentrics he interviewed – and he believes that these traits help keep them healthy. They have an over-riding curiosity that drives them on and makes them oblivious to the irritations and stresses of daily life that plague the rest of us.

'Sense of humour, creative imagination, and strong will are common characteristics of eccentrics'

'They don't try to keep up with the Joneses, they don't worry about conforming and they usually have a firm belief that they are right and the rest of the world is wrong,' Week says.

Eccentricity, he stresses, is not mental illness. In a sense it can act as a protection against more serious mental disorders, as the mild cowpox vaccine prevents a full-blown case of smallpox.

'I am already using what I've learned from my study of eccentrics in treating the patients referred to me for depression,' Weeks says, 'and I'm certainly getting better results than I was before. I tell them to loosen up – to use their sense of humour and their imagination. Neurotic patients are over-serious.'

• *Dr David Weeks, Jardine Clinic, Royal Edinburgh Hospital, Morningside Terrace, Edinburgh, EH10 5HF (tel 031 447 2011, ext 4614/4414).*

• *Dr Siegried Munser, Professor of Psychiatry, University of Vienna, has carried out a similar study.*

Sixty nine non-material needs

Margaret Chisman

Are human beings unique? Our species shares with the rest of the animal kingdom, to a greater or lesser extent, a whole list of physiological needs. Some of our non-material needs are very similar to those of higher social mammals, but we have developed them far more extensively. So if we can study these needs we might begin to get some idea of human-ness.

'We are "open-ended" creatures – and that is our glory'

The list below shows some of our non-material needs. It is not possible to make a complete list as we are not wholly definable. We are 'open-ended' creatures – and that is our glory.

The numbers do not represent any order of importance but are for reference only. There seem to be rough categories of personal needs, social and community and authority.

Personal

(1) Need to learn to speak and use language;
(2) Need to exercise reason;
(3) Need to search for truth (to research, ask questions, satisfy curiosity, to seek and solve problems);

(4) Need to explore, to take risks and return home;

(5) Need for boundaries;

(6) Need to search for meaning and purpose in life;

(7) Need to bring order out of chaos;

(8) Need to seek and to make patterns and to use our imagination;

(9) Need for beauty (to enjoy it in nature, art, music, poetry, the opposite sex);

(10) Need to develop our aptitudes and to create something;

(11) Need to feel at one with nature;

'Need to feel wholeness of being'

(12) Need to feel wholeness of being;

(13) Need to find ways of dealing with the darker side of one's nature;

(14) Need for catharsis of the emotions;

(15) Need for contrariness (to act differently from others, to take opposite sides, to feel unique);

(16) Need to be able to cope with uncertainty;

(17) Need for hope;

(18) Need to be able to make choices, to make decisions and to implement them;

(19) Need for autonomy (to resist influences, to strive for independence);

(20) Need to defend one's territory;

(21) Need to defend one's ideas;

(22) Need to feel at home on this planet;

(23) Need for transcendence of self;

Social and community

(24) Need for friendship;

(25) Need for physical and psychological 'stroking';

(26) Need for a loving, mated relationship;

(27) Need for family life;

(28) Need to have and to rear children;

(29) Need to share humour;

(30) Need to express joy in the company of others;

(31) Need to play games, physical and psychological;

(32) Need to relax, amuse oneself, seek diversions and entertainment;

(33) Need to share memories and nostalgia;

(34) Need to feel accepted;

(35) Need to feel pity and compassion and to display altruism;

(36) Need to be committed to ideas and concepts;

(37) Need to excel;

(38) Need for achievement (to overcome obstacles, to do something difficult as well and as quickly as possible);

(39) Need for recognition (to receive praise and commendation);

(40) Need to feel useful and needed, including to be able to find satisfying employment or self-employment;

'Need for a sense of community'

(41) Need for a sense of community;

(42) Need for social institutions which welcome us into the community;

(43) Need for festivals, ceremonies and celebrations;

(44) Need for rites of passage (to mark the phases of life, eg birth, puberty, adulthood, marriage, death, etc);

(45) Need for symbols and myths;

(46) Need for a vision that can inspire human idealism and heroic action;

(47) Need to practise exposition (to point, to demonstrate, to give information, explain, interpret, lecture);

'Need for a human-scale community. Need to feel human fellowship'

(48) Need for a human-scale community;

(49) Need to feel human fellowship;

(50) Need to have a moral code;

(51) Need for fairness and justice;

(52) Need to accept the call of duty;

Authority

(53) Need for dominance (to exercise authority, influence and control others);

(54) Need for a scapegoat;

(55) Need for aggression;

(56) Need to accept responsibility;

(57) Need for proselytisation (to convert others);

(58) Need for similance (to imitate or emulate others, to agree, to believe);

(59) Need for deference and respect (to admire and willingly follow a superior, to serve gladly);

(60) Need for forgiveness (absolution on repentance);

(61) Need for abasement (to comply and accept punishment, self-depreciation);

(62) Need to submit to government and the law;

(63) Need for prayer and meditation;

(64) Need for worship;

(65) Need for reverence and awe;

(66) Need to feel there is 'life' after death and that one will become nearer to God;

(67) Need for a redeemer (ie a bridge between humanity and God);

(68) Need for a reassuring, all-embracing, irrefutable explanation of everything;

(69) Need for mystery, mystical and 'magical' experiences.

In this categorisation there are grey areas; some needs fall into more than one section, and some are contradictory. This, in my opinion, does not invalidate them; the tension that this creates may be part of our growing process. Some needs may be, in fact, holding back our growth into fuller human-ness, However, I feel that we must include as many actual needs as possible in our endeavour to answer the question 'Are human beings unique?'

Some human concepts and activities seem to be a complex of simpler needs. For example, religion could include numbers 3, 5, 6, 7, 8, 9, 11, 12, 13, 14, 16, 17, 22, 23, 30, 34, 35, 36, 42, 43, 44, 45, 46, 50, 51, 52, 56, 59, 60, 63, 64, 65, 66, 67, 68 and 69. Besides applying the idea of different groupings of needs to concepts, it could apply to the requirements of different professions. Insight gained by thinking about these needs will be helpful to all of us. We will begin to understand a little of what it means to be human.

I shall be happy to engage in discussion or correspondence on these matters. In addition, if you have any more needs to add to this list I shall be glad to receive them.

Margaret Chisman, The Bungalow, near the Station, Tring, Herts, HP23 5QX (tel 044282 3281).

JILIAD for measuring happiness

Margaret Chisman

I was asked to give a talk on happiness and somewhat rashly agreed. However, the more I thought about it, the harder it became. Obviously, it is almost impossible for happiness to coexist with acute bodily discomfort – hunger, thirst, cold, pain and so on. However, the absence of these does not automatically produce happiness.

Contentment most probably consists of the satisfaction of physiological and a modest amount of psychological needs. It began to appear to me that happiness is not a static state; that it had to do with struggling, learning, developing and achieving; that it was necessary to have a goal that was neither too easy nor too difficult to attain; and that when this goal was reached, another one had to be sought.

I tried to find a unit of happiness and decided it had six faces. Each night I asked myself:

> 'Have I today: 1. experienced any Joy? 2. had any Insights? 3. Learned anything new?'

Have I today
(1) Experienced any **J**oy?
(2) Had any **I**nsights?
(3) **L**earned anything new?
(4) Made any **I**mprovements in my personality or actions?
(5) Spotted in myself any **A**nti type thinking – such as 'I couldn't do that, it's much too hard' – and managed to reformulate it positively – for example 'I know it's very hard but I'll have a good go at it'?
(6) Overcome any **D**ifficulties?

These letters (in bold type) formed a word JILIAD, so that is what I decided to call my unit. For each 'face', if I had experienced it that day, I awarded myself one sixth of a unit.

Why not, each night, see what your score is? Or you may have an entirely different approach. Please let me know.

Margaret Chisman, The Bungalow, near the Station, Tring, Herts, HP23 5QX (tel 044282 3281).

Grading experiences

Margaret Chisman

I find it helpful sometimes to grade and rate experiences. Here are some light-hearted scales and suggested units:

A measurement of feelings of guilt – a *Peccavo*:
(1) A very occasional feeling of guilt, easily suppressible;
(2) A very occasional feeling of guilt, needing an effort to divert yourself;
(3) More frequent feelings but still fairly easy to suppress;
(4). More frequent and not so easily suppressed;
(5) Very frequent feelings but still fairly easy to suppress;
(6) Very frequent but not easily suppressed;
(7) Guilt feelings so overwhelming that normal life not possible while they last.

Similar scales apply to most of the following:

- A measurement of rage or anger: an *Asper;*
- Upset due to change: a *Toffler;*
- A desire to see others suffer: a *Sado;*
- A measurement of elation: a *Eumel;*
- A scale of audience response: a *(Billy) Graham;*
- A scale for measuring pain: an *Odyne;*
- A scale for measuring level of desire for social change: a *Scargill;*
- A measurement of depression: a *Cark;*
- A measurement of dirt: a *Copra;*
- A unit of uncertainty: a *Heisenberg;*
- A unit of piety: a *Kierkegaard;*
- A unit of the amount of controversy someone arouses: a *(George) Steiner;*
- A unit of manipulation: a *(Machia)Velli;*
- A beauty scale for women: a *Milli-Helen* (enough to launch one ship);
- A unit of ambivalence: a *Janus.*

Margaret Chisman, The Bungalow, near the Station, Tring, Herts, HP23 5QX (tel 044282 3281).

Prescribing happiness

Dr Michael Fordyce, a psychologist at Edison Community College, has produced a PC computer program with automatic scoring and interpretation for therapists and counsellors to use with clients in assessing their happiness. The program also individually tailors a prescription for each client of steps that they could take to improve their long-term happiness, based on deficiencies revealed in the tests.

A decade of research has led Dr Fordyce to conclude that 'the nature of happiness is far more stable, understandable and universal than most people have ever suspected.' Most happiness tests simply measure how happy someone feels. His test goes further, in two ways, firstly by also measuring the factors that research shows contribute to long-term happiness, such as the person's personality and attitudes; and secondly, by being designed for use with a self-study course for making oneself happier.

> 'To become happier: get better organised and plan things out; develop positive, optimistic thinking; develop an outgoing social personality; and make becoming happier a higher priority'

Dr Fordyce's results suggest that among the most productive steps to take so as to become happier are: to spend more time socialising; to get better organised and to plan things out; to have lower expectations and aspirations; to develop positive, optimistic thinking; to develop an outgoing social personality; and to make becoming happier a higher priority.

Dr Fordyce envisages a day when happiness and well-being measures will become 'almost indispensable adjuncts to any investigation into human nature and the human condition.'

Dr Michael Fordyce, a psychologist at Edison Community College, 8099 College Parkway, Fort Myers, Florida 33906-6210, USA (tel 813 482 1660).

Family well-being

K.D. Kettig and M.M. Bubolz (see Note below) produced the following set of questions to help tabulate 'the perceived quality of family life'.

How would you feel about your family life if you considered only:

- The love and affection you experience?
- The closeness and sense of belonging you feel?
- The amount of respect you receive?
- Your sexual relationship?
- How comfortable it feels to be at home?
- The way household work is divided or accomplished?
- The mutual helpfulness of family members?

'How would you feel about your family life if you considered only how openly you can express feelings?'

- How openly and honestly you can express feelings?
- The kind of communication you have?
- The way decisions are made?
- The time you spend with your husband or wife?
- The things you do together?
- The amount of time the family spends together?
- The time you spend with your children?
- The material goods it enables you to enjoy?
- The way money is used?
- The amount of money available to your personal use?
- Your husband/wife?
- Your children?
- The friends it enables you to enjoy?
- Your marriage?

Note: See Rettig, K.D. and Bubolz, M.M.: 1982, 'Perceptual Indicators of Family Well-Being', Social Indicators Research 12, pp 417-438 (Kluwer Academic Publishers, Spuiboulevard 50, PO Box 17, 3300 AA, Dordrecht, Holland, tel 078 334206).

Neighbourhood quality of life

There has been a fair amount of research on this aspect of neighbourhood quality of life, but most of the Indexes resulting would not be so relevant in the third world. Darlene Russ-Eft (see Note) has developed a set of components that go to make up neighbourhood quality of life in the San Francisco Bay area, as identified by inhabitants. The components are:

- Natural beauty and natural phenomena;
- Air and noise quality;
- Population and traffic density;
- Landscape character and maintenance;
- Architectural character and maintenance;
- Housing costs and property values;
- Employment and job opportunities;
- Business and commercial facilities and services;
- Educational facilities and services;
- Recreational, cultural and social service facilities and programmes;
- Public and civic services;
- Citizen participation in local decision-making;

- Socialising and interpersonal relationships;
- Mutual assistance;
- Involvement in neigbourhood or community improvement;
- Ethnic, racial, economic and social character;
- Freedom from criminal harm.

These components were discovered by asking the inhabitants questions such as 'think about some change or development in your neighbouhood that makes your life worse' or 'think of the last time when you felt especially happy because of something that happened in your neighbourhood.'

The same painstaking research method (finding out the main factors by getting inhabitants to report what specific events in the neighbourhood had effected their quality of life) could be used to build up quality of life components for neighbourhoods elsewhere in the world, but it is hard to see how this could then result in any sort of comparable Index.

Note: See Russ-Eft, D.: 1979, 'Identifying Components Comprising Neighbourhood Quality of Life', Social Indicators Research 6, pp. 349-372 (see above for address).

Quality of life in cities

The City category in the Institute's quality of life competition was won by the Glasgow Quality of Life Group.

'Studies on quality of life ranked Edinburgh and Exeter top'

Their studies on the quality of life in UK cities ranked Edinburgh top and Birmingham bottom (London came 34th); and another on intermediate cities with populations of between 190,000 and 250,000 ranked Exeter top and Sandwell bottom. This latter survey took 19 'dimensions of quality of life' and used the results of a national opinion survey to assign these dimensions 'weightings' – thus compiling an index of 'perceived importance to the average person.' The most important characteristics of quality of life from the general public's point of view turned out to be (in order) low levels of violent and non-violent crime, good health service provision, low levels of pollution, low cost of living, good shopping facilities and easy access to areas of scenic quality.

Subsequent research has updated the survey as applied to 145 local authorities across Britain. Perth and Kinross District rated top.

Dr Robert Rogerson, Co-ordinator, Quality of Life Group, Department of Geography, the University of Strathclyde, Glasgow G1 1XN (tel 041 3552 4400 ext 3037).

An Index of Oppression
Fred Allen

It is easier to achieve consensus in defining the not-good than the good; in the same way, I think it may be easier to create an Oppression Index rather than an International Quality of Life Index. Here are a few of the sorts of issues an Oppression Index could consider:

(1) *A Vandalism Index* – simply the value of goods destroyed in every ten square miles;

(2) *An Injustice Index* – which could be a cross put on the ballot paper at each election, indicating that the voter has an unresolved grievance of a specified type;

(3) *A Stress Index* – being the weight of stress/anxiety drugs prescribed each year;

(4) *An Alcohol Index* – a look at how much booze individuals are taking and what they do on the way home. Quite a small sample would do;

(5) *A Job Satisfaction Index* – which could be an entry on the tax form to record: to what extent are you happy in your work, it is too stressful, it it boring, would you prefer a different job?

Taken together, these Indexes might make a modest Quality of Life Index. For instance, for the age group 12 to 25, absence of vandalism is probably the best indicator of personal well-being. If I had to choose a single parameter, I would choose the feeling of irremediable injustice, as I suspect the score would horrify any lawyer who regards civil law as in any way adequate.

Fred Allen, 13 Shelly Row, Cambridge CB3 OBP.

Quality of life – its underlying philosophy

Storrs McCall of the Department of Philosophy at Canada's McGill University, in a 1975 article in Social Indicators Research (see Note below), argues that the best way of approaching quality of life measurement is to measure the extent to which people's 'happiness requirements' are met – ie those requirements which are a necessary (although not sufficient) condition of anyone's happiness – those 'without which no member of the human race can be happy.'

'Measure the extent to which people's "happiness requirements" are met'

Such is the conclusion, but it is the philosophical meanderings leading up to this conclusion which make this approach stimulating. In summary:

Interest in Quality of Life represents a nostalgia for something lost – a feeling that modern industrial society, despite more affluence, communication and leisure, has not made 'any significant progress in improving man's lot.' It is, however, not clear what social scientists mean by quality of life. Is it something that pertains primarily to groups of people or to individuals and thence to groups and societies 'by a process of summation'? Is it a culture-bound concept, 'requiring that each segment of human society seek out for itself an understanding of where it conceives life's quality to lie?'

Can Quality of Life be defined in terms of the general or average happiness? McCall thinks not. Imagine a region of unutterable misery and deprivation, such as Bangladesh after a flood. Imagine people moving in who are sustained by intense religious convictions and live fulfilled existences. But, argues McCall, however many happy and fulfilled religious people move in, the region remains a low quality of life area. Quality of life consists rather in the obtaining of the necessary conditions for happiness in a given region. These are general happiness requirements which do not vary from person to person, as opposed to the idiosyncratic happiness requirements which do. Consequently, from McCall's quality of life perspective,

it is no use asking individuals the typical research question 'taken altogether ... would you say you are very happy, pretty happy or not too happy?'

Say you were investigating quality of life at work, the aspect to measure would be the objective working conditions – with subjective job satisfaction responses to questions being merely used to indicate which working conditions are important in determining quality of life at work.

One advantage of McCall's approach, is that his general happiness requirements are the same in all cultures. The greater the percentage of people in a region for which these general happiness requirements are satisfied, the higher the level of quality of life.

But are these general happiness requirements provided for by the satisfaction of human needs, or by the satisfaction of human wants and desires? Wanting is a psychological state, needing is not. Wants tend to escalate with rising expectations, needs do not. Quality of Life measuring need-satisfaction is therefore recommended, as being more objective and transcultural.

'Asserting that quality of life in Burma must be low because they do not have bathrooms or two-car garages'

Maslow has drawn up a list of needs which he claims holds for all humans at all times and all places (Maslow's hierarchy rises from basic physiological needs, to safety, belongingness, esteem and self-actualisation needs). Maslow's needs have been considered too abstract and general to be of much use in assessing quality of life. Certainly everyone needs shelter, for instance, but merely counting shelters will not reveal much about quality of life. McCall believes that Maslow's approach could be extended satisfactorily without being culture bound. For instance, does a shelter have to have a toilet? 'Yes, for health reasons,' he answers, 'unless some equally convenient sanitary facility is available ... the needs hierarchy possesses a sufficient degree of generality that we shall not be forced into culture-bound absurdities like asserting that quality of life in Burma must be low because they do not have bathrooms or two-car garages.'

Injustice, McCall insists, is incompatible with high quality of life. In a slave society, for instance, love, esteem and self-actualisation needs are all deprived. Societies with high quality of life will in general exhibit juster and more equitable distribution patterns.

- *Note: See McCall, S.: 1975, 'Quality of Life', Social Indicators Research 2, pp 229-248 (address above).*
- *Storrs McCall, Dept. of Philosophy, McGill University, 855 Sherbrooke St West, Montreal, Quebec, Canada, H3A 2T7 (tel 514 398 6060).*

The International Index of Social Progress

The International Index of Social Progress (ISP) and the Weighted Index of Social Progress (WISP) are well-established tools developed since 1974 by Richard Estes of the University of Pennsylvania's social work faculty. They measure economic development, social and political conditions, and the ability of nations to produce welfare services for their citizens. They have become 'a way of assessing shifts over time in the capacity of nations to provide more adequately for the basic social and material needs of their populations.' All nations with over one million inhabitants are included – 98% of the world's population.

'Britain came 13th. The top ten were: Denmark, followed by Norway, Sweden, Austria, Netherlands, France, West Germany, Italy, Finland and Belgium'

In the latest survey, covering 1970 to 1990 (see Note 1 below), Britain came 13th on the ISP and 12th on the WISP out of 124 nations. The top ten in 1990 were: Denmark, followed by Norway, Sweden, Austria, Netherlands, France, West Germany, Italy, Finland and Belgium. The worst ten, ranked from the least desirable upwards, were: Ethiopia, Mozambique, Angola, Chad, Guinea, Somali, Sierra Leone, Niger, Afghanistan and Mali. The greatest lowering of social progress between 1970 and 1990 was observed within the (then) Soviet bloc, with an average 6% loss of ISP – particularly within the USSR itself (-19 per cent), 'for which sharp Index declines were observed on the Defence Effort, Political Participation, Economic, Education and Women Status sub-indexes.'

Richard Estes describes the background to a previous ISP survey in his books 'The Social Progress of Nations' (1984) and 'Trends in World Social Development' (1988) – see Note 2 below. Estes reflects that the majority of previous cross-national comparative efforts to measure quality of life or social well-being have been impaired by: serious conceptual problems, missing or unavailable data, a worldwide shortage of suitable researchers and statisticians, political tensions and governments' concerns about how the resulting data will be used.

Estes looks at previous work in some detail:

Work by the United Nations on quality of life or 'levels of living' has been biased towards a 'basic needs' approach – the extent to which the most fundamental needs of people are met, irrespective of other factors. The Organisation for Economic Cooperation and Development (the OECD, made up of 24 of the world's richest nations) has for more than a decade been planning to measure well-being within its nations, but has not so far got much beyond establishing the list of relevant social concerns. Morris D. Morris and colleagues at the Overseas Development Council in Washington have developed a Physical Quality of Life Index (PQLI) measuring infant mortality, expectation of life at birth and rates of adult literacy, but these mainly reflect only the provision of health and educational services. Studies on subjective feelings of human well-being have nearly all been on Western subjects. Estes posits the 'relative non-transferability (that is, non-equivalence) of basic psychological concepts from one culture to another' and that the interpretation of 'happiness' or 'satisfaction with life' differs among people living in entirely different societies.

The newly created 'Human Development Index' formulated by the United Nations Development Programme (UNDP), according to Estes, reflects many of the same limitations as earlier efforts: the number of factors included in

the index is too limited given the intent of the index (ie like the Physical Quality of Life Index, the Human Development Index contains only three items) and continues to place more emphasis on economic rather than *social* development.

Richard Estes' own approach in developing his Index of Social Progress was to use available data from a variety of sources to measure and aggregate 46 different factors for each nation:

- School enrolment ratio, first level;
- Per cent grade 1 enrolment completing primary school;
- School enrolment ratio, second level;
- School enrolment ratio, third level;
- Per cent adult illiteracy;
- Per cent GNP in education;
- Rate infant mortality per 1,000 liveborn;
- Population in thousands per physician;
- Life expectancy at 1 year;
- Under 5 years child mortality rates;
- Per capita daily calorie supply as % of requirement;
- Per cent children immunised at age one, DPT;
- Per cent children immunised at age one, Measles;
- Female life expectation at birth;
- Female adult literacy rate;
- Per cent married women using contraception;
- Maternal mortality rate per 100,000 live born;
- Female primary school enrolment as per cent of males;
- Female secondary school enrolment as per cent of males;
- Military expenditures as per cent of GNP;
- Per capita GNP in dollars;
- GNP per capita annual growth rate;
- Real GDP per head;
- Average annual rate of inflation;
- Per capita food production index;
- External public debt as per cent of GNP;
- Total population;
- Crude birth rate per 1,000 population;
- Crude death rate per 1,000 population;
- Rate of population increase;
- Per cent of population under 15 years;
- Per cent of population over 60 years;
- Per cent arable land mass;
- Natural disaster vulnerability index;
- Average annual deaths from natural disasters per million population;
- Violation of political rights index;
- Violations of civil liberties index;
- Composite human suffering index;

'Largest per cent sharing same mother tongue'

- Largest per cent sharing same mother tongue;
- Largest per cent sharing same basic religious belief;
- Largest per cent sharing same or similar racial/ethnic origins;
- Years since first law – old age, invalidity, death;
- Years since first law – sickness and maternity;
- Years since first law – work injury;
- Years since first law – unemployment;
- Years since first law – family allowances.

Each of the above factors is given a plus or minus sign, depending on whether more or less of it contributes towards or diminishes social progress. Estes used the Universal Declaration of Human Rights to help identify the types of humanistically orientated factors to be included in his Index of Social Progress.

'The world's socially leading nations are comparatively small in average population size'

Estes concludes that the world's socially leading nations are comparatively small in average population size (18.4 million persons), culturally homogenous, have long histories of political independence, high levels of economic cooperation and of political stability, and commit relatively few of their national resources to defence expenditure.

Estes' research survey results were rather ridiculed in the British press when first published in 1986. Thus a Times leader (17/9/86) asserted: 'Professor Estes is clearly in need of something better to do. Can anyone plumb the quality of life without taking into account the weather, the food and the wine? Can anyone really assess, in mathematical or any other terms, the value of living in Britain? The very faults which lose this country points in any theoretical league of happiness reflect a sense of freedom which Britain still manages to instil in its inhabitants.' And the Daily Mail (20/9/86), in a report on his placing of Denmark at the top of the list, commented that the Danes 'consume more tranquillisers than anyone else on earth, and have the worst psychiatric problems. Violent crime, drug abuse and alcoholism have all doubled in the last ten years. The welfare system is mainly needed to help those who crack up under the strain of paying for it.'

• *Note 1: Detailed in the Estes, R: 1992, 'At the Crossroads: Dilemmas in Social Development Toward the Year 2000 and Beyond' (New York and London: Praedger Publishers). Shorter versions are available from the author at University of Pennsylvania, School of Social Work, 3701 Locust Walk, Philadelphia 19104-6214, USA (tel 215 898 5531).*

• *Note 2: Estes, R: 1988, 'Trends in World Social Development', Praeger Publishers, New York, ISBN 0 275 92613 3 ($39-95 from Praeger Publishers, 88 Post Road West, PO Box 5007, Westport, CT 06881, USA); and Estes, R: 1984, 'The Social Progress of Nations' ($24-95 also from Praeger Publishers, New York, ISBN 0 245 91151 9).*

• *Note 3: See also Estes, R: 1986, 'Towards a Quality of Life Index', in 'The Third World: definition, theory and concept', edited by Norwine and Gonzalez, (London: George Allen and Unwin). And Estes, R: 1990, 'Development Under Different Political and Economic Systems', Social Development Issues 13 (1): 5-19.*

International Human Suffering Index

This Index won the prize in the International section of the Institute's Quality of Life competition.

'We released the International Human Suffering Index in 1987,' writes Kathleen Mazzocco of the Population Crisis Committee in Washinton DC, 'and the response from the public has been overwhelming. We estimate a US audience of 100 million to date.'

The Index is presented as a colour poster, with all the countries ranked in order, and showing the close linkage between high suffering and high rates of population increase.

Of the countries classified as part of the 'extreme human suffering' category, 24 are in Africa, 6 are in Asia, and none is in the Western hemisphere. Topping the list is Mozambique (Index rating of 95), followed by Angola, Afghanistan, Chad, Mali, Ghana, Somalia and Niger. The least suffering country is Switzerland (Index rating of 4), followed by West Germany, Luxembourg, Netherlands, and the United States, with the UK 12 places worse than Switzerland with an Index rating of 12.

'The close linkage between high suffering and high rates of population increase'

The trouble with this Index, as with other such attempts, is that it relies on statistics from the World Bank, UN and and other readily available sources, with no attempt at involving citizens in drawing up subjective measures of (dis)satisfaction. The indices conglomerated in the Index are:
• Per capita GNP;
• Average annual rate of inflation;
• Average annual growth of labour force;
• Average annual growth of urban population;
• Infant mortality rate per 1000 live births;
• Daily per capita calorie supply as percent of requirement;
• Per cent of population with access to clean drinking water;
• Energy consumption per capita;
• Adult literacy rate;
• Personal freedom.

'The index also takes note of whether citizens are free from government terror, free to travel, own property, marry and able to vote for more than one political party'

The source for this last personal freedom index is Freedom House which considers a country free if it has freedom of the press and freedom to organise, particularly to organise political parties, trade unions, businesses, religious societies and churches. The index also takes note of whether citizens are free from government terror, free to travel, own property, marry and able to vote for more than one political party.

Additional measures considered for the Suffering Index included data on pollution, unemployment, war, etc but all had some weakness, duplicated measures already chosen or did not cover enough countries.

The authors, Sharon Camp and Joseph Speidel, conclude: 'The Human Suffering Index vividly shows that the majority of the world's people must endure lives of poverty and human misery ... Development efforts such as family planning, health and education could immediately ease the suffering of millions.'

Kathleen Mazzocco, public affairs officer, Population Crisis Committee, 1120 19th Street, N.W, Suite 550, Washington, DC 20036, USA (tel 202 659 1833).

Chapter fifteen
SCIENCE, TECHNOLOGY AND ENERGY

True conservatism

Neil Postman

If anyone should ask: What improves the human spirit? What improves the quality of life? Americans are apt to offer a simple formulation: That which is new is better, that which is newest is best.

The cure for such a stupid philosophy is conservatism. A capitalist cannot afford the pleasure of conservatism, and of necessity regards tradition as an obstacle to be overcome. How the idea originated that capitalists are conservative is something of a mystery to me.

> 'The aim of the genuine conservative in a technological age is to control the fury of technology, to make it behave itself, to insist that it accommodate itself to the will and temperament of the people'

A true conservative, like myself, knows that technology always fosters radical social change. The aim of the genuine conservative in a technological age is to control the fury of technology, to make it behave itself, to insist that it accommodate itself to the will and temperament of the people.

From the book 'Conscientious Objections' by Neil Postman (Alfred Knopf & Co, 1988) reprinted in Utne Reader (Lens Publishing Co, 1624 Harmon Place, Suite 330, MN 55403, USA, tel 612 338 5040. Subs. $28).

Machines on a moral spectrum

Professor M.W. Thring

Extracts from a lecture 'Towards a Creative Society: the Philosophy of Technology', published in the Journal of the Royal Society of Arts. Professor Thring, prior to his retirement, was head of the Department of Mechanical Engineering, Queen Mary College, University of London.

We can define the moral responsibility of the engineer, technologist and applied scientist as that of serving human happiness, just as a doctor has the moral responsibility of serving human health. There should be a Hippocratic Oath for engineers to the effect that they will, as far as they are able, dedicate their work towards the increase of human happiness.

It is useful to put the machines that the engineer can develop on a moral spectrum based on the extent to which the machines help or hinder human beings to realise their potentialities and thus to lead satisfactory lives:

The Moral Spectrum of Machines

- Machines to help invalids, blind and crippled people
- Machines for medicine and surgery
- Educational machines and machines used for arts and crafts

- Machines to save labour, drudgery and danger
- Transport and communication machines
- Computers

- Prime movers
- Power conversion machines
- Cosmetic machines

- Polluting and noisy machines
- Machines for destroying or torturing people

> 'Machines primarily developed to kill, maim or hurt human beings must come at the bottom of the scale'

Machines primarily developed to kill, maim or hurt human beings, and the by-product effects of machines which harm human health or happiness by noise or chemical effluents, must come at the bottom of the scale. Equally it is clear that machines which restore some of their lost possibilities to invalids, blind or crippled people, such as automatic machines for reading aloud to the blind direct from the printed word, together with all machines to help the doctors and surgeons in their work on human health, and machines for education, should come at the top of the scale.

The use of technology to improve the destructive power of an army, typified by the first use of nuclear fission, is undoubtedly a misuse of the skill and brain of the technologist, just as clearly as would be the use of doctors to produce improved means of torturing and killing human beings. The Hippocratic Oath of the engineer and technologist must be to try always to use his skill to develop the machines higher up this moral spectrum rather than those lower down it.

> ### 'Never again should graduates of, for example, the Technische Hochschule in Germany be willing to design and build a murder factory for millions of human beings'

Mr A.Kennaway, M.I.MECH.E, commented at this lecture: Scientists must not allow themselves to be willing tools of evil policies. Never again should graduates of, for example, the Technische Hochschule in Germany be willing to design and build a murder factory for millions of human beings.
Professor M.W. Thring, Bell Farm, Brundish, Suffolk IP13 8BL (tel 037 9384 296).

Hippocratic Oath for Scientists

Nicholas Albery

An Oath for machine designers and makers should have been in place centuries ago, likewise a ban on the development of new weapons. Our religious leaders have betrayed us. The Pope most worthy of respect is Pope Innocent II, who, in the Lateran Council of 1139, forbade under anathema the use of the crossbow, at least against Catholics and other Christians. The crossbow was the new ultimate weapon of the 12th century, piercing the armour of the nobility, yet wielded by non-nobles. The Pope's edict seems to have had some effect too – King Louis VII of France, otherwise known as Louis The Pious, is recorded as having had a troop of crossbowmen before the council but not afterwards, and they were only reintroduced in France after England's Richard I had popularised their use against infidels in the Crusades.

> ### 'Pope Innocent II, in the Lateran Council of 1139, forbade under anathema the use of the crossbow'

Even today, now that most weapons are dangerous boomerangs, it is perhaps not too late to make a stand against the military and technological evils that threaten to engulf us. Professor Weeramantry in Australia has made clear that a number of interacting initiatives are needed: technology assessment boards, future scanning agencies in government departments, committees for alternative futures, centres for the study of scientific policy, committees of the bar, legislative and judicial restructuring, international covenants and treaties, court-imposed moratoriums, referenda, and restructuring education and law school curricula.

As part of this wider approach, an Institute for Social Inventions' working party has drawn up a new and shorter version of the Hippocratic Oath (see below), aimed not at doctors but at engineers, scientists (pure and applied) and the executives who employ them. As Professor Weeranmantry remarks: 'the idea of an ethic for science goes all the way back

---

Hippocratic Oath for Scientists, Engineers and Executives

I vow to practise my profession with conscience and dignity;

I will strive to apply my skills only with the utmost respect for the well-being of humanity, the earth and all its species;

I will not permit considerations of nationality, politics, prejudice or material advancement to intervene between my work and this duty to present and future generations;

I make this Oath solemnly, freely and upon my honour.

Signed _____ **Date** _____

to Francis Bacon. In Bacon's work, New Atlantis, scientists took an oath for concealing inventions and experiences which they thought fit to keep secret.' An Institute working party member, Peter Lewis, adds that history provides a notable precedent of ethical behaviour by a scientist. This is the example of Leonardo da Vinci, who (despite offering many of his military inventions to the Duke of Milan and other patrons) suppressed his work on submarines 'on account of the evil nature of men, who would practise assassination at the bottom of the sea.' By Leonardo's action the world was spared submarine warfare for 300 years. Peter Lewis acknowledges that scientists have tended in the main to see their work as an amoral and dispassionate search for truth, but considers that in recent decades a growing number have begun to ask themselves if the scientific method cannot be amended so as to incorporate an ethical component. 'Anyone who is bound by an oath such as the one we propose,' writes Lewis, 'has a powerful curb placed on their behaviour. If I break the rules, even if I have concealed my transgression from other people, *I will know what I am*, and I cannot escape from that knowledge.'

> ### 'Leonardo da Vinci suppressed his work on submarines "on account of the evil nature of men, who would practise assassination at the bottom of the ses" '

(Dr John Hart and others have proposed an amended second clause of the Oath which would then read:

'I will strive to apply my skills with the utmost respect for the well-being of humanity and *the integrity of the natural world*.' Dr Hart argues that the clause about respect for *all* the earth's species would present a difficulty for biologists and others.)

> ### 'The long term aim is that the Oath should become part of the graduation ceremony for students'

There are over a hundred eminent signatories of this Oath, including 18 Nobel Laureates – the launch signatories were Professor Maurice Wilkins CBE FRS, Abdus Salam FRS, and Sir John Kendrew, who is President of the International Council of Scientific Unions. Also lending their support are the vice-chancellors or equivalents of many prestigious universities around the world. The long term aim is that the Oath should become part of the graduation ceremony for students – there is not much hope of 'converting' the 50% of scientists already working for defence industries, who have families and mortgages to worry about, but it may be more possible to influence students in their choice of work, at the outset of their careers.

The response has been encouraging, even from other continents. For instance, most of the key staff at Auckland University have signed and they have ordered hundreds of copies for their students. The Pugwash Conference in London had a working party on this theme and Unesco are showing signs of interest.

Professor Meredith Thring, chairman of the Institute's working party and author of 'Man, Machines and Tomorrow', writes: 'No one wants pointless restriction, but too many scientific developments are posing moral problems by being big enough to involve survival or destruction. Not to face up

to defining morality now will put mankind on a level with the concentration camp officials of the Second World War: "It was not my job to think. I was only obeying orders".' The wording of the Oath is of course very general and is applicable to thoughful professionals of all sorts. The expectation is that it will provide an ethical framework for the more detailed Codes of Practice within each discipline.

Eventually, such an Oath may help reduce the social standing of technologists working in armaments and similar dubious areas – and, once aroused, there are few forces on earth more powerful than social pressure.

Probably the most important issue of them all, as far as gaining acceptance for the Oath goes, is what happens to scientists or engineers with ethics, if they obey the Oath, make a stand and lose their jobs. If the Oath became part of a profession's graduation ceremony, there might be some pressure the professional association could bring to bear on the employer. Robert Jungk and his colleagues in Austria have looked at this problem, and their initial suggestion was that any scientists leaving their research jobs for ethical reasons could receive 'conscience money' through an insurance scheme; but this turned out to be too costly. What they developed instead was a fund which people could pay into, that would finance alternative scientific institutes, to provide jobs for 'refugee' scientists. There are now four or five such institutes on the continent.

● *Copies of the Oath are available on cream card for 50p in stamps (single copy) or £7 for 100 from: The Institute for Social Inventions, 20 Heber Road, London NW2 6AA (tel 081 208 2853; fax 081 452 6434).*

● *In the States, parchment copies of the Oath are available from the American Engineers for Social Responsibility, PO Box 2785, Washington DC, 20013-2785, USA.*

● *Also available is 'The Book of Oaths' a booklet describing most of the known ethical codes for scientists, £3·95 incl. p&p from the Institute.*

● *See also Professor C.G. Weeramantry's book 'The Slumbering Sentinel', Penguin, 1983.*

● *Re the pope and the crossbow, see 'Masters, Princes and Merchants', by John W. Baldwin, Princeton, 1970, Vol 1, page 223.*

A graduate pledge of social and environmental responsibility

The following student graduate pledge campaign has been in contact with the Institute in connection with the latter's Hippocratic Oath for Scientists.

A voluntary student pledge of social and environmental responsibility, begun at Humboldt State University in Arcata, California, in 1987, has been incorporated at 18 graduation exercises, including those at Stanford University and the Massachusetts Institute of Technology.

The 20 word pledge states simply:

'I pledge to investigate thoroughly and take into account the social and environmental consequences of any job opportunity I consider.'

Nelson, one of the pledge's proponents, says that the pledge lets students 'make a commitment to themselves' about what values they do and don't want to promote.

'The pledge is inviting because it's not too dogmatic. Every student can decide for himself or herself what is required to satisfy the pledge.'

The pledge 'makes students think,' says Matt Nicodemus, co-author of the original pledge at Humboldt State. 'It lets students think not only about what job they don't want but also what kind of job they do want. It's a plan for social change.'

Nicodemus says he disagrees with critics who dismiss it as a meaningless symbolic gesture. If enough campuses around the world embrace the pledge and incorporate it in their graduation exercises, 'we can have some very material consequences on the world.'

Matt Nicodemus, Graduation Press Alliance, Box 4439, Arcata, CA 9521, USA (tel 707 826 7033).

UN Declaration of Scientific Responsibility in Relation to Nuclear Weaponry

Professor Weeramantry writes: 'I have worked out a declaration for adoption by the General Assembly of the UN in relation to the social obligations of scientists who are engaged on the making of nuclear weapons. I have sent it to every Mission at the UN and received a variety of replies. This is part of my work, 'Nuclear Weapons and Scientific Responsibility', published in the US by Longwoods Publishers of New Hampshire.'

The text of the Proposed United Nations Declaration of Scientific Responsibility in Relation to Nuclear Weaponry:

Preamble

THE GENERAL ASSEMBLY,

Recognising that in an age dominated by science and technology, it is essential that science and technology should be devoted to the service of mankind

Gravely concerned that the development and production of nuclear weapons and the nuclear arms race are endangering the future of mankind and indeed of life on this planet

Conscious that the most recent and meticulous scientific inquiries have established the probability of a nuclear winter with disastrous consequences to mankind and our planet in the event of a nuclear confrontation

Realising that the nuclear arms race would be impossible to sustain without the active cooperation of scientists and technologists

Taking account of the fact that the general principles of international law as contained in

(a) International custom

(b) The general principles of law as recognised by civilised nations

(c) Judicial decisions and the teachings of jurists

(d) International Covenants

place beyond doubt the illegality of the use of nuclear weaponry, having regard to its violation of the principles of proportionality, discrimination, aggravation of pain and suffering, nullification of a return to peace and inviolability of neutral states

'The use of nuclear weaponry would undoubtedly result in ecocide and genocide'

Aware that the use of nuclear weaponry would undoubtedly result in ecocide, genocide and, if there are any survivors, in massive inter-generational damage

Convinced that the concept of a limited nuclear war is unrealistic and a nuclear war once started is totally unlikely to be contained

Persuaded that the concepts of self-defence and deterrence have become meaningless in the context of nuclear weaponry and thus afford no justification for their production, possession, testing or deployment

Mindful that the use, production, testing, possession and deployment of nuclear weapons thus constitute a violation of international law and a crime against humanity

Recalling that this Assembly by Resolution 3384 (XXX) of 10 November 1975 proclaimed the Declaration on the Use of Scientific and Technological Progress in the Interests of Peace and for the Benefit of Mankind and has since taken numerous steps towards the implementation of this resolution, including the passing of Resolution 37/189A of 18 December 1982 calling upon all States, specialised agencies, inter-governmental and non-governmental organisations to take the necessary measures to ensure that the results of scientific and technological progress are used exclusively in the interests of international peace, for the benefit of mankind and for promoting and encouraging respect for human rights and fundamental freedoms

Noting that the Human Rights Committee of the United Nations at its 563rd meeting (twenty third session) held on 2 November 1984 in its general comment 14 (23)c/(article 6) declared that the production, testing, possession, deployment and use of nuclear weapons should be prohibited and recognised as a crime against humanity

Noting also that the said Committee in the said general comment called upon all States, whether Parties to the Covenant or not, to take urgent steps unilaterally and by agreement to rid the world of this menace

Persuaded that the legal and moral responsibility borne by scientists participating in such activities is today infinitely greater than at the time of the creation of the first nuclear weapons by reason inter alia of the greater knowledge now available of the disastrous atmospheric, agricultural, medical and social impacts of the use of nuclear weaponry, the possibility of nuclear retaliation, the enormously enhanced destructive power of current nuclear weaponry and the vast nuclear arsenals now available in the event of nuclear war

Deeply moved by the consideration that the power of science is such, in the words of the Russell-Einstein Manifesto, as to open the way to a new paradise or lead to the risk of universal death

Believing that the participation of scientists and technologists is crucial to the determination of the choice between these alternatives

Convinced that the principle of individual responsibility for crimes against humanity is well established in international law

Convinced also that superior orders do not constitute a defence in international law in regard to crimes against humanity

and *Determined* that in the light of the above circumstances a consideration of the responsibility of scientists and technologists engaged in the nuclear weapons enterprise should no longer be further delayed by the international community.

DECLARATION

This Assembly hereby reaffirms the principles that

(a) The use, production, possession, testing and deployment of nuclear weapons are contrary to international law and constitute a crime against humanity

(b) The participation in scientific or technological research in this area is contrary to international law and is a crime against humanity

> 'Those who consciously participate in the manufacture of nuclear weapons are personally guilty of a violation of international law'

(c) Those who consciously participate in the manufacture of nuclear weapons and nuclear weapons research are personally guilty of a violation of international law and of a crime against humanity and/ or of complicity in such acts

(d) Such activity is incompatible with the dominant principle underlying all scientific activity, namely service to humanity, and is therefore unethical and contrary to the express Declarations of this Assembly

and *calls upon* all scientists and technologists throughout the world to abide by the legal and ethical obligations outlined in this document and to desist from any activity involving the development, production, testing, possession, deployment or use of nuclear weapons.

Professor C.G. Weeramantry, 35 Madeline St, Glen Waverley, Victoria 3150, Australia (tel 61 3 233 2846; 61 3 565 3305 office).

Reward the invention, not the feasibility study

Adapted extract from an old but still very relevant article by James Hudson in Inc. (USA), monitored for the Institute by Roger Knights.

Instead of encouraging technological breakthroughs by rewarding performance, governments discourage them with a grants structure that rewards inaction. What are we doing about nuclear safety? Studying it. What are we doing about solar energy? Holding conferences. What are we doing about dirt smokestacks? Reassessing.

The answer to the question: 'what should we do about the whole mess in Research & Development?' is: start giving out prizes.

Instead of bestowing grants for study and research, the government should announce prizes. Prizes for finishing, not for thinking about finishing. Prizes for getting something to work – for building it, testing it, breaking it, swearing at it, and fixing it till it runs. How about, let's say, a $1-billion prize for the first large, reliably functioning coal liquefaction plant?

> 'Instead of bestowing grants for study and research, the government should announce prizes. Prizes for finishing. Prizes for getting something to work'

Prizes for successful technology would go straight into the pockets of the inventors and investors, appealing shamelessly to their prurient desire to get rich. Government would withdraw most of its funding for R&D. If the prize for actual completion of a project were fat enough, industry would put up the R&D money. And it would be a lot more selective about choosing the ideas that are most likely to work (that is, the ideas that are worthwhile) because if the idea didn't work, industry would take the loss.

> 'But above all, you fear a breakthrough more than a failure. If you make a breakthrough, there's no need for further study, so your grants stop'

Sounds mad, you say? It wouldn't if you'd been doing what I've been doing lately, which is evaluating proposals for Department of Energy R&D funding. How different government R&D is from commercial research! In commercial work there is a single test of performance – does the result sell? If it does, the R&D effort wins its prize: the profits. In government research, the only test of performance is the ability to get grants. Once you're funded to study, you get the same amount of money whether you solve the problem or not. You have to meet rigid programme requirements, surrendering the free-wheeling laboratory latitude to test things on instinct. But above all, you fear a breakthrough more than a failure. If you make a breakthrough, there's no need for further study, so your grants stop.

This is not to suggest that scientists everywhere are deliberately knocking over test tubes to stall their work. It is to state that our current system inspires only process, not performance. There is in the strictest sense *nothing* to be gained by solving a problem. There's no goal, no thrill of achievement and no personal profit. You don't even get a patent if you devise something, because the results of government-funded R&D are public property. Of course, this isn't much of a problem, because government-funded work seldom produces anything worth patenting.

For instance, why not establish a $2-million prize for the first decent tyres-to-energy project? It wouldn't be too hard to set the criteria. Let's say that, to win, the process would have to convert 500 tons of tyres to usable energy, work in two places (to prove the system had wide applications, or 'transferability') run for a year, and show an operating profit after audit. Hard, but far from impossible. And here's the key that would make it attractive to investors financing the competitors: the results of all the R&D would be proprietary, not public. So you'd get to keep the patents. If the winning system is profitable, the patents could be worth a lot. You might require the winner to license whatever technology he or she develops, so all could share it – but it would be a licence with royalties, to insure that the winner gets the greatest profit.

> 'Just be glad the government didn't decide to fund research into man-powered flight. We'd still be gluing feathers to our arms'

Isn't this a wonderful idea? I certainly think so. But I won't be surprised if it sits around for five to ten years (*Ed:* this was first published in 1980), until somebody junior enough for it to affect is senior enough to influence some money. Then, there will be five years of paper studies into the feasibility (I'd be happy to get one of the contracts!), going on and on about response of the market, environmental impact, government staff impact, methods for setting prizes and performance requirements, what colour the blueprints should be, and so on. And ten years later, there may be a demonstration involving parallel projects, with one working toward a prize and the other direct-funded. Given government lag times, that would be pretty dynamic action. So I'll see you again in 25 years. In the meantime, just be glad the government didn't decide to fund research into man-powered flight. We'd still be gluing feathers to our arms.

Necessity *not* the mother of invention

Jane Jacobs

Adapted from 'Cities and the Wealth of Nations' by Jane Jacobs (published by Ramdom House, USA, ISBN 0 394 48047 3).

An emeritus professor of the Massachusetts Institute of Technology, Cyril Stanley Smith, points out that historically, necessity has not been the mother of invention; rather, necessity opportunistically picks up invention and improvises improvements on it and new uses for it, but the roots of invention are to be found elsewhere, in motives like curiosity and especially, Smith noted, 'aesthetic curiosity.'

> 'Even wheels were at first frivolities; the most ancient known to us are parts of toys'

Metallurgy itself, he reminds us, began with hammering copper into necklace beads and other ornaments 'long before "useful" knives and weapons' were made of copper or bronze. Possibly even wheels were at first frivolities; the most ancient known to us are parts of toys. Hydraulics and many mechanical ingenuities and tricks were first developed for toys or other amusements. The chemical industry grew from the need for quantities of mordants, bleaches, and alkalies for use in the finer textiles and glass. Rockets for fun came before their military use or space travel. The first successful railroad in the world was an amusement ride in London.

'All big things grow from little things,' Smith comments, with this cautionary addition, 'but new little things are destroyed by their environments unless they are cherished for reasons more like aesthetic appreciation than practical utility.'

Psychedelics caused evolution from apes?

Terence McKenna

Adapted from an 8 page article entitled 'Plan, Plant, Planet' by Terence McKenna in Whole Earth Review No 64 (PO Box 38, Sausalito, CA 94966-9932, USA, tel 415 332 1716. Subs. $26, single issue $7).

There is a hidden factor in the evolution of human beings which is neither a 'missing link' nor a *telos* imparted from on high. I suggest that this hidden factor in the evolution of human beings, the factor which called human consciousness forth from a bipedal ape with binocular vision, involved a feedback loop with plant hallucinogens. This is not an idea that has been widely explored, though a very conservative form of this notion appears in R. Gordon Wasson's 'Soma: Divine Mushroom of Immortality' (Wasson, 1971). Wasson does not comment on the emergence of human-ness out of primates, but does suggest hallucinogenic mushrooms as the causal agent in the appearance of spiritually aware human beings and the genesis of religion.

The state of consciousness would provide a reason for foraging humans to return repeatedly to those plants, in order to re-experience their bewitching novelty. The primate gains increased visual acuity and access to the transcendent Other, ever more novel information and sensory input and behaviour, and thus is bootstrapped to higher and higher states of self-reflection.

> 'Hallucinogenic plants may have been the catalysts for everything about us that distinguishes us from other primates except perhaps the loss of body hair'

Hallucinogenic plants may have been the catalysts for everything about us that distinguishes us from other primates except perhaps the loss of body hair. Recall, projective imagination, language, naming, magical speech, dance, and a sense of religion may have emerged out of this interaction.

A twentieth century Mendel?

In the well-known words from 'Gulliver's Travels': 'whoever could make two ears of corn or two blades of grass to grow upon a spot of ground where only one grew before, would deserve better of mankind, and do more essential service to his country, than the whole race of politicians put together.' Such a man may be Roy Silson, a twentieth century Mendel of whom Darwin would have approved, an independent scientist working from his home in Tring. Through patient research into breeding records right back to the 1930s and through computer simulations, Silson has demonstrated the simple ways in which new breeding methods can maximise plant and animal improvement. One of his most surprising demonstrations shows that mainstream genetic teaching that emphasises the dangers of inbreeding is mistaken: optimum results are achieved by inbreeding at approximately the level of mating between cousins.

Silson's computers, running programmes for weeks at a time, testing breeding programmes over many generations, have confirmed his findings. His work should also return to prominence the work of three professionals from the early 1900s, all with a world wide reputation at the time, who wrote books supporting inbreeding – Hagedoorn (1939 etc), Lush (1937) and Davenport (1907); and there are also encouraging reports from the same era of scattered experiments by breeders who followed Hagedoorn's ideas on their own farms. So there is practical evidence from the past backing Silson's model, and no evidence as yet that conflicts with it – because of conventional attitudes, few researchers have experimented with intermediate rates of inbreeding.

'Mainstream genetic teaching that emphasises the dangers of inbreeding is mistaken: optimum results are achieved by inbreeding at approximately the level of mating between cousins'

A recent book by Roy Silson, with the forbidding title of 'Additive Genes in Evolution and Selection' details his theories (Greenfield Publications). In it he has also published a complete computer program (written in BASIC) which will save breeders time and money by allowing them to compare the results of a range of proposed breeding systems and to select the best for their purposes.

Silson, in the piece below, outlines his ideas and some of their implications. His additive gene model lends itself to disturbing social speculations: could it be, for instance, that the church through the ages has been ill-advised, from a genetics perspective, to discourage marriage between cousins? And were we genetically better off in the past when we lived within close-knit, partially isolated communities?

Inbreeding and additive genes

Roy Silson

Genetic effects, controlled by single pairs of genes, have been widely understood since Mendel's work was rediscovered at the turn of the century.

Textbooks demonstrate these by using the simple clearcut dominant and recessive examples that are seen with colour and pattern in plants and animals.

Since about 1910 it has been recognised that other qualities result from the total effect of many genes individually too small to be measured (see Note A below).

Many theories, often controversial, have been developed to explain the complex mixture of additive and non-additive effects seen in multiple gene systems.

Variable and/or non-linear activity by individual genes has been suggested and great emphasis placed on the concept that environment seriously affects gene activity.

About forty years ago, the author started working with large additive gene systems. These were modelled on paper and later by computer (Notes A & B).

Several decades of research have confirmed and extended the original discovery that wholly additive genes are able to produce most, if not all, of the non-additive anomalies found in real species. All of these anomalies have been shown to be due to simple mathematical interactions with no need for environmental effects or variable gene action.

Apparently many experts cannot believe that the solution is so simple. Nonetheless, no evidence has yet been seen that disproves the simple explanation.

An important anomaly is reversion to the mean which produces the often confusing effect known as heritability (Note C). For the same quality, heritability varies between populations as well as changing with time in the same population.

Natural populations show the anomalies of depression following inbreeding and heterosis (hybrid vigour) following crosses.

Inbreeding is conventionally treated as something to be avoided. The model, and evidence from real species, indicate that cousin matings are approximately optimum. Reduced inbreeding produces selection plateau (Note D).

Heritability has a high positive correlation with inbreeding.

'These concepts may be used to optimise breeding methods and to maximise plant and animal improvement'

These concepts may be used to optimise breeding methods and to maximise plant and animal improvement.

The principles developed are also important for the study of evolution. The mathematics of large additive gene systems is such that there is an almost infinite number of possible gene combinations for any additive total.

In large populations, these combinations store immense amounts of cryptic genetic information. The population mean may be moved rapidly, in almost any direction, far beyond the most extreme individuals ever previously bred.

'Conventional ideas require some form of genetic isolation to produce new species. The author has shown that, within a single large additive gene system, new species may develop in a few tens of generations'

Conventional ideas require some form of genetic isolation to produce new species. The author has shown that, within a single large additive gene system, new species may develop in a few tens of generations.

This result has major implications in understanding the fossil record with its sudden appearances of new species and the scarcity of intermediate fossils.

A single additive system may intersperse millions of generations with little obvious variation, with few or many short periods of rapid or minor change. It may produce numerous new species or vary its direction as a single line.

These ideas are also important in understanding social forces. The model shows that qualities are most easily optimised in small partially isolated populations. Such populations are common in many species including humans.

Extreme human mobility is very recent. Before 1900 the author's own name occurred in only two small areas.

In such circumstances gene flow would be low with most matings being between individuals in the same or closely adjacent populations.

Crosses sometimes show heterosis but any apparent superiority is deceptive. In the second generation genes from the two sources recombine in complex ways. Typically the progeny mean crashes: some progeny may show defects unknown in either parent population. Fewer will survive to reproduce.

If avoidance of crossing is due to genetic factors such genes will become more common because more progeny are surviving from the more closely related matings.

Initial restrictions may be as simple as different courtship signals or breeding periods.

Conversely considerable evidence is being found that individuals, even of the simpler species such as amoeba, have an inherent ability to evaluate the genetic similarity of other individuals; whether reared together or not.

'Quail, for example, have been shown to prefer the theoretical optimum of cousins as mates'

Quail, for example, have been shown to prefer the theoretical optimum of cousins as mates rather than those more or less closely related.

In humans, actual experiments are difficult but much social evidence implies the existence of similar mechanisms. Murders, within families, rarely involve blood relations: cruelty is notably more common from step-parents.

At the other extreme studies have shown that married couples tend to be more similar, for a wide range of hidden as well as obvious characteristics, than random pairs of individuals from the same population. In those couples who divorce the similarities tend to be less than in those who don't.

'Studies have shown that married couples tend to be more similar than random pairs of individuals'

Racism is, conventionally, assumed to be cultural. It is more likely to be another inherent quality which reduces wide crosses.

Its reproductive aspect is clearly seen in communities where one or two foreign children have been adopted into local families. Generally accepted as infants they are suddenly rejected when they reach puberty.

It appears that society might more easily be improved if 'good' and 'bad' behaviour, within and between groups, were reconsidered in terms of inherent and unconscious control mechanisms and efforts made to minimise cultural exaggerations.

• *Note A. The book discusses additive genes only and assumes additive values of '1' or '0' for each gene. A pair of genes could be '00', '01' or '11' giving additive totals of 0, 1 and 2.*

With several pairs of genes the possible range of these additive totals, for 'n' pairs, may vary from 0 to 2n. It is theoretically important that all intermediate totals may be produced in many different ways.

• *Note B. Each quality has its own optimum additive value that may change with time and place.*

The author made the critical new assumption that selective pressures score differences from optima rather than additive values directly. With an optimum of 6, totals of 5 and 7 would both score One and be indistinguishable.

• *Note C. For each quality a population mean may be measured. From the total population the 'best' X% provide parents for a progeny generation. Both parents and progeny will have their own means.*

Although expected from simple additive theory, the progeny mean does not equal the parent mean in either simulation or practice. It shows reversion towards the mean of the original population.

The percentage of the selection differential that is actually achieved is known as 'heritability'. Its value varies within the extremes of 0% and 100%.

• *Note D. A plateau is when intense selection produces little or no change in a population mean.*

• *'Additive Genes in Evolution and Selection' by Roy Silson is obtainable from Greenfield Publications, Mayflower House, Station Road, Tring, Herts, HP23 5QX, tel 044282 381, 1989, 312 pages, ISBN 1 871508 010, paperback, £10, or ISBN 1 871508 003, hardback, £20.*

Ecotechnology Research

Mr Honda, through the Honda Foundation, donated a million pounds to the International Ecotechnology Research Centre, based in Cranfield UK, and founded in 1987. Its scientific director is Professor Peter Allen who used to work in Brussels with Nobel prize winner Ilya Prigogine (author of 'Order out of Chaos, Man's New Dialogue with Nature'). The aim of the Centre is to help humanise business through projects such as a study for the EC on the impact of technological aid in Senegal.

'It was the intuitive, random fishers ("the stochasts") who did not follow the pack ("the cartesians") who proved essential for discovering the next usable grounds'

'The main focus of fundamental research in the Centre,' says their literature, 'is to develop a better understanding of the principles and processes which underlie change in biological, ecological, social and economic systems – ie Ecotechnology.' They are interested in the dynamics of creativity and innovation. For instance, Peter Allen has co-authored a study entitled 'Dynamics of Discovery and Exploitation, the case of the Scotian Shell groundfish fisheries' (Peter Allen and McGlade, Canadian Journal of Fisheries and Aquatic Sciences 43) – which tells how the fishery grounds became overfished, and how it was the intuitive, random fishers ('the stochasts') who did not follow the pack ('the cartesians') who proved essential for discovering the next usable grounds. The conclusion drawn from work of this nature is that 'long term change is both driven by, and selects for, systems which can create and maintain an internal diversity and freedom which is incompatible with short term optimality.'

The study sums up as follows:

This concerns the question of 'discovery', of evolutionary survival and of information exchange. There is a fascinating parallel between the picture we have derived concerning fishing behaviour and that revealed by recent research into foraging behaviour in the animal kingdom, particularly in work on ant societies (Deneubourg et al 1983). The vital issue is that 'discovery' like 'invention' and 'creation' can be achieved through 'non-rational' behaviour, although subsequent exploitation may depend on 'rational' reactions. The multifaceted process of 'discovery' and 'exploitation' concerns all of us at many levels. Either as individuals or in our various roles in families, firms, institutions, communities and even nations, we must try to decide how to divide our time and effort between the performance of tasks characteristic of our present role – with known values and pay-offs – or the continued search for, and openness to, the possibilities of new roles and new pay-offs in the future.

> 'Stochasts take intellectual, emotional and financial risks by adventuring into the unknown, be it with ideas, aesthetics, personal relationships or entrepreneurial activities. Their discoveries are what nourishes society in the long run'

As individuals we can either deliberately allow ourselves to explore new paths and connections, or instead, we can organise most of the components of our lives so that we minimise such diversions which, at any given moment, have no obvious purpose. There are again two extremes: 'stochasts' and 'cartesians'. The former take intellectual, emotional and financial risks by adventuring into the unknown, be it with ideas, aesthetics, personal relationships or entrepreneurial activities. Their discoveries are what nourishes society in the long run, and assures its survival by allowing it to evolve, and to find new sources of sustenance. The 'cartesians' devote themselves to fulfilling as efficiently and completely as possible, the role they feel has been assigned to them. Their behaviour constitutes the 'backbone' of society, and offers a very necessary definition of 'normality'. The successful, long term functioning and survival of an individual, a society, a firm or a nation requires both types of behaviour, just as our example dealing with 'fishing' showed.

The whole question of 'innovation' and of management can be examined in terms of these new ideas. Old views of policy and planning as 'rationalisation', and classification, streamlining and separation of different functions must be re-examined. We need to design systems which are capable of being creative, not imposing too much rationality or too much information on them. Neither should we restrict movements or thoughts to only the known or recognised channels characterised at present by an obvious usefulness. Discovery requires freedom, while the efficient functioning of society requires cooperation and organisation. Perhaps with models such as ours, we can begin to understand and explore a new 'rationality' which encompasses both harmoniously.

The Cranfield Institute of Technology, Cranfield, Bedford MK43 OAL (tel 0234 750111; fax 0234 750163).

Rebates to customers reducing electricity consumption

The Times printed the following letter from Nicholas Albery.

The Institute for Social Inventions maintains a computer database of good ideas from around the world. One such idea from Bill Berkowitz of Arlington, Massachusetts, strikes me as a painless way for the UK government to begin alleviating the greenhouse effect: simply require the privatised companies to offer rebates to customers who reduce their total consumption by fixed percentages from the previous year.

Reply from the Secretary of State for Energy

John Wakeman, the then Secretary of State for Energy, replied in part:

While inefficient users have to pay unnecessarily high bills, efficient users already benefit directly from the savings resulting from their own decisions.

It could clearly distort these end-use decisions if consumers were simply paid for not using electricity, by whatever means. And its impact on the costs of the suppliers would be differential, depending, for example, on whether savings were made at peak.

Rebates will, however, be a matter for commercial decision by the supply company concerned.

John Wakeman, Dept of Energy, 1 Palace St, London SW1E 5HE (tel 071 238 3290).

Rebates for American energy savers

Adapted from the Economist.

Changes in the price-setting formulas by the state regulators are one of the big reasons for the electicity utilities new-found enthusiasm for conservation. They are now allowed to recover ten per cent of the 'avoided costs' of having to provide new power stations and generating capacity: ie to make price increases that let it claw back ten per cent of the savings its customers achieve through conservation. Thus Duke Power in the Carolinas presents its customers with a cheque for $50 when they install an energy-efficient refrigerator. And it gives credits of about $25m a year to the power-hungry mills in return for their agreeing to have their power supplies interrupted at times of peak load (with thirty minutes' warning).

> 'Power-hungry mills agreeing to have their power supplies interrupted at times of peak load'

It is reckoned that by the year 2000 the electricity utilities conservation programmes in the States will save 45,000 megawatts – more than four times the electricity needed to power New York City in peak periods.

Abandon standing charges

E. Turnbull writes in part:

Standing charges are obviously a regressive tax, ensuring that those who save fuel most are penalised most – for example my one therm's consumption of gas during a quarter costs me in aggregate £7·96 per therm. Likewise with the £100 car licence fee, light users pay the same as heavy fuel users.

> 'Standing charges are obviously a regressive tax, ensuring that those who save fuel most are penalised most'

E. Turnbull, Taman, 38 Elsdon Road, Gosforth, Northumberland, NE3 1HY.

Energy loans

Guy Dauncey

Adapted extract from a booklet of ideas by Guy Dauncey.

Reducing emissions of carbon dioxide is a financial problem: how can we persuade households and businesses to make the necessary investments in energy-efficient technologies? A Four-Way Energy Loan arrangement could make the difference:

(1) Retailers sell energy-saving appliances and equipment with 100% loan arrangements covering purchase and installation;

(2) A bank or credit union advances the loans to the retailer;

(3) Consumers pay their power bills at higher, pegged 'pre-efficient' levels;

(4) The utility uses the energy-saving difference to repay the loans.

> 'Consumers pay their power bills at higher, pegged "pre-efficient" levels; the energy-saving difference repaying the loans'

In this way, consumers could walk into a shop and walk out with new energy-saving equipment without paying a penny. When the loans were repaid, power bills would fall to their new low levels, and stay there.

Booklet available from Guy Dauncey, 2069 Kings Road, Victoria, British Columbia, Canada V8R 2P6 (tel 604 592 4472 h; 592 4473 w, tel and fax).

Fluorescent lamps changed free of charge

Adapted extract from an article by Jeremy Cherfas in the Guardian, monitored for the Institute by Marion Schmidt.

The Taunton Municipal Lighting Plant in Massachusetts leases compact fluorescent lamps to customers for 20 cents a month, and replaces them free of charge: the customer enjoys lower bills; the utility saves the cost of extra supplies; and the atmosphere, almost as a side-effect, is relieved of a considerable burden of carbon dioxide.

> 'The Taunton Municipal Lighting Plant leases compact fluorescent lamps to customers for 20 cents a month'

On the west coast of the States, utilities have joined forces to offer a fee (perhaps $100) to refrigerator manufacturers who sell the first 100,000 refrigerators that beat the current average energy efficiency by two-thirds: this reduces the cost of tooling up for production, and encourages sales drives; the utilities pay only if the manufacturers reach the target.

Less towel washing in hotels

Item in Brigitte magazine (Germany) monitored for the Institute by Josefine Speyer.

The Silence Hotel group, with about 300 hotels in Europe, are putting up notices in hotel bathrooms explaining to guests that towels will only be replaced daily if they are left on the floor; and that guests wishing to help save energy in this way can do so by leaving their towels on the handrails.

Muscle power into electricity

David Haaren and Kathy Abbott

Adapted extract from publicity leaflets.

We live in a small house on 14 acres of land in Southern Vermont in the States. The house is located a mile from utilities in a wooded, sloping area. Three photovoltaic panels, which produce 65 watts in full sun, charge our two deep cycle batteries. An exercise bike and generator are also used to charge the batteries. A gas refrigerator and stove and wood help provide for our other needs.

> 'An exercise bike and generator are also used to charge the batteries'

The batteries power a variety of appliances: a dozen incandescent bulbs, five fluorescent lights, a TV, video cassette player, stereo water pump (our supply is gravity), fan, Makita cordless tools, vacuum cleaner, weed-wacker, typewriter and an inverter for a computer, printer and movie projector. We find that the pedalled generator is enough to provide the necessary boost to take our system through the winter. We prefer pedalling to a noisy and polluting gas generator.

The power transmission is incredibly efficient, as evidenced by the length of time it takes for the flywheel to slow down once it's going. The permanent-magnet generator converts most of the pedal power into useful electricity.

With this system you can pedal-charge a 12 volt battery at up to 15 amps. The generator is rated to deliver 5 amps continuously and is more efficient at easier cruising rates, say 3 amps.

> 'Quiet enough so that you can read or converse while pedalling'

The pedal system consists of a Schwinn DX 900 exercise bike and a Thermax generator, mounted with what we will call a Haaren aluminium bracket. Power transmission from

Schwinn's large flywheel to the generator is accomplished using Berg sprockets and plastic chain. This steel reinforced plastic chain runs on precision sprocket gears and is efficient and quiet, quiet enough so that you can read or converse while pedalling.

We can offer a kit to retrofit the Schwinn DX 900 or we can assemble a complete machine.

David Haaren and Kathy Abbott, Pedal Systems, Box 6, Westminster Station, VT 05159, USA.

Science Fiction – can it work?

George Hay

The biggest problem about getting science fiction applied in what is laughingly called 'the real world' is the old Catch-22. It is best exemplified by Arthur C. Clarke's explanation of why he is not rather better off than he actually is. When he first had the idea of the communications satellite, he tried to get it patented. 'Come, come, Mr Clarke,' said the people at the Patent Office. 'We're a serious outfit, we haven't got time to waste on fantastic ideas like this.' Years later, when the first satellite (with which Arthur was actively involved) actually went up, and the nations were queuing to get their own satellites up, Arthur went back to the Patent Office. 'But, Mr Clarke,' they said, 'the satellite already exists. You should have come to us earlier.'

'The A-Bomb (H.G. Wells) and the tank (Major-General Swinton) were described originally in sf stories'

See what I mean? If you try to convince someone to apply sf, they say, 'Oh, that's science fiction. I mean, you can't actually *do* it. Maybe in the year 2000...' If you point out to them that ideas as disparate as the water-bed (Robert Heinlein), the dracone (Frank Herbert), the A-Bomb (H.G. Wells) and the tank (Major-General Swinton) were all described originally in sf stories, they just blink, and then look away from you. There can be precious few people who do not know what a television set is – but how many know that the word 'television' was coined by an sf editor (Hugo Gernshack) in the early years of this century?

I am not saying that sf cannot be applied. As you can see from the examples I have cited, it *has* been applied. What I want to get across here are two key points: firstly, if you wish to get someone to make use of an sf idea, check first whether to him or her the word 'sf' is simply a synonym for 'fantasy' or 'impossible'. If it is, do not mention sf. Call it futurology, or lateral thinking or any term you wish, as long as it is one he will feel safe with – something *respectable*.

Secondly, there are as many sf ideas in the genre that deal with the soft sciences – sociology, linguistics, political science, etc – as there are ones that deal with hardware, and these are mostly constructive, not destructive. I know that the 'Star Wars' system (which harks back to dear old Doc Smith's 'Lensman' stories of the 1930s) is supposed to protect us, but some of us may have doubts about this. How about something

completely different? For example, Suzette Haden Elgin, a current sf author, has created 'a language for women by a woman', Laadan. I know no more about it than that it exists, but I cannot help feeling that a discussion about Laadan might be more helpful than one about lasers in the sky...

'How many people know that the famous crescents of Bath were designed from an idea in an sf novel?'

It is important to grasp that sf speaks to the heart and soul, and does not consist merely of delayed adolescents in uniforms playing with death-rays – and can speak effectively, at that. How many people know that the famous crescents of Bath were designed from an idea in an sf novel – Thomas More's 'Utopia'? That H. G. Wells wrote a novel mentioning robot-induced unemployment in 1913, or that G. K. Chesterton wrote one in 1909 dealing with the nastier implications of psychiatry? Speaking of H. G. Wells – it is not well enough known that the introduction of the Declaration of Human Rights was really down to him, and could, not unfairly, be described as sf for its day. How's that for a social invention?

Good enough, you may say – but how about something fresh out of science fiction, something we could set about here and now without having either to invent or fund some vastly expensive technological whatsit? Well, I could mention the Argo Venture, formulated in 1984 by Lord Young of Dartington, the object of which is to set up a one-year simulation of the start-up of a Mars colony, in an isolated environment, and for which there have already been hundreds of volunteers. The social invention I would propose is an adaptation of an idea put out a year or two back by Frederick Pohl in his novel, 'The Years of the City', in which he deals with the future of New York. It would take more space than I have here to go into it properly, but basically, it could not be more simple – a real-time electronic voting system for dealing with current big city issues (or small-city either, for that matter). All the technology already exists – we are *already* the wired society. There could of course be problems with local authority ordinances, but, if there were goodwill from the local politicos, these could be dealt with – if there were not, then the general public might have to be seriously consulted. But then, that is what it is all about!

• *George Hay (founder of the Science Fiction Foundation), 53b All Saints Street, Hastings, East Sussex, TN34 3BN (tel 0424 420634).*

• *The Science Fiction Foundation, Polytechnic of East London, Longbridge Road, Dagenham, Essex, RM8 2AS.*

Can life survive the end of the universe?

Allen Tough

Adapted extract from a book entitled 'Crucial Questions About the Future' by Allen Tough, published by the University Press of America (4720 Boston Way, Lanham MD 20706, USA, tel 301 459 3366), 1991, ISBN 0 8191 8275 3, distributed in the UK by Eurospan, 3 Henrietta St, London WC2E 8LU.

If we look far enough into the future, we can imagine the end of our physical universe, at least in any form that would support human life as we know it. We can imagine the universe expanding for ever, becoming colder and colder, until finally it is completely frozen, quiet and barren. Alternatively we can imagine it collapsing inwardly, becoming hotter and hotter, ending in a 'Big Crunch'.

'Life detached from flesh and blood and embodied in networks of superconducting circuitry or in interstellar dust clouds'

Can life and intelligence somehow survive if the physical universe meets either of these fates? Intelligent life will have countless billions of years to advance and change before there is any need to adjust to the various stages of the 'end' of the physical universe. By that time, at least in some parts of the universe, intelligent life may have progressed so much that it can figure out how to avoid the extermination of all life, knowledge, intelligence and wisdom. Indeed, Freeman Dyson and Michael Michaud have already explored some possible ways of achieving this. For instance, a huge, cooperative, galactic or intergalactic project may find some method of altering the physical universe (or one portion of it) in some powerful and massive way that will enable life to continue. A second possibility is that life itself will change and adapt in ways that will permit it to continue for ever. If it is true 'that life is organisation rather than substance, then it makes sense to imagine life detached from flesh and blood and embodied in networks of superconducting circuitry or in interstellar dust clouds' (Dyson). Alternatively, some way may be found to break out of this universe into another one, either existing parallel to it or arising subsequent to it. Perhaps the best of our knowledge, intelligence, consciousness or life can be transferred to another universe.

Allen Tough, Adult Education Dept, OISE (University of Toronto, 252 Bloor Street West, Toronto, ON, Canada M5S 1V6 (tel 416 968 7246; fax 926 4725).

Chapter sixteen

TRANSPORT

Smart Cars, a proposal for a radically new transport system

Nicholas Saunders

Nearly everyone now agrees that private cars are not the answer to transport needs of the future because they are extravagant on fuel, cause enormous pollution and are dangerous. Instead, it is being suggested, we should use buses and trains.

First, I want to convince the reader that people will not switch to buses and trains, whether monorail or 'bullet'. The reason is that people are basically selfish and will only change to something that suits them better. Private cars take some beating – always ready to take you anywhere, whenever you want, right from your door to your destination – with your personal comforts such as sounds and privacy and almost complete security from the outside world. It is clear that most people who can afford a car will not give it up voluntarily in favour of efficient and cheap public transport, as can be seen in countries such as France. Forcing people to give up their cars, or taxing them off the roads, will never be politically popular, although such measures may have to be adopted in the short-term. The long-term answer is to provide something better – not as perceived by the worthy few, but by ordinary, selfish people.

'A pollution-free and noise-free transport system that is within our reach'

Second, I want to show that there are alternatives to buses and trains. For instance, a friend suggested converting surplus cruise missiles to person carriers – they can already take off and find their way to the destination avoiding other aircraft and obstacles, so all they need to be taught is how to land! I won't stick my neck out to promote that, but at least it is in the right direction – forward. In fact, technology has opened up the way to enormous untapped choices for future transport systems that have so far been largely ignored. Sadly, few people have the imagination to visualise anything other than a modification of what they have already experienced, and fewer still have the ability to assess which fantasies are practical.

Thirdly, I am going to describe my own realisable vision. This is not an invention, as it is based on bits of existing technology; nor is it a system ready to be built, as it would take a great deal of development. It is merely an example of a pollution-free and noise-free transport system that is within our reach.

The system would consist of a network of tubes about two metres in diameter in which the cars, about the size of the back of a London taxi, would run underground or above ground (depending on whether the increased cost would be justified by the environmental savings). Links up to about 200 mph could follow ground tracks like roads and railways, but very high speed links would require specially straight tracks, probably suspended above ground like a suspension bridge. Windows in the tubes would allow the traveller to see out. The speed would not only be controlled by the track, it would be decided by the designers and be fixed for every point on the track, enabling cars to run very close together without bumping into each other. This raises a safety issue in traditional engineering terms – stopping distance between cars in an emergency. The answer is that you don't need stopping distance between cars any more than you do between the carriages of a train, because each car is magnetically locked into a slot, like being hooked onto a moving chain. But what if the current fails? The cars fit the tube closely, so that the air between them moves at the same speed and would act like springs preventing them from crashing together: this is proven safety technology from lifts.

'The cars would be suspended by magnetism providing a smooth and silent ride'

The cars would have no engines or even wheels – instead the track would provide the propulsion using electricity, by means of built-in linear induction and linear synchronous motors. The cars would be suspended by magnetism providing a smooth and silent ride. The overall effect would be to make the cars cheap but the track expensive. (The Germans and Japanese have trial high speed trains using similar technology.)

I envisage stations being at about the same spacing as bus stops are at present, though as prosperity grew people might afford their own. And I hope that each station would be manned by staff able to offer assistance if required; to deliver mail and goods to homes; and to hire out trolleys and low speed electric cars. In fact, I have a much broader vision in which these stations become the new local social centres because everyone passes through them, and they could become the base units of the political system.

'The car would be routed through the network in much the same way as a telephone call'

To make a journey, passengers would go to the nearest station where there would always be at least one car waiting. He or she would get in, insert a credit-type card, dial the destination and the car would be routed through the network in much the same way as a telephone call. Once on a journey, the traveller could stop at a service area just like on a motorway.

At junctions, tracks would run adjacent and at the same speed, analogous to slip roads on a motorway. Between the two running tracks would be an intermediate transfer track. Cars changing track would transfer straight across if there were a slot available immediately adjacent, or accelerate on the transfer track to an empty slot. With correct programming there would always be a slot reserved, because congestion would be predicted and cars diverted, just as happens with telephone calls. As a further fail-safe feature, each track would form a complete loop, so that if a car did not leave a track for any reason it would be able to carry on round.

At each station, which would have its own loop of track, cars would come up like lifts to a small shop-front-style station at street level. They would pass through a detector to check them for weight and damage (and possibly even be scanned for explosives) before being allowed to leave the station's loop and return to the main track. Anyone finding a car dirty or vandalised would dial in a code that would send it to a depot – where it could be repaired and the previous user traced via their fare card. Additional detectors would check cars running on the tracks and divert those that were untrackworthy. Similarly, the state of the track would be constantly monitored by specially equipped cars.

'In country areas, where the nearest station may be several miles away, people would still use road cars'

In country areas, where the nearest station may be several miles away, people would still use road cars to get to the station and to make local journeys. However, as these journeys would be short, I envisage that it would eventually be acceptable to allow only battery-driven electric cars – slow and safe, and unable to travel far without re-charging.

Empty cars would return to the track. Whilst every station would have at least one waiting, there would be more diverted to particular areas to deal with rush hours, etc. Like any system it would have limited capacity but this could be increased by adding new tracks, stations and high speed links.

Goods would be carried in much the same way. A goods car would carry a normal fork-lift pallet load up to about a ton. Special cars could be called for longer loads, and some (such as tankers) would be privately owned. Every factory and warehouse would have its own station, and the staff at public stations would be able to deliver goods locally. Although this would require far more vehicles to carry the same goods as by lorry, the environmental impact would be less than at present because a high speed six foot tube could carry more than a twelve foot motorway lane. There would be an enormous economic advantage for business, as both people and goods could be expected to arrive within an hour or so of being despatched. Not only would the saving of time spent travelling save money, but there would be a vast saving in distribution depots, warehousing and handling of goods. For example, a manufacturer of biscuits could despatch direct to each supermarket, while a washing machine chosen from a showroom could be delivered direct from the factory by the time the customer got home.

'The invaluable saving in road accidents and casualties is another major advantage of the system'

The environmental advantages would be vast compared to roads. Apart from the fuel and pollution aspects, very little land would be required as one six foot tube track could carry the same as about 30 motorway lanes at 200mph (more at higher speeds). This compares very favourably with high speed trains. The invaluable saving in road accidents and casualties is another major advantage of the system.

The development costs of this new system would be high, but thereafter the capital and running costs should be lower than for new motorways or for above ground or underground railway lines: the tunnels required are narrow, the cars are engineless, small and cheap, and electricity can be produced from any energy source.

The problem with any new and potentially international system is how you begin. Suitable model trials in the UK could include extensions to existing tube lines – such as in South London, replacing suburban bus services. As more of these Smart Car tubes were built, they could be joined by fast links so as to form an independent system.

If such developments come about, one of the social implications will be to reduce the divisions in the UK between North and South, making commuting to work possible from almost anywhere in the country.

Nicholas Saunders, top floor, 14 Neal's Yard, London WC2H 9DP (tel 071 836 9404; fax 071 379 0135).

Fuel from water

Berit Pegg-Karlsson in Polperro, Cornwall, is the Swedish-born director of the British-Scandinavian Association for Wind and Hydrogen Power, backed by the Pure Energy Trust, of which self-sufficiency writer John Seymour is the main trustee. Pegg-Karlsson plans to popularise in Britain the very successful hydrogen 'Welgas' experiment financed in the town of Harnosand by the Swedish steel industry, SAAB and other firms. In Harnosand, Olaf Tegstrom designed and lived in a house where the electricity came from a small computer-controlled Danish windmill in the garden. The electricity was used to electrolyse filtered water into its constituents, hydrogen and oxygen, with the hydrogen gas used for cooking and heating the house and as fuel for a SAAB car. The car is non-polluting as the exhaust consists almost entirely of water vapour, and the safe storage problem has been solved, with the gas absorbed to form a metal hydride and released as required. Indeed in West Berlin, thanks to government subsidies for fuels that did not cause acid rain, Daimler Benz has built a filling station where various converted vehicles can be filled with hydrogen, produced from town gas.

> 'The electricity was used to electrolyse filtered water into its constituents, hydrogen and oxygen, with the hydrogen gas used for cooking and heating the house and as fuel for a SAAB car'

Sooner or later, Pegg-Karlsson believes, hydrogen will become the world's prime provider of energy, a technological revolution that would solve the problem of atmospheric pollution, at the same time as gradually replacing nuclear power. Hydrogen is an excellent fuel with an energy content three to four times higher than oil, and it can be produced from all known energy sources, besides being a by-product of many industrial processes.

Having hosted seminars for scientists and others on the subject in Sweden, Pegg-Karlsson now wants to do the same in Britain, and the city council of Uppsala in Sweden is interested in forming links with a British city such as Bristol, to share ideas and to conduct joint hydrogen projects. The Pure Energy Trust is also attempting to obtain funding for a minibus to run on hydrogen derived from a 20kw wind turbine and electrolysis unit.

> 'Hydrogen power is Jules Vernes' old dream come true – using water as a fuel'

Pegg-Karlsson is enthusiastic about her Association's potential: 'Humanity can today create what a few years ago was thought of as a very distant future society. And it's all about positive development, caring for the earth and taking steps towards a sustainable future society. Hydrogen power is Jules Vernes' old dream come true – using water as a fuel. The technology is already available. It is largely a question of people and politicians taking brave decisions.'

An information package is available for a minimum £2-50 donation from the Pure Energy Trust, Fairview, Polperro, Looe, Cornwall, PL13 2RB (tel 0503 72143; fax 0503 72063).

A hydrogen car at less than 1p a mile

Adapted from an article in the Daily Mail by Michael Kemp and in the Times by Kevin Eason.

A new fuel cell, patented as the Laser-Cell-TM, costing £2,000, has been developed by Dr Roger Billings (who invented the first home personal computer and double-sided floppy disk). When his fuel cell is plugged into the electric

mains it extracts hydrogen from water over an eight hour period and stores the gas harmlessly in powdered metals, where it cannot explode or ignite.

The fuel cell can then be switched into 'reverse' and turn the hydrogen into electricity to power the electric motor driving the car. Dr Billings' invention could have much wider applications, using hydrogen for home electrical needs and for trucks, buses, trains, boats, submarines and aircraft.

The cell is a third the size of a Fiesta petrol engine and has no moving parts, nothing to service and a life of over 250,000 miles. 60 to 80 per cent of the hydrogen is turned into electricity, compared with the fuel-to-power ratio of a petrol engine of 30 per cent.

> 'Fast and quiet, a hydrogen car costs less than 1p a mile to run and is also environmentally friendly. The only exhaust is water vapour'

Fast and quiet, a hydrogen car costs less than 1p a mile to run and is also environmentally friendly. The only exhaust is water vapour. A model using the new technology could be on sale for under £20,000 by 1993.

A petrol-driven Fiesta costs 33.5p a mile to run but in the prototype hydrogen vehicle, two gallons of water provide enough hydrogen for a 300-mile drive and the car has a potential top speed of 80mph.

Dr Roger Billings, Director, Academy of Science, Kansas, USA.

Solving London's traffic problems

Nicholas Saunders

The first item in this chapter describes Saunders' long-term possible solution to the problem of cars and traffic. In this item he tackles the problem in the short-term.

The following scheme would suit any UK government which wanted to show that it can do something imaginative about London's traffic problems. Although not in outline very novel, it is comprehensive in its scope – with advantages for all the various vested interests:

Introduction

This is a scheme that would enable people to travel to, and within, the central London area freely. The savings, in terms of valuable time at present lost in traffic delays, would be of enormous financial benefit; while the reduction in noice, air pollution and frustration would be of great social benefit.

Summary

As a preliminary, the public would be made aware just how anti-social and uneconomic the present traffic chaos is. Then most private car users would be persuaded to use public transport – by means of strict controls and heavy penalties. At the same time, public transport would be greatly improved, and extended to cater for those who used to commute by car.

The costs of introducing and running the system would be recouped from the resulting increased revenue. Vested interests would not suffer, and the public in general would benefit greatly.

Preliminary awareness campaign

A series of ads – on TV and in the newspapers – would make people aware of just how bad the present situation is. There could be an ad of a frustrated-looking person in a traffic jam captioned: 'If you add up the time lost in London's traffic chaos, it would be equivalent to seven people's entire working lives *every day*.'

> ### 'If you add up the time lost in London's traffic chaos, it would be equivalent to seven people's entire working lives every day'

Another ad could show that, if the roads were cleared enough for buses to double their average speed, then the *same* bus fleet could carry *twice* as many people *twice* as fast with *half* the time waiting at stops – at about *half* the fare.

The aim of the campaign would be to make people aware that a vast improvement is practical; that the new system will work better for everyone – and that private car use in the centre is anti-social – and will not be tolerated when the new system starts.

Commuter transport

A survey of car commuters would be commissioned and used to decide on the location of periphery car parks. These would be built next to tube stations if possible, and new bus routes would be provided if the surveys showed that they were needed.

Off-street parking

A survey would be made of all off-street parking facilities. The owners would be informed of a new tax – of, say, £100 per day per car – for cars entering their car park between 8.00am and 10.30am. They would be liable to pay this tax, on penalty of very heavy fines. However, owners would benefit in two ways. They would be able to charge much higher parking fees after 10.30am corresponding to higher meter charges; and they would be given planning permission for change of use to other uses which would often be more profitable.

> ### 'A survey would be made of all off-street parking facilities. The owners would be informed of a new tax – of, say, £100 per day per car – for cars entering their car park between 8.00am and 10.30am'

On-street parking

The existing regulations would be very strictly imposed, with greatly increased fines, besides the prohibition on parking at meters between 8.00 and 10.30am. This would entail the retraining of traffic wardens (who at present only give six tickets a day on average), and altering the regulations to make it impractical to avoid paying fines. Traffic wardens should be re-equipped so that they can instantly report the number of an illegally parked car on their radio; and if that car is on a list of ones with unpaid fines (or is stolen or has no tax), then it would be listed for wheel clamps or towing away.

Stopping and loading

Loading restrictions would be reassessed and in some cases made more liberal (such as after pedestrian crossings). However, these would be strictly enforced on penalty of heavy fines for even short stops. Traffic wardens could perhaps carry cameras to provide evidence of offences. Taxis would not be allowed to stop where they cause obstruction – the taxi drivers' cooperation would be solicited and should be obtained, since they will benefit greatly from the end to congestion.

> ### 'Traffic wardens could perhaps carry cameras to provide evidence of offences'

Public transport

Buses would be rescheduled (at twice the present average speed?), and re-routed, if surveys show a more efficient service would result. Bus crews would be given a tactfully run retraining scheme to deal with the new conditions, and a bonus related to the number of passenger miles they provide each week. In this way, the crews of buses that run off-schedule in 'bunches' would lose out, while those who provide a good service would gain.

> ### 'Bus crews would be a bonus related to the number of passenger miles they provide each week'

Nicholas Saunders, top floor, 14 Neal's Yard, London WC2 (tel 071 836 9404; fax 071 379 0135).

Bar codes on sides of cars

Nicholas Saunders

Enlarged versions of the bar codes used on product wrappers for reading at supermarket tills could be required on the side of vehicles in the UK. Vehicles coming into those city centre areas with traffic problems would pass through files of posts which would register different numbers of units to be billed – with a high rate, for instance, for Piccadilly at peak time.

This would be a fair way of charging for road usage and congestion; it would be easy to implement since the technology is already well developed; and it would be hard to tamper with the bar codes compared with alternative means such as magnetic codes, since they could be visually inspected.

Administratively, they could be supplied with an adhesive backing in place of the annual licence disk; or at ports of entry for foreign visitors.

Nicholas Saunders – see above for address.

Compulsory travel passes for university students

Adapted extract from an article in the Seattle Times by Peyton Whitely (USA), monitored for the Institute by Roger Knights.

The University of Washington is considering a proposal that every student, whether or not they would individually benefit, should pay about $22-50 extra every quarter for a 'Universal Transportation Pass', entitling them to unlimited travel on the metro and buses. Their present problem is that more than 35,000 people go to classes daily, but there are only 12,300 parking spaces. In the debate on this issue, it was pointed out that the 8,000 students who walk to university would get a poor deal, but one person spoke up to say that she would happily pay for the pass even though she would never use it – by public transport, it would take her three hours' commuting each day to make the two changes on her journey.

Compulsory travel pass scheme for the UK
Roy Simpson

Public transport has a great deal of spare capacity (but not everywhere and not at all times). This is a resource running to waste. When this spare capacity is made available, eg to a pensioner with an off-peak travel pass, this has a real money value to the recipient, but, as it comes from a resource otherwise running to waste, the cost to the community is very little – an arrangement that is very satisfactory to both sides.

The concept of a compulsory public transport travel pass for motorists (extending the concept behind the university scheme outlined above) would maximise the service public transport can give to the country, and would reduce the pressure on the community of public motoring, but without overburdening the system by allowing unlimited free travel.

As a general principle, local off-peak travel would be unrestricted, but longer journeys would be restricted, using computerised accounting, to a limited number per month, varying according to length of journey, place visited and so on. Commuters might be restricted to a specified journey at peak hours.

'Motorists would automatically pay for their travel pass along with the car tax (and perhaps for their family also)'

Motorists would automatically pay for their pass along with the car tax (and perhaps for their family also). The licence badge on the windscreen would show the type of pass issued. Motorists wishing to enter a city centre or other congested area, would be free to do so subject to car parking charges and provided that they had paid for a pass entitling them to enter the area by public transport.

These measures would greatly reduce the traffic flow whilst using minimum compulsion. Children, senior citizens, the low paid etc would get their passes via the social security system. 'One-off' journeys not covered by a pass would of course be paid for.

Roy Simpson, Chacewater, 13 Dalmore Avenue, Claygate, Surrey KT10 OHQ (tel 0372 65073).

Paying drivers to car-pool
Jim Fox

Adapted extract

Solo commuters are major contributors to traffic congestion. Car-pooling is a simple solution.

'Car-pool drivers would have the chance to win million-dollar prizes'

I propose rewarding car-pool drivers for giving two poolers a ride to work. During the commute, pool drivers would receive $5 at toll booths entering a city and an additional $5 leaving, or $200 a month, plus the chance to win million-dollar prizes.

Drivers deserve this money for the extra gas and effort needed to give two poolers a ride. Solo commuters would pay a $5 toll entering and leaving the city during commute hours, a small price to pay considering the time they save during their total commute.

Vehicles with two people would not pay any toll. During non-commute hours, the $5 toll would not exist. This $5 toll would fund the system. If this worked, commute traffic into cities would decrease by about half.

A dollar from each toll collected would go into a progressive super jackpot. Randomly, jackpots worth $100 or $1,000 or even $1 million would be awarded to poolers, to be split between the driver and riders.

A rider could go to a neighbourhood 'PoolStop' with his colour-coded destination sign and almost instantly get a ride. Women, if they preferred, would only pool with other women. For security, poolers would be issued computerised IDs that could be verified at PoolStop scanner stations. A computer would record who commuted together, which could be recalled in the event of a problem.

'Instant Ride' computerised phone matching system

I am also developing an 'Instant Ride' computerised telephone matching system. All that a potential pooler has to do is to dial the Ride Line and use the telephone keypad to punch in his destination code. The potential pooler would then listen to messages from people offering or needing a ride.

By pressing a key on the telephone, the computer would dial the person who left the message, putting the two people instantly in contact. Since the computer dialled the phone, the privacy of the poolers is ensured. A ride is just a phone call away.

Jim Fox, PO Box 2354, San Anselmo, CA 94960, USA (tel 415 454 7089; 415 897 0220 days; 898 0831 fax).

Car Sharers' Credit Card Club
Roger Martin

Adapted from a paper by Roger Martin.

This proposal is for a system of small government payments to drivers to encourage them both to give lifts. A meter in cars would record the identity card number of those seeking lifts, and the total mileage of the lift.

Pro-rata with the number of miles of club-member lifts given, drivers would be given credits against the following year's licence fee, or a net cash payment for larger mileages.

> ### 'Drivers would be given credits against the following year's licence fee'

Editorial comment

Apart from the bureaucracy and machinery involved, the main snag with this scheme seems to be the ease with which fake mileage claims could be run up, which no system of 'government inspectors', as proposed, could do much about. The Californian proposal of lottery prizes for car-sharing drivers passing though toll booths or check-points (see above) seems preferable – but not, maintains Roger Martin, for the UK:

'There is no pre-existing network of road toll-booths in Britain. I believe my own proposal is more appropriate as well as being cheaper and more flexible, although some kind of lottery could doubtless be tacked onto my scheme as an additional incentive.'

For the full 5 page paper on the car sharers' credit club, contact Roger Martin, Coxley House, Upper Coxley, Wells, Somerset BA5 1QP (tel 0749 72180).

Auctioning the right to have cars

Adapted extract from an article by Brian James in the Times.

Each quarter the Singapore government works out how many new cars it can permit in Singapore (based on numbers scrapped and roads progress) and allocates so many certificates to the four classes of private car, goods vehicle and motorcycles. Would-be owners get a form and make their bid for a Certificate of Entitlement to Purchase a new car.

In the first quarter, Singapore is to permit 14,000 new vehicles. In the family car category, 8,944 citizens bid for 4,583 certificates. The highest bid was more than £4,000, the lowest 33p. Officials counted from the top and the 4,583rd best bid was £1,007. As the lowest successful bid, this set the price for all certificates sold in this category.

> ### 'The 4,583rd best bid was £1,007. As the lowest successful bid, this set the price for all certificates sold'

Would not this system militate against the lower-paid? 'A little,' said Mrs Maria Choy, director of the Land (Transport) Division, 'but we have fine public transport ... the forecast was that as the economy boomed we would be moving towards 350,00 private cars on the island. The government tried to control the growth by taxes but it was all guesswork. So we decided on this approach. Let the government decide how many cars we could tolerate. Let the public decide the price they were prepared to pay to own one of them.'

Speeding up the Piccadilly line to Heathrow

Nicholas Saunders

Adapted extracts from a longer paper.

Improving the Piccadilly underground line to Heathrow would be a swifter (and vastly less expensive) way of improving access to the airport than the planned new British Rail link from Paddington to Heathrow; and it would also of course provide an improved service for Piccadilly line users. It would be worth doing whether or not the BR link is built.

The present Piccadilly underground line, unlike the planned BR Paddington-Heathrow link, serves central London directly, and connects to all British Rail termini via a maximum single change to another underground line.

However, the journey to Piccadilly Circus takes 45 minutes. Without laying extra rails, the service could be speeded up by separating the Uxbridge branch at Acton Town. Trains would not stop at some stations, so that passengers to them would have to change – but an increased frequency of service could nevertheless give these passengers a quicker service overall.

I propose that any one train should stop at only two of the eight stops between Acton Town and Heathrow – say the first and fifth; with the next train stopping at the second and sixth, etc. No trains would stop at Barons Court and Gloucester Road, which are served by parallel lines. This would save eight stops per journey. Additionally, by separating the Uxbridge branch, delays due to coordination at the Acton Town junction are eliminated.

> ### 'Any one train should stop at only two of the eight stops between Acton Town and Heathrow'

At present, trains stop for about 25 seconds to allow passengers to get on and off. In addition, each stop delays them about a further 30 seconds in slowing and accelerating. Thus cutting out eight stops would save eight minutes.

Another cause of delays at present is waiting time for passengers getting on or off – this is worst at busy times, thus delaying following trains and causing more overcrowding and so more delay. An immediate and simple aid would be loudspeaker announcements telling passengers the name of the next station and which side the doors will open.

Upgrading the Piccadilly underground line in these ways would provide a service to Heathrow that was slower than the planned BR link to Paddington, but might provide faster overall journey times for travellers needing central London or other railway stations and more convenience for most airport passengers. It should be possible to get the journey time from Heathrow to Piccadilly Circus down to about 35 minutes.

Nicholas Saunders – see above for address.

Faster tube platforms

The Institute for Social Inventions proposes that London Transport and other operators of underground train networks provide a series of simple small notices on the tube wall on the other side of the rails, facing the traveller waiting on the platform. One notice, for instance, might carry a message to the effect that 'Boarding the train at this point on the platform will give you the least walk the far end, if you are planning to change for the Bakerloo line at Paddington'; another might say that this was the best spot for those going to Holland Park Station. And so on. The notices need not be precisely in the correct location, as this might otherwise interfere with the advertisements (or they could be above the advertisements). They would not only save the traveller's time, but would alleviate the rush and congestion on the platform the other end.

> 'Boarding the train at this point on the platform will give you the least walk the far end, if you are planning to change for the Bakerloo line at Paddington'

This small and inexpensive innovation, requiring minimal upkeep, would help persuade the public that London Transport's orientation is towards caring for its customers.

Improving trains for babies and children

Steven Burkeman

Safe baby seats that locked into place could be made available to parents on Intercity services. The seats would not need to be stored on the trains – just as a wheelchair-bound passenger gives advance notice to British Rail who then arrange for a wheelchair to be available and for the passenger to be escorted to an appropriate place on the train, so the same principle could apply to the use of baby seats. The seat could be made theft-proof by locking it into place for later unlocking by the guard.

Steven Burkeman, 8 Whitby Avenue, York YO3 OET (tel 0904 425499 h; 0904 627810 w). Ed: An irrelevant aside: there is a debate in the States as to whether baby seats on planes should be made compulsory – with fears that if they are, parents will avoid planes for statistically riskier forms of transport, in order not to have to pay for the plane seat that the new baby seat will occupy. The end result would be that more babies would be injured or die.

Children's carriages on the trains

Nicholas Albery

Some of the intercity trains in Switzerland have children's carriages sponsored by companies. In the children's compartment, there are table tops with game boards on them, lots of baby bottles in evidence, and a separate partitioned play area for older children, with benches and telephones with recorded stories, and a safe rocking horse and lego table.

> 'A separate partitioned play area for children on trains'

Nicholas Albery, 20 Heber Road, London NW2 6AA (tel 081 208 2853; fax 081 452 6434).

Comment by British Rail

Adapted extract from response by T.J. Anning, Intercity National Retail Manager

We are seeking to be innovative in our dealings with our equipment but this must be tempered with the need to remain profitable in the future.

We examined the question of children's carriages some three years ago and went as far as to design a play area such as you describe. Whilst this would be a very useful and good aspiration, it has to be held up against commercial considerations.

T.J. Anning, Intercity, British Railways Board, Euston House, 24 Eversholt Street, London NW1 1DZ (tel 071 928 5151; fax 071 922 4163).

Cars piggybacked onto juggernauts

Denis Midgley

My grandfather had a bee in his bonnet. He worked on the railways around the turn of this century and was impressed by the containers of those days. These were small enough to travel by horse and cart or by goods wagon from door to door.

He wanted all goods to be moved in this way. He would lecture me on the advantages and would endlessly deplore the excess of manual labour that went into loading and unloading small packages at docks, goods yards and factory gates.

His dream has come true. And in a most impressive way in terms of the size of our juggernauts and their containers.

Goods traffic has indeed become coordinated, integrated and rationalised.

We should now turn our attention to a similar coordination of passengers.

The penalty for pioneering railways was that tunnels, tracks and stock were all of a near-diminutive Isle-of-Man quaint size. In a similar trap, our modern cars too closely fit the lesser roads. A temporary sacrifice is needed. After all, what is the advantage in sitting beside one's partner on a car journey? Is it akin to a double seat at the cinema?

If we redesign the popular car to be smaller, say by placing its occupants in line astern, we could achieve the following integration:

• For start and end of journey, fan-in and fan-out, using the private small car.

> 'On the juggernaut, escape into a corridor and enjoy a lounge, video and drink'

• For medium journeys over first-class roads, piggyback the car onto a juggernaut, escape into a corridor on the juggernaut, and enjoy a lounge, video and drink.

• For long journeys, piggyback the car onto a small-scale Chunnel type of drive on/off railcoach and again escape into a corridor to relax.

Features of the system

• Use of existing capital investment in simple road/rail infrastructure.

• Compatibility with old, small and appropriate technologies.

Probable features of the small car

• Wholly or partly electric
• Steerable/spinnable/manoeuvrable to new high standards – the Institute of Electrical Engineers (IEE) publications show how front and rear steering and mid-ship idle wheels achieve this.
• Pollution-free hydrogen fuel.
• Comfortable turning without side-slip in the IEE design.
• Easily packable into piggyback hold.
• Variable geometry – insert a midriff to carry four instead of two.

Denis Midgley, 20 Elvaston Avenue, Hornsea, East Yorkshire HU18 1HA (tel 0964 533435).

Insurance sold with petrol

This proposal comes from Paul Blankinship in Vallejo, California:

'By buying a gallon of gasoline, a driver is buying a unit insurance for the time that the gasoline is in the car'

40% of California's drivers are uninsured. The core of my proposal is to bundle costs for gasoline and insurance. By buying a gallon of gasoline, a driver is buying a unit insurance for the period of time that the gasoline is in the car. Gasoline stations would display both the brand of gasoline and the brand of insurance company. Prices for both would be displayed. (The retailer would select which insurance company to ally his station with.)

The consumer benefits by having a fixed cost of insurance that is directly related to their driving. If you normally take alternative forms of transportation but use a car for occasional trips, you have a much lower insurance cost.

The consumer benefits too by having greater competition for his insurance money. Insurance costs per gallon would be clearly posted, allowing much easier comparison shopping. There would also be a reduction in the inherent racial bias of insurance costs. Often lower income areas have a higher insurance cost which shifts the highest burden onto those who can least afford it. This plan would make for truer risk sharing.

The consumer is guaranteed protection in the event of an accident. If a car has gasoline, it is insured. Of course, this implies that the insurance system works under a no-fault rule. Regardless of fault, you are fully covered.

'The incentive for drivers to get into more fuel-efficient cars would increase dramatically'

The increase in gasoline costs would be beneficial. Because higher gas mileage would equal higher insurance mileage, the incentive for drivers to get into more fuel-efficient cars would increase dramatically. An increase in alternative forms of transportation and in mass transit could be expected.

A simple way to manage the system might be to issue a computer-coded driver's licence which would be needed to refuel. In addition to establishing who the most recent insurance carrier is, the driver could be ordered to surrender his card if serious driving violations occur. This would make it more difficult for more dangerous drivers to get on the road, reducing risk, and possibly insurance cost.

This idea is flexible. The basic concept can be stretched to add new taxes (for example taxes for mass transit or health care). And driver's licences could be coded to reflect certain risk factors (such as age or driving record).

All the main parties involved can gain by this idea:

Gasoline retailers would be induced to participate because they would have a second profitable enterprise – insurance. Depending on the cost of insurance-per-mile retailers could perhaps make an additional profit of 50-100%.

Insurance companies would be attracted to the idea because currently uninsured drivers would be paying insurance. (Such companies would also continue to supply additional comprehensive cover.)

There would be secondary savings to the government from not having to pay for property and health care costs incurred by uninsured motorists.

Paul Blankinship, 1661 Gateway Drive, Vallejo, California 94589, USA (tel 707 645 7445).

Oil company buys up old cars to clear smog

Adapted extract from an item by Martin Walker in the Guardian.

In what is being hailed as an imaginative and cost-effective anti-pollution measure, the California-based Unocal oil corporation is spending $5 million to buy up 7,000 old cars for recycling.

'Offering the owners of old bangers $700 in cash, and a one-month free bus pass'

Advertisements are being posted across Los Angeles offering the owners of old bangers $700 in cash, and a one-month free bus pass in return for their polluting old heaps.

'Thirty per cent of smog is coming from pre-1975 automobiles,' says Unocal chairman Richard Stegemeier. 'If you want to make a big impact in a hurry, this is by far the quickest and most cost-effective way.'

Unocal has opened a central junkyard employing 30 people, equipped to process 12 cars each hour, 40 hours a week.

Auctioning unsold airline tickets

Adapted extract from Insight (USA), monitored for the Institute by Roger Knights.

The San Francisco firm Marketel International Inc. is attempting to set up an electronic market for airline tickets that would enable potential passengers and travel agents to submit bids for seats. The requests would list destinations and desired departure date and time, as well as what the consumer is willing to pay. Airlines would plug into the system to pick the bids they want to accept, thus enabling them to earn some money from seats that would otherwise remain empty. Marketel plans to make its money by charging less than $10 for every bid placed and a similar fee for each bid accepted by a vendor.

> 'Passengers would list destinations and desired departure date and time, as well as what they are willing to pay'

The company hopes to begin offering the computerised service next spring through such reservations systems as American Airlines' Sabre and United Airlines' Apollo, both used extensively by travel agents in the States, but Bill Perell, Marketel's co-founder, acknowledges that no agreements have been reached. The plan also calls for customers with personal computers to be able to place their bids directly on the data base through various home computer services.

The Last Minute Club

The travel industry has created a new way to market excess capacity and airline seats. The Last Minute Club of Toronto (an example of lateral thinking in its own right) has started to market 'mystery weekends' to a surprise resort in the Caribbean. Travellers are only told at the airport about plans for their final destination.

Applied Thinking Digest, 116 Galley Avenue, Toronto, Ontario M6R 1H1, Canada (tel 416 533 9667). Subs $45.

Comment by Nicholas Albery

A third possibility would be to have a small auction booth at each airport where last minute tickets to particular destinations would be auctioned off, leaving just time to book in luggage and to board the plane. This way people would have more control over their destination, there would be the thrill of trying to pick up a bargain at the auction, airlines would be less at risk of discounting tickets they could have sold at the regular price and they will get the best price possible in the circumstances.

> 'A small auction room at each airport where last minute tickets to particular destinations would be auctioned off'

Nicholas Albery, 20 Heber Road, London NW2 6AA (tel 081 208 2853; fax 081 452 6434).

Better express coach network

The Institute for Social Inventions proposed a network of express coaches in the UK going up and down motorways only, stopping briefly at motorway service stations en route, at an airport-style interchange, where passengers would change to local buses. (The coaches would ideally be designed for luggage to accompany the passenger inside the coach, to reduce time spent at stops.)

This led to a working party on the issue, and to a variant scheme proposed by Professor Pat Willmore of the Department of Cybernetics at the University of Reading, who writes:

'The salient point is that the interchange stations should be developed at the motorway exits instead of the service stations, as the former provide the real points of connection between the motorways and other roads.'

Professor Willmore has suggested that the scheme could be tested by means of a pilot project on the M4 at Exit 11.

> 'Time lost to a coach in stopping and starting would be less than two minutes, as compared with some twenty minutes in getting in and out of a town centre'

The existing density of coaches on, for instance, the M4 motorway would provide about a 10 minute service in each direction and the target for time lost to a coach in stopping and starting would be less than two minutes, as compared with some twenty minutes in getting in and out of a town centre.

At the London end of the M4, Hammersmith underground station (saving another 20 minutes as compared with the journey through traffic to Victoria Coach Station) would be the natural London terminal, and an orbital coach service round the M25 would be the way of connecting the M4 service with those on other motorways. The M4/M25 intersection would become the coach station for Heathrow, with specialised shuttles serving the airport terminals.

Postscript

A similar scheme has been implemented by Milton Keynes Borough Council in its Coachway interchange to connecting buses. 'But it is rather dismal with few facilities,' writes Simon Norton. 'At least if interchanges were sited at existing service station, one could get something to eat.'

• *Professor Willmore, 'Inverdene', Reading Road, Burghfield Common, Berks RG7 3BT. His full paper on buses is entitled 'A Unifying Strategy for Public Passenger Transport'.*

• *Simon Norton in his paper 'The Missing Link' proposes the extension of the scheme to provide a network of cross-country buses that would give rural areas direct access to the inter-city coach and rail networks. Simon Norton's address is 6 Hertford Street, Cambridge, CB4 3AG (tel 0223 312654).*

Roof roads

David Stephens

David Stephens, a consultant building engineer, has been arguing the case for constructing purpose-made roof road buildings for 20 years or more – see for instance a four page article in the New Scientist, June 26th 1969, pp 683 ff. Here is his proposal in favour of such roads in Wales:

Wales needs better roads, especially a North/South connection to motorway standard. A linear building supporting a road on its roof is apt for hilly country: the road stays level or suffers only gentle gradients, while the ground rises and falls beneath. Construction costs provide useful buildings, instead of being wasted on earth moving for embankments and cuttings.

> 'Roof roads would be better in every respect than surface roads; for example land take and costs are less than half that of separate roads and buildings'

Roof roads would be better in every respect than surface roads; for example land take and costs are less than half that of separate roads and buildings; the buildings beneath would be unbelievably quiet and could be used even for housing; and noise levels and other pollution emitted to adjacent neighbourhoods would be less than from fast or hilly conventional roads.

The floor beneath a roof road would provide not only parking and goods servicing for the roof road buildings, but an easy conduit for services such as water and district heating mains, and perhaps a small automatic railway transporting coal and rubbish to combined heat and power stations along the roof road. The human activity along the road would support a bus service. Both the roof road buildings and adjacent communities would benefit from its services.

Roof road buildings are a good investment for the future, unlike conventional motorways. The heated buildings, probably with a simple steel frame, have an indefinite potential life, and when petroleum supplies become short, electric trams and battery electric vehicles can provide energy economical transport of people and goods.

Location within a roof road building would be attractive for both businesses and residences, with their countryside views and nearby first class road connection to North and South Wales and the national motorway network. This unique development could be very attractive to property interests. The road could thus be built with private capital, at no cost to the taxpayer.

David Stephens, Tir Gaia Solar Village, Rhayader, Powys LD6 5AG (tel 0597 810929).

Services under pavements not roads

Nicholas Saunders

Nicholas Saunders presents an idea which is by no means new, but which is innovative in its details:

To avoid the constant digging up and filling in of holes in the road for the installation, repair and renewal of telephone, gas, electricity and water services, there should be permanent channels installed just under the pavement of cities, about one metre deep and 80cms wide.

> 'To avoid the constant digging up and filling of holes in the road for the installation, repair and renewal of telephone, gas, electricity and water services, there should be permanent channels installed just under the pavement'

These would form a network under every pavement, linked by similar channels crossing streets. They would be concrete, with loose paving stones on top. Services would run along one side wall, with connections to buildings made through the wall.

To gain access, all that would be required would be to lift the paving slabs and replace them. In some cases, it would be possible to carry out inspections by crawling along without lifting many slabs. The slabs would be designed to allow plenty of ventilation by means of small gaps between them. The channel would be drained to avoid flooding.

Where major roads are crossed, slightly larger tunnels could be used to avoid any interference to the traffic. This would also enable the tarmac road surface to continue above the services.

A further advantage would be to enable the installation of new services. In Denmark, for instance, they have recently installed rubbish-burning plants that provide hot water which is piped to the houses.

I believe that such a scheme would be economic in itself, apart from the improvement in the quality of life that would be brought about by eliminating pneumatic drills and dangerous holes.

Nicholas Saunders, top floor, 14 Neal's Yard, London WC2H 9DP (tel 071 836 9404; fax 071 379 0135).

Neighbourhood car rental (Berlin)

From an unidentified cutting sent to the Institute.

Car sharing has been shown to work in Berlin, with forty neighbours sharing three cars. With adequate public transport, these people find a car a necessity only a few times a month. On these occasions they call up the neighbourhood car rental Stadt Auto and reserve one of the three cars stationed on the block where they live. They each have keys to all three vehicles and reckon on an 80 per cent chance of obtaining a car.

> 'Forty neighbours have keys to all three vehicles and reckon on an 80 per cent chance of obtaining a car'

Established by Markus Peterson, Stadt Auto is 'not a great money maker, but it works.' It is used mainly for leisure, shopping and moving heavy items, never for rush-hour commuting. The service has a sliding scale of costs according to the time and place of use. For Berlin travel the rate is about £1·06 per hour on weekdays and 70p in the evening or at the weekends. A charge of roughly £13 per day is levied for travel outside Berlin. There is no charge per kilometre but users must buy their own fuel.

The two-family car (UK)

Adapted from an article in the Independent by Andrew Bibby.

The Kendon family in Sheffield share the use of a second hand Volkswagen Passat with friends who live nearby, with whom they split the cost of purchase and share the running costs. Both households have signed a written agreement, laying down for instance that each family is entitled to two weeks' uninterrupted use each year. At other times, each family has responsibility for the car for a week at a time. 'If you need to use the car in your own week, you have priority,' says Adrian Kendon, 'but if you want to use it in the other family's week then you have to arrange it with them, or hire a car.'

There is an agreed 5p charge payable to a joint bank account for each mile driven, and the families settle up on expenses, including petrol, once a month. The car is insured in one person's name, with the other participants listed as named drivers. The AA car breakdown service requires a member of each family to be full members, even if sharing one car. A cheaper option is to choose a scheme where the car, not the driver, is insured, such as the Environmental Transport Association, using GESA Assistance.

Town-Welcome Lay-bys

Colin Gentles

I travel around quite a lot. On the outskirts of every town there is a need for a lay-by with a decent loo, unvandalised payphone, town plan and directory of industry, commerce and facilities, plus ample space to leave one's car and with a shuttle bus into town. Could these not be cooperative ventures between, for instance, the tourist boards, the AA or RAC, the local authorities and places such as Little Chefs?

Colin Gentles, 41 Thames Mead, Crowmarsh Gifford, Wallingford, Oxon (tel 0491 37778).

Compass bearings on signs

Anne Greenwood

I prefer to know the general direction in which I am going when there is any distance involved. Hence I would like a simple compass bearing to be added to some signs which would lead you in the direction you want. Names, unless they are familiar, are an irrelevance. This would be particularly useful in some country areas where many roads lead to villages by different routes. But it would be good in London too I think.

Anne Greenwood, 120 Emmanuel Road, London SW12 HSO.

Car-free cycling

Nicholas Albery

One of the least known aspects of cycling is that it is possible and exhilarating to bicycle, hardly meeting a motor vehicle all the way, from say Ladbroke Grove to Kew, Slough, Hemel Hempstead or Birmingham – simply by buying a £3 permit from British Waterways (7th Floor, Gresham House, 53 Clarendon Road, Watford, Herts) which gives access to the canal towpaths. The route requires an adventurous spirit – occasionally cyclists fall off the narrow paths into the canal, there are motorbike barriers where the bike has to be carried, punctures are frequent, buckled wheels a possibility, fishermen with their rods across the path represent an occasional obstacle, and teenage gangs have been known to use cyclists for airgun target practice.

> 'It is possible and exhilarating to bicycle along canal towpaths, hardly meeting a motor vehicle all the way, from Ladbroke Grove to Kew, or Birmingham'

But given the dangers of cycling along main roads, and the very high costs of regular cycle paths (£32,000 was spent recently on one short stretch circumventing the Shepherds Bush roundabout), it would seem that a relatively small investment – perhaps financed by a more substantial cycle permit fee – could widen the towpaths and improve their surfaces, along the 2,000 miles of British Waterways; and the constant passing of cyclists would provide greater surveillance for the barge owners who at present suffer from frequent vandalism.

These paths could then form a link with the disused railway lines now being converted into cycle tracks. Many stretches of the canal, such as that from Peachey Common to Slough, are very derelict on both banks, and would be further improved by canalside housing – or by homeless people being allowed to rent barge accommodation, with regular canal taxis offering transport to city centres. Our canals are still a very underused resource. How many tourists, for instance, appreciate that Birmingham has more canals than Venice?

Non-impotence-causing bike seats

Adapted extract from an item in 'Which? way to Health'.

It seems that there could be a need to develop softer cycle seats without a hard, narrow central ridge, to avoid compression of the nerves leading to the genitals, if the following complaint does indeed occur 'more commonly than is recognised.'

A long-distance cycle race had near disastrous results for a 27 year old man whose case was reported in the British Medical Journal. The man was suffering from secondary erectile impotence after taking part in a 200km cycle race five months previously. He was not used to cycling long distances and was forced to stop only 32 km into the race because of severe pain and an urgent need to urinate. On doing so he noticed that 'his penis was completely shrivelled and had lost all sensation.' The pain then subsided and he was able to finish the race despite further frequent stops.

After the race the man, who had previously enjoyed normal sexual function, suffered total loss of erections for three weeks as well as impaired penile sensation. Doctors at the local hospital concluded that the hard narrow saddle of the cycle had probably led to the compression of the nerves. Although only one other case of 'short-term erectile impotence' has been reported, they believe this condition to be a lot more common than is recognised.

> 'After the cycle race the man, who had previously enjoyed normal sexual function, suffered total loss of erections '

Three months later the cyclist had fully recovered.

'Which? way to Health' (subs. from The Consumers' Association, PO Box 44, Hertford SG14 1SH).

Pneumatic bike seats

Howard Noyes

I have designed a bicycle seat for women and men who aren't masochists. It is pneumatic, prototyped and patented (US 4, 611, 851). A sample is available for those interested in manufacture anywhere outside the States. It is called the Derriair, of all things.

> 'I have designed a bicycle seat for women and men who aren't masochists. It is pneumatic and patented'

Anyone interested in manufacturing the seat in Europe should get in touch with me.

Howard Noyes, The Carriage House, Whaley Abbey, Clash, County Wicklow, Ireland.

Bike with wheelchair on front

Neatwork in Berwickshire are distributing a bike with a detachable wheelchair on the front (which acts as the front wheels of the bike). It is 'a wheelchair tandem that lets a wheelchair user and a friend ride together in comfort and style. You can chat together as you move along, and the chair user is active and involved – map reading, indicating, taking photos – and there's no more lifting in and out of cars to do.'

This 'Duet' bike is imported from Germany, where 400 have been made, with some 30 sold in Britain to date, at prices from £1,800. Any profits made by Neatwork are going to help make an activity centre in the Scottish borders for families with disabled members.

Neatwork, the Lees Stables, Coldstream, Berwickshire TD12 4NN (tel 0890 3456; fax 0890 2709). Neatwork also sell bike trailers, bike child trailers and other unusual bike products.

Hitch-hiker safety postcards

Adapted by Nicholas Albery from a suggestion by Celia Fremlin.

To help reduce the risk of women hitch-hikers being molested or raped, it might help if they were hitching, whenever possible, from beside a postbox. They would have a supply of postcards, addressed to a friend, and would write down the spot from which they are hitching and the date and time. If about to accept a lift they would complete the card by writing down the vehicle's number and then posting it – and the friend would know to raise the alarm if not receiving subsequent news of the hitch-hiker's safe arrival. The driver's knowledge that the card was posted would act as a deterrent to assault.

There could be a network of such postboxes at the main hitching points, perhaps with their installation financed by a charity such as the Suzy Lamplugh Trust (set up after the disappearance of Diana Lamplugh's daughter).

> 'If about to accept a lift they would complete the postcard by writing down the vehicle's number and then posting it'

In the absence of a postbox, hitch-hikers could give the cards to passers-by or fellow hitchers to post or could leave them on the wayside in a small transparent envelope marked 'Urgent. Please Post The Card Inside.'

Celia Fremlin, 11 Parkhill Road, London NW3.

Hitch-hikers' raffle tickets

P.M. Bailey

This scheme used to operate in Eastern Europe. The idea was that potential travellers could buy books of lottery style tickets from a central state monitoring organisation, then hitch wherever they liked, giving every driver a ticket. At the end of the month a draw would be held to reward the lucky winner. It promotes the pooling of cars, and legitimises the hitcher above the level of scrounger.

P.M. Bailey, 44 Sparrowmire Lane, Hallgarth, Kendal, Cumbria (tel 0539 733204).

Tips from California

Nicholas Saunders noticed several good small transport social inventions in California, which he felt could be adopted in the UK. For instance, his host was caught going over a 'stop' sign and was given a choice of a big fine or a small one (and no offence appearing on his record) if he attended eight hours of 'traffic school' (one Yellow Pages ad for recognised traffic schools claimed 'Why groan? – laugh your way through traffic school.' They employed only 'top rate' comedians).

Saunders also liked the way that drivers on the main streets are alerted to the names of the next street crossing theirs by signs attached to lamposts.

Eye signs on the road

David Wade

So as to reduce accidents – amongst tourists, children and others – when crossing streets, white eyes and eyebrows, with the pupils painted in indicating which way to look, would be painted on the road surface.

David Wade is a writer of books on Islamic design. He suggests that 'ambi-perplexity' – his term for the confusion people have in telling their left from their right, which is the 'bane of all drill sergeants' – is a far more widespread condition than is generally recognised.

Children, tourists and sufferers from 'ambi-perplexity' all have their lives endangered, especially when crossing one-way streets, with traffic coming from an unexpected direction.

'Look Left' or 'Look Right' signs are not readily taken in, and the arrows sometimes used, although more direct, are ambiguous, because they can be taken to indicate the direction of traffic.

Wade suggests that eyes and pupils painted on the roads would save lives and would add to the growing stock of what Wade terms the 'international pictogram language', found on road signs, cleaning labels and so on, which is fast becoming like 'a Chinese esperanto of the eye.'

> **'Look Left or Look Right signs are not readily taken in, and the arrows sometimes used, although more direct, are ambiguous, because they can be taken to indicate the direction of traffic'**

David Wade, Plas Tylwych, Tylwych, near Llanidloes, Powys, Wales (tel 0597 88627). This scheme won a Social Inventions Award.

Comment by Mr M.J.Read

Mr M.J.Read, the director of road safety at the Royal Society for the Prevention of Accidents, comments: 'This suggestion is both simple and complete. We receive many many 'bright ideas', most of which are commendable in that they are trying to tackle the terrible road accident problem. Most, however, are usually impracticable for a variety of reasons. I have pleasure, therefore in commending this proposal.'

Pedestrians crossing roads on sleeping policemen

Mayer Hillman

Rather than the *vehicle* being uninterrupted at each road intersection, what is required is an uninterrupted *pedestrian* network consisting of linked pavements. To achieve this, two elements of the traffic engineer's bag of tricks can be integrated – the pedestrian crossing and the road hump (sleeping policeman). Pedestrians then walk across broad-topped humps which are the width of conventional crossings, and are paved and at the same level as the pavement. Likewise, the full 'square' of road intersections is raised and paved at pavement level. The effects of this is to create the continuous pedestrian network.

> **'The full 'square' of road intersections is raised and paved at pavement level. The effects of this is to create the continuous pedestrian network'**

At present, the pedestrian network in our towns and cities is interrupted at every road section, This is because in terms of the continuity of surfacing and minimising of delay, priority has traditionally been given to wheeled traffic. As a consequence, pedestrians are obliged to run the gauntlet of moving vehicles when they wish to get from one 'safe haven' of pavement to the next. Alternatively, usually by making a detour, they may be able to use a pedestrian crossing where they can cross with some greater, through not absolute confidence – nearly 10 per cent of pedestrian casualties occur on these crossings.

In an age when it is becoming increasingly recognised that the more journeys that can be made on foot rather than by motorised means, the better is the public interest served on social, economic, environmental, energy-saving, and equity grounds, there is a strong case for re-ordering this priority.

Evidence from the UK and the continent shows that drivers have to reduce their speed sharply to mount road humps and that they drive slowly and considerately when traversing paved areas. Whilst drivers would incur a few seconds' delay at each pedestrian crossing, this new arrangement would ensure greater convenience for people getting about on foot as well as, of course, making it much safer for them. It would also give parents concerned about the risk of their children being injured in a road accident the confidence they have been losing at an alarming rate to permit them to make the school and other journeys on their own. The idea is just now beginning to be adopted in such places as Covent Garden in London and in York.

> **'Drivers have to reduce their speed sharply to mount road humps and they drive slowly and considerately when traversing paved areas'**

Dr Mayer Hillman, Senior Fellow, Policy Studies Institute, 100 Park Village East, London NW1 3SR (tel 071 387 2171; fax 071 388 0914).

Chapter seventeen

COMMUNICATIONS

Diffusion of social inventions

Adapted extract from 'Spreading Personal Growth in Society' (published by the Artemis Trust) which provides an overview of the theories about how innovations are best diffused in society.

The cure for scurvy is one example of numerous documented cases of extremely important innovations which might have been expected to have succeeded quickly, but which did not.

> 'Scurvy was responsible for extremely high death rates in the Navy. Its prevention, by eating citrus fruits, was discovered in 1601, but the innovation was not adopted in the British navy until 1795'

Scurvy was responsible for extremely high death rates in the Navy. Its prevention, by eating citrus fruits, was discovered in 1601. Further successful experiments took place in 1747, but the innovation was not adopted in the British Navy until 1795, 194 years after the discovery. Scurvy was immediately wiped out, but it took a further 70 years for the Merchant Navy to adopt the cure...

We cannot emphasise this strongly enough: our studies show that a common cause for lack of success is that the practitioner or change agent attempting to promote an activity fails to find out how the potential adopters perceive it...

For an innovation to succeed, there must be an absence of incompatability with society's attitudes and mores, but this is not enough. There must also be the positive characteristics of meeting people's immediate and particular needs, being easy to try, and with good availability and clearly observable results...

Opinion leaders are crucial in spreading the word about the value of an innovation or growth activity. They either make an idea so acceptable that it spreads quickly through the network or else they give it the kiss of death. How do you identify opinion leaders? By asking a few people in any particular network who is the person whose opinion they value, a consensus will become clear...

A rough rule of thumb is that personal contact produces eight attendees (to personal growth workshops) for every one generated by impersonal communications...

To persuade someone to adopt an innovation, the most effective way is generally to tell stories, for instance the case history of someone who had adopted the activity with successful results. Here it is important that the case history is about someone with whom the potential adoptee can identify...

Research shows that when 10 to 25% of the population has adopted an innovation, the whole process becomes self-sustaining. From this point onwards, there is so much forward momentum that the idea catches on like wildfire through personal networks; little effort is needed to encourage more and more people to adopt it.

The booklet is directed at humanistic psychology practitioners wishing to increase the size of their practice, but, as these extracts show, it has a wider relevance for any aspiring social inventor. 'Spreading Personal Growth in Society', published by the Artemis Trust, 19 Park Hill, Ealing, London W5 2JS (tel 081 997 9401), £5.

Innovation Diffusion Game

Alan Atkisson and In Context magazine have designed an Innovation Diffusion Game for playing by 25 or more players, where a problem is set for participants to converse about (such as 'shopping as a compulsion'). Each person is given not only a part to play, from 'innovator' to 'mainstreamer' to 'iconoclast', but also suggestions about the sorts of things to say.

> 'Each person is given a part to play, from "innovator" to "mainstreamer" to "iconoclast" '

They then all mill around conversing from within their roles, with the audience ('muses of imagination') offering suggestions to the innovator. The innovator's suggestions (eg 'carol singing to replace shopping') either make progress or don't. At the end of not more than 20 minutes, the facilitator calls a halt, and the audience discusses what it has learnt about how innovations get, or don't get, adopted in society.

The innovation diffusion theories which the game should help to demonstrate include:

• that an idea has the best chance of getting adopted if it shows: an easily perceivable advantage over present methods; compatibility with existing mores; simplicity; triability in small ways, without having to make a complete plunge; and easily discernible positive results.

• that innovations start with an innovator, often a single individual with a new idea; then spreads through the work of change agents targeting opinion leaders; then if it reaches a critical mass – with about 15% of the population accepting the idea – it takes off irreversibly, with a life of its own.

The parts which have to be assigned at the start of the game are:

• The spiritual recluse (1 player);
• The curmudgeon (1 player);
• The innovator (1 player);
• The iconoclast (1 player);
• The change agent (2 players);
• The reactionary (2 players);
• The transformer (3 players);
• The laggard (3 players);
• The mainstreamer (6 players).

For a 5 page article detailing the game, see In Context magazine No. 28, $7 from In Context, PO Box 11470, Bainbridge Island, WA 98110, USA (tel 206 842 0216; fax 206 842 5208). Subs $25.

The Encyclopedia of 13,167 World Problems

'The Encyclopedia of World Problems and Human Potential' is a two-volume compendium on 13,167 'world problems' recognised by official and unofficial international bodies. The descriptions include 'counter-claims' (denying the significance of the problem from other perspectives) and the network of 80,000 relationships to other problems. The second volume focuses on the human and conceptual resources available to analyse the problems and to put them in new contexts, so as to be able to respond more appropriately to them.

The Encyclopedia, now in its third edition, is produced by the Union of International Associations as a complement to its three-volume Yearbook of International Organisations (which describes some 20,000 international bodies and the relations between them).

The Human Potential volume includes descriptions of 1,300 concepts of human development and of 2,700 modes of awareness (states of consciousness) from every discipline and culture (including over 900 from Buddhism), with over 15,000 links and pathways between them. There is also a section on ways to transform conferences. Other sections cover 2,200 constructive and destructive values, 700 concepts of conceptual integration, and the use of metaphors and patterns to help visualise problems from new and creative perspectives.

The editor's own bias seems to be that the world is too miraculous to be fully describable within the language of any single conceptual framework, however sophisticated, and that the nearest approximation is to alternate between 'essentially incommensurable perspectives.'

'The world is too miraculous to be fully describable within the language of any single conceptual framework'

The Encyclopedia (published by K.G. Saur Ltd, 1991, ISBN 3 10842 7, price £259) is edited by Anthony Judge at the Union of International Associations, 40 Rue Washington, Brussels B 1050, Belgium (tel 32 2 640 1808; fax 32 2 649 3269).

Next moves by the Encyclopedia's editor

Anthony Judge writes:

We are exploring two strategies to take us forward:

(a) **Graphics**: We believe that there is a great need for appropriate graphics to interrelate the fragmented features of our perceptual universe. We see this challenge as a problem of marrying computer abilities to manipulate data and to represent it graphically, with the problem of transforming such representations into psychologically meaningful ones.

We believe that superficial images of 'One Earth' and the 'Global Village' may be necessary, but they are certainly not sufficient to engender appropriate change. Equally we believe that sophisticated models, meaningful only to specialists, are not appropriately constrained by the need to render them meaningful enough in a highly politicised world for a real use to be made of them. It is the meaningful marriage between these two mutually hostile approaches that excites us.

(b) **Use of metaphors**: Given the low probability that major institutionalised programmes will make significant breakthroughs, and do more than limit the increasing damage to the world, the question is whether people can be empowered in new ways to perceive the opportunity for more innovative and appropriate responses. We consider metaphors one of the major unexplored resources, and the challenge of designing and 'delivering' metaphors to be one of great significance at this time (as indicated in our Encyclopedia section on the question). We are developing a project on this, hopefully with the United Nations University.

Reinventing your metaphoric habitat

Anthony Judge

Adapted extract from a fax from Anthony Judge, editor of the Encyclopedia of World Problems, (see entry above).

Most people do not question the obligation to live in a world whose nature and structure has been articulated by the experts of today and of the past. From this comfortable perspective realities are imposed upon us and our universe is designed for us. Like the fish in the depths of the ocean, we live under a weight of explanations and received opinions which tends to crush the slightest gleam of imagination and alternative understanding.

But maybe the world we think we live in can more fruitfully be understood as a metaphor in which we have got trapped.

'For those labouring in a bureaucracy, it can be reconfigured imaginatively as the Court of Louis XIV'

In this light we are each free (within limits) to design our own metaphoric habitats. For those labouring in a bureaucracy, it can be reconfigured imaginatively as the Court of Louis XIV – replete with courtiers, courtesans and people pissing in the corners!

Many corporations are locked into a pattern of military, sporting and physiological metaphors.

And who obliged you to think of yourself as 'human'? Feel free therefore to consider yourself a visitor from a distant galaxy and enjoy the amazing behaviour of the range of species you encounter during your visit here.

Are you despairing over your degree of spiritual enlightenment? Explore the fact that you have already achieved full enlightenment and are simply indulging in the illusion of searching for it – rather like a cat chasing its tail! If the 'insane' can be Napoleons and God, what is to stop you enjoying a change of status, provided it does not trap you? Try being an unrecognised genius or a billionaire from Sirius. Cultivate those who belong to the same species as yourself and develop your own unique language and garb.

How does casting metaphors differ from casting spells? Or maybe you can be a shapeshifter, modifying your form to respond to different environments. How about re-imagining the vehicle in which you are travelling as a spaceship? Do you have any contract requiring you to buy into realities which you find alienating – and to whose design you have not consciously contributed?

Join the metaphoric diaspora (Slogan: 'Have metaphor, will travel'). The product of the future will be intriguing metaphors that rearticulate your lifestyle.

Anthony Judge, Union of International Associations, rue Washington 40, 1050 Brussels, Belgium (tel 32 2 640 1808; fax 32 2 649 3269).

Problem maps like star maps

Phyllis J. O' Rourke

Adapted extract from an article from the newsletter Cassiopedia-2048 about the Encyclopedia of World Problems and Human Potential.

The social sciences have long needed a methodology for exploring the dynamic relationships between competing and incompatible ideas for solving world problems.

'Network problem maps are needed so that the relationships among problems, values, and human development can be visualised'

In order to develop a dynamic conceptual foundation appropriate to the global order of the future, network problem maps are needed so that the relationships among problems, values, and human development can be visualised and discussed among various communities, particularly to show relationships among location of resources, population density, regions of growth and economic development, political systems, differences in laws and other features of social systems which vary across cultures.

Discussing global problems today is fragmented and chaotic, as would be any discussion of space travel without star maps and telescopes describing the territory to be covered. Without such problem maps, it is extremely difficult, if not impossible, to work in concert, locally or globally, to galvanise political will for action.

Once such network problem maps are developed, they could be bound in atlases to help individuals, communities and nations visualise relationships, distances and differences among problem territories. Global decision making could then be grounded in an accurate understanding of locally perceived problems, and local communities could act in concert toward mutually beneficial solutions to common problems.

Phyllis J. O'Rourke, c/o O'Rourke & Associates, PO Box 889, Lyons, Colorado 80540, USA (tel 303 823 5677).

How are the Institute's forecasts for the nineties getting on?

Some of the Institute for Social Inventions' forecasts for the nineties (drawn up with help from the Institute's consultants and published in December '89) turned out to be prescient, although the majority have yet to (and may never) come about. Thus of its forecasts specifically for 1991, the at-least-half-right predictions were as follows:

• 'The key battle of our times is between the decentralists and the centralisers, and happily the various decentralist Davids around the world are defeating the Goliaths, whose empires of power are crumbling. This irresistible process will continue to gather pace during 1991: the Baltic republics will regain their independence, Yugoslavia will disintegrate into its constituent republics, and perestroika will sweep through the African continent, particularly Malawi, Zimbabwe and Zambia.'

In the event: correct in outline, although of the three African countries named, only Zambia experienced this perestroika.

• 'The most depressing clashes in 1991 will be, not between the Davids and their Goliaths, but between these Davids and their own dwarf Davids – for the newly autonomous nations will prove unwilling to give sufficient autonomy to their own minority groups; civil war and ethnic turmoil are on the horizon for 1991, with places such as South Ossetia in Georgia, Gagauz in Moldavia and Kosovo in Yugoslavia as likely flashpoints.'

In the event: the flashpoints were elsewhere, but the general tendency has been sadly as prepared for by the Institute; in the same month that the civil war broke out in Yugoslavia, it published the book 'Can Civil Wars be Avoided?' by Dr David Chapman.

• 'As for the Gulf situation, war with Iraq seems likely in February, but should end within weeks with Iraq's defeat. The bigger danger is the instability of Islam ... So, for instance, Egyptian involvement in the war with Iraq, or fundamentalism in Algeria could lead to Islamic civil wars in 1991.'

In the event: the ground war with Iraq did take place in February '91 and ended in days with Iraq's defeat. There were no civil wars in Islamic countries, apart from inside Iraq itself, although there were violent clashes with fundamentalists, street disturbances and killings in Algiers.

• '[There will be growing environmental] ... concern (at present voiced almost solely by Dr Clube of Oxford's Dept. of Astrophysics) about the fragmentation of the Taurid-Arietid meteor stream and cometary core; there will be growing anxiety about ... the danger of ice ages resulting from a "cometary winter" caused by the impact on the planet of Tunguska-scale bodies.'

In the event: this concern hardly achieved a high public prominence during the year, but it is spreading slowly: there was an international conference of more than 160 planetary scientists, astronomers and engineers in San Jaun Capistrano, California, on the dangers of near-Earth asteroids:

'Half the earth's population might die after an asteroid a mile across had collided'

David Morrison of Nasa's Ames Research Centre was reported in the Times as saying: 'we're talking about almost unbelievable widespread death and destruction.' Half the earth's population might die after an asteroid a mile across had collided and damaged the climate and farming, he said.

Dr Morrison said that such an asteroid hit the earth every 300,000 to one million years. The risk was greater than that of being killed by fireworks, tornados, volcanic eruptions, nuclear accidents or terrorism.

Astronomers want more early-warning telescopes like the American Spacewatch camera, at Kitt Peak, Arizona. Dr Bailey said that six of these telescopes, costing £250,000 to £500,000, should be placed at different longitudes and latitudes to observe asteroids and to measure their orbits accurately. This could give us years of warning, allowing us to take action, perhaps by blasting the incoming asteroid with nuclear explosives.

Predictions for the nineties

Of the longer-term predictions for the nineties published by the Institute in December '89 the following seem to have been on the right tracks:

• 'As for nationalism, "you ain't seen nothing yet", with the prospect of a dozen Northern Irelands [in Eastern Europe and elsewhere] and a new role for NATO and the Warsaw Pact trying jointly to curb these outbreaks.'

• (An Institute prediction published in the Times in December '88:) 'In Eastern Europe there will be emerging confederations of small nations'

• 'There will be a rise in very right-wing anti-immigration movements in Europe.'

• 'Russia to follow the path of Eastern Europe towards democracy before the end of 1990, and to suffer the same upheavals.'

In the event: this forecast about Russia was premature by a few months.

The main predictions for the nineties which have not yet happened, but which the Institute stands by, include:

'Hong Kong will never be handed back to the Chinese. By the due date, China will itself have convulsed its way out of communism, and will allow Hong Kong and Tibet their independence'

• 'Hong Kong will never be handed back to the Chinese. By the due date, China will itself have convulsed its way out of communism, and will allow Hong Kong and Tibet their independence.'

• 'A collapse of the Common Market – unable to take the strains of accommodating Eastern Europe, the Tower of Babel at Brussels will collapse, with the EC at best remaining as a Commonwealth of Europe.'

• 'There will be further moves towards cantonising South Africa along Swiss lines, and this Swiss cantonisation model will begin to be adopted in Eastern Europe, as a way of tackling the problems of ethnic conflict.'

• 'There will be an independent Scotland and an independent Northern Ireland.'

• 'There will be an outbreak of nuclear or chemical terrorist blackmail against a European city' (with the dire consequences outlined in 'Social Inventions' Journal No. 19, page 8).

• 'Sell your Channel tunnel shares. The tunnel will not last ten years, given its vulnerability to terrorists, and its symbolic value to them.'

New Paradigms Newsletter

Alan Mayne

At the present time of rapid changes and serious crises in the human situation, it has become more important than ever before to bring into being new ideas, new thinking and new visions that can lead mankind through its present difficulties towards the next stage of evolution.

Never before, as far as I know, has there been a publication such as mine that provides a regular broad introductory survey of the whole range of New Paradigms ideas – covering as many aspects of life as possible in a way that can be understood by the intelligent general reader.

Ed: Mayne's Newsletter has covered topics such as Complementary Medicine, Aspects of Democracy, World Views, Parascience and Quantum Physics, New Paradigms in Biology and the Future of Intelligence. Here is a sample paragraph from this last-mentioned article – the author is Victor Serebriakoff:

The world system is like a great brain, which is self-actualising and enormously penetrating. Political parties have no real control over this system at all; almost everything that they do makes matters worse! Even computers are beginning to 'talk to each other' to control the market without human intervention. It is as if some giant intelligence were trying to take over the planet.

Subscription enquiries to: New Paradigms Publications, Alan Mayne, 29 Fairford Crescent, Downhead Park, Milton Keynes, MK15 9AF (tel 0908 607022; urgent calls only).

Social forecasts

Simon Nicholson

I propose that we initiate regular Social and Cultural Forecasts on TV. Almost the only frequent futures broadcast on TV at present is the weather forecast, mostly it is news of the past. Young people particularly see the future as largely dominated by mass media and especially by TV News. It seems clear that all of us are socially conditioned not to have future thoughts, and, if the ideas are future-based, to ignore them.

I believe we need a revolution, a new way of looking at life and culture, a deeper understanding of the fact that all of us can help make the branches of the 'futures tree.'

The late Simon Nicholson used to run future workshops with children around the world.

Better World Society

American Ted Turner, who owns television stations as well as professional sports teams, formed the Better World Society, with the aim of putting the power of television to work in constructive ways.

The Society produces, acquires, commissions and distributes programming on global issues, and attempts to instil hope and to point viewers toward constructive involvement in those issues.

The Better World Society is a non-profit international membership organisation. Contributions and fees are used to meet programming and production costs, and also bring the members a newsletter and resource guides.

Better World Society, 1100 17th Street NW, Suite 502, Washington DC 20036, USA (tel 202 331 3770).

Greensat

Greensat is a fairly penniless network of Green broadcasters who have gained access to an underused TV satellite (the Olympus one) for broadcasting green documentaries and interviews throughout Europe, building up a BBC-style public service broadcasting that looks at ecological issues in depth, with extended interviews, coverage of Green conferences, etc. (At present it broadcasts on Mondays, 9 to 11.30am, and is mainly received outside Britain.)

> **'Greensat is a fairly penniless network of Green broadcasters who have gained free access to an underused TV satellite'**

The London-based company, a cooperative of 40 broadcasters, environmentalists, technicians and charity organisers, is also applying to the IBA for permission to broadcast free programming on one of the Marcopolo satellite channels.

Director George Rumens writes:

The project has the definite aim of developing a whole European 'Green' channel to itself within a couple of years, although this has yet to catch the interest of substantial sponsors.

The idea of 'narrowcasting' is that the programming will develop a thin dedicated audience of opinion-formers spread over many countries.

We are starting a flagship series called 'The Green News' which will be an in-depth examination of green issues. Another series will be on third world development and yet another on human rights. We are free from the normal constraints of broadcast television in that:

• We can go into great detail. We joke that we interview the world's experts until they drop: a recent interview with the wave energy expert, Dr Stephen Salter, lasted two and a half hours.

• We rarely script a programme.

• We are free to cover nebulous subjects which do not fall within normal broadcast categories. For example, we have covered the Pugwash conference in London and the Fellows conference at the Findhorn Community in Scotland.

• We give a voice to those who are routinely excluded from the media – for example the voice of women worldwide, as in our thirteen part series 'Women and Development'.

• At times of international crisis, we are able to take the longer term view, and to collect material for a comprehensive documentary. During the Gulf crisis we were able to gather about ten hours of film on the great thinkers assembled in London.

• We are not a campaign. We are a forum for discussion whereby representatives from campaign groups, academia and industry can see if they have common areas of agreement.

We feel that we are laying the ground rules for a new public service channel for the whole of Europe, one that is dedicated to our greatest social and environmental concerns.

Greensat, 34 Tredegar Square, Bow, London E3 5AE (tel George Rumens 081 981 3758; Felicity Mawson tel 0376 519 847; Jane Taylor tel 0446 773333).

Fifteen hours of quality ITV per week

Mary Ann Sieghart

The following suggestion is adapted from an article in the Times.

Opening up the airwaves is a fine idea. But the UK government should make sure that the quality of programmes on existing channels does not deteriorate. Should we despair? Not yet. There is a solution that any government could adopt in future without betraying free-market principles:

Instead of telling aspiring bidders at the ITV franchise auction that they must pass a quality threshold, the new ITC should let them bid on the basis that they can schedule as many game shows, soap operas and B-movies as they like. The winning company should, in theory, end up paying more than it would otherwise have done for the franchise because it has a licence to maximise its audience.

> ### 'Cream off the extra money the bidder has paid, and give it to a venture modelled on today's Channel 4'

But it should also be asked to set aside, say, 15 hours of its schedules per week (and not all in the early hours of the morning) for programmes which cannot necessarily finance themselves through advertising revenues. The ITC should cream off the extra money the bidder has paid, and give it to a venture modelled on today's Channel 4. That venture would consist solely of editors who would use the money to commission independent producers – or even ITV companies – to deliver high-quality programmes that would not otherwise be made.

The result: the Treasury pays out no extra money, Britain retains its reputation for excellent television, and, above all, the viewer has the greatest possible choice.

Mary Ann Sieghart, the Times, 1 Pennington St, London E1 (tel 071 782 5000).

Advertising checklist – Social Desirability Ratings (SDR)

Ad agencies, consumer panels, school classes and other members of the public can use the following checklist to provide an approximate rating for particular advertisements by giving marks in response to each of the following five questions. Thus an ad can achieve a total final Social Desirability Rating ranging from 0 (exceptionally poor) through 50 (average) to 100 (exceptionally good):

> ### 'Does the ad promote habits that are liable to prove safe, healthy and desirable'

Safety

(1) To what extent does the ad promote habits that are liable to prove **safe, healthy and desirable** for adults or children or society in general or the environment? (Marks up to 50 for this)

Balance

(2) To what extent is the ad usefully informative, in a **balanced and truthful** way, rather than relying on image building or exaggeration? (Marks up to 20 for this)

Beauty

(3) To what extent does the ad **enhance the quality of life** through its beauty, humour or artistry? (Marks up to 10 for this)

Decency

(4) To what extent does the ad achieve its effects without gratuitously **exploiting men's or women's bodies**, sex, seduction or violence? (Marks up to 10 for this)

Tolerance

(4) To what extent does the ad successfully avoid using racism, class or religious **divisiveness** or stereotyping to achieve its effects? (Marks up to 10 for this)

• *This is an early draft and readers are invited to send in their suggested improvements, or to send in clippings of ads to which they have applied these ratings, with comments, to the Institute for Social Inventions, 20 Heber Road, London NW2 6AA (tel 081 208 2853; fax 081 452 6434).*

• *These proposals were first drafted by Dr Andrew Herxheimer and arose from an Advertising Association President's lecture which David Puttnam gave, in which he appealed to the advertising industry to work for the common good in a much broader way than they mostly do.*

• *Dr Andrew Herxheimer, 9 Park Crescent, London N3 2NL (tel 081 346 5470; fax 081 346 0407).*

• *David Puttnam, Enigma Productions, Pinewood Studios, Pinewood Road, Iver Heath, Bucks, SL0 0NH (tel 0753 630555).*

A tax to discourage unapproved ads

Dr David Chapman

Extracted from a paper by Dr David Chapman on 'Consumer Information and the Control of Advertising', prepared for submission to the Green Party, and which slightly softens their draconian policy of 'limiting advertising to the informative, classified kind.'

There is little doubt that advertising is a major cause of the excessive and wasteful use of resources in our present society. Advertising stimulates the desire to consume, so that to satisfy this, people work more and earn more. More is consumed, and more damage is done to the environment. But at the same time, people get less satisfaction from this greater consumption. For much of advertising works by playing on people's anxieties and fears, and makes them insecure, envious of each other, and discontented with what they already have. People are persuaded to buy, for reasons such as status, goods which give them little satisfaction; and then to buy more.

Our aim needs to be to live better on less. Advertising makes us live worse on more.

> ### 'Normal advertising would be highly taxed, at two rates. The lower rate would apply to advertisements which were approved by a representative committee of consumer representatives'

I propose that advertisements should be taxed, except for such categories as small ads for one-off sales of second-hand goods, etc. Normal advertising, directly by the sellers, would still be allowed, in any medium used at present. But it would be highly taxed, at two rates. The lower rate would apply to advertisements which were approved by a representative committee of consumer representatives. The higher rate would be for the others. The consumer representatives could if they wished, write, or otherwise make, their own comment on an advertisement, and next to it.

The proposal is that consumer representatives should be elected by the consumers, ie by vote of everyone above a certain minimum age (which should be much lower than that for parliamentary elections). The candidates would stand in multi-member constituencies. They may if they wish stand as members of a named group, either an existing one, or one specially formed for this purpose, eg the Green Consumers, Friends of the Earth, etc. Voting is preferential, ie voters indicate their first, second, third, etc preferences, as far as they wish. In the counting, votes in a constituency are first allocated to their first preference. The candidate with fewest votes is eliminated, and his or her votes are transferred each to their next-preferred candidate. The candidate who then has fewest votes is eliminated, and so on, until there is the correct number of candidates to be elected for the constituency.

• *Dr David Chapman goes on to describe how each consumer representative would be given a salary and newspaper space, both national and local, in proportion to his/her votes. The salary and space would be paid for by the state. They could publish Which? style reports on goods, with many sellers coming to rely on these reports rather than normal advertising.*

• *Dr David Chapman, Democracy Design Forum, Coles Centre, Buxhall, Stowmarket, Suffolk IP14 3EB (tel 0449 736 223).*

Microfiche Publishing

John Zube of Libertarian MicroFiche Publishing in Australia, believes that many people could afford to publish their own specialist books using a microfiche service bureau. Main public libraries in the UK have microfiche readers (or one can be bought second-hand from about £100); and on the more expensive models (costing from about £600 second-hand) photocopies can be taken from the machine. Some microfiche readers can even be used in bed, projecting the page onto the ceiling.

> 'Using this modern and affordable technology (via a service bureau), you too could afford to publish every year, dozens of books, magazines or newsletters'

Microfiche books could be sent to colleagues for free, or sold to libraries. Since 1978, for instance, John Zube, with a shoestring budget and working part-time, has become the largest publisher of libertarian books in the world, with over 500 titles in his catalogue, selling at over 100 pages per microfiche for one Australian dollar. 'The books I produce,' says Zube, 'are largely out of print or with no copyright claimed. Any author who publishes a new work through me does so on a non-exclusive basis and is free to revoke permission to me at any time if a regular book publisher becomes interested.'

Zube stresses that 'using this modern and affordable technology (via a service bureau), you too could afford to publish every year, dozens of books, magazines or newsletters.'

John Zube, Libertarian MicroFiche Publishing, 7 Oxley Street, Berrima, NSW, Australia 2577 (tel 048 771 436). Send £5 cash note for catalogue and sample microfiche book (indicate your specialist area of interest). Sources of secondhand equipment and microfiche service bureaux can be found in the Yellow Pages under 'microfilm'.

Translation by phone in 140 languages

Adapted from an item in Newsweek.

The American phone company AT&T now offers a service called Language Line, whereby anyone with a credit card and prepared to pay $3·50 per minute can set up via the operator a conference call between themselves and a client – with the AT&T translator for the language of their choice.

> 'Set up via the operator a conference call between themselves and a client – with the AT&T translator for the language of their choice'

More than 140 languages are on offer, including less familiar ones such as Wolo, Punjabi and Tajiki. Users of the Language Line include schools for their parent-teacher conferences and police trying to cope with foreign language neighbourhoods.

Computerised info resource network

Chris Garner

The proposal is for a national network of computerised information centres, called LOGOS. Each local database would contain: an amplified What's On for the area, comprehensive and up-to-the-minute; information on community affairs; a skills exchange; jobs; a yellow pages. It could be open to drop-in enquiries, telephone and postal enquiries, access by home computers, disk copy service, radio and TV link-ups, Ceefax, CB radio, video transcriptions and printed publications.

Each centre could be based on a postcode area. Thus the main centre for Bournemouth would be known as 'BH1', with satellite centres added as the network develops (BH2, BH3, etc). Ultimately the network could extend, through satellite connections, to major centres throughout the world.

Whereas information technology is used extensively for business and scientific purposes, little attention has been paid to its application to what might be termed 'social' issues. An important area is being overlooked, and this may help to explain why so many people feel apathy, if not antipathy, towards the new technology. They do not see how it relates to their needs. LOGOS could do this in a practical and positive manner.

Digested from a longer paper submitted by Chris Garner, Information and Communication Services, 216 Newhaven Road, Edinburgh EH6 4QE (tel 031 552 8360).

Many-to-Manys

Ann Weiser

Action Linkage have set up 'Many-to-Manys' postal discussion groups, described in the following extracts from a Whole Earth Review article by Action Linkage director Ann Weiser.

Discussion groups that meet by mail are a cheap, accessible means of group communication. They are computer conferences without the computer. We call them Many-to-Manys (M2Ms).

> 'Each person writes a letter about the same topic and sends it to the editor. The editor adds his or her own letter, photocopies the letters and sends a set to each member – a group conversation by mail'

The simple recipe goes like this: a M2M usually has from twenty to fifty members. One person is the Organising Editor. By a given deadline, each person writes a letter about the same topic and sends it to the editor. The editor adds his or her own letter and a cover page listing the members and setting the next deadline, photocopies the letters and sends a set to each member – so it becomes a continuing, participatory, interactive group conversation by mail.

Each person sends the editor a deposit, usually $5 a time, to be used for their own postage and copying costs. The editor keeps track of the money and lets the participants know when they need to send more. Depending on the number of people who write each time, and how cheaply the editor can get copying done where he or she lives, M2Ms can range in cost from 50c to $1-50 per person per issue – a lot cheaper than computer conferences.

This format, unlike the 'One to Many' communication of a newsletter allows 'Many-to-Many' communication, hence the name. Altogether, Action Linkage has about fourteen M2Ms. People when they join can immediately talk with other people all over the country (and some in other countries) through M2Ms on topics ranging from 'designing a new civilisation' to 'libraries' and 'learning'. We even have a 'computer M2M', showing that computers and M2Ms can coexist peaceably. We also have 'The M2M on M2Ms', which discusses ways to improve the M2M form. There are lots of ideas for improving the ability of M2M groups to focus on tasks together, develop topics, and create consensus on issues. And we're just beginning.

M2Ms currently on offer are: career options, communication, community-regional, computers and society, cooperatives and community, designing a new civilisation, economics, general discussion, international linkage, knowledge systems on computer, libraries, learning, meaningful contact with other groups, mind and consciousness, peace studies and spirituality.

• *Action Linkage, 5825 Telegraph Avenue #45, Oakland, CA 94609 (tel 415 654 4819). Action Linkage membership costs $50 (plus $10 for airmail) – 'You may choose your own discount on memberships if money is a primary problem.'*

• *Whole Earth Review, 27 Gate Five Road, Sausalito, CA 94965, USA (tel 415 332 1716). Subs. $32.*

The Circle Letter

Rhoda Weber Mack

The circle letter is useful for keeping community with scattered friends and colleagues. We use this for our eight sibling family, to keep the common conversation intact. Here's how: write your own letter, and mail it with a list of mail stops to the next in line, who inserts his or her own letter along with yours, to the next stop. Etcetera all the way back to you. Now, read the fat contents with relish, withdraw your old letter, add a new one, and mail it on. Full circle.

My old letters add up to a diary of our days, forgotten moments with our children, moods of summer afternoons or wintry mornings long ago when I sat down to add my commentary to the family circle letter.

> 'Write your own letter, and mail it with a list of mail stops to the next in line, who inserts his or her own letter along with yours, to the next stop. Etcetera all the way back to you. Now, read the fat contents with relish, withdraw your old letter, add a new one, and mail it on. Full circle'

Extracted from the Whole Earth Review (subs. details in previous item).

Computer matched group members

Tony Judge proposes the computer matching of individuals who wish to join a social network, and who would then be allocated to groups of between 7 and 15 people. They could specify the type of group they were looking for (social action, artistic, travel, intellectual, etc) or types of people (introverts, extraverts, etc). They would meet privately; and after each meeting their individual questionnaire replies to the computer HQ would indicate their preference for the next meeting, for example:

• If so and so is still in the group, I do not want to participate.

• Unless at least X existing members continue, I do not want to participate.

• Unless so and so is in I do not want to participate.

Resulting mini-groups could, if they wished, be matched with others or with newcomers by the HQ, which might also be able to supply group dynamic experts to groups wanting such assistance. For the members the group process itself would anyway be a very rich learning experience, facilitating the emergence of many mature, self-aware, self-motivated groups.

Tony Judge makes a number of interesting points:

• Such a network would take the load off the average two-person relationship, where other interactions outside the couple often remain either superficial, vicarious or illicit.

• 'Stronger' groups would be more capable of integrating divergent tendencies.

• Presumably the more mature a group becomes, the more it will tend to formulate and implement innovative programmes of wider social significance.

• This idea, with analogies to computer dating, could be taken up by enterprising city groups; or it could be tried out at large group conferences.

Extracted from a detailed four page proposal by Tony Judge, Union of International Associations, rue Washington 40, 1050 Brussels, Belgium (tel 32 2 640 1808; fax 32 2 649 3269).

Projects and Ideas Exchange (PIE)

An Institute for Social Inventions' afternoon meeting was used as an experiment for a new way to structure meetings, called Projects and Ideas Exchange (PIE). Proposed by Dr David Chapman, and modelled on the cards that ladies used to have at balls to be able to book in gentlemen for particular dances, it was like a structured cocktail party. It provided booking forms which allowed for 23 'brief encounters' or quarter hour mini-meetings within the space of two and a half hours; and was generally agreed to have been a most stimulating afternoon. Topics that won their way through to the final 23 from the many proposed in the initial voting circle (each person could volunteer three topics) ranged from the nature of the self (is it discontinuous?), to male liberation (why are men so repressed and depressed?), to language and behaviour (people saying one thing and meaning another), to shanty towns for the UK (how to enable them?), to money & credit cards (what future in store for them?), to death (how to prepare for it?).

'Modelled on the cards that ladies used to have at balls'

PIE may be the answer for your potentially dull conference or party – often at ordinary gatherings there is no easy way a person can find others who are interested in the same things, or can get to talk about what is really important to them.

Dr David Chapman has now streamlined the PIE procedure, having written a computer program in both microsoft and BBC BASIC (which also runs on the Apple Mac) to optimise the arrangements, and is willing, for a negotiable fee, to act as consultant or to provide the software for your PIE meeting. How the Computerised PIE operates for a group of 20 or so in practice is as follows:

The group sits in a circle, and after the introductions, each person in turn briefly describes up to three topics (projects, ideas, problems – anything) that he or she wants to discuss with others. Each topic has a number and participants note down the number and beside it they record the extent to which they feel like discussing that topic by giving a mark from 1 to 9. At the end these scores are marked up on a master sheet (the participants also being identified by number). During the meal break, these details are fed into a computer, which is also given the number of rooms available and their seating capacity. It then comes up with the optimum arrangement of sessions, so that participants get as much of what they want as possible. The schedule print-out is posted up for all to see.

Dr Chapman's software is designed at present for meetings

of up to 100 people, but could readily be extended to a larger number.

Dr David Chapman, Democracy Design Forum, Coles Centre, Buxhall, Stowmarket, Suffolk IP14 3EB (tel 0449 736 223).

Structuring a conference for 310 people in 38 minutes

Harrison Owen

Adapted from a paper entitled 'Open Space Technology Comes of Age', monitored for the Institute by Tony Judge, this approach is a more free-for-all variant of the previous item.

Open Space Technology (if in fact it is a technology) began in frustration, almost as a joke, in 1982. After having organised a major international gathering complete with papers and presenters, I came to the interesting realisation that what I, and many other participants, enjoyed the most were the coffee breaks. My conclusion? There must be a better way.

Recently, using my Open Space method, 310 executives and line managers self-organised a three day meeting to deal with the future of their 30,000 person agency in 38 minutes flat, creating 32 workshops and a thick pack of proceedings, all with no advance preparation.

'All participants sign up for whatever appeals'

The mechanisms for the creation of Open Space are two, and simple in the extreme: The Camp Sign-Up Board and the Village Market Place. Each participant is invited to identify any issue or opportunity around the given theme that they would like to take personal responsibility for developing. They give it a short title on a small piece of paper, indicating time and place, and post it on the wall. After every person has posted whatever they have in mind, the Village Market Place opens and all participants are invited to sign up for whatever appeals. When conflicts of space or schedule arise, the interested parties negotiate solutions while the rest of the group goes about its business. And nobody is in charge. Everybody is.

People, treated as free and responsible, are quite capable of inspired performances.

Harrison Owen, H.H. Owen and Company, 7808 River Falls Drive, Potomac MD 20854, USA (tel or fax 301 469 9269). 'Learning in Open Space', a 25 minute video that includes the mechanics of an Open Space event is available for $65. (Ed: it might be as well to specify European VHS or whatever your video takes.)

Checklist for evaluating conferences

Margaret Chisman

Extracts from a 10 page article.

It is all too easy for conference organisers to pay insufficient attention to small details. It is often an accumulation of trivial nuisances that spoil a conference. I have drawn up, over the years, my own, quite idiosyncratic, check list, with each point rated on a five point scale:

(1) **Organisation**: (a) Adequacy of travel instructions. (b) Easy access to the venue by public transport. (c) Satisfactory arrangements for accommodation. (d) Comprehensive lists of conference attenders which include names, addresses and affiliations. (e) Adequate identification of fellow participants by some form of name tab.

> 'It is often an accumulation of trivial nuisances that spoil a conference. I have drawn up, over the years, my own, quite idiosyncratic, check list, with each point rated on a five point scale'

(2) **Comfort**: (a) Adequate transport between accommodation and conference hall(s). (b) Easy access from room entrance(s) to every seat. (c) Style and comfort of chairs; including adequate leg room. (d) Toilets within easy reach. (e) Good organisation of tea and coffee breaks. (f) Each seat with effective lighting. (g) Adequate control of temperature and ventilation. (h) Well-designed acoustics. (i) A PA system that works properly when required. (j) Film, slide and overhead projectors that operate without fuss.

(3) **Content**: (a) Does the chairman keep control of the meeting in an unobtrusive way or use the position to obtain a captive audience, for an unfair share of the time, in order to air personal views? (b) Do the formal speakers keep to their subject? (c) Have they been selected to cover the subject from a wide variety of angles? (d) Is there adequate accompanying documentation; well presented and easily available? (e) Is the audience encouraged to participate and to develop new insights by lateral thinking and brainstorming?

(4) **Interaction**: (a) Does the timetable allow sufficient time and opportunity for discussion and for questioning the speakers? (b) Are informal groupings encouraged by attention to the natural flow of the participants around the conference in relation to groupings of suitable armchairs?

(5) **Interpreters**: These should be selected so that the interpreter always speaks using the language of his or her country of birth.

(6) **Discussion groups**: I am of the opinion that no conference is completely successful when confined to plenary sessions. Discussion groups are essential.

(7) **Bedrooms**: (a) Are the beds comfortable? (b) Are extra blankets available? (c) Is the general lighting adequate for study or reading reports? (d) Is there a bedside lamp and bedside table? (e) Is it possible to open the windows? Can they be fixed open in several positions? (f) What is the level of traffic noise? (g) Are external noises excluded: other doors being closed, loud conversations and footsteps in the corridor? (h) Does each bedroom contain a comfortable armchair? (i) Is there a table and chair suitable for writing? (j) Is toilet accommodation en suite? If not, what facilities are included, a washbasin, hot water, a shaver point, good lighting at a mirror? If WC and bathroom are shared, how remote are they? (k) Are there individual room controls of temperature? (l) Is there provision for making hot drinks and for filling a hot water bottle?

(8) **Meals**: (a) Is there a choice of menu? If not, are the dishes of sufficiently wide appeal? (b) Are special diets available? (c) If waiter service is provided is it efficient rather than rushed or tardy? (d) Is the food temperature satisfactory? (e) Are the portions adequate but not too generous? (f) Is the dining room insulated for noise? (g) Is it adequately ventilated? (h) Is there at least part of the room set aside for non-smokers?

(9) **Social**: (a) There should be a place where those liking exuberant, boisterous groups can gather as well as quiet lounges with islands of easily-moved armchairs for those who prefer low-voiced discussion.

(b) Do events and outings provide a new experience of local cultural activities?

(10) **The Unexpected**: This final category is hard to define. (a) It is the occurrence of some unplanned exciting event, such as the arrival of an eminent person. (b) It is having some new and startling insights. (c) It is the beginning of a new friendship, the start of a new business relationship, or, most exciting of all, meeting someone who later becomes your spouse.

I keep a file for 'Outcomes of Conferences'; not world-shattering decisions but what the conference has done for me. Of particular importance is my record of people met with whom I wish to keep in contact. For me conferences and meetings provide a considerable source of inspiration.

Margaret Chisman, The Bungalow, Near the Station, Tring, Herts, HP23 5QX (tel 044282 3281).

Voting 1 to 9 on database contents

Over 1,500 Atari, Amiga or ST computer users (and soon PC users too) are linked through their telephone modems to a service called Compunet. Founded in 1984, it seems to be still the only database that encourages every user to review items, by allowing them to allocate marks from one to nine. The average (to the first significant place) is displayed back to the users, along with the number of people who have voted in this way.

> 'The average mark is displayed back to the users, along with the number of people who have voted in this way'

It is a very necessary development. The problem with most electronic publishing is not so much that there is no quality control – it is fine that anyone can publish anything – but that there is no grading by the readers; and so you are overwhelmed with trash waiting to be read and end up not reading any of it, because there is no way of quickly picking out the gems.

> 'The problem with most electronic publishing is that there is no way of quickly picking out the gems'

Compunet is over 25% under 18s and is mainly for games, comments, jokes, etc. Its director, Nick Green, envisages that the computerised grading system could have much wider applications – for instance in a large firm there could be voluntary accountability, with people describing their job and saying how well they are getting on, and readers giving grades.

Nick Green, Compunet, 5 North Villas, London NW1 9BJ (tel 071 267 7677). Compunet costs £12 per quarter, with telephone charges extra. Test demo on 071 284 4068. You need scrolling Teletype software (8 bit, no parity, 1 stop bit).

Meeting view-sampling machines

Keith England

Each person in a business or committee meeting could be equipped with a control knob with positions 3,2,1,0,-1,-2,-3 signifying from being wholly in favour (3) to abstention (0) to being totally opposed (-3). *(Ed:* these devices could be similar to the electronic ones now being used in TV game shows where the studio audience vote for their favourites.)

The simple central computer display would then read out the vote, indicating the strength of the support for the motion. This represents value added to a decision at very little cost. Additionally the method is quicker than counting hands or a secret ballot. And at present the thinking of each person is devalued by the simple adversarial yes-no vote and by the lack of ability to express an opinion accurately, or to indicate depth of feeling.

> 'At present the thinking of each person is devalued by the simple adversarial yes-no vote and the lack of ability to express an opinion accurately, or to indicate depth of feeling'

There are other uses which would probably become commonplace. If members continuously adjusted their knobs then the chairman could see instantaneously the existing degree of support and could cease the discussion when the voters were already convinced without further time-wasting discussion. Where a chairman felt that a contribution was irrelevant, he or she could obtain a snap decision and would then be in a far more assured position to end that particular speech.

Keith England, Langdale, Jordans, Beaconsfield, Bucks HP9 2ST (tel 02407 5816).

Comment by Professor Stafford Beer

Professor Stafford Beer writes that he proposed a similar Algedonic Meter for use in Chile in 1971 – his son, Simon, constructed a trial system. The best reference is Beer's book 'Brain of the Firm', (published by John Wiley, 2nd edition, 1981, pp 278-286), which contains a fascinating account of his cybernetics work for the Allende government in Chile. Here are relevant extracts from the book:

The algedonic meter is at last an attempt to provide a metric for Aristotle's eudemony, or 'state of general well being.' It is a simple analogue device, with interleaved segments in different colours. Thus to turn the central knob changes the proportion of the 'happy/unhappy' display – and also the electrical input to the circle of which this meter is a member.

Someone holding an algedonic meter sets the display by moving the pointer anywhere on a continuous scale between total disquiet and total satisfaction. She/he does not have to explain anything – only to respond algedonically, which people may be observed to do all the time.

There could be an official locale, housing a television set and a properly constituted sample of people, having one meter between (say) three. The meters drive a simple electrical system, which sums the voltage for this locale.

Now: when a broadcast is taking place, the people's eudemony is indicated on a meter in the TV studio – which everyone (those in the studio and the public) can see. The studio meter is driven by the sum of the people's meters. This closes the algedonic loop...

> 'People would be able to participate in arguments broadcast from the People's Assembly by the continuous registration of a combined degree of satisfaction with events'

People would be able to participate in arguments broadcast from the People's Assembly – not by responding to questions hurled at them over the air, for this route leads to logical reductionism and to political demagoguery, but by the continous registration of a combined degree of satisfaction with events. It has to be noted that not only would the meter be visible to those present in the Assembly, but also to the public whose meter it is...

The problem at present is that the government communicates directly with the undifferentiated mass of the people as if it were speaking to the individual, and creates the illusion in the home that it is. The context of this false dialogue is that the individual is also supplied by the new media with a proliferation of information and misinformation about things – as soon as they happen.

We see this effect as:

• Massive amplification of variety, insofar as single-sentence utterances may be developed into hour-long simulations of imagined consequences.

• Massive changes in dynamic periodicity: the government is reporting to the nation daily, instead of accounting for itself at election times.

But the return loop does not change. The variety that the people generate is attenuated as before. This situation attempts to disobey the Law of Requisite Variety, and disbalances the homeostatic equilibrium in both richness and in period.

Then it is predictable that the people, thus affected, will build up pressures in the system that can no longer be released – because the filtering capacity cannot contain the flow.

> 'This is bound to lead to unrest: demonstrations, agitation, perhaps violence, possibly revolt...'

This is bound to lead to unrest: demonstrations, agitation, perhaps violence, possibly revolt...

(My algedonic meter experiments) were alas, not finally undertaken by the time that the (Allende) government fell...At any rate, I hope that new experiments on these lines will be facilitated somewhere. A plausible experiment, for example, would be to equip a conference hall with closed algedonic loops: would the speaker become yet more steadily boring and obscure as the summation meter steadily dropped – for all to see?

Professor Stafford Beer, 34 Palmerston Square, Toronto, Ontario, M6G 2S7, Canada (tel 416 535 0396).

Editorial comment

One requirement for a device for use in meetings is that it should be under the table, operated ideally by foot – at least in its Boreometer mode. For the average person, it seems to take too much courage above the table – it would be like interrupting the speaker to tell him or her that you are bored; although Beer says that an individual in Manchester called James Baldwin used an above-table cube with six coloured faces, simply exhibiting one of the faces to the speaker, depending on mood.

The brain has evolved to decipher faces faster than any other information. The most effective view-sampling device therefore might be a computer-programmed face on the monitor which scowls or smiles broadly or slightly or not at all in proportion to the votes of those with access to it (to be backed up by a corresponding numerical total displayed on the side of the screen, for whenever a precise record required).

Comment by Valerie Yule

I have long wanted a console for speakers with say 144 red-lit buttons. As members of the audience freak out, they can press a button at their seat, and one of the console lights goes on. When 144 people are bored, the whole console flashes. Or, less technologically, there could be little pennants at seats, which can be flagged down when you stop listening.

> 'Churches could be lit by candles at each seat. As the congregation flags, they snuff out their candle, until the whole place is in darkness and the preacher gets the message'

Or churches could be lit by candles at each seat. As the congregation flags, they snuff out their candle, until the whole place is in darkness and the preacher gets the message.

(*Ed:* I think you should also be allowed to light a second candle if you are finding the sermon particularly inspiring. It needs to be more than just a negatively indicating device.)

Valerie Yule, 57 Waimarie Drive, Mount Waverley, Victoria, Australia 3149 (tel 807 4315).

Shorter meetings

Vincent Nolan

A way of shortening business meetings considerably is to put the name of the person who asked to have an item included on the agenda, and the length of time it is expected to take to discuss it. In this way, the person who called the meeting, or that particular part of it, can always be readily identified. The 'owner' of the agenda item is also asked what specifically he or she wants from the other people present – ideas for solving the problem, advice and opinions, information, or support for a

decision already taken. The objective is to make sure that everyone knows the purpose of each discussion and what is expected from them all through the meeting.

> 'The "owner" of the agenda item is also asked what specifically he or she wants from the other people present – ideas for solving the problem, advice and opinions, or information'

The time taken on each item is reported to the group at the end, which tends in the long run still further to reduce the length of meetings, as the 'owners' of agenda items begin to feel responsible for how the time under their control is used.

Vincent Nolan, Synectics Ltd, Fernville House, Midland Road, Hemel Hempstead, Hertfordshire HP2 5BH (tel 0442 247152). For more details, see Nolan's book 'Communication', published by Sphere Books.

Putting both hands up in a meeting

Lynn Carneson-McGregor, a social psychologist and senior partner in a management consultancy called Decision Development, demonstrated to a Dartington Conference in Devon an interesting way of getting a very large audience to participate more fully: you put one hand up if you 'resonate' with what someone is asking or you put both hands up if you have an answer, suggestion or positive contribution. In her case it went something like this:

• 'What for your life is a crucial question you want to work on?' The person she asked the question of said 'Mine is how to find time to do all I need to do.'

• 'If somebody asks a question and you can identify with it, you put a hand up.' Quite a few people put a hand up, so Carneson-McGregor could then see that it was a question worth pursuing.

The person then repeated the question and Carneson-McGregor continued:

• 'If anyone has suggestions or contributions or answers to give, please put both hands up.' She then numbered those who had both hands up, '1, 2, 3, 4,' so they knew when it would be their turn to talk.

It made for an involved feeling, yet within an orderly discussion.

> 'Those with an experience to share, please raise both hands'

Another way of using this technique in, for instance, a discussion period after a talk, is to say: 'those with questions, please put one hand up; those with an experience to share, please raise both hands.' This way it is easier to develop the mix between 'information' and 'sharing' which suits the particular meeting.

Lynn Carneson-McGregor, Decision Development, 34 Courthope Road, London NW3 2LD (tel 071 485 9938; fax 071 267 2183).

Community Counselling Circles

Taking part in a Community Counselling Circles group led by the unorthodox Freudian analyst John Southgate is an enlivening experience. It is the most dynamic advance in working with large groups since Foulkes:

Community Counselling Circles is a new design for training large groups. The main problem in large groups normally is the lack of a feeling of safety and mutual support. Here the atmosphere in the group is improved by sitting in four concentric circles.

> ## 'The innermost circle is treated as a single person "client", and this group free associates, with all the other circles as its therapists'

The innermost circle is treated as a single person 'client', and this group free associates, with all the other circles as its therapists – the second circle concentrating on noticing the emotional climate; the third circle on any material that might be to do with parental and family relationships; and the fourth circle on organisational problems in life and work.

The whole group resembles an individual's psychical world, and the members learn about the innermost dynamics of individual people, at the same time as being educated in group dynamics and the way communities operate.

Community Counselling Circles are being developed and used in area health authorities, social work training and in universities and polytechnics. Settings where they have been tried include group and management training, amongst psychiatric workers, district nurses, cooperatives and communities, local government groups, women's and ethnic groups.

> ## 'The whole group resembles an individual's psychical world, and the members learn about the innermost dynamics of individual people'

John Southgate, 12 Nassington Road, London NW3 (tel 071 794 4306). A book, 'Community Counselling Circles' by John Southgate, published by the Institute for Social Inventions (20 Heber Road, London NW2 6AA, tel 081 208 2853; fax 081 452 6434) – at £6-95 including post and packing, or £9-95 to libraries and institutions – makes the approach available to group leaders and teachers, using over 260 diagrams and looking at its roots in Zen writings and in the works of Paulo Freire, Lacan, Freud and others, ISBN 0 948826 00 2.

Debates in the year 2490

Anthony Judge

Adapted extract from a 12 page paper entitled 'The Aesthetics of Governance ... in the Year 2490'.

One stimulus for this proposal has been the poverty of imagination associated with fictional and dramatic scenarios of how executive councils function in the distant future – as reflected in science fiction films and books. Even when entities gather from 'the 100 galaxies', thousands of years hence, their encounter (even through 'holographic projections') still seems to be modelled on the United Nations Security Council or its unfortunate imitations.

In the year 2049, my gathering of the wise may best be imagined as blending the characteristics of policy councils as we now know them with those of an arts workshop, a poetry reading, a classical music concert, a theatre, a folk song-fest and a dance, together with other dimensions we would have difficulty recognising.

For instance, their 'business graphics' could have musical variants. People would be able to hear the various harmonies which provided integration to any policy represented, and they could hear the dissonances which challenged that harmony – whether as a stimulus to social growth or as a potential crisis. And their gatherings could be sophisticated psychodramas in which participants took the role of factions or constituencies rather than personalities.

> ## 'In any gathering the aim would be to use aesthetic devices (music, colour, drama, etc) to register the different perspectives represented'

In any gathering the aim would be to use aesthetic devices (music, colour, drama, etc) to register the different perspectives represented (and their associated dynamics), to provide a conceptual scaffolding to hold their relationships as they developed during the event, and to suggest directions through which richer harmonies could be explored. In contrast to the present preoccupation with a majority or consensus vote, the outcome would be expressed by a pattern or tapestry of views.

Likewise the policies emerging from these gatherings would ensure that opposite perspectives were brought into play at appropriate times to correct for programmatic weaknesses resulting from the excesses of any one insight or set of priorities.

What I am proposing should happen would call for long-term commitment by many – perhaps equivalent to the Apollo programme – in order to escape from the conceptual gravity well in which we are struck.

Anthony Judge, Union of International Associations, 40 rue Washington, B-1050 Brussels, Belgium (tel 32 2 640 18 08; fax 32 2 649 32 69).

Dream Network Bulletin

'Dream Network Bulletin' is a quarterly newsletter published by Helen Roberta Ossana of Port Townsend, Washington, USA, and exists for the purpose of integrating dreamwork into family and culture by way of disseminating information which helps in understanding the meaning of our dreams.

The bulletin prints classified ads for relevant literature, research on related topics, and advertising dream groups new and old. The bulletin also contains and invites articles about dreams, dream groups, creative 'enactments' and accounts of personal transformation in working with dreams.

A sample issue of the bulletin costs $5, subs $28 from Dream Network Bulletin, PO Box 1321, Port Townsend, WA 98368, USA (tel 206 385 3735).

Collecting readers' letters as an obsession

Roman Baczynski

Roman Baczynski is the editor and publisher of 'Discontent and Liberal Opinion – Non-partisan readers' letters to British local newspapers since the late 1960s' (published by Metaballon Books). He writes: 'The dominance of economics in the political debate is as unhealthy as the dominance of sex and violence on our film screens. Thus everyday life is denied access to debate and imagination, robbing us of vital data we need for a comprehensive critique of society. I seek to collate peoples' observations and experiences as found in the printed word toward what Walter Benjamin called a Magical Encyclopedia.' The following is extracted from the preface and introduction to Baczynski's book:

When I started collecting readers' letters, it was no more than a hobby but one so absorbing that it became an obsession and I started eventually doing it full time. What fascinated me most were the things that upset people in everyday life. If the subjects most commonly raised in readers' letters columns in local newspapers were to be judged for their efficacy to generate a positive discontent that would in turn lead to some creative solution to a pressing problem, then the likelihood of such an outcome would have to be considered remote.

> **'All degeneration begins with taking big things seriously and regarding it as self-evident that little things should not be taken seriously'**

Yet how else can we tell what is wrong with our society unless we consider the whole range of people's complaints? Because many of these seem petty they are not taken seriously, especially by politicians only interested in problems that they can solve. But as Herman Hesse said: 'All degeneration begins with taking big things seriously and regarding it as self-evident that little things should not be taken seriously' ('Reflections', Cape, 1977).

> **'Relatively minor hassles, the minor daily annoyances, often have greater effect on health than do the large-scale traumas in life'**

Sociology can be subdivided into many branches, but of the 32 listed in the Encyclopaedia of Higher Education, nowhere does the Sociology of Everyday Life get a mention. By writing letters to their local newspapers, people are using one of the few options for protesting and letting off steam that are available to them. For example, under our legal system there is not the slightest recourse that can be taken against personal insults. (Insult is not recognised as a real injury.) Recently, however, a survey carried out by the University of California, Berkeley, found that 'relatively minor hassles, the minor yet frequent annoyances we experience daily, often have greater effect on health than do the large-scale traumas in life.'

When it comes to matters dealing with everyday life, everyone's opinions ought to be equally valid. In order that the 'experts' may have more material on which to expound their theories it would seem natural that ordinary people's experiences should be taken more account of. The lack of space devoted to readers' letters in newspapers and the subsequent lack of attention paid to those that have been published is therefore disquieting to say the least.

The following is from a sample letter in the anthology, from A.Hodgson in the Nelson Leader:

Surely the council should be setting a good example on how to save fuel by not having men driving around all day spraying our dandelions with a chemical mess. The dandelion may be a weed to the lawn fanatic and council worker, but it has a long and interesting history as a medicinal plant and as a foodstuff.

Roman Baczynski, 21 Lancaster Gardens, London W13 9JY (tel 081 567 3213). 'Discontent and Liberal Opinion – Non-partisan readers' letters to British newspapers since the late 1960s' is published by Meteballon Books, ISBN 0 9512511 0 8, 1987, £9·95.

'Dear Sir', a magazine written by its readers

Faith Hines

Adapted extract from publicity material.

Disgusted of Tunbridge Wells has come into his or her own at last. The contents of a recently founded publication consists entirely of letters to the editor.

Disgusted, who used to thunder only in the confines of the Times letters columns, and then only if the editor considered his effusion of sufficient merit, can now write to 'Dear Sir' and make sure his or her views are read and discussed by an audience worthy of his talents – everyone a letter writer.

'Dear Sir', thought up by ideas merchant Faith Hines and edited by Fleet Street veteran Johnnie Johnson, costs £15·86 for a year's supply (13 issues).

'Dear Sir' will include the cream of letters from the media on a variety of topical issues plus letters written directly to the editor.

Also planned are visits to the offices of national newspapers and magazines for its readers, and dinners, luncheons, even teas, hosted by eminent writers at elite venues.

There will be an award for Letter Writer of the Year and a trophy for weekly papers for the Letters Page of the Year.

'Dear Sir', 54 Frant Road, Royal Tunbridge Wells, Kent TN2 5LJ (tel 0892 26705; fax 0732 457681).

Bisociation – the Fractal Method

Keith Hudson

> *'I have yet to see any idea, however complicated, which when you looked at it the right way, did not become still more complicated.' Poul Anderson*

There are several excellent (and enjoyable) techniques for developing new ideas in groups – for example, synectics or brainstorming – but very few have been described for use by the individual working alone. However, whether concepts are created by individuals or groups, the process is exactly the same and has been described by many writers through the ages (for instance by Aristotle in 'Prior Analytics' and Koestler in 'Act of Creation').

'The central principle is to find common connections between separate objects (or concepts). Koestler called it bisociation'

The central principle is to find common connections between separate objects (or concepts). Koestler called it 'bisociation' and that is the term I tend to use. It is also known as lateral thinking (Edward de Bono) or divergent thinking (Liam Hudson) but these are essentially concepts themselves (and an encouragement to 'free up') rather than techniques in their own right.

However, there is a problem with bisociation. Before making the connections, do you analyse the objects (or concepts) to the finest detail or do you use the objects (or concepts) in their entirety? If you do the first (as the cortex automatically does in the process of perception), then you end up with such an astronomical list of elements that the necessary bisociations take impossibly long to perform in a conscious and systematic way. On the other hand, if you try to bisociate complete objects (for example, an elephant and a lawn-mower) or complete concepts (for example, democracy and neo-Darwinism), you have a task that may take you weeks or years. (And, unless you are a philosopher, it is better not to use concepts as starters anyway.)

Some sort of intermediate method of analysing (or fractionating) objects is therefore necessary in order to arrive at a procedure which is both productive but not too tedious or lengthy. The entities that I use are called 'fractals'. These are shrewd guesses from cognitive science as to the partial stages that are involved in the perceptual and conceptual processing in the cortex (for more about fractals, see the note at the end of this article).

In this summary, I will only give a partial list of some of the fractals I use. These are some of the more generalised ones taken from the three main analytical areas found in the cortex:

Visual

(1) Shape (overall, distinctive parts, size, etc);

(2) Colour (overall, distinctive parts, luminosity, shading, etc);

(3) Distance (causal and spatial relationships with others, etc);

(4) Movement (direction, speed, locomotion, etc);

Somatic

(5) Tactility (touch, texture, pressure, temperature, sharpness, etc);

(6) Muscularity (effort, weight, posture, (a)symmetry, etc);

Auditory

(7) Loudness (power, percussiveness, etc);

(8) Pitch (tone, quality, harmonics, etc);

(9) Naturalness (musicality, aesthetics, acceptability, etc);

(10) Communication (speech, code, threat or other emotive signs, etc).

'It is very important to choose a pair of objects at random and not to make prior judgements as to their suitability'

Let us now look at the Fractal Method in practice. First of all, it is very important to choose a pair of objects at random and not to make prior judgements as to their suitability. An excellent method is to choose two items at random from an encyclopaedia or an illustrated dictionary (the Oxford Children's Illustrated is ideal – the colour photos and artwork are superb). The next step is to identify fractals in each object and, taking each fractal in turn, to find the common connection – however nonsensical it may be. Write the ideas down as they arise in 'stream of consciousness' manner with no attempt at evaluation. (That will be done on a separate occasion.)

'I had been cutting the lawn and I determined to bisociate the lawnmower with the first object I would see on television when I went indoors. It happened to be a circus elephant!'

Here is an example from real life. I had been cutting the lawn and I determined to bisociate the lawnmower with the first object I would see on television when I went indoors. It happened to be a circus elephant!

What follows are the actual notes derived from Fractal 1:

'The shape of an elephant – so different from a lawn-mower! – how would you put handles on an elephant? – or ears on a lawn-mower? – the trunk of an elephant is its most distinctive part – what about that of the lawn-mower? – the grass-collecting box, I guess (if only because mine is falling apart) – all right then, let me bisociate a trunk with a grass-box – what does a trunk do? – well, in circuses, they'll suck up water and then spray it over the clowns – or they can wash themselves – they can spray each other – water shoots out at great speed, long distance – could this be done with grass chippings? – why not? – suck them in a trunk-like tube and spray them away from the lawn...'

And so on – part of several pages of notes that I made in the next hour or so. Typically, two random objects, when analysed into fractals and then re-combined, will produce about 200 partial ideas and 30 to 50 complete ideas in a session of a couple of hours or so.

'Starting with the first random pair ("isthmus" and "chicken coop"), and choosing others when I needed them, I developed over 4,000 partial ideas'

What are the disadvantages of the Fractal Method? Firstly, it is hard mental work (particularly in the first ten minutes or so, but it gradually becomes more enjoyable). Secondly, when you look at the results on a later occasion, 90 per cent of the ideas will be seen to be impracticable, not to say ridiculous. But do not be surprised about this – this occurs for all creativity methods. (However, there are always compensations. Ideas which seemed laughable when they were originally created often take on a practical air during assessment.) Thirdly, of the remaining ten per cent (the ones that look sound and practicable), you will discover that most of these will have already been discovered. (And, indeed, some of them will have been used for many years! For example, looking through my pile of notes, I saw that I had virtually rediscovered the combine harvester!) Fourthly (once again, this applies to all methods) more ideas for tangible objects and products are produced than for intangible services or concepts.

Despite the fact that the human brain is capable of the most abstract ideas (for example, mathematics or quantum physics), nevertheless, it remains the case that our cortex is happiest when 'objectifying' things. This stood us in good stead during most of our evolution, so it is a strong bias.

However, to summarise, the big advantage is that, by using the Fractal Method, and given sufficient motivation and time, an individual working by himself or herself can systematically create unlimited numbers of ideas. I once carried out a week-long test of this method (two three-hour sessions per day) using my favourite children's illustrated dictionary. Starting with the first random pair ('isthmus' and 'chicken coop'), and choosing others when I needed them, I developed over 4,000 partial ideas, over 350 complete ideas, and consumed half a ream of A4 paper and three ballpoints. After a day's rest and two more days of evaluation, I ended up with five reasonable-looking ideas, of which two were useful in other areas of my work and three were practicable ones. Two of the latter were handed on to an inventor friend and one of these, I gather, now has commercial promise.

So the Fractal Method, while practical, does have its cost – time and energy. As the economists say, there is no such thing as a free lunch.

There is, of course, no reason why the Fractal Method should not be used in group sessions, too, so long as there is a good rapporteur or secretary. I should be delighted to hear from any individual or group who tries this method out – I am on the look-out for successful examples for a book.

Footnote re fractals: The word 'fractal' cannot yet be found in a dictionary because it has a very recent conceptual origin, and, even now, is in the process of clarification. It shares some part of its meaning with 'fraction' – that is, a fractal is a part of a whole – but it also contains the richer notion that it 'enfolds' some significant part of the meaning or form of the whole from which it has been derived. A fractal can be regarded as both a 'reductionist' and a 'holistic' version of the whole. Thus, a branch of a tree can be considered, not as a 'chopped off' fraction of a tree but as a sort of tree itself – containing many of the features and functions of its parent tree.

'Human consciousness may be considered to be a fractal of the universe'

Fractals are beginning to turn up in many areas of science – both practically and conceptually. In computer problems, recursive programming can be used to describe solutions in terms of easier or smaller versions of the same question. In graphic terms, a large curve can be described in smaller curves. An ice molecule is a fractal of a snowflake. In mathematics (differential calculus) an integral is a fractal of an equation. In biology, a DNA molecule is a fractal of the mature life-form that will ultimately develop from it. In a hologram, one small area of it contains the essence of the whole. In modern physics, a single quantum event (such as the release of a photon from an electron) 'enfolds' almost all the fundamental problems of philosophy (such as causality and meaningfulness) so that modern 'hidden variable' theoreticians such as David Bohm are seeking even 'deeper', 'sub-quantum' fractals that also contain the essence of the whole (the 'implicate order'). Human consciousness may be considered to be a fractal of the universe.

Similarly, the fractals that are used in my Fractal Method have the simultaneous meaning that they are reduced parts of the whole (so that enough permutations can be manufactured between them) but also retain sufficient conceptual relationship (with the whole) so that what is produced – by way of ideas – are practical rather than highly abstract (and thus not immediately usable). The Fractal Method can therefore be considered as a pragmatic 'middle way' between the sorts of comprehensive, fundamental ideas that only turn up once every few decades (such as evolution and relativity), and the infinite number of trivial ideas that can be produced by permutating the smallest constituent parts of the original items chosen.

The Fractal Method gives us some freedom in partially unravelling our existing, tightly constrained mental concepts and allowing re-combinations. There is absolutely no reason in principle why this should not be aplied to social innovation as well as to conceptual or product innovation.

Keith Hudson, 6 Upper Camden Place, Bath, BA1 5HX (tel 0225 442377; fax 0225 447727).

Ways of improving brainstorming

The normal rules for brainstorming are simply to come up with as many ideas as possible, with as little self-censorship or group evaluation as possible (at least during the 'ideas' part of the session).

Peter Evans and Geoff Deehan, in a book called 'The Keys to Creativity' (published by Grafton Books, £12·95), survey the research evidence and conclude that traditional brain-storming practices can be improved:

• By using personal analogy charades as in Synectics (one group member, for instance, acts as the deodorant that the others are trying to find new names for);

• By using sequencing (going round the circle asking for ideas, to prevent domination by one or two members);

'Brainstorming can be improved by subjecting ideas to critical analysis and evaluation as they crop up'

• By subjecting ideas to critical analysis and evaluation as they crop up (fewer ideas are produced this way, but their quality tends to be higher);

• By encouraging individuals to brainstorm on their own, using a group merely for warming-up first.

An options market for ideas

Henry Petroski

Adapted excerpt from 'Beyond Engineering – Essays and Other Attempts to Figure Without Equations' (published by St Martin's Press, New York), monitored for the Institute by Roger Knights.

I propose an options market in which the underlying securities would not be sides of beef or shares of stock but ideas – the fruits of creative thinking – a Higher Options Exchange. This is how it would work:

'Anyone who conceives an idea could approach one or more brokers on the Higher Options Exchange'

Anyone who conceives an idea that he or she reasonably expects to bring to fruition in a specified period of time could approach one or more brokers on the Higher Options Exchange and put forth a proposal outlining the idea and the potential financial gain to be realised from it.

Higher Options Exchange

Wednesday, September 7, 1988
Closing prices of all higher options. Sales unit is 100 shares.

	a – not traded				b – not offered	
	Oct		Jan		Apr	
Option	Vol	Last	Vol	Last	Vol	Last
Best Seller	170	11.5	b	b	24	7
Better Mousetrap	b	b	a	a	1	1.5
Broadway hit	75	12.5	32	7.25	b	b
Gold record	16	33.33	45	78	1	0.87
Good 5c cigar	b	b	7	98	b	b
Great novel	100	.25	12	3	3	12.25
Latest fad	150	70	200	50.5	90	37.25

A broker, having become interested in representing a promising idea, would then submit to the conceiver contracts for exclusive rights to offer a specified number of options in the idea. The contract would typically specify a fixed, one-time fee for the trading right. But particularly promising ideas might command more attractive contracts, especially if there were competition among brokers to represent an idea.

Upon reaching an agreement with the conceiver, a broker would prepare a prospectus describing the idea and the tangible product expected therefrom, the expected date of realisation of the idea (which would also be the expiration date of the option), and the financial potential of the idea. The prospectus would also specify the percentage of royalties that the conceiver is willing to share with an option holder.

Once an idea option were listed, the conventional free market system would take over to set daily prices, which would be reported along with other market transactions in the customary media. Ideas would be expected to conform to quarterly fruition dates to coincide with the Higher Options Exchange option expiration dates.

There would be no trading in underlying stocks; the price of an idea option would be affected primarily by rumours of the creator's progress or lack thereof.

Should a creator fail to bring an idea to fruition before the expiration date, the holders of the options would retain the claim to a prorated share of any future royalties realised from the idea. This would prevent the creator from delaying so as to retain all rights.

The creative individual offering an idea obviously benefits by raising capital with which to realise the idea. This capital would come principally from the negotiated price the broker pays for the right to offer the option on the Higher Options Exchange. But particularly promising ideas might earn their creators a cut of the broker's commission on all sales that resulted in an increase in the option's price.

'The option buyer expects to share in substantial royalties'

The broker expects to recoup the initial outlay to the conceiver and more, of course, through sales of options alone. The option buyer expects to share in substantial royalties. Potentially everyone is a winner.

Brain Clubs

Tony Buzan's Brain Club is designed to encourage its members to build up a range of mental and physical skills through the Brain Club Curriculum and through book reading, tapes, practice, competition, networking and mentors. For those who wish, accomplishment levels in the different skill areas may be graded and certified. Its international members live in the UK, Sweden, Finland, Belgium, USA and Canada and they organise meetings when required.

Tony Buzan is the author of books such as 'Use Your Head' and 'Use Your Memory'. The curriculum is potentially quite tough: for example master grade 1 in speed reading goes to those who can read 1,000 words per minute with 70% comprehension, with master grade 10 for those reading 10,000 words per minute. And those of us who find it hard to remember 20 items on a tea tray may be daunted by the Master 10 requirement to memorise 10,000 useful items.

Brain Club membership costs £67 for the first year. Contact Buzan Centres Ltd, Suite Two, Cardian House, 37 Waterloo Road, Winton, Bournemouth, Dorset, BH9 1BD (tel 0202 533593; fax 0202 534572).

Creative Slip Writing

Charles Clark

Adapted extract

Creative Slip Writing provides a remarkably simple process for getting ideas from constituents that can lead to significant improvement in the quality of service, more enthusiastic, motivated staff, and increased gifts from constituents by volunteers who have used the creative process.

How it works: each participant is given a pad of paper. The group leader presents a problem or simply asks for ideas for improving a service. He or she asks each person in the group to write on a slip of paper their ideas, without pre-judging them, one idea to a slip, within a five minute time limit. The papers are collected, the ideas categorised, all are then copied and the results returned to the group quickly for further discussion – either as a big group or by categories in workshop settings. Alternatively, the ideas may be given to key staff to develop further or to implement directly. All the ideas can be deposited in the leader's idea bank.

The benefits: This method allows the collection of many ideas from a vast reservoir of constituents in a relatively short period of time. The anonymity leads to honest and near 100 per cent participation. It works even in auditoriums with fixed seating. Participants can be energised to reach organisational goals.

Charles Clark, 623 Grant Street, Kent, Ohio 44240, USA (tel 216 673 1875).

HyperCard

HyperCard is a piece of software supplied free with the Apple Mac computer, which allows virtual computer illiterates to design their own programs using a language more similar to English than previous more arcane programming languages; and users can make tree-like structures of their thoughts as they branch out, connecting the different personalised screen-cards of their own mini-encyclopaedias in any way desired. Douglas Adams, author of 'The Hitchhiker's Guide to the Galaxy', has written that HyperCard may prove as significant a step forward as the invention of the first tool. The following are extracts from an interview with HyperCard's creator, Bill Atkinson, from the book 'The Complete HyperCard Handbook' by Danny Goodman (Bantam Computer Books):

'HyperCard may prove as significant a step forward as the invention of the first tool'

ATKINSON: What HyperCard is all about is sharing information. A program's soul has a lot to do with the people who are making it and what they're thinking about as they're making it. We're not doing this to make money. We're not doing it to make Apple happy. We're making this because we want to share something. One of the things I find myself sharing is my understanding of programming. I find I'm a very good programmer and that I know something about computer graphics. Those two things I can teach by example in HyperCard.

HyperCard is an authoring tool and an information organiser. You can use it to create stacks of information to share with other people or to read stacks of information made by other people. The HyperTalk language is sort of a humane starting point for people who want control of their computer and are not interested in programming per se. You can use it as a hub for launching documents and applications. I worked out a way to make searching about 200 times faster than a more obvious way. The thing I'm most excited about is HyperCard's 'opening up' potential. You know, we talk about open architecture hardware. Well, this is open architecture software where, really, you go inside a stack that somebody else wrote and look and see how it was done and modify it and tweak it a little to tune it for your uses and learn from what someone else has done.

'The Complete HyperCard Handbook' by Danny Goodman (720 pages, published by Bantam Computer Books, 1987, ISBN 0 553 34391-2, £27·95; available in the UK from Computer Bookshop Birmingham, 30 Lincoln Road, Olton, Birmingham B27 6TA, tel 021 706 1250).

Coin-through-the-wall-phones
Nicholas Saunders

This idea is to attach coin-operated pay phones to the outside walls of buildings, with a small hole the size of a coin drilled through the wall so that coins are collected inside the building.

'A small hole drilled through the wall so that coins are collected inside the building'

In areas of high vandalism, these phones would be offered to shopkeepers on a profit basis, so that shopkeepers would collect more money than the charge for calls made. It would therefore be in the interests of the shopkeeper to see that the phone were kept in good condition.

Installation: The concept of drilling a hole through a house wall large enough to take coins may sound off-putting, but in fact this can be done without causing damage in a few minutes using a standard large drill. A trained installer with the right equipment would be able to make a neat job in a couple of hours.

At present British Telecom is obliged to supply public phones, but expect to lose several thousand pounds per box over a six year period in vandalism and other costs. BT could thus afford to offer cheap or free installation of such proposed phones.

Obstruction: Most shops have a forecourt, part of the pavement where they may put ice-cream signs and the like. The phones would be over this area and would require no change in the law. Less obstruction would be caused than with existing call boxes.

Construction: I envisage a very compact design based on some wall phones now sold – the receiver, push buttons, coin slot and display could all be vertically arranged under an arched rain cover some six inches overall. This would allow use in situations where the shopfront is mainly openings with only narrow pillars.

Nicholas Saunders, top floor, 14 Neal's Yard, London WC2H 9DP (tel 071 836 9404; fax 071 379 0135).

Return to sender stickers for junk mail
Eric Walker

I have got fed up with all the junk mail that I get. I wrote off months ago to the Mail Preference body to try to stop it, but there does not seem to be any let up.

So I had labels with a message printed by Able-Label:

> **RETURN TO SENDER!**
> Message to sender. Please delete my name from your mailing list and save yourself money and cut the wastage of paper.

I just stick them over my address on the offending mail and pop them back in a letterbox. It may not do any good but I feel better for it!

I can supply them for £1 per 100, or people can order 1,000 direct from Able-Label for £3·25, and can give them out as presents to their friends.

• *Able-Label, Steeple Print Ltd, 5 Mallards Close, Earls Barton, Northampton (tel 0604 810781).*

• *Eric Walker's address is Exchange Value Video Club, Nacton, Ipswich, IP10 OJZ (tel 0473 717088).*

The Neal's Yard DeskTop Publishing launderette

Nicholas Albery

The Institute for Social Inventions promotes new and imaginative projects which improve the quality of life. One such, in my opinion, is the DeskTop Publishing 'launderette', run by Institute director Nicholas Saunders, in Covent Garden. Here you can either get a 'service wash' or you can do it yourself, using the latest Apple Mac machines with giant screens, the latest software, scanner, laser printer and typesetting.

> *'You can either get a "service wash" or you can do it yourself, using the latest Apple Mac machines with giant screens and the latest software'*

I have an aversion to Cow Gum glue and the fumes it gives off, so I am delighted that now I can avoid pasting up altogether. I take in my proof-read word processed disk and on one occasion I was able to lay out a simple book of 600 pages in three ten-hour days at the DTP 'launderette', using the very simple Pagemaker application. At the DIY rate, the cost is £6 per hour (£7-50 at peak times) and 50p per laser print, a total with VAT for my book of £441.

Where else can you laserset and lay out a huge book for 73.5p a page, with artwork ready to send off to the printers within three days? It works out more expensive initially whilst you are learning how to use the machines – it is £1 each time you need assistance, and £25 an hour if you need someone to sit with you all the time or to do it for you. But since the manuals are on the whole fairly easy to follow, I think most people could soon learn enough to be getting on with. There is an interactive program they let people use free which takes about two hours and familiarises users with the Apple Mac machine; and after that the cheapest and most sensible route into desktop publishing would probably be to use the Getting Started tutorial to teach yourself Pagemaker 4 – this should take about 4 hours and cost about £40, with occasional assistance from the staff.

The Institute is using the place for its ISI Publishing (tel 081 208 2853), where we offer to typeset and print people's books within six weeks and at cut-price rates – 1000 copies of a 128 page laminated A5 paperback can cost under £2,000 this way (including layout, printing and delivery), if authors are prepared to type simple style codes into their word processed text, for rapid transfer to Pagemaker 4 (which will use Pagemaker's 'Read Tags' facility to add font styles when placing the text).

The Neal's Yard Desk Top Publishing Studio, the first floor, 14 Neal's Yard (through an alleyway off Monmouth St), London WC2 (tel 071 379 5113). Although there are 10 workstations there, it is as well to book in before going.

High tech suburban offices, rentable by the hour

Clive Akerman

Anyone who commutes into or across London will have noticed that, as London becomes more prosperous, the journey takes longer and becomes more unpleasant (or perhaps I am just getting old and crotchety!). Yet, for many of us, 'work' consists in the main of chattering away at a computer or computer terminal – jobs which can be done practically anywhere, given a modest investment in equipment. However, while we, or our employers, might be able to afford small computers and cheap modems and access to electronic mail services and the like, we all also need occasional access to secretarial assistance, photocopiers, maybe laser printers or slide-making equipment, facsimile machines and the like.

In addition, not everyone has the space or the desire to clutter up their homes with computers and the detritus which surrounds us at work. We also 'go to work' for social reasons, including a dose of 'daily divorce', without which many relationships run into difficulties.

> *'Suppose that suites of small offices were set up in or near areas inhabited by commuters. They would act like the nursery units for small businesses, but, rather than being rented by the year, would also be available by the half-day or day'*

The Neal's Yard DeskTop Publishing Studio in Covent Garden provides the germ of an idea which might enable us to avoid the worst of the commute, yet still get away from home during working hours. Suppose that suites of small offices were set up in or near areas inhabited by commuters. They would act like the 'nursery units' set up to encourage and assist small businesses, but, rather than being rented by the year, would also be available by the half-day or day. They would be equipped with computers and the usual office facilities, including shared secretarial and other staff. Some offices might be suitable for an individual and others for small informal meetings. These latter would not compete, except at the margin, with established conference centres such as are provided by many hotels, but would rather be intended to replace the in-office meeting room where a handful of colleagues discuss projects in hand or hold regular reviews of progress and plans.

Employers who made regular use of such dispersed offices would naturally be able to reduce the size of their central facilities – though would no doubt maintain some central space for meetings and for work not do-able at home. Individuals would commute or use their local studio-office as needed. Savings in central space, in fares and in time would be used to pay for studio rentals.

These payments could be brought to good social use. For suppose the studios were constructed in vacant schools or parts of schools, or in other public property. Then, not only would the urge to dispose of the property, and its other uses within the community, be reduced, but surpluses could be used to improve the facilities available to the community.

I have always argued that schools, being already owned by the community, should be upgraded to become total community resources, with education of children being one of a wide range of facilities offered. Here we have a means to finance some of them.

So far as I can judge, such studio offices, located near the homes of commuters, offer benefits to the commuters and to their employers; they will be a source of jobs (well suited to part-time workers); they would enable disabled and other workers unable or unwilling to commute every day a degree of equality of opportunity; they would reduce the strain on the transport system. The losers – since every change leads to losers as well as gainers – would be the petrol companies, the motor industry and public transport.

Another group who might wish to join in are what, for want of a better word, we might call 'anti-commuters' – those who live in the inner suburbs and would find a trip to the outer areas more comfortable than a trip inwards. (Some years ago I drove out along the M1 for 15 miles each morning in considerable comfort, at least compared with the poor sods in the London-bound carriageway. The distance was irrelevant since the journey rarely met anything approaching a hold-up apart from the last half-mile into the centre of St Albans and thence to the office.)

> 'Anti-commuters – those who live in the inner suburbs and would find a trip to the outer areas more comfortable than a trip inwards'

Clive Akerman, 92 Sandbrook Road, London N16 OSP (tel 071 241 0866).

Rural 'telecottages' in Sweden

This project, actually under way, has similarities with the proposals of Clive Akerman, above. The details are extracted from 'Ledis', a newsletter about local economic development, put out by the Planning Exchange (3 Worsley Road, Worsley, Manchester M28 4NN, tel 061 727 8677; fax 061 727 8675).

Origins

The first telecottage in Sweden opened in 1985 at Vemdalen, a village in the north of the country not far from the Norwegian border. The man responsible for initiating this scheme, Henning Albrechtsen, was inspired a few months earlier by Jan Michel,

a Danish speaker at a seminar on economic development in rural regions.

The aim of setting up this first telecottage was to make jobs, vocational training and service facilities available to people in this remote part of Sweden (where there is less than one inhabitant per square kilometre); and to do this by providing access to a variety of computers and modern telecommunications equipment for anyone willing to invest time and energy by learning how to use them.

> 'About 40 telecottages are in the course of being set up in Scandinavia, and approximately half are already in operation; and as many as 75 countries have already joined a world-wide organisation, the International Union of Telecottages'

Today, less than four years later, about 40 telecottages are in the course of being set up in Scandinavia, with approximately half already in operation. The Association of Nordic Telecottages (FILIN) has been formed to foster cooperation and as many as 75 countries have already joined a world-wide organisation, the International Union of Telecottages (TCI).

Activities

The telecottage infoteque combines the functions of a training centre, library, post office, telecom shop and communications centre, with courses in the use of computers and telecommunications equipment. As a service unit, the telecottage is able to assist local firms with letter writing, book keeping, translations, etc, whilst functioning as an office for small businesses, and providing advice on the purchase of computers and software. FILIN is opening marketing offices in the larger cities of Scandinavia in order to gather work from large companies and agencies, for feeding out to the telecottages.

Finance

In the case of the Vemdalen telecottage, the initial finance (approximately 1m Swedish kroner) came from the government, Swedish Telecom and the local council. It has managed to cover its running costs in a short period of time, bringing in a monthly income of as much as 150,000 kroner.

From the beginning, the initiators of the project wanted to create a number of jobs where people could sit at home, each working with their own computer connected to the main computer in the telecottage. The unions worried that the workers might be exploited in their low-paid isolation. A solution was adopted whereby these individuals became members of the telecottage staff, working at home if they prefer to do so, but with the choice of working alongside their colleagues in the telecottage. As employees, their rights are thus assured as are their social contacts.

TCI and FILIN, Box 54, S.820 92 Vemdalen, Sweden (tel 46 684 30453). Christer Lundberg is helping the islanders of the northern archipelago outside Gothenburg to set up their own telecottages; his address is Div. for Industrial Architecture and Planning, Chalmers University of Technology, S. 412 96 Goteborg, Sweden (tel 46 31 722478).

Using your fax to stop torture

Amnesty International are recruiting people with fax or telex machines to join their urgent action network. Torture of political prisoners tends to happen in the early days of their imprisonment so fast action is essential. By joining the network you agree to take on the number of cases per year that you specify, and to spend up to an hour or so per case sending off a fax about it to the relevant authorities.

The Urgent Action Coordinator, Amnesty International British Section, 99-119 Rosebery Avenue, London EC1R 4RE (tel 071 278 6000).

Fax machines at postal sorting offices

Nicholas Albery

The Royal Mail service over the next twenty years will lose almost all its letters business to fax machines; but in the shorter term it could get some of this fax traffic for itself by equipping every sorting office with a publicised 0898 fax number. This Telecom service would charge the fax sender at 33p (off-peak) to 44p (peak rate) per minute. Royal Mail's 50% share of receipts from this would cover the cost of the local sorting office sending the fax on to the local customer by first class post.

> 'The Royal Mail will lose almost all its letters business to fax machines; but it could get some of this fax traffic for itself by equipping every sorting office with a publicised 0898 fax number'

Members of the public locally without their own fax machines could put the sorting office's fax number on their notepaper. And to send a fax this way you would fill in a standardised front page fax form, to be obtainable from any post office, with the address in a set place on the form, so the sorting office could easily place the fax in a window-style envelope.

Nicholas Albery, 20 Heber Road, London NW2 6AA (tel 081 208 2853; fax 081 452 6434).

QED, a high participation suggestion scheme

Most workplace suggestion schemes get about 5% of the workforce putting in ideas. The QED scheme claims to raise this to about 75%, and does so by putting the workforce into competing small teams (of up to 12 members) with funny names and a league table; using humour so people will not feel silly about having ideas; plastering the workplace with dramatic stickers about the scheme; going for quantity not quality of ideas, over a concentrated four weeks, with small prizes for every idea submitted (a mug, supplemented by a random prize draw); public announcements and recognition; and persuading the employer to try QED in the first place by distributing a cassette tape in which employers who have tried QED tell of their successful experience.

'Small prizes for every idea submitted'

Nick Thornely, the QED managing director, has identified what he terms the 'non-financial motivating factors' which the scheme makes use of: curiosity, surprise, recognition, publicity, pride, status, fear (of not taking part), money, greed, challenge, involvement, humour, leadership, planning and having a deadline.

'The "non-financial motivating factors": curiosity, surprise, recognition, publicity, pride, status, fear (of not taking part), money, greed, challenge, involvement, humour, leadership, planning and having a deadline'

Some of the biggest firms have called QED in – Vickers, GEC, RTZ, etc – and now health authorities are beginning to. The charge is a rather stiff minimum £15,000 but they guarantee to return any shortfall if the firm does not save at least this much. Such a sum would obviously be beyond many smaller firms and organisations, but there seems no reason why they should not design a similar approach for their own use.

QED, Industrial Motivation Ltd, 40 High Street, Thornbury, Bristol BS12 2AJ (tel 0454 418855).

Chapter eighteen

ARTS AND LEISURE

The Academic Inn

The London-based Academic Inn, founded by John Papworth, editor of Fourth World Review, hosts occasional dinner discussions for up to 100 people in a hall in St John's Wood. It is an opportunity not so much to hear a lecture but more to meet and debate at length with well-known figures in a convivial atmosphere. Past speakers have included Ivan Illich, Auberon Waugh, John Seymour, Rudolf Bahro, Lord Young of Dartington and Jean Liedloff. A paper by the speaker is circulated by mail in advance and at the dinner the speaker speaks for half an hour or so to remind people of it, before the questions and answers begin.

The Academic Inn concept was originally suggested on a somewhat different basis by Professor Leopold Kohr, author of 'The Breakdown of Nations', who wrote that 'the first universities of the Western World, the academies of ancient Athens, started out as fellowships of the drinking table.' He proposed to rescue the modern pub from its decline by putting good conversation on the menu, with the pub announcing, for instance, that 'Samuel Johnson (or rather his nearest equivalent amongst today's conversationalists) has his beer every day at 7pm at table 2.' That would be his only duty. 'From then on the chain reaction of conversation, sparked by musing silence or animated talk, will continue into dinner and after-dinner hours.'

'Having held forth on the subject for two decades,' writes Professor Kohr, 'I have rarely encountered a person whose enthusiasm could not be aroused *upon the instant* by the thought of such an institution.'

John Papworth, The Academic Inn, 24 Abercorn Place, London NW8 9XP (tel 071 286 4366).

Book-Pals

Stephen Rogers

Have you got favourite books that you would love to discuss in depth with other enthusiasts? Selected library books could have a contact sheet pasted in the back. People wanting to meet those drawn to the same work could enter their names and contact details.

I have often felt the urge to get in touch with those who have underlined and dog-eared the very pages I found significant. My proposal would be the next best thing – it would certainly provide a new means by which people could relate to each other.

> 'Selected library books could have a contact sheet pasted in the back. People wanting to meet those drawn to the same work could enter their names and contact details'

Stephen Rogers, 7 Avenue des Eglantines 24, 1970 Wezembeek-Oppern, Belgium.

Responses and reply

Mrs B. Jones, Spinney Cottage, Birchwood Lane, Chaldon, Near Caterham, Surrey, writes:

What an excellent idea. Not only does it help the librarian to know how popular or unpopular the books are, but there seems no better way of making congenial friends than to share the same taste in reading and learning. Just a short phone call and a lasting new friendship could be made, because a similar taste for reading usually shows common interests and compatible temperaments.

Response from Radio 4 programme

This 'Book-Pals' idea was taken up from the Institute for Social Inventions' Guardian column by BBC Radio 4's 'You and Yours'. They broadcast the views of three members of the public, all in favour, and those of Susan Cook, a librarian at the Porchester library off Westbourne Grove:

I don't mean to be a wet blanket, but when I first read the article I was really horrified because there are problems associated with this sort of idea: the main one that springs to mind is that people would be encouraged to start writing in the body of the book; and the second one which is very important is that personal names and phone numbers could be used in a way that wasn't anticipated; and the last one is that I feel that people would start scribbling notes on the page that weren't acceptable to the majority of people.

Reply by Nicholas Albery

(1) Would it encourage people to scribble in the body of books? It could well have the opposite effect, giving people a legitimate space to express their interest; a trial would demonstrate one way or the other.

(2) As to the danger associated with people giving their names and phone numbers:

(a) People are already prepared to take this risk of expressing their interests and giving their addresses or phone numbers in magazines such as Loot, so there is no reason why they should shy away from doing the same with this scheme;

(b) At the top of the pasted-in page could be a notice from the library warning that readers are advised to arrange to meet up first in a neutral venue such as a pub;

(c) As a further protection for those that want it, the library could offer a self-financing box number service, forwarding contact mail;

(d) The pasted-in pages could go initially into selected academic or similar books, and not into semi-pornographic or other dubious books;

(e) The scheme could be given an initial trial in a library used solely by students who are unlikely to feel at risk from fellow students.

(3) People might scribble obscene or objectionable comments, Cook fears. If the pasted-in page had a note to the effect 'please report objectionable graffiti to the library,' it could then be blacked out with a felt-tip pen or a fresh page pasted in. The previous borrower is likely to be the offender, and the risk of being identified in this way is likely to deter.

The Institute would be delighted to hear from any librarian prepared to consider a trial of the above scheme.

Share-a-Pet

Item in the Examiner (USA), monitored for the Institute by Roger Knights.

Jo Smith could not take proper care of her dog, Mota, but she didn't want to give him away or put him to sleep. So she hit on a novel idea: share him.

> 'Pet to share, Four year old Bichon Frise. Owner travels and would like to share with loving older couple'

Jo Placed an ad in a Chicago newspaper: 'Pet to share, Four year old Bichon Frise. Owner travels and would like to share with loving older couple.'

Story-teller cafes

Story-teller cafes are beginning to spread in Sweden. Anyone can take the floor and tell a story. Often two or three professional reasonably well-known authors or radio or TV personalities are involved to get the ball rolling. All sit round a table. These cafe evenings have been organised by Liv i Sverige (Life in Sweden), who have linked up with the Stockholm Centre for Folk Culture.

The Centre for Folk Culture's phone number in Stockholm is 46 8 205502. Item monitored for the Institute by Marilyn Mehlmann and the Swedish Institute for Social Inventions.

Chess tents in the park
Malena Griffiths

Lots of children and adults play chess. Venues are always cheap, scruffy and unpleasant. A large tent (black and white checked) could be temporarily put up in Hyde Park, Regents Park, etc as a place to play chess.

I have also contacted British Rail to find available space in major railway stations spread in different parts of the country to be used for Chess Centres.

Malena Griffiths, Flat 19, 17 Broad Court, London WC2B 5QN (tel 071 240 0556).

Female urinals with hoses

Adapted extract from the Examiner (USA), monitored for the Institute by Roger Knights; and from a story developed from Institute information by Jonathan Sale in the Independent on Sunday.

Four restaurants in the town of Pensacola, Florida, have installed new female urinals, and if they are well received, more will be installed in public places, to reduce queues for female toilets.

> 'The "She-inal" resembles a urinal for men, but has a hose attached to it. Women stand in front of the urinal and pull the hose towards them'

The device, called the 'She-inal', designed by Urinette Inc., resembles a urinal for men, but has a hose attached to it and is enclosed by partitions. Because the cubicles are narrower than traditional toilets, more can be fitted into the same space; and because users do not have to undress as much, the process is quicker and queues move faster.

Women stand in front of the urinal, pull the hose towards them and a piece of tissue (for wiping dry) drops down. When finished, the user hangs the hose up and flushes.

'It's an issue whose time has come,' says Janet Marie Smith, vice-president of planning and development for the Baltimore's Memorial Stadium, who has considered the installation of She-inals. 'It is embarrassing to see women queuing up around the corner waiting to use the restrooms.'

A Glamour magazine reporter concluded 'I found the She-inal very easy to use. It would be great for expectant mothers who find it hard to squat.' It is also expected to prove easy to use for the wheelchair-bound of both sexes and for children defeated by the height of the normal toilet seat.

Urinette Inc., 7012 Pine Forest Road, Pensacola, FL 32526, USA (tel 904 944 9779; fax 904 944 9778).

Let's Talk stickers

Denis O' Brien

People who would like to talk on an impromptu basis in public could wear a 'Let's Talk' badge or sticker. Others seeing the sign would be able to open conversation without fear of feeling presumptuous or rude or interfering. The cost of the stickers could be paid for by advertising. Humour could be integrated into the concept, for example, 'I am a Charlton Chatterer,' 'Tetley Talker' or 'Sainsbury Stutterer'.

> 'Trains, buses, shops and other public and private places could start to buzz with chatter'

Trains, buses, shops and other public and private places could start to buzz with chatter. Each journey to work could be exciting, unpredictable and human. There could be even be special talking and non-talking compartments on the tube.

Once the idea is made public, I could see it as a subject of much media interest. The Sun would print a photo of two people talking, British Gas would sponsor 'Will Sid Please Talk to Me' stickers. Being British, we would all use the excuse of talking (rather jokingly) about the scheme as an entree to more serious conversation.

Denis O'Brien, 20 Brookscroft, Linton Glade, Forestdale, Addington, Croydon, Surrey CRO 9NA (tel 081 657 4148).

Singing families

Valerie Yule would like the UK to copy the popular Chinese 'Singing Families' TV competition. In fact she would like not only a televised show to find the Singing Family of the Year, but also other TV contests for Over-Fifties, Work-Place Singers, Pub Singers, etc.

> 'It is astonishing how many people today never enjoy singing, when in the past and the world over singing together or alone has always been one of the great pleasures of life'

'It is astonishing how many people today never enjoy singing,' says Valerie Yule, 'when in the past and the world over singing together or alone has always been one of the great pleasures of life. Drunks used to be able to sing all of 'Sweet Adeline', now they can only manage the first phrase of a song. Particularly in places of high unemployment, being able to sing, and knowing the words of the songs, are pleasures that cannot be taken away. It is also good physical exercise. People who meet anywhere could have singing as a sideline.'

A condition of the television contests, Yule adds, would be that no line could be repeated more than once in any verse or chorus, and that all choruses must have different verses in between, as a guard against totally mindless pap; and the songs would be subtitled, so that viewers could learn to sing them too.

Valerie Yule, 57 Waimairie Drive, Mount Waverley, Victoria, Australia 3149 (tel 807 4315).

Walk Parties

Nicholas Albery

This is my suggestion for a cheaper, simpler, healthier alternative to a dinner or drinks party, and one that I find suits all ages from about 9 to 75: for the last two or three years I have organised a walk party for almost every Saturday. On Mondays I spend some three quarters of an hour sending out to about 25 friends (and to people I need to meet for work reasons) an invitation to a walk, within an hour or so by train from London. I send them a photocopy of the walk details and a map – normally culled from one of the walk books (the best is the 'Which?' book of walks), or from looking at possible footpaths in the Ordnance Survey. We go rain or shine, and normally there are between 4 and 17 of us, the numbers depending mainly on the weather.

> 'A cheaper, simpler, healthier alternative to a dinner party, and one suited to any ages from about 9 to 75'

We tend to walk about 8 miles, stopping for lunch at a pub and having a cream tea somewhere afterwards. It is a wonderful day out, with the walking stimulating conversation and an anarchic spirit. Sometimes we have medium fast walks just for the adults, and other times leisurely rambles, accompanied by dogs, children, even babies, and (once) a parrot. Since everyone pays their own way, my total outlay each week in organising the party is about £7-50 for stamps, envelopes, labels and photocopying. It has to be a Saturday not a Sunday, as there often seem to be engineering works on the railways on Sunday and the pubs tend not to serve meals.

Nicholas Albery, 20 Heber Road, London NW2 6AA (tel 081 208 2853; fax 081 452 6434).

Paying party guests

Nicholas Saunders

A type of party common in Denmark but not yet common in the UK is one in which the host gets the guests to pay. The guests are, of course, told when invited, and even approximately how much it will cost. The advantage is that the most elaborate feast with live music, or a whole weekend in the country, is affordable by everyone.

Nicholas Saunders, top floor, 14 Neal's Yard, London WC2H 9DP (tel 071 836 9404; fax 071 379 0135).

From mass festivals to human-scale fairs

Nicholas Saunders

Nicholas Saunders proposes ways to bring a 'human scale' back to mass summer festivals.

Several summer festivals in the UK such as the Glastonbury Festival and the Elephant Fair in Cornwall have in recent years grown out of hand, becoming so large that they attract too many dubious customers and too much trouble both on site and with neighbours.

Possible ways for organisers to reduce the scale and to change the tone of these events include:

• Closing down for a year to allow expectations to fade;

• Advertising them to sound slightly soppy and off-putting to the hard cases; with an orientation towards children, perhaps by calling them Children's Fairs; and if necessary not letting in unaccompanied adults;

• Not advertising any big name attractions;

• Holding them the same weekends as mass festivals or events elsewhere that will draw away the rough customers;

• Admittance only (or at a reduced price) to those wearing fancy dress;

• Stalls on site to sell only products that the stallholders have made themselves;

• No cars or motorbikes on site;

• No amplified music;

• If necessary have regular small fairs, rather than big annual events.

Nicholas Saunders, top floor, 14 Neal's Yard, London WC2H 9DP (tel 071 836 9404; fax 071 379 0135).

Oak Dragon Camps

The Oak Dragon Camps run from May to September each year. The number of campers ranges from forty to 100, and a camp is like an 'open-university-in-a-field.' There is a particular theme to each camp, such as alternative healing, music and dance, Green arts, etc, and they last eight to ten days, taking place at various sites in Wales, England and Cornwall.

'The special thing about Oak Dragon is that it is not a course,' say the organisers, 'it is an experiential journey in how to learn together, on all levels, not just the academic.' As people acclimatise, they are encouraged to propose activities and involve themselves in the running of the camp. There are frequent 'pow-wows', circular meetings at which important issues and deep feelings can be aired and discussed. Oak Dragon 'welcomes all spiritual paths with heart, honours our differences and rejoices in what we can share, adopting a policy of "both/and" rather than "either/or". Oak Dragon is involved with the spiritual aspect of our love of the earth as well as the ecological and Green political, and seeks to unite these various ways in which we involve ourselves with the earth. There is potential for each person to plant seeds of positive change, with far-reaching effects.'

> 'A camp is like an "open-university-in-a-field". There is a particular theme to each camp, such as alternative healing, music and dance"

People need to bring their own tents and sleeping gear; Oak Dragon provides marquees and geodesic domes for workshops, children's facilities, a cafe with healthy vegetarian food, toilets and hot showers. No dogs are allowed, as the camps are situated in farmers' fields.

SAE for details to Oak Dragon Project, Elfane, Mynyddcerrig, near Llanelli, Dyfed, SA15 5BD (tel 0269 870959).

Irish Organic Farm Guesthouses

Irish organic farmers and growers are opening their houses to visitors as part of the Irish Organic Farmers and Growers Association. 'Now you can stay in a big house, farmhouse, cottage or hostel and eat good food wherever you go. In every house you will find a personal welcome and the best of home grown food or other carefully selected produce.' For example:

'Moneygold is a traditional stone cottage set beside the mountains and the sea. 20kms of beaches. Safe swimming, lagoon, islands and sand dunes. Indoor gym and sauna 1km. Organic farm with Connemara ponies. We teach riding, also English for foreign students. Traditional music. Bed and Breakfast from £12, hostel beds at £5 per night. Tel 071 63337.'

For descriptions of the seven places on the circuit, contact Gillies Macbain, Cranagh Castle, Templemore, County Tipperary, Ireland (tel 0504 53104). (Cranagh Castle is itself on the list from £4 a night for hostel accommodation, with private rooms also available. It offers introductory courses in the walled organic garden.)

Railway carriage holiday cottages on old viaducts

Adapted extract from an article by Marcus Binney in the Times.

Stephen Weeks has come up with a commercial proposition for saving the old vast British Rail viaducts that has found acceptance with environmentalists (although local councils remain dubious): place eight old railway carriages on the viaducts and use them as holiday cottages. Replicas of famous engines such as the Mallard will be used and old 1950s or 60s carriages, repainted in the livery of the old line.

The carriages will be self-contained cottages of 500 square feet with a large living and dining room, kitchen, bathroom and two bedrooms. Each site will have its own caretaker.

> 'The holiday trains will offer spectacular views in places where planning permission would never have been given for a new hotel'

The holiday trains will offer spectacular views in places where planning permission would never have been given for a new hotel or holiday village; and Weeks is confident that all sites are safe and secure for children.

He is negotiating for nine viaducts and expressing interest in a dozen more; all his candidates are double-tracked viaducts, so that carriages can stand on the northerly side and visitors drive up and sit outside on the south. The BR Property Board and the Railway Heritage Trust have together offered £80,000 towards the costs of renovating his first acquisition, Monmouth Troy over the River Wye.

In the past the only major takers for redundant viaducts have been local authorities or the organisation Sustrans, usually because they want to open up a footpath or cycle way.

50 fine listed viaducts are available to local trusts or those with acceptable ideas on how to use them.

For further information contact David Lawrence of the BR Property Board (tel 0904 626262) or John Grimshaw of Sustrans (0272 268893).

100 Year Diary

The title page of the '20th Century Diary', published by Annabel Greaves, announces that this is 'a year-dated scrapbook album for you and your family to fill in with pictures and memories of our life and times. Now you can dance through the century, recount the sorrows and celebrate the joys.' The diary runs from 1900 to 2000, and, except for the years 1901 to 1929, each year has a lined, blank page to itself, headed with a few events to jog the memory. For example, 1985 is headed 'End of miners' strike, Band Aid and Live Aid, Gorbachev becomes Soviet leader, mass production of micro-chips begins in Texas, privatisation of British Telecom, cold wet summer and long warm winter.'

The diary can be an excuse for people to get together: whole families, classes, clubs or villages can add photos, cuttings from magazines and personal reminiscences. 'The luckiest families,' writes publisher Annabel Greaves, 'can consult a relation who is ninety – perhaps ask them to write a page or two. I think it could benefit lonely people – researching their century and following up favourite interests.'

Just over 2,000 diaries have been printed.

'20th Century Diary', published by 20th Century Diaries, Severels, Runcton, Chichester, Sussex PO20 6PS (tel 0243 786406), 1991, 100 looseleaf A4 pages in ring binder cover, £15·95 including p&p.

A diary of personal commitments

Omar Mahmoud

Adapted from a longer submission.

This proposal is that people could write in their diaries the commitments that they make each day as they go through experiences that lead to such decisions. These commitments could range from simple family matters ('I'll not change my baby's sleeping time') to business interactions ('I'll not send an angry letter the day I write it'), to social or political issues.

The purpose of such a diary is to benefit from important events and thoughts of our daily life, so that our future is always better than our past.

Those who are keen on living up to their commitments and principles can share their diary with their spouses, children or their friends, so as to transform their personal commitments into social ones.

Building on this idea, those events and commitments of a general nature from a number of contributors could then be published in a diary with two pages per day; one telling a story and the other left for users to record their own.

I plan to start my Diary of Personal Commitments. I'll be willing to share some of my insights with others.

Omar Mahmoud, 16 Route de Meyrin, 1202 Geneva, Switzerland.

Setting priorities from inside outwards

Stephen L. Holliday

Adapted extract from a letter to the Institute.

The ever-increasing complexity of modern life gives rise to ever-increasing conflict with regard to priorities. Some of the many things left undone turn out to be things we realise should have been top priority.

The solution is a clear hierarchy which is simple enough to be applied without ambiguity, yet provides a valid and personally satisfying basis for judgement and action.

The solution is to start at the centre of one's life and to work gradually outward:

(1) First priority is the interior of one's own body: health and fitness (physical and mental).

(2) Second priority is the exterior of one's body: personal hygiene; grooming; clothing.

(3) Next are things that relate to personal living quarters: making the bed; hanging up clothes; fixing the alarm clock.

(4) Next come all immediate family needs, both physical and emotional.

(5) Now consider things that are contained within the rest of the living area: kitchen; living room, etc.

(6) After that come the personal property and facilities that lie just outside the living area: vehicle maintenance; garage maintenance; yard work.

(7) Then come things dealing with other daily environments: workplace; co-workers; neighbours; close relatives.

(8) Now you can attempt to squeeze in things that require going beyond the daily 'track': specialised shopping; personal correspondence; travel and vacations; distant relatives.

(9) Politics.

Every now and then something will assert itself with enough importance that it requires attention before its usual rank in the hierarchy – 'the exception that proves the rule.' (Don't forget to vote if it's election day!) A good way to deal with this is to abandon the hierarchy completely for a day; the universe, as well as the human spirit, craves a little reshuffling now and then.

Stephen L. Holliday, 12441 Short Avenue, Apt. 7, Los Angeles, CA 90066, USA (tel 213 306 4518).

A Mini-Mind Gym

A number of computer software programs designed to enhance creativity, self-understanding, personal well-being and thinking are emerging, mainly from California. For instance, the Mindware catalogue contains programs such as 'Brainstorming Made Easy' (made easy if not cheap: for IBM machines, $74·95). This asks for your ideas and then reorganises and displays them in all their possible combinations, offering you a new perspective on your task each time you press a key. The program 'Combine Timeless Wisdom with Modern Science' (for IBM machines, $149) checks your rational answers against your biofeedback readings (as measured by placing two of your fingers on the mouse attachment) to see if 'your answers differ from your deeper emotional responses as revealed by biofeedback.' The goal of the program is to process your responses in a way that leads you to 'serenity'. To get there, you pick adjectives describing how you feel, which are linked by the program to a matching 'personality'.

> 'The computer program checks your rational answers against your biofeedback readings to see if your answers differ from your deeper emotional responses as revealed by biofeedback'

Other programs analyse dreams, teach muscle control and compute sexual compatibility. Timothy Leary has designed a game called Mind Mirror, in which gaining 'emotional insight' gives credit in the realm of 'social interaction', and you are scored as to your bioenergy, emotions, mental ability and social interactions.

Mindware catalogue, $2, 1803 Mission Street, Suite 414, Santa Cruz, CA 95060, USA. Information originally from an item by Bruce Eisner in the Omni WholeMind Newsletter, WholeMind, PO Box 11208, Des Moines, IA 50347, USA. Subs. $24.

Quality video club

> 'Beat the Devil – this I think is almost the funniest film I have ever seen. I must have watched it five or six times and it never palls'

The best of today's and classic movies are available by mail (at £5 each for one week) from the Exchange Value Video Club started by film enthusiast Eric Walker. He writes:

I have been interested in film ever since as a child I used to collect Pathescope Monthly free from our photographic shop in Nottingham and to dream of having my own collection.

Later my wife and I founded a charity called Concord Films Council which for many years has been one of the main suppliers of educational films to schools and colleges throughout the country.

In 1985 I took early retirement and decided to start this video library of worthwhile films which in general are not easily available from local video shops. So far it has succeeded in using up most of my pension, but as I did not start it with the idea of making a fortune out of it, this has not worrried me.

The library contains over 600 titles, everything from Amadeus and Gandhi to Shakespeare Wallah and Les Enfants du Paradis. Here are some of my own recommendations:

'Ashes and Diamonds' so stunned me that coming out of the cinema I found my car would not start. After my wife and two friends had pushed for quarter of a mile, I found I had not switched the ignition on. 'The Blue Angel' – a milestone in the development of the cinema. 'Beat the Devil' – this I think is almost the funniest film I have ever seen. I must have watched it five or six times and it never palls. 'The Unknown Chaplin' – each night I eagerly awaited this when it was originally shown on TV.

The system works as follows: send off £1·50 for the catalogue and supplements. In the catalogue is a £1 voucher to set against the normal hire charge of £5 (this £5 covers postage both ways). A returnable deposit of £20 is held for the duration of membership.

Exchange Value Video Club, Nacton, Ipswich IP10 OJZ (tel 0473 717088).

Plastic bag art

Nicholas Saunders reports that an upmarket Danish supermarket chain owned by the Co-op sponsors living Danish artists by reproducing their works of art on their carrier bags – with the name of the shop on the side panel, not over the artwork, plus a little box giving details about the artist. 'The quality of colour printing on plastic is really excellent nowadays,' says Saunders 'and this way the bags tend to have a longer life – some even end up framed on people's walls.'

> 'The Co-op sponsors living Danish artists by reproducing their works of art on their carrier bags, with the name of the shop on a side panel, not over the artwork, plus a little box giving details about the artist'

Nicholas Saunders, top floor, 14 Neal's Yard, London WC2H 9DP (tel 071 836 9404; fax 071 379 0135).

Poetry carved into London pavements

The following is adapted from an article in the Illustrated London News entitled '50 ways to improve London':

Featureless monoliths, bare pavements and dreary walkways could be greatly improved if they were inscribed with relevant extracts from novels, plays and poetry – stamped in concrete, carved in stone, turning every stroll into a literary adventure – just as poetry was engraved on pavements along the Jubilee Gardens, set there during the Festival of Britain in 1951; and just as poetry has featured in advertising spaces on the London Underground and on Dublin billboards.

Extracts from works which never mention London could also be used as long as they were relevant to their location. Thus we could see psalms in the pavements of Ludgate Hill on the way to St Paul's, Confucius and Lao Tzu in Chinatown, and on Greek Street a sprinkling of Plato.

The Transformation Game
Martin Leith

The Transformation Game comes as a basic boxed set for two to four players or as a workshop led by a trained facilitator. It was developed at the Findhorn Foundation, a holistic education community based in Scotland. The game provides the means of looking at your life – and a specific life issue – in a new light. Each participant starts by choosing a playing focus – an outcome that he or she would like to achieve by playing the game.

As I look back, there is one game which I found particularly memorable. It started off in the usual way. We had a meditational 'attunement', spent some time clarifying playing purposes, and filled Personal Unconscious envelopes with Angel cards, Insight cards and Setback cards. All three players were born without difficulty, receiving a red Physical Level scorecard, and taking a Guardian Angel from their envelope (such as the Angel of Creativity, Faith or Purpose) to support them in their game.

A player moves from one level to the next – in this case from the Physical to the Emotional – by a throw of the dice, landing on one of the eleven different life squares (Insight, Angel, Miracle, Service, etc) and receiving cards which slot into spaces on the scorecard. When the spaces have been filled, the player moves to the next level. Two of the players moved effortlessly to the Emotional Level but the third remained stuck on the Physical Level for much of the game. Now this was an interesting situation, because she had chosen as her Playing Focus 'I intend to develop fruitful action.' And her action was being thwarted by the absence of a Service Token that she needed to fill the remaining slot on her scorecard. She had had two Miracles (providing an over-abundance of Grace) and passed up two opportunities to serve another player and thereby obtain the vital Service Token. And she had virtually the whole set of 96 Physical Level Awareness Tokens spilling from her scorecard in all directions. Here was her life spread before her. 'I suppose I'm not ready to move yet. It's my karma,' she said. I pointed out that karma is a Sanskrit word meaning 'action' and yelled at her, 'Do someone a bloody service and get off this damned Level NOW!' She looked horrified. But her next turn got her unstuck and on to the Emotional Level. And today there's no stopping her – she is one of the most dynamic, action-orientated people I know. That is how the Transformation Game works.

I usually facilitate these game workshops in people's homes and offices (including one for a group of managers at a large British petroleum company) and they last from four hours to at least a day.

Martin Leith, 5 Dryden Street, London WC2E 9NB (tel 071 829 8361; fax 071 240 5600).

Boxing – blows below the collar only

Rev. John Worthington

In boxing, just as the belt is the line *below* which a blow may not be landed, so the collar should be the line *above* which a blow may not be landed.

'Evidence that blows to the head can trigger future Alzheimer's Disease'

There is growing disquiet about the head injuries sustained by professional and amateur boxers, and recent evidence that blows to the head can trigger future Alzheimer's Disease.

Among changes to the rules of boxing in the past 150 or so years have been:
(1) The introduction of rounds, instead of a continuous fight until one man could fight no more or was knocked out. (2) The banning of bare knuckle fights with the introduction of muffled hands, and then boxing gloves. (Fists as well as heads could be damaged for life.) (3) The banning of head butting. (4) The introduction of not hitting below the belt.

None of the above were easily accepted by the fancy at the time.

The main vested interests affected by this new proposal are boxers, boxing promoters, bookmakers, manufacturers and ancillary workers. They should all realise that boxing is on shaky ground. The anti-boxing lobby is alive and may get stronger, but if those interested in the continuance of boxing will take on board this 'limited target' idea, their financial stake in boxing will be safe.

Boxers will never again have the dread of a 'bad' brain scan or permanent eye damage hanging over them.

Boxing will continue to meet the needs of the aggressive spirit of the public and of young men. Amateur boxing would be happy to fall into line and might well increase in popularity in the services and schools.

If a spirited lead is given by the United Kingdom with this idea, it will no doubt be followed worldwide.

Rev. John Worthington, Moorland Cottage, Godshill, Fordingbridge, Hampshire SP6 2LG (tel 0425 654448).

DIY tutors

Alan Stern

Alan Stern's proposal for DIY tutors is entitled 'The Institute for Domestic Engineering Advancement and Learning' (IDEAL):
IDEAL's aim would be to enrol students who wish to learn the skills of 'domestic engineering', and hence, to develop and keep their homes, contents and attachments, in an attractive, comfortable and well-maintained condition.

'The tutor would offer practical tutorials in DIY, in the student's own home'

IDEAL would create a register of independent consultant craftsmen or tutors, in much the same way as the Open University maintains a local tutor and counsellor network. The IDEAL tutor would offer practical tutorials, in the student's own home or place of development, with the objective of helping that student become both proficient and self-sufficient with respect to the developmental problem at hand. Examples of domestic engineering skills that could be taught at such tutorials include: painting and decorating, plumbing, wiring and electrical installation, general household and building repairs, to both internal and external fixtures and fittings as well as furniture, mechanical appliances, motors and bicycles, plus guidance in gardening and horticultural projects.

'Not to do the job itself but to teach the student how to do it for themselves'

This new educational institution would be financed by student fees paid (via IDEAL) to the tutor, matching the market rate for the standard job. The tutors would, in effect, be paid not to do the job itself but to teach the student how to do it for themselves.

IDEAL will need to take steps to deal with issues such as the selection and ongoing quality control of tutors, and establishment of criteria for student assessment and the awarding of a diploma in domestic engineering (Dip. Dom. Eng.).

Initial funding and the foundation of IDEAL could well find benefaction from one or more of the several large retail DIY chains such as Homebase, Texas, B&Q, Do-It-All and Wickes, etc, who would all benefit from both a financial and public relations perspective, as they help to create a nation of DIYers.

IDEAL would in turn serve an ever-growing market of home owners, desperate to know everything there is to know about DIY, but afraid to experiment on their own.

To summarise the benefits of IDEAL:

(1) Society would become more self-sufficient on the DIY front resulting in renovated, revitalised and refurbished communities.

(2) Legitimately skilled and empathetic local craftsmen would find a growing and grateful market, that would continue to employ their tutorial service, as new skills are required to tackle ever more demanding domestic engineering tasks. Moreover, their image and community standing would be enhanced by their IDEAL tutor status, no doubt resulting in increased job satisfaction.

(3) Industry and commerce would find a new and potentially lucrative outlet for its social responsibility policies.

The chairman of Wickes Building Supplies, W. J. McGrath, has responded encouragingly to the scheme: 'We would be delighted to discuss the possibility of developing our current innovation, product development and design department into a far more proactive Wickes institute.'

Alan Stern, 5 Walker Close, London N11 1AQ (tel 081 361 5323).

Holidays in the Past

Tony Ryder

Adapted extract from a submission to the Institute.

A 'Holiday in the Past' organisation, using a tiny and remote Greek island, could offer an experience of the past: through the windows, out in the harbour, travellers who had booked in would see the flickering flames and the shape of the galley that would take them to the Polis next day. Greek servants would wake the visitors and serve an ancient-style breakfast. Belongings could be carried to the quayside by slaves (if the visitors could afford them). The galley would be rowed to the other side of the island.

There would be a wall around the Polis, an open air Agora, shops, a town hall or office, barracks, fishing boats, etc. The buildings would be furnished and decorated in the correct style, circa 300 BC.

Only food of that era would be available (rough bread, wine, fish, honey, etc). Teachers would tell stories (pre 300 BC) and maybe teach ancient Greek. Artisans would practise and teach their craft – woodwork, painting, pottery, sculpture, cooking, jewellery, building.

Quite a bit of the work in building up the Polis could be done by the visitors too.

Such a holiday away from the twentieth century might be of particular interest initially to teachers and students of history, archaeologists, writers and actors.

Tony Ryder, 70 Rowheath Road, Kings Norton B30 2EX (tel 021 459 4468).

Shock Third World holidays

Adapted extract from a submission to the Institute.

'For unhappy Westerners suffering from "rat race desperatis", therapy could consist of a few weeks' visit to the grinding daily realities of a Third World country'

For unhappy Westerners suffering from 'rat race desperatis', therapy could consist of a few weeks' visit to the grinding daily realities of a Third World country – based on the premise that one cannot really appreciate something without experiencing its opposite.

The objective would be to experience the Third World existence and not to see the exotic and historical sites. For example, if we take Egypt, where I come from, the programme would include:

• A one-star hotel (bed and cockroaches), all meals to consist of horse beans and salad;

• A minimum dose of two rides on public transport each day;

• A visit to a government office to get some official papers issued such as a visa extension;

• A visit to a public hospital for whatever excuse;

• A one-week stay in the 'City of the Dead' (one and a half million people in Cairo live in the cemeteries);

• A stay in a village in rural Upper Egypt.

This therapy will work in three main ways: It will be a real human experience; the Westerner will appreciate the good things in life in the West; and will develop an interest in the Third World and hence a purpose in life – net, the trip should result in a paradigm shift of life and happiness.

The trips should be organised by a cultural travel club, jointly by the Western and Third World country, with nominal amounts paid to receiving families in the Third World country.

The proposal is based on my experiences in two extreme countries: Egypt, where I was born and grew up; and Switzerland, where I have been living for six years. Per capita income in Egypt is less than $500 per annum while that of Switzerland is $26,000, one of the highest in the world. On the other hand, the consumption of jokes and laughter, a measure of relaxation if not satisfaction, is much higher in Egypt. When an Egyptian meets a friend or an acquaintance, the first question is 'What's the latest joke?' In Switzerland the only place to find a joke is a book entitled 'Swiss jokes ... they exist'!

Omar Mahmoud, 16 Route De Mayrin, 1202 Geneva, Switzerland.

Sustainable Tourism

North-South Travel is recommended in the 'Global Consumer Guide' as a travel agency for cheap flights. It covenants all its profits to a trust supporting projects in developing countries. 'We offer discounted flights worldwide,' writes North-South Travel. 'Often we can match a quote you may have been given and then, because of our charitable status, you may prefer to use us.' It has also opened its own tourist-hotel in Suffolk; and has launched 'Travel Friends Inter-National', which seeks to relate travellers and tourists in Britain to people and organisations in destination countries.

> ## 'Travel with trekking companies that use kerosene, make no open fires, put on warm clothes instead, limit hot showers to two per week'

Tourism Concern is another organisation trying to promote responsible and sustainable tourism – in this case through a charter, codes, presence at conferences and publications. A sample item in its newsletter contains conservation tips for trekkers in Nepal, such as 'Conserve firewood; use stoves, stay at lodges that use kerosene or fuel efficient wood stoves, travel with trekking companies that use kerosene, make no open fires, put on warm clothes instead, limit hot showers to two per week and make sure your porters have warm clothing.'

'The Responsive Travellers' Handbook – A Guide to Ethical Travel World-Wide' has been published by the Centre for the Advancement of Responsive Travel on a subscription basis of £5 per year, but is available only to members of Tourism Concern (£12 per year) or Travel Friends Inter-National (£10 to join).

Finally, Equations is a group concerned with the impact of tourism on India and South East Asia and publishes reports such as 'The Impact of Tourism on India's Environment'.

* *North-South Travel Ltd, Moulsham Mill Centre, Parkway, Chelmsford, Essex CM2 7PX (tel 0245 492882).*
* *Tourism Concern, Froebel College, Roehampton Lane, London SW15 5PU (tel 081 878 9053).*
* *Interface, Moulsham Mill, Parkway, Chelmsford, Essex CM2 7PX (tel 0245 492882).*
* *Centre for the Advancement of Responsive Travel (Roger Millman, director), 70 Dry Hill Park Road, Tonbridge, Kent TN10 3BX (tel 0732 352757).*
* *Equations, 96, IInd Main, 'H' Colony, Indiranager Stage 1, Bangalore 560 038, India (tel 812 542313; fax 812 542627, attn. 020).*

Chapter nineteen

INTERNATIONAL AND DEVELOPING WORLD

Dismember the superpowers

Peter Cadogan

'War is the health of the State,' ran Ralph Bourne's famous precept from World War I days. And it is true. The nation state is a modern horror of a mere 500 years' vintage. The essential unit of civilisation is the city state as it was known to the classical Greeks and to the Middle Ages and Renaissance Europe. The centralised government of the modern nation state uses the issues of war and imperial rivalry to build its militarism and its bureaucracy – never more than in the case of today's superpowers.

Genuine democracy needs to be face-to-face as between governors and governed and this is only possible on the city regional scale. There can be no grass-roots democracy so long as we are brainwashed into believing that democracy equals Westminster and Whitehall. With multiple parliaments and multiple No 10's democracy becomes feasible again. West Germany has 11 'länder', Italy has 20 regions and Switzerland has 26 cantons, all with extensive powers. We and the French are miles behind.

Back in the early seventies we could and should have discussed English regionalism when the subject of Scots and Welsh nationalism came up. It was side-stepped. The trouble is that no main political party is in favour of it, since all are committed to London centralism. The serious debate and organisation have to begin outside the party political orbit.

The new imperative is a new political dimension based on volunteers and principled professionals and where decision-making is regionalised. It has been slowly emerging from the 'alternative' movements of the last 30 years and is currently underwritten by the Church's endorsement of 'compassion and justice' as the values of the future. There is new thinking about 'counter-economics' and a widespread development of cooperative and other responses to mass unemployment. Decentralist extra-Westminster democracy is slowly surfacing.

It is up to people, every freedom-and-peace movement, to make their very specific contribution to the slow dismemberment of the superpower empires from within. When the process is complete and the last of the Caesars has been laid to rest, the problems of the world will be reduced to the level of the soluble.

> 'When the process is complete and the last of the Caesars has been laid to rest, the problems of the world will be reduced to the level of the soluble'

Peter Cadogan, East-West Peace People, 3 Hinchinbrook House, Greville Road, London NW6 (tel 071 328 3709).

Unrepresented Nations and Peoples Organisation

Information in part from a report by Sarah Lambert in the Times.

In 1991, 14 groups united to form the Unrepresented Nations and Peoples organisation – a sort of alternative United Nations. The 14-strong core included Estonians and Latvians (who have since, of course, achieved their independence) and West Papuans and Tartars. The Masai, the Karen of Burma and Eritreans came to the special session in The Hague as observers and would like full membership.

The principles behind this new body are those of respect for human rights, for the right to self-determination, for democratic principles, and for the protection of the environment. Each member pledges to try to solve conflicts without violence.

As a group they hope to run information networks and management training schemes and to pool their contacts. The organisation has a long list of academic, legal and political experts prepared to help advise and support the organisation. They have established an Urgent Action Council to intervene at the request of members and their groups who are threatened by state violence and bloody conflicts. They believe that the mechanisms of existing bodies are too slow to anticipate and to act on crises before they happen.

The criteria for peoples seeking membership are that:
(1) They are a distinct group; (2) They have their own

culture; (3) they have their own language; and (4) they are not members of the UN.

Founding Secretary General Van Walt Van Praag, Unrepresented Nations and Peoples Organisations, 347 Dolores St, Suite 206, San Francisco, CA 94110, USA tel 415 626 0995; fax 415 626 0865).

The shire as the fundamental unit of government

Adapted extracts from a review in 'Reason' (USA), by Donald Boudreaux, of 'The Vermont Papers' by Frank Bryan and John McClaughry ($18-95, published by Chelsea Green Publishing Company, PO Box 130, Post Mills, Vermont 05058, USA, tel 802 333 9073); review monitored for the Institute by Roger Knights.

The authors of 'The Vermont Papers' propose that the fundamental unit of state government be the 'shire' – a geographic region small enough to ensure that its members share similar values and perspectives and, hence, a genuine sense of citizenship. They claim that the number of citizens in the optimal-size shire is 10,000.

> **'Each town in a shire will hold town meetings at which citizens vote for town officers, state senators, and for shire reeves who will represent the town in the Shire-Moot'**

Each town in a shire will hold town meetings at which citizens vote for town officers, state senators, and for (archaically named) shire 'reeves' who will represent the town in the shire legislature, called the 'Shire-Moot'. The Shire-Moot will have all legislative authority for the shire, as well as the right to elect a shire council. The shire council, along with a hired shire manager, will administer the day-to-day business of the shire. A system of shire courts will replace the existing state superior and district courts, with shire judges elected by the Shire-Moot. Each shire will be part of a federation of shires, much as the several states in the United States are now part of a federation of state governments.

The state government has a definite place in the Bryan-McClaughry plan, but its role would be greatly reduced in scope from the role it currently plays. Significantly, 'delegated powers go to the state, reserved powers to the shires ... always with the presumption that power resides in the shires.'

The state government will be 'radically smaller,' concentrating its efforts on protecting the environment, providing technical services to the shires, and conducting state 'foreign policy' – mainly state relations with other states and with Washington DC. The shire will remain the fundamental unit of government.

The authors correctly understand that, all other things being equal, smaller and more localised governments – because of competition from other jurisdictions – simply cannot get away with being as tyrannical and redistributionist as more centralised regimes.

If we applaud the market system for supplying individuals with their favourite flavour of ice cream, consistency requires

that we applaud a political system that supplies each person with his or her preferred style of community life, without violating the rights of others.

> **'If we applaud the market system for supplying individuals with their favourite flavour of ice cream, consistency requires that we applaud a political system that supplies each person with his or her preferred style of community life'**

The address for John McClaughry, the book's co-author, is: Institute for Liberty and Community, Concord, Vermont 05824, USA (tel 802 695 2555).

Europe of Many Circles

'Europe of Many Circles – Constructing a Wider Europe' by Richard Body, published by New European Publications Ltd, 14-16 Carroun Road, London SW8 1JT, £14-95, ISBN 1 872410 01 4.

'Europe of Many Circles' is the first book that reveals how it is possible to return to a 'human scale' Europe, one that relishes the smallness of even its smallest Liechtensteinian-size members, and that would not for a moment dilute their ethnic and cultural diversity. It is a book that celebrates Leopold Kohr's vision of applying 'small is beautiful' to nation-state size; and a book that is in tune with the break-up of the Soviet empire in Eastern Europe and out of tune with the Dellorian EC fat cats. It argues, quite simply, that 'small nation states should decide for themselves what is most appropriate for themselves; and when they decide for themselves that their interests converge with one or more neighbouring nation-states, then a circle of interest can be formed, and within that circle they can act together for the common advantage of the people who live in the circle.' An example Body gives is that of patents: European countries, including three non-EC members, have quietly and successfully agreed a common patent policy for new inventions.

So: let there be simply ad-hoc groupings for particular purposes, rather than some massively over-centralised EC bureaucracy. 'Accountability, as a principle of parliamentary democracy,' Body writes, 'must itself be on a human scale. The size of a constituency is crucial to its practicality; and no matter how hard the Euro MP tried, his accountability to 500,000 constituents could only be a sham and a charade.'

The Russian Republic itself must dissolve

John Papworth

The dissolution of the Soviet Empire shows that its peoples have begun to grasp that the key to the control of their destinies in democratic terms lies not in unity but in division.

Yet one paramount danger that remains lies in the disproportionate size of the Russian Republic, with its 147 million population against the less than 10 million of most other republics.

This is the kind of disbalance which enabled Prussia to unite and dominate Germany under Bismarck and which led to two world wars, just as other such unities in Britain, France and Italy prompted these countries to policies of imperial expansion and their inevitable outcome in monster wars.

If peace is to prevail among the newly liberated peoples of the Russian Empire it is imperative that the first rule of peaceful coexistence should be observed: that no single nation should be so large as to enable it to dominate the others.

The Russian Republic stretches from Eastern Europe to the Pacific. In ethnic terms it is an imperial power rather than a nation, and it will be a test of their democratic sincerity to see how they will resolve this problem in accordance with the wishes of the many nationalities in the republic.

Similar principles of division need to be applied to the other giant republics of Uzbekistan (20.3m), Kazakshstan (16m) and the Ukraine (51.7m). Nor need we concern ourselves with questions of the economic viability of small units. The Baltic nations were a byword for prosperity and peacefulness before the communist take-over; and just as the really wealthy countries of Asia – Hong Kong, Singapore, Taiwan and South Korea – are the smallest, so in Europe it is the minuscule nations such as the Scandinavians, which are amongst the most prosperous. When will we learn that smallness is not a bar to prosperity but a condition for it?

John Papworth, Fourth World Review, 24 Abercorn Place, London NW8 9XP (tel 071 286 4366). Subscriptions to the Fourth World Review cost £10.

Welcoming a Balkanised Europe

John Papworth

The old order changeth indeed and in Europe just now faster than anywhere. But in all sorts of ways it seems to be a change back towards the past rather than towards some brilliant new dawn, and it is a past which fills many commentators with the gloomiest forebodings as they dilate on nationalism, ethnic struggles, 'Balkanisation', turmoil, conflict, violence, and, just round a corner signposted 'a Reunited Germany', the shadow of another world war.

Such feelings seem to be based on faulty reasoning and a false view of history. Before the Second World War, and even more before the First, 'Balkanisation' became a synonym for nationalist turbulence and political instability for two main reasons. The first related to the fact that many legitimate nationalist aspirations were frustrated by undemocratic systems of government, and the second to the way in which each of the 'great powers' sought to use these frustrated aspirations to serve its own interests and to deny possible advantages to its rivals. One observer concluded:

'There's not a nation in Europe but labours
To toady itself and humbug its neighbours.'

This has caused many people to conclude that nationalism is a dirty word and bound to lead to endless discord and political disruption as a matter of course, but is this borne out by the facts?

The history of Scandinavia is one of continual war, conquest, suppression and nationalistic resurgence, until, that is, the idea of democracy took hold. Today, as twentieth century political standards go, they are models of good government, peaceful, stable, moderate and, as the Brundtland Report might suggest, able to address problems in terms to which the world community is ready to listen.

And does not the record of Switzerland suggest a similar lesson? European history is in part a record of frequent conflict between French, German and Italian speaking peoples; why then have the same linguistic peoples been able to dwell in perfect harmony within the Swiss Confederation? Switzerland can justly claim to be one of Europe's oldest democracies, and in many ways its system of government gives its varied peoples a far more effective voice in political matters than that of many other countries which can claim to be democratic.

It will be noted that in both these examples that not only has the factor of democracy been of importance in establishing the peaceful conditions which prevail, so too has been the principle of non-interference in their affairs by outside powers. But there is also a third factor which has helped to achieve these results, and it is one which is highly relevant to the turmoil through which much of Eastern Europe is now passing.

'There is a quite extraordinary disposition to assume that unity brings with it prosperity and stability'

In both cases their peoples have not sought to solve their problems on the basis of some form of unity, rather have they actively promoted the principle of division. There is a quite extraordinary disposition to assume that unity brings with it prosperity and stability and that division is either impossible or impracticable and the prelude to anarchy and misery, when in fact exactly the opposite is the case.

The small nations of Scandinavia, each of which has a population less than the number of the inhabitants of London, and in two cases less than half the number of which London might boast, are not poor, they are among the most prosperous nations on earth! The same may be said for Switzerland, its six or seven million people live in a haven of prosperity, stability and political sanity, not because they are united, for the very name of 'Switzerland' is shorthand for the Swiss Confederation, meaning a confederation of self-governing cantons, each of which can leave the confederation if it so wishes, and where citizens of a single canton can divide themselves into two cantons if they are, as they have been, so minded.

It will be noted that no outside power has imposed any 'settlement' on any of these peoples in order to bring about the system which prevails; the governing systems, the boundaries and the allocation of constitutional powers and prerogatives have been decided by the peoples themselves, and the key to their well-being resides in the fact that, having decided what they wanted, they proceeded to get it and can continue to claim that they have now got it.

There is a tendency to assume in the case of Switzerland that the country is well governed simply because it is rich, but as Professor Leopold Kohr pointed out in his 'Breakdown of Nations', first published over forty years ago, this is to get things the wrong way round; Switzerland is not well governed because it is rich, it is rich because it is well governed. One may add that it is well governed because it has rejected the principle of centralised unity and pursued the path of non-centralised diversity.

Is there not here a key to the solution to the turbulence through which much of Europe is now passing? The evidence is abundant that smallness of size, far from being a barrier to prosperity and peace, is a factor which enables them to be promoted. So, far from fearing the further division of Europe into its ethnic parts, why not embrace the principle of democratic self-determination in every case where people are seeking to assert their identities?

This brings us to the problem of Germany, a problem which the Congress of Vienna tried, and failed, to solve in 1814; it was a failure which played its part in the events leading to two world wars. The size of Prussia was out of proportion to that of the other German states and the size of the Bismarckian-unified Germany was out of proportion to many of its neighbouring countries. The Prussian Bismarck's enforced unification of the German kingdoms, principalities and grand duchies was a direct consequence of the rigid centralisation imposed on France by Napoleon (which in turn can be said to have its origins in the centralised iron rule of the English Tudors).

'When proportion is ignored, so that one or more countries are too large proportionally to others, conflict is inevitable'

In the politics of peacekeeping, proportion is all, and when proportion is ignored, so that one or more countries are too large proportionally to others, conflict is inevitable and war something difficult to avoid. This is the lesson that Europe must at some stage digest; that power, to be robbed of its capacity for violence, needs to be fragmented into numerous small units so that if any one of them should opt for war the consequences would be modest in scale and containable, rather than result in a tragedy of global dimensions.

The old political framework will no longer serve for the new Europe that is emerging, even less will it be served by the old ideas on which that framework is based. For instance, there is no reason at all, apart from entrenched old fogeyism in the realm of ideas, why Ireland should not be divided into a number of self-governing provinces on the lines of the Swiss cantons, with a confederal-type government having absolutely minimal powers which are strictly defined and controlled by the provinces.

'A super-sovereign states of Europe would create another immense and uncontrollable power bloc on the world stage'

The same sort of thinking needs to be applied to other parts of Europe. Europe, as Mrs Thatcher used rightly to affirm, is not a country and never will be. The attempts by her old adversary Mr Heath and others to create a super-sovereign states of Europe, moves now happily in retreat as the dangers of such an approach – which would create another immense and uncontrollable power bloc on the world stage and result in an inevitable increase in the tensions and phobias about

security and all the attendant prospects of increased global conflict endemic to such a scale – are increasingly recognised.

A Europe organised on the basis of democratic division and non-centralisation will still need functionally unified organs of government, but these need be no more than what common sense indicates is required and, no less important, they need not all be located in a single centre. Its transport commission could be in Lyons, its health commission in Birmingham, its postal and communications commission in Geneva and so on, and all firmly under the control of elected representatives from the different provinces, counties or cantons.

'The Europe that once existed of many small city states gave it the only sublime glories it has ever known'

Of course such an approach involves a radical restructuring of its large existing countries, of Russia and Germany, no less than of Britain, France and Italy, into smaller and more manageable units, but before such proposals are dismissed out of hand as mere map dreaming, let it be recalled that the European malaise is fundamentally a malaise of power, power out of control and producing results which continue to threaten the demise of our entire civilisation. And let it be also recalled that the Europe that once existed of many small city states gave it the only sublime glories it has ever known.

John Papworth, 24 Abercorn Place, London NW8 9XP (tel 071 286 4366).

Protecting minorities in the emerging democracies

Vernon Bogdanor

Adapted extracts from a paper prepared for a symposium in Malta for Eastern European politicians and constitution designers.

Personal federalism

In the modern world, ethnic relationships tend to transcend geography. For countries where minorities are not territorially concentrated, it might be worth adapting the principle of what has been called 'personal federalism'.

'Non-territorial associations were entrusted with the administration of cultural affairs, while political and economic questions were dealt with on a multi-ethnic basis'

The idea of personal federalism is an invention of the Social Democrat, Karl Renner, in the Austro-Hungarian Empire at the beginning of the 20th century when the principle of nationalism within the Empire was coming to be recognised. Since it was not possible, in the Empire, to attach nationality to a given territory, an alternative solution had to be found. This was achieved by dividing the state into 'associations' each of which comprised only individuals of the same nationality.

These non-territorial associations were entrusted with the administration of cultural affairs, while political and economic questions were dealt with on a multi-ethnic basis, through national and regional institutions. A similar model was adopted in Lithuania in the inter-war years in an effort to conciliate that country's German and Jewish minorities; also in the Lebanon in 1943 and Cyprus in 1960, although these two latter examples can hardly be cited as successful illustrations of the operation of personal federalism.

Minorities within government

As a further precaution, the principle of power-sharing can be introduced into the executive level of government. This is achieved, for example, in Switzerland, where, by convention, the government, which is not responsible to the legislature, keeps a minimum of two seats for the French-speaking cantons, and ensures that there is a balanced representation of religious and linguistic groups. In Belgium, the Constitution (Article 86b) requires that 'with the possible exception of the Prime Minister, the Cabinet comprises an equal number of French-speaking and Dutch-speaking ministers,' thus over-representing the Francophone minority; while in Canada, convention rather than constitutional rule ensures that cabinets balance Anglophones and Francophones. In the Austrian *Länder* – with the exception of Voralberg – power-sharing at executive level is secured in a novel way. Each *Land* parliament, itself elected by proportional representation, elects a *Land* executive by proportional representation also.

> 'Each *Land* parliament, itself elected by proportional representation, elects a *Land* executive by proportional representation also'

Minority vetoes v. strong government

The emphasis on power-sharing can be strengthened by requiring weighted majorities for certain measures of constitutional change or measures affecting the interests of particular groups. In Belgium, for example, each chamber is divided into two linguistic groups, one Flemish and one Francophone. Article 107d of the Constitution requires that certain laws 'be passed with a majority vote within each linguistic group of both Houses, providing the majority of the members of each group are present and on condition that the total votes in favour of the two linguistic groups attain two thirds of the votes cast.'

> 'To take away from governments their power to do evil may also be to take away their power to do good'

In addition, the Constitution provides for an 'alarm bell' procedure (Article 38b) for laws not requiring a special majority, excluding the budget. In the case of such laws, three quarters of the members of one of the linguistic groups 'may declare that the provisions of a draft or proposed bill which it specifies are of such a nature as to have a serious effect on relations between the communities.' In such cases, the cabinet, in which, as we have seen, each linguistic group enjoys parity of

representation, reconsiders the bill, and parliamentary consideration of it is suspended for thirty days. A suspensive veto of this kind has the virtue of protecting the interests of particular groups while avoiding the dangers of inflexibility to which an absolute veto can give rise. For too frequent recourse to the veto can make government immobilist so that no decisions at all are taken. Overuse of the veto by the Turkish legislators on tax bills was indeed a major reason for the failure of the 1960 Cyprus constitution in 1963, and, in general, the scope of any constitutional vetoes should be as narrow as is consistent with a feeling of security for the various groups. 'The veto power,' it has been said, 'must be regarded as a kind of emergency brake,' not as part of the normal machinery of government. (Arend Lijphart: 'Consociation: The Model and its Application in Divided Societies', in Desmond Rea, ed., political Cooperation in Divided Societies, Dublin 1982, p. 177.)

This is then the danger in such consensus-creating devices. The constitution should not give so much weight to the need to secure consensus that the outcome is deadlock and immobilism. It must recognise the importance of creating a government strong enough to resolve complex socio-economic problems and to act effectively. In the inter-war period, the collapse of democratic governments in Central Europe was due at least as much to the fact that they were unable to take strong action in the face of unemployment as to the failure to achieve a consensus amongst different groups. Power-sharing democracies may prevent measures that are offensive to minorities; but they may also prevent the necessary measures being taken to resolve fundamental problems. To take away from governments their power to do evil may also be to take away their power to do good. It is one of the oldest of political dilemmas, and shows just how difficult it will be for the emergent democracies of Central and Eastern Europe and the old Soviet Union to find the precise point of balance between strong government and the protection of minorities. They might perhaps be comforted by the knowledge that none of the long-established democracies has found the perfect answer to this question either.

Vernon Bogdanor, Brasenose College, Oxford OX1 4AJ (tel 0865 277830).

Avoiding civil wars – new constitutions for emerging democracies

David Chapman

The following innovatory suggestions come from 'Can Civil Wars be Avoided – Electoral and Constitutional Models for Ethnically Divided Counties' by Dr David Chapman (published by the Institute for Social Inventions, 1991, ISBN 0 948826 26 6, £7-95, or £12-95 libraries and institutions). Its ideas are applicable not only to the emerging democracies around the world, such as the old Soviet Union and Eastern Europe, but also to established democracies such as the UK. The Institute has initiated two international conferences for East European constitution designers and politicians to forward the kind of ideas in this book; and has helped establish the East Europe Constitution Design Forum to provide continuing assistance to the new democracies.

Parties needing to gain votes in all areas

The key proposal in the book -- and one that if widely adopted could do more to prevent ethnic turmoil and civil wars than any other measure available – is that of **Local Balance Representation**. This is a system for use in countries where the different ethnic groups are to some extent geographically segregated. Local Balance Representation penalises a party by loss of seats, if in some areas of the country it gets few or no votes. Thus each party is given the incentive to get votes from the areas occupied by each ethnic group, and so to become an inter-ethnic party, appealing to each group. A government formed by such a party would be responsive to each of the ethnic groups in the country, whether it were a majority or a minority. The system is applicable for a newly democratic South Africa, Israel-Palestine, Northern Ireland, the Baltic republics, Georgia, Czechoslovakia, Bulgaria, tribally divided countries in Africa and others besides.

> 'Local Balance Representation penalises a party by loss of seats, if in some areas of the country it gets few or no votes'

In more detail, how this new system would operate is that a party's seats would depend on its degree of support in its 'lowest tenth'. This 'lowest tenth' is worked out as follow: the whole country is divided into small areas or neighbourhoods, with the exact boundaries not being crucial, so normally any naturally homogeneous areas with about 1,000 or so inhabitants could be used; and the percentage of votes that a party gets is calculated for each area. The lowest tenth is that ten per cent of these areas in which the party has its lowest percentage; the party then loses seats if it has a percentage of votes in the lowest tenth which is less than three quarters of its percentage over the whole country.

> 'If widely adopted could do more to prevent ethnic turmoil and civil wars than any other measure available'

No weak coalition governments

Direct Election of Government would give single-party government, where no party has a majority of seats. One party is elected, directly by the people, to be the sole government party. The method of election, a development of that of Condorcet, tends to elect a moderate government, one whose policy is near to the centre of the country's political spectrum, and widely responsive to the different sections of the electorate. The party elected as government is awarded a block of extra votes in the parliament, so as to give it a majority of votes if not of seats, so enabling it to govern. This avoids the problems linked to weak coalition government, while giving single-party government by a party acceptable to the electorate as a whole.

Single-member constituencies even with Proportional Representation

Uninomal Proportional Representation (UPR) is a proposal that would give each MP his or her own single-member constituency. To achieve this, the country is divided into small electoral areas of perhaps a few thousand electors. A party assigns to each of its candidates a constituency composed of a number of these areas, seeking to make the constituency of such size that the candidate gets a quota of votes, ie just enough to be elected. UPR thus combines at least some of the advantages of the present UK system, with those of the usual forms of PR.

Building in a bias towards decentralisation

Progressive Federalism is a proposal for allocating powers and functions between central, regional and local levels of government in such a way as to give a bias towards decentralisation. Instead of being fixed by a more or less rigid constitution (as under the usual type of federalism), the powers of any set of lower-level governments can be changed at any time by negotiation between them and the higher-level government involved. In case of disagreement between them, the powers of the lower level are decided by a national commission elected by all the elected representatives at that level, over the whole country. There is a commission for each level of government below the centre, and in case of disagreement between *them*, the lower-level one has primacy.

Thus the scheme can be expected over time gradually to transfer powers to the lower levels as they become ready to exercise them. It could be used either by countries which were already federal, to allow the powers of the centre to be gradually adjusted, or by a unitary state such as the UK, to bring about a gradual federalisation of the country.

Local elections first for new parties emerging out of communism

This proposal is to hold a series of **elections in sequence**, starting with the most local level and ending with the national assembly level, and throughout to give parties state aid in proportion to previous votes, to help them to fight the next stage and to increase their support. This is designed for a newly democratising country, to enable weak and poorly organised emerging parties to develop rapidly, so as to form an effective opposition to any dominant and well organised party, if one exists.

Fixed terms plus emergency elections

Fixed term elections on mandatory dates are proposed, but also allowing the government to call an extra early emergency election. Thus, since the next fixed election would still be held, the government would have no incentive to call an early election purely for its own electoral advantage.

Dr David Chapman, Democracy Design Forum, Coles Centre, Buxhall, Stowmarket, Suffolk IP14 3EB (tel 0449 736 223).

A new type of directly elected president

Professor Peter Jambrek, a member of the Slovenian constitutional court, has put forward a way of electing presidents that would protect ethnic minorities. This was subsequently elaborated as a joint paper by Professor Jambrek and Dr David Chapman.

In this version, the president would be elected directly by the people, using a Chapman variation of the Condorcet method which would tend to elect a moderate candidate nearest to the centre, one who appealed to wide sections of the electorate and to the minority groups.

'The president's only substantial power would be to select the prime minister, who can then only be rejected by a two-thirds majority of parliament'

The president's only substantial power would be to select the prime minister, who can then only be rejected by a two-thirds majority of parliament (and then only if they propose a replacement candidate).

The prime minister appoints cabinet members, who may or may not be MPs, with candidates subject to the same parliamentary veto.

The government is not obliged to resign if it is defeated on any one issue and would normally simply adjust the proposed legislation until it got the required support.

This would have the added advantage of giving more stable government than is usually obtained under proportional representation, by avoiding unstable coalitions.

• *Dr David Chapman – see above for address.*

• *Professor Peter Jambrek's address is Pravna Fakulteta, Univerza Edvarda Kardelja, Trg osvoboditve 11, 61000 Ljubljana, Slovenia, Yugoslavia (tel 061 331 611; fax 61 331 734).*

Exporting the Swiss constitution

Nicholas Albery

The Institute for Social Inventions initiated a symposium for Eastern European politicians and constitution designers which took place in Lausanne in 1990, financed by the Swiss government and organised by the Swiss Institute of Comparative Law. I had always admired the Swiss constitution from afar, and I felt that the 50 or so constitutional experts from Eastern Europe who were present for the three days of deliberations could only have benefited from the painstaking immersion into every aspect of the Swiss system. The Swiss, with typical, if misplaced, modesty, made no efforts to 'sell' their constitutional set-up to the Easterners and were scrupulous in drawing attention to Switzerland's failings.

Positive aspects

I learnt a great deal at this symposium as to the essential ingredients that have made the Swiss constitution so suitable for export to troubled 'hot spots' around the world.

• The most vital aspect of all, I believe, is the rural Swiss commune at the village level, each with a couple of thousand inhabitants enjoying a fair degree of autonomy. These communes have their own constitutions and some meet once a year to debate and vote at open meetings.

'In Switzerland, final sovereignty resides clearly with the people, and so there is not the same chasm of distrust between governors and governed that is apparent in most other countries'

• The main constitutional safeguard against over-mighty government is the right of the Swiss citizen to gather between 50,000 and 100,000 signatures, depending on circumstances, so as to trigger a referendum on a heartfelt topic. These referenda are relatively popular. The average Swiss citizen can vote perhaps three to five times a year in federal referenda, once every two years on a cantonal issue, and once every three years in a communal referendum. There is virtually no limit to the odd and diverse topics that citizens can attempt to add to the constitution in this way. Thus article 32 forbids the sale of absinthe and there was even an (unsuccessful) referendum recently that would have required the abolition of the Swiss army. In Switzerland, final sovereignty resides clearly with the people, and so there is not the same chasm of distrust between governors and governed that is apparent in most other countries.

'Minorities are safeguarded in that a referendum once passed by the voters must also be passed by a majority of the cantons'

• Furthermore, minorities are safeguarded in that a referendum once passed by the voters must also be passed by a majority of the cantons. As for minorities within cantons, those that feel sufficiently oppressed can follow the example of the Jura, who through a complex series of referenda broke away to form their own canton. Although the Swiss constitution makes no allowance for secession, we were assured that if Jura had wanted to leave the federation and join France instead, it would not have been prevented from doing so; in practice such a misguided impulse would not have survived a closer look at the centralised nature of the Napoleonic French system.

• At the federal level, sweetness and light between the different language groups is preserved by reserving each of them a permanent place in the cabinet. And presidential ambitions are curtailed by having a presidency that rotates amongst the seven ministers. Many Swiss do not even know who their current president happens to be. (Uruguay once copied the Swiss constitution only for its president to rebel at his lack of power, with an army coup promoting him to military dictator.)

Improving the Swiss constitution

How could the Swiss constitution be improved by a country in Eastern Europe or elsewhere seeking to adopt it for their purposes? What are the failings of the Swiss system?

• It all works so slowly. A Swiss referendum can take four or five years to achieve its by then obsolete aim. No commercial business could succeed that took four years to make a simple yes/no decision. A total revision of the Swiss constitution has been under way for 25 years, and the end is still not in sight.

I suggest that to prevent the constitution become over-encrusted with obsolete elements, any additions should lapse automatically after a hundred years unless renewed; and also that the whole referendum process should be dragged into the modern era by devoting in-depth television programmes to referenda debates, followed by voting within a few weeks.

'Give lottery tickets to all those who turn up to vote'

• People in Switzerland apparently feel that they suffer from a surfeit of democracy, with apathy spreading amongst the young and the working classes. On several occasions only just over 20% of the electorate have bothered to vote in a referendum. It might be worth trying Peter Mucci's idea to attract working class voters in particular: give lottery tickets to all those who turn up to vote.

• The lowest turnouts are for referenda on abstract constitutional issues 'beloved by law professors.' The highest turnouts are for issues that hit the Swiss citizen in the pocket. The suspicion lurks that the Swiss refused to join the United Nations less for reasons of principle than because it was going to cost them – they prefer to buy into particular programmes à la carte – which might indeed be a sensible way for other nations to fund the UN whilst keeping firm control of the purse strings.

'The Swiss prefer to buy into particular UN programmes à la carte – which might indeed be a sensible way for other nations to fund the UN whilst keeping firm control of the purse strings'

• Cities need subdividing into a network of communes. John Papworth in the Fourth World Review has highlighted the lack of political subdivision within Swiss urban communes. A city commune of half a million voters is absurdly large compared with its rural counterpart. Perhaps this lack of meaningful representation has contributed to the alienation of the young, reflected in the fact that the Swiss have the highest proportion of drug addicts (and AIDS victims) of any country in Europe.

• A tax on the size of firms is needed to control the powers of the large corporations, which otherwise tend to ride roughshod through any constitutional or other safeguards.

• The main present threat to the Swiss constitution is an external one. There are signs that the Swiss economy may be heading for troubled times, as multinationals and banks (pressured by the United States into becoming no longer so secret) move elsewhere in search of the European community market. It is on the horizon that financial fears may push the Swiss into the Common Market, a move that would not only, I believe, diminish their long-term prosperity, but would also homogenise their cantonal diversity and replace a highly evolved system of local autonomy and human scale government with dictates from Brussels.

I am sure that the Swiss 'peasant' farm in the mountains visited by our coachload of East European constitution designers would not survive amongst the EC's industrialised farms. The 82 year old grandfather sang and yodelled for us, saying that he felt like a millionaire, his gold was his life in the mountains and his bevy of grandchildren. His son, with occasional help from the neighbours, looked after forty cows. It is, I believe, as good a test as any as to whether a country's agriculture is sufficiently human scale to find out if the cows have individual names. In this case each had not only a name over her stall ('Amoureuse', 'Bourgeoise', etc) but a posy of flowers and a heavy bell waiting for the ceremonial autumnal descent to lower lands. I bought a distinctive Gruyere cheese that would probably not have met EC pasteurisation standards, and I learnt that farming is more heavily subsidised in Switzerland than even the EC would allow, for it has to take into account the difficult mountainous nature of the terrain.

The dangers of world government

Switzerland's cautious approach to the United Nations made me think some more about the Fourth World distaste for a strong world government or a strong United Nations. The Fourth World position is roughly this: a World Government would inevitably become just one more tyrannous empire, even more remote and inaccessible than the present superpowers.

To quote from the book I co-edited – 'How to Save the World – A Guide to the Politics of Scale':

'We believe that the movement we are supporting for a new localism in world affairs, involving as it does the breakdown of giant nations, needs to be balanced by a sane internationalism.

'We must evolve criteria and safeguards for the federalist and transnational structures that are necessary to confront the complexity of the planet's problems.

'Any form of political or economic power which is not controlled by those affected by it is a threat to peace, or freedom or both. Questions that need to be asked centre on control:

• Who appoints whom?
• Who elects whom?
• Who hires and fires?

'Who decides policy? Who settles the budget?'

• Who decides policy?
• Who settles the budget?
• Who checks the books?
• And who controls those who make these decisions?'

Criteria for sane transnational structures

My exemplar of a sane transnational structure is not the slightly grotesque United Nations but rather the humble international postal union which is based in Berne and quietly gets on with the specialist job of facilitating international mail. Thus my criteria for worthwhile global organisations would include:

• They should be based in various places around the world, not all in one country.

• They should have an incentive to dissolve once their specialist task is completed.

• They should be separate organisations, with separate names, and not under one central or global authority, whether United Nations, World Parliament or similar.

• They should wherever possible consist of concerned

professionals and experts getting together on an ad hoc basis, subject to national political supervision and interest group lobbying as required. Thus the international postal union could continue to be based in Switzerland, with a centre for tackling transnational pollution in Kenya, and regional commissions for human rights. There would also at times no doubt need to be ad hoc regional poolings of national armies or militias for service in emergencies, as in the grouping of countries that confronted Iraq – a grouping which could have taken place without the blessing of the United Nations.

• These transnational bodies should have as little power as possible.

• They should incorporate the principle of subsidiarity, leaving powers devolved to the most local levels possible.

'Communism's doomed love affair with the curse of bigness'

Communism's internationalism was not the least of its failings. Internationalism was all part of communism's doomed love affair with the mass scale, with the curse of bigness. Politicians and constitution designers have an obligation to learn the principles of scale, as must architects, town planners, engineers, industrialists, economists and all those who have blighted this century with their over-bloated giantism.

• *The Fourth World Review, 24 Abercorn Place, London NW8 9XP (tel 071 286 4366). Subs £10.*

• *'The Swiss Constitution – Can it be Exported' by Nicholas Gillett, is available for £8-50 incl. p&p from YES, 14 Frederick Place, Clifton, Bristol BS8 1AS.*

What rights should local areas have?

Nicholas Albery

The next task facing many of the newly emerging democracies in Eastern Europe, the old Soviet Union and elsewhere, now that the national elements of their constitutions are largely settled, is to frame constitutional laws for local government. As a contribution to the debate as to whether greater autonomy for neighbourhoods could help protect minority groups, I drew up the following provocatively decentralist 'rights for neighbourhoods'. A critique of these points by Professor Dietrich Kappeler (a teacher of administrative, constitutional and international law living in Malta) is followed by my response.

Albery: At the level of the municipality or parish council or urban neighbourhood (population groups normally of between 500 and 15,000 people) the municipality should have the following rights (either on its own or in joint operation with other municipalities of its own choosing) – provided that it is democratically governed and subject to any national or international laws protecting human or minority rights.

(1) The right to establish its own governing council or form of government.

Kappeler's response: This is very important and should be non-controversial.

(2) The right to pass its own laws.

Kappeler: This right should be limited to matters related to

cohabitation within the community and relations with similar communities and super-imposed entities, to the extent that the latter do not regulate such inter-community affairs.

Albery: My own view is that the community's laws should take precedence over the laws of other levels of government, except in so far as freely acceded to by that community or as determined by the Decentralisation Commission – see point 11 – or in so far as they relate to basic human or minority rights as enshrined in international conventions.

(3) The right to place taxes on its inhabitants, its businesses, its imports and exports and its resources.

Kappeler: The right of taxation to cover community expenses should exist, but this should not prevent taxation rights of superimposed entities for the financing of their own activities. No taxation of 'imports and exports' should be allowed, as this would create intolerable obstacles to the free flow of goods and services.

Albery: Taxation could be at the community level, with part of the tax remitted to the other levels, in so far as freely acceded to by that community, or as determined by the Decentralisation Commission (point 11). Taxation of imports and exports might indeed hinder trade, in which case a community might decide not to impose such taxes, but it should retain the right to do so – for instance to discriminate against goods from multinational firms. Encouraging communities to become more self-reliant is as or more important than encouraging free trade.

(4) The right to establish its own banks or credit unions.

Kappeler: At the planned level of 500 to 15,000 people, no bank or credit union could function. So this right is pointless.

Albery: Of course credit unions can function with less than 15,000 people. Many are far smaller than this, with mere hundreds of members. And banks too can operate successfully at this level of population – witness the bank in the Vatican, a country with a population of under 1,000.

(5) The right to issue its own currency, in so far as this does not counterfeit other currency issued elsewhere.

Kappeler: At a time when currencies are becoming worldwide so as to eliminate unnecessary complications, such a right should be shunned at all costs. The size of the planned communities would moreover make its exercise illusory.

Albery: Currencies can indeed be issued at the community level, and will, I forecast, increasingly be so issued. Again, the Vatican issues its own currency, despite its population of under 1,000. And the Wörgl shilling, issued by the small town of Wörgl in Austria in the early 1930s, helped it to overcome the effects of the depression and to decrease unemployment – and only came to an end when other towns wanted to copy Wörgl, and the Austrian State Bank stepped in and prohibited the currency. With the new computer networks, there will be many more such experiments – indeed the Institute for Social Inventions published a book on the need for such 'electronic nodes' by Conrad Hopman (entitled 'The Book of Future Changes') and the software already exists; these community nodes could then link up electronically whilst retaining their individuality. Exchanges between multiple versions of computerised money are simple. Similar experiments have taken place in a number of communities using so-called Green Pounds or Green Dollars (see the chapter on 'New Money Systems' in this book).

Any such measures which increase the divisions between economies are to be welcomed. It is like having watertight compartments on the Titanic, for then a local economic crash cannot sweep as easily and catastrophically through the world economy.

> **'Divisions between economies are to be welcomed. It is like having watertight compartments on the Titanic, for then a local economic crash cannot sweep as easily through the world economy'**

(6) The right to use its own languages in all its affairs.

Kappeler: This right is self-evident, subject to the need to communicate with other communities and superimposed entities in a language acceptable to both sides.

(7) The right to establish its own schools, according to its own curricula and teaching practices.

Kappeler: This right should be exercised within a much larger framework as regards the determination of curricula and requirements for degrees and diplomas. Otherwise these would lack recognition beyond the narrow confines of the community.

Albery: The right of a community to its own school curricula is worth safeguarding. Countries at present manage to recognise each other's educational qualifications without having standardised curricula.

(8) The right to establish its own police force.

Kappeler: This right is self-evident, but its implementation might be beyond the human and financial resources of very small communities.

Albery: I fail to see why a small community should be unable to establish its own police force, even if this were to consist of just one neighbourhood warden. Again, the Vatican manages to have its own police force (indeed its own army!). And there are increasing moves towards neighbourhood vigilante or Guardian Angel-type forces, which are best regulated at the neighbourhood level.

(9) A community shall have the right to establish its own newspapers, radio or TV stations or other forms of media, in so far as these do not interfere with media transmissions from other sources within the region; and with the Decentralisation Commission (in point 11) adjudicating any dispute between communities over wavelengths, etc.

(10) The right to establish its own public transport systems and to control its own roads and transport networks.

Kappeler: Such a right could only be exercised by the largest of the contemplated communities and even then they might find it an excessive financial burden.

(11) The right to select representatives to a Decentralisation Commission made up of representatives from all the other municipalities throughout the nation, which would be wholly responsible for deciding which functions – besides those described above – could be allowed to be provided at the municipality level and which should remain with higher levels of government; and it would adjudicate in any dispute between these higher levels of government and any particular municipality.

Kappeler: Such a body would presumably have to exist alongside the elected parliament of the superimposed entity or as a second chamber of it.

(12) The municipality shall have the right to secede from higher levels of government or from the nation itself – if a majority of its inhabitants so decide in a referendum.

Kappeler: Such a right should not be granted outside truly exceptional circumstances, as it is likely to be grossly abused. Any rich neighbourhood of a city complex (eg Chelsea in London) would secede in order to escape sharing the problems and financial burdens of the others, with results that can be imagined.

> **'It is open to the surrounding regions to discriminate economically against a rich neighbourhood that opts out'**

Albery: The right to secession is indeed a tricky point (choosing Pimlico rather than Chelsea as the example would make this more vivid for all those who have seen the film 'Passport to Pimlico'). As for a rich area using secession as an excuse to evade paying part of its wealth to other poorer areas, (a) there is little evidence that in the long-term involuntary redistribution is healthy, either for the donor region or the recipient, and (b) it is open to the surrounding regions to discriminate economically against a rich neighbourhood that opts out, so there would be natural checks and balances against extreme forms of greed (or environmental pollution, etc).

> **'Any group that can form a village, can form a stable and sovereign society'**

My favourite references on this subject are 'Human Scale' by Kirkpatrick Sale (published by Secker and Warburg 1980, particularly pages 413-415) and 'The Breakdown of Nations' by Leopold Kohr (published by EP Dutton 1978, copyright 1957; available for £5-50 including p&p from Schumacher Book Service, Ford House, Hartland, Bideford, N.Devon, UK; particularly pages 106-108). For instance, Kohr writes: 'Any group that can form a village, can form a stable and sovereign society. A country such as Andorra, with a present population of less than seven thousand, has led a perfectly healthy and undisturbed existence since the time of Charlemagne.'

And Sale writes that 'Lucca (in Tuscany) became one of the fiercely independent republics in the thirteenth century – with a population of perhaps 10,000 to 12,000 – and for the next 400 years, it was one of the most prosperous places on the entire Italian peninsula ... It was a major banking centre ... Union with successively larger territories served mostly to impoverish the once resplendent republic, and today it is a forgotten backwater.'

Nicholas Albery, 20 Heber Road, London NW2 6AA (tel 081 208 2853; fax 081 452 6434).

South African cantonisation

Remarkable proposals for cantonising South Africa along Swiss lines are put forward in the books 'South Africa – The Solution', 'Let the People Govern' and 'The Heart of the Nation – Regional and Community Government in the New South Africa'. The first of these books was a No.1 non-fiction bestseller in South Africa. Its authors, Leon Louw and Frances

Kendall, spell out in convincing detail how decision-making in South Africa could be decentralised initially to the present magisterial districts (which have an average population of 80,000 each), leading to the formation of some one hundred cantons within a national confederation, with an unconditional one-person-one-vote universal franchise; with the additional safeguards of a Bill of Rights to protect minorities, the abolition of governmental apartheid, complete freedom of movement between cantons and, by referendum, the right of a canton to secede from the confederation (or to be expelled). Communist cantons could co-exist with conservative or laissez-faire cantons – people will be free to 'vote with their feet.'

> '**Communist cantons could co-exist with conservative or laissez-faire cantons – people will be free to "vote with their feet"** '

The central government would keep a mere five administrative functions: foreign affairs, national finance, national defence, infrastructure and international affairs.

Groundswell

Gail Day

Groundswell was formed as a back-up movement to these books. Gail Day, its coordinator, writes about how it has progressed.

Groundswell is a non-profit educational organisation. It was founded to bring about constitutional change based on the ideas in the books by Leon Louw and Frances Kendall. It has accomplished an extraordinary amount with limited funds. 'South Africa – The Solution' (which has sold in excess of 80,000 copies) has been translated into Afrikaans. We have produced a video based on the book, and summaries of the book have been translated into Zulu, Xhosa, Tswana and Sotho.

Frances Kendall and Leon Louw have now twice been nominated for the Nobel Peace Prize and are sought after as speakers by groups ranging from the President's Council to the KwaZulu executive. Through Louw and Kendall, we have presented evidence to the South African Law Commission on their Bill of Rights and on a democratic constitution, and we have networked successfully with key people in the forefront of the political debate. Diverse leaders are publicly proclaiming their support for some or all of our ideas. Moreover, government is being limited through privatisation and deregulation, and South Africans across the political spectrum are beginning to appreciate the importance of local decision-making and the referendum.

We organise 'Solution Parties'. These are small informal gatherings at which Groundswell's proposals are presented and debated. They are hosted by members of the public in their homes, offices and clubs (over 500 have been held to date). They are free of charge. A survey has shown that 60% of people once they have attended such a house party would opt for a devolved federation for South Africa – as opposed to 14% of non-attenders. We run regular Speakers' Forum workshops to train members to do presentations at house parties.

Groundswell's 'Project Stand Tall' is a series of seminars, two per month, subsidised by the business community and aimed at the man in the street. At these full-day seminars we deal with issues such as redistribution, affirmative action, privatisation, direct democracy, proportional representation, devolution and other issues vital for South Africa's future.

- *The book 'South Africa – The Solution' is available from the Institute for Social Inventions, 20 Heber Road, London NW2 6AA (tel 081 208 2853; fax 081 452 6434) for £7 incl. p&p. The Groundswell movement received a main Social Inventions Award from the Institute.*
- *Groundswell's address is PO Box 92385, Norwood 2117, Johannesburg, South Africa (tel 27 11 442 7247; fax 27 11 442 7247).*
- *Frances Kendall's address is 57 Glenrose Road, Melrose 2196, Johannesburg (tel 27 11 442 8898).*
- *The video mentioned is available on VHS for 84 rands from Teevision, P.O. Box 7473, Johannesburg 2000 (tel 011 402 1400 ext. 23).*

Four regions in Ireland

A Gandhi Summer School in Oxfordshire has argued that Ireland historically has four regions – Ulster, Leinster, Munster and Connaught – and has proposed that increased sovereignty for these quarters would serve to reduce fears of London and Dublin.

Full statement from Peter Cadogan, 3 Hinchinbrook House, Greville Road, London NW6 5UP (tel 071 328 3709).

Two states, one holy land

John Whitbeck, an American lawyer living in Paris, has had the following framework for peace published in the Jerusalem Post and Ha'aretz (Israel), Al-Fajr (Palestine), the Los Angeles Times and the Christian Science Monitor (USA), the Middle East International (UK), the Irish Times, the International Herald Tribune, Al-Qabas (Kuwait) and Al-Yamamah (Saudi Arabia). He has discussed it personally with prominent Palestinians, including Yasser Arafat, as well as with Israeli peace activists and Israeli generals.

Israel needs to recognise that its self-interest lies in launching a peace offensive and promptly declaring its willingness to consider some form of two-state solution and to negotiate a comprehensive peace not just with its neighbours but, most importantly, with the Palestinian people.

Contrary to common wisdom, sharing the Holy Land is not a zero-sum game, in which any development advantageous to one side must be disadvantageous to the other. One can envisage a society in which, by severing political and voting rights from economic and social rights in a negotiated settlement, both the legitimate national aspirations of Palestinians and the legitimate security interests of Israelis could be simultaneously satisfied.

The non-negotiable minimum for both peoples of the Holy Land is their own self-determination as peoples and nations – that they can have a state of their own in the land they both love, including at least some share of Jerusalem, and that never again will anyone else govern them.

This is not impossible. The Holy Land could be a single economic and social unit encompassing two sovereign states and one Holy City. Jerusalem could form an undivided part of both states, be the capital of both states and be governed by an autonomous, elected municipal council.

'All current residents of the Holy Land could be given the choice of Israeli or Palestinian citizenship'

All current residents of the Holy Land could be given the choice of Israeli or Palestinian citizenship, thus determining which state's elections they would vote in and which state's passport they would carry. Each state could have its own 'law of return', conferring citizenship on persons not currently resident in the Holy Land.

Borders would have to be drawn on maps but would not have to exist on the ground. The free, non-discriminatory movement of people and products within the Holy Land could be a fundamental principle subject to one major exception: to ensure that each state would always maintain its national character, the right of residence in each Holy Land state could be limited to that state's citizens, to citizens of the other state residing there on an agreed future date, and to their descendants.

As an essential counterpart to the absence of border controls within the Holy Land, Israel could retain the right to participate in immigration controls at the frontiers of the Palestinian state, with any visitors restricted to the Palestinian state and found in Israel facing penalties.

'The Palestinian state could be fully demilitarised, with only local police forces and United Nations peace-keeping forces allowed to bear arms'

To ease Israeli security concerns, the Palestinian state could be fully demilitarised, with only local police forces and United Nations peace-keeping forces allowed to bear arms.

The settlement agreement could be guaranteed by the United Nations and relevant states, with international tribunals to arbitrate disputes regarding compliance with its terms.

Jerusalem's status poses the toughest problem for any settlement plan, causing many to assume that no settlement acceptable to both sides can ever be reached. When the UN General Assembly adopted Resolution 181 in 1947, it addressed the problem by suggesting an international status for Jerusalem, with neither the Jewish nor the Arab state to have sovereignty over the city. Yet the concept of joint undivided sovereignty, while rare, is not without precedent.

Chandigarh is the undivided capital of two Indian states. Until German reunification, the western sectors of Berlin, under American, British and French sovereignty, were jointly administered by an autonomous, elected senate. For more than 70 years, Vanuatu (formerly the New Hebrides) was under the joint undivided sovereignty of Britain and France.

As a joint capital, Jerusalem could have Israeli government offices principally in its Western sector, Palestinian government offices principally in its Eastern sector and municipal offices in both. To the extent that either state wished to control persons or goods passing into it from the other state, this could be done at the points of exit from, rather than the points of entry to, Jerusalem. In a context of peace, particularly one coupled with economic union, the need for such controls would be minimal.

'Israel would finally achieve international recognition of Jerusalem as its capital'

In a sense, Jerusalem can be viewed as a cake which could be sliced either vertically or horizontally. Either way, the Palestinians would get half the cake, but, while most Israelis could never voluntarily swallow a vertical slice, they might just be able to swallow a horizontal slice. Indeed, by doing so, Israel would finally achieve international recognition of Jerusalem as its capital. A capital city is both a municipality on the ground and a symbol in hearts and minds. Shared in this way, Jerusalem could be a symbol of reconciliation and hope for Jews, Muslims, Christians and the world as a whole.

Such a framework would address in ways advantageous to both sides the three principal practical problems on the road to peace – Jerusalem (through joint sovereignty over an undivided city), settlers (through a separation of citizenship rights from residential rights in a regime of free access to the entire Holy Land for all citizens of both states, under which no one would be compelled to move) and borders (through a structure of relations between the two states so open that the precise placement of borders would no longer be such a contentious issue and the pre-1967 borders – subject only to the expanded borders of Jerusalem, under joint sovereignty – might well be acceptable to most Israelis, as they would certainly be to most Palestinians).

For Israelis, the threat of one day living in a state with a majority of Arab voters, or an inescapable resemblance to pre-1990 South Africa, would be replaced by the assurance of living in a democratic state with fewer Arab voters than today. The Israelis' security would be enhanced by assuaging, rather than continuing to aggravate, the Palestinians' grievances. By escaping from the role (so tragic in the light of Jewish history) of oppressors and enforcers of injustice, Israel would save its soul and its dream.

For all Palestinians, human dignity would be restored. They would cease to be a people treated (and not only by Israelis) as pariahs uniquely unworthy of basic human rights. For those in exile, an internationally accepted Palestinian citizenship, a Palestianian passport and a right to return, if only to visit, would have enormous significance.

And if the Palestinians themselves accepted a settlement, few, if any, Arab states would continue to reject Israel. If a Palestinian flag were peacefully raised over Palestinian government offices in Jerusalem, few Arab eyes would still see Israel through a veil of hatred.

Acceptance and implementation of such a framework for peace would require a moral, spiritual and psychological transformation for both Israelis and Palestinians. Yet, given the decades of hatred, bitterness and distrust, *any* settlement would require such a transformation. Precisely because such a transformation would be so difficult, it is far more likely to be achieved if both peoples can be inspired by a truly compelling vision of a new society of peaceful coexistence, mutual respect and human dignity, in which both peoples are winners, than if they are left to contemplate painful programmes for a new partition and an angry separation in which both peoples must regard themselves, to a considerable degree, as admitting defeat.

Israelis, Palestinians and the true friends of both must join the search for a compelling vision of a society so much better than the status quo that both Israelis and Palestinians are inspired to accept in their hearts and minds that peace is both desirable and attainable, that the Holy Land can be shared, that a winner-take-all approach produces only losers, that both Israelis and Palestinians must be winners or both will continue to be losers and that there is a common destination at which both peoples would be satisfied to arrive and to live together.

John Whitbeck, 150 rue de l'Université, 75007 Paris, France (tel 010 331 4266 0319 w; fax 4266 3591; tel 4555 0658 h). His proposals won a Social Inventions Award.

A new Palestinian homeland within Egypt from reclaimed desert

Anthony Cooney

Adapted extract from a suggestion to the Institute.

The Jewish population and the Palestinian Dispersion cannot both fit into the former territory of Palestine. Desert land could however be reclaimed to create a new sovereign state within Egypt, linked to a small Palestinian 'Home State' in Samaria. A canal, about half the length of the Suez canal, but as wide and as deep to facilitate navigation, built from El Alamein to the Qattara Depression, would create a large inland sea from a land area at present uninhabitable. The expanse of water would modify the climate of its littoral and would offer immediate opportunities for fishing and salt manufacture.

Israel may be sufficiently convinced that peace is always cheaper than war to lend its expertise in reclaiming the desert. Egypt would need to be persuaded to yield territory at present uninhabited and waste to a new state within its borders.

Anthony Cooney, 17 Hadassah Grove, Liverpool L17 8XH.

Comment by Robert Hart

These comments come from Robert Hart, an expert on agroforestry, who is featured in the Ecology and Environment chapter of this book.

Egypt has in fact already carried out large-scale reclamation schemes in the Western Desert. Richard St. Barbe Baker describes two such schemes in his book 'Sahara Conquest': one largely dependent on irrigation channels originating from the Nile, and the other tapping groundwater resources used by the Ancient Egyptians and Romans. Boreholes had been drilled as deep as 3,600 feet.

Irrigation schemes in many parts of the world have proved unsatisfactory owing to the evaporation of the water and salination of the soil. Consequently, in modern reclamation schemes, more emphasis is placed on the planting of drought-resistant trees and shrubs, of which at least 500 species are known. These provide 'nurse conditions' for more delicate plants, such as fruit trees and cereals. Large sections of the Negev, one of the most arid areas in the world, have been reclaimed by this method. There is abundant experience to indicate that most of the desert regions of North Africa and the Middle East could be reclaimed at far less than the cost of the armaments that have been accumulated in the area. Thus a vast new 'Green Zone' could be established, in which millions of Palestinians and other displaced people could find homes, decent living conditions and abundant food. Mineral-rich desert sands, once cultivated, can achieve high degrees of fertility and grow some of the most nutritious vegetation in the world. People with their basic needs thus fully satisfied and living creative lives would feel less urge to perform acts of violence against their neighbours.

Thus the politicians are faced with two fundamental choices: to continue their present policies of prevarication, rivalry, intrigue and merely tinkering with deep-rooted problems – policies which will do nothing to halt the cycle of violence – or to adapt a great imaginative, comprehensive, cooperative design that would benefit all.

Robert Hart, Highwood Hill, Rushbury, near Church Stretton, Shropshire SY6 7DE (tel 06943 342).

The State Dowry concept for relieving population pressure

Guy Yeoman

Adapted from the book 'Africa's Mountains of the Moon' by Guy Yeoman, published by Hamish Hamilton/Elm Tree Books (1989, £25). The Institute for Social Inventions wants to help ensure that this scheme is taken up as a pilot project by one of the major aid agencies.

Summary

Current benefits of Western financial aid to Kenya are largely illusory, since any increase in national wealth benefits only a small proportion of the population, while for the majority of people it is cancelled by the high birth rate. It is suggested that switching aid funds directly to women of childbearing age in the form of State Dowry payments, as an incentive to restrict family size, is the only practicable way of *rapidly* stabilising the population. Such a system could have substantial welfare benefits for women and children as well as enhancing women's liberation, and it is the essential first step towards a sustainable agriculture and fundamental environmental conservation.

It is emphasised that the proposal is to be regarded as an emergency measure in the face of a crisis, to make possible the other necessary long-term measures of education and poverty reduction.

> 'Switching aid funds directly to women of childbearing age in the form of State Dowry payments, as an incentive to restrict family size, is the only practicable way of *rapidly* stabilising the population'

Biological cataclysm

In 1925 Norway had almost exactly the same population as Kenya. Sixty years later, her population has scarcely increased by half; it is now virtually stable and her people enjoy a degree of social well-being which is hardly surpassed elsewhere in the world. In the same period, Kenya's population has multiplied ten times, and in spite of all the commendable efforts of the Kenyans, no substantial impact has been made on the widespread poverty, while the country has suffered enormous environmental deterioration. Kenya, and many other countries in the Third World, are heading for biological cataclysm.

The attempts to transplant Western birth control tactics to Africa have so far largely failed. The reason for this is the widely different ethos of African society. In a situation where the male's machismo demands children, family restriction advice addressed to men is unlikely to be heeded; and if addressed to women, is only likely to be effective in a form that is going to put them in a stronger position in the face of male dominance. The problem thus becomes a question of what can be done for African women, not just to provide them with a contraceptive option, but to provide an incentive to take up this option that is stronger than the strong male pressure to ignore it.

The dowry

At present, throughout Africa, a dowry or bride-price is paid by the parents of a young man to those of a girl whom they wish their son to marry. Consequently there is great pressure to marry a girl off as early as possible, and for her to justify her 'price' by becoming pregnant as soon as possible.

There is only one time in an African woman's life when she is in a position to call the shots: this is in the pre-marital period, when the dowry is under negotiation. I suggest that she should be offered some form of personal wealth that could on the one hand give her negotiating power in the choice of a husband or, on the other, finance the option of delaying or refusing marriage. The extent of such wealth and the manner of its provision would be dictated by what was found to be necessary to outweigh the existing social pressure for her to marry early.

> 'Every woman on reaching the age of, say, 16 without becoming pregnant, would become eligible for a regular cash allowance. The payments would cease as soon as it was established that she was pregnant'

I propose that the State, riding in a sense on the back of the traditional dowry system, should introduce a 'State Dowry'. Under this, every woman on reaching the age of, say, 16 without becoming pregnant, would become eligible for a regular cash allowance. The payments would cease as soon as it was established that she was pregnant, but would resume again after a further period of non-pregnancy. There would thus be a strong incentive for her and her parents to delay marriage, and after marriage, for her and her husband to delay conception.

Uplifting the village economy

Would such a system be unacceptably expensive? One way of answering this is to say that it would effectually cost nothing. All that we would be doing would be to alter the direction of the flow of money. At present, money flows from the West to governments or agencies, and thence through the hands of ministries and departments, to contractors and managers who are all too often incompetent or corrupt, with little benefit to rural communities. This procedure, whereby multi-billion dollar sums are poured away, must be regarded as unacceptably expensive, wasteful and demoralising. Under the State Dowry system, the same sort of volume of cash would go directly to peasant families through post office accounts or cooperative women's groups. For the first time, the African agriculturalist (and women are the primary agriculturalists) would be free to decide for herself how she wished to be 'developed'. Whether more or less wisely saved or spent (and my belief is that rural women would spend it wisely, provided they could keep it in their own hands), the money would find its way into uplifting the village economy, which is something most aid schemes signally fail to do.

> 'For the first time, the African agriculturalist (and women are the primary agriculturalists) would be free to decide for herself how she wished to be "developed"'

No money would be wasted. Cash would only be paid out where it was being successful in persuading a woman to limit her family; where the scheme failed to do this, money would not be paid out.

Dr Raymond Crotty, of the School of Systems and Data Studies at Trinity College, Dublin, has called my attention to the similar proposal in his book 'Ireland in Crisis'. His computations show that, on the basis of the current annual Western aid to the Third World, adequate funding would be available to halve the present birth-rate. This would, for example, meet the recent plea of President Moi of Kenya, to reduce the average Kenyan family from eight to four children.

Practicalities

While in the early days of such a system, women might find it difficult to ensure absolute control over dowry payments, the very existence of the scheme could act as a stimulus to the advance of feminine power and the development of women's organisations. These would eventually lead to recipients achieving a large measure of control over funds paid in their name. A possible outcome of this could be a moderation of the present oppression of women and a hardening of their attitude to such institutions as child marriage, polygamy and female circumcision.

> 'A possible outcome of this could be a moderation of the present oppression of women and a hardening of their attitude to such institutions as child marriage, polygamy and female circumcision'

Such an idea would obviously take off slowly and cash requirements in the early days would be small. The concept could of course be pilot-tested on a scale as small as desired in order to find out the best administrative system. It is easy to point out difficulties: the solutions must be found by trial and error. A pilot scheme could also determine the size of monthly payment needed to offset the present social pressures on women to start a family early in life and to have frequent babies.

It will be appreciated that we would in effect be creating a child allowance system without the incentive to have children that such a system entails. The funds paid to discourage women from starting a pregnancy would in fact enhance the welfare of any existing child, or a child to come in the future. The chances of the survival of such well-spaced and well-provisioned children would be much greater than is commonly the case at present. One may note that while all societies accept the concept of paying people to do things, we in the West increasingly pay people *not* to do things. The principle has been widely used for controlling agricultural production and for encouraging conservation policies. In the final analysis it will be seen that we would simply be reinforcing every woman's inalienable right to say no.

The actual logistics of providing the necessary family planning services are sometimes spoken of as a stumbling block, but I do not share this view. We should get away from the idea that sophisticated clinics with highly trained staff are necessary. Village shops, free dispensing machines and barefoot advisers should provide a service at the very simplest level. In the early days, we should not feel behoven to provide the near 100 per cent guarantee against conception that is the norm in the West. In the early stages the widespread adoption of the male condom would be unlikely, but recent prototype development of a female condom points the way to future possibilities.

AIDS

Any discussion of future population trends in Africa would be unrealistic if it did not take into consideration the dark shadow of AIDS that stretches across the continent as a heterosexually transmitted disease: my proposals for the dowry system should be looked at against this background. The future effect of AIDS is difficult to assess, but a recent attempt by researchers at Imperial College, London, and Princeton University, USA, concludes that is unlikely to make any major difference to current African population forecasts for several decades to come. There is to my mind one hopeful chink of light. The only measures that can be anticipated to control the AIDS pandemic are largely the same as those that will be necessary to bring about population stabilisation. AIDS will be controlled in the end by the polarisation of society according to behaviour patterns. On the one hand a sub-culture will emerge which, because it adopts a preventive approach to sex, will be virtually 'immune' to this avoidable condition. At the other pole, the disease will run its tragic course.

'AIDS will be controlled in the end by the polarisation of society according to behaviour patterns'

It should be noted that eligibility for the State Dowry would be universal, for town dwellers as well country folk, and it could be expected that it would become a major factor in promoting safe sex and the use of the male and female condom, as well as reducing prostitution and promiscuity. African urban prostitution is a response to urban poverty and male mobility and the widespread abandonment of wives and partners that has become a feature of the unstable new urban societies. By providing such women with an alternative source of finance, I believe that the forcing of them into prostitution would be reduced.

'The State Dowry would become a major factor in promoting safe sex and the use of the male and female condom as well as reducing prostitution and promiscuity'

Conclusion

All attempts to conserve the animal and plant eco-systems of Kenya will prove fruitless, and the existing structure of reserves and parks will collapse, unless a sustainable agriculture and forestry (fuel supply) can be attained. The essential precursor to this is to stabilise the human and livestock populations. All agencies, whether government or NGO, and whether concerned with social, agricultural or wildlife problems, should therefore concentrate their resources and energies on this vital primary objective.

Progress so far

The State Dowry concept received a Social Inventions Award for the best proposal to assist developing countries. This money has been used to initiate a small feasibility study in Kenya.

In the UK, Mrs Jo Hanson has been promoting the initiative through leaflets and other work.
- *Guy Yeoman, Crowden Lea, Upper Booth, Edale, Derbyshire, via Sheffield S30 2ZJ (tel 0433 670284).*
- *Jo Hanson, 71B Effra Road, London SW2 1BZ (tel 071 733 0910).*
- *Raymond Crotty, School of Systems and Data Studies, University of Dublin, Trinity College, Dublin 2, Ireland (tel Dublin 772941). Crotty's piece on population stabilisation appears in his book 'Ireland in Crisis' (Brandon, Dingle, 1986).*

Kenya: £15 a month for life if only 2 children

Dr S. Mohindra

Guy Yeoman's State Dowry project (see above) proposes a reverse-targeted child allowance system as an incentive to women in Kenya to space their child-bearing more; these comments are by a Kenyan Indian living in Cheshire.

'If a girl from age 10 were paid say £20 a month until the birth of the first child, £15 until the second and £10 until the third, then nearly all would accept a lifelong bounty and stop at two'

The State Dowry scheme is excellent and eminently workable. A slight modification may make it simpler to administer.

If a girl from age 10 were paid say £20 a month until the birth of the first child, £15 until the second and £10 until the third, then nearly all would accept a lifelong bounty and stop at two. If a girl agreed to be sterilised after two she could be paid £15 for life plus say a £200 bonus.

Now there are 5 billion people in the world, 2 billion live in the West or China; leaving 3 billion in the Third World. Of these 1.5 billion are females and perhaps .75 billion outside the age range.

If *all* became eligible, thereby stabilising world population once and for all, £20 for .75 billion will cost £15 billion a month. This may seem a lot but is only about 5% of the Western defence budget or less than 1% of the total budget – a small price to pay to save the planet.

Also the transfer of this sum *doubling* family income will create big new markets and eliminate poverty.

The horribly rapid population growth is very soon going to create havoc. It is essential that we all agree to a common scheme and put pressure on individuals and governments to fund it. Also we should press the Tory and Labour parties to pledge *not* to increase child benefit after the third child to set an example.

We as individuals could start this scheme by sponsoring individual women. Even one woman covered like this in each village enjoying a doubling of her family's income would create a tremendous psychological effect. Other women in the village would postpone the second or third child in order to become eligible when more funds became available for their lifelong wealth.

As a Kenyan Indian I know of the problems that a doubling of population every 17 years in Kenya has created.

Dr S. Mohindra, 11 Eaton Drive, Alderley Edge, Cheshire SK9 7RA (tel 0625 582798).

Comment by Valerie Yule

Adapted extracts from Yule's suggestions.

The problem is so complex that it needs tackling from many directions at once, such as:

• Guaranteed old age pensions for those with two or less surviving children;

• Encouraging more sources of honour and prestige for every man, so that they have more sources of pride than begetting a lot of children;

• Compulsory insurance deducted from wages until earners are 25, when they can collect and marry, to encourage a social custom of later marriages;

• Parents over the age of 25 to be paid monthly bonuses for the first and second children until these are aged six (when mothers may reasonably work again) but no bonuses for further children. So you are wise not to have your first child until you are 25.

Valerie Yule, 57 Waimarie Drive, Mount Waverley, Victoria, Australia 3149 (tel 807 4315).

Payments to girls in the States

An adapted extract from an American newspaper, the Sun, monitored for the Institute by Roger Knights.

Teenage girls are paid $1 a day not to get pregnant by a planned parenthood group in Denver, Colorado. All the girls have to do for their money is to show up for a weekly 'rap session' at the planned parenthood clinic.

So far, about a dozen youngsters have made a habit of picking up the $7 weekly reward for not reproducing.

One 16 year old client had an abortion when she was only 13, but now she has earned nearly $500 by keeping herself from getting pregnant again.

> **'Teenage girls are paid $1 a day not to get pregnant by a planned parenthood group in Denver. All the girls have to do for their money is to show up for a weekly "rap session" at the planned parenthood clinic'**

Between 30 and 50 per cent of American youngsters who become pregnant are likely to conceive again before they are 18, they note, but only one of the 18 participants in the Denver programme has had a repeat pregnancy.

The Rocky Mountain Planned Parenthood, Denver, Colorado, USA (tel 303 832 5069).

Best Buys from the Third World

Each chapter of 'The Global Consumer – Best Buys to Help the Third World' (compiled by the New Consumer organisation) has recommended choices for those consumers who wish to take into account the effect of their purchases on the developing world, such as:

• B&Q and Texas seem to have gone furthest in developing a policy on hardwood sourcing; go there for preference.

> **'Bananas are a good crop as they can be intercropped with food crops, have nutritional value, are labour intensive, require very little capital outlay and can be harvested all year round'**

• Bananas are a good crop as they can be intercropped with food crops, have nutritional value (unlike tea leaves or cocoa pods), are labour intensive, and are suitable for smallholder production as they require very little capital outlay and can be harvested all year round. Geest and Windward Islands bananas are a good choice. Fyffes' Honduran bananas come second.

• The ideal Third World cash crop is one that can be eaten if times are hard, does not compete for land or labour with food production, can be processed locally to create jobs, is environmentally benign and fetches a good price. Cotton is one crop that comes out pretty badly measured against these criteria, while peanuts compare favourably.

• Overall, the Co-op is the supermarket to try first, on the basis of its social policies generally, and with respect to development and the Third World issues in particular.

• If you are intending to buy electronic products look first at Technics, Panasonic, JVC, Sony and Hitachi.

• Best Buy tea and coffee come from organisations like Traidcraft, Oxfam Trading and Equal Exchange.

• For oils, soaps and detergents, Best Buy products are Ecover detergents and Body Shop personal care products.

- *'The Global Consumer' by Phil Wells and Mandy Jetter, published as a Gollancz Paperback Original, £5·99, ISBN 0 575 05000 4.*
- *New Consumer, 52 Elswick Road, Newcastle upon Tyne NE4 6JH (tel 091 272 1148; fax 091 272 1615).*

Fair Trade Mark for ethical Third World produce

Information from 'The Global Consumer' (publishing details in previous item).

1992 saw the introduction of the 'Fair Trade Mark'. This guarantees that the brand carrying the Fair Trade Mark has been sourced and supplied from the Third World in a way that provides the producer with a better deal than is the norm. The mark will be administered and promoted by a number of development agencies, campaign groups and alternative trading organisations, who were inspired by a similar and very successful scheme in the Netherlands, and who will soon be setting up an independent foundation. Look out for the Fair Trade Mark, particularly on coffee, tea and honey.

An article by Gail Counsell in the Independent (adapted below) explained how the Dutch scheme works.

Any commercial Dutch or Belgian coffee roaster can use the Max Havelaar brand name – the equivalent there of the Fair Trade Mark – provided it agrees to purchase its beans from a list of approved small Third World coffee growers. The scheme has captured a three per cent market share in less than three years.

> 'It agrees to purchase its beans from a list of approved small Third World coffee growers'

The scheme has its flaws. The attempt to set a minimum floor price is probably doomed to failure given the fluctuating nature of the world price for coffee. Moreover, all attempts to 'fix' prices lead to trouble in the long run: as the failure of pacts from tin to cocoa – including in 1989, coffee – have demonstrated. Also, traders, who dominate the coffee market, form a useful function balancing and smoothing the market and establishing a true price. Some effort will have to be made to include them in the system if it is to really take off.

Giving food surpluses without undermining local farmers

Dr David Chapman

One way for the EC and America to distribute their food surpluses is simply to transport the food to the areas of food shortage and to distribute it free to those in need. But this tends to disrupt what local food production there is, causing food prices to collapse and putting local farmers out of business.

However, it seems possible to design a method of distributing surplus food so as not to undermine local agriculture:

The donor country or agency transferring the surplus food, should not give it away but should sell it, and do this through whatever market channels the recipient country has been using already. But before the donor does this, it should estimate:

- How much in local currency it is likely to receive for the food; and
- By how much this release of foreign food on to the local market is likely to reduce the price received by the local farmers for their produce.

> 'The donor would pay, preferably in advance of the sale of the food, a compensation to the farmers of at least as much as they were expected to lose'

The donor would then pay, preferably in advance of the sale of the food, a compensation to the farmers of at least as much as they were expected to lose. This could perhaps be given as a payment of so much per hectare of cultivated land, with perhaps a ceiling amount per holding, in order not unduly to benefit large farmers.

The rest of the expected revenue from sale of the food could be distributed as:

- Cash aid (or perhaps wages to do public works, etc) to destitute or poor people, whether farmers or not;
- Special aid to farmers whose food production had collapsed, to enable them to get production going again; and
- Conditional aid to farmers, paying them to adopt more ecologically sustainable methods, such as tree-planting, anti-erosion contour walls, or whatever was appropriate to the area.

The local currency for this would be purchased with the donor's currency on the currency exchange market. The revenue from the sale of the food could then be used either to finance the next cycle of food aid (if there was to be one) or to change back into the donor's currency so that the donor could then be partly recouped for its original expenditure.

Thus it seems that a scheme such as this could immediately benefit the hungry people, and also, far from undermining the local agriculture, could actually enable it to increase its food production – and not only in the short term, but on a sustainable basis.

Dr David Chapman, Democracy Design Forum, Coles Centre, Buxhall, Stowmarket, Suffolk, IP14 3EB (tel 0449 736 223).

Village Aid

An imaginative Third World aid project is being piloted by the Institute of Cultural Affairs (ICA), whereby a Westerner contributes a regular sum monthly or annually to sponsor a particular village activist in Kenya, receiving in return regular reports describing the self-help development work in the villages. So far there are about fifty sponsors, and more are sought. The ICA is already co-ordinating the work of 'Village Volunteers' in 500 villages in Kenya.

> 'A Westerner contributes a regular sum monthly or annually to sponsor a particular village activist in Kenya'

Village Volunteers are those who have dedicated themselves to the building of a better future for the villages of Kenya by working alongside fellow villagers. The ICA provides up to six months' intensive training in development approaches, and practical and leadership skills, and then the Village Volunteers work in teams of two or three in the villages helping to draw up action plans and to organise neighbourhood task groups.

There is a growing attitude among many villages that the government or other aid agencies will bring about development for them, often resulting in the stifling of local initiative and a dependency on programes that are inappropriate and unwanted. Village Volunteers offers an alternative.

> 'A spotlight needs to be placed on the successes in development. A means must be found for massively accelerating the development of approaches that work'

The ICA have also produced a series of three volumes of an international directory of 'What's Working in Rural Development'. The first contains the names, addresses and descriptions of 290 projects, sponsored by various agencies, ending with an analysis of the key factors that these successful projects share in common. It costs £15 from the ICA. As they write: 'A spotlight needs to be placed on the successes in development, so that hope in the future can be founded realistically on past experience. A means must be found for massively accelerating the development of approaches that work.'

Institute of Cultural Affairs, PO Box 505, London N19 3YX, (please write, tel media only, 081 567 9883).

Chickens for Children

Chickens for Children is a scheme in Northern Kenya whereby disabled children can build chicken coops, and are then helped to purchase local hens and a rooster. The eggs are bought off the children for use in the local hospital and elsewhere, and the children use their income to purchase necessities for their families.

> 'Disabled children are helped to purchase local hens and a rooster'

Alison Curtis, 33 Chemin du Caudoz, 1009 Pully, Switzerland (fax 030 31426).

Wonderboxes & Simply Living

'Simply Living, the Story of Compassion and the Wonderbox', by Anne Pearce, published by Box Publications at the author's address: Box-Aid, Orchard Cottage, 11 Hill Top Lane, Saffron Walden, Essex CB11 4AS (tel 0799 23321); 1989, ISBN 1 85421 061 9, 239 pages, £6·95.

Anne Pearce tells the inspiring story of how she and her friends gradually discovered their latent creativity whilst working with the Quakers and an organisation called Compassion in the poorest parts of South Africa and amongst the Crossroads shanty town dwellers. One of their first and most enduring creations was the Wonderbox, consisting of two cushions filled with polystyrene beans, which are used to envelop a cooking pot, as with a haybox. A pot of food is brought to the boil, then tucked between the cushions to prevent the heat escaping, and left to continue cooking away for two or more hours, without using any further fuel – and thus saving paraffin or trees.

For many Africans, the loss of tree cover is changing rain patterns and causing deserts to encroach, and many African women are having to walk miles to obtain wood from trees. It took ten years of effort, but homemade Wonderboxes during that time spread widely amongst the South African blacks. And for us in the pampered industrial countries, the Wonderbox could be relevant, helping us cut back our contribution to the greenhouse effect.

> 'The Wonderbox, consisting of two cushions filled with polystyrene beans, which are used to envelop a cooking pot, as with a haybox'

Upgrading shanty town life

Other schemes followed in profusion at Compassion. They developed, for instance, a very neat way of making bread without an oven and for keeping it fresh much longer than normal. The dough was simply placed in a plastic bag; once it had risen in the Wonderbox, the neck of the bag was twisted to exclude air, and a knot tied in the bag. This was then boiled for 20 minutes, followed by an hour or so in the Wonderbox; and finally a second knot in the plastic bag helped keep the bread sterile and fresh for a long time.

> 'A very neat way of making bread without an oven and for keeping it fresh much longer than normal. The dough was simply placed in a plastic bag. This was then boiled for 20 minutes'

In between feeding malnourished children with soya beans, and helping Crossroads women learn to use waste carpet yarn for knitting on large needles made of wood dowling, they demonstrated how to make a tiny and efficient Wonder Oven using a paraffin tin, and helped upgrade the squatter camp with buildings made of chicken wire attached to wooden uprights, backed with discarded plastic and then covered with cement.

Their UK-based charity, Box-Aid, employs no staff but continues their efforts, resulting in new schemes to produce Wonderboxes in Bangladesh, Brazil, India and Africa. And Pearce and Co continuously dream up new uses for the Wonderboxes: for lying on, as foot warmers, cool-boxes for drinks, replacement under-blankets in hospitals, etc. Perhaps 'New Uses for a Wonderbox' could even provide a change from that traditional brainstorming exercise of thinking up unusual uses for a brick.

Wonderboxes are available in the UK at £16 (plus £2-50 p&p) from Wonderbox Products, c/o Anne Pearce (address above).

Engineers' aid to developing world villages

Professor Meredith Thring, engineer, is helping set up an organisation called Power Aid, which will work with the Intermediate Technology Development Group and others to develop renewable energy pilot projects in villages in the developing world.

'To develop renewable energy pilot projects in villages in the developing world'

Engineers would make contact with an engineering organisation in the chosen country. They would then select a suitable village or slum for a project. If villagers were enthusiastic then work would start – on anything from a windmill to a solar concentrator or leaf fractionation system.

Thring writes that 'Power Aid looks hopeful now that the World Bank has begun to realise that its giant projects do not help the poor and land the countries in vast debts.'

Prof. Meredith Thring, Bell Farm, The Street, Brundish, Suffolk IP13 8BL (tel 037 9384 296).

Grameen Banks for the poorest of the poor

Guy Dauncey

The Grameen Bank was set up in 1977 by Muhammad Yunus. Instead of insisting on personal collateral, the Grameen Bank asks landless villagers to form into groups of 50 people of the same sex – Bangladesh being a Muslim country – and then to form into smaller groups of five. The ten groups of five each meet regularly with a bank worker for training, and with each other to discuss their business ideas. Each loan has to be approved by a smaller group of five, by the larger group and finally by the bank's officer in the field; Grameen does not believe in having huge city banks. Two people in a small group can then apply for a loan. The average loan size is £35, equivalent to about £5,000 in Britain, given the annual incomes of landless peasants. Women borrowers use their loans for such things as buying a milch cow, paddy husking and cattle fattening, while men tend to invest in paddy and rice trading, cattle fattening and setting up grocery shops. After six weeks, if the first two have been regular in their payments, the next two members get their loan, and after another six weeks, the final member. The loans are not analysed by the bank – they leave it up to the villagers to do the analysis. As they depend on each other's success in repaying them, the system works. The default rate is only 2.7% – a 97.3% on-time repayment record, and in recent years the bank has made a profit on its activities.

The bank is active in 15,000 villages, employing 8,000 workers, and lending to half a million people, and it is growing all the time. Grameen banking operations are being developed in India, and in South America, where people in 60 cities and towns in 12 countries are benefiting from loans organised by Accion International. The South Shore Bank in Chicago is experimenting in rural Arkansas with Grameen principles, linked to other community economic development strategies. The annalists of the twenty-third century may be able to write that for the poorer people on the earth the invention of social collateral and peer-group lending was the single most significant economic breakthrough of the twentieth century.

'The annalists of the twenty-third century may be able to write that for the poorer people on the earth the invention of social collateral and peer-group lending was the single most significant economic breakthrough of the twentieth century'

• *Extracted from Guy Dauncey's book, 'After the Crash – The Emergence of the Rainbow Economy' (published by Green Print/ Merlin Press, 10 Malden Road, London NW5 3HR, tel 071 267 3399, 1988, £6-99, 312 pages, ISBN 1-85425-004-3).*

• *The South Shore Bank in Chicago is tel 312 288 1000.*

• *Grameen Dialogue, newsletter of the Grameen Trust (Grameen Trust, Mirpur Two, Dhaka 1216, Bangladesh, tel 880-2-801138; fax 880-2-803559).*

Ashoka funding for innovators in the developing world

'Ashoka Innovators for the Public' is an unusual American grant-making programme which since 1981 has funded individuals in the developing world rather than projects. It has funded 'indigenous people who are public service entrepreneurs'. At present these are some 250 'Ashoka Fellows' working in Thailand, Brazil, Mexico, Nepal, Pakistan, India, Indonesia, Zimbabwe and Bangladesh, and receiving about $200 per month of support for a one to four year period. They are selected for their creativity, entrepreneurial skills, ethical fibre and likely social impact; and they in turn help suggest other possible 'Fellows' and give each other help and collaboration.

'Indigenous people who are public service entrepreneurs are selected for their creativity, entrepreneurial skills, ethical fibre and likely social impact'

The Ashoka organisation writes: 'We far prefer to have one exceptional person with an important idea than a thousand hard-working, genuinely altruistic workers. We do not want to help start a new school or clinic; we want to do everything possible to help someone who's launching a better way of teaching, ie an idea that can spread way beyond the school where it is first demonstrated.' Ashoka prefers to give its support when the person is ready to launch his or her vision, but before it is a demonstrated success. So for instance, Mary Allegretti in Brazil was supported to follow through her proposal for creating 'extractive reserves' in the Amazon (where instead of giving one person extensive ownership, a legal form more appropriate for agriculture, users would be given long-term geographically overlapping rights – subject to environmental safeguards – for such uses as rubber tapping and fishing).

> ### 'We far prefer to have one exceptional person with an important idea than a thousand hard-working workers'

Bill Drayton, Ashoka's founder, says that his purpose was to help create an association that would give moral and financial help to social innovators with a practical vision for social change and the stamina to carry it out. 'There's very little support for these visionaries in society ... those people who spot the opportunities for positive social change and can't rest until it's happened.'

> ### 'Moral and financial help to social innovators with a practical vision for social change and the stamina to carry it out'

Damon Valentino, Communications Coordinator, Ashoka Innovators for the Public, 1200 North Nash Street, Arlington, Virginia 22209, USA (tel 202 628 0370; fax 202 628 0376).

The Trickle Up Programme

Adapted extract from a leaflet and from an item by Francis Kinsman in Resurgence (No. 139).

The Trickle Up Programme, founded by Glen and Mildred Leet, has provided poor people in ninety-nine countries with seed money to help them realise their dreams.

> ### 'If groups are willing to invest a thousand or more hours of their unemployed time, they may apply for a grant of US$100 to start a business'

The conditions are that if groups of five or more people are willing to invest a thousand or more hours of their unemployed time, they may apply for a Trickle Up Programme grant of US$100, to be paid in two $50 instalments, to establish a profit-making enterprise. This must be one:

(1) That they have planned themselves;

(2) For which they have or can secure any necessary approvals or resources;

(3) Where the 1,000 hours of self-employment can be completed within three months;

(4) Where a profit is anticipated;

(5) Where not less than 20% of the profit will be reinvested;

(6) Where continuing and expanding levels of self-employment are anticipated; and

(7) For which they will send reports on their enterprise and results to Trickle Up Programme.

The Programme seeks to involve young people who have never had a job; and women, many of whom have never earned money for the work they do. There are over 183 types of Trickle Up Programme enterprises, ranging from auto repairs to vegetable raising.

Trickle Up Programme, 54 Riverside Drive, New York, NY 10024, USA (tel 212 362 7958).

Ladakh – a global model

'Every year, more than 10,000 tourists visit Ladakh,' writes Helena Norberg-Hodge, who has worked among the Ladakhis in Kashmir, on the borders of Tibet, for the last 14 years. 'The picture most Ladakhis have of life in the West is a very distorted one. Having seen it only in its seemingly attractive form of digital watches and camera-laden tourists (who spend – in the Ladakhi context – the equivalent of $150,000 a day!), by contrast their own lives seem slow, primitive and inefficient. They are made to feel stupid for being farmers, and for getting their hands dirty. Our educational programme is helping to correct some of these misconceptions. We are showing them the parallels between the new 'post-industrial' age of which Westerners speak and what they – the Ladakhis – already have. We have to encourage young Ladakhis to maintain respect for their own culture.'

> ### 'The picture most Ladakhis have of life in the West is a very distorted one. Having seen it only in its seemingly attractive form of digital watches and camera-laden tourists (who spend – in the Ladakhi context – the equivalent of $150,000 a day!), by contrast their own lives seem slow, primitive and inefficient'

Her newsletter tells how progress has been maintained. The son-in-law of Ladakh's Queen has become full-time director of the Ladakh Ecological Development Group, and his wife is coordinator of its handicrafts programme. There is increasing demand for the Ladakh Project's solar greenhouses, Trombe walls, ram pumps and improved water mills. The exhibition at the Centre for Ecological Development in Leh provides a graphic representation of how life could be in Leh if development is not carefully controlled. There is also a game which allows children to see the effects of increasing economic dependence on the outside world. A new indigenous group has started called the Students' Educational and Cultural Movement of Ladakh, founded primarily as a means of promoting the traditional culture. Its young founders, all in their 20s, come from the very segment of Ladakhi society which is most at risk from the region's modernisation.

Helena Norberg-Hodge is sometimes available to give lectures or slide shows about Ladakh in the UK. She makes a most interesting presentation of her subject.

Helena Norberg-Hodge, the Ladakh Project, 21 Victoria Square, Clifton, Bristol BS8 4LS, tel 0272 731575. Above item excerpted from 'How to Save the World' (available from the Institute for £4-95 incl. p&p) and from the Ladakh Project Winter '89 newsletter (available for a donation from the Ladakh Project). Also available from the Ladakh Project are a video 'Development, a Better Way?' (£20) and other publications: 'Ladakh in a Global Context – Energy', 'Ecological Steps Towards a Sustainable Future' and 'Ecology and Principles for Sustainable Development', all at £5 each; and, for a donation, a short pamphlet, 'Guidelines for Visitors to Ladakh'.

Right Governance Awards to governments

Gregory Wright

My proposal: a Right Governance Award (RGA) would be given yearly or biannually by an international coalition of non-governmental organisations to one or more nations whose governance fulfils the parameters of the coalition's consensus definition of good, enlightened, progressive, just, intelligent, sustainable governance.

The Right Governance Award to nations would be given in the spirit of the Right Livelihood Award to individuals and organisations.

> 'A Right Governance Award would be given to one or more nations where the governance was good, enlightened, progressive, just, intelligent and sustainable'

Some of the qualifying defining parameters of a 'well-governed' nation might include positive key measurements of public health, welfare and education, a certain reasonable distribution of wealth, a modest size of armed forces and military budget, sensible environmental policies, honesty and integrity of elections, an institutionalised respect for the basic human and civil rights of all groups, equality of all under the law, a low proportion of the population in incarceration, and an arguably positive effect of the nation on other nations and peoples (eg exported pollution, arms, and refugees would be debits; well-designed foreign aid programmes, helpful participation in the UN and its agencies and in regional organisations, peace-brokering efforts, useful export products, a reasonably even balance of trade, trained emigrants and polite visitors abroad would be credits).

An important relativism: each government would be evaluated in the context of its region of the world or by the standards of its continent.

A Right Governance Award hopefully would help set a standard to which governments would strive in their management of their countries, a standard which their own citizens and their neighbours would expect and demand.

And the RGA would help put the idea 'in the air' that there is a reasonably objective yardstick against which the quality of a government can be measured.

Ed: Perhaps an Award could be given to the most improved nation since the previous ceremony.

> 'Well-designed foreign aid programmes, helpful participation in the UN and its agencies, useful export products, a reasonably even balance of trade, trained emigrants and polite visitors abroad would be credits'

Gregory Wright, 14161 Riverside Drive, #3, Sherman Oaks, CA 91423, USA (tel 818 784 0325).

Ten commandments for extra-planetary travellers

Nicholas Albery

What an unsavoury character Christopher Columbus was, at least as described by Kirkpatrick Sale in 'The Conquest of Paradise'. And the Europe from which he came was itself 'petty, racist, morbid, disillusioned, violent and arrogant.'

Columbus landed on an island in the Antilles inhabited by the Taino people, and proceeded to enslave them, with 'unchecked Spanish ruffians embarking on daily raids of rape, pillage, robbery and murder.' In 1500 a second expedition arrived and, seeing the ravages Columbus had allowed, sent him home in chains. The devastation continued however: within a generation the Taino were driven from their islands; and within a century they were extinct.

> 'There is in my opinion no better people and no better land in the world. They love their neighbours as themselves, and their way of speaking is the sweetest in the world, always gentle and smiling'

And yet these were the people Columbus had described on his first landfall as 'so affectionate, they have so little greed .. and there is in my opinion no better people and no better land in the world. They love their neighbours as themselves, and their way of speaking is the sweetest in the world, always gentle and smiling. Both men and women go naked as their mothers bore them; but ... their behaviour to one another is very good and their king keeps marvellous state, yet with a certain kind of modesty that is a pleasure to behold, as is everything else here.'

During the next century the Spanish from the Old World were responsible for the deaths of upwards of 15 million of the New Worlders. Paradise had been expelled.

This tragic incursion set me thinking. One day our race, if it survives, may feel its destiny is to leave the solar system before our sun expires, and to go in search of other habitable solar systems. What lessons can be learnt from Columbus' errors? For the crew setting off for Alpha Centauri, what Ten Commandments would be appropriate? Here is my version.

'For the crew setting off for Alpha Centauri, what Ten Commandments would be appropriate?'

(1) Thou shalt not travel beyond thine own solar system without first studying the history of previous explorers and of their tragic impact on the beings they encountered.

(2) Thou shalt not assume that human culture is superior or treat intelligent beings from other solar systems as less than human, for that way lies genocide.

(3) Thou shalt eat as low down the IQ chain as possible, in case thou ever needst a moral argument to persuade more intelligent beings from other planets not to eat thyself.

(3) Thou shalt approach other species as if thou wert a mass of infections and a bearer of plagues.

(4) Thou shalt have ecologists who respect ecological diversity in charge of thine explorations.

(5) Thou shalt simply observe on arrival, and take minimal action, until thou art fully in tune with the ways and rituals of the inhabitants.

(6) Thou shalt have no sexual intercourse with other species.

(7) Thou shalt stay hidden and make minimal direct contact with the inhabitants of other planets, if there is any danger of thy culture overwhelming theirs.

'Thou shalt leave any planet visited in at least as good a condition as when thou hast arrived'

(8) Thou shalt leave any planet visited in at least as good a condition as when thou hast arrived.

(9) Thou shalt take up as small and unobtrusive a space as possible on any planet where thou stayst long-term, and thou shalt go away if not made welcome, whether at the outset or at any time thereafter.

(10) Thou shalt not take advantage of the innocence or naivety of any extra-terrestrial beings.

• *Nicholas Albery, 20 Heber Road, London NW2 6AA (tel 081 208 853; fax 081 452 6434).*

• *'The Conquest of Paradise – Christopher Columbus and the Columbian Legacy', by Kirkpatrick Sale, published by Hodder and Stoughton (47 Bedford Sq, London WC1B 3DP), hardback, 1991, £17-95, ISBN 0 340 53383 8.*

Chapter twenty

PEACE SCHEMES

War redundant by 2005

Peter Cadogan

History is an account of wars, recoveries from war and the preparations for war – no more so than at the present time. In 1794 Kant produced his 'Perpetual Peace' in which he predicted that wars would continue until they ceased to be feasible and became too expensive. After some 200 years he is now about to be proved right. The cost of war preparations is doing impossible things to all the main global powers. It will bring them to their knees. The effect for us may be comparable. There is no way that Green priorities and militarism can cohabit. A quarter of our civil servants and half our R&D are in the service of the Ministry of Defence. The distortion is lethal.

> 'In 1794 Kant produced his Perpetual Peace in which he predicted that wars would continue until they ceased to be feasible and became too expensive. After some 200 years he is now about to be proved right'

Wars are not being won any more, they are being stopped, called off, as too expensive in both human and monetary terms. The Gulf war is the classic case. The redundancy of war puts demilitarisation, not disarmament, on the agenda. We can now proceed to demilitarise both sides of Europe and North America, when once the Russian and American peoples have dealt with their own military-industrial complexes. These are the political showdowns that the world awaits.

The historical record shows that the major cultural changes take 60-90 years, eg Copernicus to Galileo, the story of the steam engine or parliamentary reform or votes for women. At any given moment we are somewhere in the middle of any number of these cultural cycles. If the international war cycle began to wind up in 1945, that means that such wars can be finally disposed of by the year 2005.

Adapted from an article in BAR by Peter Cadogan, of 3 Hinchinbrook House, Greville Road, London NW6 5UP (tel 071 328 3709).

Editorial comment

In the present circumstances of civil wars and threats of many more such, the best way for the various main military powers to promote peace might be to agree between themselves a certain set procedure for setting up an ultra-democratic state, which any new small would-be nations must go through, if they wish their borders to be guaranteed by these powers. The conflict between Serbia and Croatia would never have escalated if NATO, Russia, etc had had such normative procedures in place, warning both Serbia and Croatia in advance of exactly the conditions that they would be required to accept. Sensible criteria for the international community to announce might include, for instance, that it would recognise and guarantee the security of any small would-be nation as long as:

• It has more than 100,000 inhabitants.

• A referendum (to be supervised by the international community) is on offer to the inhabitants, with a majority vote required for independence.

• A democratic and cantonised system (on the Swiss model) is proposed along with adequate protection for minorities, including Local Balance Representation as an electoral system for the territory if it has different ethnic groups which are to some extent geographically segregated (see David Chapman's article on 'Avoiding Civil Wars' in the chapter on International and Developing World for details of this).

• It guarantees to accept the right to secede of any yet-smaller territory within this new country which can likewise meet these criteria.

New Armageddon weapons

'Military history teaches us an important lesson,' warns statistician Peter Lewis: 'If a particular weapon system is to be stopped, it needs to be stopped *early*. The further advanced a weapon system becomes, the more difficult is its suppression. Once a programme has been funded, jobs and careers become linked to it. Bureaucratic inertia takes over. The best time to tackle a weapon is almost before it has left the inventor's mind.'

In a paper, 'The Road from Armageddon', Lewis describes a number of horrifying possible future weapons, about which military speculation has already begun. Some are for the distant future and require assembly in outer space, for instance *anti-matter bombs* ('the force of the explosion would be equivalent to 43 MT per kilogram of anti-matter destroyed, an efficiency far in excess of uranium or any other nuclear explosive') or *black hole bombs* ('military theorists have started to speculate about the possibility of using small black holes as weapons, by cutting off their supply of fresh material electrically').

'Ethnic weapons designed to exploit naturally occurring differences in vulnerability among specific population groups'

More readily feasible are *transuranic weapons*, the use of the isotope californium-252 to produce a nuclear bullet with a force of between one ton and 700 tons of TNT. There has been a fifty-year programme of research into *genetic weapons* or *race bombs* by scientists, and with the development of genetic engineering techniques in the last two decades, there is a danger that someone may make a breakthrough which could lead to these weapons becoming feasible – an American military manual describes the possibility of 'ethnic weapons designed to exploit naturally occurring differences in vulnerability among specific population groups.' And for thirty years already there have been experiments with *infrasonic radiation weapons*, with at least two experimenters suffering severe injuries (the Hungarian government reported that 'calculations have shown that the destruction of human beings would require considerably less expenditure by infrasound weapons than by any existing type of weapon of mass destruction').

Lewis urges the need for groups such as Scientists Against Nuclear Arms to broaden their perspective so as to help ward off the grave threat posed by new weapon systems. Then, as soon as research developed to a point where scientists became aware of possible weaponry applications, draft international agreements and conventions could be prepared to help restrain future military development.

Peter Lewis, Romneya, St Chad's Avenue, Midsomer Norton, Bath, Avon BA3 2HG (tel 0761 413316).

Court finds nuclear weapons to be illegal

In 1988, three judges, Rubin, Boyle and Weston, at the end of the first judicial tribunal ever to address the issue of the legality of nuclear weapons, declared, in Judge Rubin's words: 'that the international rules of war apply to nuclear weapons and their use in warfare and that in all cases the threat or use of those weapons in ways forbidden by the international humanitarian rules of warfare is of sufficient interest to the general international community to justify that community in taking legal measures to prevent it. I therefore grant to the Plaintiffs an injunction forbidding the threat or use of nuclear weapons in any way violative of international law.' Concurring with Judge Rubin, Judge Weston delineated six 'core rules' of international law regarding nuclear weapons:

• First, that it is prohibited to use weapons or tactics that cause unnecessary and/or aggravated devastation and suffering;

'It is prohibited to use weapons that cause indiscriminate harm as between combatants and civilian personnel'

• Second, that it is prohibited to use weapons or tactics that cause indiscriminate harm as between combatants and non-combatant military and civilian personnel;

• Third, that it is prohibited to effect reprisals that are disproportionate to their antecedent provocation or to legitimate military objectives, or that are disrespectful of persons, institutions, and resources otherwise protected by the laws of war;

• Fourth, that it is prohibited to use weapons or tactics that cause widespread, long-term and severe damage to the natural environment;

• Fifth, that it is prohibited to use weapons or tactics that violate the jurisdiction of non-participating States; and

• Sixth, that it is prohibited to use asphyxiating, poisonous or other gases, and all analogous liquids, materials or devices, including bacteriological methods of warfare.

Judge Boyle stated in his turn that:

'Under article 38(1)(d) of the Statute of the International Court of Justice, this Opinion' – by himself and his two fellow judges – ' constitutes a "subsidiary means for the determination of rules of law". It could therefore be relied upon by some future international war crimes tribunal.' This case has thus become the seminal case in the field, and could be referred to by litigants in any country.

The trial was the result of an initiative by Leon Vickman, a Californian attorney, for whom it became clear, after some research, that bringing a lawsuit about nuclear weapons in the United States would not result in a ruling on the merits, since domestic courts consider such matters to be 'political questions' which require abstention. It also seemed futile to him to turn to the International Court of Justice in the Hague, since defendants in any suit must agree to the jurisdiction of the Court and only nations can sue.

'The lawsuit was filed soon thereafter, on behalf of all the persons of Earth, against 28 nuclear nations'

Leon Vickman describes his six-year battle in a new pamphlet 'Why Nuclear Weapons Are Illegal' (published by the Nuclear Age Peace Foundation), from which the following is extracted:

'It was necessary to search for a court that was empowered to hear such matters. And it came to pass that such a court was in a formative stage, within a provisional world government, called the Federation of Earth. Under its Constitution, a complete court system could be formed. Upon the author's urging, a Bill was passed at the Federation's First Provisional World Parliament in Brighton, UK, in 1982, establishing such a court in Los Angeles. The lawsuit was filed soon thereafter, on behalf of all the persons of Earth, against 28 'nuclear' nations. The defendants were divided into three groups: the superpowers, the nuclear host nations, and the nuclear-capable nations.

Every step of the process was conducted with meticulous care to conform to generally accepted legal procedures. The defendant nations were served numerous times with legal pleadings. (India was the only state to file a responsive pleading, stating it was against the use of nuclear weapons.) Attorney Gaither Kodis of Bellevue, Washington, was appointed to serve as an amicus to the Court, representing the viewpoint of the defendants in briefs and oral argument.

During the almost six-year duration of the lawsuit, perhaps the most dramatic event, other than the court hearing itself, was the appointment of three highly qualified judges to the panel that was to decide the case: Judge Francis A. Boyle, Professor of International Law at the University of Illinois Law School at Champagne, Judge Alfred P. Rubin, Professor of International Law at the School of Law and Diplomacy at Tufts University, and Judge Burns H. Weston, Professor of International Law at the University of Iowa School of Law. The fact that the three judges are leading experts in the field of nuclear weapons law resulted in the three lengthy written opinions by the judges having a far reaching legal effect.'

The principal cause of action on the court summons stated: 'Plaintiffs are informed and believe and on said basis allege that the following defendants possess nuclear weapons that are poised for use against human population centres, as well as numerous other target areas which inevitably drastically affect human populations: China (People's Republic), France, Union of Soviet Socialist Republics, United Kingdom and the United States.' The finding against the defendants could prove influential, concludes Leon Vickman:

'We are a people of law. We now have the law on the most horrible of weapons. Let us observe it'

'It will only take a few persons to start a peaceful international protest against nuclear weapons that can ultimately impact on the very core of nuclear policy. Remember the pioneering work of Linus Pauling against atmospheric testing, and the crusade of Helen Caldicott against nuclear arsenals ... We are a people of law. We now have the law on the most horrible of weapons. Let us observe it.'

'Why Nuclear Weapons Are Illegal', by Leon Vickman, is booklet number 20 (12 pages) published by the Nuclear Age Peace Foundation, 1187 Coast Village Road, Suite 123, Santa Barbara, CA 93108, USA. See also the article on the UN Declaration of Scientific Responsibility in Relation to Nuclear Weaponry in the chapter on Science, Technology and Energy in this encyclopaedia.

Debating international conflict

Nicholas Albery

In the Falklands War (although less so in the Gulf War), the general public in the combatant countries did not have readily available both countries' in-depth perspective on the conflict as it developed. As an aid to understanding, the Security Council of the UN could require and finance both parties to an imminent conflict to place full page ads of a fixed number of words in the main newspapers of both sides and a dozen other principal newspapers globally, stating their position in numbered points. Each side would then have to reply to these point-by-point in a second series of ads; with a final third ad in reply to the reply. Then, so far as reason has a part to play in this sphere, it should be clearer to the general public and to world opinion which side has the better case.

Nicholas Albery, 20 Heber Road, London NW2 6AA (tel 081 208 2853; fax 081 452 6434).

Britain as a medical research centre

Fred Allen

Fred Allen is an Aikido expert.

An alternative 21st century strategy for deterrence against nuclear attack, and less expensive than Star Wars, would be to spend *half* the defence budget on making Britain indispensable to the rest of the world, through developing Britain as a centre for high tech medical facilities.

'Spend half the defence budget on making Britain indispensable to the rest of the world, as a centre for high tech medical facilities'

By gradually transferring the money from the defence budget to advanced medical research and facilities, Britain would become a nation that the rest of the world would want to remain unharmed. More UK jobs would result than from equivalent spending on nuclear systems which are mainly imported; and industry would benefit by having the latest medical technology to exploit and export, for by concentrating on one area we could become world leaders.

I am afraid that some modern fanatic will try to import nuclear bombs into this country by the heroin route, with retaliation deterrence being quite impracticable against fundamentalist Islamic or other fanatics, and in any case the source of the attack may not be known. So whereas no one can keep all suicide fanatics out, we can make them not want to come in. If their friends or fellow nationals had received high tech medical treatment in Britain, they would be likely to refrain from attack – just as the Argentinians told the captain of HMS Endurance during the Falklands War that they would not try to sink his ship because they had eaten dinner with him.

Respect for medicine and fear of illness has deterred aggression in the past: for instance, the Jewish biochemist Professor Warburg was unmolested throughout the whole Nazi era because Hitler feared cancer more than he feared the Jews.

I should emphasise that only half the defence budget is to be transferred. This leaves us, however, with more than half the security, as it is well known that defensive security is non-linear and doubling a budget merely adds a small increment.

And, although I think we should consider a citizen army, like the Swiss, I do not believe that we could do it until the Catholics and Protestants settle their differences.

With my scheme it is part of the logic that other countries must not be able to be self-sufficient in this sphere: the defence medical work would have to be treated more like the drug industry, with the end results made freely available, but with others relying on us through not knowing the details of the methods used. It would be work with huge machines because these are what the defence contractors make at present, and the reason for medical work to replace defence work is that it keeps the defence contractors solvent; and people want to pay for it with taxes.

Aid to the poor world (or any other altruistic scheme) cannot meet these criteria. Since the cholera epidemic and the Chadwick Act, the British people have expressed a determination to pay for public health.

> **'There is a saying in the martial art of Aikido that "you have won, only when your enemy no longer wishes to attack"'**

Britain would in this way be providing a service to the world. There is a saying in the martial art of Aikido that 'you have won, only when your enemy no longer wishes to attack.'

Fred Allen, 13 Shelly Row, Cambridge, CB3 0BP. This proposal won a Social Inventions Award.

Some ideas to prevent World War III

Stephen Salter

Adapted extract from a paper.

To be successful, any scheme for multilateral disarmament should proceed by small steps, should convince both sides that each has bettered the other, and, most importantly, should not become embroiled in the difficulties of weapon comparison. I propose a mechanism which has these three characteristics. Indeed, it can turn to advantage the inevitable differences of opinion about weapons of the two sides. It is based on the 'I cut – you choose' rule by which children can divide a cake.

> **'A scheme for multilateral disarmament based on the "I cut – you choose" rule by which children can divide a cake'**

My proposal would work for weapons of all sorts and between any two countries of comparable power, but take as an example two nuclear powers. Each side begins by assigning a number to each separable nuclear device in its armoury. This number, the 'military value percentage', is chosen by the weapon owner to represent his view of the usefulness of the item as a part of his entire inventory. The sum of all the numbers of each side is equal to one hundred. To take an example, if Side A decided that the 350 missiles in their 'Class X' system represented, say, 15 per cent of their nuclear strength, then the military value of each would be 0.04292 per cent.

It would be extraordinary if the values of usefulness chosen by one side were in exact agreement with the magnitude of threat felt by the other. Indeed, we may expect that the weapons with accurate terminal guidance and short launch times, which are suitable for pre-emptive first strikes, will induce a feeling of threat in their victims which is much greater than the feeling of comfort they offer to their owners. On the other hand, second-strike weapons are valuable deterrents and provide a large feeling of security, but do not pose a threat in proportion. This difference of opinion provides the incentive for the disarmament process and ensures that both sides can believe that they have secured an advantage.

The first reduction should be very small. Let us suppose that it is a step of about one per cent. Each side picks from the list of its opponent the most threatening items with total military value percentage not exceeding this 'table limit'. The selections may be announced simultaneously and small differences carried forward as credits for a second round.

If Side B happened to decide that the 'Class X' missile was the most serious threat, they would request as a first move that the number of missiles be reduced by 23. Meanwhile Side A would pick the most threatening one per cent of weapons from Side B's list. Side B would be quite indifferent about Side A's choice because the numbers would have been chosen to make any one per cent selection equal, in their view, to any other.

Either side may wish to distort the percentage values it declares. But because the sum total is always equal to one hundred, a reduction is quite legitimate, but the ploy may backfire and lead to the loss of good weapons at less than their face value.

It is also possible to design rules which allow for the updating of weapons. For example, if Side A insists on the introduction of some new missiles, it may do so provided that it also declares a military value percentage for them. Side B may then, without loss to its armoury, remove items to that same value from any part of Side A's inventory including the new ones. Side A will not want the new ones to be instantly lost and so will have to put a higher than true value on them. It will therefore have to give up rather more of its obsolete inventory. This rule would encourage the evolution of new weapons which provide high perceived security for low perceived threat – a most desirable feature.

Stephen Salter, Department of Mechanical Engineering, School of Engineering, The King's Buildings, University of Edinburgh, Mayfield Road, Edinburgh, EH9 3JL, Scotland (tel 031 667 1081 ext 3276). This scheme won a Social Inventions Award. 'Some Ideas to Stop World War III' by Salter is available from the Institute for £1-55.

Extensions of 'cake-sharing' disarmament

Peter Lewis

Adapted extract from a paper

One of the more attractive features of 'cake-sharing' disarmament (see previous item) is that the procedure between the sides is semi-automated, with the conflict *between* them becoming instead a conflict *within* them. The various military factions will argue their respective cases within their own countries. But in this situation there is an authority (the President) who can finally give a ruling which will settle any dispute. Furthermore, this situation is one that the disputants can trust, since the President is just as patriotic as they are.

Salter's ideas can be extended in several new directions.

(1) **Multiple powers:** Full disarmament would require the participation of more than two powers. Salter's procedure can be adapted to cope.

If there were say 100 nations or groups of allies taking part, then each would start by forming its forces into 10,000 packages. Each group would then select one package from each of the other 99 groups, thereby achieving an approximate one per cent reduction in total. The problem of two nations selecting the same package from one of the opposing lists can be overcome by having the nations select sequentially rather than simultaneously – then rotating the order in which the nations choose between rounds, or having a different order of choosing for each of the lists.

> 'What are the minimum levels of forces required to sustain stability within and between states, assuming all states had minimum forces?'

(2) **Minimum force levels:** What are the minimum levels of forces required to sustain stability within and between states, assuming all states had minimum forces?

Further research is required to assess this, but when these numbers have been derived, these forces would be excluded from the bargaining process. All forces in excess of these minima would be packaged and bargained as before.

The military powers need to divert some effort into researching ways of structuring their negotiations. The resources required are derisorily small in comparison with expenditure on armaments, and the potential benefits are massive.

Peter Lewis, Romneya, St Chad's Avenue, Midsomer Norton, Bath, BA3 2HG (tel 0761 413316).

Soldiers for civilian development

Alec Dickson

Assuming that defence forces are not going to be totally dissolved or abandoned in the near future, can we to some extent 'tame' them or 'domesticate' them by seeing them increasingly as being capable of fulfilling developmental roles?

> 'A humanitarian or developmental role would help to make defence forces popular with the civil population'

Probably only the defence forces of the then Soviet Union had the resources in transport and manpower to bring any kind of relief to the Chernobyl nuclear disaster. Probably only aircraft of the RAF (and German Air Force) were able to drop supplies to the starving population in Ethiopia.

Apart from emergencies of this kind (and flooding around Hamburg three years ago) there are many tasks in development which can best be met by trained, disciplined, mobile units. This role can be interesting for officers and men in the defence forces. It can influence attitudes. Some projects (for example the problems of the receding waters of Lake Chad) could be undertaken on an international basis. This humanitarian or developmental role would help to make defence forces popular with the civil population (and military service more acceptable to conscripts in, say, Latin America). It does not need radical legislation to bring this about. It does not mean making generals redundant. But gradually a change in attitude and in perspective might be expected. It makes sense.

Alec Dickson, 19 Blenheim Road, London W4 IVB (tel 081 994 7437).

20 minutes a week for peace and the environment

Adapted from an item by Phil Catalfo in Whole Earth Review, PO Box 38, Sausalito, CA 94966-9932. Subs. $33.

20/20 Vision's agenda is 'practical peacemaking and protecting the environment', concentrating on defence spending and reversing the arms race, but the model could be applied to virtually any issue where grassroots citizen involvement is at a premium. Subscribers (a $20 per year service fee is requested but not required) are guaranteed that they will not need to commit more than twenty minutes to carry out that month's action – usually, writing or phoning a legislator. Subscribers are assured that the recommended action will make the best possible use of their twenty minutes that month. Local people form a core group of five to ten members who commit themselves to four to five hours per month each, researching legislative issues affecting constituents, and recommending a lobbying action on a particular issue. The ultimate goal is to have many different area projects.

> 'They will not need to commit more than twenty minutes to carry out that month's action'

It works. Influential legislators are influenced, and wrongheaded government actions (such as the American Air Force's plan to install a Ground Wave Emergency Network tower in a local community) are averted.

20/20 Vision, 130 Cottage St, Amherst, MA 01002, USA (tel 413 549 4555).

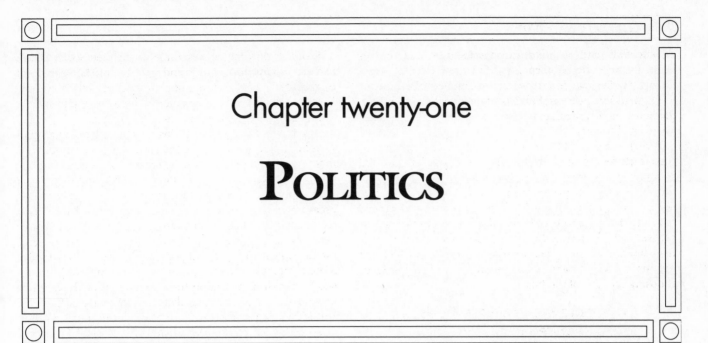

Chapter twenty-one

POLITICS

Ten political 'commandments'

Nicholas Albery

Many people are pessimistic about the future, believing that the established 'political-industrial-military complex' cannot and will not allow the radical decentralist and ecological transformations required. The reasoning is hard to fault, and there may well be only an outside chance of peaceful change happening in time. It is as if a miracle were needed. And yet it is not irrational to expect a miracle: today's society would seem magically (if insanely) transformed to a past citizen dragged instantly 200, 100 or even 50 years forward into our present. The future is almost bound to be weirder than we can imagine, rather than a straightforward continuation of present trends – and today's seemingly puny David-versus-Goliath style efforts may well turn out to have had a catalytic and positive effect.

One such effort is that of the Fourth World movement for 'small nations, small communities and a human scale,' whose long-term strategy for change seems not only desirable but also just conceivably feasible:

A long-term strategy for change

(1) There would need to be a widespread and well-funded education and publicity campaign by the Greens, the Fourth World movement and others to show how Schumacher's 'Small is Beautiful' ideas can be applied to the political system – for instance, making sure that no politician or student of politics is unaware of the ten Principles of Scale drawn up by Professor Leopold Kohr and Kirkpatrick Sale. I would like to see these principles published as a poster. They state as follows:

The Principles of Scale

The Beanstalk Principle: For every animal, object, institution or system, there is an optimal limit beyond which it ought not to grow.

The Law of Peripheral Neglect: Governmental concern, like marital fidelity or gravitational pull, diminishes with the square of the distance.

'The Law of Peripheral Neglect: Governmental concern, like marital fidelity or gravitational pull, diminishes with the square of the distance'

The Law of Government Size: Ethnic and social misery increase in direct proportion to the size and power of the central government of a nation or state.

Lucca's Law: Other things being equal, territories will be richer when small and independent than when large and dependent.

The Principle of Limits: Social problems tend to grow at a geometric rate, while the ability of humans to deal with them, if it can be extended at all, grows only at an arithmetic rate.

The Population Principle: As the size of a population doubles, its complexity – the amount of information exchanged and decisions required – quadruples, with consequent increases in stress and dislocation and mechanisms of social control.

The Velocity Theory of Population ('Slow is Beautiful'): The mass of a population increases not only numerically, through birth, but through increases in the velocity with which it moves.

The Self-Reliance Principle: Highly self-reliant local communities are less likely to get involved in large-scale violence than those whose existence depend on worldwide systems of trade.

The Principles of Warfare: (a) The severity of war always increases with an increase in state power; (b) War centralises the state by providing an excuse for an increased state power and the means by which to achieve it.

The Law of Critical Power: Critical power is the volume of power that gives a country's leaders reason to believe that they cannot be checked by the power available to any antagonist or combination of antagonists. Its accumulation is the inevitable cause of war.

(See the references below for the background to these laws.)

To which I suppose could be added an eleventh principle, modestly entitled:

Albery's Law of Inevitability: High technology superpowers are inherently unstable and their fragmentation is inevitable within a relatively short time span. The main variable is the violence with which this transformation occurs. (Thus a return to a human scale is guaranteed, even if, at worst, it is a nightmare world of radiated tribes eking out a post-nuclear existence.)

The breakdown of nations

The education campaign would also focus on two main practical policies for achieving a politics of the human scale, both derived from Leopold Kohr's work:

(a) No nation or federation should have more than about 12 million inhabitants.

(b) Within the nation there needs to be a Swiss-style non-centralised structure, with villages and neighbourhoods having as much autonomy as possible within a federation of cantons or counties.

The neighbourhood

(2) Greens or others with policies of this nature would need not only to present them at national election time, but also, as is already beginning to happen, to focus on putting human scale ideas into practice at the local neighbourhood, parish and county levels – in movements for creating urban parishes, smaller schools, locally controlled banks and credit unions, barter currencies and the like. So that if and when a break-up of the centralised nation state occurs, local people are as experienced as possible in running their own affairs.

National elections

(3) In the UK, Greens and others could campaign at national elections on a platform of dividing the UK into half a dozen independent nation states. It took the Labour Party less than fifty years from its founding for it to be elected, despite the UK's lack of proportional representation. It may well take a Greenish party less time, as civilisation continues its downward rush with more events of Chernobylian proportions. And given that their first act on election would be to honour their manifesto commitment to divide the UK into independent nations, the obstructive power of civil servants to carry on the same old policies would be much reduced.

Multinationals

(4) Taxation would need to be altered to make it advantageous for multinational and large companies to divide gradually into independently run units, with incentives for companies to become as small in size as their particular industry allows. (See Shann Turnbull's tax scheme for 'Humanising Corporations' in the chapter on Taxation.)

Superpower size reductions

> 'Russia, China, India and other megastates giving independence to their constituent parts'

(5) At the international level, there would have to be negotiations for multilateral and balanced reductions in bloc size – with Russia, China, India and other megastates giving independence to their constituent parts at the same rate as the USA gives independence to its states, and the EC to its member countries.

First step

But the first step would have to be a widespread educational debate and campaign, on the lines of the influential campaign for a Swiss-style constitution in South Africa run by the Groundswell group there. Human scale policies would be implemented readily enough once the underlying Kohr philosophy were taken to heart. In Kohr's words:

'The young people of today have yet to grasp that the unprecedented change that has overtaken our time concerns not the *nature* of our social difficulties, but their *scale*.

> 'The more united we become, the closer we get to the critical mass and density at which, as in a uranium bomb, our very compactness will lead to the explosion we try to avert'

'The real conflict of today is between Man and Mass, the Individual and Society, the Citizen and the State, the Big and the Small Community, between David and Goliath...And the more united we become, the closer we get to the critical mass and density at which, as in a uranium bomb, our very compactness will lead to the explosion we try to avert.'

• *Nicholas Albery, the Institute for Social Inventions, 20 Heber Road, London NW2 6AA (tel 081 208 2853; fax 081 452 6434).*

• *The Principles of Scale are examined in detail in the 300 page compendium 'How to Save the World, A Guide to the Laws of Scale', particularly pages 29 to 43. Available from the Institute for £4-95 incl. p&p.*

• *'Human Scale' by Kirkpatrick Sale is a 559 page book published by Secker and Warburg, 1980, £4-95.*

• *A sub to the Fourth World Review, which covers these issues, costs £10 from 24 Abercorn Place, London NW8 9XP (tel 071 286 4366).*

Collapse – the Christmas Tree Syndrome

Clive Akerman

Certain social systems disintegrate under their own weight. The Roman Empire for certain; the Spanish Empire perhaps – its disintegration was aided and abetted by a certain Corsican! – the British Empire perhaps for other reasons; with the Soviet Empire as the most recent example of a similar collapse. In each case the disintegration is unwillingly and unwittingly aided and abetted by the bureaucracies of the empire, fighting to maintain an unsustainable *status quo ante*. Perturbations and mutations arise throughout the empire, and it all falls apart.

This collapse is also true of many other systems. I call it the 'Christmas Tree Syndrome', and a simple example is provided by the typical computer application. It begins simple, elegant and economical. Then users come along and say 'very nice, but...' and request enhancements. So new bits are bolted on, like decorations on a Christmas Tree. These too attract comments of the 'very nice, but...' genre, so more decorations are tacked on. After a time the application becomes unmaintainable and, in effect, collapses under its own weight and complexity. The system engineers then redesign the system, putting back the elegance and apparent simplicity of the original, but on a bigger and more sophisticated scale. The process continues to iterate until the application is no longer needed.

> 'New bits are bolted on, like decorations on a Christmas Tree. After a time the application becomes unmaintainable and, in effect, collapses under its own weight and complexity'

I suspect that similar processes are repeated in many human (and possibly other natural) enterprises.

We have seen, for example, the regulations relating to social security payments grow in complexity over the years until the system began to fall apart – not, in my view, due to the evil intentions of the government of the time, merely due to intrinsic complexity brought on by well-intentioned tinkering by generations of well-intentioned people. Now it is being rethought and simplified.

The bureaucratic structures of the EC and the overly complicated regulatory structures of the London financial markets are other examples of over-burdened Christmas Trees which will, no doubt, at some time fall over.

Clive Akerman, 92 Sandbrook Road, London N16 0SP (tel 071 241 0866).

Green parish councils

Bob Finch

Adapted extract from Econews, Rhiw Goch, Aberaeron, Dyfed SA46 0HR (tel 0545 571405).

Parish councils are the smallest unit of local government. They put the town hall on people's doorsteps. They are more accessible and more accountable than any other part of local government. More importantly, they are the most participatory and, therefore, the most democratic institutions in the British political system. Campaigns by the Green Party for urban parish councils would generate a great deal of publicity. Greens could publish a monthly newsletter in each parish to keep people informed about what was happening and to outline policies they would like to implement. The Greens will need to set up parish parties – these should become the basic unit of the party, incontrovertible proof that it believed in devolution, community politics and power to the people. Parish councils will force the Green Party down to the grassroots.

> 'The Greens will need to set up parish parties – these should become the basic unit of the part'

Bob Finch, 46 Albany Street, Spring Bank, Hull, HU3 1PL.

Independent local Green parties – a model constitution

Mark Kinzley has designed an elegant constitution for local Green parties, one that is radically decentralist and that would allow the transformation of the UK Green Party into a confederation of local parties. These local parties would themselves be federal bodies made up of semi-autonomous ward branches. His constitution also guards against takeover by unrepresentative factions by requiring postal ballots for selections of candidates (using a single transferable voting system) – although perhaps there should be a further safeguard through requiring changes to the constitution to be confirmed by a ballot, rather than simply passed at a meeting.

The key element of independence in Kinzley's scheme is financial: the local parties would administer their own memberships and collect the fees, deciding for themselves what proportion of these fees to remit to the national office, rather than the other way round, as at present.

Redbridge Green Party exercised this financial independence briefly in 1990 and, possibly as a result, Kinzley as their candidate scored the largest number of votes of any Green candidate in outer London in the local elections.

Mark Kinzley, 7 Gaysham Avenue, Gants Hill, Ilford, Essex IG2 6TH (tel 081 550 3383).

Sequential size boycott

Gillies Macbain

Many alternative ideas are based on the premise that the world is mistaken in the direction that it is taking, and the very word 'alternative' seems to carry this implication wrapped up within it.

On the other hand many of the people who sympathise with the ideas, cannot see an immediate or effective route from where the world is, to where they feel it ought to be. The task of agreeing in advance upon a blueprint for a replacement world, under the conditions of a rapidly shifting context, is more than any practical person would undertake. Nor is there any holistic way of 'laboratory' testing a proposed new sustainable culture.

A route has to be proposed, rather than a destination, and that route begins from where the world finds itself this morning.

Rigidly defined alternative goals cannot be dictated. The alternative thinkers should concentrate on maintaining the social environment in which evolution is possible.

The first of these conditions is liberty.

Without liberty there is no variation. Without variation there is no advantage. Without advantage there is no competition. Without competition there is no evolution. Without evolution there is no life.

Liberty: we must assume that we have a fair measure of liberty or we would not now be proposing social inventions.

Diversity: the next step in facilitating evolution is to ensure variation and diversity.

A simple but potentially devastating idea is proposed...

A sequential size boycott.

A consumer of goods or services cannot always afford to disengage from every technology or organisation of which he or she disapproves, or has reservations about. In any case, many institutions remain necessary, pending the provision of some substitute, or development of some alternative.

> 'In a sequential size boycott, the consumer boycotts the largest of a group of multinationals in any particular field, for example breweries, and continues to enjoy the products of the remainder'

In a sequential size boycott, the consumer boycotts the largest of a group of multinationals in any particular field, for example breweries, and continues to enjoy the products of the remainder.

While the remainder are in no way ecologically or morally superior to the largest individual unit, the process of agglomeration is put into reverse, and the tide turned.

The immediately advantageous position for a producer to hold would be second largest producer, size being reckoned in units of production (number of bottles per year).

The second largest producer would also have a dilemma: whether or not to go for one extremely profitable year, mopping up the customers who disengage from number one; for they would then inherit the leadership – and the boycott – in the next financial year.

Their computers would quickly tell them – allowing for the percentage success of the boycotting – to throttle back, or more effectively, to break up the company into smaller, still perhaps profitable, decentralised units, competing and evolving.

An undertaking to do this could of course cause the boycott to be lifted, pending the reorganisation.

So, raise your glass – having checked the label on the bottle first – to Life, Liberty, Diversity, Evolution and the Sequential Size Boycott.

Gillies Macbain, Cranagh Castle, Templemore, Co. Tipperary, Ireland (tel 0504 53104).

Hierarchies of ten

Professor Meredith Thring

Professor Meredith Thring presents a simple hierarchical structure in his book 'Machines – Masters or Slaves of Man' (published by Peter Peregrinus Ltd, Southgate House, Stevenage, Herts SG1 1HQ).

Sir Lawrence Bragg when he was in charge of the Cavendish Laboratory formulated the 'Rule of six to the power of n', according to which each person can only give adequate real attention to the work and problems of six people reporting directly to him. This number six is not exact as it depends on how much other work the person has and how much attention his group members require, but certainly ten or twelve is the upper limit for direct leadership.

I will try to adapt the idea of Sir Lawrence Bragg as a possible means of solving the problem of how the individual can have a say (and a feeling he has a say) in government and also the problem of choosing wise leaders.

I suggest that it might be possible to make a democratic hierarchy in some such way as the following. People are divided regionally by place of home into groups of one thousand adults who vote every five years to choose ten of their number to represent them regionally. Each of these ten has the responsibility to see each of his one hundred people at least once a year in small groups and to discuss all kinds of political issues with them. These ten choose one of their number who represents them on the county scale (one million people). The thousand regional councillors on the County Council choose ten to do the regular work after listening to speeches by all those out of the one thousand who wish to stand for higher office. The National Parliament is formed from the tens of each of the counties.

> 'Each person can only give adequate real attention to the work and problems of six people reporting directly to him'

Professor Meredith Thring, Bell Farm, Brundish, Suffolk, IP13 8BL (tel 037 9384 296).

The power of pre-election questionnaires

Guy Dauncey

Adapted extracts from an article and notes by Guy Dauncey

For the municipal elections in the Greater Victoria area of British Columbia, a group calling itself Voters for a Responsible Community drew up a lengthy pre-election questionnaire with some 100 questions on possible policy initiatives, which was circulated to all candidates. In Victoria, 70 per cent of the candidates responded. Five of the seven subsequently elected indicated they would support initiatives for:

- Bike Lanes;
- A Council of Elders;
- A Greening of Businesses;
- The phasing out of the city's use of toxic pesticides and herbicides;
- The development of a rapid light rail transit scheme;
- Environmentally friendly sewage treatment facilities;
- A permanent elected youth council.

The task of achieving such an agenda would be massive, with each proposal involving research, meetings and a mass of paperwork. But a host of community and environmental groups could work with the council on these issues.

> 'It allows community groups to put up radical policies and to see which go on to get majority support from the elected candidates'

So one of the advantages of this pre-election questionnaire is that it allows community groups to put up radical and positive policies in large numbers and to see which go on to get majority support from the elected candidates of whatever political persuasion. It is then possible to inform these politicians that they do indeed have a potential majority on these policies and that they can press ahead and implement them.

For those who might be wondering 'Could we do this ourselves?' here are some of the nuts and bolts:

• In August 1990 a 'Green City' meeting shared in a large circle their personal visions of a 'Green Victoria' and then ideas for turning visions into action.

• In September, a second community meeting resulted in the choice of twelve questionnaire areas, and the establishment of working groups and a committee. An auction of promises raised $500 ('I'll cook an evening meal for four people'; 'I'll do a water-colour painting of your house'). Another $500 came from a donation.

• The committee met at least weekly until the November elections. A Consistency Committee spent hours scanning, screening and polishing the questions. A draft questionnaire was delivered by hand to 100 local groups inviting their endorsement within five days, and their advice on major errors or omissions. The questionnaire was printed and delivered by hand to every candidate for office. In the week that followed, the committee members phoned every candidate to deal with questions and to encourage them to deliver or fax their response sheet. This consisted of a score-box for each of the twelve areas, scoring A = 2, B = 1, C = 0, D = -1, where A = 'active support,' B = 'would vote for this,' C = 'I don't know,' D = 'I would vote against.'

A computer database should have been used to record the scores, as hours were spent checking and re-checking the 8,000+ responses for errors.

The scoring system was probably critical in winning the attention of the media, without which the whole campaign might have failed. The media credibility may have persuaded some candidates to answer.

With this exercise, every candidate for office was educated, and their sights were raised in a very cost-effective way. A wide cross-section of the community was helped to articulate a comprehensive vision for the future of the region; and the published results provide a powerful lever for people who wish to see a more socially and environmentally responsible Victoria.

• *A 26 page report is available for $2-80 from Voters for a Responsible Community, 202 Montreal St, Victoria, BC V8V 1Z2, Canada (tel 604 384 2878; fax 604 592 4473).*

• *Guy Dauncey, 2069 Kings Road, Victoria, BC V8R 2P6, Canada (tel 604 592 4472 h; 592 4473 w, tel and fax).*

Extra voting power proportional to votes won

Hugh Warren

Representative democracy is best served by electing representatives by preferential transferable vote, and, in the body to which they are elected, whether parliament or elsewhere, using modern technological means to allow them the same number of votes as they themselves obtained in their election.

It might be argued that in the Trades Union Congress, the representatives of the various Unions are, in effect, already given the voting power of the number of persons they represent.

But what is unsatisfactory about the TUC way of doing things is that the representatives from the Unions are elected from single representative constituencies, with all the shortcomings that such a method generates.

'Allow them the same number of votes as they themselves obtained in their election'

With the preferential transferable vote proposed, the voter simply marks the candidates on the ballot paper in order of preference. In the count, after the first preference votes have been counted, the candidate with the least votes is eliminated, and the votes cast for that candidate transferred to the voters' second preferences. This process is repeated until the number of candidates is reduced to the number to be elected.

In subsequent councils, by giving the representatives as many votes as they won in their election, we are recognising that they are voting as the representatives of those who elected them.

The same philosophy clearly applies to parliamentary elections, by interpreting what has above been called a 'council', as the 'batch' of representatives that a multi-member constituency would return to parliament. The MPs would all have as many votes in parliament as they won in their election. In this way every citizen would have an influence on every decision taken by parliament.

Hugh Warren, 19 Rectory Road, Farnborough, GU14 7BU (tel 0252 545175).

Electing representatives by jury system

Russell Simmons

Adapted extract from an item by Russell Simmons in 'People's Almanac No. 2', USA (published by Bantam Books).

Maybe the way to restore the government to the people is to make it truly representative once again.

'Why not view serving in the legislative branch of government as a responsibility of every citizen, just as each citizen has the duty to serve on a jury?'

Why not view serving in the legislative branch of government as a responsibility of every citizen, just as each citizen has the duty to serve on a jury? Names of candidates could be drawn in much the same way that jurors' names are selected. A random sample would ensure a far better representation of minorities, women, and the various levels of our economic strata than our present system could ever hope to provide.

'It would mean the demise of political parties as we know them'

It would mean the demise of political parties as we know them. It would mean that our legislative bodies would consist of citizens not beholden to any special group or interest. The preposterous expense of election campaigns would be eliminated, and the campaign period could be drastically shortened. We could get down to the real business of running the government for the people who pay for it.

This kind of representative government would silence the office-holders who are forever telling us that to get competent legislators we have to offer them higher salaries. In any state in the union, there are thousands of capable and honest people who could serve with distinction in the legislative positions now held by professional politicians, and would be glad to do so. Nor would they think the present salaries are too low.

Such a proposal as this would never be adopted at the federal level, or even the state level, but perhaps some municipal government might have the courage to try it as a pilot project. If it turned out to be as successful as I think it would be, the idea might catch on and eventually be tried at higher levels of government.

All MPs as leadership candidates

Dr David Chapman

From a paper distributed by the Institute for Social Inventions to relevant members of the Conservative Party hierarchy.

This paper proposes a way out for the Conservative Party from the nightmare of its leadership election procedure (and could also to advantage be used by the other parties). The last Conservative leadership contest was too complicated and protracted, and its working created great disruption and discord. On top of that, it cannot be relied on to elect the right person – after all the effort and disturbance, in theory there could well have been someone else whom a majority would prefer to whoever was elected as leader.

'The Conservative Party's leadership election procedure is too complicated and protracted, and its working creates great disruption and discord'

How then could this happen? One way is that this right person – the one preferred by a majority to any other person – might be a cabinet minister, who was thus unable, out of loyalty, to stand against the existing leader. Thus if either Mrs Thatcher or Mr Heseltine had been elected in the first ballot, though we would never have known for sure, a majority might nevertheless have preferred to have had one of the cabinet ministers as the leader.

Another way a candidate could be majority-preferred and still lose is on the third ballot. This could even have happened in the last election, if a third ballot had been held. According to the rules, three candidates stand in the third ballot, and MPs can give second as well as first preferences. Thus in this hypothetical third ballot, Hurd could well have got back the votes of those of his sympathisers who, seeking a quick decision on the second ballot, are reported to have voted for Major. Suppose that Hurd still got fewest first preferences, but obtained the second preferences of those who voted first for

Heseltine, and of those who voted for Major. By the rules, Hurd would be eliminated, and have the votes of his first-preference supporters transferred to their second preferences, and presumably Major would have been elected. But a majority (the Heseltine and Hurd supporters) would have preferred Hurd to Major, and another majority would have preferred Hurd to Heseltine.

Fortunately, however, there is a method of election which the Conservative Party could use in future, which would avoid such mistaken results, and would also be much less disruptive, and less protracted.

'Conservative MPs are automatically listed on the ballot paper as candidates for the leadership, without their having to put their names forward'

The first feature of this method is that Conservative MPs are automatically listed on the ballot paper as candidates for the leadership, without their having to put their names forward, or having to be nominated. Thus Hurd and Major would have been candidates from the start, without being open to any accusations of disloyalty. When voting, an MP would then put as many names in order of preference as he or she felt inclined.

'The votes are sorted and counted, to find out if there is one candidate who is preferred to each other candidate by a majority of those expressing a preference between the two of them'

The winning candidate is then found by a variation of the Condorcet method (first proposed by the French philosopher Condorcet in 1785). The votes are sorted and counted, to find out if there is one candidate who is preferred to each other candidate by a majority of those expressing a preference between the two of them. For example, if Hurd were preferred by a majority to Major, and to Heseltine, as described above, and also to each other candidate, Hurd would be elected.

It would be possible, if the Conservative Party so wished, to keep the present 15 per cent rule, and require the winner to get this 15 per cent margin over each other candidate. If no one did so, another ballot would have to be held, at which only a bare majority would be needed.

'A stronger incentive to run the party as the majority of the party's MPs preferred'

What then are the advantages for any party that adopts this new method of electing the leader? First, there would be no need for open challenges to, or campaigns against, the current leader, so that there would be less disruption and bad feeling, and less harm to the party's electoral prospects. Second, because of the wider field of alternative candidates, the prospect of this more effective competition in the future would give the leader – at all times, not just when a leadership election was coming up – a stronger incentive to run the party as the majority of the party's MPs preferred. Third, any leader who lost the MPs' confidence, for whatever reason, would soon be replaced, relatively quietly and without bitter strife or disruption. Fourth, the methods currently used by the Conservatives and others virtually compel MPs to engage in tactical voting. But with the new method, the best way for any set of MPs to influence the result in the direction they want, would nearly always be to vote according to their true preferences. Lastly, the candidate elected would in general be that one who was preferred by a majority to the other candidates, a result which is by no means guaranteed by the present method of election.

David Chapman, Democracy Design Forum, Coles Centre, Buxhall, Stowmarket, Suffolk IP14 3EB (tel 0449 736 223).

Secret voting in parliament

George Webb

George Webb has proposed that it would break the party system stranglehold if MPs voted secretly in parliament. Here are his answers to the obvious objections.

'If MPs voted in secret, we wouldn't know which way our MP had voted.'

Answer: 'It is his duty to prefer your interest to his own. But his unbiased opinion, his mature judgement, his enlightened conscience, he ought not to sacrifice to you, to any man, or to any set of men living...and he betrays you, instead of serving you, if he sacrifices it to your opinion' (Burke, Bohn, pp. 446 ff).

> **'his unbiased opinion, his mature judgement, his enlightened conscience, he ought not to sacrifice to you, to any man, or to any set of men living'**

An MP can best serve your interest by promoting your petitions, ensuring that they receive the attention of parliament, are negotiated freely and subjected to impartial arbitration when they reach parliament. Then the initiative for legislation comes from the people and is judged not by its source but on its merits. This is government *by* the people, which party government is not and cannot be.

Government by petition ('the inherent right of every commoner in England') was stultified by a series of Standing Orders between 1832 and 1878, expressing the impatience of party governments with the voice of the people (Erskine May Ed. XIX, 1976, Ch. XXXII).

'A Communist might gain election by posing as a Conservative.'

Answer: An MP could not propose Communist measures of substance because only ministers can propose bills involving the expenditure of public money (S.O. 78). Any resolution such an MP put to the House (a) would betray his or her treachery, which could lead to prosecution for false pretences; and (b) would win support on its merits since no question of party politics can arise if MPs vote secretly.

'It might be easier to corrupt an MP if he voted secretly.'

Answer: The voting public were regularly intimidated, bribed and bemused with ballyhoo until 1872 when they were made to vote secretly. At by-elections and elections thereafter there has been no such corruption ('Elimination of Corrupt Practices in British Elections', O'Leary, OUP, pp. 85 ff). How do you bribe a person to vote one way or the other when it cannot be demonstrated and you cannot find out, which way he or she has voted?

> **'Under the present system MPs have sold their votes wholesale and in advance'**

Yet under the present system MPs have sold their votes wholesale and in advance.

'Without the Labour Party to fund the election of poorer people, people of independent means would predominate'

Answer: Nothing in what is proposed can prevent a Labour Party or trade union supporting or rewarding a candidate as they please. All that the secret ballot does is to prevent them compelling the MP to vote as ordered. The MP must, of course, promote their petitions for the legislation they need or want, which party government now largely prevents the MP from doing.

> **'The MP must promote their petitions'**

'Will a secret ballot weaken Government policies?'

Answer: The initiative for legislation will tend to come from the people rather than from the civil service. Every step in this direction represents 'an access of strength to the government' (Gladstone on Reform Bill, 1868). Ministers will enjoy security of tenure for as long as they retain, by their own merits and without party political animosities to weaken and distract them, the support of the House and of their electors. (At present, ministers are often puppets in the hands of their departmental civil service; whereas, when dealing with petitions, 'parliament...conducts enquiries for its own information' (May, op cit p. 859), and will no doubt unveil the arcana imperii that frustrate so many ministers.

'Wouldn't PR achieve the same?'

Answer: Under any system of party government, the role of the parties is at the expense of government by the people. When a secret vote is adopted, parties will have to take their place in the queue like everyone else. But the queue will not be lengthened. When 'the pestilential influence of party animosities' is abated, then a small committee, say three MPs, will be enough to examine and arbitrate upon points still in dispute when petitions are brought into parliament. This multiplies parliamentary time by some two hundred, and, provided any MP may raise any matter in the full House, no harm is done.

'Would it not be sufficient to insist on a free vote?'

Answer: The party whip can be applied after the vote as easily as before. It is only one, and not the most offensive way in which governments corrupt MPs, so that if we prevent its overuse we merely make matters worse. Only when MPs cannot reveal which way they are going to vote or have voted, and nobody can discover it – only then are MPs forced to vote on the merits of what is laid before them, in the light of all the arguments they have heard for and against, without regard to the source of the proposals – whether it comes from the united outcry of 59,999,999 sturdy Britons, or the one remaining weak-kneed scoundrel who may, after all, be in the right.

George Webb, 94 Shrubland St, Leamington, Warwicks, CV31 3BD.

Editorial comment

The Economist has suggested a compromise variant: believing, as it does, that constituents have a right to know how their MPs voted, it suggests the publication of voting lists with a lag of four months. This delay would weaken the party whips' power, as the relevant bill would have ended its Commons passage, or been lost,within this four months. The power of the whips might be weakened still further by only publishing the voting lists when an election had been called.

Short-ReinDemocracy

JonathanGray

Claims that the UK's electoral system is a democratic one can be readily challenged on many counts and there is an urgent need for a fundamental change. I consider that Proportional Representation as presently proposed and understood is no more than a step in the right direction. I should therefore like to put forward a suggestion for an alternative electoral system in line with the political perspectives and democratic principles of the Green movement as I understand them.

It represents an attempt to evolve a more truly democratic model. For want of a better label I have called it 'Short-Rein Democracy', since its built-in accountability would enable the electorate to keep politicians 'on a short rein' without unduly restricting movement and progress in their governmental actitivities.

A notable feature of the system would be the absence of general elections. This would facilitate an uninterrupted continuity of governmental activities. As a consequence, every MP would occupy his or her seat in parliament for an indefinite period which could only be terminated in one of three ways; by death, by voluntary retirement or by a special 'recall to account' procedure explained below.

To ensure that the allegiance of MPs would be to their constituents exclusively, they would be expressly forbidden by law to have any direct involvement or connection with any political party or with any commercial organisation. This should make them independent in every sense and their salaries as MPs would be set at a level designed to reinforce such independence.

> 'An official notice recalling the MP to the constituency to account for his or her actions or decisions in the House'

Since every MP would be truly independent, political parties would no longer be in a position to govern the country, although political parties would still have an important role to play in the political scene, but as campaigning pressure groups rather than as executive power structures.

With such independence, it would be each MP's personal responsibility to decide which way to vote in the House on any particular issue – without the imperative or guidance of any party whip. Naturally, he or she would be expected to bear the interests and feelings of constituents in mind when making such decisions, even though, in the end, any decision must be a personal one. However, if MPs value their constituents' confidence and continued support, they would be wise to vote in accordance with their understanding of the prevalent constituency feeling.

Under the 'recall to account' procedure, an official notice recalling the MP to the constituency to account for his or her actions or decisions in the House could be served by an appropriate number of dissatisfied constituents. Such a notice, to be legally valid, would have to be signed by a significant proportion of the constituency's electorate; a proportion specified by statute and set at a level low enough to afford the constituents a reasonable degree of control of their MP, yet high enough to avoid facilitating the disruptive tactics of any small but vigorous minority group. As a further safeguard against such disruptive elements, any constituent signing such a notice would not be permitted by law to sign another such notice for a period of, say, two years.

On receipt of the notice, the MP would have to choose whether to resign his or her seat voluntarily, or to return to the constituency and go for re-election against any other candidates who may present themselves for election. This latter course would afford the MP the opportunity to face the critics in his or her constituency, explain his actions and try to justify them. By describing the context of his actions and discussing the issues involved more fully, he or she might even convince the critics that a certain stance was the right one in the circumstances. In which case, he or she would stand a good chance of being re-elected for a further indefinite period.

However, in order to provide a further safeguard against frivolous and irresponsible abuse and to establish some degree of stability, any 'challenging' alternative candidate in such an election would be required to poll at least two-thirds of the vote to unseat the challenged MP. Such a requirement would also help to avoid a continuing state of stressful indecision for an MP whose constituency is seen to be almost equally divided politically.

In my view, if we are to manage human society in a manner that is more responsible and responsive to the ecological parameters of the planet, we need to be able to curb the pernicious excesses of powerful minorities. An essential prerequisite of that is a much greater degree of real democracy, and I believe that an electoral system such as my suggested 'Short-Rein Democracy', operating within a Green economy, would achieve that. There is now an urgent need for a wider debate and discussion of these topics.

Jonathan Gray, c/o Green Drum magazine, ('the environmental quarterly for people who care'), 18 Cofton Lake Road, Birmingham B45 8PL (tel 021 445 2576). The above is extracted from issue 57 of Green Drum. £3-50 subs.

Government by binding contract

Tony Judge

Adapted extract from a suggestion to the Institute.

Consider the possibility that the programme presented by each political party to the electorate could take the form of a draft contract – a legal contract rather than simply a social contract. During the run-up to the election parties would each be free to modify their proposal in the light of feedback from the electorate and from opposing parties. But their proposal would become final (and 'frozen') at some period prior to the election (say one month). The proposal now constitutes a commitment (or formal 'tender'). If this 'bid' is accepted by the electorate, in that the proposing party comes into power as a result of election, the commitment then takes the form of a binding legal contract between the party and the highest power in the land, namely the crown or presidency.

> 'The programme presented by each political party could take the form of a legal contract. This makes it much more difficult to renege on commitments'

This makes it much more difficult for the government to renege on commitments. The form of the contract could, amongst other things, provide for time clauses in relation to such commitments and the kinds of penalties to be imposed on the contracting party if it is found to be in default. Clearly 'escape' clauses could be explicitly built into the original contract to provide for unforeseen emergencies. Clauses could be included to define the status of commitments made subsequent to the election.

In the event of a coalition of parties forming the government, again the principle of participation in any such coalition could be outlined in the original proposal of each party. The coalition would then be defined by a further contract linking the original contracts on which the electorate had expressed itself. Legal form is then given to 'letters of agreement', with appropriate termination clauses.

To clarify the feasibility of this proposal, a detailed study is required of the appropriate 'rules of tender' and the kinds of contract which could be formulated and the degree of freedom required by contracting parties; also of importance is the relationship of privatised government to a permanent civil service. Similar studies could be made for local government.

Why should elected representatives, whether individually or collectively, be immune from prosecution?

Tony Judge, Union of International Associations, rue Washington 40, 1050 Brussels, Belgium (tel 32 2 640 41 09; fax 32 2 649 32 69).

Editorial comment

An analogous approach was amusingly described by Bernard Levin in the Times: Mr Harries, an entrepreneur living in Cardiff, sued the Conservative government in the High Court for a million pounds of compensation. His case was that the government during the late eighties and early nineties negligently ran the economy in a way which they knew, or ought to have known, would be deleterious to all those who depended on it (particularly by not keeping proper control over the Bank of England, with interest rates almost doubling); and that by their negligence, they thus ruined his businesses and rendered themselves liable to damages.

> 'His High Court case was that the government ran the economy in a way which they knew, or ought to have known, would be deleterious'

Social Policy Bonds

This proposal, detailed in a 15 page paper, was put forward by Ronnie Horesh whilst working as a policy analyst in the Ministry of Agriculture in New Zealand. It won a Political Social Inventions Award.

Government objectives could be achieved more efficiently by issuing bonds which could be redeemed for a fixed sum only when the goal is achieved.

The bonds could be traded on the open market at whatever prices they would fetch. For example, there could be an issue of a £10 bond that was redeemable only when unemployment went below 3 per cent for a sustained period. This £10 bond would initially be auctioned – maybe for a price as low as 10p.

> 'There could be a £10 bond that was redeemable only when unemployment went below 3 per cent'

The bond would increase in value as the objective came closer to being met.

The effect of issuing such bonds would be to give some of the responsibility for getting down unemployment to the bond-holders, and to take it away from cumbersome government departments; and would provide the incentive for bond-holders to take measures to hasten the reduction in unemployment – with those who knew they could do most towards the goal being the most likely to acquire the bonds.

Measures taken could include defraying recruitment costs to enterprises; supplementing prospective employees' income; finding jobs for unemployed people; and offsetting job training and transfer costs.

In the health area, indicators such a life expectancy, infant mortality and disability could be targeted.

Bond-holders would get involved in preventive medicine to try to ensure that these goals were met sooner.

> 'Apart from providing greater efficiency in social policy delivery, the bonds would guarantee stability and increase the transparency of policy objectives'

Apart from providing greater efficiency in social policy delivery, the bonds would guarantee stability and increase the transparency of policy objectives.

The potential benefits to the disadvantaged would be significant. At present, the system is inherently cynical: the solution of a social problem by a government institution would lead to the dissolution of that institution – there is no relationship between the solution of problems and the rewards to those employed to solve them. Contracting out 'long-term' social services is not the answer; nor is privatisation, as private agencies have private objectives which may not coincide with social objectives.

Social Policy Bonds could be used for instance to target:

• The number of homeless (or the number of new approved housing units completed, or occupancy rates of the existing housing stock);

- Pollution (nationally averaged levels of water or air pollution);
- Education: target results to be achieved in basic literacy and numeracy tests taken by children.

The efficiency of these bonds could be tested initially by allocating the same sums of money as are currently allocated for a particular social objective to the redemption of Social Policy Bonds which target the identical objective. The maximum cost to the government of the issue would then be set so as not to exceed the expenditure that would anyway have been incurred in pursuit of the same objective.

Ronnie Horesh, c/o 12 George St, Chester CH1 3EQ (tel 0244 319510).

Two Sir Humphreys

Dr David Chapman

The standing joke of the TV series 'Yes, Prime Minister' is that the permanent secretary Sir Humphrey manipulates the prime minister. But in fact this is serious – in so far as the politicians are not in control of the affairs of the nation, our democratic control is weakened.

> 'In any ministry, in addition to the head of its civil service of a ministry, there should be appointed an alternate head with similar qualifications'

To deal with this problem, I propose that in any ministry, in addition to the head of its civil service, there should be appointed an *alternate* head with similar qualifications. The alternate would get at least the salary the head gets now, and the head a greater salary still.

The alternate would be independent of the head, and have full access to all information and all persons in the ministry and elsewhere, to which the head has access.

The source of the minister's control is that at any time he may promote the alternate to be head, and demote the head to be alternate.

Sir Humphrey exerts his influence by concealing the nature and even the existence of options that the minister would prefer if he knew of them. But with a well-informed alternate seeking to replace him, this strategy would not be viable, since the alternate has an incentive to inform the minister of any attractive option which is being concealed.

Quite apart from deterring concealment, this competition would encourage adaptiveness and creativity – the alternate would continually seek for better ways in which the department could be run, and the head would do the same to avoid demotion.

The alternate should prove more useful than an outside consultant brought in by the minister, because of his greater permanence and experience, and because he can be called on to put his recommendations into practice. The scheme differs from the USA 'spoils system' in that the alternate has no more party political allegiance than the head, and would be no more likely to be promoted by an incoming government than by any other.

This scheme of alternates could be used in other contexts as well, such as the following:

(1) Alternates could be appointed to heads of large sub-departments, thus giving the overall head more control of his own organisation;

(2) It could be used for government agencies other than ministries;

(3) Or for the head of an organisation such as a charity, to enable a board of governors, who would tend to be part-time and amateur, to exert more effective control;

(4) Or for the head of a cooperative or a trade union. The controlling body could be either an elected council, or the whole membership, voting in a kind of election where the loser stays on as an alternate.

Dr David Chapman, Democracy Design Forum, Coles Centre, Buxhall, Stowmarket, Suffolk, IP14 3EB (tel 0449 736 223).

Ministry of Ideas

Edward de Bono in Today newspaper once asked 'Isn't it time we had a Ministry of Ideas?' For de Bono there is the 'technology' of concepts of use and value. 'We need to treat "concept R&D" in as serious a manner as we treat technical R&D.'

De Bono believes it would be a vote-winner for a prime minister to set up a formal and visible Concept R&D department, a Ministry of Ideas, which could provide provocative new ideas and 'take the flak'.

He gives several examples of the kinds of ideas the Ministry could come up with: how about a 'new industrial animal for enterprises with sales of less than say £500,000? There would be an imputed tax of 25% of sales. Against this there would be a flat allowance of say £15,000 per employee. The paperwork associated with wages and employment would all be handled by a local wages office (on a fee basis). This concept would provide incentives to employ people profitably and also reduce the viscosity of paperwork that is so debilitating to young enterprises.'

> 'A levy rather than a ban on TV violence, with say a £5,000 fee per personalised killing, £3,000 for an impersonal shoot-out (not per corpse)'

De Bono also suggests a levy rather than a ban on TV violence, with say a £5,000 fee per personalised killing, £3,000 for an impersonal shoot-out (not per corpse); and £1,000 per assault, with the money going to a victims' fund, and the producer under new pressure to assess the 'dramatic necessity' of violence.

Referenda via banks

Bo Tsang

Several people have submitted ideas similar to the following to the Institute. This version comes from Bo Tsang, 90 Geraint Street, Liverpool L8 8HQ.

As a contribution to society, banks and building societies should bear the costs of referenda conducted using their cashpoint machines. Each registered voter would be issued with a plastic voting card containing their national insurance number or other form of identity.

> 'As a contribution to society, banks and building societies should bear the costs of referenda conducted using their cashpoint machines'

Counting would be extremely rapid and there would be no spoilt votes. But just as the idea of universal and women's suffrage was opposed, there are many vested interests that would oppose an 'electronic democracy', not least MPs, who would see much of their power stripped away. One sop to them might be that an issue could only be proposed for referendum by an MP, who would need the support of two thirds of the House.

A TV referendum experiment

Adapted extract from an article monitored for the Institute by Duane Elgin (PO Box 820, Menlo Park, Ca 94026, USA). What is described is not a new idea, but this particular experiment represents more or less the state of the art.

The Woodlands is a new community of approximately 4,000 people outside Houston, Texas. About 850 of its residents are subscribers to the Woodlands cable TV system. Like several other cable TV systems which are cropping up in communities all over the USA, the one in the Woodlands is a two-way system whereby home viewers can register their reaction to programmes through their channel selector. Each number of the channel selector represents a code announced before the programme begins. The responses are automatically fed into the computer at the cable TV station. But the system in the Woodlands is the only one in the US that has been used for on-the-spot opinion polling. During community meetings, where issues are discussed by local officials and politicians, the audience response is shown on a screen every five or ten minutes at the meeting itself. It is a successful two-way conversation by means of which the public is able to give a prompt response to whatever issues it may agree or disagree with.

> 'channel 2 means "approve"; channel 4 means "disapprove"; channel 6 means "talk faster, provide less detail"; channel 9 means "talk slower, provide more detail, important issue"; channel 11 means "change the subject" '

A typical meeting may go something like this. Before the meeting begins, the station announces the code to be used: channel 2 means 'approve'; channel 4 means 'disapprove'; channel 6 means 'talk faster, provide less detail'; channel 9 means 'talk slower, provide more detail, important issue';

channel 11 means 'change the subject'; and channel 13 means 'talk louder'. When the speaker notes on the screen that 60% of the viewers disagree with what he or she is saying, the speaker will usually try to explain what he or she has said in a manner geared toward audience opinion. Similarly, the speaker will change the subject if the audience indicates the topic is uninteresting or unimportant, and will provide more time and detail to issues the audience wants to hear about.

The Woodlands cable TV system has also made a breakthrough in obtaining emergency aid services for its subscribers. Each home with the cable is automatically wired to the local fire department, police department, and emergency medical aid unit. These public safety services are obtained through using a standard channel selector designated for the specific emergency. Since the system has been in use there has not been one successful burglary in homes with the cable. The two local insurance carriers have reduced their fees to policy owners with the cable by 25%.

The installation fee for the cable is $300, and there is a monthly service charge of $5. Tocom Industries of Houston is currently the only manufacturer of the computer mechanism used in the Woodlands system. But it seems likely that the idea will be spreading throughout the US; and that the benefits more than justify the cost.

Extra voting power for the knowledgeable
Fred Allen

Fred Allen extends the previous idea in a probably undesirable direction.

I invented the cash dispenser at the time of the Suez crisis but never thought of it as a banking tool, I thought of it for promoting democracy. It asks you objective background questions relevant to the referendum decision and the more you get right, the more your vote is worth. In Ireland it would bypass the social problem of one man one vote for a representative, and in all situations where a gerrymandered democratic majority is the objective. The Pope might as well end his opposition to birth control as a family of eight ignorant catholics could be out-voted by one educated atheist. Nothing would so motivate people to learn as the certainty that knowledge is power, and nothing is easier than to find out than whether people really know, using multiple choice questions.

> 'It asks you objective background questions relevant to the referendum decision and the more you get right, the more your vote is worth'

Fred Allen, 13 Shelly Row, Cambridge, CB3 OBP.

Making bureaucracy pay for delays
Nicholas Albery

British bureaucracy sometimes rivals Third World bureaucracy for delay, rudeness and complacency. The London passport office took six months to renew my passport, including losing my application form after cashing my cheque. It took patience and a phone with automatic repeat dialling for me to be able to get through to them. Their advertised numbers were and no doubt still are almost continuously engaged – for any suffering reader I pass on some of the ex-directory numbers that should connect you to a supervisor: 071 271 8594, 071 271 8505 and 071 271 8599. Phoning seems to work better than letters: they cheerfully admitted to me that it was taking them three weeks even to open mail, let alone deal with it.

'When my passport finally arrived, I sent them an invoice for £15 for my time for the estimated three hours I had spent chasing them up by phone and letter'

When my passport finally arrived, I sent them an invoice for a modest £15 for my time for the estimated three hours I had spent chasing them up by phone and letter, and asked for a further £4·53 for my material costs, including phone bill and stamps. Before the month was up I received a cheque for the full amount as 'reimbursement for the difficulties you incurred in obtaining a passport' and as an 'ex-gratia payment in full and final settlement.'

I advise anyone else who has been made to wait overlong by bureaucracy to charge for their time. The paymasters for these organisations must be made to realise that allowing their services to be run on minimum budgets so that they are then overwhelmed by demand is not acceptable. A change of attitude is also required – and the Citizen's Charter is a step in right direction. As Stuart Conger puts it in 'Social Inventions' (Saskatchewan Newstart), social agencies, like businesses, 'must proclaim the customer king.' The emphasis must be on building the self-image of clients rather than humiliating them, and the orientation must be towards pleasure rather than puritanism. Every government department and social services agency needs a unit solely concerned with trying out new and improved ways of delivering their services to the public.

Nicholas Albery, 20 Heber Road, London NW2 6AA (tel 081 208 2853; fax 081 452 6434).

Chapter twenty-two

SPIRITUALITY AND CULTS

Aspects of a Wisdom Culture

Ken Wilber

Ken Wilber in 'Up From Eden' (Routledge and Kegan Paul 1983) lists the following possible aspects of a future Wisdom Culture – quoted by Richard Slaughter in 'Future Vision in the Nuclear Age' (Futures journal).

- Vivid understanding of common humanity and brother/sisterhood;
- Move beyond roles based on physical differences of skin colour and sex;
- Growth of mental/psychic clarity;
- Balanced use of rationality and intuition;
- Consciousness recognised in each soul and throughout creation;

> 'Higher motivations alter economic incentives and theory; education becomes a discipline in transcendence, body to mind to soul'

- Higher motivations alter economic incentives and theory;
- Methods and institutions to cure emotional disease and foster growth of consciousness;
- Education becomes a discipline in transcendence, body to mind to soul;
- Technology as an aid to transcendence, not a substitute for it;
- Electronic media as vehicles of bonding consciousness and unity;
- Outer space as a projection of inner psychic space;
- Appropriate technology to free material exchanges from chronic oppression;
- Cultural/national differences set against background of universal consciousness;
- All people as ultimately one in spirit, and incentives to actualise this;
- Transcendent unity of all religions;
- To govern, politicians demonstrate understanding and mastery of body/mind/soul/spirit.

God's Eco-Laws

Ulf Christiensen

Extracted from articles in 'Vision Seeker and Sharer' Nos 5 & 6, published by Rainbow Publications, 15 St Julitta, Bodmin, Cornwall PL30 5ED (£1-10, subs £4-40).

God's Eco-Laws are plain and simple and can be read straight out of nature. American Indian and Pacific Island Pantheists, Samoyeds and Eskimos point to nature as their supreme bible. Shameless sinners, billions of us, have broken the fundamental aims and laws of the Great Plan such as:

(1) The rule (aim/law) of increasing balance and justice;
(2) of increasing harmony and beauty;
(3) of increasing diversity and individuality;
(4) of ever-evolving biology and health;
(5) of increasing self-control, knowledge and wisdom;

> 'The law of increasing diversity and individuality and ever more differentiated decentralisation'

(6) of ever more differentiated decentralisation;
(7) the principles of evolution rather than revolution.

I have prayed for a respite from the effects of global aggression so that social innovators and sensible problem solvers can have an opportunity. Once I listed thousands of outstanding problem-solvers and world citizens. These individuals are 'saved' in the sense that they perceive much more of the ultimate reality behind the stage-like reality most people see. They are nearer to God. To evolve from the human-made eco-catastrophes, half-hells and spiritual shambles we have caused in defiance of God, we have now to recreate that part of God's creation that our techno-civilisation has so recklessly despoiled. This evolutionary task could fill life with meaning for hundreds of generations to follow. For God's sake, our human and material resources, our energies and business profits must be invested in Nature-restoration schemes, recycling schemes (turning waste into our biggest resource), health schemes in the widest sense and beauty-restoration (every eyesore is a pain for ever).

We have the innovations and technologies available to raise our daily ethics to the level of our religions. Britain, for example, is not just a fourth-rate nation, full of industrial debris and depressing inner-city slums. It is also the finest cultural oasis in the world.

It is within human power to create a world of shining beauty and transcendent glory.

Ulf Bygdinn Christiensen, Bygdinn House, Byjdoy Alle 26, 0265 Oslo 2, Norway (tel 02 43 02 99). 'One of my many social innovations is for computerised bartering between locally stocked warehouses owned by, and run for, human-sized communities. There are four times too many people on earth and we need to re-establish nature's most lavish production system, permaculture, with its principle of complete recycling. Britain with its BBC can help stimulate global enthusiasm for tackling such concerns.'

How to rate a guru?

In the wake of scandals surrounding the Bhagwan and Hare Krishna religions in the States, the Institute for Social Inventions is compiling a list of questions that a would-be disciple could ask before joining up with a guru or new cult. The total of 'yes' answers to questions such as the following could provide a rough-and-ready comparative 'rating' of gurus:

(1) Is what the guru offers free?

(2) Is the guru relatively poor? – ie not having personal control (or control in practice) over more wealth than is needed for him or her to live in normal comfort and dignity?

(3) Is it unnecessary to join the organisation in order to have access to the teachings (are there books, tapes, open meetings, etc that transmit the knowledge needed)?

(4) Is it easy to leave the guru; are ex-disciples treated satisfactorily; and are 'opponents' of the guru treated fairly?

> **'Is there respect for quality in the work of the guru's organisation (no ugly architecture for instance)?'**

(5) Does the guru refrain from sexual involvement with the disciples?

(6) Is free contact allowed with families and friends?

(7) Is there respect for quality in the work of the guru's organisation (no ugly architecture for instance)?

(8) Are the guru's words in harmony with past spiritual insights, such as contained in Huxley's 'Perennial Philosophy' anthology?

(9) Is the organisation non-authoritarian – are there signs of democracy, for instance, or of questioning and debate and thinking for oneself being welcomed?

(10) Is the guru's legitimacy anchored in a tradition that points back to previous gurus, rather than the guru claiming to be the sole arbiter of his or her legitimacy?

(11) Does the guru avoid claiming to be a perfect master, offering the only route to enlightenment? Is he open about his own 'feet of clay', if he has them?

(12) Does the guru recognise that his or her authority is 'phase-specific', eg lasting only long enough to bring you up to his or her level of understanding?

(13) Does the guru's organisation, in its methods and in all aspects of its daily regime, successfully avoid psychologically coercive or brainwashing-style techniques?

(14) Do the guru's or organisation's replies to these questions agree with evidence from other sources? – for instance, ask the Cult Information Centre for their perspective (Ian Haworth, BCM Cults, London WC1N 3XX, tel 081 651 3322).

(15) Does the guru have less than 1,000 signed-up disciples? (Gurus with large followings seem to be more prone to succumb to the temptations of power.)

'Guru Quotient' ratings table

Percentaging the positive answers to these questions – based on the available literature, with additional information from present and past disciples (and answering the questions as if all the gurus rated were still alive) – produces the following very approximate table:

- Bhagwan (Osho) 17 (out of 100);
- Maharishi 23;
- Leonard Orr of the Rebirthing movement 53;
- Swami Bhaktivedanta of the Hare Krishna movement 60;
- Krishnamurti 73;
- Stephen Gaskin (from the Tennessee farm commune) 77.

These ratings do not of course necessarily reflect what a disciple can learn from a particular guru, they are more an indication of how 'safe' the guru is. Potential disciples would be well advised to steer clear of becoming organisationally involved with 'low GQ' gurus. It is after all a very basic check-list: almost all traditional gurus for the last three thousand years would have had little difficulty in scoring in the 70s and above.

Please send improved checklist questions (or examples of trying out the test on a guru that you know) to 'Guru Quotients', c/o the Institute for Social Inventions, 20 Heber Road, London NW2 6AA (tel 081 208 2853; fax 081 452 6434).

Bhagwan's low Guru Rating queried
Swami Anand Subhuti

In the above table, Bhagwan's rough-and-ready GQ (Guru Quotient) came out at 17 out of 100. Swami Anand Subhuti writes in response from Bhagwan (Osho)'s commune in Poona, India.

Your advice on how to rate a guru contains a fatal flaw which invalidates your conclusions.

The reasons why people seek gurus and spiritual masters in the first place is because they have become disillusioned with Christianity and its bankrupt system of belief and morality.

It does not make any sense to use Christian criteria to judge a non-Christian guru. Yet your checklist is filled with old, rotten Christian ideas.

Why should a guru be 'relatively poor'? Just because Jesus Christ exalted poverty? What is wrong with being rich? Has the Christian idea of 'blessed are the poor' helped humanity in any way over the last 2,000 years?

Why should a guru's teachings be free? Is he supposed to be running a different version of the Salvation Army?

Why should he abstain from sexual involvement with his disciples? Because Christian saints are supposed to be celibate? Because of the perverted Christian idea that the spirit is holy but the pleasures of the flesh are evil?

The fact that Krishnamurti scored high on this test is a

condemnation of him, not a compliment. And the fact that my own spiritual master, Osho (Bhagwan), rated low comes as a blessed relief. Christianity has done immense harm to millions of people. Nobody in their right mind wants to find another Jesus Christ.

Swami Anand Subhuti, Osho Commune International, 17 Koregaon Park, Pune 411 001, MS, India.

Editorial comment

The guru ratings give a good indication of whether it is relatively safe to become organisationally involved with the guru. I do not think that many of the neighbours of the Bhagwan's commune in the States who were threatened with poisoning, or those members of the commune who were nearly murdered, would argue that Bhagwan's leadership had proved particularly safe or even wise. The biography of him by one of his closest followers makes sorry reading indeed.

Subhuti asks why Bhagwan or any other guru should 'abstain from sexual involvement with his disciples'. Recent history seems to show that gurus such as Bhagwan who get sexually involved with their disciples go seriously astray in the end. It is a bit like a therapist making love with a client; there are so many transference issues involved that it may seem like a free choice without coercion for the client, but is most unlikely to be so in fact.

And what is wrong with Bhagwan being super-rich with his huge fleet of Rolls Royces? Firstly, gurus show no signs of being immune to the rule that power tends to corrupt and absolute power corrupts absolutely; and secondly, a guru sets an example to his or her disciples, and the planet needs examples of conspicuous consumption as much as it needs a hole in the ozone layer.

Gurus hot & cold, structured & unstructured

Andrew Rawlinson

Adapted extract from a letter to the Institute.

I am writing a book about Western gurus and have developed a model of comparative religion (see the article 'The Yogi and the Mystic', edited by K. Werner, published by Curzon Press, 1989)

In this model the various spiritual teachings can be mapped as in the diagram below. This model is directly relevant to the question of a teacher's reliability and your Guru Quotient.

Hot

Hot Structured

The teaching: The teaching is never given all at once but only when necessary and then only in cryptic form. This is typical of all forms of esotericism. The teacher as magician or the one who knows the secret.
Examples: Hindu tantra, gnosticism, Gurdjieff (who also had some cool structured exercises).
Spiritual practice: a series of leaps or initiations.
Transmission: by ordeal.
Images: magician, gambler.
The message: **JUMP!**

Hot Unstructured

The teaching: There is no teaching – only love and submission. The teacher as servant of God or embodiment of God.
Examples: Meher Baba: 'I come not to teach but to awaken'. Subud.
Spiritual practice: submission.
Transmission: a gift.
Images: lover, martyr.
The message: **SUBMIT!**

Structured ——————— Unstructured

Cool Structured

The teaching: The teaching is open and complete but there's no point in reading p.100 before you read p.1. The teacher as clear discriminator or guide.
Examples: Patanjali's 'Yoga Sutras'.
Spiritual practice: graduated and gentle.
Transmission: learning how to use the map.
Images: yogi, craftsmen.
The message: **WORK!**

Cool Unstructured

The teaching: The teaching is constantly given (the same truth over and over again) but no one understands it. The teacher embodies truth.
Examples: Ramana Mahrashi, Taoism and Zen.
Spiritual practice: just realise.
Transmission: none – truth already exists.
Image: sage, hermit.
The message: **LET GO!**

Cool

Andrew Rawlinson continues:

Essentially, the Guru Quotient is a *Cool* evaluation, tending somewhat towards the *Cool Structured*. There is nothing wrong with this in itself, of course, but it *is* one-sided; the Hot idea (both *Structured* and *Unstructured*) can be just as compelling as the *Cool* but it is based on different axioms.

What has tended to happen, I think, is that the liberal, humanistic middle-classes (who are themselves drawing on a Western tradition that is in the *Cool Structured* quarter of the model) have a deep suspicion of poor-quality teachers of the *Hot* persuasion. But good-quality exponents also exist (eg Ramakrishna; Meher Baba; Neem Karoli Baba, Ram Dass's master – see Ram Dass's 'Miracle of Love', Dutton, NY, 1979).

'One should also beware of using high-quality *Cool* values to discredit poor-quality *Hot* teachers'

Of course, it is always possible to provide a *Cool* critique of high-quality *Hot* teachings or teachers. But then one has to accept the consequences – eg dumping the notions of divine will, submission, grace, etc, all of which have their place in all the major religions. It is easy to see how this would appeal to an intelligent humanist but even so it is not something that should be done lightly. And on top of that, one should also beware of using high-quality *Cool* values to discredit poor-quality *Hot* teachers.

By analogy, there is a world of difference between European classical music and American blues. But comparing the best examples of each – say, Mozart and Billie Holiday – can be instructive even if, in the end, one ends up saying that one genre is superior to the other. But comparing poor examples – say, early Mendelssohn and Barry White or Luther Vandross in their 'blues' mode – with each other really doesn't get us anywhere. And as for comparing a good example of one genre with a poor-quality example of another – that's either a rigged comparison or an ignorant one.

The essential point, I think, is that (a) there are different kinds of good quality; and (b) comparing these different kinds cannot be done by people who don't actually see the different kinds of quality – like someone who can't appreciate Mozart (my son) or Billie Holiday (my mother-in-law). The result is that they can't really converse about music but only about certain forms of it.

Andrew Rawlinson, Meregill, Bentham, Lancaster LA2 7AN (tel 05242 61185).

Editorial comment

This is a fascinating and illuminating classification scheme; but nevertheless the ignorant and abusable beginner on the trail and at the bottom of the power mountain would still benefit from having (if necessary four different) ways to help sense who are the charlatan gurus in each quadrant.

And I still maintain that a disciple, however *Hot* the guru yearned for may be, would be well advised before or between jumping head first into the guru's influence, to take a *Cool, unstructured* look at what's going on – just as Wordsworth recommended the recollection of emotion in tranquillity. Very few people are permanently in just one of the four quadrants that Rawlinson depicts and they might as well therefore take advantage of the insights and perspectives available from whichever quadrant they temporarily find themselves in.

Response from Andrew Rawlinson
Adapted extract from a second letter to the Institute.

'Gurdjieff ran his groups like a slightly batty sergeant major; and he had children by several of his students'

As for detecting frauds in the four categories, it is a matter of how well each ideal is upheld. For example, Gurdjieff was a *Hot Structured* teacher: he enjoyed spending money (especially other people's); he ran his groups like a slightly batty sergeant major; and he had children by several of his students. Now what I'm saying is that the appropriate question (or rather the *first* appropriate question) isn't 'Is this out of order?' but 'Did Gurdjieff live up to the standards of a *Hot Structured* teacher?' (which means that he is bound to be challenging, disturbing and constantly trying to wake people up). If the answer is Yes, then he's high quality and one can only argue that he's out of order by applying a critique from another category. And we can do that – but then we should be aware of what we are doing. If the answer is No, then he's poor quality and it's highly likely that he misused money, power and sex – according to the *Hot Structured* ideal, that is.

So what I'd say about gurus, teachers or groups is: don't get involved with the *Hot* ones unless you can hold your own. If a guru is out to shake me up, it helps if I can say 'Get lost!' And if he chucks me out – fine. In short, take responsibility for yourself and your own actions. But on the other hand, it may well be that in being asked to give money, certain attachments and obsessions are revealed to me and that I'd be grateful for it. It may be that being forced through an intense practice (as in Zen *sesshin*) breaks down barriers of resistance that I could not have breached on my own – and I could be grateful for that, too.

It's not that I'm against warnings about gurus; rather, that behind these warnings may be a need for security that is unexamined and which is actually frightened of taking risks – a sort of stodgy bourgeois goo that is in favour of God, queen and country without examining what any of them mean. Of course, I don't deny that the *Cool Structured* ideal, which is based on clarity, fairness, balance and so forth, has its excellence. But this is *high quality;* the bourgeois goo is *poor quality*.

Editorial comment

This smacks of special pleading for Gurdjieff and his ilk. Since there are *high-quality Hot Structured* gurus who behave neither immorally nor unethically, why bend over backwards to make excuses for those who have feet of clay? And there seem to be very few cases of disciples being able to stand up to a guru, as Rawlinson advises. Their overpowering charisma is often how they came to accepted as gurus in the first place.

'Why bend over backwards to make excuses for those who have feet of clay?'

Celebration of Life Group

MargaretChisman

The Celebration of Life Group was set up by a small group of friends who believed that it was possible to devise secular ceremonies which would give expression to the affirmation of our delight in the world; in our optimism that we can change ourselves and reach out to fulfilment; that the emotions generally thought to be exclusive to religion – worship, awe, wonder, faith, self-transcendence and hope – could be experienced through our ceremony; and that it could refresh the dry spaces of the spirit and generate a desire to help each other as friends.

'To give expression to the affirmation of our delight in the world'

We meet about six times a year in members' homes, commencing with a meal. One or other of us will have devised a ceremony suited to the theme selected in advance for the evening. We arrange a framework of specific actions, but allow spaces to be filled by each of us as desired. To the richness of our interpretation we add music, poetry, sound, light, incense, paintings, sculpture – anything that gives insight, delight, and helps the emotions to play a positive role in our lives.

Some of the themes we have explored include: to thine own self be true; celebrate something you hope will happen; inspiration in our lives; a happiness ritual; successes and failures in our love lives; turning points; altered states of consciousness; symbols.

Margaret Chisman, The Bungalow, near the Station, Tring, Herts, HP23 5QX (tel 0442 82 3281). If you would like to know more about the group and to be invited to its next meeting, please make contact.

The Constant Instant

Michael Hildred

Michael Hildred wrote in a letter to the Institute: 'I think this is a social invention, a sort of bench mark for thought. The awful recognition of the question, "Is that which I am doing at this instant of my time worthy of being for ever?" There seems to be no way that I can communicate the feeling of excitement and heightened awareness that the concept induces in me.'

'Is this instant of my time worthy of being for ever?'

There needs to be a new understanding amongst those wishing to change things. I offer four new observations (at least new to me):

(1) The Universe is a Constant Instant. Every instant is 'forever' for having been at all. (2) The size of an idea bears no relationship to the time given thinking of it. (3) Conceptual thought is like the universe was before matter gave it time or space. (4) Our relationship to the universe of seeming matter is similar to our relationship to our own subconscious – both are total recorders except that our subsconscious recorder is not yet as reliable or as factual as that of matter.

To expand on these four observations:

(1) An example is that of astronomers listening and thinking that they had found the echo of the original Big Bang still ringing in radio waves. So that is one instant that has been fairly constant in its cause and effect ever since.

A couple of years ago, scientists managed to achieve star heat of 15 million degrees for a billionth of a second with lasers. It was over in a flash but will for ever remain as a high point of achievement. Photographs are a recognition that we can capture an instant of time and freeze it. Dr Wilder Penfield, Montreal's famous neuro-surgeon, found that by stimulating different parts of the brain, it had total recall of sight, sound, smell, in fact a practical re-living of an event.

'Christians hope for a second life, when this one is for ever already'

Thomas Aquinas spoke of the 'Eternal Present', yet Christians hope for a second life, when this one is for ever already. I do not know how we got it so wrong in the first place. The Constant Instant theory provides a new realisation which enhances every person's place in his or her universe and opens up a new appreciation of being. It should lend a degree of importance to all our lives.

(2) We can think 'atom' or 'universe'. Therefore you can think 'for ever' before you do something that changes 'for ever'. The mind, with practically infinite capacity, compresses its ideas and thoughts into material action and in reverse sees the universe in the drop of dew on a rose petal.

Many years ago, I tried to illustrate this 'size of an idea' concept in Vermont: to show the children of Swanton that the whole world is in their back garden I wrote around the world and obtained eighty-five stones – from the road to the Parthenon, from the road to the pyramids, a stone blessed by a shinto priest, etc. These were built into a cairn, so that people could touch many parts of the world right there in Swanton.

The stones had been separate from a time before the planet was formed and had lain roughly where they were for some four billion years and now 'in a flash' they were cemented together and likely to remain roughly in the Swanton area for the next umpteen billion years.

I can only hope that future geologists, archaeologists or visitors from elsewhere will realise that they are looking at a conscious materialisation of a concept.

The fact that we do the same sort of thing every day in a supermarket is inclined to elude us.

'Humanity is the universe becoming aware of itself'

(3) We create our own time and space just by being. We know that part of our physical brain is much like that of a crocodile: primitive, vaguely sensory and instinctive, but we seem to have added a few distinct layers to the point where we can now be aware of being aware. How much further we need to go in brain size development I do not know. Maybe it is just a case of looking at all the stimuli that are stored in all our brains as if they were a haphazard scattering of iron filings only requiring a little magnet to give them realignment and purpose. I have tried to invent such a magnet.

(4) As Carl Sagan said, 'humanity is the universe becoming aware of itself'. A hundred and sixty one billion miles back

down the track of this planet, Christ pointed out the same concept that man was the light of the world. Both these statements, nearly two thousand years apart, are becoming part of your life as you read them and incidentally illustrating the theory-proving statement, 'my words will be with you for ever'. You cannot do anything that is *not* for ever.

The principle of every instant becoming constant or a space-time continuum has allowed us to get where we are more by accident than design, hence our sudden global recognition of the consequences of not having been aware of the damage we are doing to the only planet we have to live on.

Did we really say to ourselves 'Let us build a world brain that would work at the speed of light bringing true the prophecy that "the son of man will go from East to West as summer lightning" ' and then invent radio and satellite TV to link the ten billion neurons in the heads of six billion people and add computers for good measure?

Instant communication and the ability to record and recall means that we are literally living in a constant instant.

Add to this Fritjof Capra's estimate that the average speed of an electron around a nucleus is 650 miles per second, which means that everything, including us, is being reassembled every split second.

To take a film of a person's seventy-year life but with the film going through the gate of the camera at 650 miles per second instead of the usual two feet per second, would take more than a billion years to watch. A sort of time equivalent of E equals Mc^2.

We cannot move a split second back into the past or a split second forward into the future. We can only be synchronistically aware of the strange phenomenon that suddenly allows the split second of now to become eternally permanent. The concept has been around in man's intuition for a long time but it is only in our now that communications and science and intuition have come together to allow the recognition of the principle of the constant instant – changing our perception in the prophetic twinkling of an eye. It is possible on a world that is only a seventh of a second big.

Michael Hildred, Flint Lodge, 2 Villiers Road, Southsea, Hants PO5 2HQ (tel 0705 734 829).

Converting church galleries

Rev. Graham of Aberdeen suggests converting church galleries for wider community use as restaurants, museums, creches, etc. 'In these days when the vast majority of church buildings lie empty most of the week, or are very sparingly used,' he writes, 'we believe that social innovation could take place by converting the galleries of these churches, largely unneeded for congregational purposes, into areas suitable for daily community use.' His church in Aberdeen now houses, amongst other community activities, a Family Museum about life in the Holy Land three thousand years ago.

He writes that creating level areas in galleries can be achieved by laying joists on the highest of the stepped areas, running them to the gallery edge, and covering them with chipboard. Safety is achieved by using old pew seats as timber to raise the gallery edge to the required 1.1m height.

Rev. A.D.M. Graham, 22 Osborne Place, Aberdeen AB2 4DA (tel 0224 648041).

Green Spirituality: suggestions for groups

Margaret Chisman

A few sample adapted extracts from a 5 page paper for people thinking of forming Green Spirituality groups (available from the author at the address below for 80p in stamps).

Aspects to explore

• Is Green spirituality different from other spirituality?
• Is the idea of Green spirituality the beginning of a new religion?
• In what essential ways does Green spirituality differ from other Green activity?
• What is the opposite of spirituality?

When discussing what you expect from the group, the convener could throw in a few ideas to stimulate thinking. These could include:

• What do you feel is lacking in the Green movement that would be fulfilled by Green spirituality?
• What is lacking in your own life that you think Green spirituality would fulfil?
• Have you ever experienced feelings of exaltation? Or vague yearnings or even what could be called spiritual hunger?

Exercises

• Between now and when you come together again, take a walk round your locality with a 'Green hat' on and look at everything with a new eye. And try linking it to a profession or role, imagining yourself as Green teacher, Green parent, Green local councillor, etc.
• Devise your own Green credo or Desiderata.

'Write your own Green ten commandments'

• Formulate your own personal Green covenant between humans and the planet Earth, or between humans and God.
• Make a list of what you are going to promise to try your best to achieve. You could compare your covenants after an interval of some months.
• Devise your own Green grace before meals.
• What about an evening of music that expresses for you some of your feelings about Green spirituality?
• Or how about an evening of extracts from books or articles about Green spirituality?
• You could try to write some Green haiku. Here is one of mine:

Great cathedrals now
Are banks and supermarkets.
Metamorphosis?

• Imagine you are the Queen, the Archbishop of Canterbury or the Prime Minister. A magic wand has given you three wishes to lay down Green moral edicts or parliamentary laws. What would you choose?
• Devise a Green Christmas party.

Margaret Chisman, The Bungalow, near the Station, Tring, Herts H23 5QX (tel 0442 82 3281).

Chapter twenty-three

OLD AGE

Is ageing necessary?

Robert Hart

'All my faculties are as good as ever, and in the highest perfection: my understanding clearer and brighter than ever, my judgement sound, my memory tenacious, my spirits good, and my voice, the first thing that is apt to fail others, grown so strong and sonorous that I cannot help chanting out loud my prayers morning and night'. So wrote Luigi Cornaro, a Venetian scholar and agriculturalist, in 1562 at the age of 95, in a treatise called 'The Joys of Old Age'.

This treatise, together with two others on health and longevity that he wrote at the ages of 83 and 86, are, in all respects but one – that of diet – in tune with the most up-to-date thinking, and are an inspiring testimony to the possibility of leading a full and happy life to an advanced age. (His writings are published in paperback by Thorsons under the title 'How to Live 100 Years'.)

The first rule of longevity is 'never retire', but live creatively, constantly striving to expand your mental horizons. At the age of 95 Cornaro was promoting marshland reclamation and harbour improvement schemes for the Venetian republic. He was also writing treatises on agriculture and architecture.

Music

The second rule of longevity is harmonious living, and music is an outstanding aid to that. The human being is intended by nature to be a singer. The head has three pairs of sinuses, the only known function of which is to act as resonators corresponding to the three 'registers' of the singing voice. If they are not used for that purpose, they tend to get clogged with mucus, causing headaches and catarrhal troubles. Everyone should take singing lessons, as singing is one of the most health-promoting of all activities.

'Singing is one of the most health-promoting of all activities'

The ancient Italian bel canto system of voice production has affinities with yoga and is of religious origin. Like yoga, it involves breath control and meditation. Through a narrowly trumpet-shaped mouth the lungs should be filled with air, while the diaphragm, the powerful muscle between the ribs and the solar plexus, should be drawn in to the limit of capacity. A column of air should then be forced gently but firmly from the base of the lungs through the throat and up into the head, finally being allowed to escape softly through the nostrils. This process not only helps to develop the voice but also leads to a heightened state of consciousness, promoting calm, clear, constructive thinking and an intensification of sensitivity.

Creative thinking

Continuous, constructive thinking is the third rule of longevity. To achieve this, another ancient technique, which has been rediscovered by modern psychology, is essential. It is the art of transmuting negative conditions, emotions and impulses into positive achievements. Cornaro gives an example of this. At an advanced age he actually welcomed the loss of a considerable part of his income by crooked dealing, as it gave him the opportunity of finding a means of more than repairing the loss by the application of his agricultural skills. In a letter to a friend he wrote, 'I have been to the test and have proved to all that I can turn misfortune to advantage and derive additional benefit from reverses.'

'Continuous, constructive thinking is the third rule of longevity. The bold acceptance of problems as challenges to be overcome leads to inner strength'

It is widely recognised today that the prime aim of life should be self-development towards the goal of mental, physical, emotional and spiritual wholeness. This is a full-time occupation, which leaves no time for depression, self-pity, irritation and other negative states which play havoc with one's constitution. We are constantly advised by health counsellors to avoid tension. This does not mean closing our eyes to problems, running away from them or trying to suppress them. The effect of these is to force problems to sink into the subconscious, where they fester and sooner or later cause mental and physical disturbances and disease. If we are to avoid tension, the first essential is to face up to our problems fearlessly and clear-sightedly, dispersing the mist of vague fears and anxieties which often makes them seem bigger than they really are. The bold acceptance of problems as challenges to be overcome leads to inner strength.

Paradoxically, the tensing and flexing of our mental and physical muscles which the overcoming of problems involves, leads to a relaxation of mental tension. We all have greater potentialities than we realise. The determination to find some solution to even the most obdurate and deep-seated of problems has the effect of releasing hidden talents and capacities. Our struggles should not be against the problems but for some constructive, integrative goal, in the light of which the problems will be transcended and lose their urgency, before being solved.

The human system, far more intricate and elaborate than any computer, spaceship or other machine devised by man, has infinite potentialities for development. It is said that most of us employ only five per cent of our brain cells. Doctors know a lot about disease but very little about health. There can be no doubt that if some of the expertise concentrated on disease germs, drugs and vaccines were switched to the study of the human as a whole – body, mind, soul and spirit – means could be found of enormously expanding talents and longevity.

Nutrition

The science of nutrition is still in its infancy, at any rate as far as the medical profession is concerned. Few doctors or lay people recognise the full implications of the fact that our bodies, including the most sensitive organs, such as the brain, heart and nerves, are made of the food we eat. Engineers go to extreme lengths to select the right alloys for some delicate machine. How much more efficient would the human machine be if equal care were taken in selecting the best raw materials for its construction and repair? The latest nutritional research indicates that the ideal diet for positive health and longevity is one comprising a high proportion of raw, organically grown fruit, vegetables, nuts and herbs. Such a diet avoids the build-up of acid, fatty substances which clog the system and are the main cause of degenerative diseases, such as arthritis. Older people should progressively reduce their intake of proteins and calories, which overload the system, hindering the free flow of the restorative factors which constitute the body's healing and health-promoting armoury. Age research with animals has shown that low-calorie diets can extend 'normal' life-spans by an astonishing three hundred per cent.

> 'The ideal diet for positive health and longevity is one comprising a high proportion of raw, organically grown fruit, vegetables, nuts and herbs'

The value of experience

It must be admitted that the process of building up disease resistance and positive health demands continuous vigilance, effort and self-discipline, and many people are tempted to ask, 'Is it worth it'? Cornaro had the answer in his dissertation on 'The Joys of Old Age'. Present-day Western civilisation, with its cult of youth, seems largely to have forgotten one basic fact which was clear to Cornaro, the Renaissance man: the value of experience. While young people can sometimes acquire intellectual and manual skills with amazing speed, the most important lessons of an evolving life, those connected with the emotional and spiritual nature and human relations, generally take decades to imbibe. There is no substitute for experience. However wide one's theoretical knowledge, unless it is backed up by a wide and deep fund of practical experience, it is virtually useless.

One of the supreme needs of the present age is mature wisdom and the inner strength derived from it. War, violence, crime, drug-taking and other forms of perversity so prevalent today are all symptoms of emotional immaturity, instability and insecurity. No satisfaction on earth can compare with that gained from a continuous struggle to face up to and overcome life's problems on the basis of a reliable value system.

Robert Hart, Highwood Hill, Rushbury, near Church Stretton, Shropshire SY6 7DE (tel 06943 342).

One's age is one's private property

Adapted extract from 'Life After Work – The Arrival of the Ageless Society' by Michael Young and Tom Schuller, published by HarperCollins, 1991, £16.

> 'Age would become information which people would not be required to give to the State or anyone else, nor others allowed to pass on, except for census purposes'

It is a central paradox of modern society that so much has been achieved, so effectively, to reduce the injury done to people by biological ageing, and so little the injury done by social ageing. In the longer run, this unnecessary insult can be reduced in a decisive manner only by a radically new approach: by regarding the ages of adults as something very personal to them, their private property, which they are entitled to privacy about, a private matter to be taken out of the public and placed in the private domain. This will require bringing age within the scope of an extended Data Protection Act which goes well beyond what is stored in computers: their age would become information which people would not be required to give to the State or anyone else, nor others allowed to pass on without permission, except for census purposes where individuals would not be identified.

The consequences would be far-reaching. Pensions would have to be abandoned along with age-enumeration, at any rate collectively organised pensions tied to ages of eligibility; and a social wage would have to be introduced in their place. A Social Wage or National Dividend has not, as far as we know, been advocated before in order to eliminate both age discrimination and age privilege. The wage would be enough to live on, even if at a modest level. Whatever the level decided upon, it would be paid to each individual adult whether it were needed or not, just as pensions are now paid to both rich and poor. But it would be taxable as part of a person's income so that wealthier people would in effect return the wage to the exchequer in the form of taxes. There would be no means test for old people or anyone else except that which belongs by its very nature to income tax.

The sole remaining ageist compulsion would be that children would have to start school at five or before. But we see no good reason to compel pupils to remain in secondary school until they are sixteen. It surely makes more sense to give the option to young teenagers to leave school if they wish to do so. We settle on the age of thirteen, which has the justification that this is now around the general age of puberty. From that time on, all information about their ages would be out of government records at Somerset House and elsewhere.

'Every teenager would be given vouchers entitling them to eight further years of education at whatever age they wanted it'

Every teenager would be given vouchers entitling them to eight further years of education at whatever age they wanted it, from fourteen onwards. Spending on education would thus have to rise, but the prize would be very great: life-long education could at last become a fact instead of a dream.

Our premise is that age has become one of the organising principles of modern society, and as such has been carried so far as to inflict serious psychological injury on millions of people. We are proposing a new negative freedom – freedom from a kind of interference which stops people behaving more fully in accord with that part of themselves which does not change with age. The young and the old – with unnecessary barriers removed – would be able to join the mainstream of society and to leave behind the segregation which has been forced upon them.

Age specialisation is no longer appropriate now that older people are living so much longer than they once did and adulthood comes to younger people so much earlier than it did. Neither younger nor older any longer fit the stereotypes of childhood and old age which social control imposed. People are ready for the next big shift in society, the generation shift, to follow on the gender shift.

'Someone whose time is not their own has therefore been deprived of something much more intrinsic than property'

Time is not an extension of the person, it is part of the person; 'Time is a condition a priori,' Kant said, 'of all phenomena whatsoever.' Someone whose time is not their own has therefore been deprived of something much more intrinsic than property, and yet it has not by and large been resisted nearly so strongly. So much of people's time has been handed over to organisations which on an unprecedented scale require the timetables of millions upon millions of people to be synchronised with the utmost precision. A city is a giant clock which all its citizens have to obey. But the stage is now set for a retreat from mass society, and for greater variety, greater idiosyncrasy, greater individuality and perhaps greater fulfilment.

Marketed drug is a youth serum

Adapted extracts from items in the National Enquirer (USA), by Jay Gourley, and the Examiner (USA) by Don Vaughan, monitored for the Institute by Roger Knights. Similar reports are emerging of scientific experiments demonstrating the longevity-enhancing value of certain herb essences, particularly Thyme.

Human trials are now under way with Deprenyl, a prescription drug used in the treatment of Parkinson's disease, to test claims that it enhances longevity. It has side effects if taken in large doses, cautions Dr William Tatton, a molecular and cell biologist at the University of Toronto (where the drug has been studied), but, he adds, 'after adequate testing, in ten to fifteen years, this drug might be taken by everyone, starting at age 40.'

'Rats lived to the human equivalent of 120 to 150 years'

Deprenyl's potential as a life extender came to light when Dr Joseph Knoll conducted a rat study at the pharmacology department of the Semmelweis University of Medicine in Budapest, Hungary. When Deprenyl was given to rats at an age equivalent to people 65 years old, all of them outlived rats the same age who did not get the drug. They lived to the human equivalent of 120 to 150 years, and they regained a youthful appearance, activity and virility for much of their lives.

Deprenyl blocks an enzyme that neutralises the dopamine brain chemicals. The dopamines help transmit nerve signals throughout the brain, and some scientists believe that as long as the brain is supplied with them, it will not degenerate.

Dr Knoll is very much an outsider in recommending that people 45 years and older take two 5 milligram tablets of Deprenyl every week (as he himself does).

Pre-Retirement Day Release
Anthony Dyke

I propose Day Release Into Voluntary Easy Retirement (DRIVER). My suggestion is that firms give 'day release' (as is given, for learning purposes, to apprentices and other young people) to those members of staff who will be due for retirement in two years' time.

'Firms should give day release to those members of staff who will be due for retirement in two years' time'

Far too many otherwise fit people die very soon after being retired from a lifetime of honest work. Most of the reasons for their deaths can be associated with the shock of suddenly being without a life-style – without friends, pattern of living, reason for going on, identity, or usefulness.

With the DRIVER scheme, older employees on their days off will be encouraged to search for, discover and develop their unused natural talents. This can include suitable clubs, societies and organisations, where new friends can be made.

Skilled guidance from a trained personnel officer in the case of large firms, or from Social Services in other cases, could consist of control and encouragement. A basic daily diary would help to plan the days off, and a simple progress chart can be used for checking that all goes well. Part-time voluntary work can be encouraged, as well as private enterprise where conditions allow.

A side-benefit for large organisations, would be the opportunities for understudies to gain experience for one or two days a week. The scheme would also create jobs in every area of the social services, and in the larger organisations who participate in the scheme.

If this DRIVER scheme is backed by the state, then many more jobs would be created in order to cover the lost man-hours over the country as a whole.

So, we have a scheme that not only saves lives, and enriches the lives of older people, but will create new jobs. There is also the added benefit of saving otherwise prematurely bereaved families from a great deal of grief.

Anthony Dyke, 11 Belfield Avenue, Marldon, Paignton, South Devon, TQ3 1NU (tel 0803 553128).

A movement for holidays in the sun

Brian Walden in the Sunday Times suggested that 'every voluntary body dealing with the aged, every trade union in the land and every local authority, should make a winter in the sun for the elderly a priority item on its agenda.

'All that is needed is some cooperation between different agencies to coordinate the exodus. Its administrative costs would be offset by savings elsewhere. Who knows, we might find that it paid to build facilities abroad and staff them for so worthwhile a purpose.'

New Horizons Trust

Modelled on a Canadian government programme of the same name, New Horizons offers grants of up to £5,000 to groups who satisfy these conditions:

(a) There must be at least ten people in the group and half of them must be aged 60 or over;

'Involving about one third of the retired population'

(b) They must identify a new project which uses the skills and experience of group members to meet a community need.

'If the project sounds like fun, so much the better!' Over 200 projects have been given grants so far. The parent project in Canada, started in 1972, has funded more than 16,000 projects, involving about one third of the retired population of Canada.

UK projects given money to date include a Vietnamese Elderly Club in Cambridge; pre-retirement courses on local radio in York; a talking newspaper for the blind in West Yorkshire, with tapes of news from local papers; the creation of a ten mile Darwin's Walk around Lichfield, in memory of Erasmus Darwin who practised as a doctor there 200 years ago; an answercall telephone system in Redruth offering emergency help to those activating their pendant alarms; and a group of pensioners in Bollington converting an old church into an arts centre.

New Horizons Trust, Paramount House, 290-292 Brighton Road, South Croydon, CR2 6AG (tel 081 666 0201).

Dark Horse Venture for Over 60s

Mary Thomas

'The Dark Horse Venture was initiated when Mary Thomas, a retired teacher, walked into Age Concern's Liverpool office with her vision and an enormous amount of enthusiasm. She recruited the invaluable Miss Pearl Clark, whose experience with the Duke of Edinburgh Award scheme was essential. Together they developed the scheme' – (from 'Third Age' newsletter).

The Dark Horse Venture for retired people is a totally new idea. It aims to provide new opportunities for individual self-discovery by offering an overall framework for the development of interests, enthusiasms and involvement in non-competitive activities.

All you have to do is to select an activity you have never tried before and become involved in it on a regular basis for just twelve months. Examples include: sharing skills with young people; qualifying in first aid, lifesaving, etc; fundraising; giving practical help of any kind; learning a musical instrument, lace making, quilting, marquetry, upholstery, writing; and getting out and about – rambling, orienteering, youth hostelling, travelling or dancing.

During this time you will be able to benefit from the guidance and advice of *a person of your choice* – someone who has professional training or experience in the activity you have chosen.

To enter you simply purchase a Personal Journal which contains details of what you have to do and space in which to record your achievements. Dark Horse Venture Certificates will be awarded on the basis of progress and performance for each activity. There is no limit to the number of single subject certificates that you can enter and win. Those who have been awarded one certificate from each of the three activity categories can apply for the Gold Seal Certificate.

Everyone is a dark horse. This scheme is an antidote to loneliness and boredom.

Mary Thomas, The Dark Horse Venture, Unit D54, South West Brunswick Dock, Liverpool L3 4BD (tel 051 709 8999).

Help for Pensioners from the Retired (HelPeR)

Hugh Stapleton

Adapted from a submission to the Institute.

Proposal: the formation of a nationwide professional aid source – HelPeR (standing for 'Help for Pensioners from the Retired').

Objective: to provide assistance to old-age pensioners, disabled persons, widows, the infirm and the destitute.

'Coordinate the services of retired qualified persons in a number of recognised professions, such as plumbers, electricians, engineers, carpenters'

Service: HelPeR would coordinate the services not merely of retired executives (as with the organisation REACH) but of retired qualified persons in a number of jobs, such as plumbers, electricians, engineers, carpenters, solicitors, builders, bankers, commercial accountants, etc.

System: HelPeR would provide for the carrying out of certain tasks for persons unable to pay for them, to be done by professionals. These jobs might include:

repairs to plumbing or domestic appliances; wiring a bedside lamp; fixing a shelf; repairing a door-bell; unblocking a drain; sweeping a chimney; cutting kindling; advising on income tax, benefits and allowances; making a will; planning requirements; the filling in of official forms; coping with finances, or dealing with insurance, rates or investments; writing letters, and caring for other relatives. (There are many other tasks that might apply locally.)

Operation: recruitment to HelPeR would be only from retired, qualified professional persons. No payment for services rendered would be accepted.

Any donations received would be pooled in a fund to purchase tools and necessary materials and no HelPeR volunteer would benefit financially in any way. Where a problem was beyond the scope of HelPeR, efforts would be made to obtain the best solution at the least possible cost.

Every pensioner would be issued with the address and telephone number of the HelPeR team in their area. These would also be supplied to Women's Institutes, old people's centres, Citizen's Advice Bureaux, church councils, etc.

Coordination of the HelPeR scheme would be by the County or District Council.

A set of regulations would be drawn up which would govern the actions of every participant in the HelPeR scheme – both the professional volunteers and the beneficiaries.

Funding: this should come initially from local councils to cover publicity, postage, printing, etc, the DSS and from individual contributions.

Hugh Stapleton, Glenbervie, Mary's Well, Illogan, Redruth, Cornwall TR16 4EG (tel 0209 842201 and 717111).

Grannycare shops

MargaretChisman

Adapted from a submission to the Institute.

I suggest a new chain of shops called Vint Age, as a Grannycare version of Mothercare shops, which would become a focus and provide a real service to pensioners. The age market is growing and many a younger relative would be glad to shop with a specialised firm for presents for their older relatives. These shops could also provide refreshments in the afternoons in surroundings with no shiny plastic, Muzak or fruit machines.

I suggest also that a company be set up with a name such as Vint Age Toys, to research into and manufacture toys for older folk (which could be sold in the Vint Age shops). For instance, it should not be technologically impossible to produce a curled-up, natural-looking cat, powered by solar batteries, that would purr when stroked, move its claws and fit nicely in one's lap. Not all older folk are in a position to keep a pet, but they have been shown to benefit from stroking furry, responsive animals. Why not? Businessmen have clever executive toys and children invent their own if deprived.

Margaret Chisman, The Bungalow, near the Station, Tring, Herts, HP23 5QX (tel 044282 3281).

Bringing elderly people into schools

CSV have launched their Open Doors programme, whereby elderly people are encouraged to take an active part in schools. In the pilot project, at Benwell Primary School in Newcastle, the elders taught and participated in corn dolly making, french knitting, paper bead making and cookery. A group of elders joined in the school assembly once each fortnight and they were invited to any 'special events' at the school. They also joined together in drama activities to help make the past seem more alive.

'Tom Callaghan had actually attended the school as a child. Most of his life had been spent as a tramp on the road'

For instance, Tom Callaghan had actually attended the school as a child. Most of his life had been spent as a tramp on the road. He was introduced to the class as a tramp who wanted to get into the workhouse they were managing. 'How could I find it difficult to play a role which I had played in real life?' Tom remarked, and the teacher told how 'the children, and myself, of course, had very stereotyped ideas about what we thought a tramp should be.' First of all he recounted what life was like being out on the streets, and the children wrote stories for him. The drama led to Tom doing other things with the children, helping them with their manuscripts and even going on field trips with them.

A tape slide show and a report about 'Open Doors' are available from Eileen Flemming, CSV Education, 237 Pentonville Road, London N1 9NJ (tel 071 278 6601).

Linking young and old

Adapted extracts from Time (USA), monitored for the Institute by Roger Knights.

• A day-care centre for young and old alike has been set up by Stride Rite Corporation of Cambridge, Massachussetts, who are the first private company to establish this type of facility. The $700,000 pilot programme consists of adjoining centres that allow easy mingling and interaction between 55 children, from 18 months to five years old, and 24 elders over

60. Separated only by windows and hallways, the old and the young have plenty of opportunities to visit one another. Shared activities such as cooking and birthday parties are planned by the staff, but informal get-togethers happen spontaneously.

> 'Separated only by windows and hallways, the old and the young have plenty of opportunities to visit one another'

• Linking Lifetimes is a programme which brings retirees together with at-risk teenagers. It is being launched in nine US cities.

• In Omaha and seven other cities, elderly volunteers visit regularly with chronically ill children in a programme called Family Friends.

• At the Point Park College Children's School in Pittsburgh, some pre-schoolers are being taught about ageing by staff members, who are all over 55. The teachers use activities like planting seeds to illustrate the stages of the life cycle.

> 'Toddlers from a local day-care centre spend time with Alzheimer's patients after being read such books as "Grandpa Doesn't Know It's Me" '

• In one Pennsylvania programme, toddlers from a local day-care centre spend time with Alzheimer's patients after being read such books as 'Grandpa Doesn't Know It's Me'.

• Youngsters also learn that death is a natural component of life. Generations Together is developing a curriculum dealing with separation and loss. It will help children cope not only with an elderly companion's demise but also with other issues, like their parents' divorce or the loss of a favourite pet.

Grandparents for latch-key kids

Adapted extract from Lawrence-Journal World (USA).

33 stringently selected volunteer housebound grannies and grandpas in Chicago run a telephone advice service for latch-key kids, from 3pm to 6pm daily. Between 300 to 500 calls per month are handled, covering subjects such as attack from bullies and girls who think they are pregnant.

The service uses a commercial answering service and a well-publicised phone number, with the calls transferred though to an on-duty volunteer at home, without re-dialling.

Grandparents keep a daily log of the calls and evaluate questions and answers at the end of each day to a clinical psychologist who is a staff member.

Topics are discussed at three conferences per year for the participating grandparents. They are also put through a training programme, with written materials to be learned and procedures to be practised in simulated calls.

To preserve anonymity, only first names are used on the phone, with participants discouraged from giving addresses.

The programme has been running for more than two years and is now going national.

Adoptive grandparents for single parents

Vivienne Marks

From a letter to the Institute.

I would like to see a different approach in cases where a young girl becomes pregnant and, for one reason or another, does not have the support of family.

> 'Adopting the *mother* and taking a grandparents' role in respect of the child'

Why not allow not-so-young couples to foster the girl with the ultimate idea of adopting the *mother* and taking a grandparents' role in respect of the child?

> 'Enable the girl to continue schooling'

This would:

(a) Give the girl security and support during pregnancy;

(b) Avoid the problems for mother and child consequent on parting them, or of being a one-parent family; and

(c) Enable the girl to continue schooling or training where appropriate, or to start a career.

There must surely be some couples around who have missed out on parenthood and would be mature enough to take the two to their hearts. If the relationship did not work out in the long run, the mother would be free, at the age of 18, to leave, but it would still have been a worthwhile experience for the couple, even with the danger of being hurt. The rewards of success would be great.

Vivienne Marks, Little Grove Cottage, Waldron, Heathfield, East Sussex TN21 ORB (tel 043 53 2840).

Elderly sharing housing with younger housemates

Adapted extract from an article in Newsweek (USA), monitored for the Institute by Roger Knights.

77 year old widower Walter Smith, threatened by escalating property taxes in Vermont, and by house maintenance costs, now shares the extra rooms in his house with housemates – a middle-aged couple, an old farmhand and a college student. He was matched with them by a Vermont project called SHARE (Shared Housing Alternatives for Rural Elders). Sharing can keep an elderly person from going to a nursing home; Walter Smith's housemates keep track of him and he reciprocates.

> 'Sharing can keep an elderly person from going to a nursing home'

A similar group called Philadelphia Match can place a person in shared housing for a cost of about $500. By comparison, the US Department of Housing and Urban Development's average cost for a new unit of housing comes closer to $70,000. So it is a very cost-effective way of creating housing.

Care and Repair

The organisation Care and Repair has produced a guide entitled 'Improving Matters' to enable people to set up and run agencies which advise elderly, younger disabled and other low-income households. These agencies organise the finance and building work to make repairs and adaptations possible.

A Care and Repair worker comments that 'a disproportionate amount of Britain's oldest and poorest housing is occupied by elderly people, many of whom have worked a lifetime to own their own homes, only to find that it all turns to nightmare as the costs of maintenance and repair outstrip declining disposable income.'

> 'A disproportionate amount of Britain's oldest and poorest housing is occupied by elderly people – the costs of maintenance and repair outstrip their declining disposable income'

Care and Repair will advise those willing to set up services and support staff. It provides a regular newsletter.

'Improving Matters' is published by Care and Repair and is available at £10 (incl. p&p) from 22a The Ropewalk, Nottingham NG1 5DT (tel 0602 799091; fax 0602 859457).

Mother/Father Swap

Patricia Troop

People who have an elderly parent living with them might swap (probably temporarily) their parent, thus giving a change which might prove refreshing from all participants' points of view.

> 'People who have an elderly parent living with them might swap (probably temporarily) their parent, thus giving a change which might prove refreshing'

To get this idea going one would need some form of publicity and an agency, or a column in 'Exchange and Mart', 'Loot' or a daily or evening or local paper.

If I had the inclination to go into business I could set up an agency myself, because I think that in the long run it would be profitable.

One way of introducing the idea would be a short talk on Woman's Hour, but actually one would probably need to get one or two people to try it out first, so that experience would show likely hazards and benefits and provide the initial impetus to get others to try.

Eventually, local Social Services might run a register of names of those willing to move or be moved for a period of time – two weeks, a month or whatever.

Patricia Troop, 42 Elizabeth St, London SW1W 9NZ (tel 071 730 5189).

The Pet Fostering Service Scotland

Kathleen Grieve MBE

The Pet Fostering Service Scotland got off the ground in February 1985 and was created to fill a very real gap in provision for elderly pet owners who find themselves in a crisis situation such as illness.

> 'Pet fostering for when, for any reason, the owner is temporarily unable to care for the animal'

Current research indicates that elderly people in particular can benefit socially, physically and psychologically from a relationship with a pet, but many are deterred from owning a companion animal by their worry as to what would happen to it if they were to take ill. The Pet Fostering Service Scotland was created to remove the worry and the stress which arises when, for any reason, the owner is temporarily unable to care for the animal. It is also designed to reduce the stress which the pet undergoes through separation from its owner.

316 volunteers throughout Scotland have offered their homes and foster care to animals in this situation. Social work departments and health boards have been advised of the service which is already widely used and appreciated. The only cost to the owner is for food. This is part of a policy designed to keep the owner in touch with the pet throughout the period of separation. Those who undertake the fostering service are encouraged to keep in touch with the owner either by letter or where possible by visiting, with or without the pet, depending upon the enlightenment of the hospital authorities. Some long-term friendships have been established and this has been a bonus.

In the event of the owner's death or being too frail to care for the pet on discharge from hospital, or perhaps being put into residential care where no pets are allowed, arrangements for adoption are made, and in twelve cases the fosterer has adopted the pet in his or her care. The pet has found a loving home but the Pet Fostering Service has lost one.

Without the help of the Scottish Health Education Group and of Network Scotland Ltd, which provided free accommodation and the use of facilities, the Service could not have developed as it has. Help the Aged has made a generous grant and support has also come from Pedigree pet food and the Tailwaggers Club Trust. Glasgow University Vet Students adopted the Service as one of their charities.

Since its inception, over 1,000 approaches have been made to the service – by community and hospital social workers, doctors, home-makers, health visitors, nurses, homeless units, prisons, wardens in sheltered housing, relatives, etc. More than 800 pets have been fostered, some more than once; advice has been given and other arrangements made in over 500 cases, and many requests for help in walking a dog have been met.

The reasons for fostering have varied from illness to bereavement, from homelessness to short-term prison sentences, from short rehabilitation holidays arranged by social workers, to removal of a dog at a doctor's request to identify an allergy. The main thrust has been, and will continue to be, towards elderly owners and their companion animals.

Organisers for Pet Fostering Service Scotland have now been appointed for almost all the regions in Scotland and for the divisions of Strathclyde. These are responsible for arranging fosterings locally – each organiser has been provided with a telephone answering machine and appropriate forms to record requests for help, the reasons for the request, the duration of fosterings and comments on the outcome.

The co-ordinator of the Pet Fostering Service Scotland is Mrs Shelly Constantine, Arrats Mill, Brechin, Angus, Scotland (tel 067 481 356). Mrs Kathleen Grieve MBE, who helped initiate the service, is at 13 Montgomerie Terrace, Ayr KA7 1JL, Scotland (tel 0292 261768). The service won a Social Inventions Award.

The indoor milk indicator

To help the milkman and the householder, the indoor milk indicator consists of large red numbers, about four inches high, which can be hung up inside a window, facing outwards, to indicate how many pints of milk to leave (with '0' meaning 'no milk today' and '?' meaning 'please call or see message').

'It can be seen by the milkman from his vehicle'

The advantages are: it avoids the vandalism and tampering that affect outdoor indicators; it suits the aged or infirm, who otherwise have to go outside in the cold, wet or dark; and it can be seen by the milkman from his vehicle before reaching your door.

'I invented the Hang-Up Milk Indicator,' writes Mr Smith, 'when I carried out a milk round and experienced the many problems faced by householders, particularly the aged and infirm.' He has a prototype kit and would like help putting it on the market.

A.J.Smith, 58 Eastwood Road, Bramley, Surrey, GU5 ODU.

Rehearsing for old age

A workshop for nurses at Victoria Hospital, Accrington, Lancashire, gave nurses an insight into the feelings of elderly patients. Frances Biley reported in the Nursing Times: 'Participants were asked to tie their legs together, place cotton wool plugs in their ears and wear spectacles with the lenses obscured. Music was played, a TV turned on and I was pulled out of my chair, led about the room and introduced to people. I was left to wander aimlessly about, painfully bumping into furniture, before being pushed into a chair. All sense of time was lost, my feelings became introverted and I began to resent any intrusion into my own safe world.'

'Participants were asked to tie their legs together, place cotton wool plugs in their ears and wear spectacles with the lenses obscured'

After the half hour exercise, Biley and her colleagues realised the necessity for change in their approach to the care of their elderly patients.

Touch and teddy bears for the elderly
Mrs Burnes

Something cuddly, preferably teddy bears, should be given to the very elderly patients who revert to childlike needs in geriatric wards and old people's homes.

My aunt at 97, who was fortunate enough to be in a private home with all the comforts, had her teddy bear (purchased when she was admitted) always on her lap. Another elderly relative, who had been in a geriatric ward for many years, only showed any recognition or delight when her hand was held. Nurses have so little time to hold hands; something soft and cuddly would begin to fill the gap. Perhaps the parliamentary Lords and Commons Bear Den, which collects bears for children in hospital, could extend the good work.

I am sure that you are also aware of the success of volunteers, taking their dogs to visit old people's homes. 'Something to touch' has proved a great success.

Mrs Burnes, 5 Firlands, Harmans Water, Bracknell, Berkshire RG12 3SB (tel 0344 425294).

Visits to the elderly from P.A.T. Dogs
Michaela Edridge

Adapted from a piece by Edridge, with additional information from the Examiner (USA), monitored for the Institute by Roger Knights.

An old lady is sitting in a lounge in a home for the elderly. She is totally withdrawn into herself. She has no friends and no relations to visit her, except maybe once a year.

She has given up talking to anyone, she has nothing left to live for. Her past life has faded into a blur, so even her memories are shadows. Every single day is the same as the one before.

'One day something unusual happens that she cannot help noticing. There is a dog in the room, a large golden dog that wags its tail'

One day something unusual happens that she cannot help noticing. There is a dog in the room, a large golden dog that wags its tail and comes up to nuzzle her hand. She cries, because suddenly she remembers her old dog and how she had to leave it when she came to the home. But the tears are a release, and the dog becomes her friend who comes to see her every week, with the kind lady who owns him.

The dog is a P.A.T. Dog, a PRO-Dog Active Therapy visiting dog, one of over 4,500 who regularly visit the sick, the elderly, the mentally disturbed, the blind, the deaf, in homes and hospitals all over the United Kingdom.

The whole thing started in 1976 when Lesley Scott Ordish, a magistrate and freelance journalist, decided to form a national charity to counteract the growing intolerance to dogs in our society; to promote better understanding and attitudes; to encourage better dog ownership; to take educational programmes into schools; and to provide medical and veterinary advice and information in a realistic and useful way. PRO Dogs stands for Public Relations Organisation for Dogs.

In June 1983, the first pilot for PAT Dogs took place in Derbyshire. Even Lesley Scott Ordish could not have dreamed that this would grow to the extent that PRO-Dogs have now registered over 4,500 PAT Dogs. These dogs are temperament-tested, registered and provided with an identification disc, and are then sent to visit homes and hospitals nearby. There are local PAT Dog coordinators in most areas to ensure that everything runs smoothly. The coordinators are in touch with all the homes and all the visiting teams.

> **'When a patient looks at a dog, strokes him and talks to him, the blood pressure goes down, temperature decreases and a sense of well-being increases'**

PAT Dog visiting fulfils a very important need. So many people have to part with their pets when they go into homes. Many of them become withdrawn, morose and unhappy. On many occasions the visits have changed the lives and improved the happiness of the elderly in institutions. It gives them a point of communication, and it has been proved and well documented that physical contact with a pet is therapeutic. An inherent trait in humans is the need for attachment to others. Visiting dogs, who always visit on a regular basis, provide that attachment. When a patient looks at a dog, strokes him and talks to him, the blood pressure goes down, temperature decreases and a sense of well-being increases. PAT Dogs provide the undiscriminating affection that everyone needs.

Likewise in the States there are 8,000 registered therapy dogs, according to Paula Cingota, who runs the San Diego branch of Therapy Dogs International, each insured for $1 million, and with some working with terminal cancer patients in hospices.

- *Lesley Scott-Ordish, Rocky Bank, 4 New Road, Ditton, Maidstone, Kent ME20 7AD (tel 0730 848499). This scheme was a highly commended Social Inventions Award winner.*
- *Michaela Edridge, 267 Hillbury Road, Warlingham, Surrey CR3 9TL.*
- *Society for Companion Animal Studies, c/o Anne Docherty, The Mews Cottage, 7 Botanic Crescent Lane, Glasgow G20 8AA (tel 041 9452088).*

Bedtime service

Louise Close

We have pioneered this service for putting people to bed in the inner city in Belfast.

The service is coordinated by an organiser, but depends on volunteers who feel they can commit some time in the evenings on a regular basis to befriend and aid an elderly person with their bed-time routine.

Some elderly people who live alone find the effort of getting to bed too much and rely on family or nursing services. This may mean they have to be in bed at an early hour, or it may mean a constant strain on even the most caring of relatives.

The Bedtime Service aims to relieve relatives and allow the elderly person to retire at a more appropriate hour.

> **'Volunteers commit some time in the evenings on a regular basis to befriend and aid an elderly person with their bed-time routine'**

Louise Close, Bedtime Service, Bryson House, 28 Bedford Street, Belfast, BT2 7FE (tel 0232 325835 ext 29).

National Bed Line

National Bed Line provides useful information, mainly to welfare organisations, on the availability of patient and residential vacancies in the private sector (residential homes, nursing homes and private hospitals nationally). The service is free of charge and 'calls are answered by experienced nurses and additional information on the Homes is available, such as fees, number of floors, lifts, etc.'

National Bed Line, tel 0626 51896.

Checklist of questions for residential homes

The following are a list of questions that are worth bearing in mind when selecting or evaluating a particular residential home (whether it is a home for the elderly or established for therapeutic, medical or other reasons).

This checklist is drawn from a much longer list prepared by one of the Institute's correspondents, who has asked, for professional reasons, to remain anonymous. It is designed primarily for use by official visitors to residential homes run by local authorities and statutory agencies.

(1) What activities are residents engaged in at the time of your visit?

(2) How do residents seem to respond to your visit? Interested? Pleased? Apathetic? Resentful? Resigned?

(3) How many residents have significant contact with family, friends or former neighbours?

(4) How many go away at least some weekends?

(5) Do residents hold their own room and front door keys? If not, how are nights out managed?

(6) Do residents have their own coffee mugs?

(7) Do residents have any say in choice of decor?

(8) How many residents have single rooms? Can they bring their own belongings? How much storage space does each resident have?

(9) Are menus clearly posted? What allowances are made for special diets? Are residents allowed in the kitchen?

(10) What facilities exist for residents to make snacks or drinks out of hours?

(11) Is there a payphone? If not, can residents receive calls?

(12) Are there quiet areas where residents can read, study, meet visitors, etc?

(13) Does each resident have a drawer that will lock?

(14) Does the home smell of urine, disinfectant and polish,

or like an ordinary home?

(15) What is the staff-resident ratio?

(16) Do the care staff wear overalls or 'civvies'?

(17) Is there 'parity' in the way staff address residents and vice versa: ie if staff use residents' christian names, do residents use staff christian names also?

'Does the home smell of urine, disinfectant and polish, or like an ordinary home?'

(18) Are residents observably talking to each other?

(19) Is there a 'Friends' support group?

(20) Do reports of the home's social activities appear in the local press?

(21) Is there provision for residents' friends and relatives to meet with the resident privately? Is there, at low cost, a guest room for overnight or weekend visits?

(22) Are prospective residents encouraged to make an overnight or weekend stay before deciding to come into residence?

(23) Are the expressions 'good boy!' or 'good girl!' used in connection with adult residents?

(24) Do residents have a grievance procedure and is it made clear to them what it is?

(25) Is there a suggestions box?

(26) What contacts exist with the local neighbours, shop-keepers, churches, pubs, etc?

(27) What links exist with, for example, the local further education college, practising artists, schools, local radio, community service volunteers?

(28) Are questionnaires ever issued to residents for their evaluation of the service they receive?

A cardinal feature of all institutions is their tendency to take on a life of their own. Thus each establishment has, in addition to its overt task, a hidden agenda: the securing of its own survival and the perpetuation of its own ethos and norms. Residents who subscribe or at least conform to these are considered 'good'. Those who do not, are seen as 'having problems'.

Any residential worker knows the extent of the power of the principal officer, officer-in-charge or matron of the establishment. Even progressive local authorities whose professional managers have clearly defined the tasks of each establishment and who monitor closely their performance, often find it difficult to ascertain exactly what is going on in their minds at any particular time. The power of the people in charge is not absolute, but in relation to their residents it is enormous.

It is difficult to over-estimate the defensiveness of both the staffs and the senior and middle managements of council-provided homes. Perhaps admitting to shortcomings, failures and mistakes in the provision and running of a home carries emotive connotations of being a bad parent and this makes objective assessment difficult.

The checklist could in time form the basis of a data-collecting exercise and could prove to be an effective 'change agent' within individual homes.

The suggestion at present, however, is to read through the checklist before a visit, and then discard it. A little gentle probing, in residential life, goes a long way. Abrasive and over-detailed interrogations could be counter-productive.

Residents rule – OK?

Dr David Chapman

The media have revealed the neglect, bad conditions and even serious abuse and violence, suffered by residents in at least some of the privately owned homes for the elderly. The government is providing £500 million a year for this private care, and is clearly not getting good value for the money. Various suggestions have been made to remedy this, such as: more effective inspection; an independent complaints procedure for residents; better selection and training of managers of homes; and greater firmness by local authorities in shutting down homes where abuse occurs.

But helpful though these suggestions may be, they do not get to the root of the problem, which is that the home receives from the DHSS an unconditional £130 per week per resident, however well or badly the residents are treated. The home thus has little incentive to provide better conditions than that minimum (evidently very low) which would avoid getting the home closed down.

'A bonus fund, to be divided between the different homes according to how well they were rated by their respective residents'

I therefore propose that the home should unconditionally receive only part of the payment – let us say £100. The remaining £30 should go into a 'bonus fund', to be divided between the different homes according to how well they were rated by their respective residents. Thus while the average home would still get £130, an unsatisfactory home would get less, and a good one more.

The residents of a home would be given (perhaps once a month or once a quarter) the opportunity of recording a rating, between zero and 100, reflecting the satisfaction of the resident with the running of the home. It would be given in a secret ballot, run by some impartial outside body (perhaps Age Concern), to avoid any chance of pressure on residents from the management of the home. In giving his/her rating, a resident may be assisted by another person, who could be a relative or friend, or another resident, but must not, of course, be one of the home staff.

For each home, its average rating would be calculated. The home would then receive a share of the bonus fund in proportion to its number of residents, multiplied by its average rating.

Persons should be allowed to choose at which home they should live and they should be allowed to change from one home to another without difficulty. To help them in this choice, the average rating of each home should be made publicly known and a Consumers' Guide could be published. Thus dissatisfied residents would tend to move from homes with a low rating to homes with a high rating. An unsatisfactory home would not only get a lower payment per resident, but would also tend actually to lose its residents, and this would put added pressure on it to improve its conditions.

But, it has been objected, would not the scheme deter the management from taking measures which were good for the residents, even though against their wishes? This seems a somewhat paternalistic objection. If the staff think they know what is best, they should seek as far as possible to convince the residents before taking action.

Again, it has been objected that a confused elderly person might be incapable of making a sensible rating. But in this situation, the rating could be made by a relative or friend, according to their judgement of how well the person was being treated. In any case, there is no reason to deny the non-confused majority the opportunity to affect the conditions under which they have to live.

The case for the scheme is that it would give each home a strong incentive to provide conditions agreeable to its residents. It would seek a higher rating, not only to get higher payments, but also to get public recognition of its good work. This scheme seems likely to bring about a great increase in the welfare of our old people, in return for increasing public spending only by the small amount needed to conduct the ratings ballot.

David Chapman, Democracy Design Forum, Coles Centre, Buxhall, Stowmarket, Suffolk IP14 3EB (tel 0449 736 223).

Alternative suggestions by David Scott

David Scott argues that Dr Chapman's scheme would be 'costly to administer, with increased bureaucracy and serious reduction in cash flow' for needy 'poor' homes; and that there would also be the danger of residents voting in favour of mediocre accommodation without having other institutions to compare with. He makes a number of alternative proposals:

• An award for homes which meet high standards. Inspections by a panel coupled to a controlled questionnaire to residents and staff. Also a certificate of good residential care, and a Queen's Award for services to the elderly or handicapped.

> 'A certificate of good residential care, and a Queen's Award for services to the elderly'

• Regular inspection of all residential homes by an independent panel of local people to include Age Concern, local nurses, and other elderly people. Include local authority residential homes and provide the panel of visitors with the power to close all unsatisfactory accommodation, or to take over the management.

• Training for managers and staff to be compulsory and only certificated persons to be allowed to manage (after a reasonable transition period).

• Define standards of food, hygiene, laundry, bedding and so on, and appoint a senior executive of Trust House Forte to administer the programme of basic standards in the manner adopted by franchise holders such as 'Little Chef'.

• Encourage WRVS, Red Cross and St John Ambulance to participate in the day to day management of all local residential homes in order to harness local experience and skills for the benefit of the community.

• All residential homes in receipt of public funds to be fully accountable by annual budget, and audited quarterly out-turn figures to an independent local committee for residential homes drawn from local caring agencies, including representation by residents or their next of kin.

David Scott, National Association of Almshouses, Billingbear Lodge, Wokingham, Berkshire RG11 5RU tel 0344 52922).

Response by David Chapman

David Scott objects that my proposals would be costly and bureaucratic, and then goes on to propose a raft of highly expensive measures whereby some external bureaucracy could inspect homes, impose training, define and administer standards of food and materials, audit the accounts and so on. The fundamental problem is the utter powerlessness of old people in these homes under the present structure. Scott's proposals, if we could afford them, would do nothing to correct this.

Homes for the elderly who share same interests
Gregory Wright

Why not establish nursing homes and senior residences which accept residents based on their sharing a range of interests, hobbies, past careers and backgrounds? For example, there could be a Gardeners' Home, an Artists' Home, a Readers' Home, an Animal Lovers' Home. The residents of these themed homes might find life a lot more worth continuing, and more conducive to personal growth and health in an environment of shared interests and accumulated knowledge. The staff could be selected according to *their* similar interests too.

Gregory Wright, 14161 Riverside Drive, #3, Sherman Oaks, California 91423, USA (tel 818 784 0325).

Group homes for elderly people from black and racial minorities
Robin Currie

This social invention has established a new approach to community care for elderly people from racial minorities. The scheme has arisen out of an awareness of the failure of existing provision to meet individual needs adequately and sensitively.

Research showed that there was an extremely low take-up of welfare services by black elderly people. When they were unable to continue to live at home, the option of residential care was of a traditional kind in an old people's home, where care staff and other residents had little understanding of someone with a different cultural background, diet and language. Frail, elderly people were therefore often being faced with an isolated existence in an alien environment.

> 'The house was designed around the needs of the three individual people who would be living there. This necessitated for example the provision of a prayer room'

The new scheme set up by PSS (the Liverpool Personal Service Society) provides a social worker who works closely with recognised racial minority community associations and housing associations to establish small (three or four bedded) sheltered group homes for elderly people in the Liverpool area. The scheme aims to provide flexibility, with the design of the accommodation and the level of care provided varying according to need. In the first stage of the scheme, which has been set up with the Somali community, the house was designed around the needs of the three individual people who would be living there. This necessitated, for example, the provision of a prayer room. It has also meant that a Somali carer is employed to visit and provide help to the residents on a daily basis. The carer is able to talk with the residents in their own language, and understands their dietary and cultural needs.

The Society has now opened similar homes for elderly people from the Caribbean community and one for Chinese elderly.

The extent of the need for the provision of meals and care within the homes will be dependent on individual circumstances. Provision can be increased, if and when people become more frail, and may, if necessary, include a resident carer. One of the attractive features of the scheme is that it will enable a range of care to be provided within one particular setting. It offers an important opportunity to develop forms of care that are sensitive to individual language, cultural and religious differences, and that are responsive to the expressed needs of elderly people from racial minority groups.

Robin Currie, director, PSS, 18-28 Seel Street, Liverpool L1 4BE (tel 051 707 0131). This scheme won a Social Inventions Award.

Nature reserves with homes for the retired

Stanley Slee

Extracts from a proposal for a scheme for retired owner occupiers – but one that could easily be adapted for subsidised, rented or institutionalised accommodation.

This idea has come to me as I have been trying to come to terms with the fact that much as we still prize our home, and the space, beauty and birdlife that we have enjoyed here for over thirty years, we no longer need the spacious converted barn and enormous garden, and are no longer physically capable of looking after them adequately. However, having said this, I find it difficult even to consider the idea of spending the rest of my life in a tiny house or flat with little or no garden and no intimate relationship with any wildlife or practical association with the desperate needs and problems of our environment.

> 'What a joy it would be to move into a smaller dwelling unit, set within a newly created, tiny bird sanctuary and nature reserve'

What a joy it would be (for the elderly) to move into a smaller dwelling unit, set within a newly created, tiny bird sanctuary and nature reserve.

The project would be self-financing by the sale of these dwelling units, a dozen or so per reserve. The title deeds would grant exclusive rights to the ownership of the dwelling unit and the relatively small private garden area immediately surrounding it, together with an entitlement to share in the use and enjoyment of the whole of the wildlife area of the reserve, and membership of the committee of 'fellow owners', responsible for the planning and management of the whole project.

The residents would quickly form a homogenous group, working together (if they had the ability and the inclination), creating and maintaining the surroundings – which could also make a suitable setting for stroke patients or the disabled. I anticipate that there would be a rush of applicants for places, once the first of these projects had become fully functional.

Within each reserve it would be necessary to construct a network of sound, all-weather walkways, each wide enough to accommodate wheelchairs, and these would criss-cross the whole of the area and link in all the dwelling units. Some of these walkways could be bordered by plants set out to provide a feast of colour or scent, with the effect accentuated by interplanting spectacular garden varieties of native trees, shrubs and climbers.

It will be essential to include within the nature reserve a selection of realistic small glades and varied patches of impenetrable thickets. The immediate aim must be to reproduce a wide range of settings within which a variety of resident birds and returning migrants might be attracted, and where all suitable varieties of native plants will flourish, act as hosts and sustain all possible varieties of native insects.

Stanley Slee, French's Farm, Hempstead, Saffron Walden, Essex CB10 2NZ (tel 079986 284). This proposal won a Social Inventions Award.

Housing for carers

Christian Claridge

This is a proposal for Medically Assisted Sheltered Housing (MASH), for couples where one falls sick and needs professional care – and would otherwise have been admitted to a long-stay hospital.

The local authorities, district health authorities or housing associations could provide flats or bungalows for rent near hospitals or health centres. The couple move in. Financially, they may either be eligible for housing benefit or have sold a property and bought an annuity (which provides the income to pay the rent) or have arranged a reversionary mortgage.

The sick partner would be cared for not only by the spouse but also by a nurse. The spouse would cook, clean (with the aid of a home help if applicable) and would be there to feed their sick partner if necessary. The nurse would bed-make with the aid of the spouse, would help give the patient a bath and all the necessary treatment.

An estimated nurse to patient ratio of 7.32 per 12 patients would be required, as against 1 per 2.5 patients in a long-stay hospital.

The carers of the sick would have communal areas to use: a restaurant and sitting room. There could be film shows, entertainments, whist drives and organised outings to keep up interest and morale – all organised by the fit for the less fit; with perhaps one of the fit acting as general secretary of the housing association.

The atmosphere would not be institutional but rather

residential with club facilities. Long-stay hospitalisation leads to lack of personal caring, loss of control of daily living, boredom, disorientation then confusion and even incontinence.

And one of the saddest sights is an old man staggering up to hospital to visit an old wife and just sitting by her in the alien atmosphere, uncommunicating, unoccupied.

> ## 'One of the saddest sights is an old man staggering up to hospital to visit an old wife and just sitting by her in the alien atmosphere, uncommunicating, unoccupied'

Christian Claridge, St Martin's House, St Martin's Avenue, Canterbury, Kent (tel 0227 464241).

Retirement Security

Retirement Security have a very sheltered housing scheme, aiming to keep people independent until they die, although not targeted on those who would otherwise be in hospital.

Retirement Security, run by Bob Bessell, has built three developments of 40 to 55 units in Stratford-upon-Avon, Redditch, Wokingham, Hove, Milton Keynes and Sutton Coldfield, with others building in Reading, Hinckley, Lewes, and planned in Manchester and Northampton.

Each of the developments observes the same rules: no unit is on more than one floor, all corridors, doors and lifts are wheelchair-wide and physical aids are a standard feature. Owners own their services as a cooperative, which the company runs for them. Three wardens alternate day-time duties and one stays at night. One half-day's home help is included in the service charge and there is a restaurant on site. In addition to buying their property (ranging from £50,000 in the North to £119,000 in the South), each owner pays a £36 a week service charge. Residents can stay until they die.

Retirement Security, 15 Boult St, Reading, Berks (tel 0734 503745; fax 0734 508729).

Magic Me

'We need heroes. We need people whom we revere, whose values we internalise and whose actions we emulate,' says Bill Berkowitz, author of 'Local Heroes – the Rebirth of Heroism in America'. He has interviewed 22 'ordinary' Americans who lacked any extraordinary resources or expertise at the outset, and yet whose heroic actions have helped to transform their communities. One of his hero's local initiatives has since been copied internationally:

Kathy Levin founded her 'Magic Me' organisation in Baltimore in 1982. 'Magic Me' trains children aged 10 to 13 to make contact with residents in homes for elderly people.

Levin had been distressed to find that many people in their fifties were no longer visiting their relatives in homes, and 'it occurred to me,' she says, 'wouldn't it be fun to teach a little group of kids who could grow up to be fifty year olds who could see through the wrinkles and tears from an early age and really see nursing homes differently?' She wanted to reassure children that 'it's really valid to stay in touch with the part of you that's scared about being mortal. The old and the isolated keep us vulnerable and raw and feeling and unpredictable and alive. To me that's the essence of our humanness, scary and delightful.'

From a background in advertising, Levin knew that she needed to give her project just the right image to attract the kids. She lured them with a trendy Magic Me T-shirt of a purple child juggling a rainbow; and she wrote and staged a Magic Me musical for the kids (the latest version of which has songs by twenty top Broadway composers). 1,500 kids watched her first performance – 'many of them were crying and happy and really excited by it.'

The next stage was to hold training seminars in the classroom, where she answered some of their worst fears about the project, such as 'what happens if somebody dies when we're with them'; and she got them to experience some of the limitations of age, by putting them in wheelchairs and having them bind their hands, and walk around with weights on their legs, blindfolded, and with cotton wool in their ears.

> ## 'Four or five of the residents get up out of their wheelchairs and move and dance with the children to the Michael Jackson music'

At last they were ready for their first visit to a home. Music was playing. 10 year old Mac looks his elderly partner in the eye and says, 'Oh well, if you can't move your left side, it doesn't matter, you got a whole right side. Come on, I bet you can, I know you can.' Four or five of the residents get up out of their wheelchairs and move and dance with the children to the Michael Jackson music. It was for Levin a very moving moment: 'I think that human beings have an urge to transcend the bodily. The creative arts seem a quick way of doing this. Magic Me inspires children too to discover magic within themselves and thereby to transcend. When you see yourself in a wrinkled face you are expanded. When you have found your magic powers, you can release those of others.' For such children, says Levin, 'the mere thought of abandoning their aged relatives would be as repulsive as cutting off one's own arm.'

> ## 'When you see yourself in a wrinkled face you are expanded. When you have found your magic powers, you can release those of others'

Magic Me in the UK

In the UK, Magic Me works with children in Islington, Tower Hamlets and Westminster, using many art forms. Magic Me is now a registered UK charity and is active in homes and long-stay hospitals across Tower Hamlets. It seems to be succeeding on a long-term basis without depending entirely on Levin's own charisma and energy.

- *Susan Langford, Magic Me UK, Mile End Hospital, Bancroft Road, London E1 4DG (tel 071 377 7878).*
- *Magic Me USA, 808 North Charles Street, Baltimore, Maryland 21201, USA (tel 301 837 0900).*
- *'Local Heroes – The Rebirth of Heroism in America' by Bill Berkowitz, containing a long interview with Kathy Levin, is published by Lexington Books, D.C. Heath and Company, 125 Spring Street, Lexington, Massachusetts 02173, USA.*

Memory Box personal museums

Yvonne Malik

Many of us have keepsakes – things of no monetary value, but sentimental or nostalgic mementoes which stimulate our memories, such as old photos, letters, coins, tickets, keys, trinkets, crockery, ornaments, holiday souvenirs, scarves, ties, medals, certificates. Individually, they may seem small or insignificant, but put together in a display, these same objects could become a decorative and pleasing Personal Museum.

> 'The Memory (exhibition display) Boxes could be converted sewing boxes, tool boxes (the type which open up into two or three tiers), circular tea trays, or shallow suitcases'

The arrangements could be displayed inexpensively in, for instance, sewing boxes, biscuit tins, tool boxes (the type which open up into two or three tiers), circular tea trays, or shallow suitcases. These can be repainted and make excellent holders for three dimensional objects.

When we are old, is it necessary for us to sit like potted plants in silent immobile rows, communicating nothing of what we have been, like empty people waiting for the end?

Retirement and rest homes await many of us, offering little means of expressing life's experiences or of taking a pride in having survived at all.

With Memory Boxes we would have 'something to show for it.' An answer to several needs. The opportunity to communicate in non-verbal ways that: 'I was here; I did this; I learnt that; I did and do exist and live.' It answers too the need for reassurance in visual terms, emphasising, stimulating and drawing attention (through memories) to the length of life experienced (rather than the shorter length still anticipated).

Language is no barrier (unlike oral history). Pride can be taken in a tangible expression of one's past.

The collecting and putting together of possible objects could take place in our homes, by a group of friends, or could be carried out in a day centre, as part of art therapy, where the camaraderie of others similarly involved, could stimulate and encourage those with less initial confidence.

The participants will be surprised and pleased with the results, which could be exhibited in local libraries, etc, as a way of generating more awareness and interest from others – particularly those of the same generation.

Yvonne Malik has made her own Memory Box as an example. Her address is: 145 Walker Street, Rhodes, near Middleton, Manchester M24 4QF (tel 061 643 1461). This scheme was highly commended in the Social Inventions Awards.

Chapter twenty-four

DEATH AND DYING

The Natural Death Centre

Nicholas Albery

The Natural Death Centre is part of an educational charity and was launched in 1991, by four of us, all psychotherapists, who are its directors. It has as its overall aim to help improve 'the quality of dying'. It does so in three main ways:

Firstly, helping break the taboo about freely discussing death and dying – through dinner-discussions for all ages, meetings and contacts with the media.

Secondly, encouraging people to prepare for dying well in advance – through:

• All day workshops entitled 'Exploring Our Own Death';

• One-day course for those looking after a dying person at home (and for nurses);

• Collecting and publicising accounts of near-death experiences and dignified natural deaths;

• Helping people draw up 'living wills' which state how much high-tech medical intervention they want if suffering from a terminal illness;

• (In the longer term) building up a network of people, preferably people who have had near-death experiences themselves, who can act as informal 'midwives for the dying' and can give counselling and spiritual help (if desired) to the dying person and the family;

Thirdly, helping the average family take back control of the process of dying from the big institutions – through:

• Generating more support for those dying at home, both from the authorities and the surrounding neighbourhood, so that the majority of people can die at home in familiar surroundings, rather than in hospitals;

• Researching into the alleviation of suffering for the dying; and into alternatives to euthanasia such as fasting;

• Preparing a manual, 'The Natural Death Handbook';

• Drawing up a 'Declaration of the Dying Person's Rights';

• Campaigning with the Office of Fair Trading and others to ensure that funeral wholesalers and undertakers will supply just coffins, without charging an excessive mark-up, to those members of the public who wish to organise a funeral themselves; for a regulation similar to the 1984 American one compelling all funeral directors to give price breakdowns on request over the phone and written price lists to visitors; and for a Natural Death Law giving legal recognition to 'Living Wills'.

• Acting as a consumer body, available by phone or letter, for unbiased information, referrals and recommendations about, for instance, who are the good healers, counsellors, undertakers, etc throughout the UK, ideas and suggestions for new funeral rituals and how to get a cheap, green or 'DIY' funeral (see the article on this last below).

• Helping people to set up their own independently run Natural Death networks in their own regions or countries.

The Natural Death Centre, 20 Heber Road, London NW2 6AA (tel 081 208 2853; fax 081 452 6434). The Natural Death Handbook (published September 1993) can be ordered from this address for £13-95, incl. p&p.

How to support a dying person

The following are extracts from an interview by Libby Purves with Dr Robert Buckman in the Times about his book 'I Don't Know What to Say – How to Help and Support Someone who is Dying', published by Papermac, £6-95.

Six years ago Dr Buckman nearly died himself of a rare auto-immune disease. He recovered, and the experience gave him a certain strength in dealing with the pain of other people's last days, and above all a passionate desire to communicate one fact that he – although a determined atheist – sees as centrally important. 'Death ends life, but it does not rob it of its meaning. If you want to kill someone, you take the meaning from their life. When you're dying, you need to know that you have been, and will go on being, valuable.'

Above all he urges people to listen when the dying person wants to discuss funerals, or resuscitation or terminal pain, or how the family will get on without him, and to avoid at all costs phrases like 'Don't talk about that now.' He discusses with uncomfortable clarity the psychological pros and cons of trying for endless miracle cures from alternative medicines. 'The attitude of "I'll go anywhere and I'll try anything" has a price tag. The price is the loss of time to be close to each other, and the loss of that tenderness and sensitivity that might have been allowed to grow.'

He has seen as many ways of dying as there are of living. 'Let your friend go out of life in his own way: it may not be your way or the way you would like to see, and it may not be the way you read about in a book or magazine, but it's his way and consistent with the way he's lived his life.'

Scalp massage for the dying

Margaret Ryder

Last year a friend of mine died of cancer. She found it very difficult to open up or to ask for much. I offered to give her scalp massage. She loved it. She said it made her feel wonderful and I did it for her for many of her last days. It made her feel relaxed and cared for and sometimes she talked easily and personally – although I never pushed her to.

It was wonderful for me to have something to offer which she really wanted.

I think this idea could be valuable for other people. I did in fact go by invitation to a hospice where I demonstrated head massage to staff. They all loved it and decided firstly, to do it for one another; secondly, to help visitors to do it where they and the patients liked the idea; and thirdly, to help patients who wanted to do it for one another.

Some of the merits of the idea, in addition to those I have mentioned, are that patients do not have to undress, which would be a barrier for some. At the hospice I showed them head, neck, face and shoulder massage. Different people like all or some of these. Only a very few do not like any. This massage offers an easy way to have loving physical contact. It gives the patient a relaxing time and I suspect that many will find it a good time to talk: relaxed, loved, but not always looked at. (Some people, as a parallel example, will talk on a car journey where they have company but are not looked at.) It is easy to do once they have had it explained or (better) shown to them.

I have seen so many people sitting next to a dying person having run out of things to do, say or offer, and I feel that this idea might mean a lot to many people.

Margaret Ryder, c/o the Natural Death Centre, 20 Heber Road, London NW2 6AA (tel 081 208 2853; fax 081 452 6434).

Musical midwifery for the dying

Therese Schroeder-Sheker

Adapted extract from 'The Luminous Wound', an article printed in an interesting anthology of spiritual preparations for death published as a special issue of Caduceus magazine, Summer 1991, £2-50 (or £11-75 sub) from Caduceus, 38 Russell Terrace, Leamington Spa, Warks CV31 1HE, tel 0926 451897.

I call this work musical-sacramental-midwifery. I first began singing and playing for people who were near their transition when I was a mere girl, full of naivety and intuition, and had very little life experience. Now as a grown woman who has experienced so many kinds of death and tended the deaths of countless men and women, people urge me to write about some of the personal experiences about which I've remained silent.

'I began leaning down to his left ear and singing gregorian chant'

The first time that I was ever actually present and alone with someone who was in fact dying is the first time that I ever really experienced silence, and an indescribably delicate kind of light. The man was struggling, frightened, unable to breathe. No more respirators, dilators, tracheotomies or medicines could resolve his disintegrated lungs. He could take no more in, could swallow no more, and in his complete weariness, there was almost nothing he could return to the world. I climbed into his hospital bed and propped myself behind him in midwifery position, my head and heart lined up behind his, my legs folded near his waist, and I held his frail body by the elbows and suspended his weight. At first I held us both in interior prayer, but soon began leaning down to his left ear and singing gregorian chant almost pianissimo: the *Kyrie* from *the Mass of the Angels*, and *Adoro te devote*, the *Ubicaritas*, the *Salve Regina*.

'He immediately nestled in my arms and began to breathe regularly'

He immediately nestled in my arms and began to breathe regularly, and we, as a team, breathed together. It was as if the way in which sound anointed him now made up for the ways in which he had never been touched or returned touch while living the life of a man. The chants seemed to bring him balance, dissolving fears, and compensating for those issues still full of sting. How could they do anything less? These chants are the language of love. They carry the flaming power of hundreds of years and thousands of chanters who have sung these prayers before. It seemed that the two of us were not alone in that room. When his heart ceased to beat, I stayed still for long moments. Almost twenty years later, the silence that replaced his struggle and that was present in his room has continued to penetrate the core of my life, birthing stages of hearing that even now flower at unexpected times and places.

When you are really peacefully present with someone whose time has come, all that matters is that they shine through the matrix. People ask if a midwife knows fear or sorrow: none of that exists if you are with the dying person. It's their time, not yours. Any burden or sorrow or wounds of your own disappear. You hold the person and keep vigil while they quietly, almost invisibly, shimmer an indescribable membrane of light. If there is no tenderness in the room, this film dissolves unnoticed. If a midwife is practising inner emptiness, and is capable of profound stillness, she can guard this gossamer film for a moment or an hour. When a dying person's stillness fills the entire room, you can gently let go and lay them to rest. Then you thank them, again and gain, for affirming what is so bright.

Chalice midwives employ harp and voice in assisting the process of death and dying in home, hospital and hospice settings. Readers interested in recordings, publications or the Chalice of Repose training programme and internship may contact them at 4121 Grove Street, Denver, Colorado 80211 USA (tel 303 494 2643; fax 303 433 9053).

Dolphin 'therapy' for a dying child

Allegra Taylor

Adapted extract from a very moving book 'Acquainted with the Night – A Year on the Frontiers of Death' by Allegra Taylor, published 1989 by Fontana, £3-99, ISBN 0 00 637249 X.

This tale of transition and transformation was told me by Robert White, an American factory worker from North Carolina. The story had begun when Robert and his wife went to visit their daughter Lee in hospital as they did every evening.

'It's not easy to die when you are fifteen, but Lee had already accepted her fate,' said Robert. As he spoke, his eyes were full of tears and he could barely keep his voice steady. 'She knew she had an illness that would not spare her. She knew that in spite of their finest efforts the doctors couldn't save her. She suffered a lot but never complained. This particular evening she seemed tranquil and composed but suddenly she said, "Mama, Daddy – I think I'm going to die soon and I'm afraid. I know I'm going to a better world than this one and I'm longing for some peace at last but it's hard to accept the idea that I'm going to die at only fifteen."

'We could have lied, telling her of course she wasn't going to die, but we didn't have the heart. Somehow her courage was worth more than our pretence. We just cuddled her and cried together. Then she said, "I always dreamed of falling in love, getting married, having kids ... but above all I would have liked to work in a big marine park with dolphins. I've loved them and wanted to know more about them since I was little. I still dream of swimming with them free and happy in the open sea." She'd never ask for anything, but now she said with all the strength that she could muster, "Daddy, I want to swim in the open sea among the dolphins just once. Maybe then I wouldn't be so scared of dying."

'It seemed like an absurd, impossible dream but she, who had given up just about everything else, hung on to it.

'My wife and I talked it over and decided to do everything we could. We had heard of a research centre in the Florida Keys and we phoned them. "Come at once," they said. But that was easier said than done. Lee's illness had used up all our savings and we had no idea how we would be able to afford air tickets to Florida. Then our six year old, Emily, mentioned that she'd seen something on television about a foundation that grants the wishes of very sick children. She'd actually written down the telephone number in her diary because it seemed like magic to her.

'I didn't want to listen. I thought it sounded like a fairy tale or a very sick joke and I gave in only when Emily started crying and accusing me of not really wanting to help Lee. So I phoned the number and three days later we were all on our way. Emily felt a bit like a fairy god-mother who had solved all our problems with a wave of her magic wand.

'When we arrived at Grass Key, Lee was pale and terribly thin. The chemotherapy she'd been having had made all her hair fall out and she looked ghastly, but she didn't want to rest for a minute and begged us to take her straight to the dolphins. It was an unforgettable scene. When she got into the water, Lee was already so weak she hardly had the strength to move. We had to put her in a wet suit so she wouldn't get cold and a life preserver to keep her afloat.

'I towed her out towards the two dolphins, Nat and Tursi, who were frolicking around about thirty feet away from us. At first they seemed distracted and uninterested but when Lee called them softly by name they responded without hesitation. Nat came over first, raised his head and gave her a kiss on the end of her nose. Then Tursi came over and greeted her with a flurry of little high-pitched squeaks of joy. A second later they picked her up with their mighty fins and carried her out to sea with them.

"It feels like I'm flying!" cried Lee, laughing with delight, I hadn't heard her laugh like that since before she became ill. I could hardly believe it was true, but there she was gripping Nat's fin and challenging the wind and the immensity of the ocean. The dolphins stayed with Lee for more than an hour, always tender, always attentive, never using any unnecessary force, always responsive to her wishes.

'Maybe it's true that they are more intelligent and sensitive creatures than man. I know for certain that those marvellous dolphins understood that Lee was dying and wanted to console her as she faced her great journey into the unknown. From the moment they took her in hand they never left her alone for a second. They got her to play and obeyed her commands with a sweetness that was magical. In their company Lee found for one last time the enthusiasm and the will to live. She was strong and happy like she used to be, At one point she shouted, 'The dolphins have healed me, Daddy!"

'It was as if she had been reborn'

'There are no words to describe the effect that swim had on her. When she got out of the water it was as if she had been reborn.

'The next day she was too weak to get out of bed. She didn't even want to talk, but when I took her hand she squeezed it and whispered, "Daddy, don't be sad for me. I'll never be afraid again. The dolphins have made me understand that I have nothing to fear." Then she said, "I know I'm going to die tonight. Promise me that you'll cremate my body and scatter my ashes in the sea where the dolphins live. They have left me with a great feeling of peace in my heart and I know they will be with me on the long journey that lies ahead." Just before dawn she woke and said, "Hold me, Daddy, I'm so cold." And she died like that in my arms a few minutes later – passing from sleep to death without a ripple. I only realised her suffering was over because her body became colder and heavier.

'We cremated her as she wanted and went out the next day to scatter her ashes in the ocean amongst the dolphins. We were all crying, I'm not ashamed to say; not just my wife and I and our three other children, but even the sailors on the boat that had taken us out into the bay. Suddenly, through our tears, we saw the great arching silver shapes of Nat and Tursi leaping out of the water ahead of us. They had come to take our daughter home.'

- *Allegra Taylor, 6 Amyand Park Gardens, Twickenham TW1 3HS (tel 081 892 3172).*
- *In the UK, the Starlight Foundation, 8a Bloomsbury Square, London WC1A 2LP (tel 071 430 1642; fax 071 430 1482) is a registered charity which tries to grant the wishes of children who are 'chronically, critically or terminally ill.'*
- *Re dolphin therapy in the UK, particularly its striking results in cases of depression, contact Dr Horace Dobbs, Operation Sunflower, International Dolphin Watch, Parklands, North Ferriby, Humberside HU14 3ET, UK, tel 0482 634895; fax 0482 634914. To become a member and to receive the Dolphin newsletter send £8 (£4 under 16).*

Starvation is a gentle way to go

Geoffrey Cannon

Adapted extract from 'The Good Fight, The Life and Work of Caroline Walker', bestselling food campaigner and co-author of 'The Food Scandal', by Geoffrey Cannon, published by Ebury Press, 20 Vauxhall Bridge Road, London SW1V 2SA, 1989, £4-99, ISBN 0 7126 3769 9.

Just as there are societies to encourage home births, so there should be societies for home deaths. Being looked after at home is more trouble, of course, just as home cooking takes more time. But dying in hospital, as most people now do, stuck full of tubes in white rooms, surrounded by suffering and strangers, with those you love kept at the end of a telephone, is a sad and bad ending. Caroline thought being sent to hospital to die is like being put in a skip (no disrespect to builders or doctors).

At home in August, Caroline finished planting our garden, with seeds and bulbs identified with little flags, so I would know what to expect next spring and summer. She gave two interviews: one at the beginning of the month, for the Guardian on her sense of death, as we ate lunch; the other from her bed, at the end of the month, for BBC Radio 4's Food Programme on the meaning of her work.

Our home filled with family and friends and flowers. Pain was the only uncertainty. The surgeons had warned me that obstruction caused by the cancer would eventually be horribly painful. Not so; Dr Anne Naysmith, consultant at our local community hospital, a woman about Caroline's age, disagreed; and with a careful cocktail of drugs, Caroline rested at home, and took responsibility for her death, simply by stopping eating, two weeks before she died. Around midnight as her last day began, she foresaw her death. How was it – what did the thought feel like? 'Oh, *lovely*,' she said; and we laughed. And it was lovely to be with her when she died.

'Caroline took responsibility for her death, simply by stopping eating'

So, here after all is more advice. Starvation is a gentle way to let go. Find a general practitioner who will be your friend. And share.

'I want to share with you why I shall always be grateful to Caroline,' wrote a friend. 'She could always make me laugh, with her wonderful sense of the absurd and her sharp wit. But it was the last few months of her life that were a real inspiration to me. She showed me that the time of dying can be an enriching and growing experience.'

Cheap, green and 'DIY' funerals

Green, no-frills burial ground

Nick Evans, a gardener and builder and ex-sales manager in Shropshire, is seeking to purchase a two or three acre field near Ludlow, subject to planning permission that will allow him to turn it into a green, no-frills burial ground for 100 plots. Disgusted by all the trimmings and waste at a family funeral he attended, he is trying to encourage funerals without hearses etc, where the body will be buried in the simplest coffin, and with only trees and memorial plaques on the trees, and no gravestones, so that the site will look as natural as possible. The aim is to cut the expenses involved in funerals, to have funerals 'without fuss but with dignity', and to make it a burial ground suitable particularly for people who want a non-religious burial and for Greens.

'Memorial plaques on the trees'

Nick Evans, The Bell House, Wooferton, Ludlow, Shropshire SY8 4AL (tel 058472 342)

Fruit tree planted over body

Steven Levine

Extracted from 'Who Dies' by Steven Levine (published by Gateway Books, Bath) and quoted in 'Funerals and How to Improve Them' by Dr Tony Walter (published by Hodder and Stoughton).

Often, in the back country of Montana, a hole will be dug and the body, in a plain pine coffin or perhaps just wrapped in a tie-dyed cloth, will be lowered into the ground. Instead of a tombstone, a fruit tree is planted over the body. The roots are nourished by the return of that body into the earth from which it was sustained. And in the years to follow, eating the fruit from that tree will be like partaking in that loved one. It touches on the ritual of the Eucharist.

Memorial groves

Jonathon Porritt

Adapted extract from the Daily Telegraph.

My recommendation to the DoE would be to think laterally. There has been a lot of talk about new community forests since the government recently committed £70 million to support a new scheme from the Countryside Commission. The obvious answer is to set aside special 'memorial groves' where every new burial plot would be planted with three or four hardwood saplings, provided free by the Forestry Commission. The combination of built-in fertiliser, plus unlimited tender loving care from the relatives, would pretty well guarantee a thriving woodland in next to no time.

Making our own coffins

Barbara Huellin

My husband, aged 77, has recently finished building our coffins. We have spent a most enlightening few months organising and preparing for our deaths.

The coffins are made in blockboard at a cost of about £50 each (not including our time). They are painted green and have nautical-looking rope handles (from the ship-chandlers). The coffins are stored in the workroom. We have booked a double-decker site in the local Council cemetery for £100 to which we intend that family and friends shall physically bear us. We are leaving the commemorative gravestone for our survivors to add if they wish, so that they have something they can do.

Barbara Huelin, 69 Kingston Road, Oxford OX2 6RJ (tel 0865 511527).

A cheap coffin by mail order

James Gibson is an independently minded funeral director in Bolton who specialises in lavish funerals with horses and glass-sided carriages. But he is also about the only funeral director prepared to sell coffins to members of the public without too outrageous a mark-up. His cheapest version costs £45 including handles and lining, plus £21 extra for delivery in a large cardboard box anywhere in the UK. One person has complained about very slow processing of her order by Gibson, so plan well ahead!

James Gibson (tel 0204 655869). More expensive, quoting about £60 for their cheapest coffin, are the funeral directors Hartley and Near, in Grimsby (tel 0472 250150).

Cheapest funerals in the UK?

T. Finn in Plymouth is a retired insurance agent and ex-Royal Marine. He gets his coffins from James Gibson (see above) and will sell these on to local people, or he will arrange a very basic funeral for those who do not want DIY. He will merely add 10% to the final total for his services. So with £76 for a coffin, £127 for a cremation fee, £57 for the medical fees, £50 for the estate car, and £77 for catering, coffin carrying and flowers, the total with his percentage would come to about £300. And at a simple £10 per hour rate he can also help with wills and probate.

T. Finn, 21 Alfred Road, Plymouth PL2 1QB (tel 0752 560819). Readers are invited to let the Natural Death Centre (tel 081 208 2853) have their evaluation of Finn's services, if used. Which? magazine say the average funeral costs £920, all-in.

Burials on your own land

It is possible to arrange burials on your own land. One of the directors of the Institute for Social Inventions did this by setting aside a part of her large back garden in perpetuity for her husband's grave, so that this part was not sold with the rest of the house and grounds. In practice, unusual burials like this are only likely to be allowed if there are no neighbours within a hundred yards and no objections from them, and no nearby watercourses. You will need to make contact with your local planning authority and environmental health department.

For further information about any of the above, or about sea burials, contact the Natural Death Centre, 20 Heber Road, London NW2 6AA (tel 081 208 2853; fax 081 452 6434).

Memorials by Artists

Memorials by Artists puts you in touch with an artist who will design and make a fine memorial. These range from beautifully lettered headstones to ceramic tiles. The project was initiated by Harriet Frazer of Saxmundham in Suffolk, and was highly commended in the Social Inventions Awards. Harriet Frazer writes:

Memorials by Artists is a new venture which arranges commissions with many of the best letter cutters and memorial artists working in Britain.

The idea behind Memorials by Artists arose from my own experience in trying to find someone to make a good headstone for my daughter who died in 1985. I discovered that it was still possible to have a memorial that was well designed, beautifully carved and with fine lettering. The whole process of finding this out took a long time, and involved a great deal of searching and trial and error – in deciding what we wanted, in finding someone to design and carve the stone and discovering what was allowed by the church authorities.

'Puts you in touch with a high-quality memorial artist who can design a headstone for a grave'

It then struck me that I could use this experience to advise other people who might be in a similar situation. I have built up a register of artists throughout Britain, all of whom I have met and whose work I know. They include many well-established figures in letter cutting, glass engraving and memorial design, together with younger artists who have been recommended to me.

Although the majority of memorials will probably continue to be made in stone, many other possibilities exist. I have a register of artists working in other media who will make private or public memorials of any description. One could commission, for instance, a single ceramic tile, a pane or a whole window of engraved or stained glass, a stone seat, a wooden bench, a sundial, a bird bath, a sculpture, a fountain or a folly.

Memorials by Artists will, I hope, help to increase public awareness of the possibilities for memorial design and encourage artists and craftsmen and women who work in stone and other materials.

Memorials by Artists will take responsibility for the job being done, from the first contact up to the fixing of the memorial. This of course does not exclude clients from being involved in the project as much as they wish.

A finely produced 40 page booklet is available for £3. This contains 20 pages of photographs and several articles, for example, 'A History of Memorial Design', epitaphs, suitable stones, etc. Harriet Frazer, Memorials by Artists, Snape Priory, Saxmundham, Suffolk IP17 1SA (tel 0728 88 8934).

Ashes and annual wake in pub

From 'You and Yours', BBC Radio 4.

For a payment of between £50 and £5,000, the Packhorse pub in Bewdley, Herefordshire, is offering regular customers that it will place their ashes behind tiles in the pub and hold a wake in their honour when they die and once a year thereafter. £50 would buy a customer a tile by the urinals, £5,000 a spot close to the fire. The landlord, Coln O'Rourke, hopes that in due course there will be a wake celebration almost every night.

'It will place their ashes behind tiles in the pub and hold a wake in their honour when they die and once a year thereafter'

Coln O'Rourke, Packhorse Pub, High St, Bewdley, Near Kidderminster, Hereford (tel 0299 403 762).

Chapter twenty-five
PROMOTING SOCIAL INVENTIONS

Social and Political Experiment Districts

Gregory Wright

Particular counties, townships and districts, college towns, small cities and other identifiable jurisdictions within nations might, in the course of daily living, perform a distinct service to their own and other nations – and to themselves – by volunteering to try out and learn the effects of certain mostly untried social, economic and political arrangements, these to be decided by consensus in local elections.

> 'Particular districts volunteering to try out and learn the effects of certain mostly untried social, economic and political arrangements'

The national government would first hold a referendum or election to decide if, say, a two-thirds majority would like their area declared, for a set length of time (say, five to ten years) a Social and Political Experiment District (SPED).

An adventurous and well-educated populace might vote for this, such as a college town, or a rural enclave of 'counter-culture' types.

Proposals for programmes and experimental laws to try in a SPED would be voted on three times: firstly, should a given idea be considered further? secondly, does the proposal need alternative versions to be shaped and presented? and thirdly, to try or drop the final version of the proposal?

The benefits for SPED inhabitants could include:
• Tax relief from the central government in recognition of the risks residents would be taking;
• Government start-up money for some of the innovative experiments;
• Rotating heads of local government;
• Prestige and a sense of increased group and personal meaningfulness, helping determine future trends in the larger society;
• Benefits from particular experimental projects that work as intended.

Examples of the sorts of projects that could be tried abound in the Institute's publications. Further possible examples include:
• Car-free and car-limited regions;
• Self-planned independent study programmes in schools;
• Basic income schemes;
• Weekly TV-free days;
• Total redesign of street and other exteriors through massive public arts programmes.

Gregory Wright, 14161 Riverside Drive, #3, Sherman Oaks, CA 91423, USA (tel 818 784 0325).

Comment by David Hall

Comment by David Hall, Director, Town and Country Planning Association, 17 Carlton House Terrace, London SW1Y 5AS.

It does seem a very intriguing concept. If such SPEDs existed in this country, then they would provide a very useful method of introducing, on a strictly democratic basis, community innovation of all kinds and the development of the 'bottom-up' approach generally. Obviously, there is enormous scope.

My only reservation would be that for what might be quite a major upheaval for a community rather more than a two-thirds majority should be necessary before a SPED was established. Perhaps 75% or 80% would be better.

Future Workshops Consultancy

Guy Dauncey in his book 'After the Crash – The Emergence of the Rainbow Economy' (Green Print/Merlin Press, £6-99) provides an excellent overview of future workshops.

A future workshop is a social invention which could have as profound an effect on human progress as any other yet invented. It is a participatory process which enables people to get together to explore any issue which concerns them, and to develop creative approaches which please them. It releases people's resourcefulness and invites them to take part in creating the kind of future they want.

'A future workshop is a social invention which could have as profound an effect on human progress as any other yet invented'

The person who has contributed most to the invention is the Austrian writer Robert Jungk, a refugee from the Nazis in the 1930s, who saw how disastrous the results can be when people experience powerlessness:

'At present the future is being colonised by a tiny group of people,' writes Jungk, 'with citizens moving into a future shaped by this elite. I believe that we should not go blindly into this future.'

One of Jungk's early future workshops was run in the coal-mining village of Eisenheim, in Germany. The village was scheduled to be torn down and replaced with modern, high-rise buildings which would bring increased incomes to the developers. The villagers were resisting, but their leaders were being labelled troublemakers and reactionaries who were opposed to change. The villagers felt frustrated and full of bitterness at their powerlessness.

With help from a socially committed planner who lived nearby, they cleaned and painted an old coal wash-house for use as a meeting room, and in the course of one day they then held a future workshop, during which they produced dozens of proposals for a modernisation programme in keeping with their needs. They voiced their frustrations and pent-up anger, and worked in small groups with large sheets of paper, dreaming up ideas they wanted to see in their village. No one had ever consulted them before – their ideas had lain idle all these years. The coal mine owned their houses, and told them what to do. They wanted to set up a park, a lending library, a youth centre and a local newspaper, and to have a notice board where people could post up their complaints about the estate management's negligence and harassment. They wanted to create a meeting place where German and foreign workers could get together, and they considered what could be done for pedestrians, and how the sewers and drains could be restored to working order. Eisenheim, they felt, could become a model for other communities by enhancing its own cultural life, by providing more ways for people to get to know each other, and by continuously involving all its residents.

'As long as the villagers remained defensive, they were on the losing side. When they came up with constructive proposals, the authorities had to give way'

As long as the villagers remained defensive, they were on the losing side. When they came up with constructive proposals, the authorities had to give way. The village was saved, and a programme of renewal and restoration was put into action following their ideas.

The future workshop comes in five phases:

• Phase 1, the *Preparatory Phase*, occurs before the workshop begins, when people are invited to a briefing session so that they know what they will be attending. If the workshop is happening over a weekend, then it starts with:

• Phase 2, the *Critique Phase*, happens on the Friday night.

People take time to share their frustrations, irritations and difficulties, which are written on sheets of paper and stuck on the walls.

• Phase 3, the *Creative Phase*, takes place on Saturday. Focusing on their main items of worry, people now let their imaginations roll, dreaming up hundreds of ideas which they would like to see take place, using the brainstorming technique.

'The future workshop liberates the spirit that has been sleeping, and the awakened spirit then begins to create a new reality'

• Phase 4 is the *Implementation Phase*, which starts on Saturday and continues on Sunday. Time is now spent giving detailed attention to the ideas which received the most support. Plans need to be drawn up, working groups formed and arrangements made for follow-up. The miracle of birth is over and the long childhood of a community development project begins. The months and years that follow involve labour, trial, experiment and endless learning. The future workshop liberates the spirit that has been sleeping, and the awakened spirit then begins to create a new reality.

• Phase 5 is the *Action Phase* which takes place over the following months and years. Opposition may have to be overcome and internal tensions resolved and lessons learnt from successes and failures.

During the workshop, people grow in confidence, and their horizons stretch.

Robert Jungk writes: 'In the fantasy phase of a workshop on "Alternative Forms of Work" we were taking a short break. A woman broke the silence by saying "I'm sorry, but I have say something. I don't know about the rest of you, but I've not felt so well in years as during the last couple of hours. That's all I wanted to say. I just had to get it off my chest."

'The workshop is not just another problem-solving method – it may have a lasting impact on the participants, turning them into activists for social change'

'Many workshop participants, even if they have never been politically minded, become committed in a quite personal way to the search for a more basic restructuring of society. The workshop is not just another problem-solving method – it may have a lasting impact on the participants, turning them into activists for social change.'

Through childhood, and in school, college or training, we are rarely invited to contribute our creativity in an open-ended way. We get used to a method of learning which is one-way, in which someone else has the knowledge and expertise. The systems of state examinations allow a few people through the barriers to power and influence, and they then become the experts. The powers-that-be would have us believe that those who do badly at school are simply less intelligent. In this way, people grow used to the idea that someone else will always govern them, be their boss and determine the future of their community. This is why the future workshop is such a critical invention.

'Individuals get an opportunity to spread their wings,' writes Jungk, 'and they discover what they are capable of when serving a larger cause. In the process, their self-confidence grows as they come to realise that they are capable of constructive planning, and thus take their first steps towards adding more meaning to their lives.'

The Aberdeen hill-farmers, instead of becoming depressed and committing suicide under the pressure of mounting bills, might decide, through holding a future workshop, to help each other with their emotional strains and worries, to set up a debt-management advisory service, to explore ways in which they could reduce their loss-making operations, to diversify into new operations, to experiment with new crops and organic approaches, to develop the tourist potential of their area, to establish a local development agency to pursue their plans further – and so on.

The running of a successful future workshop requires group leaders who understand the facilitator style of leadership, and who are sensitive to the realities of long-term community development. Workshops could be encouraged by locating people who possess these skills and asking them to train a group of local people, who would then become a permanent resource. These people could get in touch with community groups and organisations and interest them in holding workshops as part of a wider community awakening strategy.

• *The book 'Future Workshops – How to create desirable futures' by Robert Jungk is published by the Institute for Social Inventions, 20 Heber Road, London NW2 6AA (tel 081 208 2853; fax 081 452 6434) at £4·95.*

• *Guy Dauncey, 2069 Kings Road, Victoria, BC V8R 2P6, Canada (tel 604 592 4472 h; 604 592 4473 w and fax).*

The Futures Circle

The Futures Circle are an interesting new design by Leif Drambo in Sweden. Each Circle will consist of five to eight people, with a trainer. The groups will use adult education facilities to debate future issues and then to design a project. Drambo trains the trainers, and equips each one with a special briefcase containing a cassette, a video, various publications and a Life-style Game he has designed. The latter gives players life choices, allowing them to make mistakes and to try again.

The Swedish labour movement has financed the cost of half of these suitcases, and Drambo hopes to start 5,000 Futures Circles within three years. Already he has trained 25 trainers and he is negotiating the introduction of Future Circles with 30 commune local authorities in the North of Sweden. There will be a prize for the best project undertaken by a Futures Circle – the prize probably consisting of a free trip to the EPCOT 'Experimental Prototype Community Of Tomorrow' in Orlando, Florida. The following extracts from his introductory booklet have been translated by Marilyn Mehlmann of the Swedish Institute for Social Inventions (SISU). Any organisation prepared to consider translating the whole suitcase package and the Life-style game into English and helping to distribute it, is invited to make contact. Extracts from Leif Drambo's description of his project follow.

The future is created by you. This is your right – and your duty. If you do not do it, someone else will on your behalf. And you may not like it. By taking part in Futures Circles you can actively influence the course of events. Tomorrow is born of today's decisions and actions. It does not just happen: it is created here and now. And creation is always an act based on knowledge.

No one knows what the future holds. It is truly unknown. What we can do is to prepare ourselves for the unknown – for the future. By learning to discuss and understand probable, possible and desirable futures we increase our ability to cope with uncertainty. The processes of change are inevitable, but we can see to it that they are constructive.

'To create the future you need tools: knowledge, experience, insights, methods'

To create the future you need tools: knowledge, experience, insights, methods. The Futures Circle is designed to give you these. It gives no patent solutions, no panaceas, but tools to help you create a desirable future. It is also a forum where different ideas, knowledge and experience can meet – the future is a group product.

The objectives of a Futures Circle are development and renewal, for you, your place of work, organisation, company, authority, residential area, school, association, borough, region, country. Each circle must determine its own focus. You can network electronically or otherwise with other circles, arrange conferences locally or regionally or even nationally. You can develop exhibitions or futures workshops.

The first thing you will find in your Futures Toolkit is a little book, Introduction to Futures. It describes three different styles of future: the probable, the possible and the desirable. Combined in a special way, these three styles give you 'the four stories', where the future is the new story. The book concludes by helping you to write your own story of the future.

The briefcase also contains four cassette lectures: *Twelve transformations* is about the most important factors that are likely to affect every individual and activity in the future. *The information age* concerns what is happening as we shift out of the industrial era. *Visions* shows how visionary thinking can be used as a powerful management tool to form and create a desired future. *The knowledge society* describes one such vision, and teaches how to test new possibilities and to create what we truly want to create.

A Jonathan Livingston Seagull videotape is included for relaxation and to encourage the formation of pictures in the inner eye – and to encourage answers to the questions: What are your dreams? What are your opportunities, here and now?

The next main course is a book, Infotopia, which takes a trip backwards in time to meet some of the foremost Utopian visionaries. But you will also be confronted with the possibilities and risks of modern technology. How will working life be affected by new technology?

Then it is time for a diversion, a party game that is more than a game. *Life-style* has no winners or losers. The point is to live a life from the age of 20 to the age of 80 as happily as possible. The game is played by drawing cards from special packs, including a pack of 54 scenario cards and 96 experience cards. You will find yourself confronted with a large variety of events and situations. Some will affect you personally, whereas others affect society around you – economically, politically, technically, culturally and so on. It is not always easy to reach a decision. But then, who said that life should be easy?

Next follow eight exercises in visionary thinking such as *Me – ten years on* and *City of the Future*, designed to help develop your social imagination and problem-solving abilities, and to give a basis for discussing value judgements concerning future developments.

Scenarios are also included: an article from a paper published in 1999, and a description of a future family.

An embryo Futures Data Base, 'Infoteque', is included, for you to add your own information to as it accrues. The need for new tools will become apparent as the circles progress. Only our imagination sets the limits. Imagine too if all circles could communicate with each other via electronic mail to exchange experience, information and knowledge. Each new circle could get a head start by tapping in to the problems, solutions and methods of other circles. This may not be just a dream – industry is beginning to talk of installing computer terminals free or very cheaply in almost every home, along the lines of the French experiment.

So far we have been concerned with *how* to study the future. Now is the time to decide *what* you want to renew or develop, in other words to select a focus for the circle's activities. The possible range is very wide. Here are some examples:

Working life
Politics, welfare, democracy and influence
Industry
Economics and resources
Education and research
Environment and ecology
Peace and security
Values and life-styles
Science and technology
Mass media
Culture and leisure
Health, nutrition, dwellings

The briefcase then introduces you to *Future Methods in 8 steps* to help organise the work of the circle to achieve its desired results. The essential point is to select a focus which feels relevant and important for all members of the circle. Future studies are intended to bring into being the potential of the here and now. Projects need to develop new possibilities or to solve old problems, so as to move from now to a perhaps previously 'impossible' future.

Leif Drambo, Effekta Future AB, Box 3445, 16203 Stock-holm-Vallingby, Sweden (tel 010 46 8 387300).

Global Action Plan for The Earth

Chris Church

Global Action Plan for the Earth (GAP) is working for a cleaner and safer environment in nine countries. GAP's activities are based around the 'Eco-Team programme'. There is no shortage of books that tell you *what* to do to help the environment, but the Eco-Team programme uses a workbook that shows you *how* to change things.

During the six month programme an Eco-Team – it can be a family, a family and neighbours, or perhaps a group of friends – works together to cut pollution and waste, save energy and save money too. There are six chapters in the workbook – one for each month of the programme.

Each month teams send in 'feedback sheets' listing what they have done. The national office collates the information and lets everyone know how the whole programme is going. After six months, team members' homes will be running more efficiently and they will have learnt ways to cut pollution and save money.

Eco-Teams are running in America, Canada and Germany and are starting up in Britain and other European countries. In America a survey shows that a family that has been through the Eco-Team programme will save each year a total of $1,200, 3,120 lbs of garbage, 73,000 gallons of water, ten trees, ten tonnes of carbon dioxide and 600 gallons of petrol – while at the same time improving its quality of life.

GAP-UK is setting up our first Eco-Teams in 1992. Anyone can form their own Eco-Team – the only expense is the money spent on the workbook. If you would like to be involved, as an individual or an organisation, let us know and we can keep you informed. No one can save the planet on their own – but GAP gives everyone a chance to make a difference.

• *Global Action Plan for the Earth, c/o Chris Church, GAP-UK, PO Box 893, London E5 9RU (tel 081 806 1836).*

• *GAP-USA, c/o David Gershon (GAP's founder), 57A Krumville Road, Olivebridge, NY 12461, USA (tel 914 657 8081; fax 914 657 8044).*

An electronic Global Suggestions Box

Gregory Wright

Adapted from a 21 page package.

My proposal is for IdeaNet, an electronic and print Global Suggestions Box, a linking-up of as many as possible of the idea-gathering organisations (IGOs we may call them) around the world.

> 'A linking-up of as many as possible of the idea-gathering organisations around the world'

Already existing computer networks such as USENET, BITNET, PeaceNet, EcoNet or SeniorNet – and new emerging networks – could be used to link these IGOs up.

Idea Gathering Organisations

Gregory Wright includes a 14 page listing of IGOs. Amongst the more interesting-sounding ones are:

• Macrocosm USA, Sandi Brockway and Carl Moodispaugh, Box 969, Cambria, CA 93428, USA (tel 805 927 8030). 'A clearing-house for progressive and pioneering efforts, projects and organisations.'

• Planetwork, Ed and Jennifer Moffet, PO Box 804, Ketchum, ID 83340, USA. 'A clearing-house for earth-friendly ideas.'

• ElfNet, Box 6844, Malibu, CA 90264, USA (tel 310 317 1411). A bulletin board for facilitating 'evolving global intelligence of leading future-creators of Planet Earth.'

• Forum 2000, PB 5140 Majorstua, 0301 Oslo 3, Norway (tel 02 13 85 85 53 40 14). Coordinator Sven Bjork. 'Organiser and channel for new ideas.'

Gregory Wright, 14161 Riverside Drive #3, Sherman Oaks, CA 91423, USA (tel 818 784 0325).

Collecting urban innovations

David Hutchinson, London Co-ordinator, Mega-Cities Project, writes:

The purpose of the Mega-Cities project is to identify innovations which are helping to make cities, and particularly the very largest cities (the 'mega-cities'), better places to live and work in; and to disseminate information about these innovations so that they can be adopted in other places.

> 'The purpose of the project is to identify innovations which are helping to make cities, and particularly the very largest cities (the "mega-cities"), better places to live and work in'

The project derives from three basic ideas:

• A growing proportion of the world's population lives in cities and some of the fastest growing are already the largest. However, relatively little attention has so far been paid by the aid and development agencies to these cities, their problems and their opportunities.

• The mega-cities share particular problems and offer opportunities in addition to those which are common to all urban areas.

• Most studies of the largest cities focus on the problems and pay relatively little attention to one of the most positive aspects, the vast amount of innovation which is taking place. Some of the innovations are city specific but many could be copied or adapted for use in other cities if only there was some way of knowing about them.

The innovations may be an individual product or piece of equipment; a design, engineering or construction process or procedure; or it could be an organisational or administrative innovation. The innovation must, however, have been put into practice and found to be workable to qualify, not just be a 'bright idea.'

The project is already under way in four Latin American cities: Rio de Janeiro, Sao Paulo, Buenos Aires, and Mexico City as well as in Los Angeles and New York. Nairobi, Tokyo, Beijing and Bangkok have all expressed a desire to become involved. Dr Janice Perlman, the originator of the project has visited the latter three cities and helped launch it in London too.

Several American foundations and large businesses have contributed funds towards the coordination of the project in New York. It already has the support of the World Health Organisation, the World Bank and the UN Habitat. However, each participating city is expected to raise its own funds. Each has, or will have, a steering committee, and a full-time coordinator with administrative and research support.

Among the innovations that the New York Mega-Cities Project has documented (says an article in the New York City Tribune) are:

• *R2 B2 Recycling Project.* R2 B2 is a private recycling centre on Carter Avenue in the Bronx which is subsidised by the Department of Sanitation. The centre pays people for their garbage and recycles it. This programme of 'Cash-for-Trash' supplements income, creates 20 full-time jobs for neighbourhood residents and provides inexpensive recycled goods to South Bronx businesses. It also helps to solve New York's garbage problem, providing an alternative method of disposal.

• *Glassphalt Road Paving Material.* The Department of Transportation has begun using Glassphalt – 20 per cent recycled glass and 80 per cent asphalt – to repave roads. This technological innovation will foster a huge demand for recycled garbage.

David Hutchinson, London Co-ordinator, Mega-Cities Project, c/o London Research Centre, 81 Black Prince Road, London SE1 7SZ (tel 071 735 4250; fax 071 261 1710).

Community Action Network (USA)

The 'American Values Community Action Network' in New York advertises as 'the only national and international Idea Exchange Library. In cooperation with advertising and its media, it shares practical solutions to people problems with communities, volunteer group, government, clubs, schools and individuals ... an invaluable resource available on request to all'.

Their president Miles David, and their chairman Norman Glenn, used their long experience of the media in the States to recruit to the 'formation committee' the chief executives of key advertising and publishing associations. A telephone survey was conducted without charge by R.H. Bruskin to discover what problems most concerned Americans. The percentages of private citizens who expressed themselves as willing to do volunteer work on specific problems were as follows:

• Drunk driving (64.5%)
• Child abuse (62.1%)
• Missing and runaway children (62%)
• Rape and other sex crimes (56%)
• Drug and alcohol abuse (55.5%)
• Medical care (54.3%)
• Teenage suicide (53.7%)
• Burglary and street crime (53.5%)
• Problems of the elderly (52.3%)
• The hungry and the homeless (51.8%)
• Education system inadequacies (44.9%)
• Problems of the handicapped (43.7%)
• Criminal justice inadequacies (43.6%)
• Adult unemployment (35.9%)
• Environmental problems (35.4%)
• Inadequate affordable housing (32.2%)
• Family problems (31.1%)
• Youth unemployment (31.1%)
• Occupational and product safety (29%)
• Business neglect of community (21.3%)

They decided to focus only on these problems and to use their media contacts to advertise for media coverage of solutions, netting some thousand entries for their catalogue of headlines, a 'Can Do!' Databank Catalogue of 'Hundreds of Ideas to Change Your World'. This will be published as 20 separate booklets in 20 problem categories.

> **'Senior Gleaners, citizens over 50 years of age who operate warehouses in the San Fernando Valley from which they dispense donated food that would otherwise have gone to waste, helping feed 63,000 people'**

They offer prizes for the best media coverage of community projects. One winner was an article in the Christian Science Monitor about 'Senior Gleaners', citizens over 50 years of age who operate warehouses in the San Fernando Valley from which they dispense donated food that would otherwise have gone to waste, helping feed 63,000 people.

Some of the more intriguing media articles listed in the catalogue are, for example:

229. Drunk driving. Hotel rewards groups who designate one person in the party as the non-drinking driver.

293. Drunk driving. TV spot with taxi company's offer of a free ride home.

135. Missing and runaway children. Strategies for protecting children from kidnapping.

> **'Problems of the elderly. Love Exchange (grade-school pen pals) and Homeshare (youthful "roomers")'**

8. Problems of the elderly. Love Exchange (grade-school pen pals for the elderly) and Homeshare (youthful 'roomers' living in an old person's house), Tulip Street ('senior centre').

87. Problems of the handicapped. Tender Loving Zoo takes animals to shut-ins and to the handicapped.

127. Problems of the neighbourhood. Albert Einstein Medical Centre's Capuchin Monkey Project provides trained pets to assist quadriplegics.

American Values Community Action Network, Suite 1203, 211 E. 43rd Street, New York, NY 10017, USA (tel 212 818 1360).

The Giraffe Project

The Giraffe Project in the States gives commendations to people who 'stick their necks out' for the common good, whether it is restoring an old barge under the Brooklyn Bridge into a concert centre, or developing a herb-growing enterprise in the South Bronx.

Ann Medlock, the founder and president of the Giraffe Project (which now has a staff of twelve) writes that 'a critical mass of grassroots citizen-activists can renew our communities, end poverty, clean up the environment and create a peaceful world.' Their Giraffe Schools Programme 'provides children with the stories of real people who as Giraffes live exciting lives. This role model approach will help children look forward to living such lives themselves.'

There is also a Giraffe Project office in Moscow with a staff of eight Russians.

The Giraffe Project, POB 759 197 Second Street, Langley, WA 98260, Whidbey Island, USA (tel 206 221 7989; fax 206 221 7817).

The Brain Exchange

Joy-Lily of the San Francisco Brain Exchange writes: 'I define creativity as "the artful and innovative solving of problems in all spheres of life." There are several ways to solve problems creatively. My personal favourite is to get help from other people. Why struggle alone? The most enjoyable and dynamic form of group problem solving I have found is brainstorming – the process where quantities of ideas are offered with no criticism. Only later are the ideas analysed to find realistic solutions.'

During 1989, the Brain Exchange offered brainstorming salons once a month, sometimes with themes, such as defusing domestic dilemmas, humour, career transition, healing and women only. The Brain Exchange 'staff' consisted of Lee Glickstein and Joy-Lily, who sent out details of meetings to a mailing list of about 600 people. $5 was charged at the door (which paid expenses), with meetings in private homes and attendance ranging from five to 25 people.

'A local radio station,' wrote Lee, 'has been inviting us to brainstorm ideas on the air with listeners every other month. Most callers want us to solve their problems, and fewer have ideas for the earlier callers, which is what we want from them. But we inspire some people with our attitude about "considering the possibilities".'

How to start a brainstorming salon

Lee gives tips to those trying to start brainstorming groups in their own localities:
- Introduce it to friends as a game;
- Advertise in newspapers, local business publications;
- Speak with Chamber of Commerce and other business organisations;
- Stick with a regular meeting schedule no matter how small you start and you will attract the right people;
- Invite journalists; it's a good story for them;
- Call a meeting to discuss a particular local problem;
- Make it a big event by flying in famous brainstormers to lead a meeting;
- Throw a potluck where everyone brings their favourite food and favourite problem;
- Have a meeting on the subject of how to meet romantic partners;
- Brainstorm on a radio call-in show.

> **'Common element enjoyed by people who define themselves as basically happy: the willingness to embrace change, an acceptance of others as they are, and the openness to explore a range of possibilities in life'**

How to brainstorm

Another San Francisco group researched the common elements enjoyed by people who define themselves as basically happy... (It seems that) the road to peace of mind is paved with the willingness to embrace change, an acceptance of others as they are, and the openness to explore a range of possibilities in life. Brainstorming is a seriously playful exercise toward these ends. The actual ideas – stimulating, ridiculous, useful, whimsical as they may be – are not as important as the positive attitude the game fosters.

Joy-Lily describes how to brainstorm, with slightly different guidelines from the ones normally used by the Institute for Social Inventions:

Try it with your friends, family or co-workers. Here are our guidelines.

(1) Keep ideas brief, don't tell stories;

(2) Give only one idea per turn;

(3) Speak in the imperative ('do this, try that', instead of 'have you considered...?');

(4) Make it safe by not criticising or 'yes butting' anybody's idea (including your own before you speak);

(5) Make your thinking as funny or as silly as possible;

(6) Piggyback (build) on previous ideas freely;

(7) When it's your question, write down all ideas without evaluating them, and don't speak during the brainstorm.

(*Ed*. Many perfectly successful brainstorming groups do not follow guidelines 2, 3 or 7.)

We notice that some people habitually critique ideas thrown their way. Whether with frowns or 'I've tried that already's, these pre-judgers cast a stifling gloom over the room. But anyone who acccepts all suggestions as gifts (you wouldn't say 'I have one of those already, yuck') has already solved the bulk of the problem.

Afterwards, Lee follows up the brainstorming with an evaluation process in which the following four questions are asked, with ideas offered, brainstorm-style:

(1) What's good about this idea?

(2) What's wrong with this idea?

(3) How can these problems be overcome?

(4) What new ideas are suggested by this evaluation process?

The Institute for Social Inventions hosts occasional brainstormings, but has ambitions to start a similar regular Brainstorming Salon in London, as an active alternative to going to the cinema, and with themes advertised in What's On, City Limits and Time Out.

Joy-Lily, The Brain Exchange, 4215 Army Street, San Francisco, CA 94131, USA (tel 415 826 8248).

International Futures Library

The International Futures Library in Salzburg claims to be the 'first public library specialising in the collection, interdisciplinary networking and distribution of future-oriented information.' Set up by Robert Jungk, author of 'The Nuclear State' and winner of the Right Livelihood Award, it has a staff of three and funding from the Salzburg and state authorities.

The library's future survey quarterly Pro Zukunft is published in German, but it would like to do an English version.

Catalogue of Hope

The International Futures Library has assembled over 600 reports of social inventions and social experiments from around the world. A first selection of 51 has been published under the title 'Katalog der Hoffnung' by the prestigious German publishing house Luchterhand (Frankfurt). It is edited by Robert Jungk and the library.

There are plans to publish similar collections of encouraging ideas at least every second year. The printed as well as unprinted reports will be preserved in a 'Data Bank of Hope', accessible to all those who are looking for good ideas and living examples of a more just, human and sustainable world.

The International Futures Library is at Imbergstrasse 2, Salzburg A 5020, Austria (tel 43-662 73206).

The National Suggestions Centre

The nearest UK precursor body to the Institute for Social Inventions was the National Suggestions Centre (later renamed the National Innovations Centre) and its magazine 'What?', which was founded by Michael Young in 1968 and lasted until it ran out of funds in 1974. The Centre's first director was Richard Luce, now high up in the Conservative hierarchy, and the Centre had a budget of over £35,000 a year and about half a dozen staff.

In the first two and a half years of its existence it received some 10,000 suggestions from the public and, amongst the ideas that it helped put into action, were National Heritage (for the improvement of museums), WAM (Working Association of Mothers), decimal braille and charity postage stamps. In the later stages of its work, the Centre decided to concentrate on building up a 'Community Innovations Register' of already existing innovations in the field of health and welfare, whilst running down the suggestions side of its work and ceasing to publish its magazine.

> 'The National Suggestions Centre failed because we did not have enough skilled people who were able to get the good ideas put into practice'

Michael Young, in a letter to the Institute, writes:

'The main reason the National Suggestions Centre failed was because we did not have enough skilled people who were able to get the good ideas put into practice. For the most part, it really needed a great deal of innovative skill to see what the best approach was in each case.

'I remember I must have spent several hundred hours just in trying to persuade the Electricity Council to go for an experiment with tokens for electricity meters which had an enormous advantage over coins. I failed. I took it up later when I was chairman of the National Consumer Council and had a bit more weight behind me, and, after an even greater effort, they were persuaded and the first trials of the tokens in the North of England turned out well.

'It's not exactly an earth-shaking issue but it took about 15 years to get the authorities to budge, even though we knew that they worked like a charm in Japan. The idea is pretty well as good as it ever was and there ought to be much more use of such non-cash-like tokens. Since the tokens are self-destruct, no money has to be collected and no money is vulnerable to theft. Also they have their cash flow problems eased because the money is up front. The concept has since been used with Phonecards but it has much wider possibilities for all sorts of coin boxes.

'Some things just fell into our lap like National Heritage, which was pretty well fully formed when we took it on and it has gone extremely well ever since.

'I do not think there was anything wrong with our idea but just the lack of the right people with the right sort of nous.'

Michael Young, The Institute of Community Studies, 18 Victoria Park Square, Bethnal Green, London E2 9PF (tel 081 980 6263).

Response from Nicholas Albery

Nicholas Albery of the Institute for Social Inventions wrote in reply to Michael Young.

I am trying to see what other lessons I learn for our Institute from the relative failure of the National Suggestions/Innovations Centre – apart from the factors mentioned in your letter. To judge by the scanty remaining evidence:

• I think the new baby required looking after longer by you as initiator. It needed people with a track record of successful social innovation steering it, supported by a team of similarly innovative people.

• It seems to have been a mistake to drop the magazine and the contact with the public.

• The venture was perhaps too paternalistic towards the public, at least at the outset: we will do your idea for you, rather than supporting a person in taking it further themselves; like a hospital that takes the baby away from the mother rather than leaving it by her side for breastfeeding.

• There was no evidence of an attempt to build up a club-like network of socially innovative people.

• The overseas network to let you know of socially innovative projects that could be implemented in the UK does not seem to have materialised.

• There was no educational work with the aim of showing people ways to become more innovative for themselves, by running workshops, etc. No one appreciated the value of the 10,000 suggestions from this perspective of encouraging people to start thinking of better directions for society – even if you considered the suggestions themselves to be not so good.

• There was no setting of criteria to help people judge whether their suggestions were as finely tuned as they might be.

• There was not enough focusing on neighbourhood schemes that people could carry out without government or bureaucratic approval.

• Most crucially, there was no serious attempt to make the Centre financially self-supporting within the lifetime of the grants.

This is probably all too harsh, building up an unreliable picture from the fragments that remain. And it neglects the substantial achievements – a highish circulation magazine, thousands of suggestions and several good projects.

Nicholas Albery, 20 Heber Road, London NW2 6AA (tel 081 208 2853; fax 081 452 6434).

Social inventions in specialist magazines
Nigel Bradley

Editors of weekly and monthly magazines should dedicate one to four pages of their publications to social inventions and specialist ideas from their readers.

The Institute for Social Inventions cannot possibly process, appraise and disseminate all the good ideas in these specialist areas. The results overall could be of national importance.

Nigel Bradley, 91 Hawksley Avenue, Chesterfield, Derbyshire S40 4TJ (tel 0246 208473).

Institute Fellows
Valerie Yule

I propose that the title Fellow of the Institute for Social Inventions, FSI, should be conferred on those whose outstanding social inventions have been in practice successfully for at least four years.

> **'Very few innovations last as long as four years, but this is what really matters. "Between the idea and the action falls the shadow" '**

Most social inventions remain ideas only. Some social inventions get put into practice. Very few innovations last as long as four years, but this is what really matters. 'Between the idea and the action falls the shadow' (T.S. Eliot).

A great deal of effort goes into encouraging the young to have ideas – but astonishingly little into showing them the importance of the hard work and persistence required actually to put them into practice – and to persist in the work required beyond the first few years of disillusion and frustration.

Valerie Yule, 57 Waimarie Drive, Mount Waverley, Victoria, Australia 3149 (tel 807 4315).

Collecting social inventions
John Zube

To indicate my interest in 'social inventions' and the need to collect, register and market them:

(1) My father (Kurt Zube, Auwaldstr. 7, D-7800 Freiburg, Br., Germany) designed his Ideas Archive project in 1939, tried to realise it in the late forties and early fifties in Austria and Germany and wrote it up in a book.

I have been involved with this idea since 1949, and have made my own collection of social reform ideas, using microfiche publishing *(Ed: see this encyclopaedia's chapter on Communications for more on this).*

Since 1952 I was particularly influenced by the treasury of social reform and individual liberty ideas which Ulrich von Beckerath (1882-1969) gathered in a life-long effort from the age of 16.

I have given up on conventional publishers. If I had to approach a thousand of them to get one book temporarily printed, for that outlay I could microfiche 10-100 titles.

> **'I have given up on conventional publishers. If I had to approach a thousand of them to get one book temporarily printed, for that outlay I could microfiche 10-100 titles'**

(2) In my microfiched Peace Plans 61-63 I pondered the need for an ideal volunteer militia for the protection of human rights – for which Cromwell's Ironsides, at least in England itself, set not a bad precedent: rightful, limited, and very discriminating force.

(3) I have microfiched material too on the need too for 'Panarchy', a social organisation that would be self-correcting, peace-, freedom- and wealth-promoting. My microfiche deal with the organisational aspects and requirements of individual sovereignty, individual secessionism, voluntarism and personal law.

(4) For the clarification of first principles, I have microfiched (in Peace Plans 589/590) over a hundred private declarations of individual rights (such as P.B.Shelley's), as alternatives to the all-too-limited governmental bills of rights.

(5) I have finally finished preparing a newsletter plus microfiche on 'Monetary Freedom'.

(6) I have publicised the use and potential of micrographics.

(7) Another iron I try to keep in the fire is: a total denationalisation programme for expropriating the worst ex-propriators, with the assets ending up as transferable assets in the hands of private citizens, free of charge, to be used by them however they please.

(8) Another approach I advocate: a revival of free juries and true direct democracy and local self-government. I would have enjoyed the local self-government that free Englishmen once enjoyed, according to J.Toulmin Smith ('Local Self-Government and Centralisation', my first microfiched reprint).

(9) My most hopeless approach: an attempt through my 'Peace Plans' publications to drum some sense into those involved in the peace movements. There are a handful of sharp thinkers and activists that are worthwhile from my point of view, such as Gene Sharpe and Brian Martin, but the rest are almost hopeless muddleheads and ignoramuses.

(10) Since people have fallen so often for the wrong slogans and catch phrases, I am involved in publishing counter-wordings, 'Slogans for Peace'.

(11) Related to this is my planned 'Encyclopaedia of the Best Refutations of Common Errors, Myths and Prejudices that are Obstacles to Social Progress'. These errors, etc together form something like a common and primitive religion that is the enemy of almost all that is good in humans.

(12) I am preparing a 'Redensarten' handbook: benefiting from the numerous mistakes I make in my arguments with others, I will list ways of making a point skilfully, persuasively, politely or sometimes aggressively.

(13) I am microfiching all the literature and experience concerning ending the 'organised antagonism' of the employer–employee relationship.

(14) I made attempts to start a club of utopists, of those interested in social utopias as opposed to science fiction. Pip Wilson, in Sydney, has been trying for the last two or three years to start such a club, but has not found enough supporters. There may, initially, only be enough people for it worldwide.

Finally: the German Reichsbank, during the Great Depression, got some 100,000 proposals for ending the depression. Ideas still today need registering and marketing properly. Thus do I very much welcome the Institute for Social Inventions as a new associate in this effort. However, I hold that you are very optimistic if you think you could abstract and review all of them in conventional publishing.

> **'Nature is also very profuse with seeds. Most do not fall on fertile ground. None are properly marketed, not even wheat or eggs'**

Who knows, someone sometime might follow one of the hints in this outpouring of mine. Nature is also very profuse with seeds. Most do not fall on fertile ground. None are properly marketed, not even wheat or eggs.

John Zube, 7 Oxley Street, Berrima, NSW 2577, Australia (tel 48 771 436).

A Catalan organisation for promoting social innovation

Marti Olivella

Adapted extract from a letter to the Institute.

In 1990, a group connected to the Catalan Centre d'Estudis Joan Bardina began Ecoconcern as an association for the fostering of social innovation – especially for the designing of new institutional frameworks, alternatives to the present monetary system, in-depth studies of participatory democracy and ways of reducing land speculation.

Our group has diverse backgrounds (engineers, economists, journalists and businessmen) and we interact with 150 people in Catalonia and we send information to 150 international addresses.

We would like to learn from the experience of the Institute for Social Inventions in London (what legal form would be best? how can we obtain financial support?), and, as far as possible, to introduce your work in our country, or to set up joint training, research or publishing projects.

Marti Olivella, Secretary, EcoConcern, Can Riu, 08540 Centelles, Catalonia, Spain (tel 34 3 881 08 42; fax 881 13 21).

Centre for Social Innovation, Vienna

Dr Josef Hochgerner

The Centre for Social Innovation is working to develop and promote social innovations in the following: 'Work and Technology', 'Mobility and Housing', 'Environmental Policies' and 'European Research Cooperation'. It works in an educational and advisory capacity with local, governmental and international organisations.

Dr Josef Hochgerner, Zentrum für soziale Innovation (ZSI), Plösslgasse 2, A-1041 Vienna, Austria (tel and fax 43 1 504 2060 and 43 2252 55886).

Radio Social Inventions in Australia

Valerie Yule

Adapted from a letter about ABC Australia's very tentative hopes for a social inventions radio series in Australia. Valerie Yule is helping with advice for this.

There are ways of presenting social inventions on Australian radio to fit almost any budget, from lots to practically nothing. Even the social inventions competition could be run on a shoestring, with a Shoestring Award. All is not done for money,

I see a desperate need for Australians to develop more initiative, thinking, enterprise and sense of humour, and for young Australians to get that infection too. I would like to see, from any small beginning at all, extension of social inventing to a Radio 'Today's Invention', with some TV and video demonstrations of succesful inventions, a newspaper feature, and possibly an Australian journal, and an Annual Skillolympics under the guise of attracting tourists (which is currently an excuse for introducing any sort of social evil) but actually to get Australian minds out of mothballs.

I would see Australian social inventions as being fairly pragmatic as well as often funny, and not getting into philosophies like the UK Institute – at least not at first. Each session could include one far-out item, however, which could arouse lively comments. Topical problems could also be set, for new solutions that have not been attempted yet.

Valerie Yule, 57 Waimarie Drive, Mount Waverley, Victoria, Australia 3149 (tel 807 4315).

Social inventions Danish-style

In Copenhagen, the Centre for Social Inventions ('Center for Social Udvikling'), started independently from the UK Institute for Social Inventions but in the same year, 1985, has a much larger budget than that of the Institute, with £200,000 a year from the Egmont Petersen Foundation and £200,000 a year from the Danish Ministry of Social Affairs. Their work runs in parallel in many respects – like the UK Institute, they too work in schools, mostly with 16 to 18 year olds, who are encouraged to find out for themselves about particular problems in their local environment. For instance, a recent class chose to equip itself with wheelchairs and tried to make its way around Copenhagen and into libraries and other public buildings, learning to empathise with the obstacles faced by the handicapped in their daily lives.

Where the Centre particularly scores over the UK Institute is that whenever any person or group contacts them with an idea for a project, they can afford to jump in the car to visit them. With paid consultants in the main regions of Denmark, they have now visited and encouraged some 300 projects in this way. For instance, when an 85 year old pensioner contacted them wanting to do something for fellow pensioners, they visited her and helped her work up a scheme where the elderly could have flats together rather than go into a home, and then helped her to tour around the country telling others of her plans. And one of their associates, Per Hensen, during the winter cold spell, helped a group of alcoholics in Copenhagen obtain their own caravan in which to set up a drinking club, with club rules set by themselves, such as that they wanted the police to visit three times a day and to have easier access to treatment.

> 'Whenever any person or group contacts them with an idea for a project, they can afford to jump in the car to visit them'

News of the Danish Centre has spread like a bushfire without advertising, since people know that they have the ear of the Egmont Foundation, with its £3m a year to give away. Ole Dahl, the administrator of the Egmont Foundation, who first thought of the idea for the Centre and gathered together 30 experienced 'project makers' to discuss it, stresses that the Centre is administered entirely independently of the Foundation, but that any charitable foundation, whether in Denmark or the UK, would feel the benefit of having independent consultants such as the Centre's out in the field helping projects clarify their ideas, reach out to possible participants and draw up sound budgets and action and evaluation plans. 'Applications to the Foundation,' says Dahl, 'have been of much higher quality than before.' Projects do need experienced encouragers to help them through the initial hurdles and the bureaucratic jungle.

Center for Social Udvikling, c/o Ole Dahl, Egmont H. Petersen Foundation, Frdberg Runddel 1, Copenhagen, Denmark (tel 45 31 86 36 44).

Swedish social inventions

Hans Lavonius, of the Swedish Institute for Social Inventions (SISU), wrote to the UK Institute in 1987:

'Some friends of mine read in a Swedish newspaper about Nicholas Albery's visit to Stockholm. We became very inspired by learning about the work your Institute has done in the field of social inventions. We feel strongly that this is a challenging field with enormous possibilities of achieving positive changes in this world of ours.

'So now, inspired by your work, we have begun to found a Swedish Institute for Social Inventions. Everything is about to start, with a few ideas to date and a lot of work to do to get things going. We are considering ways of raising money, ways of evaluating inventions, the appropriate form for our organisation and so on.'

Progress

The Swedish Institute is going strongly. It has awarded prizes in its own competition each year, it has issued 16 magazines, and it has evolved a two-pronged organisational structure of a foundation and a members' association.

Amongst its many initiatives, it has brought the theory and practice of permaculture to the Scandinavian countries and has formed the Swedish Global Action Programme committee. The latter is concerned with mobilising individuals to modify their life-styles in order to achieve the aims set out in the Brundtland report on the environment.

'Mobilising individuals to modify their life-styles'

Marilyn Mehlmann, SISU, Peter Myndes Backe 12, 5 tr, 118 46 Stockholm, Sweden (tel 08772 45 87; fax 08 642 26 41).

Ecological and Social Innovations in Germany

A charitable company for researching, supporting and publishing ecological and social innovations has been started in Germany. It is the idea of Professor Declan Kennedy and Professor Dr Margrit Kennedy, the couple who introduced Permaculture to Germany in 1981 and to many other European countries since. Declan is Irish and was a professor of urban infrastructure and former vice-president of the Technical University of Berlin. Margrit is German and a professor for resource-saving building techniques at the Architectural Department of the University of Hannover.

• *DANA, Prof. Declan Kennedy, Ginsterweg 5, DW-3074 Steyerberg, Germany (tel 49 5764; fax 49 5764 2368).*

• *There is also a separate and rather quieter initiative in Giessen, called the German Society for the Development and Promotion of Social Inventions. Contact Hubert Meyer, Deutsche Gesellschaft zur Entwicklung und Förderung Sozialer Erfindungen e.v., Löberstrasse 25, D-6300 Giessen, Germany (tel 0641 75255).*

Moscow Foundation for Social Innovations

Gennady Alferenko started the Foundation for Social Innovations in Moscow in 1987 having read a translation of a UK article about the London Institute for Social Inventions. It has undertaken many imaginative activities: it has brought together American veterans from the Vietnam War and Soviet veterans from the Afghan War; and has arranged meetings between Alaskan and Siberian Eskimos. It has also been busy setting up new business initiatives, and has a support office in California.

'It has brought together American veterans from the Vietnam War and Soviet veterans from the Afghan War'

The Foundation for Social Innovations is on the second floor of the Hotel Yaroslavskay, Yaroslaskaya St, 4 Bldg. 8, 129243 Moscow (tel 217 6035 or 217 6021 – Nelly Grigoriyan speaks English; fax 217 6033; in the States their contact phone numbers are 415 931 2593 or 415 265 7021).

The Body Shop Department of Social Inventions

Jeremy Sherman

The Body Shop's head office in West Sussex has a department devoted to developing the company's social and environmental mission. Distinct from the company's Environmental Department whose mission is to 'clean up after ourselves,' the Department of Social Inventions' objective is to 'clean up more than our own share of the mess' through campaigning, local volunteer work and capers that 'promote the extraordinary into all pockets of the company.'

'Promote the extraordinary into all pockets of the company'

The department provides a volunteer job referral service to all 1,435 employees, entitled by company policy to spend a paid half-day every month at the volunteer work of their choice.

The department houses a large and growing compilation of quotations on activism, social change and current events which the company dips into to find messages to print in huge block letters on lorries, billboards, parking lots, company cars and 'any other blank space we can find.' The company cars sport large warning labels like those found on cigarette packets: 'Global Warming: Cars cause 80% of all air pollution and severe life-threatening climate change.'

Department initiatives include a UK-wide campaign to collect 100,000 old keys from customers to use in a joint campaign with Shelter to get the government to provide 100,000 additional homes a year at affordable rental rates. The keys will be transformed into a huge sculpture to be presented to the government.

The Department of Social Inventions is developing a series of free action alerts to be distributed in branches of The Body Shop on a number of important social and environmental issues. Each action alert will describe problems such as global warming, suggest a solution, and encourage customers to take a specific action. The action alerts can be updated easily, enabling rapid response to current events.

On the wackier side, the department is forming an employee African Drumming group and hopes one day to create the longest corporate conga line in world history.

'The Department of Social Inventions has launched a programme to train a specialist in social inventions in each branch of The Body Shop worldwide'

In The Body Shop head franchise offices around the world, small Departments of Social Inventions are cropping up. The Department of Social Inventions has launched a programme to train a specialist in social inventions in each branch of The Body Shop worldwide.

Jeremy Sherman, Department of Social Inventions, The Body Shop International plc, Watersmead, Littlehampton, West Sussex BN17 6LS (tel 0903 731500; fax 0903 726250).

INDEX

This Index contains surnames of inventors and contributors, The Book of Visions'
title for their scheme and names of organisations